90 0813173 8

KV-585-715

WITHDRAWN
FROM
UNIVERSITY OF PLYMOUTH

The Semantic Web for Knowledge and Data Management: Technologies and Practices

Zongmin Ma
Northeastern University, China

Huaiqing Wang
City University of Hong Kong, Hong Kong

INFORMATION SCIENCE REFERENCE

Hershey · New York

Director of Editorial Content: Kristin Klinger
Senior Managing Editor: Jennifer Neidig
Managing Editor: Jamie Snavely
Assistant Managing Editor: Carole Coulson
Typesetter: Sean Woznicki
Cover Design: Lisa Tosheff
Printed at: Yurchak Printing Inc.

Published in the United States of America by
Information Science Reference (an imprint of IGI Global)
701 E. Chocolate Avenue, Suite 200
Hershey PA 17033
Tel: 717-533-8845
Fax: 717-533-8661
E-mail: cust@igi-global.com
Web site: http://www.igi-global.com

and in the United Kingdom by
Information Science Reference (an imprint of IGI Global)
3 Henrietta Street
Covent Garden
London WC2E 8LU
Tel: 44 20 7240 0856
Fax: 44 20 7379 0609
Web site: http://www.eurospanbookstore.com

Library of Congress Cataloging-in-Publication Data

The Semantic Web for knowledge and data management : technologies and practices / Zongmin Ma and Huaiqing Wang, editors.

p. cm.

Summary: "This book discusses the Semantic Web, as an extension of the current World Wide Web in which information is given well-defined, better enabling computers and people to work in cooperation"--Provided by publisher.
Includes bibliographical references and index.

ISBN 978-1-60566-028-8 (hbk.) -- ISBN 978-1-60566-029-5 (ebook)
1. Semantic Web. I. Ma, Zongmin, 1965- II. Wang, Huaiqing.
TK5105.88815.S434 2009
025.04--dc22

2008010316

British Cataloguing in Publication Data
A Cataloguing in Publication record for this book is available from the British Library.

Editorial Advisory Board

Table of Contents

Chapter VI
Automatic Semantic Annotation Using Machine Learning 106
Jie Tang, Tsinghua University, Beijing, China
Duo Zhang, University of Illinois, Urbana-Champaign, USA
Limin Yao, Tsinghua University, Beijing, China
Yi Li, Tsinghua University, Beijing, China

Section II

Chapter VII
Paving the Way to an Effective and Efficient Retrieval of Data over
Semantic Overlay Networks 151
Federica Mandreoli, University of Modena and Reggio Emilia, Italy
Riccardo Martoglia, University of Modena and Reggio Emilia, Italy
Wilma Penzo, University of Bologna, Italy
Simona Sassatelli, University of Modena and Reggio Emilia, Italy
Giorgio Villani, University of Modena and Reggio Emilia, Italy

Chapter VIII
SWARMS: A Platform for Domain Knowledge Management and Applications 176
Jie Tang, Tsinghua University, Beijing, China
Bangyong Liang, NEC Labs, China
Juanzi Li, Tsinghua University, Beijing, China

Chapter IX
Modeling and Querying XML-Based P2P Information Systems:
A Semantics-Based Approach 207
Alfredo Cuzzocrea, University of Calabria, Italy

Section III

Chapter X
Applying Semantic Web to E-Tourism 243
Danica Damljanović, University of Sheffield, UK
Vladan Devedžić, University of Belgrade, Serbia

Chapter XI
Semantic Web in Ubiquitous Mobile Communications 266
Anna V. Zhdanova, The Telecommunications Research Center Vienna, Austria
Ning Li, University of Surrey, UK
Klaus Moessner, University of Surrey, UK

Detailed Table of Contents

Section I

This chapter defines a hierarchical clustering algorithm namely Contextual Concept Discovery (CCD), based on an incremental use of the partitioning algorithm Kmeans, guided by a structural contextual definition and providing a web driven evaluation task to support the domain experts. The CCD algorithm is implemented and tested to incrementally extract the ontological concepts. It is shown that the context-based hierarchical algorithm gives better results than a usual context definition and an existing clustering method.

Based on fuzzy set theory, this chapter reviews the existing proposals for extending the theoretical counterpart of the Semantic Web languages, description logics (DLs), and the languages themselves. The expressive power of the fuzzy DLs formalism and its syntax and semantic, knowledge base, the decidability of the tableaux algorithm and its computational complexity as well as the fuzzy extension to OWL are discussed.

Chapter III
Improving Storage Concepts for Semantic Models and Ontologies 38
Edgar R. Weippl, Vienna University of Technology, Austria
Markus D. Klemen, Vienna University of Technology, Austria
Stefan Raffeiner, Vienna University of Technology, Austria

This chapter presents an improved database schema to store ontologies. More specifically, it proposes an intuitive and efficient way of storing arbitrary relationships, shows that their database schema is well suited to store both RDF and Topic Maps, and explains why it is more efficient by comparing it to other approaches.

Chapter IV
Ontologies and Intelligent Agents: A Powerful Bond 49
Kostas Kolomvatsos, National and Kapodistrian University of Athens, Greece
Stathes Hadjiefthymiades, National and Kapodistrian University of Athens, Greece

This chapter provides an exhaustive description of fundamentals regarding the combination of the Semantic Web and intelligent agent technologies. It is shown that agents build ontologies and agents integrate ontologies in an automatic way.

Chapter V
Probabilistic Models for the Semantic Web: A Survey 74
Livia Predoiu, University of Mannheim, Germany
Heiner Stuckenschmidt, University of Mannheim, Germany

Focusing on probabilistic approaches for representing uncertain information on the Semantic Web, this chapter surveys existing proposals for extending semantic web languages or formalisms underlying Semantic Web languages in terms of their expressive power, reasoning capabilities as well as their suitability for supporting typical tasks associated with the Semantic Web.

Chapter VI
Automatic Semantic Annotation Using Machine Learning 106
Jie Tang, Tsinghua University, Beijing, China
Duo Zhang, University of Illinois, Urbana-Champaign, USA
Limin Yao, Tsinghua University, Beijing, China
Yi Li, Tsinghua University, Beijing, China

This chapter studies the problems of semantic annotation and introduces the state-of-the-art methods for dealing with the problems. It also gives a brief survey of the developed systems based on the methods. Several real-world applications of semantic annotation are introduced as well.

Section II

This chapter presents a semantic infrastructure for routing queries effectively in a network of SONs (Semantic Overlay Networks). The chapter defines a fully distributed indexing mechanism which summarizes the semantics underlying whole subnetworks, in order to be able to locate the semantically best directions to forward a query to. It is demonstrated through a rich set of experiments that the proposed routing mechanism overtakes algorithms which are usually limited to the only knowledge of the peers directly connected to the querying peer.

This chapter describes the architecture and the main features of SWARMS, a platform for domain knowledge management. The platform aims at providing services for (1) efficiently storing and accessing the ontological information; (2) visualizing the networking structure in the ontological data; (3) searching and mining the semantic data.

This chapter first focuses its attention on the definition and the formalization of the XML-based P2P Information Systems class, also deriving interesting properties on such systems. Then the chapter presents a knowledge-representation-and-management-based framework that can efficiently process knowledge and support advanced IR techniques in XML-based P2P Information Systems.

Section III

Chapter X
Applying Semantic Web to E-Tourism 243
Danica Damljanović, University of Sheffield, UK
Vladan Devedžić, University of Belgrade, Serbia

This chapter presents Travel Guides - a prototype system for tourism management to illustrate how semantic web technologies combined with traditional E-Tourism applications help integration of tourism sources dispersed on the Web, and enable creating sophisticated user profiles.

Chapter XI
Semantic Web in Ubiquitous Mobile Communications 266
Anna V. Zhdanova, The Telecommunications Research Center Vienna, Austria
Ning Li, University of Surrey, UK
Klaus Moessner, University of Surrey, UK

This chapter provides background information on the Semantic Web field, discusses other research fields that bring semantics into play for reaching the ontology-enabled ubiquitous mobile communication vision, and exemplifies the state of the art of ontology development and use in telecommunication projects.

Chapter XII
Design Diagrams as Ontological Sources: Ontology Extraction and Utilization for Software Asset Reuse 288
Kalapriya Kannan, IBM India Research Labs, India
Biplav Srivastava, IBM India Research Labs, India

This chapter discusses how semantic web technologies can help solution-building organizations achieve software reuse by first learning ontologies from design diagrams of existing solutions and then using them to create design diagrams for new solutions. The proposed technique, called OntExtract, extracts domain ontology information (entities and their relationship(s)) from class diagrams and further refines the extracted information using diagrams that express dynamic interactions among entities such as sequence diagram.

Compilation of References 316

About the Contributors 359

Index 365

Preface

The World Wide Web (WWW) has drastically changed the availability of electronically accessible information. Currently the WWW is the biggest information repository around the world and the most convenient means for information sharing and exchange. While the current Web provides access to an enormous amount of information, it is currently only human-readable. It is increasingly difficult to find, access, present and maintain the information required by a wide variety of users. In response to this problem, the Semantic Web was proposed by Time Berners-Lee, Director of the World Wide Web Consortium. The Semantic Web is defined as "an extension of the current World Wide Web in which information is given well-defined, better enabling computers and people to work in cooperation". The Semantic Web allows the explicit representation of the semantics of the data so that it is machine interpretable. Therefore, the Semantic Web will enable a knowledge-based web and facilities the use of agent-based technology to better mine and filter information needs expressed by information consumers.

The Semantic Web is generally built on syntaxes which use URIs to represent data, usually in triple based structures: that is, many triples of URI data that can be held in databases, or interchanged in the World Wide Web using a set of particular syntaxes developed especially for the task. These syntaxes are called Resource Description Framework (RDF) syntaxes. The layer above the syntax is the simple datatyping model. The RDF Schema (RDFS) is designed to be a simple datatyping model for the RDF. The Web Ontology Language (OWL) is a language as an ontology language based upon the RDF. OWL takes the RDF Schema a step further, by giving us more in-depth properties and classes. The next step in the architecture of the Semantic Web is trust and proof.

Being the next generation Internet technology, the Semantic Web is typically application-oriented. With advances and in-deep applications of computer and Internet technologies in data and knowledge intensive domains, the Semantic Web for knowledge and data management is emerging as a new discipline. The research and development of knowledge and data management in the Semantic Web are receiving increasing attention. The requirements of large-scale deployment and interoperability of the Semantic Web represent a major challenge to data and knowledge management, which raises a number of issues and requirements regarding how to represent, create, manage and use both ontologies as shared knowledge representations, but also large volumes of metadata records used to annotate Web resources of a diverse kind. So the Semantic Web for knowledge and data management is a field which must be investigated by academic researchers together with developers and users both from database, artificial intelligence, and software and knowledge engineering areas.

This book focuses on the following issues of the Semantic Web: the theory aspect of the Semantic Web and ontology, data management and processing in the Semantic Web, ontology and knowledge management, and Semantic Web-based applications, aiming at providing a single account of technologies and practices in the Semantic Web for knowledge and data management. The objective of the book is to provide the state of the art information to academics, researchers and industry practitioners who are involved or interested in the study, use, design and development of advanced and emerging the Semantic Web technologies with ultimate aim to empower individuals and organizations in building competencies for exploiting the opportunities of the data and knowledge society. This book presents the latest research and application results in the Semantic Web. The different chapters in the book have been contributed by different authors and provide possible solutions for the different types of technological problems concerning the Semantic Web for knowledge and data management.

INTRODUCTION

This book which consists of twelve chapters is organized into three major sections. The first section discusses the issues of the Semantic Web and ontologies in the first six chapters. The next three chapters covering the Semantic Web for data and knowledge management comprise the second section. The third section containing the final three chapters focuses on the applications of the Semantic Web.

First of all, we take a look at the issues of the Semantic Web and ontologies.

Research in ontology learning had always separated between ontology building and evaluation tasks. Moreover, it had used for example a sentence, a syntactic structure or a set of words to establish the context of a word. However, this research avoids accounting for the structure of the document and the relation between the contexts. Lobna Karoui combines these elements to generate an appropriate context definition for each word. Based on the context, she proposes an unsupervised hierarchical clustering algorithm that, in the same time, extracts and evaluates the ontological concepts. The results show that her concept discovery approach improves the conceptual quality and the relevance of the extracted ontological concepts, provides a support for the domain experts and facilitates the evaluation task for them.

In the Semantic Web context, information would be retrieved, processed, shared, reused and aligned in the maximum automatic way possible. The experience with such applications in the Semantic Web has shown that these are rarely a matter of true or false but rather procedures that require degrees of relatedness, similarity, or ranking. Apart from the wealth of applications that are inherently imprecise, information itself is many times imprecise or vague. In order to be able to represent and reason with such type of information in the Semantic Web, different general approaches for extending semantic web languages with the ability to represent imprecision and uncertainty has been explored. Hailong Wang *et al.* focus their attention on fuzzy extension approaches which are based on fuzzy set theory. They review the existing proposals for extending the theoretical counterpart of the semantic web languages, description logics (*DLs*), and the languages themselves. The expressive power of the fuzzy *DLs* formalism and its syntax and semantic, knowledge base, the decidability of the tableaux algorithm and its computational complexity as well as the fuzzy extension to OWL are discussed.

Ontologies are more commonly used today but still little consideration is given of how to efficiently store them. Edgar R. Weippl, Markus D. Klemen and Stefan Raffeiner present an improved database schema to store ontologies. More specifically, they propose an intuitive and efficient way of storing arbitrary relationships, show that their database schema is well suited to store both RDF and Topic Maps, and explain why it is more efficient by comparing it to other approaches. The proposed approach is built on reliable and efficient relational database management systems (RDBMS). It can be easily implemented for other systems and due to its vendor independence existing data can be migrated from one RDBMS to another relatively easy.

The emerged form of information with computer-processable meaning (semantics) as presented in the framework of the Semantic Web (SW) facilitates machines to access it more efficiently. Information is semantically annotated in order to ease the discovery and retrieval of knowledge. Ontologies are the basic element of the SW. They carry knowledge about a domain and enable interoperability between different resources. Another technology that draws considerable attention nowadays is the technology of Intelligent Agents. Intelligent agents act on behalf of a user to complete tasks and may adapt their behavior to achieve their objectives. Kostas Kolomvatsos and Stathes Hadjiefthymiades provide an exhaustive description of fundamentals regarding the combination of SW and intelligent agent technologies.

Recently, there has been an increasing interest in formalisms for representing uncertain information on the Semantic Web. This interest is triggered by the observation that knowledge on the web is not always crisp and we have to be able to deal with incomplete, inconsistent and vague information. The treatment of this kind of information requires new approaches for knowledge representation and reasoning on the web as existing Semantic Web languages are based on classical logic which is known to be inadequate for representing uncertainty in many cases. While different general approaches for extending Semantic Web languages with the ability to represent uncertainty are explored, Livia Predoiu and Heiner Stuckenschmidt focus their attention on probabilistic approaches. They survey existing proposals for extending semantic web languages or formalisms underlying Semantic Web languages in terms of their expressive power, reasoning capabilities as well as their suitability for supporting typical tasks associated with the Semantic Web.

The Semantic Web provides a common framework that allows data to be shared and reused across applications, enterprises, and community boundaries. However, lack of annotated semantic data is a bottleneck to make the Semantic Web vision a reality. Therefore, it is indeed necessary to automate the process of semantic annotation. In the past few years, there was a rapid expansion of activities in the semantic annotation area. Many methods have been proposed for automating the annotation process. However, due to the heterogeneity and the lack of structure of the Web data, automated discovery of the targeted or unexpected knowledge information still present many challenging research problems. Jie Tang *et al.* study the problems of semantic annotation and introduce the state-of-the-art methods for dealing with the problems. They also give a brief survey of the developed systems based on the methods. Several real-world applications of semantic annotation are introduced as well.

The next section takes look at the data and knowledge management with the Semantic Web and ontologies.

In a Peer-to-Peer (P2P) system, a Semantic Overlay Network (SON) models a network of peers whose connections are influenced by the peers' content, so that semantically related peers connect with each other. This is very common in P2P communities, where peers share common interests, and a peer can belong to more than one SON, depending on its own interests. Querying such a kind of systems is not an easy task: The retrieval of relevant data can not rely on flooding approaches which forward a query to the overall network. A way of selecting which peers are more likely to provide relevant answers is necessary to support more efficient and effective query processing strategies. Federica Mandreoli *et al.* present a semantic infrastructure for routing queries effectively in a network of SONs. Peers are semantically rich, in that peers' content is modelled with a schema on their local data, and peers are related each other through semantic mappings defined between their own schemas. A query is routed through the network by means of a sequence of reformulations, according to the semantic mappings encountered in the routing path. As reformulations may lead to semantic approximations, they define a fully distributed indexing mechanism which *summarizes the semantics* underlying whole subnetworks, in order to be able to locate the *semantically best* directions to forward a query to. They demonstrate through a rich set of experiments that their routing mechanism overtakes algorithms which are usually limited to the only knowledge of the peers directly connected to the querying peer, and that their approach is successful in a SONs scenario.

Jie Tang *et al.* describe the architecture and the main features of SWARMS, a platform for domain knowledge management. The platform aims at providing services for (1) efficiently storing and accessing the ontological information; (2) visualizing the networking structure in the ontological data; (3) searching and mining the semantic data. One advantage of the system is that it provides a suite of components for not only supporting efficient semantic data storage but also searching and mining the semantics. Another advantage is that the system supports visualization in the process of search and mining, which would greatly help a normal user to understand the knowledge inside the ontological data. SWARMS can be easily customized to adapt to different domains. The system has been applied to several domains, such as News, Software, and Social Network. The authors present the performance evaluations of the system.

Knowledge representation and management techniques can be efficiently used to improve data modeling and IR functionalities of P2P Information Systems, which have recently attracted a lot of attention from both industrial and academic research communities. These functionalities can be achieved by pushing semantics in both data and queries, and exploiting the derived expressiveness to improve file sharing primitives and lookup mechanisms made available by first-generation P2P systems. XML-based P2P Information Systems are a more specific instance of this class of systems, where the overall data domain is composed by very large, Internet-like distributed XML repositories from which users extract useful knowledge by means of IR methods implemented on top of XML join queries against the repositories. Alfredo Cuzzocrea first focuses his attention on the definition and the formalization of the XML-based P2P Information Systems class, also deriving interesting properties on such systems, and then he presents a knowledge-representation-and-management-based framework, enriched via semantics, that allows us to efficiently process knowledge and support advanced IR techniques in XML-based P2P Information Systems, thus achieving the definition of the so-called Semantically-Augmented XML-based P2P Information Systems.

In the third section, we see the application aspects of the Semantic Web.

Traditional E-Tourism applications store data internally in a form that is not interoperable with similar systems. Hence, tourist agents spend plenty of time updating data about vacation packages in order to provide good service to their clients. On the other hand, their clients spend plenty of time searching for the 'perfect' vacation package as the data about tourist offers are not integrated and are available from different spots on the Web. Danica Damljanović and Vladan Devedžić develop Travel Guides - a prototype system for tourism management to illustrate how semantic web technologies combined with traditional E-Tourism applications help integration of tourism sources dispersed on the Web, and enable creating sophisticated user profiles. Maintaining quality user profiles enables system personalization and adaptivity of the content shown to the user. The core of this system is in ontologies – they enable machine readable and machine understandable representation of the data and more importantly reasoning.

The world becomes ubiquitous, and mobile communication platforms become oriented towards integration with the web, getting benefits from the large amount of information available there, and creation of the new types of value-added services. Semantic and ontology technologies are seen as being able to advance the seamless integration of the mobile and the Web worlds. Anna V. Zhdanova, Ning Li and Klaus Moessner present the overall state of the art ontology-related developments in mobile communication systems, namely, the work towards construction, sharing and maintenance of ontologies for mobile communications, reuse and application of ontologies and existing Semantic Web technologies in the prototypes. Social, collaborative and technical challenges experienced in the project showcase the need in alignment of ontology experts' work across the mobile communication projects to establish the best practices in the area and drive standardization efforts. They indicate certain milestones in integration of Semantic Web-based intelligence with Mobile Communications, such as performing ontology construction, matching, and evolution in mobile service systems and alignment with existing heterogeneous data models.

Ontology is a basic building block for the Semantic Web. An active line of research in semantic web is focused on how to build and evolve ontologies using the information from different ontological sources inherent in the domain. A large part of the IT industry uses software engineering methodologies to build software solutions that solve real-world problems. For them, instead of creating solutions from scratch, reusing previously built software as much as possible is a business-imperative today. As part of their projects, they use design diagrams to capture various facets of the software development process. Kalapriya Kannan and Biplav Srivastava discuss how semantic web technologies can help solution-building organizations achieve software reuse by first learning ontologies from design diagrams of existing solutions and then using them to create design diagrams for new solutions. Their technique, called OntExtract, extracts domain ontology information (entities and their relationship(s)) from class diagrams and further refines the extracted information using diagrams that express dynamic interactions among entities such as sequence diagram. A proof of concept implementations is also developed as a Plug-in over a commercial development environment IBM's Rational Software Architect.

Zongmin Ma and Huaiqing Wang
Editors

Acknowledgment

The editors wish to thank all of the authors for their insights and excellent contributions to this book and would like to acknowledge the help of all involved in the collation and review process of the book, without whose support the project could not have been satisfactorily completed. Most of the authors of chapters included in this book also served as referees for chapters written by other authors. Thanks go to all those who provided constructive and comprehensive reviews.

A further special note of thanks goes to all the staff at IGI Global, whose contributions throughout the whole process from inception of the initial idea to final publication have been invaluable. Special thanks also go to the publishing team at IGI Global. This book would not have been possible without the ongoing professional support from IGI Global.

The idea of editing this volume stems from the initial research work that the editors did in past several years. The assistances and facilities of Northeastern University and City University of Hong Kong, China, are deemed important, and are highly appreciated. The research work of Zongmin Ma supported by the *Program for New Century Excellent Talents in University* (NCET-05-0288).

Zongmin Ma and Huaiqing Wang
Editors
January, 2008

Section I

Chapter I
Contextual Hierarchy Driven Ontology Learning

Lobna Karoui
Ecole Supérieure d'Electricité, France

ABSTRACT

Research in ontology learning had always separated between ontology building and evaluation tasks. Moreover, it had used for example a sentence, a syntactic structure or a set of words to establish the context of a word. However, this research avoids accounting for the structure of the document and the relation between the contexts. In our work, we combine these elements to generate an appropriate context definition for each word. Based on the context, we propose an unsupervised hierarchical clustering algorithm that, in the same time, extracts and evaluates the ontological concepts. Our results show that our concept discovery approach improves the conceptual quality and the relevance of the extracted ontological concepts, provides a support for the domain experts and facilitates the evaluation task for them.

INTRODUCTION

Some current work in data annotation, data integration, information retrieval, building multi-agents application, semantic web services depends on ontologies. The development and the deployment of these applications are related to the richness of the conceptualization inside the ontology. Moreover, giving a semantic to the web can be realized in an incremental manner by using the ontology vocabulary. In this paper, we focus on the use of context in the ontology learning process. Until now, most works have investigated various issues of ontology building such as methodology of ontology extraction and ontology evaluation but separately. In our research, we are interested in defining an approach that permits, at the same time, to extract and evaluate the ontological concepts by using the notion of "context". Generally, the idea of defining the context of a word is limited to a sentence, a syntactic structure, a set of words or a set of sentences without tacking into account the document's structure and the relation between the contexts. In this work, we combine these elements to establish an appropriate context definition for each word. So, our contributions are to propose firstly a new context definition that takes into account the document characteristics and secondly to define a new approach that not only extracts the ontological concepts but also evaluates them. This approach is based on our proposed context definition that takes into account the position of a word inside the HTML structure and the relation between the deduced contexts in the HTML document. For this purpose, we propose an unsupervised hierarchical clustering algorithm namely Contextual Concept Discovery (CCD) based on an incremental use of the partitioning Kmeans algorithm, guided by a structural context and producing a support for an easy evaluation task. Our context definition is based on the html structure and the location of each word in the documents. Each context is deduced from the various analyses included in the pre-processing step (Karoui et al., 2006). This explicitly contextual representation, titled contextual hierarchy, guides the clustering algorithm to delimit the context of each word by improving the word weighting, the words pair's similarity and the semantically closer cooccurent selection for each word. By performing an incremental process and by recursively dividing each cluster, the CCD algorithm refines the context of each word cluster. It improves the conceptual quality of the extracted concepts. The CCD algorithm offers the choice between either an automatic execution or a user interactive one. In order to help the domain expert during the evaluation task, the last part of the CCD algorithm exploits a web collection and extracts the existing contexts. This information is used to compute the credibility degree associated to each word cluster in order to inform about it and facilitate the experts' semantic interpretation. So, the CCD algorithm extracts the domain concepts and proposes a quantitative and a qualitative evaluation for the experts. Our evaluation proposition permits the ontology reuse and evolution since the informing elements that support the experts' interpretation are driven by the web changes and are stored with the experts' comments for a later use. We experiment the contextual clustering algorithm on French html document corpus related to the tourism domain. The results show that our algorithm improves the relevance of the extracted concepts in comparison with a simple Kmeans. Also, our observations and discussions with experts confirm that our evaluation process helps and assists the user.

The remainder of the paper is organized as follows: section 2 presents the state of the art related, sections 3 answers the question: What is the impact of the context on the intelligent interpretation, section 4 presents defines the context and the Contextual Concept Discovery" (CCD) algorithm, section 5 experiments our algorithm proposition and section 6 concludes and gives our future directions.

RELATED WORK

Ontology is "a specification of a conceptualization" (Gruber, 1993). Ontology learning systems as defined in (Faure, 1998; Chalendar, 2000; Meadche, 2001) have different purposes. Many of them extract concepts and relationships from a collection of documents related to a specific domain in order to either construct ontology or enhance it. For this they use a conceptual clustering (Faure and Nedellec, 1998), linguistic approach (Navigli, 1998; Chalendar and Grau, 2000), statistic one (Maedche et al, 2000; Srinivassan, 1992). In this related work, we present an overview of the context in some domains that are related to our research (since the notion of context is used in many other domains that are not close to our work such as physic, mathematical models, etc.). We focus on the use of context in the ontology learning. Then, we expose some ideas about the ontology evaluation.

Context in Some Domains

In this research, our aim is to discover the concepts that belong to a domain ontology by using the notion of "context". The concepts that constitute an ontology are named "ontological concepts". In order to improve the conceptual quality of those concepts, we use the context of each word. According to the Oxford English Dictionary (http://www.askoxford.com/), the term context has two meanings: (1) the words around the word, phrase, statement and so one used to help explain the meaning and (2) the general conditions in which an event, action, and so on takes place. In the following sections, we explain how this notion has been used in some domains related to our research.

Context in Word Sense Disambiguation

In this field, context is used either as a micro context or a topical context. As a micro context, Yarowsky (1993) experiments different small window (the larger one is 4 words). He affirms that these micro contexts are sufficient for local ambiguities. Similarly, Leacock and al (1996) shows that the best performance in their tests is due to a local window of +-3 words. As topical context, Yarowsky (1992) has used a 100-word window in order to extract the related words. Voorhees and al (1993) define the context as two sentence window. Others use either +- a big number of words inside the window such as Gale and al (1992) (+- 50 words) or sections of the documents (Brown et al., 1991).

Context in Machine Learning

Turney (1996) was one of the first to explicitly acknowledge the problem of context in learning. He gives a formal definition of contextual and context sensitive features. His approach was motivated by resolving the learning problems related to the fact that testing examples were governed by a different **context** than the training examples from which the **concepts** are deduced. These features are used for a normalization task and defined manually. However, in Widmer (1996), the author presents a method to automatically detect the contextual attributes in an on-line learning approach. These determined features are used during the learning setting. Other researches work on the speech recognition task by using the speaker's accent, the sound and the information, the electrocardiogram data and the patient's identity to realize a heart disease diagnostics, etc.

Context in Ontology Learning

Faure and Nédellec (1998) describe a system called ASIUM where a cooperative conceptual clustering is applied to technical texts using syntactic parser to produce an acyclic conceptual graph of clusters. Basic clusters are formed by words that occur with the same verb after the same preposition. In Chalendar and Grau (2000), the authors design a system titled SVETLAN. This system learns noun categories from texts by using Sylex tool. Consequently, nouns having the same role with the same verb inside the same syntactic context are homogenous and belong to the same class. Input data are semantic domain and its thematic entities learned automatically by using SEGAPSITH. The difference between ASIUM and SVETLAN is that this later is independent of the expert intervention and the text nature. TEXT-TO-ONTO (Meadche and Stabb, 2001) is an ontology learning environment which has a bookshop of learning methods such as formal concept analysis, association rules which permit to extract concepts, taxonomic relations and non taxonomic relations, linguistic tool (analyzer) and heuristics. WebOntEx (Han, 2000) system's goal is to extract semi automatically ontology by analyzing Web pages of the same specific domain. Knowledge extraction is based on HTML tags (B, h1), lemmatization tags (verb, name) and conceptual tags (entity, attribute) using WordNet and a logic inductive programming method. However, this methodology requires a long manual task during which the designer manually develops a kernel ontology and extracts generic patterns from domain Web pages. OntoMiner (Davulcu, 1998) analyzes sets of domain specific web sites and generates taxonomy of particular concepts and their instances. This tool uses HTML regularities within web documents in order to generate a hierarchical semantic structure encoded in XML. It explores directories of home pages in order to detect key domain concepts and relations between them. OntoLearn (Navigli, 1998) is a tool based on linguistic and semantic techniques. It extracts domain terminology from Web documents by using a linguistic processor and a syntactic parser. The semantic interpretation task consists in finding the appropriate WordNet concept for each term.

Discussion

For TEXT-TO-ONTO, ASIUM, SVETLAN and OntoLearn systems, the linguistic context of the term is defined using syntactic dependencies. This context definition limited to a linguistic one is not sufficient because the word context exceeds the phrase i.e. the word can exist in the paragraph with other meaning. With the WebOntEx and OntoMiner systems, the authors consider respectively the HTML tags (separately without studying the relations between them) and the home page directories as contexts. We also remark that the context can be an existing ontology, domain expert, some visual information, some rules, some words around a target object (window), one or a set of sentences or one syntactic structure (verb group, nominal group). For all these definitions, the document structure is rarely taken into account. Also, the relations between these contexts (for one application) are not considered. In our work, we deal with these issues to improve the ontological concept discovery (extraction and evaluation). For us, the context is a set of circumstances (situations) which surround the studied object and reflects its concrete environment. It provides an active background for a learning activity and an appropriate support for a semantic interpretation. In this study, the studied object is a word, the learning activity is a clustering task, the semantic interpretation is the evaluation and labeling of the word clusters and the context definition is deduced from the html structure (HTML tags and the relations between them). In our work, the contribution is not only to adapt a clustering algorithm to the ontology learning domain (like many other researches) but also to define a new context definition that takes into account the document structure and the word position in the related contexts .More details are explained in our algorithm (section 4).

Ontology Evaluation

Ontology evaluation remains a real problem in the area of the semantic web. There is no standard methodology or approach to evaluate ontology. This is due to the fact that the ontology learning depends on several aspects such as the purpose of the ontology building, the application (s) using the ontology, the entities constituting the ontology, the kind of ontology (domain ontology, task ontology, etc.), etc. In this survey, we present research related to the evaluation of concepts which constitutes the ontology.

A concept is "A general idea derived or inferred from specific instances or occurrences" (http://www.thefreedictionary.com). Discovering concepts implies having a vocabulary for which the idea of the concept is deduced. Therefore, the ontology engineer can evaluate each or both of the vocabulary and extracted concepts. In order to evaluate the vocabulary, Meadche and Staab (2002) proposed an approach that aims to evaluate the lexical and vocabulary level of an ontology. They have defined a similarity measure in order to compare two strings: one provided from the produced ontology and the other one from an existing ontology. In (Brewster et al., 2004), the authors evaluate their lexical by using WordNet and precision and recall measures. Based on this vocabulary, ontology building approaches applying clustering methods to obtain word clusters as potential future concepts. So, the question is how to evaluate these clusters. In the clustering process, the quality of a cluster is generally based on homogeneity or compactness. In (Vazirgiannis et al., 2003), some criteria for the statistical evaluation of unsupervised learners have been defined. However, the ontology learning applications cannot rely on these standards defined for other applications. Moreover, cluster homogeneity does not imply that the words in the cluster are semantically closer or that the associated label satisfies the domain expert. For the concepts extraction, the evaluation is more challenging. In (Holsapple et Joshi, 2005), the authors proposed an evaluation method based on a collaborative manual ontology engineers in order to maintain the suggestions resulting from the maximum number of experts. Navigli and al (2004) proposed a qualitative evaluation by multiple domain experts that answer to a questionnaire in which they evaluate the quality of the discovered concepts. In (Holsapple et Joshi, 2005; Navigli and al., 2004), the concept evaluation is based on a human intervention which is a painful task. In other research (Meadche and Staab, 2002; Brewster et al., 2004; Vazirgiannis et al., 2003), the evaluation and the labeling process is based on statistic measures, a thesaurus, an existing ontology or an application. Generally, we remark that thesaurus doesn't cover all specific aspects of a domain. Also, the evaluation based on an existing ontology is not sufficient because, in some fields, ontology does not exist or does not contain all the concepts founded in the produced ontology. Moreover, it is not evident to find an application that uses the produced ontology.

As a conclusion, we can say that the evaluation is a difficult task. That is why we deal with this issue. In the following section, we analyze the impact of the context on the interpretation in order to facilitate the experts' evaluation.

CONTEXT AND THE INTELLIGENT INTERPRETATION

The evaluation problem is defined as the process that clarifies the transition from what it is 'written' to what it is 'thought' i.e. eliminates the fuzzy and unpredictable character of the interpretation. In our research, we deal with the issue of evaluating the concept extracted from word clusters resulting from a clustering method. So, the expert tries to give a semantic label to a group of words by finding the relations between them. But this task remains difficult for the expert. That is why we propose to give complementary information either for the single units (words), or for all the words of a cluster considered as a group or for both of them. To provide this useful information, we use the contexts of the words of each cluster. So, what is the impact of the context on the experts' evaluation task?

In this analysis, we explain how the context affects the intelligent interpretation in at least five different ways.

First, recognizing the context allows the user to make predictions about the possible meanings of some elements. Contextual information provides top-down predictions that permits recognition of revealing elements based on partial knowledge about them and it can serve as source of hypotheses about the meanings of words not yet known.

Second, contexts modulate interpretation by setting some parameters or suggestions to orient the reasoning. It limits the words' ambiguities in function of other related contexts which are more general or more specific. For example, when a person hears me saying (Brézillon, 1993): "I heard a lion roar in my office this morning'", he can suppose that I am speaking about my boss, so it is necessary to introduce explicitly some piece of knowledge such as adding the following sentence: "I work in a university near a zoo that can be seen from the window of my office." We note that within these two sentences, the listener knows that I speak about a real lion and not my boss. So the context (first sentence) allows a first interpretation and the second one adjusts it in order to achieve the right one.

Third, context helps user focus his attention. The user have often many interpretations, consequently he needs some way for determining which of his interpretation is the most appropriate one, which differs depending on the context. For example, having the sentence "in the east region of USA, The means of accommodation are comfortable" allows the user to have different interpretations about the word "accommodation" so it could be a medical accommodation for doctors or a social accommodation for helping poor people or a tourism accommodation for tourist. It could also be just a hotel as accommodation or hotel and camping or other kind of accommodation. So this context is insufficient to guide the user's interpretation. But by giving supplementary information like "the east region of USA is a touristic one and the means of accommodations are comfortable.", the user knows that it is a tourism accommodation so we can have as sub concepts hotels, camping and so one.

Fourth, context influences the user's choice of the appropriate meaning of the word. For example, in French language the word "pêche" which could be translated in English as "peach" or "fishing" has two meanings, so there is an ambiguity. But, by having the word "sea" in the same context or in related contexts, the user chooses the meaning of fishing rather than peach because the word "sea" which is an element of the context had influenced the user's choice.

Fifth, context determines how the user can discover implicit meanings. For example, let us take these two sentences: "Mrs Smith reserves a hotel in Florida and decides to go by car. Since, he can not be separated from his dog; he decides to take it with him instead of leaving it to his neighbour." Within this context, the existing information allow the user to discover that the hotel that Mr. smith chooses accepts animals and has a parking in spite of these two information are not said explicitly. So, we can consider accepting animals and having parking as property to the concept "hotel".

We are conscious now that the context has a real impact on the semantic interpretation. These ideas are applied in our algorithm (section 4.2).

THE CONTEXTUAL CONCEPT DISCOVERY ALGORITHM

Our algorithm proposition is constituted of three parts which are: a structural context definition, a clustering process to group the semantic words together and a web driven evaluation task based on various context types with a quantitative criterion (credibility degree).

The Context Definition

In this section, we focus on the selection of the semantically closer cooccurrents and the word weighting process. Generally, if two words appear together in a phrase or a document, we attribute them either the value 1 (i.e. present in this context) or another value between 0 and 1. In the two cases, the context (phrase, document, etc.) could be appropriate to some words but not all the words of a corpus. For example, we consider the three phrases: "USA gives a lot of lodging possibilities. In the north east region, it offers hotels and residences. Also, it gives various leisure activities." If we fix the context to a sentence, we find that 'lodging' and 'hotel', which belong to the same concept, have the value 0 because they don't belong to the same sentence. If we fix the context to a window whose size is 14 words, we find that 'residence' and 'leisure' have a value while they do not belong to the same concept (residence belong to the concept 'lodging' and 'leisure' is another concept). So, 'leisure' should not be a cooccurrent to 'residence'. For these reasons, we believe that the context should be refined in order to take more into account the location of the word.

Actually our challenge is to answer correctly the question: how can we give a weighting that effectively illustrates the importance of a term in its domain and characterizes its relations with other words?

Let us go back to our corpus and the various analyses performed on the HTML documents. We note that there exist relations between the existing HTML elements. For instance: <h1> → <p> (heading → paragraph). We also note that key tags (defined tags like <keywords>, <glossary>, etc.) and <title> are related to other existing HTML elements. For example: <TITLE_URL> (header of a hyperlink) → <H1> (headings of a part of document). The first group of links is physical noted P.L because it depends on the structure of the HTML document. But the second group shows a logical link (L.L) that is not always visible (elements are not necessarily consecutives). In order to represent links between tags, we define two new concepts: contextual hierarchy (C.H) based on HTML elements and link co-occurrence (L.C). A contextual hierarchy is a tag hierarchy. It illustrates possible relations existing within HTML documents and between them.

When we find two terms in the same context unit (paragraph, text), we speak about co-occurrence between these two words in a unit related to the context. In our study, the concept of context is variable, so we do not fix the context during the process but we define a new concept which is a contextual hierarchy represented explicitly. By taking this structure into account, we can define a link between terms, if they appear in the same block-level tag (<p>, <td>, etc.). In this case, the link is a neighbourhood co-occurrence (N.C) and the context is limited to the tag. However, if they appear in different tags that are related by a physical or a logical link defined in the contextual hierarchy, we define the concept of link co-occurrence (see Figure 1). In this second case, the context is the association of the two related tags. The neighbourhood co-occurrence permits finding the word's cooccurrents in a unique context while a link cooccurrence depends on the word position in a context and the relation between this context and the other existent ones. So, it is a generic context that will be instantiated according to the location of the term in HTML tags (for example the context can take various values since it could be in one case the tag <B> and in another case the association of <H1> and <TITLE>).

The structural context definition represents the term's adaptability in its corpus. The associated

Figure 1. Examples of contexts use and their deduced cooccurrents

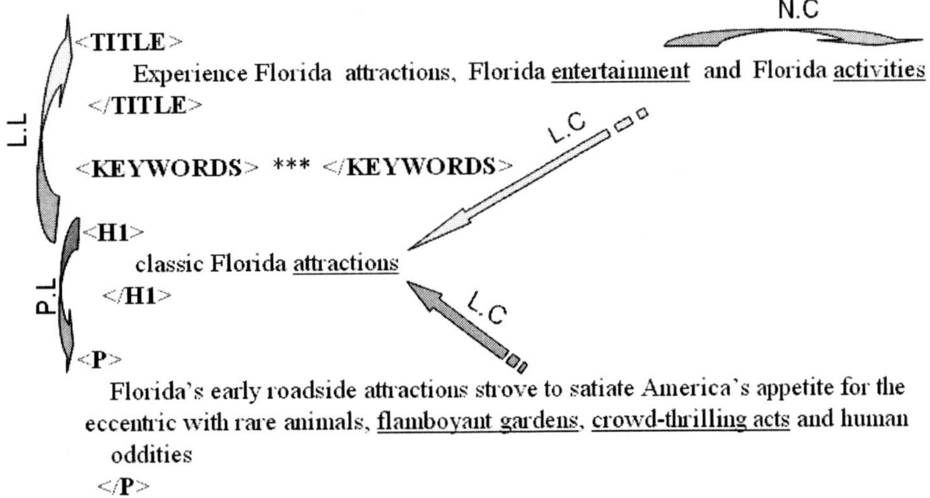

contextual model respects the word location in order to take a multitude of term situations into account when computing its weight. The term weighting is computed by applying the Equivalence Index defined by Michelet (1988) (Ci: term occurrence; Cij: terms cooccurrences):

$$E_{ij} = C2_{ij} / (C_i \times C_j) \qquad (1)$$

The Fundamental Directives of the Evaluation Task

Our idea is as follows: looking through the Web in order to understand the meaning of each word or two words together and so on could be a solution but why?

This task is a contextualization operation. Brézillon (1999) says: Context is what gives meaning to data and contextualization is the process of interpreting data, transforming data to information.

In order to extract concepts, terms are selected from their context in order to group them, but they are presented to the knowledge engineer or the expert domain without any context after a decontextualization process that's why the evaluation step is always difficult. McCarthy (1993) says that decontextualization is to abstract a piece of knowledge from contexts into a more general context that cover the initial context. In our case, for each cluster the general context is the domain (tourism). But this information is not sufficient to evaluate a cluster and to give it a semantic tag.

A solution for ensuring an easy analysis requires a big collection of web documents related to the same studied domain and extracting several contexts from them.

The context granularities degrees: Our hypothesis is having words in the same context imply that they share common information which permit to attribute an appropriate concept for these terms. In this case a context is an appropriate support for a semantic interpretation i.e. it limits the associated knowledge of each word and gives a background for the evaluation and labeling task. In order to explain this idea, we take the sentence: the possible accommodations in the east region of USA are hotels and residences. Within this example, when we limit the context to the association of 'hotels' and 'residences' by the conjunction 'and', we deduce that 'hotels' and 'residences' belongs to the same concept. However, when we limit the context to the entire sentence, we can say that the associated concept to these two words is 'accommodation'. So, thanks to the contextualization task, we can deduce either the meaning of each word, or the semantic association between some words or the concept associated to some words. Taking into account a static context i.e. only one such as a sentence for all the word clusters is not sufficient since in some case the sentence does not contain all the words of a cluster. That's why, our evaluation is not restricted to a unique context on the contrary it depends on various granularity levels which are applied and considered consecutively. The several contexts defined from the domain web documents are provided by two sources. The first one is a linguistic analysis that permits to give us the various nominal groups and verbal groups. It also procures the various word associations by a preposition (of, on, etc.) or a co-coordinating conjunction (and, or, etc.). The second source is a documentary analysis that permits to give us the various sections of phrases (part of a phrase finished by a punctuation like ';' or ','), the sentences, the paragraphs and the documents. So, we have two types of contexts which are a linguistic context and a documentary context. By using the first one, we obtain the close words of our target terms. By using the second one, the context is more generalized than the linguistic one and the information deduced will be either complementary information or completely new information for the words of a cluster.

Our context definition is dynamic since it depends on the presence of the target words in one context. For example, with a cluster with four words and by using two nominal groups, we find that these words are associated and we can give them a concept so we are not obliged to look for their documentary context. But, when the 8 words on a cluster do not belong to one of the four results of the linguistic context, we are obliged to look deeply into the documentary context. So, the expert evaluation thanks to our contextualization process is easier than the existing ones and it is done by respecting this order for each word clusters: (1) Linguistic context (Nominal groups based context, Verbal groups based context, Prepositional groups based context, Conjunctional groups based context); (2) Documentary context (Sections of phrase based context, sentences based context, paragraphs based context, documents based context).

In order to present a context analysis example, in the following sentence the possible accommodations are hotels and residences, we find that are hotels and residences is the verbal group and the possible accommodations is the nominal group. So this sentence which is a context contains two contexts.

Algorithmic Principles

In this section, we present an unsupervised hierarchical clustering algorithm namely Contextual Concept Discovery (CCD) to extract ontological concepts from HTML documents. It is based on an incremental use of the partitioning algorithm Kmeans (McQueen, 1967) and is driven by the structural contexts in which words occur. We chose Kmeans because it is an unsupervised algorithm able to classify a huge volume of objects within a short execution time. The algorithm description is given in Figure 2. The different notations used in the CCD algorithm are given in Table 1.

The clustering algorithm proceeds in an incremental manner. It computes the occurrences of each word and selects their semantically closer cooccurrents according to the context definition. Then, it divides the clusters obtained at each step in order to refine the context of each group of words. So, the algorithm refines at the same time the context of a word and the context of each cluster.

Table 1. Notations used by the CCD algorithm

F	The file of the dataset
WC	The set of word **clusters** WC ={C1, C2, C3, …, CT} with T: the total number of **clusters**
K	The number of **clusters**
P	The highest number of words per **cluster** accepted by the user
M	The possible number of words belonging to one **cluster** as a complementary information which is defined and accepted by the user
S	The similarity measure
Di	The word distribution into the various **clusters** Ci with Di ={C1, C2, C3, …, Ci}
Ci	A word **cluster** belonging to Di As Ci Є Di
Word-Number (Ci)	The number of words in the **cluster** Ci
W i	Each word belonging to Ci So Ci = {W 1, W 2 , …, W i}
Cc-c	The **cluster** that has the closest centroid to the target word W i

Figure 2. The Contextual Concept Discovery Algorithm

```
0: Algorithm Contextual-Concepts-Discovery (In: F, K, P, M, S, Out: WC)
1: Apply our Context definition and compute the occurrences of the population {/*Step 0*/}
2: Di ← Φ {/* Step 1*/}
3: Choose sporadically the K first centers
4: Assign each word to the cluster that has the closest centroid
5: Recalculate the positions of the centroids
6: if (the positions of the centroids did not change) then
7: go to the step 10
8: else
9: go to the step 4.
10: Di ← Di U {C1, C2, C3, …, Ck}
11: For all Ci Є Di do {/* Step 2*/}
12: if (Word-Number (Ci) ≤ P) then
13: WC ← WC U {Ci}
14: Di ← Di \ {Ci}
15: else
16: Di ← Di \ {Ci}
17: Unbolt the words Wi belonging to the cluster Ci
18: Compute the value of K
19: Go to the steps 3, 4, 5 and 6
20: For all Ci Є WC do {/* Step 3*/}
21: if (Word-Number (Ci) = 1 and Wi Є Ci) then
22: Calculate the position of Wi to the existing centroids of the clusters Ci Є WC
23: if (Word-Number (Cc-c) > P+M) then
24: Choose another cluster Cc-c that has the following closest centroid
25: Go to the step 20
26: else
27: WC ← WC \ {Cc-c, Ci}
28: Assign Wi to the cluster Cc-c
29: WC ← WC U {Cc-c}
30: Form a collection of web documents related to the domain {/* Step 4*/}
31: Process the corpus
32: Analyze the corpus
33: Extract the various contexts
34: For each Context type Do
35: For all Ci Є WC Do
36: Find the cooccurrents of the cluster Ci in each sample of the chosen context
37: Compute the Credibility Degree of the cluster Ci
38: Go to step 35
39: Go to step 34
40: Return (WC) + the different credibility degrees associated to each context and each cluster Ci of WC
41: End
```

Also, it offers to the user the possibility to choose either a complete automatic execution or an interactive one. If he/she decides the first execution manner, he/she should either define some parameters or choose the default ones resulting from our empirical experiments. These parameters are: the highest number of words per cluster P, the accepted margin M representing an additional number of words in a resulting cluster accepted by the user and the similarity measure S. If he prefers to evaluate the intermediate word clusters, he should choose the interactive execution. In this case, the algorithm allows him to analyze the word cluster at the end of each intermediate clustering in order to define the value of k' and to decide whether he prefers to continue within an interactive execution or to run an automatic one for the rest of the clustering process. In the interactive execution, the process takes longer than the automatic one but it offers an opportunity to the user to intervene in order to obtain better hierarchical word clusters.

As input to this algorithm, the user should first choose the input dataset. Secondly, he should define the number of clusters K, and chooses whether he prefers an automatic execution or an interactive one. An automatic execution of our algorithm is defined in four steps:

- **Step 0:** Applying the context definition. In this step, the algorithm takes into account the data file in which we find the word and their outbuilding to the html tags. Based on this input, it applies the context definition and returns a file containing the candidates (words), their cooccurrents (attributes) and their associated weightings.
- **Step 1:** Executing the first Kmeans. The goal of this step is to execute the kmeans algorithm in order to obtain the first word distribution Di. We obtain k word clusters.

These steps 0 and 1 concern the application of the structural context which is deduced from the various analyses, computed from the dataset F and stored in a matrix and the execution of the partitioning algorithm to obtain the first k clusters.

- **Step 2:** Performing the hierarchical clustering. This step finds clusters respecting the criterion defined by the user: the P value. For each intermediate execution of kmeans, we should define the value K' which represents the number of clusters related to the words of a cluster that could be divided. In an automatic execution of the algorithm, this value is not defined by the user but computed by the system. We implement a proportional function that automatically defines the value of K'. Based on several empirical experiments and the domain experts' knowledge, we define a proportional link needed for our function. By using this information and solving the following equation, we can compute the value of K'. The useful equation, which is applied in any domain, is:

  K' = a *ln (Word-Number (Ci)* b)
  (2)

  If the number of words in a cluster (Word-Number (Ci)) is less than (1/b), the value of K' will not be computed but defined as 2. When the number of words per cluster Ci is less or equal to P, we include the cluster Ci to the set WC.
- **Step 3:** Affecting the single word to the formed clusters. When applying the division process, we can obtain clusters with only one word. Our idea is to automatically associate each word alone in a cluster resulting from step 2. Another problem appears when the algorithm affects too many words to the same cluster (by respecting the similarity). In this case and for a little number of clusters, we can obtain clusters with a great number of words. If a word is assigned to a cluster already containing P+M words, the CCD algorithm will choose the cluster which is the closest centroid to the target word.

Choosing an interactive process implies applying the same steps but with the user intervention firstly after step 1 and during step 2 and 3. The clustering method adopts a vector-space model and represents a term as a vector containing attributes that belong to the corpus and are stored in a matrix. In step 2, if a cluster is divided, the algorithm allows to refine the context of each cluster by taking into account only the associated attributes of its belonging words. By applying this method, the similarity computed better represents the association degree between each two words. By applying the step 3, it avoids the cases of having only one word in a **cluster** and those containing the majority of the single words.

- **Step 4:** Evaluating the word clusters. To obtain a domain web collection of French documents, we use a cleaner (for example HTTrack Website Copier). Then, we treat them thanks to the pre-processing step of our system. This last cleans and structures the collected web pages. Then, we perform various analyses (Karoui et al., 2006). Now, the problem is that the expert is incapable, even when he is given all the results of the analysis, to find the possible association of the targets words, especially when working on a big *corpus*. In order to facilitate this process, we define a semantic index which represents the credibility of the target words' association in relation with the different contexts. This index is named credibility degree. It is computed for each word cluster and for each context definition in an automated way. More details about this criterion and its importance are provided in sub section titled the impact of the credibility degree.

In the following section, we experiment with the Contextual Concept Discovery algorithm.

EXPERIMENTAL EVALUATION OF THE CONTEXTUAL CONCEPT DISCOVERY ALGORITHM (CCD)

Our objective is to extract and evaluate the ontological concepts.

- **Source of information.** In our experiments, we use HTML documents (600 pages) collected from the Canada tourism web sites. Those documents (French language) contain some HTML structure. We collect them by using the HTTrack Website Copier. Since we aim to perform an incrementally concept extraction process, we start the process with key and title tags to give an outline of the domain's semantic information. These terms are those chosen by the site designer as keywords, document titles, glossaries, etc. Our dataset is composed of 872 words. So, our general context is the first two levels of the contextual model (key tags + title tags+ headings tags). In the following research, this method will progressively integrate all the html elements and the terms of the corpus in order to obtain more domain concepts.
- **Experimental protocol.** We perform two experiments. Firstly, we compare between two contextual definitions which are a simple window and our context definition. Our new context definition improves the words' pairs weighting and the words' pair's similarities. These results are presented in (Karoui et al., 2006) in which we explain clearly the advantage of our context. Secondly, we keep our context definition and we apply it with two algorithms which are Kmeans and CCD. We evaluate the CCD algorithm results by comparing them to those obtained by the Kmeans one. We chose the Euclidian distance as a similarity measure. The Kmeans algorithm distributes them in 156 clusters. The CCD algorithm is experimented with various values for each parameter. We present an automatic execution while respectively applying to k, P and M the values of 20, 10 and 22 (more significant results). We obtain 162 clusters.
- **Evaluation protocol.** Our evaluation process is applied within a close interaction with the domain experts. Firstly, we execute the Kmeans algorithm and the three first steps of the CCD algorithm. The obtained results are presented to two domain experts. Indi-

vidually, each of them evaluates and labels manually the word clusters (318 clusters). Then, they work together in order to discuss about the results, their label propositions and to give us only one evaluation and labelling result about which they agree. After this first evaluation step, we have discussed with them, analysed their results and defined four criteria which are the word distribution, the semantic interpretation, the extracted concepts and the generality degree of the extracted concepts. Secondly, in order to evaluate the impact of the evaluation step of our algorithm, we complete the execution of the CCD algorithm (Step4). Then, we present the results to two other domain experts. They maintain the same evaluation protocol which is a manually one and they provide their results, remarks and conclusions. For us, we have remarked that the second evaluation is easier and faster than the first one. The conclusions of the experts confirm our remarks.

Comparison Between Kmeans and the CCD Algorithm

We start by presenting the four criteria with the first evaluation step. Then, we present the impact of our parameters (P and M) in the results.

Word Distribution: With the Kmeans algorithm, we have 13% of our initial words that are grouped together. While with the CCD algorithm, we obtain only 3.66% of our initial set of words in the same cluster.

Semantic Interpretation: The domain expert notes that there are three types of word clusters which are advisable clusters, improper clusters and unknown clusters. Advisable clusters are those for which the expert is able to associate a label and in which words belonging to the same group are close semantically. Improper clusters are either those with an amount of words having no relation with the principle extracted concept, or those containing more than one concept. Unknown clusters are clusters where words do not have any semantically relation and the expert could not find any semantic interpretation. Thanks to the P and the M values, in each word cluster, the percentage of noisy elements decreases a lot. As a consequence, the percentage of unknown and improper clusters is reduced (respectively 20. 51% and 26. 28% for the kmeans algorithm versus only 14. 81% and 16. 66% for the CCD algorithm). Moreover, we obtain 68.52% advisable clusters with the CCD algorithm which is more important than only 53.2% with the Kmeans one (see Table 2).

Extracted Concepts: We take into account only the advisable clusters in the two cases and we compute the precision. In our study, Precision is the ratio of relevant words having between them a great semantic similarity with the total words for a given cluster. By applying this criterion, we obtain respectively 86.18% and 86.61% with the kmeans algorithm and the CCD one.

Generality Degree of the Extracted Concepts: Another element which affects the concept's quality is the level of generality for a concept. In order to evaluate the generality degree of the concepts, we focus only on concepts extracted from the

Table 2. The detail of the extracted concepts

	Advisable **clusters**	Improper **clusters**	Unknown **clusters**
Kmeans Algorithm	53. 2 %	26. 28 %	20. 51 %
CCD Algorithm	68.52%	16.66%	14.81%

advisable clusters. We based our manual evaluation on the OMT thesaurus (1999). It contains generic and open terms presenting general key domain concepts. In our experiments, we obtain respectively with the kmeans algorithm and the CCD one 78.31% and 85.58% general concepts. Also, we remark that the clusters obtained with the CCD algorithm are more enhanced than with the Kmeans algorithm. For example, we find with the Kmeans algorithm the cluster C1 :{Event, festival, music} while with the CCD one we obtain C2:{Event, festival, music, party}.

The impact of the P parameter and the step 2 of the CCD Algorithm: A first execution of the kmeans algorithm with 20 clusters (step1) gives a cluster having 68.69% of the initial set of words. By defining the P parameter, we decide to divide the word clusters and consequently to perform an intermediate clustering based only on the common attributes of the P words. So, we refine the context of this cluster and we obtain better results thanks to new similarities between the P words. For example, with the kmeans algorithm, we found the word civilization with a big set of words without any relation between them, but with the CCD algorithm, we found it in a cluster where there are words semantically similar like archaeology, ethnology, etc.

The impact of the step 3 of the CCD Algorithm: The CCD algorithm allows assigning these single words to the existing clusters. We remarked that some words are assigned to the appropriate cluster. For example before and after the step 3, we obtain respectively the clusters {Academy, club, golfer} and {Academy, club, golfer, golf}.

We now present the importance of the credibility degree criterion in the evaluation task, especially to facilitate the semantic interpretations of the results by the domain experts.

The Evaluation Step

In this section, we expose the contribution of our evaluation step included in the CCD algorithm.

The impact of the Credibility Degree: Let us take some resulting word cluster in order to explain concretely the credibility degree's importance:

Our Credibility Degree Computation criterion is executed on a set of word clusters in order to compute their credibility degrees. For instance, with the example 1 (Table 3) and according to one context definition (nominal groups or sentence), the algorithm finds all the possible combination in the context i.e. tries to find the four words (academy, golf, golfer, club), then the association of three words and so on. For each found association, it presents the associated words and gives a degree representing how many times this type of association is found. For example, with the same example, it finds two possible associations with three words which are {academy, golf, golfer} and {golf, golfer, club} so the credibility degree is 3_2 i.e. two associations of three words.

Our criterion has several functionalities which are:

- Finding the associations between some words in order to facilitate the labelling step. With Example 5, our criterion finds only the association that permits the user to give a label by him self like 'excursion on foot'.
- Finding at the same time the available association in the context and the concept (Example 2, the concept is 'civilization').
- Detecting the noisy elements in a cluster and either delete them or move them to

Table 3. Examples of term clusters

Examples	Word Clusters
Example 1	academy, golf, golfer, club
Example 2	Civilization, archeology, ethnology, people
Example 3	Park, national, cliff, rock
Example 4	Cult, church, evangelization, memory, religious, sanctuary
Example 5	excursion, foot, person
Example 6	Hiker, gorges

another cluster. For instance, in Example 5, the word 'hiker' is found inside the several association returned by our algorithm and corresponding to 'excursion' and 'foot' but the problem is that this word belongs to the Example 6. Our evaluation process decides to remove it from example 6 and include it into example 5 because no association is found related to the other words of cluster 6. If the words exist in two associations related to two clusters, the CDD algorithm presents the word using the red colour to announce a possible ambiguous situation.

- Enhancing a cluster by other words from the associations. For Example 3, we can enrich the group by the word nature and inheritance and find the concept which is 'natural inheritance'.

Since our evaluation task is based on various context definitions, if the user does not find a connection between some words by using the linguistic contexts, he can analyse the provided association by the documentary contexts in which the probability to find more relation is bigger than with the first context type (Example 4).

Thanks to the credibility degrees computed for each cluster and for each context, the user obtains an amount of information useful and in some cases sufficient to manipulate (delete word, remove word, etc.), evaluate and label the cluster. For example, for a same cluster, if he finds the three credibility degrees (5_1, 4_3, 3_8, 2_{15}) which are a quantitative indications, he starts by analysing the association with 5 words. If it is not sufficient, he analyses the three associations of four words (4_3) and so on. If the information returned by our algorithm to this cluster and for one context is not enough, he can look to the other credibility degrees provided by the other contexts by respecting the previous order (linguistic context type then documentary context one).

So, our web driven concept evaluation method provides two revealing aspects: the qualitative ones based on the word associations deduced from the various contexts and the quantitative ones resulting from the computed credibility degree index. The qualitative evaluation provides a semantic support for an easy user interpretation. Moreover, our proposition, based on a large collection of domain web documents, several context definitions and different granularity degrees, permits to an ordinary user to help the expert by manipulating the word clusters and giving him semantic tags as suggestions. Consequently, the expert should decide on the appropriateness of these labels as well as clusters homogeneities which are not labeled. Moreover, our algorithm assures ontology reuse and evolution since the elements on which the expert's interpretations are based (the provided word associations) depend on the web changes. For example, when the web documents change, the various extracted contexts change too and the results of the mapping operation between the words belonging to the clusters and the contexts are updated. This resulting information about the word clusters is presented to the experts in order to help them during the evaluation task. Then, they are stored with the experts' comments in order to be reused by another expert either during the same period or later (after some months or years depending on the frequency of updates). Also, thanks to our context based hierarchical clustering, the CDD algorithm follows the document changes whether it is at the level of the structure or the content.

Our results are presented to the user in a HTML format (Figure 3).

Discussion

In a previous work, we have compared different clustering algorithms (kohonen, EM, etc.) to kmeans and we have remarked that all of them give as results big clusters. Those clusters contain a lot of noisy words and consequently their evaluation by the expert is very difficult. That is why we have decided to define a new clustering

Figure 3. An extract from the resulting file related to a group nominal context

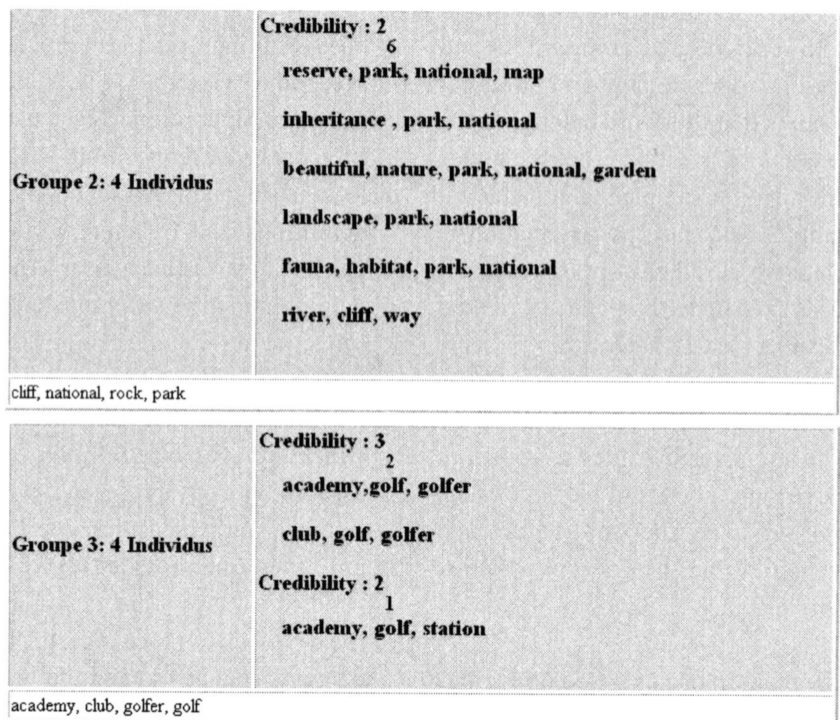

algorithm in order to resolve this problem and compare it, as first experiments, to the kmeans one. In this section, we have shown that the clustering method guided by the structural context definition gives better results than the simple kmeans (with a usual context definition). The generic context is based on a contextual hierarchy constituted by the HTML links. In order to keep our method functional, we should have a minimum structure in the documents. However, the structure analysis adapts the context definition by taking into account most of the used HTML tags. Moreover, the absence of some HTML tags does not affect the functionality of our method. For example, if we do not have the sub title tag <H1>, the method can be applied since it is incremental and searches the word's cooccurrents in other lower levels of the C.H (in the tags <p>, <td>, etc.). In addition, when the tag <title>, which permits to initiate the clustering process and gives future concepts, is not present, we have other HTML key tags which provide information. In this work, we can not use the precision and the recall since we used a collected domain pages which have not pre-clusters. But our architecture [18] provide a pre-treatment component treating the HTML documents, so the hierarchical clustering method named CCD can be applied either in a benchmark related to one specific domain (in this case we can apply the precision and the recall measure since we have classified terms) or a domain collection either collected by the researcher or given by a third party (institution, industry, etc.).

CONCLUSION

It is important to discover and organize the available knowledge about an application domain in a coherent manner. In this paper, we defined a hierarchical clustering algorithm namely Contextual Concept Discovery (CCD), based on an incremental use of the partitioning algorithm Kmeans, guided by a structural contextual definition and providing a web driven evaluation task to support the domain experts. The CCD algorithm proceeds in an incremental manner to refine the context and to improve the conceptual quality of each word cluster. The last functionality of our algorithm is a new evaluation method based on a large web collection and different contexts extracted from it. We implement and experiment the CCD algorithm to incrementally extract the ontological concepts. We show that the context-based hierarchical algorithm gives better results than a usual context definition and an existing clustering method. Moreover, our evaluation process permits to help either an ordinary user (knowledge engineer) or the expert to take the right decision about the semantic homogeneity of a cluster. So, we have defined an algorithm that at the same time extracts the domain concepts, evaluates them and considers their contexts during the two activities. In our research, the CCD algorithm is defined for the ontology building. But, it is important in many other applications like information retrieval, annotation, multi-agent systems, etc. For the information retrieval research, first, discovering knowledge inside the documents is very important. By using our algorithm, we can extract their concepts and evaluate them in order to understand their content. Second, we should refine the user request. The CCD algorithm discovers the domain concepts that can be used to replace the keywords from the requests. For the annotation, we need also discovering concepts from web documents by using our algorithm. As a perspective, we will define and experiment (with the CCD algorithm) a linguistic context and a documentary context combined with the structural one and apply them to words belonging to the HTML tags in order to enhance the set of extracted concepts, obtain more specific concepts and take into account other types of documents such as textual ones. We will develop ideas related to the instance and relation discovery. Also, we are going to pursue the reflection to develop our evaluation method that will be based on some synthetic criteria computed by considering the notion of 'contextualization'.

FUTURE RESEARCH DIRECTIONS

In this chapter, we defined a hierarchical clustering algorithm namely Contextual Concept Discovery (CCD). It is guided by a structural context definition and provides a web driven evaluation. It proceeds in an incremental manner to refine the context and improve the conceptual quality of each word cluster. The last functionality of our algorithm is a new evaluation method based on a large web collection and different contexts extracted from it. We implement and experiment the CCD algorithm to incrementally extract the ontological concepts. We show that the context-based hierarchical algorithm gives better results than a usual context definition and an existing clustering method. Moreover, our evaluation process helps either an ordinary user (knowledge engineer) or the expert to take the right decision about the semantic homogeneity of a cluster. So, we have defined an algorithm that at the same time extracts the domain concepts, evaluates them and considers their contexts during the two activities. In our research, the CCD algorithm is used for the ontology building. But, it is important in many other applications like information retrieval, annotation, multi-agent systems, etc. For the information retrieval research, we need to refine the user request. The CCD algorithm discovers the domain concepts that can be used to replace the keywords from the requests. For the annotation, we also need to locate concepts in web documents by using our algorithm. Recently, we defined an evaluation method based on some synthetic criteria computed by considering the notion of 'contextualization'. In addition, we are working on relation extraction and concept hierarchy evaluation. We are developing an application that visualizes the concept hierarchy and evaluates it either automatically or manually. We now plan to define and experiment (with the CCD algorithm) linguistic, documentary and structural contexts and apply them to other HTML documents. We also will take into account other types of document such as textual ones. Later, we hope to link this work together - concept extraction and evaluation, hierarchy evaluation and visualization and relation extraction - as a unique application useful for the semantic web community. The background of this research is related to the notion of 'context', the ontology learning (that contains the concept extraction) and the ontology evaluation. In the related work, I present some research related to these three subjects. In the readings section, I add more references related to these topics and others such as relation extraction, the use of context in other domains, some measures to extract concepts, etc.

REFERENCES

Brewster, C., Alani, H., Dasmahapatra, S. & Wilks, Y. (2004). Data Driven Ontology Evaluation. *Proceedings of Int. Conf. on Language Resources and Evaluation*, Lisbon.

Brézillon, P. (1999). *Context in problem solving: A survey.* The Knowledge Engineering Review, Volume: 14, Issue: 1, Pages: 1-34.

Brézillon, P. (1993). *Context in Artificial Intelligence: II. Key elements of contexts.* Computer and AI.

Brown, S., Peter, F., Della, P., Vincent, J. & Mercer Robert, L. (1991). Word sense disambiguation using statistical methods. *Proceedings of the 29th Annual Meeting of Association for Computational Linguistics*, Berkeley, California.

Chalendar, G. & Grau, B. (2000). SVETLAN A system to classify nouns in context. *Proceedings of the ECAI 2000 Workshop on Ontology Learning.*

Davulcu, H., Vadrevu, S. & Nagarajan, S. (1998). OntoMiner: Boostrapping ontologies from overlapping domain specific web sites. In AAAI'98/IAAI'98 *Proceedings of the 15th National Conference on Artificial Intelligence* and the *10th Conference on Innovative Applications of Artificial Intelligence.*

Faure, D., Nedellec, C. & Rouveirol, C. (1998). *Acquisition of semantic knowledge uing machine learning methods: the system ASIUM.* Technical report number ICS-TR-88-16, inference and learning group, University of Paris-sud.

Gale, W.A., Church, K.W., & Yarowsky, D. (1992a). Using bilingual materials to develop word sense disambiguation methods. *Proceedings of the International Conference on Theoretical and Methodological Issues in Machine Translation*, 101-112.

Gruber, T.R. (1993). Towards Principles for the Design of Ontologies used for Knowledge sharing. In N. Guarino & R. Poli (Eds), *Formal Ontology in Conceptual Analysis and Knowledge Representation.* Deventer, the Netherlands: Kluwer Academic Publishers.

Han, H. & Elmasri, R (2000). *Architecture of WebOntEx: A system for automatic extraction of ontologies from the Web.* WCM 2000.

Karoui, L., Bennacer, N. & Aufaure, M-A. (2006). Extraction de concepts guidée par le contexte. *XIIème Rencontres de la Société Francophone de Classification SFC'06*, pp 119-123.

Kiyota, Y. & Kurohashi, S. (2001). Automatic summarization of Japanese sentences and its application to a WWW KWIC index. *Proceedings of the 2001 Symposium on applications and the internet*, page 120.

MacQueen, J. (1967). Some methods for classification and analysis of multivariate observations. *Proceedings of 5th Berkeley Symposium on Mathematics, Statistics and Probability*, 1:281- 298, 1967.

Meadche, A. & Staab S. (2001). Ontology learning for the semantic Web. *IEEE Journal on Intelligent Systems*, Vol. 16, No. 2, 72-79.

Meadche, A & Staab, S. (2002). Measuring similarity between ontologies. *Proc. CIKM 2002*. LNAI vol.2473.

Michelet, B. (1988). *L'analyse des associations*. Doctoral thesis, Université de Paris VII, UFR de Chimie, Paris.

Navigli, R., Velardi, P., Cucchiarelli, A. & Neri, F. (2004). Quantitative and qualitative evaluation of the ontolearn ontology learning system. In *Proc. Of ECAI-2004 Workshop on Ontology Learning and Population*, Valencia, Spain.

Navigli, R. & Velardi, P. (1998). Learning domain ontologies from document warehousees and dedicated web sites. In *AAAI'98/IAAI'98 Proceedings of the 15th National Conference on Artificial Intelligence* and the *10th Conference on Innovative Applications of Artificial Intelligence*.

Paslaru Bontas, E. (2005). Using context information to improve ontology reuse. Doctoral Workshop at the *17th Conference on Advanced Information Systems Engineering CAiSE'05*.

Thesauus on tourism and leisure activities (1999). First edition copyright Secretariat of state for tourism of France and World Tourism Organisation.

Padmini, S. (1992). Thesaurus construction. In William B. Frakes & Ricardo Baeza-yates (Eds.), *Information retrieval: data structures and algorithms*, 161-218. New York: Prentice-Hall.

Turney, P. (1996). The management of context-sensitive features: A review of strategies. *Proceedings of the ICML-96 Workshop on Learning in Context-Sensitive Domains*, pp. 53-69.

Vazirgiannis, M., Halkidi, M. & Gunopoulos, D. (2003). *Uncertaintly handling and quality assessmen in data mining*. Springer.

Voorhes, E-M. (1993). Using WordNet to disambiguate word senses for text retrieval. *ACM SIGIR Conference on Research and Development in Information Retrieval*, Pittsburgh, Pennsylvania, 171-180.

Widmer, G. (1996). Recognition and exploitation of contextual clues via incremental meta-learning. *Oesterreichisches Forshungsinstitut fuer artificial intelligence*, Wien, TR-96-01.

Yarowsky, D. (1993). One sense per collocation. *Proceedings of ARPA Human Language Technology Workshop*, Princeton, New Jersey, 266-271.

Yarowsky, D. (1992). Word sense disambiguation using statistical models of Roget's categories trained on large corpora. *Proceedings of the 14th International Conference on Computational Linguistics, COLING'92*, Nantes, France, 454-460.

ADDITIONAL READING

Bastien, C. (1992). The shift between logic and knowledge. *Le courier du CNRS, Numéro Spécial "sciences cognitives"*, No 79, pp.38.

Barwise, J. & Seligman, J. (1992). The rights and wrongs of natural regularity. In J. Tomberlin (ed.), *Philosophical Perspectives 8: Logic and language*. Atascadero, CA: Ridgeview.

Berland, M. & Charniak, E. (1999). Finding parts in very large corpora. In *Proc. of the 37th Annual Meeting of the Association for Computational Linguistics*.

Bruandet, M.F. (1990). Domain Knowledge Acquisition for an Intelligent Information Retrieval System : Strategies and Tools. In *Expert Systems Applications EXPERSYS - 90*, Grenoble, pp231-235.

Buitelaar, P., Olejnik, D. & Sintek, M. (2004). *A protege plug-in for ontology extraction from text based on linguistic analysis*. ESWS.

Buyukkokten, O., Garcia-Molina, H. & Paepcke, A. (2001). Accordion summarization for end-game browsing on PDAs and Cellular Phones. In *Proc. Of Conference on Human Factors in Computing Systems (CHI01)*.

Cai, D., Yu, S., Wen, J. & Ma, W. (2004). Block-based web search. *Proceedings of the 27 Annual International ACM SIGIR Conference on Research and Development in Information Retrieval*, pages 456-463.

Cilibrasi, R. & Vitanyi, P. (2006). Automatic Extraction of Meaning from the Web. *The IEEE International Symposium on Information Theory*, Seattle, WA.

Cimiano, P. & Volker, J. (2005). *Towards large-scale, open-domain and ontology-based named entity classification*. RANLP.

Claveau, V., Sebbillot, P., Fabre, C.& Bouillon, P. (2003). Learning Semantic Lexicons from a Part-of-Speech and Semantically Tagged Corpus using Inductive Logic Programming. *Journal of Machine Learning Research, special issue on ILP*.

Compton, P. & Jansen R. (1988). Knowledge in context: a strategy for expert system maintenance. In J.Siekmann (Ed), *Lecture Notes in Artificial Intelligence, Subseries in computer sciences*, Vol. 406.

Gamallo, P., Gonzalez, M., Agustini, A., Lopes, G. & de Lima, V. S. (2002). Mapping syntactic dependencies onto semantic relations. *ECAI Workshop on Machine Learning and Natural Language Processing for Ontology Engineering*, Lyon, France.

Girju, R., Badulescu, A. & Moldovan, D. (2003). Learning semantic constraints for the automatic discovery of part-whole relations. In *Proc. of the HLT- NAACL*.

Goh, C.H., Madnick, S.E. & Siegel, M.D (1994). Context interchange: overcoming the challenge of large-scale interoperable database systems in a dynamic environment. In *proceedings of the third international conference on information and knowledge management*, Gaithersburg (USA), pp. 337-346.

Grefenstette, G. (1992). Use of syntatic context to produce terms association list for text retrieval. In *Conference in Researche and Developement in Information Retrieval (SIGIR'92)*, Copenhagen, Denmarke, pages 89-97.

Guarino, N. (1998). Formal Ontologies and Information Systems. *FOIS'98*. Trento, Italy: IOS Press.

Haddad, M-H. (2002). *Extraction et impact des connaissances sur les performances des systèmes de recherche d'information*. Doctoral thesis, université joseph Fourier.

Hearst, M-A. (1992). Automatic acquisition of hyponyms from large text corpora. In *proceedings of the fourteenth international conference on computational linguistics*, Nantes, France, pages 539-545.

Holsapple, C. & Joshi, K.D. (2005). A collaborative approach to ontology design. *Communications of ACM*, Vol. 45(2) pp. 42-47.

Iria, J. & Ciravegna, F. (2005). Relation Extraction for Mining the Semantic Web. *Dagstuhl Seminar on Machine Learning for the Semantic Web*, Dagstuhl, Germany.

Karoui, L. & El Khadi, N. (2007). Relation Extraction and Validation Algorithm. *4th International Conference on Distributed Computing and Internet Technology*, LNCS volume 3347.

Karoui, L. (2006). Intelligent Ontology Learning based on Context: Answering Crucial Questions.

The IEEE International Conference on Computational Intelligence for Modelling, Control and Automation - CIMCA06, Sydney.

Karoui, L. & Aufaure, M-A (2007). Revealing Criteria for the Ontology Evaluation Task. *Special Issue of Journal of Internet Technology (JIT) on Ontology Technology and Its Applications.*

Karoui, L., Aufaure, M-A. & Bennacer, N. (2007). Analyses and Fundamental ideas for a Relation Extraction Approach. *The IEEE proceedings of the Workshop on Data Mining and Business Intelligence in conjunction with the IEEE 23rd International Conference on Data Engineering (ICDE'07)*, Turkey.

Loh, S., Wives, L. & Oliveira, J.P. (2000). Concept-based knowledge discovery in texts extracted from the web. In *SIGKDD Explorations*. Volume 2, Issue 1, Page 29.

Magnini, B., Negri, M., Pianta, E., Romano, L., Speranza, M. & Sprugnoli, R. (2005). From Text to Knowledge for the Semantic Web: the ONTOTEXT Project. *SWAP 2005, Semantic Web Applications and Perspectives*, Trento.

McCarthy, J. (1993). Notes on formalization context. *Proceedings of the 13th IJCAI*, Vol. 1, pp. 555-560.

McDonald, R., Pereira, F., Kulick, S., Winters, S., Jin, Y. & White, P. (2005). Simple Algorithms for Complex Relation Extraction with Applications to Biomedical IE. *43rd Annual Meeting of the Association for Computational Linguistics (ACL-2005)*, Ann Arbour, Michigan, pp. 491-498.

Maedche, A. (2002). *Ontology Learning for the Semantic Web.* Kluwer Academic Publishers, Norwell, MA.

Meadche, A. & Staab, S. (2001). Ontology learning for the semantic Web. *The IEEE Journal on Intelligent Systems*, Vol. 16, No. 2, pp. 72-79.

Meadche, A. & Staab, S. (2002). Measuring similarity between ontologies. *Proc. CIKM 2002.* LNAI vol.2473.

Maedche, A. & Staab, S. (2000). *Discovering conceptual relations from text.* ECAI.

Mittal, V.O & Paris, C.L. (1995). Use of context in explanations systems. *International Journal of Expert Systems with Applications*, Vol.8 No. 4, pp. 491-504.

Morin, E. (1999). Using Lexico-Syntactic Patterns to Extract Semantic Relations between Terms from Technical Corpus. In *Proceedings, 5th International Congress on Terminology and Knowledge Engineering (TKE)*, 268–278. TermNet, Innsbruck, Austria.

Nakache, J.P. & Confais, J. (2005). *Approche pragmatique de la classification : arbres hiérarchiques, partitionnements.* Editions Technip, Paris.

Nazarenko, A. (1994). *Compréhension du langage naturel : le problème de la causalité.* Doctoral thesis.

Reinberger, M.L., Spyns, P. & Pretorius, A.J. (2004). Automatic initiation of an ontology. *On the Move to Meaningful Internet Systems 2004: CoopIS, DOA, and ODBASE*, LNCS 3290, Napa, Cyprus, pp. 600-617.

Sabou, M. (2004). Extracting ontologies from software documentation: a semi-automatic method and its evaluation. *In Proceedings of the ECAI-2004 Workshop on Ontology Learning and Population (ECAI-OLP).*

Schutz, A. & Buitelaar, P. (2005). RelExt: A Tool for Relation Extraction from Text in Ontology Extension. *4th International Semantic Web Conference (ISWC-2005)*, Galway, pp. 593-606.

Schmid, H. (1994). *Probabilistic Part-of-Speech Tagging Using Decision Trees.* IMS-CL, Institut Für maschinelle Sprachverarbeitung, Universität Stuttgart, Germany.

Soderland, S. (1999). *Learning information extraction rules for semi-structured and free text.* Machine Learning.

Soo-Guan Khoo, C. (1995). *Automatic identification of causale relations in text and their use for improving precision in information retrieval.* PhD thesis.

Sciore, E., Siegel, M. & Rosenthal, A. (1992). Context interchange using meta-attributes. *Proceedings of the 1st International Conference in Information and knowledge Management*, pp. 377-386.

Smith, B. (2003). Ontology. In L. Floridi (ed.), *Blackwell Guide to the Philosophy of Computing and Information.* Oxford: Blackwell, pp. 155–166.

Spyns, P. (2005). *Evalexon: Assessing triples minedfrom texts.* Technical report 09, STAR Lab, Brussels, Belgium.

Van. Rijsbergen, C.J. (1979). *Information Retrieval.* London: Butterworths.

Robison, H.R. (1970). Computer detectable semantic structures. *Information Storage and Retrieval, 6*, 273-288.

Walther, E., Eriksson, H. & Musen, M.A. (1992). Plug-and-play: Construction of task-specific expert-system shells using sharable context ontologies. *Proceedings of the AAAI Workshop on knowledge Representation Aspects of Knowledge Acquisition*, San Jose, CA, pp. 191-198.

Yangarber, R., Grishman, R. & Tapanainen, P. (2000). Unsupervised Discovery of Scenario-Level Patterns for Information Extraction. *6th ANLP*, Seattle, pp. 282-289.

Stevenson, M. & Greenwood, M. (2005). A Semantic Approach to IE Pattern Induction. *43rd Meeting of the Association for Computational Linguistics (ACL-05)*, Ann Arbour, Michigan, p. 379-386.

Chapter II
A Review of Fuzzy Models for the Semantic Web

Hailong Wang
Northeastern University, China

Zongmin Ma
Northeastern University, China

Li Yan
Northeastern University, China

Jingwei Cheng
Northeastern University, China

ABSTRACT

In the Semantic Web context, information would be retrieved, processed, shared, reused and aligned in the maximum automatic way possible. Our experience with such applications in the Semantic Web has shown that these are rarely a matter of true or false but rather procedures that require degrees of relatedness, similarity, or ranking. Apart from the wealth of applications that are inherently imprecise, information itself is many times imprecise or vague. In order to be able to represent and reason with such type of information in the Semantic Web, different general approaches for extending semantic web languages with the ability to represent imprecision and uncertainty has been explored. In this chapter, we focus our attention on fuzzy extension approaches which are based on fuzzy set theory. We review the existing proposals for extending the theoretical counterpart of the semantic web languages, description logics (DLs), and the languages themselves. The following statements will include the expressive power of the fuzzy DLs formalism and its syntax and semantic, knowledge base, the decidability of the tableaux algorithm and its computational complexity etc. Also the fuzzy extension to OWL is discussed in this chapter.

INTRODUCTION

The Semantic Web is an extension of the current web in which the web information can be given well-defined semantic meaning, and thus enabling better cooperation between computers and people. From this point of view, we should find some methods which can describe the semantic meaning of the web. Fortunately, "ontology" can do this. The core of the Semantic Web is "ontology" which refers to a set of vocabulary to describe the conceptualization of a particular domain. Over the past few years, several ontology definition languages for the Semantic Web have emerged, including RDF(S), OIL, DAML, DAML+OIL, and OWL. Among them, OWL is the newly released standard recommended by W3C. As the Semantic Web expects, OWL has the reasoning nature because description logics (*DLs*) (Baader, 2003) are essentially the theoretical counterpart of OWL and play a crucial role in this context. *DLs* provide a logical reconstruction of object-centric and frame-based knowledge representation languages. It is a subset of first-order logic that provides sound and decidable reasoning support (Baader, 2003).

It is clear that *DLs* play a key role in the Semantic Web. As with traditional crisp logic, any sentence in OWL, being asserted facts, domain knowledge, or reasoning results, must be either true or false and nothing in between. However, most real world domains contain uncertainty knowledge and incomplete or imprecise information that is true only to a certain degree. Ontologies defined by these languages thus cannot quantify the degree of the overlap or inclusion between two concepts, and cannot support reasoning in which only partial information about a concept or individual in the domain can be obtained. Uncertainty becomes more prevalent when more than on ontologies are involved where it is often the case that a concept defined in on ontology can only find partial matches to one or more concepts in another ontology. To overcome the difficulty arising from the crisp logics, existing ontology languages need to be extended to be able to capture uncertainty knowledge about the concepts, properties and instances in the domain and to support reasoning with partial, imprecise information. Along this direction, researchers in the past have attempted to apply different formalisms such as Fuzzy logic (Zadeh, 1965), Rough set theory and Bayesian probability as well as ad hoc heuristics into ontology definition and reasoning.

In this chapter, we review existing proposals to extend semantic web languages with the capability to handle uncertain information to better deal with the situations mentioned above. There are many ways of representing and dealing with uncertainty. In this chapter, we restrict our attention to approaches that use fuzzy methods for representing uncertain information. In particular, we will not cover recent proposals for probabilistic extensions of semantic web languages. We will also not discuss non-monotonic and non-standard logics for representing uncertainty. As described above, existing Semantic Web languages are mainly based on logic and do not support representing imprecise and uncertain information. In this chapter, we therefore review a number of proposals for extending logical languages with fuzzy extensions in more details. We focused on:

1. Approaches that extend description logics which play as the theoretical counterpart of the semantic web languages.
2. Approaches that directly extend semantic web languages, in particular OWL.

In the first category, we cover fuzzy extensions of description logics which are commonly accepted as being the formal basis of OWL. Even though most approaches only cover logics that are much weaker than OWL, the methods proposed can directly be applied to the corresponding subset of OWL without changes because the description logics play as the theory counterpart of the OWL. When talking about the different approaches, we will survey them according to the expressive power from weaker to stronger. And in the following survey, we should discuss the following issues of the different approaches:

- Expressiveness of the logical language
- The syntax and semantic of the fuzzy extension to description logics
- The components of the knowledge base
- Tableaux algorithm for the description logics
- The decidability and complexity of the tableaux algorithm

Indeed, the balance of expressive power and the computability of the fuzzy extension of description logics is a hot topic of the research. Generally speaking, the more expressive of the description logic, the higher computational complexity of it, so we should consider the balance of the two factors in a real application. At last, in the latter category, we also review a number of proposals for extending the ontology description language OWL.

The chapter is structured as follows. We first present some background information on semantic web languages and related formalisms that are the basis for the logical languages used in the different approaches discussed later in the chapter. We also provide a brief introduction to fuzzy set theory which the fuzzy description logics are based on. In the mainly part of this chapter, we survey the different approaches to extend the description logics to represent the imprecise and uncertainty information according their expressive power. We also discuss proposals for fuzzy languages OWL for the semantic web. Finally, we conclude with a critical review of the state of the art and an analysis of directions for future research.

PRELIMINARIES AND BACKGROUND

Description Logics

In the last decade a substantial amount of work has been carried out in the context of Description Logics. *DLs* are a logical reconstruction of the so-called frame-based knowledge representation languages, with the aim of providing a simple well-established Tarski-style declarative semantics to capture the meaning of the most popular features of structured representation of knowledge. Nowadays, *DLs* have gained even more popularity due to their application in the context of the Semantic Web (Berners-Lee, 2001).

The recent research about description logics can be divided into three categories:

- Introducing the theoretical foundations of description logics, addressing some of the most recent developments in theoretical research in the area;
- Focusing on the implementation of knowledge representation systems based on Descriptions Logics, describing the basic functionality of a *DL* system, surveying the most influential knowledge representation systems based on descriptions, and addressing specialized implementation techniques;
- Addressing the use of description logics and of *DL*-based systems in the design of several applications of practical interest.

In the following statements, we mainly focus on the first category, especially the theoretical formalism of the description logics, with respect to the balance between its expressive power and its computational complexity. Indeed, subsequent results on the tradeoff between the expressiveness of a *DL* language and the complexity of reasoning with it, and more generally, the identification of the sources of complexity in *DL* systems, showed that a careful selection of language constructs was needed and that the reasoning services provided by the system are deeply influenced by the set of constructs provided to the user. We can thus characterize three different approaches to the implementation of reasoning services. The first can be referred to as *limited + complete*, and includes systems that are designed by restricting the set of constructs in such a way that subsumption would be computed efficiently, possibly in polynomial time. The second approach can be denoted as *expressive + incomplete*, since the idea is to provide both an expressive language and efficient reasoning. The drawback is, however, that reasoning algorithms turn out to be incomplete in these systems. After some of the sources of incompleteness were discovered, often by identifying the constructs—or, more precisely, combinations of constructs—that would require an exponential algorithm to preserve the completeness of reasoning, systems with complete reasoning algorithms were designed. Systems of this sort are therefore characterized as *expressive + complete*; they were not as efficient as those following the other approaches, but they provided a test bed for the implementation of reasoning techniques developed in the theoretical investigations, and they played an important role in stimulating comparison and benchmarking with other systems.

Now, we survey the languages of the description logics according to their expressive power with the beginning of *AL*. Elementary descriptions are atomic concepts and atomic roles (also called concept names and role names). Complex descriptions can be built from them inductively with concept constructors and role constructors. In abstract notation, we use the letters *A* and *B* for atomic concepts, the letter *R* for atomic roles, and the letters *C* and *D* for concept descriptions. Description languages are distinguished by the constructors they provide. In the sequel we shall discuss various languages from the family of *AL*-languages. The language *AL* (= attributive language) has been introduced as a minimal language that is of practical interest. The other languages of this family are extensions of *AL*.

The Basic Description Logic AL

Concept descriptions in *AL* are formed according to the following syntax rule:

$C, D ::= \top \mid$	(universal concept)
$\bot \mid$	(bottom concept)
$A \mid$	(atomic concept)
$C \sqcap D \mid$	(intersection)
$\forall R\,.\,C$	(value restriction)
$\exists R.\bot \mid$	(limited existential quantification)

In *AL*, negation can only be applied to atomic concepts, and only the top concept is allowed in the scope of an existential quantification over a role. In order to define a formal semantics of *AL*-concepts, we consider interpretations *I* that consist of a non-empty set Δ^I (the domain of the interpretation) and an interpretation function $\bullet^I$, which assigns to every atomic concept *A* a set $A^I \subseteq \Delta^I$ and to every atomic role *R* a binary relation $R^I \subseteq \Delta^I \times \Delta^I$. The interpretation function is extended to concept descriptions by the following inductive definitions:

$\top^I = \Delta^I$
$\bot^I = \Phi$
$(\neg A)^I = \Delta^I \setminus A^I$
$(C \sqcap D)^I = C^I \cap D^I$
$(\forall R\,.C)^I = \{a \in \Delta^I \mid \forall b.\ (a, b) \in R^I \rightarrow b \in C^I\}$
$(\exists R\,.\square)^I = \{a \in \Delta^I \mid \exists b.\ (a, b) \in R^I\}$

We say that two concepts *C*, *D* are equivalent, and write $C \equiv D$, if $C^I = D^I$ for all interpretations *I*.

The Family of AL-Languages

We obtain more expressive languages if we add further constructors to *AL*. The *union* of concepts (indicated by the letter U) is written as $C \sqcup D$, and interpreted as:

$(C \sqcup D)^I = C^I \cup D^I$:

Full existential quantification (indicated by the letter E) is written as $\exists R.C$, and interpreted as:

$(\exists R.C)^I = \{a \in \Delta^I \mid \exists b.\ (a, b) \in R^I \wedge b \in C^I\}$

Note that $\exists R.C$ differs from $\exists R.\bot$ in that arbitrary concepts are allowed to occur in the scope of the existential quantifier.

Number restrictions (indicated by the letter N) are written as $\geq nR$ (at-least restriction) and as $\leq nR$ (at-most restriction), where n ranges over the nonnegative integers. They are interpreted as:

$(\geq nR)^I = \{a \in \Delta^I \mid |\{b \mid (a, b) \in R^I\}| \geq n\}$

and

$(\leq nR)^I = \{a \in \Delta^I \mid |\{b \mid (a, b) \in R^I\}| \leq n\}$

respectively, where"|•|"denotes the cardinality of a set. From a semantic view point, the coding of numbers in number restrictions is immaterial. However, for the complexity analysis of inferences it can matter whether a number n is represented in binary (or decimal) notation or by a string of length n, since binary (decimal) notation allows for a more compact representation.

The *negation* of arbitrary concepts (indicated by the letter *C*, for "complement") is written as $\neg C$, and interpreted as:

$(\neg C)^I = \Delta^I \setminus C^I$

Extending *AL* by any subset of the above constructors yields a particular *AL*-language. We name each *AL*-language by a string of the form:

AL[U][E][N][C]

where a letter in the name stands for the presence of the corresponding constructor. For instance, *ALEN* is the extension of *AL* by full existential quantification and number restrictions.

The More Expressive Description Logics

There are several possibilities for extending *AL* in order to obtain a more expressive *DL*. The three most prominent are adding additional concept constructors, adding role constructors, and formulating restrictions on role interpretations. Below, we start with the third possibility, since we need to refer to restrictions on roles when defining certain concept constructors. For these extensions, we also introduce a naming scheme. Basically, each extension is assigned a letter or symbol. For concept constructors, the letters/symbols are written after the starting *AL*, for role constructors, we write the letters/symbols as superscripts, and for restrictions on the interpretation of roles as subscripts. As an example, the *DL* $ALCQ^{-1}{}_{R+}$, extends *AL* with the concept constructors negation (*C*) and qualified number restrictions (*Q*), the role constructor inverse ($^{-1}$), and the restriction that some roles are transitive($_{R+}$).

Restrictions on Role Interpretations

These restrictions enforce the interpretations of roles to satisfy certain properties, such as functionality and transitivity. We consider these two prominent examples in more detail. Others would be symmetry or connections between different roles.

i. *Functional roles.* Here one considers a subset N_F of the set of role names N_R, whose elements are called *features*. An interpretation must map features *f* to functional binary relations $f^I \subseteq \Delta^I \times \Delta^I$. *AL* extended with features is denoted by AL_f.

ii. *Transitive roles.* Here one considers a subset N_{R+} of N_R. Role names $R \in N_{R+}$ are called *transitive roles.* An interpretation must map transitive roles $R \in N_{R+}$ to transitive binary relations $R^I \subseteq \Delta^I \times \Delta^I$. *AL* extended with transitive roles is denoted by AL_{R+}.

All the *DL*s mentioned until now contain the concept constructors intersection and value restriction as a common core. *DL*s that allow for intersection of concepts and existential quantification (but not value restriction) are collected in the *EL*-family. The only constructors available in *EL* are intersection of concepts and existential quantification. Extensions of *EL* are again obtained by adding appropriate letters/symbols. In order to avoid very long names for expressive *DL*s, the abbreviation *S* was introduced for ALC_{R+}, i.e., the *DL* that extends *ALC* by transitive roles. Prominent members of the *S*-family are *SIN* (which extends ALC_{R+} with number restrictions and inverse roles), *SHIF* (which extends ALC_{R+} with role hierarchies, inverse roles, and number restrictions of the form $\leq 1R$), and *SHIQ* (which extends ALC_{R+} with role hierarchies, inverse roles, and qualified number restrictions). Actually, the *DL*s *SIN*, *SHIF*, and *SHIQ* are somewhat less expressive than indicated by their name since the use of roles in number restrictions is restricted: roles that have a transitive sub-role must not occur in number restrictions.

Description Logics with Data Type Representation

A drawback that all *DL*s introduced until now share is that all the knowledge must be represented on the abstract logical level. In many applications, one would like to be able to refer to concrete domains and predefined predicates on these domains when defining concepts. To solve the problem, Baader and Hanschke prompt two extensions (Hanschke, 1992; Haarslev et al., 1999). In the two papers, the definition of *concrete domain* is given and a tableau-based algorithm for deciding consistency of *ALC*(*D*)-ABoxes for admissible *D* was introduced in (Baader & Hanschke, 1991). The algorithm has an additional rule that treats existential predicate restrictions according to their semantics. The main new feature is that, in addition to the usual "abstract" clashes, there may be concrete ones, that is, one must test whether the given combination of concrete predicate assertions is non-contradictory. This is the reason why we must require that the satisfiability problem for *D* is decidable. As described in (Baader and Hanschke, 1991), the algorithm is not in PSpace. Using techniques similar to the ones employed for *ALC* it can be shown, however, that the algorithm can be modified such that it needs only polynomial space (Lutz, 1999), provided that the satisfiability procedure for *D* is in PSpace. In the presence of acyclic TBoxes, reasoning in *ALC*(*D*) may become NExpTime-hard even for rather simple concrete domains with a polynomial satisfiability problem (Lutz, 2001).

The more expressive description logics *SHOQ*(*D*) which can represent data information is proposed in (Horrocks, 2001). Although *SHOQ*(*D*) is rather expressive, it has a very serious limitation on data types; that is, it does not support customised data types. It has been pointed out that many potential users will not adopt it unless this limitation is overcome. Pan and Horrocks release a series of papers about data types to solve the problem, in (Pan & Horrocks, 2006; Pan, 2007). In the two papers, they summarize the limitations of OWL datatyping and propose the data type approach. For example, the *SHIQ*(*G*) and *SHOQ*(*G*) *DL*s presented in (Pan & Horrocks, 2006; Pan, 2007) can support user-defined data type and user-defined data type predicates.

Fuzzy Set Theory

Fuzzy data is originally described as fuzzy set (Zadeh, 1965). Let *U* be a universe of discourse, then a fuzzy value on *U* is characterized by a fuzzy set F in U. A membership function μ_F: $U \rightarrow [0, 1]$ is defined for the fuzzy set F, where $\mu_F(u)$, for each $u \in U$, denotes the degree of membership of u in the fuzzy set F. Thus the fuzzy set F is described as follows:

$$F = \{\mu_F(u_1)/u_1, \mu_F(u_2)/u_2, ..., \mu_F(u_n)/u_n\}$$

When the $\mu_F(u)$ above is explained to be a measure of the possibility that a variable X has the value u in this approach, where X takes values in U, a fuzzy value is described by a possibility distribution π_X. Let π_X and F be the possibility distribution representation and the fuzzy set representation for a fuzzy value, respectively. In the fuzzy set theory, each object $u_i \in U$ is assigned a single value between 0 and 1, called the degree of membership, where U is a universe of discourse.

Fuzzy set theory is the theory basis for fuzzy extensions to description logics to represent imprecise and uncertain information.

FUZZY EXTENSIONS OF SEMANTIC WEB LANGUAGES

Extensions of Description Logics

Much work has been carried out towards combining fuzzy logic and description logics during the last decade. The initial idea was presented by Yen in (Yen, 1991), where a structural subsumption algorithm was provided in order to perform reasoning. The following statements will illustrate all the fuzzy extensions to *DL*s from weaker to stronger in expressive power.

The Family of FALC Languages

ALC is the basic format of the description logics. Reasoning in fuzzy *ALC* was latter presented in (Straccia, 2001), as well as in other approaches (Straccia, 1998), where an additional concept constructor, called membership manipulator was included in the extended language. In all these approaches tableaux decision procedures were presented for performing reasoning services. The operations used to interpret the concept constructors in all these approaches were the same ones as in our context. (Tresp & Molitor, 1998) contains complete algorithms for solving these inference problems in the respective fuzzy extension of *ALC*. Although both algorithms are extensions of the usual tableau-based algorithm for ALC, they differ considerably. For example, the algorithm in (Tresp & Molitor, 1998) introduces numerical variables for the degrees, and produces a linear optimization problem, which must be solved in place of the usual clash test. In contrast, (Straccia, 2001) deals with the membership degrees within his tableau-based algorithm.

The Fuzzy Description Logic *FALC*

Definition. Let N_I , N_C and N_R be three disjoint sets: N_I is a set of individual names, N_C is a set of fuzzy concept names and N_R is a set of fuzzy role names. Fuzzy *ALC*-concepts are defined as:

$$C, D ::= \bot | \top | A | \neg C | C \cup D | C \cap D | \exists R.C | \forall R.C;$$

Here $A \in N_C$, $R \in N_R$. Fuzzy *ALC* semantics is defined by a fuzzy interpretation $I = <\Delta^I, \cdot^I>$, Here Δ^I is a nonempty set and $\cdot^I$ is an function which maps every $a \in N_I$ to an element $a^I \in \Delta^I$, maps every $A \in N_C$ into a function $A^I : \Delta^I \rightarrow [0, 1]$, and maps every $R \in N_R$ into a function $R^I : \Delta^I \times \Delta^I \rightarrow [0, 1]$.

Furthermore, for any fuzzy *ALC*-concepts C and D, $R \in N_R$ and $x \in \Delta^I$, we have:

$\top^I(x) = 1;$
$\bot^I(x) = 0;$
$(\neg C)^I(x) = 1 - C^I(x);$
$(C \cap D)^I(x) = C^I(x) \wedge D^I(x);$
$(C \cup D)^I(x) = C^I(x) \vee D^I(x));$
$(\exists R.C)^I(x) = sup_{y \in \Delta I} \{min (R^I(x, y), C^I(y))\};$
$(\forall R.C)^I(x) = inf_{y \in \Delta I} \{max (1 - R^I(x, y), C^I(y))\};$

With the introduction of the fuzzy sets into the classical *ALC*, the form of the knowledge base is changed accordingly.

Definition. A fuzzy *ALC* knowledge base is composed of a TBox and an ABox:

- A TBox is a finite set of terminology axioms of the form $C \subseteq D$. Any interpretation *I* satisfies $C \subseteq D$ iff for any $x \in \Delta^I$, $C^I(x) \leq D^I(x)$. *I* is a model of TBox *T* iff *I* satisfies all axioms in *T*.
- An ABox is a finite set of assertions of the form $< \alpha \bowtie n >$, Here $\bowtie \in \{>, \geq, <, \leq\}$, $n \in [0, 1]$, α (called a fuzzy assertion) is either of the form a: *C* or (*a*, *b*): $R(a,b \in N_I)$. Especially, in order to giving a uniform format of the ABox, we define: when n=1, the form $<\alpha \geq 1>$ is equivalent to $<\alpha=1>$. Concretely speaking, $<a: C \geq 1>$ means that a is determinately an individual of *C*; $<(a, b): R \geq 1>$ means that (*a*, *b*) determinately has the relationship *R*. Any interpretation *I* satisfies $<a:C \bowtie n>$ iff $C^I(a^I) \bowtie n$ and satisfies $<(a, b): R \bowtie n >$ iff $R^I(a^I, b^I) \bowtie n$. Then *I* is a model of ABox *A* iff *I* satisfies all assertions in *A*.

Reasoning algorithms for *FALC* and their proofs can be found in (Straccia, 2001). It can be seen from syntax and semantics presented above that the entailment and subsumption relationships may hold to some degree in the interval [0, 1]. Complete algorithms for reasoning in *FALC* have been presented, that is, we have devised algorithms for solving the entailment problem, the subsumption problem as well as the best truth-value bound problem. The complexity result shows that the additional expressive power has no impact from a computational complexity point of view.

The Fuzzy Description Logic ALC_{FM}

The *DL* language used was a sub-language of the basic *DL ALC*. The main idea underlying the fuzzy extensions of description logics proposed in (Tresp & Molitor, 1998) is to leave the syntax as it is, but to use fuzzy logic for defining the semantics. Thus, an interpretation now assigns fuzzy sets to concepts and roles, i.e., concept names *A* are interpreted by membership degree functions of the form A^I: $\Delta^I \rightarrow [0, 1]$, and role names *R* by membership degree functions of the form R^I: $\Delta^I \times \Delta^I \rightarrow [0, 1]$. The interpretation of the Boolean operators and the quantifiers must then be extended from {0, 1} to the interval [0, 1].

Tresp & Molitor (1998) also propose an extension of the syntax by so-called manipulators, which are unary operators that can be applied to concepts. Examples of manipulators could be "*mostly*", "*more or less*", or "*very*". For example, if *Tall* is a concept (standing for the fuzzy set of all tall persons), then *VeryTall*, which is obtained by applying the manipulator *Very* to the concept *Tall*, is a new concept (standing for the fuzzy set of all *very tall* persons). Intuitively, the manipulators modify the membership degree functions of the concepts they are applied to appropriately. In our example, the membership function for *VeryTall* should have its largest values at larger heights than the membership function for *Tall*. Formally, the semantics of manipulators is defined by a function that maps membership degree functions to membership degree functions. The manipulators considered in (Tresp & Molitor, 1998) are, however, of a very restricted form. Lets us now consider what kind of inference problems are of interest in this context. (Yen, 1991) considers crisp subsumption of fuzzy concepts, i.e., given two concepts *C*, *D* defined in the fuzzy *DL*, he is interested in the question whether $C^I(d) \leq D^I(d)$ for all fuzzy interpretations *I* and $d \in \Delta^I$. Thus, the subsumption relationship itself is not fuzzified. He describes a structural subsumption algorithm for a rather small fuzzy *DL*, which is almost identical to the subsumption algorithm for the corresponding classical *DL*. In contrast, (Tresp & Molitor, 1998) are interested in determining fuzzy subsumption between fuzzy concepts, i.e., given concepts *C*, *D*, they want to know to which degree *C* is a subset of *D*. In (Tresp & Molitor, 1998), also ABoxes are considered, where the ABox assertions are equipped with a degree.

Fuzzy Description Logics with Hedges and Modifiers

Reasoning in fuzzy *ALC* was also presented in other approaches (Hölldobler, 2002; 2003; 2004; 2005; 2006), where an additional concept constructor, called membership manipulator was included in the extended language. In all these approaches tableaux decision procedures were presented for performing reasoning services. (Hölldobler, 2002) presents a fuzzy description logic ALC_{FH}, where primitive concepts are modified by means of hedges. ALC_{FH} is strictly more expressive than Fuzzy *ALC* defined in (Straccia, 2001). The paper shows that given a linearly ordered set of hedges primitive concepts can be modified to any desired degree by prefixing them with appropriate chains of hedges. Furthermore, it defines a decision procedure for the unsatisfiability problem in ALC_{FH}, and discusses truth bounds, expressivity as well as complexity issues.

Strictly speaking, the language defined by (Tresp & Molitor, 1998) is more expressive, as we do not consider concept modifiers. From a semantics point of view, the extension to Tresp and Molitor's language is quite straightforward. But, the cost that we have to pay for this increasing expressive power is that, from a computational complexity and algorithms point of view, things changes radically. The fuzzy extension to *ALC* can be used as a basis both for extending existing *DL* based systems and for further research. In this latter case, there are several open points. For instance, it is not clear yet how to reason both in case of fuzzy specialisation of the general form $C \sqsubseteq D$ and in the case cycles are allowed in a fuzzy KB. Another interesting topic for further research concerns the semantics of fuzzy connectives. While for a huge number of proposals given in the literature their impact from a semantics point of view is well understood, the question how they impact from a computational complexity and algorithms point of view remains still open.

According to the above statements, the family of fuzzy *ALC* description logics can be summaried in Table 1.

The More Expressive Fuzzy Description Logics

However, *FALC* offers limited expressive power of complex fuzzy information. Some discussions about reducing *FALC* into classical *ALC* and providing a tableau for *FALC* with General Concept Inclusions (GCIs) were given in (Straccia, 2004a) and (Stoilos, 2006c), respectively. In (Stoilos, 2006c), fuzzy description logics have been proposed as a language to describe structured knowledge with vague concepts. A major theoretical and computational limitation so far is the inability to deal with General Concept Inclusions (GCIs), which is an important feature of classical *DLs*. It addresses this issue and develops a calculus for fuzzy *DLs* with GCIs. (Meghini *et*

Table 1. The family of FALC languages

Fuzzy description logics	Corresponding references	Mainly discussed issues
FALC	(Straccia, 1998; 2001)	Syntax,semantics, properties and reasoning services
ALC_{FM}	(Tresp and Molitor, 1998)	Syntax,semantics and a mothod for computing the degree of subsumption
ALC_{FH}	(Hölldobler, 2002; 2003; 2004; 2005; 2006)	Syntax,semantics and reasoning services
ALC_{FL}	(Dinh-Khac, 2006)	Syntax,semantics and reasoning services

al. 1998) proposed a preliminary fuzzy *DL*, which lacks reasoning algorithm, as a modeling tool for multimedia document retrieval.

In the following statements, we survey the different formalisms of the description logics according to the concept constructors or role restrictions that have been constraint on them.

Fuzzy Description Logics with Number Restrictions

Approaches towards more expressive *DL*s, are presented in (Sánchez, D, 2004), where the *DL* is $ALCQ_F^+$. It includes fuzzy quantifiers, which is a new novel idea for fuzzy *DL*s. Unfortunately, in the approach only the semantics of the extended languages are provided and no reasoning algorithms. But in (Sánchez, D, 2006), it introduces reasoning procedures for $ALCQ_F^+$, the fuzzy description logic with extended qualified quantification. The language allows for the definition of fuzzy quantifiers of the absolute and relative kind by means of piecewise linear functions on N and Q ∩ [0, 1] respectively. In order to reason about instances, the semantics of quantified expressions is defined based on recently developed measures of the cardinality of fuzzy sets. A procedure is described to calculate the fuzzy satisfiability of a fuzzy assertion, which is a very important reasoning task. The procedure considers several different cases and provides direct solutions for the most frequent types of fuzzy assertions. In addition, (Sánchez, D, 2006) defined *independence* of fuzzy assertions and obtained some results that speed up the calculation of fuzzy satisfiability in some (the most common) cases.

The Series of F-SHOIQ

Because today quite a lot of multimedia systems and applications use knowledge representation formalisms to encode and reason with knowledge that exists within the multimedia documents, (Stoilos, 2005a) presents a more expressive fuzzy *DL* f_{KD}-*SI*. The goal of this direction is to narrow the semantic gab between the content of a multimedia object, as perceived by a human being, and as "viewed" by an information system. (Stoilos, 2005a) has extended the *DL* language *SI* with fuzzy set theory. The combination of transitive and inverse roles can capture knowledge about part-whole relationships and aggregated objects. Furthermore, the incorporation of fuzziness allows the users to encode and reason with vague and imprecise knowledge. Both these properties fit well into the framework of knowledge based multimedia processing where both part-whole relationships, as well as, imprecise and vague knowledge appear in applications like multimedia information retrieval and processing. In the latter of the paper, a tableau algorithm for checking the consistency of ABox is given and has been proved that it will terminates. (Stoilos, 2005b) provides an extension of the above f_{KD}-*SI* to an even more expressive *DL*, namely f_{KD}-*SHIN*. The paper has presented an extension of the very expressive description logic *SHIN* with fuzzy set theory. It shows the semantics as well as detailed reasoning algorithms for the extend languages. A fuzzy tableau for f_{KD}-*SHIN* ABoxes is shown and it proves the flowing lemma.

Lemma: *Let A be an* f_{KD}*-SHIN ABox and R a fuzzy RBox. Then*

1. When started for A and R the tableaux algorithm terminates
2. A has a fuzzy tableau w.r.t. R if and only if the expansion rules can be applied to A and R such that they yield a complete and clash-free completion forest.

In (Stoilos, 2006b), the syntax and semantics of fuzzy *SHOIQ* were presented and the properties of the semantics of transitivity, qualified cardinality restrictions and reasoning capabilities were investigated. (Stoilos, 2006b) extends the current state-of-the-art on fuzzy extensions to Semantic Web languages by presenting the syntax and semantics of the fuzzy-*SROIQ DL* as well as the abstract, XML syntax and semantics of a fuzzy extension to OWL 1.1. Moreover, it provides reasoning support for a fuzzy version of fuzzy-*SROIQ* by extending well-known reduction techniques of fuzzy *DLs* to classical *DLs* for the additional axioms and constructors of fuzzy-*SROIQ*.

Fuzzy Description Logics with Concrete Domain

The Semantic Web is expected to process knowledge information and data information in an intelligent and automatic way. But recent research has shown that the OWL DL ontology language is very limited in representing data information. Furthermore, the OWL DL can't process imprecision and uncertainty which widely exists in human knowledge and natural language. In (Straccia, 2004b), a fuzzy extension of *ALC(D)* (the *ALC* extended with concrete domains) was presented. The paper presents a fuzzy description logic where the representation of concept membership functions and fuzzy modifiers is allowed, together with a inference procedure based on a mixture of a tableaux and bounded mixed integer programming.

The more expressive *DLs* which can support fuzzy concrete domains is shown in (Straccia, 2005), where the language is *SHOIN(D+)*. It is the corresponding Description Logic of the ontology description language OWL DL. It shows that the representation and reasoning capabilities of fuzzy *SHOIN(D)* go clearly beyond classical *SHOIN(D)*. Interesting features are: (i) concept constructors are based on t-norm, t-conorm, negation and implication; (ii) concrete domains are fuzzy sets; (iii) fuzzy modifiers are allowed; and (iv) entailment and subsumption relationships may hold to some degree in the unit interval [0, 1]. The fuzzy concrete domain is defined as following: $(\Delta_D, \bullet^D)$ is an interpretation. $\bullet^D$ is an interpretation which assigns each concrete individual to an element in Δ_D; assigns each simple data type role $T \in \mathbf{R}_D$ to a function $T^I: \Delta^I \times \Delta_D \rightarrow [0, 1]$; assigns each n-ary predicate p to the fuzzy relation $p^D: \Delta_D{}^n \rightarrow [0,1]$ which means the relationship of data types $v_1,\ldots,v_n$ satisfies predicate p in a degree in [0,1]. Based on the definition of the fuzzy concrete domain, the fuzzy data information in the semantic web can be represented and reasoning.

According to the above statements, some more expressive fuzzy description logics can be summarized in Table 2.

Extensions of OWL

More recently, little work has been carried out towards combining fuzzy logic and the Semantic Web ontology. In (Stoilos, 2005c), the OWL web ontology language was extended with fuzzy set theory, which is called f-OWL, in order to capture, represent and reason with imprecise information. Based on a fuzzy extension to OWL called Fuzzy OWL, (Stoilos, 2006a) developed a reasoning platform, Fuzzy Reasoning Engine (FiRE), which lets

Table 2. Some important fuzzy description logics

	Representation of fuzzy terminologies and concepts					Representation of fuzzy data information		
	f-*TSL*	f-*ALCQ*$_F^+$	f-*SI*	f-*SHIN*	f-*SHOIQ*	f-*ALC*(D)	f-*SHOIQ* (D)	f-*SHOIQ* (G)
Syntax & semantic	(Yen, 2001)	(Sánchez, 2004,2006)	(Stoilos, 2005a)	(Stoilos, 2005b)	(Stoilos, 2006b)	(Straccia, 2004b)	(Straccia, 2005)	
Tableau algorithm	(Yen, 2001)	(Sánchez, 2004,2006)	(Stoilos, 2005a)	(Stoilos, 2005b)	(Stoilos, 2006b)	(Straccia, 2004b)		
Decidability	(Yen, 2001)	(Sánchez, 2006)	(Stoilos, 2005a)	(Stoilos, 2005b)	(Stoilos, 2006b)			

Fuzzy OWL capture and reason about imprecise and uncertain knowledge. Several connections between Fuzzy Logic, the Semantic Web, and its components were presented in (Stoilos, 2005c).

For most recent research issues about fuzzy logic, and more generally soft computing, in the description logics, ontologies and the Semantic Web, ones can refer to (Ma, 2006), (Sanchez, 2006a; 2006b).

DISCUSSION AND CONCLUSIONS

In this chapter, we focus our attention on the recent research achievements on fuzzy extension approaches which are based on fuzzy set theory. We survey existing proposals for extending the theoretical counterpart of the semantic web languages, description logics (*DLs*), and the languages themselves. The above statements include the expressive power of the fuzzy *DLs* formalism and its syntax and semantic, knowledge base, the decidability of the tableaux algorithm and its computational complexity etc. Also the fuzzy extension to OWL is discussed in this chapter. After reviewing all the proposals of fuzzy extensions, we find that it is a paradox in the balance between the expressive power of the *DL* formalism and its computational complexity. It is sure that the computational complexity will become more complex with the more expressive power of the *DL* formalism.

FUTURE RESEARCH DIRECTIONS

As overall conclusion, we can summarize that until recently, research has not paid much attention to fuzzy extensions to *DLs* in the area of the Semantic Web. However, it gains more and more interest and new approaches considering imprecise and uncertainty tend to emerge. Still, many of these approaches are rather half-baked and a lot of things are missing:

- Fuzzy extensions to concrete domain to support the fuzzy user-defined data type and fuzzy user-defined data type predicate. It should be pointed out that, however, the *SHIQ*(*G*) and *SHOQ*(*G*) *DLs* presented in (Pan & Horrocks, 2006; Pan, 2007) which can support the user-defined data type and user-defined data type predicate can only deal with crisp knowledge. In the real world, human knowledge and natural language have a big deal of imprecision and uncertainty, as a result, a fuzzy extension version of *DL* language which can process fuzzy data information should be developed. Especially, we should pay more attention on the fuzzy extension of user-defined data type and user-defined data type predicates.
- The computational complexity of the fuzzy tableau algorithm and the optimal technologies to the fuzzy tableau algorithm. After prompting a fuzzy tableau algorithm to an expressive *DL* language, although the decidability of the algorithm is investigated, the computational complexity is still an open problem. Furthermore, the optimal technologies can be investigated which can reduce the computational complexity of the algorithm.
- Fuzzy extensions to description logics based on vague sets. A single membership degree in the fuzzy sets is inaccurate to represent the imprecision in the membership degrees. As a result, based on vague sets (Gau, 1993), a fuzzy extension of description logic should be presented. Instead of a crisp degree of membership, two degrees of membership (lower and upper degrees of membership) are used in the newly proposed fuzzy description logic version. Its syntax, semantics and inference problems and tableaux also should be investigated.

REFERENCES

Baader, F., Calvanese, D., & McGuinness, D. (2003). *The Description Logic Handbook: Theory, Implementation and Applications.* Cambridge University Press.

Baader, F., & Hanschke P. (1991). A scheme for integrating concrete domains into concept languages. In *Proc. of the 12th Int. Joint Conf. On Artificial Intelligence (IJCAI'91)*, pp. 452–457.

Berners-Lee, T., Hendler, J., & Lassila, O. (2001). The Semantic Web. *The Scientific American*, 284 (5), 34- 43.

Dinh-Khac, D., Hölldobler, S. & Tran, D. K. (2006). The fuzzy linguistic description logic ALC_{FL}. *Proceedings of the 11th International Conference on Information Processing and Management of Uncertainty in Knowledge-Based Systems,* 2096-2103.

Gau, W. L. & Buehrer, D. J., (1993) Vague sets. *IEEE Transactions on Systems, Man, and Cybernetics,* 23 (2), 610-614.

Haarslev V., Lutz C., & Möller R. (1999). A description logicwith concrete domains and role-forming predicates. *J. of Logic and Computation*, 9(3), 351–384.

Hanschke P. (1992). Specifying role interaction in concept languages. In *Proc. of the 3rd Int. Conf. on the Principles of Knowledge Representation and Reasoning (KR'92)*, Morgan Kaufmann, Los Altos, pp. 318–329.

Horrocks I., & Sattler, U. (2001). Ontology reasoning in the SHOQ(D) description logic. *Proceedings of the 17th International Joint Conference on Artificial Intelligence (IJCAI 2001)*, pp. 199–204.

Hölldobler, S., Khang, T.D., & Störr, H.P. (2002) A fuzzy description logic with hedges as concept modifiers. In *Proceedings In Tech/VJFuzzy'2002.* pp. 25–34.

Hölldobler, S, Störr, H. P. & Tran, D. K. (2003). The fuzzy description logic ALC_{FH} with hedge algebras as concept modifiers. *Journal of Advanced Computational Intelligence and Intelligent Informatics*, 7 (3), 294-305.

Hölldobler, S., Nga, N. H. & Khang, T. D. (2005). The fuzzy description logic ALC_{FLH}. *Proceedings of the 9th IASTED International Conference on Artificial Intelligence and Soft Computing*, pp. 99-104.

Hölldobler, S., Störr, H. P., & Khang, T. D. (2004). The subsumption problem in the fuzzy description logic ALC_{FH}. *Proceedings of the 10th International Conference on Information Processing and Management of Uncertainty in Knowledge-Based Systems*, pp. 243-250.

Pan., J. Z. (2007). A Flexible Ontology Reasoning Architecture for the Semantic Web. *IEEE Transaction on Knowledge and Data Engineering.* 19(2), 246 - 260.

Pan, J. Z. & Horrocks, I. (2006). OWL-Eu: Adding Customised Data types into OWL. *Journal of Web Semantics*, 4(1), 29-49.

Lutz, C. (1999). *Reasoning with concrete domains.* In Proc. of the 16th Int. Joint Conf. on Artificial Intelligence (IJCAI'99), Stockholm, Sweden, pp. 90–95.

Lutz, C. (2001). NEXPTIME-complete description logics with concrete domains. In *Proc. of the Int. Joint Conf. on Automated Reasoning (IJCAR 2001)*, volume 2083 of Lecture Notes in Artificial Intelligence, Springer, pp. 45–60.

Meghini, C., Sebastiani F. & Straccia, U. (1997). Reasoning about the form and content for multimedia objects. *Proceedings of AAAI 1997 Spring Symposium on Intelligent Integration and Use of Text, Image, Video and Audio*, pp. 89-94.

Ma. Z. M. (2006) *Soft Computing in Ontologies and Semantic Web.* Springer-Verlag.

Sanchez, E., (2006a). *Fuzzy Logic and the Semantic Web*. Elsevier.

Sanchez, E. & Yamanoi, T. (2006b). Fuzzy ontologies for the Semantic Web. *Lecture Notes in Artificial Intelligence,* 4027: pp. 691-699.

Sánchez, D., & Tettamanzi, G. (2004). Generalizing quantification in fuzzy description logic. In *Proceedings 8th Fuzzy Days in Dortmund.*

Sánchez, D. & Tettamanzi, G. (2006). Reasoning and quantification in fuzzy description logics. *Lecture Notes in Artificial Intelligence,* 3846, pp. 81-88.

Shadbolt, N., Hall, W. & Berners-Lee, T. (2006). The Semantic Web revisited. *IEEE Intelligent Systems*, 21 (3), 96-101.

Stoilos, G., Stamou, G., & Tzouvaras, V. (2005a) A fuzzy description logic for multimedia knowledge representation. *Proceedings of the 2005 International Workshop on Multimedia and the Semantic Web.*

Stoilos, G., Stamou, G., & Tzouvaras V. (2005b) The fuzzy description logic f-SHIN. *Proceedings of the International Workshop on Uncertainty Reasoning for the Semantic Web*, pp. 67-76.

Stoilos, G., Stamou, G., & Tzouvaras, V. (2005c) Fuzzy OWL: Uncertainty and the Semantic Web. *Proceedings of the 2005 International Workshop on OWL: Experience and Directions.*

Stoilos, G., Simous, N., & Stamou, G. (2006a), Uncertainty and the Semantic Web. *IEEE Intelligent Systems,* 21 (5), 84-87.

Stoilos, G., Stamou, G. & Pan, J. Z., (2006b) Handling imprecise knowledge with fuzzy description logic. *Proceedings of the 2006 International Workshop on Description Logics.*

Stoilos, G., Straccia, U., & Stamou, G. B. (2006c). General concept inclusions in fuzzy description logics. *Proceedings of the 17th European Conference on Artificial Intelligence*, pp. 457-461.

Straccia, U. (1998). *A* fuzzy description logic. In *Proc. of the 15th Nat. Conf. on Artificial Intelligence (AAAI-98),* pp. 594–599 Madison, USA.

Straccia, U. (2001) Reasoning within fuzzy description logics. *Journal of Artificial Intelligence and Research,* 14(1), 137–166

Straccia, U. (2004a). Transforming fuzzy description logics into classical description logics. *Proceedings of the 9th European Conference on Logics in Artificial Intelligence*, pp. 385-399.

Straccia, U. (2004b). Fuzzy ALC with fuzzy concrete domains. *Proceedings of the 9th European Conference on Logics in Artificial Intelligence*, pp. 385-399.

Straccia, U. (2005). Towards a fuzzy description logic for the semantic web. In *Proceedings of the 2nd European Semantic Web Conference.*

Tresp, C., & Molitor, R. (1998). A description logic for vague knowledge. In *Proc of the 13th European Conf. on Artificial Intelligence (ECAI-98).* Brighton, England.

Yen, J. (1991). Generalising term subsumption languages to fuzzy logic. In *Proc of the 12th Int. Joint Conf on Artificial Intelligence (IJCAI-91),* pp: 472-477, Sydney, Australia

Zadeh, L. A. (1965). Fuzzy sets. *Information and Control*, 8(3), 338-353.

ADDITIONAL READING

General Logic

Ben-Ari, M. (2001). *Mathematical Logic for Computer Scientists.* Springer-Verlag.

Ebbinghaus, H.-D., Flum, J. & Thomas, W. (2007) *Mathematical Logic.* Springer-Verlag.

Enderton, H. B. (2002). *A mathematical Introduction to Logic*, 2nd edition. Academic Press.

Schoening, U. (1994). *Logic for Computer Scientists*. Birkhaeuser Verlag

Fuzzy Set Theory

Zadeh, L.A. (1978) Fuzzy sets as a basis for a theory of possibility, *Fuzzy Sets Systems*, 1(1), pp. 3-28.

Semantic Web

Antoniou, G. and Harmelen, F. V. (2003). *A Semantic Web Primer*, The MIT Press.

Description Logic

Franconi, E., *Description Logics Course Information*. http://www.cs.man.ac.uk/~franconi/dl/course/

OWL

Horrocks, I. & Patel-Schneider, P. F., van Harmelen, F. (2003). From SHIQ and RDF to OWL: The making of a web ontology language. *Journal of Web Semantics*, 1(1):7-26.

Smith, M. K., Welty, C. & McGuiness, D. L. (2004). *OWL Web Ontology Language Guide*. W3C Recommendation, from http://www.w3.org/TR/2004/REC-owl-ref-20040210/

RDF and RDF Schema

A selection of documents on RDF and RDF Schema (Specification, Use Cases, Recommended Readings, Tools, Related Technologies, etc.), from http://www.w3.org/RDF/

de Bruijn & J., Heymans, S. (2007). Logical Foundations of (e)RDF(S): Complexity and Reasoning. In *Proceedings of the International Semantic Web Conference (ISWC)*.

Chapter III
Improving Storage Concepts for Semantic Models and Ontologies

Edgar R. Weippl
Vienna University of Technology, Austria

Markus D. Klemen
Vienna University of Technology, Austria

Stefan Raffeiner
Vienna University of Technology, Austria

ABSTRACT

Ontologies are more commonly used today but still little consideration is given of how to efficiently store them. The proposed approach is built on reliable and efficient relational database management systems (RDBMS). It can be easily implemented for other systems and due to its vendor independence existing data can be migrated from one RDBMS to another relatively easy.

INTRODUCTION

During the last couple of years ontologies moved into the center of interest in mainstream computer science research. With the Internet becoming a truly global information resource, the effort required to find the right information increased, even though the quality of search engines improved considerably.

The next big step is anticipated to be the integration of semantic information of electronically available resources which will allow searches to obtain much better results. The process of building the required ontologies can either be top-down or bottom-up.

The RDF-based approach, favored by Tim Berners-Lee, strives to semantically enrich each Web page and build ontologies by integrating all the semantic information. Topic Maps, in contrast, are usually regarded as top-down approach where occurrences are linked to topics once the Topic Map exists.

A prerequisite to building large ontologies is an efficient way of storing the required data. Today, it is generally agreed that ontologies evolve over time and require maintenance. Thus both retrieval and updates need to be handled efficiently by the storage system.

In this chapter we present an improved database schema to store ontologies. More specifically, our contribution is to:

- Propose an intuitive and efficient way of storing arbitrary relationships (Section 2.1)
- Show that our database schema is well suited to store both RDF and Topic Maps (Section 2.2)
- Explain why it is more efficient by comparing it to other approaches (Section 3)

LINK-BASED SCHEMA

In this section we first explain the general idea of the improved database schema and provide an example of how concepts and relationships between them are stored. We then show how both RDF and Topic Maps can be stored, too.

Database Schema Based on a Link Table

The idea, first described in (Weippl et al 2005), is based on an architecture that uses relational database. Tables are not linked to others directly with foreign keys or by using n : m intermediary tables but via a single, generic association table referred to as the link table.

In the classical schema, adding an n : m relationship between two tables requires creating a new intermediate table to resolve the n : m relationship into a1: n and a 1 : m relationship . Our approach is to merge these intermediate tables into one link table which stores all relationships centrally.

The advantages of our approach are:

1. In contrast to classic E-R approaches, any relationship can be added without schema modifications. This allows to easily perform operations within transactions.
2. Tables and indices can be clustered to improve the speed of join operations with the central link table. In the classical model many n : m relationships exist, therefore, cluster optimizations are far more difficult and less efficient.
3. Our approach allows retrieving relationships from the link table without accessing the data dictionary. Since the data dictionary is vendor specific, the classical approach requires modifying the application for each database system.
4. If n entities exist and n : m relationships are to be established between all entities, the number of additional tables is O(n2), whereas our approach is O(1) Of course this applies only to new relationships, not new tables.

Detailed explanations on the advantages can be found in (Weippl et al 2005).

Figure 1 shows a simple database schema. Table ref1 contains the SQL statements of the following example. A new file type Document (.doc) is created with OpenOffice. An optional description is added and a relationship between the two topics is established (steps 1–4). In the same way occurrences can be linked to topics.

Steps 5–10 in Table 1 show how reification (Figure 2) can be implemented using our schema.

Our concept differs from to other approaches (Section 3) by using separate tables to store different types of entities but one central link table for all relationships. The data-centric approach, which we also refer to as the 'classical' way, uses

Figure 1. The database schema to store the information as given in Table 1

Figure 2. Reification

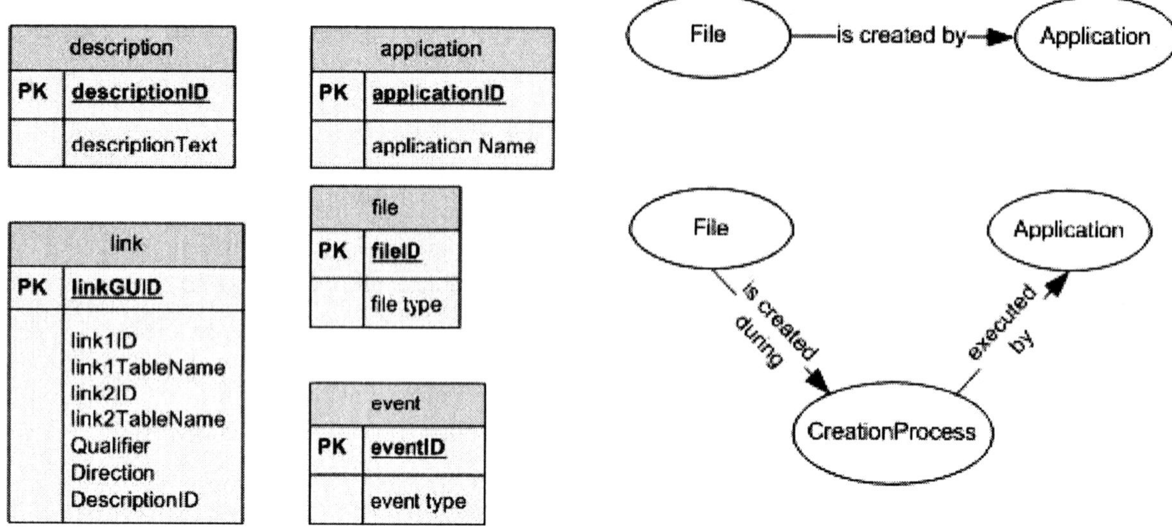

Table 1. A relationship between a document and an application is stored (steps 1–4). An example for a reification is given in the following steps

Step	SQL Command
1 2	INSERT INTO file VALUES (1, 'Document (.doc)')
3 4	INSERT INTO application VALUES (10, 'OpenOffice')
5 6	INSERT INTO description VALUES (90, 'save as
7 8	operation') INSERT INTO link VALUES (111, 1,
9 10	'file', 10, 'application', 'assocrl', '1', 90)
	INSERT INTO event VALUES (42, 'save as') INSERT
	INTO link VALUES (112, 1, 'file', 42, 'event',
	'assocrl', '1', 91) INSERT INTO link VALUES (113,
	42, 'event', 10, 'application', 'assocrl', '1',
	91) DELETE FROM link WHERE linkGUID=111 DELETE
	FROM description WHERE descriptionID=90 INSERT
	INTO description VALUES (91, 'reification')

one table for each n : m relationship. The structure-centric approach stores everything in one table (such as an RDF triple store).

The advantage compared to the data-centric approach is that we require fewer changes of the database schema during normal database operations. Adding a new type of relationship — by far the most common operation — requires no schema modification. The structure-centric approach has the same advantage but suffers from another drawback. Since everything is stored in a single (or very few) tables this table will quickly become very large and thus access slower. Numerous self-joins, which will be required, also have a negative impact on performance.

Storing Topic Maps and RDF

Even though the structure-based approach is slower during retrieval, it may make sense to implement it in a very dynamic environment where new entities, new relationships and even new types of relationships are often created. These characteristics typically apply to semantic environments such as RDF or Topic Maps. Modifying the aforementioned link-based architecture we show that the relational storage model as proposed by (Widhalm et al 2002) can be optimized in several ways helping to improve the performance and reduce the complexity of the database schema.

First and foremost we can reduce the number of tables used without the loss of data or metadata (Figures 3 and 4). By using qualifiers in the link table we can combine tables such as basename, sortname, dispname and topname into one table called name. The qualifier attribute in the link table contains information whether the name is used as basename, sortname, etc.

Following the XTM standard[1] we also no longer need the table facet. The link that connects topics and associations stores the association role as qualifier, not in a separate table. In the same way we can avoid separate tables for fvalue, locationstype, nonconforming and cassign.

Since 'everything' is a topic we do not need to explicitly store this information in a table. Instead, we propose to create a view that contains all the information (create view ... as select from ... UNION selection from ...).

The main difference between RDF and Topic Maps that is relevant to storing information is that RDF only supports relationships between two entities — RDF uses nodes and arches to build graphs of concepts and relationships between them.

This makes storage much easier and the simplest approach is to store RDF triples in the form (s, p, o) (subject, predicate and object) (Somani et al 2001).

However, RDF can be stored similarly as Topic Maps either using the 'pure' link-based approach (Section 2.1) or by modifying it analogous to what we showed for Topic Maps. All four major differences between RDF and Topic Maps can be handled by the link-based approach:

1. In RDF relationships can only be established between two resources whereas Topic Maps supports relationships between any number of topics. The link table supports an arbitrary number of links.
2. In RDF relationships are directed and only valid for one direction. In most cases this requires creating a redundant second and inverse relationship. In the link table an attribute is used to store the direction.
3. In contrast to Topic Maps, RDF does not support scopes which makes it difficult to create large ontologies by combining existing smaller ones. If scopes are required, a table (scope) needs to be added. By linking the appropriate scope via the link table, scopes can be easily handled.
4. In RDF reification is necessary if additional information needs to be attached to a relationship later on. This is not necessary for Topic Maps since everything is already reified. Reification can be performed efficiently as shown before.

EVALUATION OF OTHER STORAGE CONCEPTS

In this section we briefly look at three systems that store personal information and strive to provide semantically enriched retrieval capabilities.

We then look at existing solutions to organizing a semantic data store.

- XML databases (Section 3.2)
- Data-centric approach with relational databases (Section 3.3)

Figure 3. Storing topic maps in an RDBMS (Widhalm et al., 2002)

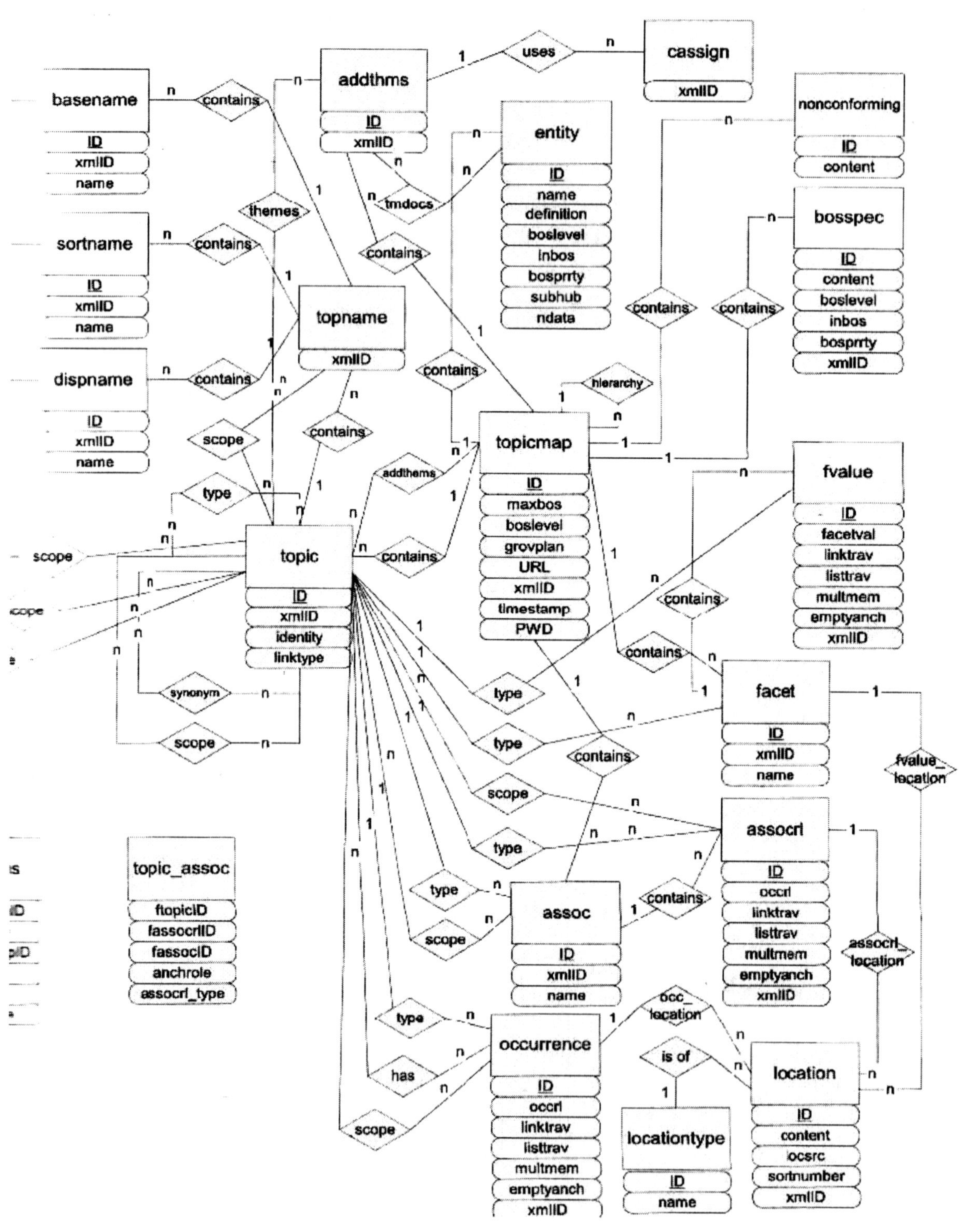

Figure 4. By storing all relationships in the link table together with a qualifier, fewer tables (compare to Figure 3) are needed but all advantages as described in (Widhalm et al., 2002) are retained

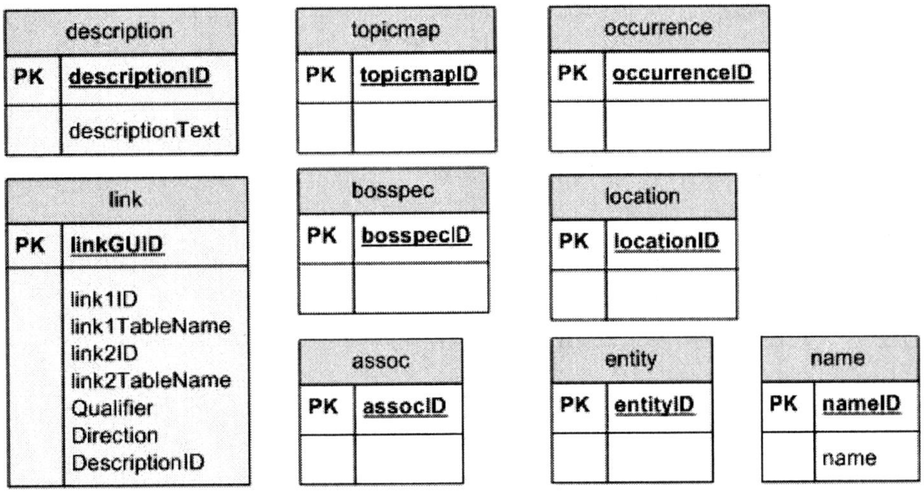

- Structure-centric approach with relational databases (Section 3.4).

Storing Personal Digital Information

Vanevar Bush's vision of the Memex (Bush 1945) — a paper that almost everyone cites when writing about semantically enriched information storage — is the basis on which projects such as Microsoft's MyLifeBits (Gemmel et al 2002) or the SemanticLIFE project (Ahmed et al 2004) build.

The authors want to build a personal digital storage that records all documents, emails, photos, videos, etc. of an individual.

MyLifeBits focuses on storing digital content in a database; unlike SemanticLIFE it does not primarily aim to semantically enrich the stored data. Instead MyLifeBits relies on future improvement of search engines and desktop search solutions. The focus of SemanticLIFE is building ontologies and discovering relationships between existing data items.

Haystack (Adar et al 1999) is a platform to visualize and maintain ontologies. The system is designed to flexibly define interactions and relationships between objects. The focus lies on the quality of the retrieval process and not on storing data.

While both systems inherently address issues of storing ontologies they do not focus on an efficient storage concept. MyLifeBits assume that MSSQL Server will provide all the needed functions without providing details on the database schema used.

XML in Oracle

Both RDF and Topic Maps (XTM) can be encoded in XML. Major relational database management systems (RDBMS) now offer ways of storing XML content.

With Oracle9i a new data type XMLType was introduced. The idea is that XML data can be stored in the database that natively supports XML. Previously XML data was often stored in an unstructured way using BLOBs or CLOBs; CLOBs are Character Large Objects and compared to BLOBs have an advantage when text is required to support different code pages.

When an XMLType is used Oracle provides several features that are specific to XML data. for

Figure 5. Data-centric approach of Sesame (Broekstra et al., 2001)

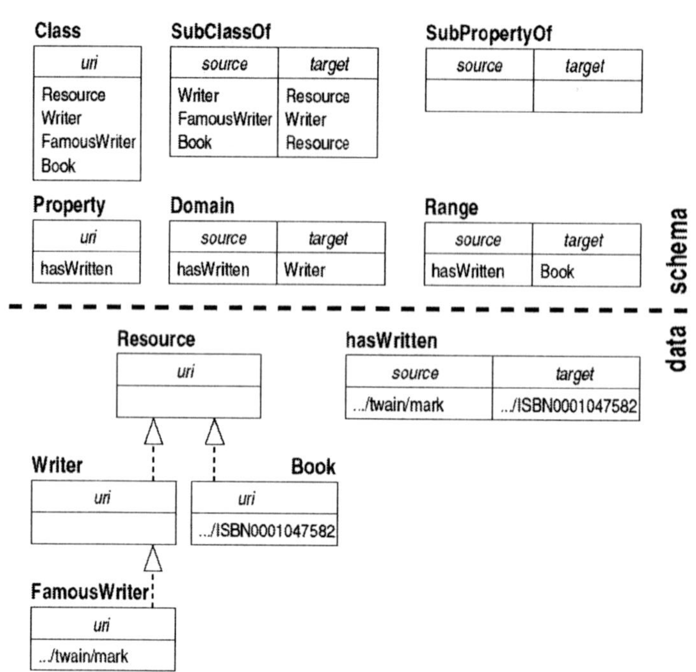

instance, XPath[2] can be used to query the stored data directly. Moreover, XSL transformations and schema validation. However, whenever XML data is modified, the XMLType requires an XML syntax check; obviously this tasks requires processing time. Dillon (Dillon 2005) reports that inserting data in an XMLtype results in an approximately 22-fold increase of processing time, even if the XML document is a very simple document:

```
<?xmlversion="1.0"?> <testTag/>
```

Oracle offers another option to store XML documents. Using the object-relational approach XML documents are decomposed into data elements when inserted into the database. The data is stored in a relational model and can be queried accordingly.[3] In addition, the original XML document can be re-assembled automatically. The obvious drawback is that the XML schema has to be registered with the database.[4]

Storing XML in an RDMS such as Oracle is a good idea if many XML documents need to be stored since the database is optimized to handle a large number of individual documents. A Topic Map, however, is a single and very large XML file; thus the database cannot handle updates to this document efficiently.

Data-Centric Approach

One approach, also known as data centric approach, is often mentioned in context with mapping XML documents to relational databases (Kuckelberg et al 2003, Bourret, Bourret 2001, Mittermeier 2003). With respect to ontologies, the process can be described as follows.

The first step is to identify the types of concepts and their properties that are to be stored in the ontology. Then, these types of concepts are mapped to according tables in a traditional RDBMS, with the previously identified properties being the fields of the tables. Finally, the instances of the classes can be inserted into the tables as rows, with one row representing one instance of a concept. This procedure is the same for subjects, relationships and all other data model entities defined by the respective standard.

In addition, several 'auxiliary' tables are needed to keep track of whether a certain table maps to a subject or to a relationship etc. This leads to the situation that the database is actually split into two 'virtual layers': the virtual 'schema layer' consists of the auxiliary tables that keep track of all classes in the ontology, whereas the virtual 'data layer' contains the tables created as instance containers for specific classes.

Such a data centric approach was for instance originally followed by the Sesame ontology framework (Broekstra et al 2001, Broekstra et al 2002) in conjunction with a PostgreSQL database. Figure 5 shows the setup of the Sesame data centric object-relational mapping.

There are two advantages that can be exploited with the data centric approach. First, query answering as well as inserting, removing and updating instance of classes is extremely inexpensive and straightforward, as there is virtually no difference to traditionally designed databases. All manipulations concerning instances are in effect nothing more than executions of data manipulation commands as they are natively provided by all RDBMS.

Second, some RDBMS like PostgreSQL offer built-in object-relational features that can be used directly for modeling class-subclass relationships etc. PostgreSQL databases offer for instance the possibility to create subtables that are connected to their parent tables through transitive relationships. This allows for creating a table for a certain class and according subtables (for subclasses of that class). The same is true for properties and subproperties, accordingly.

The main drawback of the data centric approach is that changes to the class hierarchy in an ontology are extremely expensive, as they require creating new entities in the database. For every new class (and also subclass) that is to be inserted into the ontology, a respective table has to be created, even if only a small number of instances is present. This means that changes to the class hierarchy always require data definition commands to be performed, which are expensive in almost any RDBMS.

Structure-Centric Approach

The second approach is also known as structure centric and is equally popular among Topic Map and RDF implementations. As it is the case with the data centric approach, persistency is eventually provided by a traditional RDBMS, but usually without requiring object-relational features. Opposed to the first approach, the key idea here is to map the finite number of data model concepts to according structures (tables) in the relational database. Again, the process has also been described for XML documents (Kuckelberg et al 2003, Bourret, Bourret 2001, Mittermeier 2003) but has also been specifically implemented for both Topic Map and RDF applications.

As shown in detail in Section 2.2, the Topic Map data model offers a small number of built-in concepts, like Topic, Association, Occurrence, Scope etc., whose properties are well defined. In contrast to the actual classes and instances they represent, the number and design of these built-in concepts are static (as they are standardized). Therefore, it is a straightforward task to create corresponding structures in a RDBMS and map the concepts to these structures in such a way that in the end there is one table for all topics, one table for all associations, etc. Various examples of this implementation for Topic Maps exist, e.g. (Kiyakov et al 2001, Widhalm et al 2002).

With respect to RDF, the data model consists basically only of statements, with each statement including a subject, an object and a predicate. This means that for a naive approach only one single table (with three corresponding text fields containing the respective URIs or literals) is needed to express a complete RDF graph. Due to the layout of their tables, databases configured this way are therefore commonly referred to as triple stores. They are certainly a very elegant solution for ontology persistence and are probably one of the main reasons that RDF/OWL has gained significant popularity among ontology developers. Also, many variations and improvements over the naive approach exist, mainly in order to achieve high levels of scalability.

The first advantage of the structure centric approach is its ability to allow for inexpensive, frequent changes of instance data as well as of schema information (class hierarchies). Since all assertions, including hierarchical relations, are broken down to the level of single statements, no artificial distinction between "schema layer" and "data layer" has to be made. This allows not only for representing frequently changing ontology hierarchies, but also for efficient incremental incorporation of large datasets, as no structural changes of the underlying database schema are required.

The second advantage of structure centric ontology representation is commonly found to be reported for dedicated triple stores, but also applies for Topic Map representations. Due to the fixed, rather simple architecture of the database, scalability optimizations are easy to apply, enabling the efficient storage of millions of concepts and relationships.

One main disadvantage of the structure centric approach (in the case of RDF triple stores) is encountered when retrieving statements for answering ontology queries. In order to evaluate a condition that not directly addresses the URIs or literals of the statements to be retrieved, the table containing the statement triples has to perform one or more self-joins, an operation which is expensive for large datasets (Kuckelberg et al 2003, Alexaki et al 2001). Such large datasets must be considered to occur frequently, as all information of an ontology is stored within a single triple table. It is therefore not uncommon for such a table to contain millions of triples, which have to be compared to each other even several times, depending of the nature of the query to be answered. Although various optimization efforts try to limit the negative effects of storing triples in a single table, generally worse query answering performance has to be expected compared to the object-relational approach.

CONCLUSION

We proposed an improved way of storing ontologies in a relational database so that changes of hierarchies and relationships between tables can easily be added without schema modification. The advantages of our approach are:

1. Most modifications require no data-definition language (DDL) statements; they cannot be executed within a transaction.
2. Tables and indices can be clustered to improve the speed of joins with the central link table.
3. Our approach is vendor-independent as no metadata on relationships need to be retrieved from the data dictionary.

In addition, we showed that both Topic Maps and RDF can be stored efficiently using our database schema.

FUTURE RESEARCH DIRECTIONS

Ontologies become more important as semantic is increasingly relevant not only for Search Engines, but also for Web Services and many enterprise-wide applications. Research that will be addressed includes the storage of very large ontologies with even more instances. As relational database management systems are widely deployed today, improvement in ontology-storage in RDMS will be important. Efficiently querying the database, however, is of even greater importance. While SPARQL is a good choice, major improvement still need to be made before the handling of ontologies will become as easy as using Google.

REFERENCES

Adar, E., Karger, D., & Stein, L. A. (1999). Haystack: Per-user information environments. In *Proceedings of the Conference on Information and Knowledge Management.*

Ahmed, M., Hanh, H. H., Karim, S., Khusro, S., Lanzenberger, M., Latif, K., Michlmayr, E., Khabib, M., Nguyen, H. T., Rauber, A., Schatten, A., Nguyen, M. T., & Tjoa, A. M. (2004). Semanticlife — a framework for managing information of a human lifetime. In *Proceedings of the 6th International Conference on Information Integration and Web-based Applications and Services (IIWAS).*

Alexaki, S., Christophides, V., Karvounarakis, G., & Plexousakis, D. (2001). On storing voluminous RDF descriptions: The case of web portal catalogs. In *Proceedings of the 4th International Workshop on the the Web and Databases.* ICSFORTH.

Bourret, R. (n.d.). *Xml-dbms.* Retrieved from http://www.rpbourret.com/xmldbms/readme.htm

Bourret, R. (2001). *Mapping dtds to databases.* Technical report, from http://www.xml.com/lpt/a/2001/05/09/dtdtodbs.html

Broekstra, J., Kampman, A., & van Harmelen, F. (2001). Semantics for the WWW. In *An Architecture for Storing and Querying RDF Data and Schema Information.* MIT Press, 2001, from http://www.cs.vu.nl/frankh/postscript/MIT01.pdf

Broekstra, J., Kampman, A., & van Harmelen, F. (2002). Sesame: A generic architecture for storing and querying rdf and rdf schema. In *ISWC 2002,* from http://www.openrdf.org/doc/papers/SesameISWC2002.pdf.

Bush, V. (1945). As we may think. *The Atlantic Monthly, 176(7),*101–108.

Dillon, S. (2005). Which storage xml? *Oracle Magzine, April 2005,* from http://www.oracle.com/technology/oramag/oracle/05mar/o25xmlex.html.

Gemmel, J., Bell, G., Lueder, R., Drucker, S., & Wong, C. (2002). Mylifebits: Fulfilling the memex vision. In *ACM Multimedia '02, December,* 235–238.

Kiyakov, A. K., IV. Simov, K., & Dimitrov, M. (2001). *Ontomap: Ontologies for lexical semantics.* Technical report, OntoText Lab, Sirma AI EOOD, from http://www.ontotext.com/publications/ranlp01.pdf.

Kuckelberg, A., & Krieger, R. (2003). *Efficient structure oriented storage of xml documents using ordbms.* Technical report, RWTH Aachen.

Mittermeier (2003). Naiv nativ. *iX, 42(8).*

Somani, A., Agrawal, R., & Xu, Y. (2001). Storage and querying of e-commerce data. In *Proceedings of VLDB* , Rome, Italy. From http://www.vldb.org/conf/2001/P149.pdf.

Weippl, E. R., Klemen, M., Linnert, M., Fenz, S., Goluch, G., and Tjoa, A. M. (2005). Semantic storage: A report on performance and Flexibility. *Submitted to DEXA 2005.*

Widhalm, R., & Mueck, T. (2002). *Topic Maps: Semantische Suche im Internet.* Springer Verlag.

ADDITIONAL READING

Aussenac-Gilles, N., Biebow, B., & Szulman, S. (2000). Revisiting ontology design: A methodology based on corpus analysis. In *Proceedings of the 12th European Workshop on Knowledge Acquisition, Modeling and Management EKAW '00,* 172-188. London, UK: Springer-Verlag.

Baader, F., Horrocks, I., & Sattler, U. (2005). Mechanizing Mathematical Reasoning. In *2605/2005 of Lecture Notes in Computer Science, chapter Description Logics as Ontology Languages for the Semantic Web,* 228-248. Berlin / Heidelberg, DE: Springer-Verlag.

Bernaras, A., Laresgoiti, I., & Corera, J. M. (1996). Building and reusing ontologies for electrical network applications. *ECAI,* 298-302.

Brank, J., Grobelnik, M., & Mladenic, D. (2005). A survey of ontology evaluation techniques. *SIKDD 2005 at Multiconference IS.*

Broekstra, J., & Kampman, A. (n.d.) Sesame: A Generic Architecture for Storing and Querying RDF and RDF Schema. *On-To-Knowledge Deliverable D10,* from http://sesame.aidministrator.nl.

Fernandez, M., Gomez-Perez, A., & Juristo, N. (1997). Methontology: from ontological art towards ontological engineering. In *Proceedings of the AAAI97 Spring Symposium Series on Ontological Engineering,* 33-40. Stanford, USA.

Gomez-Perez, A. (1996). A framework to verify knowledge sharing technology. *Expert Systems with Application,* 11(4), 519-529.

Krohn, U., & Davies, J. The Search Facility RDF-ferret. *On-To-Knowledge Deliverable D11,* from http://www.ontoknowledge.org .

Seaborne, A. (2001). *RDQL: A Data Oriented Query Language for RDF Models.* From http://jena.sourceforge.net/tutorial/RDQL/

The European On-To-Knowledge project (IST-1999-10132), from http://www.ontoknowledge.org.

ENDNOTES

1 http://www.topicmaps.org/xtm/1.0/

2 To retrieve, for instance, the last name of a person following XPath query could be used: select extractValue(OBJECT VALUE, '/Person/FirstName') from xmldocs;

3 For instance, select x."XMLDATA"."FirstName" from xmldocs x

4 Oracle10g provides the stored procedure DBMS XMLSCHEMA.REGISTER SCHEMA, making frequent modifications of the XML schema difficult.

Chapter IV
Ontologies and Intelligent Agents:
A Powerful Bond

Kostas Kolomvatsos
National and Kapodistrian University of Athens, Greece

Stathes Hadjiefthymiades
National and Kapodistrian University of Athens, Greece

ABSTRACT

The emerged form of information with computer-processable meaning (semantics) as presented in the framework of the Semantic Web (SW) facilitates machines to access it more efficiently. Information is semantically annotated in order to ease the discovery and retrieval of knowledge. Ontologies are the basic element of the SW. They carry knowledge about a domain and enable interoperability between different resources. Another technology that draws considerable attention nowadays is the technology of Intelligent Agents. Intelligent agents act on behalf of a user to complete tasks and may adapt their behavior to achieve their objectives. The objective of this chapter is to provide an exhaustive description of fundamentals regarding the combination of SW and intelligent agent technologies.

INTRODUCTION

The Semantic Web (SW) evolution has brought a number of changes in contemporary Computer Science. Its main characteristic is the transformation of the traditional form of information so that it is easily machine comprehensible. Ontologies, the basic component of the SW, help along this line. They facilitate the interoperability of heterogeneous information sources by providing a formalization that makes them machine accessible. Ontologies are the key for the emergence of the SW. They carry knowledge and information for reasoning.

Agents are autonomous software programs that act in dynamic and heterogeneous environments in order to satisfy their owners' needs. In the relevant literature, one can find static or mobile agents technologies with regard to their ability to move to nodes in order to find the required information. Additionally, intelligent agents can learn from the owners' behavior and adapt accordingly.

It is obvious that a combination of the agent and Semantic Web technologies may support users in searching and accessing information sources with a small involvement degree. Conventional information systems, like Information Retrieval systems, require active users who read and understand information. Currently, machines with the assistance of intelligent agents can read the semantically enriched information and extract knowledge that can satisfy the queries posed by users. Ontologies may serve in many fields of the agents' technology and offer a lot of advantages.

In this chapter, we discuss technologies related to the functional combination of both SW and intelligent agents. Initially, we discuss the main characteristics of the two technologies and describe consolidation efforts pertaining to agents and ontologies. There are numerous efforts that involve agents manipulating ontologies as well as ontologies that describe the basic characteristics of intelligent agents enriching them with semantic information. We study important issues with regard to agents and Semantic Web services. We provide an overview of the new trends in agent technology and, finally, present a case study for ontologies used for learning Agents in Multi-Agent environments.

BACKGROUND

In this section we present an introduction to the fields of software agents and ontologies. Our objective is to provide to readers basic description of the two technologies in order to discern their characteristics and importance to many application domains.

Software Agents

With the rapid evolvement of the Internet, software agents play an important role in Computer Science research. Software agents are components of software and/or hardware which are capable of acting on behalf of a user in order to accomplish tasks (Nwana, 1996). The owner of an agent may be a human or another computational entity. Tasks are posed by the agents' owners in order to fulfill their needs. There are a lot of kinds of agents. One can meet information agents that search for information sources in order to achieve their goals, mobile agents that move from an environment to another, intelligent agents that learn from their owners and the environment and so on. For a full description of these types of agents and many more, one can refer to (Nwana, 1996). Agents can be used in many domains such as information retrieval, e-learning, medical applications, games, e-commerce, etc. For a full survey one can refer in (Jennings and Wooldridge, 1998).

A lot of research is involved in agent applications and a number of construction tools have been proposed. Some of them are: AgentBuilder (Reticular Systems, 1999), MOLE (Straber, Baumann and Hohl, 1997), Open Agent Architecture (Martin, Cheyer and Moran, 1998), RETSINA (Sycara, Pannu, Williamson and Zeng, 1996), ZEUS (Nwana, Ndumu and Lee, 1998), JADE (Bellifemine, Poggi and Rimassa, 2000), etc. The most of them are based on Java. However, there are tools that use other languages as Tcl, C or C++.

In the most cases, agents must deal with complicated tasks that demand cooperation with others. A Multi-Agent System (MAS) can be defined as a loosely coupled network of problem solvers that interact to solve problems that are beyond the individual capabilities or knowledge of each problem solver (Durfee & Lesser, 1989). In such systems agents can cooperate or compete with others to complete their tasks. We must note that such systems are open which means that change over time.

The basic characteristics of an agent are (Wooldridge and Jennings, 1995):

- Autonomy
- Social Ability
- Reactivity
- Proactivity

Each agent has its own beliefs, goals and intentions in order to complete its tasks. It acts autonomously and manages its internal states. Its goals are posed after an interaction held with its owner, and continually tries to complete these targets. It may work in environments where other agents are also active. This means that agents may cooperate in order to find solutions to their problems. The interactions held between autonomous agents comprise their social ability. In these cases communication is very important. The environment where agents cooperate may change over time. Agents are able to control their internal states and adapt to the new conditions. They adjust their behaviors and may change their goals if it is necessary. This characteristic is reactivity. Finally, proactivity means that agents may take initiatives in order to reach their targets. It is an important element of agents' nature especially in cases where agents must find new ways to their targets' road.

The most important agent architectures are (Huhns and Stephens, 2004):

- **Reactive agents:** This kind of agents does not maintain information about the state of the environment but they react to current perceptions. These agents have a number of behaviors from where they choose the most appropriate in order to act in every situation.
- **BDI (Belief Desire Intention) agents:** This architecture specifies for each agent three basic elements: beliefs, goals (desires) and plans (intentions). Beliefs contain the view of an agent about the environment, other agents and of course itself. On the other hand desires and intentions include goals and plans for their accomplishment. Plans also specify when a goal must be characterized as unachievable.
- **Layered architectures:** These architectures use a set of layers. Each layer is used to provide means for reasoning tasks. Higher levels provide means for reasoning concerning general concepts while lower layers are used for reasoning in more specific concepts. Hence, lower levels provide to agents responses to immediate events as middle and higher layers enable agents to interact with others and consider the long-term effects of their behaviors.

Special cases of agents are intelligent agents. An intelligent agent is a software agent that exhibits a kind of artificial intelligence. They learn from their owners and further more they learn from the environment where they are activated. Intelligent agents have a set of 'sensing' components through which they observe the environment and according to its conditions they take the appropriate decision. Hence, there are two extra features (over the above referred basic characteristics of a software agent) that intelligent agents have. The first is the capability to adapt to new situations formed in the environment. This is attained through specific rules which have the form:

if *condition* then *action*

On the other hand, intelligent agents have the ability to learn. Learning is achieved through mechanisms that imply the behavior analysis and the assimilation of some examples.

In conclusion, and trying to remark the elements that agents have and may be represented using ontologies we can describe an agent as an entity that is affected by two factors, as it is depicted in Figure 1.

The first factor is the internal state that an agent has and the second is the environment. Internal state depicts the opinion of the agent for all the elements of the virtual world in which it is put in (its goals and plans, other agents, the system, etc). Environment includes all the external factors that can affect the behavior of an agent. The internal and external elements, as we can see in the next sections, can be represented using ontologies giving a semantic annotation of each element. This means that agents may understand the information carried by them or taken from the environment with a way that approaches human's view of information. The benefits are many, including efficiency in goals completion or interoperability in cases when two or more agents have to cooperate in order to complete their tasks.

Intelligent agents may be used in many application scenarios. For example, a user may use an agent in order to search information or products in the Web. Let us think the case where a user communicates with its personal intelligent agent. User may pose their instructions to agent and accordingly the agent is responsible to search and find the appropriate information or product that the user wants. Furthermore, an intelligent agent has learning capabilities in order to understand and store the preferences of user. This knowledge is used in future tasks when intelligent agent is capable of adapting to user characteristics. However, there are more complicated application scenarios where agents offer many advantages. Such scenarios involve, banking applications, telecommunications systems, expert systems, etc.

Figure 1. Agent's abstract description

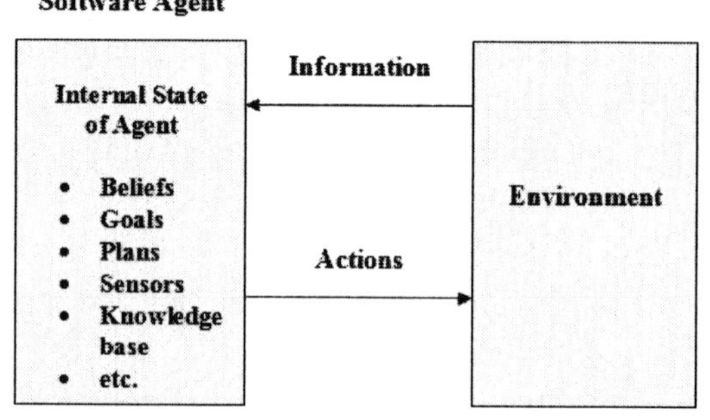

Discussion on Ontologies

In this section, we describe the main characteristics of ontologies and issues considered in the field of Ontological Engineering. It is important to understand how ontologies carry the information and how ontologies must be developed.

Ontology description languages, inference systems and implementations with reasoning capabilities have been developed to improve information retrieval and enable knowledge discovery. This is because in the Semantic Web era, ontologies are the key actors providing the means to extract information. Ontologies are widely used in domains related to e-commerce, knowledge management, information manipulation and retrieval, etc. The concept of ontology has its roots in the ancient Greek philosophers such as Parmenides and Aristotle. In our days, due to the importance that ontologies have for many disciplines a lot of definitions have been presented in the related literature. The most prominent are:

An ontology defines the basic terms and relations comprising the vocabulary of a topic area as well as the rules for combining terms and relations to define extensions to the vocabulary. (Neches et al., 1991)

An ontology is an explicit specification of a conceptualization. (Gruber, 1993)

Ontologies are defined as a formal specification of a shared conceptualization. (Borst, 1997).

An ontology is a common, shared and formal description of important concepts in a specific domain. (Fensel, 2000)

There are many more definitions for ontologies, some of them more specific and others more general. Following the above mentioned definitions, it is easy to understand that an ontology may be used to define the concepts and their relations describing a specific domain. We can note some interesting remarks for ontologies:

- Ontologies are used to describe a specific domain.
- The developer of the ontology defines the concepts that describe this domain and their relations.
- Rules are also posed in order to combine concepts and relations determining extensions to basic vocabulary.
- There is an hierarchy between concepts of the domain. Usually, this is defined through the use of the relation IS-A specifying which terms' meaning is more general than others. IS-A relation organize the ontology and appends child concepts to terms.

In (Gruber, 1993), authors specify the main components of an ontology. These are classes, relations, functions, formal axioms and instances. Table 1 shows the definition of each component while Table 2 describes a short example for the University domain.

The main role of an ontology is information annotation through which semantic interoperability is possible. They provide an explicit description of the information. From this point of view one can discern three basic models: *Single ontology approach, multiple ontology approach and hybrid approach* (Wache et al., 2001). In single ontology models, there is a global ontology which serves as a base vocabulary for the specification of semantics in the domain. Each information source must be described using terms from the global ontology. On the other hand, multiple ontologies models use the combination of many private ontologies with which the information sources are described. Hence, each data source has its own semantics. The lack of a common vocabulary is critical and the need for a combination procedure imperative. Finally, hybrid approaches allow the description of each information source using private ontologies but they are built based on a shared vocabulary in order to be comparable. The shared vocabulary contains basic terminology of the domain.

In (Auxilio and Nieto, 2003), the authors describe basic uses of ontologies. First of all, ontologies provide a means to describe data semantics with meta-information. They give the opportunity to humans or software agents to acquire knowledge through the semantic annotation of information resources. It is obvious that this is a very important issue because information will be accessible from machines, making the information retrieval process more efficient.

Another use of ontologies is the building of knowledge bases. As we saw, ontologies consist

Table 1. Ontology components

COMPONENT	DESCRIPTION
Class	Represents concepts of the domain.
Relation	Represents associations between concepts of the domain.
Function	It is a special case of relation.
Axiom	It is used to represent knowledge that cannot be defined by the other components. They serve to define sentences that are always true.
Instance	Represents individuals, following the above mentioned components.

Table 2. Example of ontology components

DOMAIN: University	
COMPONENT	EXAMPLES
Classes	Persons, Faculty, Students, Staff, Lessons, Publications, etc.
Relations	is-a, hasAdvisor, hasPosition, hasGrade, hasDuration, hasPublication, etc.
Axioms	A student cannot have salary.
Instances	Individuals representing teachers, students and staff.

of classes, relations, functions, axioms and instances. Through the use of these elements one can set a knowledge base that can be processed by users (software or humans). This knowledge base is the resource for the response in the queries posed by users. In conclusion, we can note that knowledge bases are formed by an ontology and a set of individual instances of its classes (Noy and McGuinness, 2001).

Ontologies are able to operate as repositories for semantic information describing a specific domain. They also provide means for the organization of this information. Hence, users can pose their queries acquiring knowledge described by the ontology. This knowledge is extracted through the hierarchical relation of the concepts and, of course, through their relations.

They also provide the semantic integration of different resources setting up the base for the description of each element. In this respective, one can study efforts that use a general domain ontology for the description of the concepts of each information source while others allow the use of private ontologies that is combined when it is necessary. The first method exhibits the advantage of the semantic interoperability while the second provide freedom in the ontology construction since it allows developer to construct ontologies based on their interests.

Finally, ontologies enhance the quality of the retrieved information through the semantic annotation of information. They provide means for taxonomies construction, based on which queries can be disambiguated. Through this procedure the information returned to users is more precise corresponding to their needs and their appreciation of the domain.

It is obvious from the above mentioned, that ontologies in the Semantic Web era play an important role. They allow machines to understand the annotated data and serve users approaching their appreciation of information. Nowadays, ontologies are used in many application domains. An interesting scenario based on ontologies is their use for access to heterogeneous information sources. Thus, every source is described using terms taken from an ontology. Ontologies can provide a common view of the information sources augmenting interoperability and knowledge reuse.

AGENTS FOR ONTOLOGIES

Agent technology offers a lot of advantages in Computer Science. Also, it can offer important facilities to ontologies domain. In this section we describe basic models in which agents are used in ontology manipulation.

Ontology Construction

An important aspect of the use of agents in ontology manipulation is the ontology construction. Many times agents must build an ontology in order to describe their knowledge base. Knowledge base is an essential for agents working to serve their owners. Agents reason on their knowledge base, deciding what is the most appropriate move according to environment's and users' needs. There are three approaches in which agents may be based on in order to construct their ontologies (Guan and Zhu, 2004).

The first choice is to rely on an ontology definition provider. This means that they must communicate with it in order to gain access to ontology concepts and relations. Through that procedure they are able to construct their knowledge using classes that the provider gave them. Hence, all the agents can use the same concepts given by the provider, facilitating their communication and furthermore their cooperation. In such systems, the central elements of the overall architecture are a kind of intelligent broker agent which is responsible to maintain and manage a shared contextual model (Chen, Finin and Joshi, 2003). Hence, agents are able to share contextual knowledge through the use of common ontologies communicating with the broker. Of course, communication channels and protocols are necessary in order to complete these tasks. However, this method restricts agents' autonomy as they are bounded to specific concept hierarchy. Also, this process requires time and resources.

An alternative solution is to construct their ontologies themselves. This means that an agent must observe and analyze the information exchanged in the environment and extract basic concepts and their relations in order to define fundamental elements of the constructed ontology. It concerns a tedious effort that may require the intervention of agents' owners. This complicates the whole procedure. Furthermore, the construction of an ontology demands increased intelligence from the side of the agent in order to be capable of recognizing the basic elements of the ontology. This approaches human intelligence.

The third choice is the communication with other agents working in the environment for concepts acquisition. Agents may cooperate in this direction exchanging basic terms of an ontology. This requires a specific plan of exchange as well as the honesty of the transmitting agent. In (Guan and Zhu, 2004) authors present such an example where agents cooperate for ontology exchange. They divide models for exchange according to the number of the involved agents. The models that they discuss are: unilateral, bilateral and multilateral. Agents determine the criteria for ontology exchange and proceed to the action using requests and responses in KQML (Finin, Fritzson, McKay and McEntire, 1994). For further details one can refer to the above mentioned article.

Ontology Integration

In these cases of agents' usage, usually there is one or more agents that undertake the responsibility to match two or more ontologies. The reason is that in an open and dynamic environment as a multi-agent system is, there is a large enough possibility to find agents that use different ontologies as a knowledge base. This means that an integration procedure is necessary in order to enable communications paths between them. Figure 2 depicts the described scenario.

Figure 2. A mapping agent

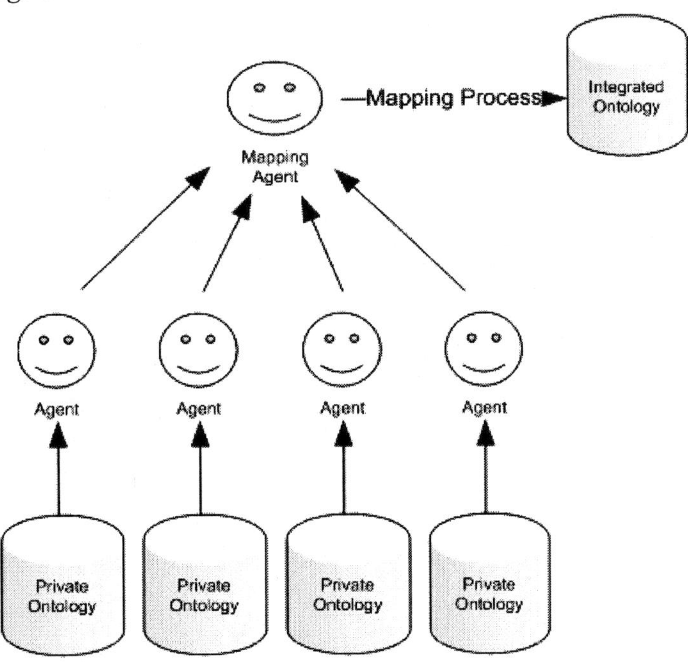

For example, in (Deen and Ponnamperuma, 2006) authors describe a system where an ontology agent integrates ontologies from source agents working in the environment. The ontology agent is comprised by four parts:

- Validator which checks if source ontologies are in the correct form
- Integrator which integrates the ontologies based on mapping methods
- Messaging part which transmits the mapping result to the source agents in order to inform them
- Query part which transforms or answers queries posed by other agents

Another effort in this research field is presented in (Li, Wu and Yang, 2005; Li, Yang and Wu, 2005). In the referred system, an integration agent is responsible to map between ontologies providing a new one, for which an ontology agent is created for handling it. The system creates new ontologies from the existing ones either extending them or combine them. The integration agent starts from the root of each ontology and counts the number of appearances of each concept. After this, it filters the unacceptable concepts related to a threshold. Through this procedure it provides a mapping result based on the number of appearances of each concept regarding to the relations that held in ontologies between concepts.

In (Elmore, Potok and Sheldon, 2003) a system is presented where an integration agent merges ontologies taken from a number of data agents. This system interacts with the user in order to choose the required data sources. A number of data agents are in front of the actual data sources providing ontology elements when needed. Integration agent is responsible to define a common ontology, with the help of the user, following a specific process. The final queries posed by the user are answered based on the merged ontology that is constructed.

Agent technology offers a lot of advantages in ontology integration. First of all, it provides a dynamic procedure that is held when the integration decides based on its knowledge. Usually, the integration process starts when changes in private ontologies are met. Furthermore, it is an automatic process that does not require manual intervention. Of course, a basic element for the success of the mapping agent is the matching algorithm which gives the final results. The matching algorithm and the matching validity threshold are issues for further study. Moreover, agents are rationale and adaptive components that may learn from this procedure. This knowledge may be applicable to the future interactions of an integration agent. Finally, we must note that new ontologies which are the results of such a process are applied immediately to a system providing an important advantage for the search of information. Due to this fact, agents that are based on different ontologies may refer to mapping peers in order to resolve the gap in their communication.

ONTOLOGIES FOR AGENTS

The use of ontologies for the description of agents' characteristics concerns the majority of research in domains where agent technology and ontologies are met. As mentioned above, ontologies enable interoperability among heterogeneous information sources. They provide knowledge on a certain domain. In this section we discuss how ontologies may assist agents in knowledge discovery. In this point, we give a short description of the benefits of ontologies in agent systems. These are:

- Ontologies provide a shared vocabulary of a domain.
- Ontologies provide the opportunity to agents to reuse knowledge associating terms and relationships.
- Agents can reason based on ontologies.
- Ontologies help in interoperability among agents working to similar domains.

Agents use information related to specific application domain. If this domain is described with an ontology that, as discussed above, provides a shared vocabulary, then it is obvious that agents may profit from this description. Agents will be able to manipulate the shared information and, furthermore, to cooperate based on common elements. Also, in the cooperation procedure, agents must know the characteristics and properties of other agents with which they interact (Zini and Sterling, 1999). This knowledge may be represented by an ontology that describes agents and their characteristics. It concerns a set of types of agents and specifications about their features. Additionally, ontologies may assist agents to ground their beliefs and actions. The internal state of an agent may be described by an ontology in order to be enriched semantically. Its knowledge base, goals and plans may be manipulated more efficiently providing to users qualitative services.

Ontologies used in agents systems may be divided in two major categories: Private and public ontologies (Sycara and Paolucci, 2003).

Private ontologies represent the domain and the internal knowledge of the agent. These elements are necessary to problem-solving by the agent. On the other hand, public ontologies are common in a number of agents working in an environment. They are independent from the internal state of each agent and represent shared knowledge helping in the cooperation.

Despite of the advantages that ontologies have in applications domains, their use has some disadvantages. Even if ontologies describe in a semantically enriched way the information, trying to reach the way that humans do, machines or software components do not have humans' perception of information and for this reason they may not judge correctly the meaning of specific data elements (Siebes and van Harmelen, 2002). Furthermore, problems may arise if two agents have different representations of information based on different ontologies. In these cases, specific models must be defined in order to handle this gap of semantic representation. This is very crucial thinking about the importance that ontologies have in commercial and research applications. Finally, we must note that maintaining an ontology in which an agent is based on, solving problems for its owners or even more providing services to others, means that the structure and the elements of the ontology are fresh and represent with the right way the domain. In different case, problems concerning the correctness of the tasks performed by agents may arise.

In the following sections we discuss the fields in which ontologies may help agents to be based on in order to fulfill their owners' needs.

Knowledge Extraction

A knowledge base provides the means for the storage, manipulation and retrieval of knowledge. It stores data in a computer readable form enhancing the automated retrieval and reasoning related to them. Knowledge bases may use ontologies in order to specify their structure and scheme. Ontologies as we referred above are explicit specifications of a domain. They provide terms describing the core elements of an environment. Concerning that agents use a knowledge base for their internal and external states, it is obvious that ontologies enrich the information manipulated by these autonomous software components. The semantically enriched information provides an advantage to agents seeking for data in order to complete their tasks. Thus, agents are able to understand information through a way that comes near to the way that a human appreciates it. This means more efficient search of information.

Ontologies explicitly specify the concepts and their hierarchy in a domain. This enriches semantically the information and defines relationships among concepts facilitating the reasoning process. The most common relationship among concepts in an ontology is the relation IS-A that defines a parental relationship. Of course, a number of types of relationships may be defined depending on the application field. The knowledge base is built using the instances of the ontology wrapping the actual data sources. With this process each agent depends on a semantic framework that provides him with the necessary information to reason and decide how to react in different situations. Hence, ontological elements may be used to describe every aspect of an agent. An ontology may be used for the description of agents' beliefs, goals, messages and intentions as we can see in Figure 3 (general description of the use of ontologies). We remind that beliefs show what the agent knows, desires represent what the agents tries to achieve and intentions shows the plan of the agent in order to achieve the current goal. Furthermore, ontologies may be used for the description of other agents' characteristics. At every time of agent's life, it observes the environment and reasons about its and others' behavior taking the appropriate decision about its next moves. When an event occurs, the agent looks at its knowledge base for relevant plans and for each of them examines its appropriateness to the new situation. After this, it selects the most appropriate and starts its execution. Additionally, at every moment of its life it decides which goal must pursue and of course how to pursue it. It concerns a very important and dynamic procedure that evolves over time until agent reaches the final goal. We must note that its knowledge base may be expanded adding more classes (concepts), new features in classes, new constraints, new relations and more instances.

Agent Communication and Collaboration

Another important field in which ontologies may offer significant advantages is in agents' communication. Communication is the basis of cooperation. Agents working in open environments and having specific capabilities may need others' help in order to solve their problems. The communication model specified by FIPA (http://www.fipa.org) is based on speech act theory (Searle, 1969). Agents are able to communicate using asynchronous messages that declare communicative acts. The language used for this reason is ACL (Agent Communication Language) (FIPA, 2002). However, ACL does not provide a robust way for communication in open environments and does not facilitate reasoning. It is obvious that the use of ontologies may be very helpful in agents' interaction. A message content ontology helps agents to describe facts, hypotheses and predications about a domain (Van Aart, Pels, Caire and Bergenti, 2002). On the other hand, we must not forget that

Figure 3. Use of ontologies for the description of the agent's states

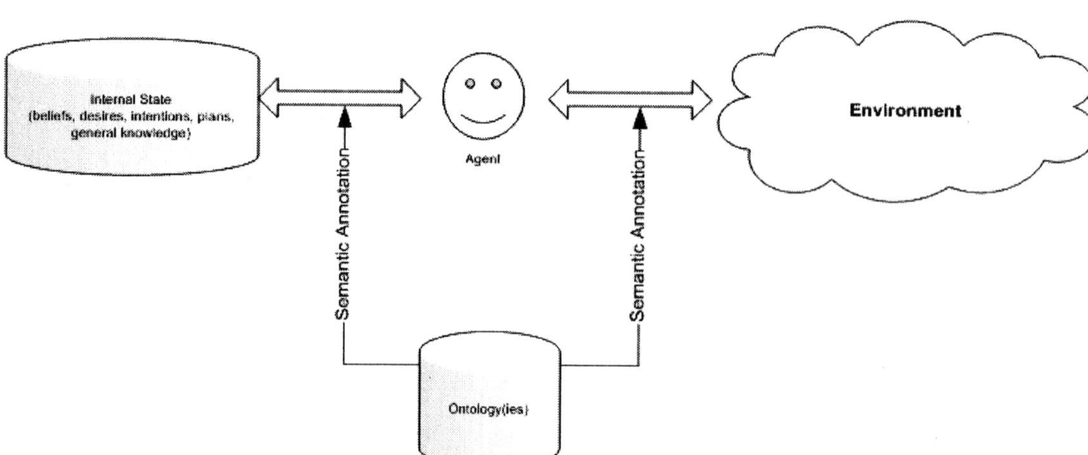

each agent may use its own private ontology in order to describe its knowledge. Each agent is built by a different developer that has a specific view of the domain. For this reason, a number of approaches have been built in order to overcome this disadvantage. The most important of them are (Stuckenschmidt and Timm, 2002):

- **Emergence of a common ontology.** It concerns an approach where using specific methods, as language games (Steels, 1998) or social networks analysis (Hamasaki, Matsuo, Nishimura and Takeda, 2007), a common ontology evolves in the system. Through language games agents are able to define the common and basic terms in which they may be based on in order to evolve the common ontology. This ontology becomes the basis of each communication held in the environment. The disadvantage is that an additional phase of interaction is required. Also, the agents involved in such a procedure may be aware of the process through which the common ontology is developed.
- **Merging ontologies.** They involve models in which a merging process leads to a common ontology which includes all the terms of the merged sub-ontologies. Usually, merging is based on a matching algorithm that examines the similarity between all the terms used in private ontologies. After this, the communication is based on the global ontology. Many similar efforts can be found in the respective literature. We indicate some of them: (Stephens and Huhns, 2001; Dou, McDermott and Peishen, 2002; Stumme, 2005; Stumme and Maedche, 2001; Noy and Musen, 2000 & 1999; Kotis and Vouros, 2004). However, this methodology suffers from the fact that the use of the global ontology bound agents, which are, as we mentioned before, autonomous software components.
- **Mapping ontologies.** It is the procedure through which mappings between concepts defined in private ontologies are defined. The success of mapping is depended on the matching process. This process requires a lot of manual effort since there is not a lot of research using automatic models. There are a lot of examples located in this research field. Some of them are: (Hendler, 2001; Prasad, Peng and Finin, 2002; Weisman, Roos and Vogt, 2002; Pinto, 1999; Pan, Ding, Yu and Peng, 2005; Mitra, Noy and Jaiswal, 2004).

For a survey on ontology integration methods one can refer in (Wache et al., 2001).

We must note that the procedure of the construction of a common representation of different private ontologies may be held by the system where agents cooperate. Such an example is presented in (Blythe, Chalupsky, Gil and McGregor, 2004). The system has the ability to translate terms used in an ontology to the others. Methods that are used may be merging or mapping, as discussed above. The registration of each agent is necessary for the mappings between ontologies to be defined. In the communication phase each message is translated into to the appropriate ontological representation.

Generally speaking, as we can see in Figure 4, agents' communication is based on a common ontology in order to have a common view of the domain.

Reasoning and Verification

In this point we outline the reasoning mechanisms that can be used by agents in order to extract useful information for their tasks. The reasoning process of an agent can be divided into two parts: firstly an agent reasons about the state of the world and secondly it reasons about the actions that performs (Lambrix and Padgham, 1998). An agent based on observations may understand

Figure 4. Agent communication framework using a common ontology

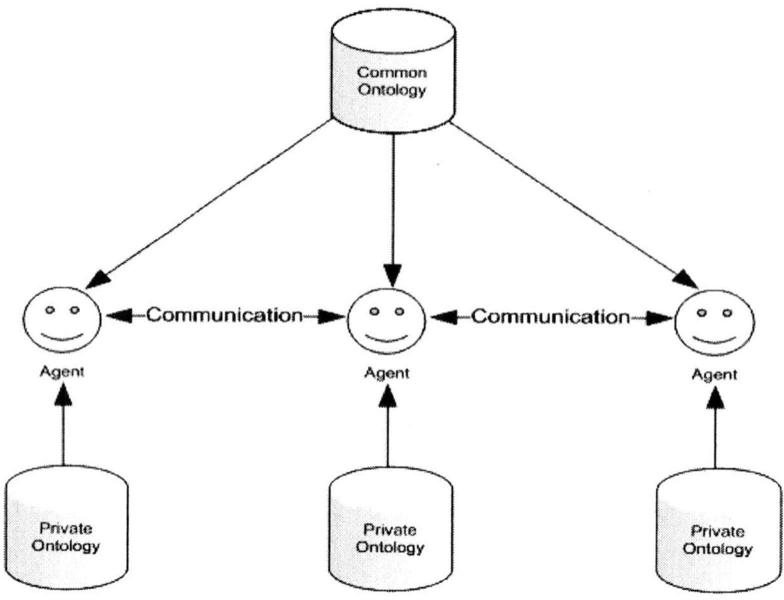

what happens in the environment and adapt its behavior. Unfortunately, this knowledge cannot be exhaustive. In a timeless way it reasons about its internal and external states and chose the appropriate action.

The simplest form of reasoning is deduction. According to deduction, knowledge is reached based on previous facts. If preconditions are true then the conclusion is also true. A simple example is the following:

If $P \rightarrow Q$ and P then Q

This formula is known as modus-ponens. Similarly, an agent may be based on specific axioms that when they are true lead to a conclusion giving him a way of reaction.

Agents have some important characteristics about how they might reason logically: their reasoning takes time and their knowledge is imperfect (Anderson, Gomaa, Grant and Perlis, 2005). Ontologies describing their content facilitate machines to process information in a semantically enriched way.

RDF (Resource Description Framework) and RDFS (RDF Schema) (W3C, 2004b) concerns basic Semantic Web Technologies. RDFS provides a framework for the definition of vocabularies used for the semantically annotation of metadata for RDF files. An RDF file is an annotation metadata repository for a specific domain. The RDF metadata framework is based on making statements about resources in the form of subject – predicate – object. While the RDF model is a simple language, more powerful languages have been presented in the Semantic Web framework. Some of them are OWL (W3C, 2004a), DAML (Quellet and Ogbuji, 2002), OIL (Klein et al., 2003), etc. Ontologies can be built using the referred technologies.

Domain ontologies specify classes for concepts and relations among them. A reasoning state of an ontology is an assignment of truth values (true or false) to a set of ground individuals (Bosse, Jonker and Treur, 2005). Knowledge that an ontology define can be easily represented by terms of Description Logics (DL) (Baader, Horrocks and Sattler, 2003). In DL each concept represents a set of individuals while roles define binary relations between them. A knowledge base in DL has two parts: the terminology (Tbox) and the assertional part (Abox). Each of them has a set of axioms. The Tbox includes axioms about the concepts and roles of the domain described describing a concept hierarchy (concept tree) while the Abox includes axioms about the individuals (instances) of each concept.

The basic inference on concept expressions in DL is *subsumption,* typically written as $C \sqsubseteq D$ (Nardi and Brachman, 2003). Subsumption is the examination if a concept D is more general than a concept C. C is subsumed by D if and only if all the instances of C are also instances of D. Hence, the concept C defines a subset of properties of the concept D. For example, the concept 'vehicle' is more general than the concept 'car'.

It is obvious that knowledge may derive through relationships that the concepts have. The relationships hierarchy is derived based on the most used relation IS-A. This relation shows the parental relation between concepts activating the inheritance of properties from the general concept to the more particular ones. Of course, the definition of other types of relations is permitted. A developer can incorporate the relations' definition in concepts' definition making subsumption the basic reasoning method. Ontology languages that use DL as an inference framework are based for reasoning in DL SHIQ (Horrocks, Sattler and Tobies, 1999). Basic mechanisms are the examination of single and multiple inheritance paths as well as the examination of constraint limitations. An alternate method for reasoning is the *satisfiability*. This means that we look if a concept definition is not the empty concept.

From the above, we conclude that an agent that has described its internal and external states with concepts taken from a domain ontology can build a knowledge base using a set of individuals. Based on observations and on its beliefs can reason using subsumption relations and satisfiability in order to extract the most appropriate action to the environment's incentives.

Agents' Capabilities Representation

In agents' discovery procedure, the matching process between agents' requests and agents' advertisements is a very crucial factor. For this reason ontologies may play an important role especially in agents' capabilities representation. Agents must advertise their capabilities in a system in order to help others to find the most appropriate partners. This is the base for cooperative problem solving. In literature, there are two main schemes for capabilities representation, explicit and implicit (Sycara and Paolucci, 2003).

Explicit methods provide direct ways through which agents advertise their capabilities. This means that ontologies, used in these methods, describe tasks performed by agents using different concepts. Explicit models provide a straightforward and fast method for capabilities presentation however they may result very large ontologies depending on the number of agents and capabilities that describe. Another important drawback of these methods is that they do not define the inputs and outputs that are necessary in order to communicate a requesting agent with the service provider agent. This is very crucial because it may impact communication efficiency.

An example of explicit capability representation is provided in Figure 5.

Implicit methods do not describe tasks performed by agents but they describe the environment first and next the result that agents can extract. Agents' tasks are defined by means posed in the domain representation. Ontologies used in these models describe the context, the type of inputs and outputs as well as the inputs and outputs with their restrictions. Implicit models provide a good enough description of the domain in which an agent is activated and they give an outline of the information needed in interaction procedure between requestors and the service

Figure 5. Explicit capability representation example

Capability c1
  Ontology University
    Class Faculty
      Slot name
      Slot address
      Slot position
      Slot office
      Slot years
      Slot salary computation
      ...

provider. On the other hand a requesting agent must infer the capabilities of the provider agent in order to cooperate. This demands an extra effort from the side of the requestor that delays the whole interaction.

An example of implicit capability representation is provided in Figure 6.

A service representation is similar to the representation of implicit capabilities. Properties of a service description could be the following:

- Service Name
- Service Description
- Type
- Protocol
- Communication Language
- Ontology
- Content Language
- Properties

As we can see in the description of a service we note all the important elements that help the requestors to retrieved and use the service. Services are very important in agents' cooperation procedure which provides the necessary information for goals completion.

In conclusion, we must note that there are efforts that combine the two above referred models.

Figure 6. Implicit capability representation example

Context: University
Input: name, position, years
Output: salary
Input-output constraints: years>=0
Description: it computes the salary of a faculty based on the years of experience.

Hence, we can find a combination that uses the ease of matching process of the explicit methods with the domain and data required by the provider from the implicit models.

ONTOLOGIES FOR LEARNING AGENTS

An interesting research area is that of learning agents in Multi-Agent environments. In a Multi-agent environment a number of agents are working for their goals completion usually through cooperation with others. These agents have a specific private knowledge, part of which is common among them. However, outside of this common knowledge they recognize additional concepts. The basic idea in learning systems is that a number of agents teach a learning agent concepts needed for their communication and hence for their cooperation. Such a scenario is depicted in Figure 7.

An interesting solution is the example-based learning. In these models 'teachers' select a number of positive or negative examples that are provided to learner in order to clarify the meaning of the examined concept. A general interaction scheme is presented in (Afsharchi and Far, 2006):

1. The learner defines what it wants to learn for a particular concept.

Figure 7. Agent Learning System

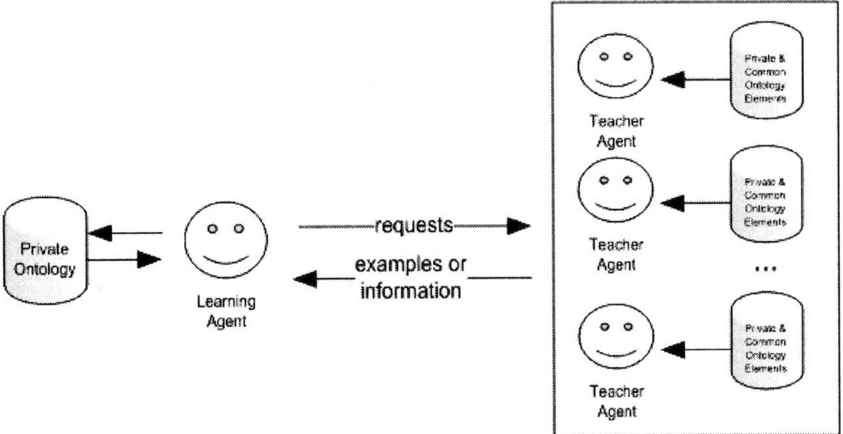

2. Each agent of the system tries to find the most appropriate example. For this, a selection procedure is performed.
3. The learner collects the answers and resolves potential conflicts.
4. The learner updates its ontology.

The most important step in this procedure is the step 2. In this step each 'teacher' tries to find in its internal knowledge base the most appropriate example for the examined concept. For this, it can use the hierarchy of its internal ontology.

In this point we present a short description of the example-based learning methods. Let us define as C the examined concept. If an agent tries to find negative examples for C then the best solution is to use the super-concept of C as a limit to these examples. This super-concept has common characteristics with C but their positive examples consist in 'near-misses' in C. Furthermore, another resource can be the siblings of C. Positive examples in siblings consist in negative for C because they are not covered by C.

Positive examples selection is easier, but it may include the subjective view of the teacher. In each teacher's knowledge base there are a number of objects that associate with the concept C as answers to queries related to it. All of them consist in positive examples for C. Teachers choose a good subset from this pool of objects and send it to learner. However, describing the concept C, teacher agent may use its point of view using features that are out of the limit of its ontology set of elements, but they consist in internal belief of the teacher.

The learner taking the descriptions of the C from the teachers extracts a final annotation and after this updates its internal ontology representation. This provides it common elements facilitating the cooperation among the team.

It is obvious that the characteristics of ontologies play an important role in this field. The ontology classes and relations among them provide the necessary information about the example selection. Learning methods use the IS-A relation as well as features and topological information of each concept and through a matching procedure defines the most appropriate examples either negative or positive. Through this process, agents that have a limited knowledge about the environment can extend their knowledge base increasing the concepts that they possess. Of course, it concerns a procedure that requires time and resources and it is affected by the number of the teacher agents and the conflicts that may be happened in the side of the learner. This can be ought to the different representations of the specific concept may have in the teachers' internal knowledge base. If this happens, the learner must resolve the conflict entering in a new communication phase with others, affecting its performance and consuming valuable time. However, it is about a challenging field that has a lot to offer in agent systems.

AGENTS AND SEMANTIC WEB SERVICES

Web is primary designed for human interpretation. In today's Web, agents cannot process and understand information that is in an unprocessed or in natural language form. However, the Semantic Web vision enables machines to understand and manipulate information in a semantically enriched way. This is also observed in the field of the Web Services (WS) (W3C, 2002). Currently, Web Services are based on XML, UDDI, WSDL and SOAP (Liu, 2003). XML (eXtensive Markup Language) provides means for markup information while UDDI (Universal Description Discovery and Integration) is a registry which involves description, discovery and integration of Web Services facilitating their use. Finally, WSDL (Web Services Definition Language) provides a mechanism for defining interfaces to Web Services as SOAP (Simple Object Access Protocol) is a protocol that facilitates Web Services to exchange data wherever they are located.

Speaking for ontologies one can allege that the most powerful use of ontologies is in the area of Web Services (Hendler, 2001). Semantic markup languages are created for semantic Web Services annotation as OWL-S (W3C, 2004c), DAML-S (The DAML Services Coalition, 2001), etc. The first use of such languages is to provide means for the service advertisements in an ontological description. Tools and agents that search for Web Services could use the hierarchy to find matches based on call/subclasses properties and their relations (Li, 2002). It is obvious that these languages enable basic actions on Web Services such as service discovery, execution, composition and interoperation (McIlraith, Son and Zeng, 2001). All these actions may be executed by an intelligent agent.

Service discovery involves the automatic search of the location of a Web Service which matches with the properties of a specific request. Semantic Web Services are marked with ontological elements facilitating the matching process. **Service execution** involves the retrieval of the results of a service that is executed by an agent. Furthermore, very important is the field of **service composition** which involves the selection and composition of a number of Web Services in order to perform a task. Similar to this is the **service interoperation** where an agent may use information taken from Web Services to perform calls to other services exchanging data through a number of services. Ontologies used in the described four tasks provide a robust and efficient way for their execution. This leads agents to retrieve the appropriate information in order to complete their tasks.

Agents and Web Services have some similarities and some differences according to their nature (Liu, 2003). First of all, both need a communication language. In agent systems it is necessary for the communication, which is the basis for the cooperation while Web Services are based on XML and SOAP in order to provide methods for services invocation. This communication language enables the exchange of messages during the calling process of an agent or a Web Service. Finally, both Web Services and agents are based on ontologies which helps them to define in a semantically way the carried knowledge for agents and the interface for services.

However, these two technologies have a number of differences. The differences are mainly located in the intelligent nature of agents. Agents have the ability to learn, adapt and move (in some cases) in order to find the appropriate information for their goals completion. In contrary, Web

Services are static, not autonomous and of course they do not change according to the needs of their environment.

In spite of the differences, the two technologies may profit from each other. Agents may use Web Services as a means for their capabilities representation using a fixed technique for description. This description provides an interface for capabilities invocation from the potential partners. Web Services may profit from the dynamic nature of agents. They can use agents' characteristics such as adaptability, flexibility or reasoning. Agents can adapt to their environment's needs according to their knowledge base which is a basic reasoning repository. They reason over time in order to provide a high performance as for their owners' needs. These characteristics give them flexibility and robustness in their goals completion.

It is obvious from the above described that the discussed technologies and their combination may provide more efficient tools for the developers in order to build flexible and robust systems. They may combine the description techniques used in Web Services field with the intelligence of agents. All these drive to a common target: the high satisfaction level of users.

BENEFITS AND SYSTEMS COMPARISON

The combination of the described technologies (intelligent agents and ontologies) offers many advantages in various application domains. Actually, the combination of the referred technologies involves the advantages of each one. Thus, the most important agent features include the autonomy to act on behalf of their users as well as the capabilities of reacting to changes that happen in the environment. Moreover, the use of ontologies to various tasks that are accomplished by the agents provides a high level of efficiency in information manipulation. For example, using ontologies, agents are capable to understand in one extent the semantically enriched information. This information is used to describe critical data concerning the knowledge that the agents have for its internal and external states or it is used to describe specific information sources or products. Thus, developers are able to deal with interoperability issues since a common view between the knowledge domains of different entities could be established. If we consider an agent that seeks products for its owner, we can discern that it can efficiently manipulate information described based on terms taken from an ontology. Hence, the agent is capable to understand the meaning of a property named 'Price', as long as providers describe their products using classes and properties taken from the ontology (class 'Product', property 'Price'). Obviously, this ontology, and its classes and properties, hides different references to the price of products (e.g. 'Value', 'Price', etc) under a common concept. Of course, the terms used in the ontology are common knowledge to the agent. Furthermore, ontologies can provide a common language in agents communication. Through this, agents that want to interact with others may learn concepts provided from an ontology and thus learn the language in which communication is held.

On the other hand, agents can help in ontologies manipulation. Due to their independent nature and their intelligence, agents are capable of manipulating ontologies in many aspects. All the important issues concerning ontologies may be implemented by agents. Such issues involve ontology construction, ontology integration, etc. Moreover, agents are capable of renovating their knowledge learning from their environment. Hence, it is possible to be able to evolve ontology concepts. In conclusion, we may note that using agents with ontologies, we combine the autonomous character of agents with the semantically enriched information provided by ontologies. Hence, the integration of information located in heterogeneous sources will be more efficient helping users to search and retrieve information and services more productively.

The most of the systems found in the relevant literature target to solve specific problems detected in the combination of intelligent agents and ontologies. For example, there is an increased effort to deal with the problem of communication between autonomous entities. Agents based on different ontologies may face problems in interactions with other members that use their own ontologies. Hence, various efforts try to deal with the mapping or the aggregation process between the different ontologies. This is going to facilitate agents because they could use the same terms in their interaction. However, the most of the proposed systems do not study in depth the cases where more than two ontologies should be mapped. Another problem that should be dealt with is information search. Ontologies solve the problem of heterogeneity because they provide a common view to different information sources. Thus, intelligent agents are able to seek more efficiently information and furthermore to be this procedure more productive related to their response to users. In the reverse direction, as mentioned, ontologies are used in agent systems to provide a semantic annotation to basic parts of the agent technology such as their capabilities, goals, etc. However, ontologies can only semantically enrich agents knowledge. This means that they can help in the direction of doing agents to understand more efficiently the information through which agents can productively serve their owners. For example, agents using ontologies are able to cooperate with the appropriate entities according to their goals and to find the most relevant information inquired by their owners.

A short comparison of a number of systems that combine ontologies and agents are presented in Table 3.

As we can discern, in ontology mapping and merging research one can find many efforts. The referred systems concern the combination of agents and ontologies, however, there are efforts that exclusively study the integration process such as (Lacher & Groh, 2001; Pinto, 1999; Noy & Musen, 2000; Wache et al., 2001).

FUTURE RESEARCH DIRECTIONS

The combination of ontologies and agent technology provide a lot of advantages in users working in open environments like the Web. However, there are some issues that need further research. First of all, a general methodology for ontology development must be defined. In the relevant literature there are tools that help a developer to construct an ontology, but the lack of a common development methodology is important. Using a common development framework, specific steps for ontology construction, manipulation and integration will be defined.

Another important issue that the combination of agents and ontologies will face is ontology integration. As explained, each developer uses its own ontology based on its point of view. This means that agents based on such ontologies and acting as front ends of information sources should utilize an integrated ontology for their interaction. This task imposes a mapping process that in some case is cumbersome. Moreover, an efficient method should be used in order to provide correct and qualitative results. In most of the cases, agents should integrate their private ontologies either resorting to a middle entity or entering to a phase of interaction with the others in order to define the connections between concepts and properties of the mapping ontologies. In this field, a general automatic method for ontology integration should be defined. The integration procedure should be held by agents in a full automatic and efficient way.

Concerning agents communication, the definition of an upper message ontology is necessary. The message ontology could provide the appropriate means for the interaction between autonomous entities as agents are. Such ontology will lead to

Table 3. Systems comparison

System	Domain	Methodology	Short Description
Expose, SHOE - Presented in (Luke et al., 1997).	Information Search	Ontology definition (SHOE) based on HTML.	Agents (Expose) parse the annotated HTML (using an ontology) and reuse their knowledge.
System presented in (Prasad et al., 2002).	Agent Communication	Mapping between two different ontologies.	Authors present a methodology for the mapping process between different ontologies used by agents.
System presented in (Weinstein & Birmingham, 1999).	Agent Communication	Mapping between two different ontologies.	Authors present a methodology for the mapping process between different ontologies.
System presented in (Stuckenschmidt & Timm, 2002).	Agent Communication	Mapping between two different ontologies.	The presented methodology maps terms taken from two ontologies in order to fill the communication gap. Authors present formal methods for the referred procedure.
CaseLP (Zini & Sterling, 1999).	Knowledge Representation	Ontology is used to describe agents knowledge.	Ontology is used to describe agents as entities as well as agents knowledge. Four kinds of agents are used. Moreover, each agent is characterized by concepts retrieved from the ontology.
System presented in (Li et al., 2005).	Ontology Integration	Ontology Mapping and Integration.	The system presented uses agent that integrates ontologies found in business scenarios. The ontologies are taken from different information sources.
System presented in (Deen & Ponnamperuma, 2006).	Ontology Integration	Ontology Integration.	Authors describe an automatic methodology for ontology integration in agent systems. This procedure is held every time a new member joins the community.

an efficient exchange of information between partners. Thus, the cooperative problem solving procedure that agents pursue in many cases becomes more productive.

Since agents use ontologies for their internal and external states description, their reasoning mechanisms are based on them. Hence, research should be held in the field of reasoning based on the context of the application domain. Context reasoning is essential for the construction of more efficient and flexible systems because it defines the characteristics of the environment where agents act. Thus, it is important to take it into consideration when agents reason about others and about their next moves. Moreover, agents work in an environment where they search for services based on a specific context. It is necessary to find the appropriate partners, information and services that are consistent with the specific context.

Finally, more attention should be paid on the use of intelligence and flexibility of agent systems through its combination with the characteristics of semantic Web Services. Web Services may represent aspects of the states of agents and their capabilities while agents may produce and act as front-end interface of Web Services. This will lead to an automatic and efficient method for services discovery and invocation.

CONCLUSION

Ontologies and agents become more and more important in computer engineering. Ontologies provide a conceptualisation of a domain defining a common view of heterogeneous information sources. This is a very important characteristic due to the nature of the Web, where information is provided by different users in different forms. A reasoning process can be based on ontologies in order to find the appropriate information that fulfils our needs. On the other hand agents are software components that act on behalf of their owners to satisfy their needs. Agents work in heterogeneous environments communicating, if it is necessary, with others in order to complete their goals. We must not forget that each agent consists in a software program that depicts the point of view of its developer.

In this chapter we described the aspects of the combination of the two referred technologies. We saw agents that build ontologies and agents that integrate ontologies in an automatic way. In this kind of models we try to take advantages of the intelligence and the flexibility that agent systems provide. We saw that ontologies are used to define the internal and external state of agents. For example, there are ontologies that are the knowledge base for agents, ontologies that are used to annotate messages in interaction procedure between agents as well as ontologies for agents' capabilities representation.

Also, we discussed the connection between agents and Web Services. Agents may profit from the fixed description techniques that Web Services provide. These techniques are well suited for agents' capabilities representation. On the other hand Web Services may profit from the dynamic characteristics of agents. Such characteristics are adaptability, flexibility or reasoning.

Of course, there are issues that must be taken into consideration in order to construct more robust systems. However, it is obvious that the combination of the examined technologies may offer a lot of advantages in the future Web.

REFERENCES

Afsharchi, M. & Far, B. H. (2006). Improving Example Selection for Agents Teaching Ontology Concepts. *In Proceedings of the 10th International Workshop on Cooperative Information Agents, CIA '06, Edinburgh, UK,* 228-242.

Anderson, M. L., Gomaa, W., Grant, J. & Perlis, D. (2005). On the Reasoning of Real-World Agents: Toward a Semantics for Active Logic. *In Proceedings of the 7th International Symposium on Logical Formalizations of Commonsense Reasoning, Corfu, Greece.*

Auxilio, M. & Nieto, M. (2003). *An Overview of Ontologies.* Technical Report, Center of Research in Information and Automation Technologies, Interactive and Cooperative Technologies Lab, Universidad de las Americas. Retrieved March 5th from http://www.starlab.vub.ac.be/ teaching/ ontologies_overview.pdf.

Baader, F., Horrocks, I. & Sattler, U. (2003). Description Logics as Ontology Languages for the Semantic Web. In D. Hutter & W. Stephan (Eds.), *Festchrift in Honor of Jorg Siekmann, Lecture notes in Artificial Intelligence.* Springer.

Bellifemine, F., Poggi, A. & Rimassa, G. (2000). Developing Multi-Agent Systems with JADE. *In Proceedings of the 7th International Workshop on Agent Theories, Architectures and Languages, Boston, MA.*

Blythe, J., Chalupsky, H., Gil, Y. & MacGregor, R. (2004). *Ontology-Based Agent Communication with Rosetta.* USC/Information Sciences Institute. Retrieved March 12th from http://www.isi.edu/expect/projects/agents/rosetta.html.

Borst, W. N. (1997). *Construction of Engineering Ontologies.* Centre for Telematica and Information

Technology, University of Tweenty. Enschede, The Netherlands.

Bosse, T., Jonker, C. M. & Treur, J. (2005). Requirements Analysis of an Agent's Reasoning Capabilities. *In Proceedings of the AOIS '05*, 48-63.

Chen, H., Finin, T. & Joshi, A. (2003). Using OWL in a Pervasive Computing Broker. *In Proceedings of the Workshop on Ontologies in Agent Systems, AAMAS '03, Melbourne, Australia.*

Deen, S. M. & Ponnaperuma, K. (2006). Dynamic Ontology Integration in a Multi-agent Environment. *In Proceedings of the 20th International Conference on Advanced Information Networking and Applications (AINA '06)*, 373-378.

Dou, D., McDermott, D. V. & Peishen, Q. (2002). Ontology Translation by Merging Ontologies and Automated Reasoning. *In Proceedings of the EKAW2002, Workshop on Ontologies for Multi-Agent Systems*, 3-18.

Durfee, E. H., & Lesser, V. (1989). Negotiating Task Decomposition and Allocation Using Partial Global Planning. In *L.* Gasser & M. Huhns (eds), *Distributed Artificial Intelligence, Vol. 2, 229-244.* San Francisco, CA: Morgan Caufmann.

Elmore, M. T., Potok, T. E. & Sheldon, F T. (2003). Dynamic Data Fusion Using An Ontology-Based Software Agent System. *In Proceedings of the 7th World Multiconference on Systemics, Cybernetics and Informatics.*

Fensel, D. (2000). The Semantic Web and its Languages. *IEEE Computer Society, 15(6)*, 67-73.

Finin, T., Fritzson, R., McKey, D. & McEntire, R. (1994). KQML as an Agent Communication Language. *In Proceedings of the 3rd International Conference on Information and Knowledge Management*, 456-463.

FIPA (2002). *FIPA ACL Message Structure Specification.* Retrieved March 12th from http://www.fipa.org/specs/fipa00061/SC00061G.html

Gruber, T. R. (1993). A Translation Approach to Portable Ontology Specification. *Knowledge Acquisition, 5(2)*, 199-220.

Guan, S. & Zhu, F. (2004). Ontology Acquisition and Exchange of Evolutionary Product-brokering Agents. *Journal of Research and Practice in Information Technology, 36(1)*, 35-46.

Hamasaki, M., Matsuo, Y., Nishimura, T. & Takeda, H. (2007). Ontology Extraction Using Social Network. *In Proceedings of the 20th International Joint Conference on Artificial Intelligence, Workshop on Semantic Web for Collaborative Knowledge Acquisition, Hyderabad, India.*

Hendler, J. (2001). Agents and the Semantic Web. *IEEE Intelligent Systems*, 30-37.

Horrocks, I., Sattler, U. & Tobies, S. (1999). Practical Reasoning for Expressive Description Logics. *In Proceedings of LPAR '99, number 1705 in LNAI, Springer-Verlag*, 161-180.

Huhns, M. & Stephens, L. M. (2004). Multiagent Systems for Internet Applications. In M. P. Singh (Ed.), *Practical Handbook of Internet Computing.* Chapman Hall and CRC Press.

Jennings, N. R. & Wooldridge, M. (1998). Applications of Intelligent Agents. In N. R. Jennings & M. J. Wooldridge (eds), *Agent Technology: Foundations, Applications and Markets.* Springer-Verlag: Heidelberg, Germany.

Klein, M., Broekstra, J., Fensel, D., van Harmelen, F. & Horrocks, I. (2003). Ontologies and Schema Languages on the Web. In D. Fensel. J. Hendler, H. Lieberman & W. Wahlster (eds), *Spinning the Semantic Web: Bringing the World Wide Web to its Full Potential.* Cambridge, MA: The MIT Press.

Kotis, K. & Vouros, G. A. (2004). The HCONE Approach to Ontology Merging. *In Proceedings of the 1st European Semantic Web Symposium,* Heraclion, Greece, 137-151.

Lacher, M. & Groh, G. (2001). Facilitating the Exchange of Explicit Knowledge through Ontology Mapping. *American Association for Artificial Intelligence, 2001.*

Lambrix, P. & Padgham, L. (1998). Using Knowledge Representation for Agent World Model. *In Proceedings of the International Conference on Multi-agent Systems, France,* 443-444.

Li, L., Wu, B. & Yang, Y. (2005). Agent-Based Ontology Integration for Ontology-Based Applications. *In Proceedings of the 2005 Australasian Ontology Workshop, Sydney, Australia,* 53-59.

Li, L., Yang, Y. & Wu, B. (2005). Agent-Based Ontology Mapping Towards Ontology Interoperability. *In Proceedings of the 18th Australian Joint Conference on Artificial Intelligence (AI '05), LNAI 3809, Springer-Verlang, Sydney, Australia,* 843-846.

Li, W. (2002). Intelligent Information Agent with Ontology on the Semantic Web. *In Proceedings of the 4th World Congress on Intelligent Control and Automation, 2(2),* 1501-1504.

Liu, D. (2003). *Agents and Web Services.* SENG609.22 Tutorial.

Luke, S., Spector, L. Rager, D. & Hendler, J. (1997). *Ontology-Based Web Agents. In Procedings of the 1st International Conference on Autonomous Agents, USA, 59-66.*

Martin, D. L., Cheyer, A. J. & Moran D. B. (1998). The Open Agent Architecture: A Framework for Building Distributed Software Systems. *Applied Artificial Intelligence, 1998.*

Mcllraith, S. A., Son, T. C. & Zeng, H. (2001). Semantic Web Services. *IEEE Intelligent Systems, March/April 2001,* 46-53.

Mitra, P., Noy, N. F. & Jaiswal, A. R. (2004). OMEN: A Probabilistic Ontology Mapping Tool. *In Proceedings of the 3rd International Conference on the Semantic Web (ISWC-2004), Workshop on Meaning Coordination and Negotiation, Hiroshima, Japan.*

Nardi, D. & Brachman, R. J. (2003). An Introduction to Description Logics. In F. Baader, D. Calvanese, D. L. McGuinness, D. Nardi & P. F. Patel-Schneider (eds), *The description Logic Handbook: Theory, Implementation, and Applications.* Cambridge University Press.

Neches, R., Fikes, R. E., Finin, T., Gruber, T. R., Senator, T. & Swarout, W. R. (1991). Enabling Technology for Knowledge Sharing. *Artificial Intelligence Magazine, 12(3),* 36-56.

Noy, F. N. & McGuinness, D. L. (2001). *Ontology Development 101: A Guide to Creating Your First Ontology.* Stanford Knowledge Systems Laboratory Technical Report KSL-01-05 and Stanford Medical Informatics Technical Report SMI-2001-0880, March.

Noy, N. F. & Musen, M. A. (1999). SMART: Automated Support for Ontology Merging and Alignment. *In Proceedings of the 12th Workshop on Knowledge Acquisition, Modelling and Management,* Banff, Canada.

Noy, N. F. & Musen, M. A. (2000). PROMPT: Algorithm and Tool for Automated Ontology Merging and Alignment. *In Proceedings of the National Conference on Artificial Intelligence,* Austin, Texas.

Nwana, H. S. (1996). Software Agents: An Overview. *The Knowledge Engineering Review, 11(3),* 1-40.

Nwana, H. S., Ndumu, D. T. & Lee L. C. (1998). ZEUS: An Advanced Toolkit for Engineering Distributed Multi-Agent Systems. *In Proceedings of the PAAM '98,* London, UK, 377-391.

Pan, R., Ding, Z., Yu, Y. & Peng, Y. (2005). A Bayesian Approach to Ontology Mapping. *In Proceedings of the 4th International Semantic Web Conference,* Galway, Ireland.

Pinto, H. S. (1999). Some Issues on Ontology Integration. *IJCAI 1999, Workshop on Ontologies and Problem Solving Methods.*

Prasad, S., Peng, Y. & Finin, T. (2002). Using Explicit Information to Map Between Two Ontologies. *In Proceedings 2nd International Workshop on Ontologies in Agent Systems,* Bologna, Italy.

Quellet, R. & Ogbuji, U. (2002). Introduction to DAML: Part I & Part II. *O' Reilly xml.com.* Retrieved March 12th from http://www.xml.com/pub/a/2002/01/30/daml1.html

Reticular Systems (1999). *AgentBuilder – An Integrated Toolkit for Constructing Intelligence Software Agents.* http://www.agentbuilder.com.

Searle, J. (1969). *Speech Acts.* Cambridge University Press.

Siebes, R. & van Harmelen, F. (2002). Ranking Agent Statements for Building Evolving Ontologies. *In Proceedings of the Workshop on Meaning Negotiation, in conjunction with the 18th National Conference on Artificial Intelligence,* Edmonton, Canada.

Steels, L. (1998). The Origins of Ontologies and Communication Conventions in Multi-Agent Systems. *Journal of Autonomous Agents and Multiagent Systems, 1(1),* 169-194.

Stephens, L. & Huhns, M. (2001). Consensus Ontologies – Reconciling the Semantics of Web Pages and Agents. *IEEE Internet Computing,* 92-95.

Straber, M., Baumann, J. & Hohl, F. (1997). Mole – A Java based Mobile Agent System. In M. Muhlhauser (eds), *Special Issues in Object Oriented Programming.* Dpunkt Verlag, 301-308.

Stuckenschmidt, H. & Timm, I. J. (2002). Adapting Communication Vocabularies Using Shared Ontologies. *In Proceedings of the 2nd International Workshop on Ontologies in Agent Systems, in conjunction with the AAMAS '02,* Bologna, Italy, 6-12.

Stumme, G. (2005). Ontology Merging with Formal Concept Analysis. In Kalfoglou Y., Schorlemmer M., Sheth A., Staab S. & Uschold (eds), *Semantic Interoperability and Integration,* Internationales Begegnungs – und Forschungszentrum fuer Informatik (IBFI), Dagstuhl, Germany.

Stumme, G. & Meadche, A. (2001). Ontology Merging for Federated Ontologies on the Semantic Web. *In Proceedings of the International Workshop on Foundations of Models for Information Integration,* Viterbo, Italy.

Sycara, K. & Paolucci, M. (2003). Ontologies in Agent Architectures. In S. Staab & R. Stuber (eds), *Handbook on Ontologies in Information Systems.* Springer-Verlag.

Sycara, K., Pannu, A., Williamson, M. & Zeng, D. (1996). Distributed Intelligent Agents. *IEEE Expert, 11(6),* 36-46.

The DAML Services Coalition (2001). *DAML-S: Semantic Markup for Web Services.* Retrieved March 12th from http://www.daml.org/services/daml-s/2001/05/daml-s.html.

Van Aart, C. Pels, R., Caire, G. & Bergenti, F. (2002). Creating and Using Ontologies in Agent Communication. *In Proceedings of the Workshop on Ontologies in Agent Systems, AAMAS '02,* Bologna, Italy.

W3C (2002). *Web Services Activity.* Available at http://www.w3.org/2002/ws.

W3C (2004a). OWL – Web Ontology Language Overview. *W3C Recommendation.* Retrieved March 12th from http://www.w3.org/TR/owl-features/.

W3C (2004b). RDF Primer. *W3C Recommendation, eds F. Manola and E. Miller.* Retrieved March 12th from http://www.w3.org/TR/rdf-primer/.

W3C (2004c). *OWL-S: Semantic Markup for Web Services*. Retrieved March 12th from http://www.w3.org/Submission/OWL-S.

Watche, H., Vogele, T., Viser, U., Stuckenschmidt, H., Schuster, G., Neumman, H. & Hubner, S. (2001). Ontology-Based Integration of Information – A Survey of Existing Approaches. *In Proceedings of the 17th International Joint Conference on Artificial Intelligence (IJCAI 2001), Workshop: Ontologies and Information Sharing*, Seattle, Washington, 108-117.

Weinstein, P. & Birmingham, W. (1999). *Agent Communication with different ontologies: height new measures of description compatability*, Technical Report CSE-TR-383-99, 7.

Weisman, F., Roos, N. & Vogt, P. (2002). Automatic Ontology Mapping for Agent Communication. *In Proceedings of the 1st International Joint Conference on Autonomous Agents and Multiagent Systems*, Bologna, Italy, 563-564.

Wooldridge, M. & Jennings, N. R. (1995). Intelligent Agents: Theory and Practice. *The Knowledge Engineering Review, 10(2)*, 115-152.

Zini, F. & Sterling, L. (1999). On Designing Ontologies for Agents. *In Proceedings of Appia-Gulp-Prode '99: Joint Conference on Declarative Programming*, L' Aquila, Italy.

ADDITIONAL READING

On Ontologies

Auxilio, M. & Nieto, M. (2003). *An Overview of Ontologies*. Technical Report, Center of Research in Information and Automation Technologies, Interactive and Cooperative Technologies Lab, Universidad de las Americas. Retrieved March 5th from http://www.starlab.vub.ac.be/ teaching/ontologies_overview.pdf.

Baader, F., Horrocks, I. & Sattler, U. (2003). Description Logics as Ontology Languages for the Semantic Web. In eds D. Hutter and W. Stephan, *Festchrift in Honor of Jorg Siekmann, Lecture notes in Artificial Intelligence*. Springer.

Brachman, R. J. & Levesque, H. J. (2004). *Knowledge Representation and Reasoning*. Morgan Kauffman Publishers.

Gomez-Perez, A., Fernandez-Lopez, M. & Corcho, O. (2004). *Ontological Engineering*. Springer-Verlag (2nd printing).

Klein, M., Broekstra, J., Fensel, D., van Harmelen, F. & Horrocks, I. (2003). Ontologies and Schema Languages on the Web. In D. Fensel. J. Hendler, H. Lieberman and W. Wahlster (eds), *Spinning the Semantic Web: Bringing the World Wide Web to its Full Potential*. The MIT Press, Cambridge, MA.

Nardi, D. & Brachman, R. J. (2003). An Introduction to Description Logics. In F. Baader, D. Calvanese, D. L. McGuinness, D. Nardi & P. F. Patel-Schneider (eds), *The description Logic Handbook: Theory, Implementation, and Applications*. Cambridge University Press.

Uschold, M. & Gruninger, M. (1996). *ONTOLOGIES: Principles, Methods and Applications*, Knowledge Engineering Review, *11(2)*, 93-155.

W3C (2004a). OWL – Web Ontology Language Overview. *W3C Recommendation*. Retrieved March 12th from http://www.w3.org/TR/owl-features/.

W3C (2004b). RDF Primer. *W3C Recommendation, eds F. Manola & E. Miller*. Retrieved March 12th from http://www.w3.org/TR/rdf-primer/.

W3C (2004c). *OWL-S: Semantic Markup for Web Services*. Retrieved March 12th from http://www.w3.org/Submission/OWL-S.

On Intelligent Agents

Bellifemine, F., Poggi, A. & Rimassa, G. (2000). Developing Multi-Agent Systems with JADE. *In Proceedings of the 7th International Workshop on Agent Theories, Architectures and Languages,* Boston, MA.

FIPA (2002). *FIPA ACL Message Structure Specification.* Retrieved March 12th from http://www.fipa.org/specs/fipa00061/SC00061G.html

Franklin, S. & Graesser, A. (1997). Is It an Agent, or Just a Program?: A Taxonomy for Autonomous Agents. In Müller, J.P., Wooldridge, M.J. & Jennings, N.R. (Eds), *Intelligent Agents III.* Springer-Verlag, Berlin.

Hendler, J. (2001). Agents and the Semantic Web. *IEEE Intelligent Systems,* 30-37.

Jennings, N. R. & Wooldridge, M. (1998). Applications of Intelligent Agents. In N. R. Jennings and M. J. Wooldridge (eds), *Agent Technology: Foundations, Applications and Markets.* Springer-Verlag: Heidelberg, Germany.

Muller, J. P. (1998). Architectures and Applications of Intelligent Agents: A Survey. *The Knowledge Engineering Review, 13(4),* 353-380. Cambridge University Press.

Nwana, H. S. (1996). Software Agents: An Overview. *The Knowledge Engineering Review, 11(3),* 1-40.

Russel, S. & Norvigm P. (1995). *Artificial Intelligence: A Modern Approach.* Prentice Hall, Inc.

Watche, H., Vogele, T., Viser, U., Stuckenschmidt, H., Schuster, G., Neumman, H. & Hubner, S. (2001). Ontology-Based Integration of Information – A Survey of Existing Approaches. *In Proceedings of the 17th International Joint Conference on Artificial Intelligence (IJCAI 2001), Workshop: Ontologies and Information Sharing,* Seattle, Washington, 108-117.

Wooldridge, M. & Jennings, N. R. (1995). Intelligent Agents: Theory and Practice. *The Knowledge Engineering Review, 10(2),* 115-152.

Wooldridge, M. J., & Jennings, N. R. (1995). Agent Theories, Architectures, and Languages: A Survey. *In Intelligent Agents: ECAI-94 Workshop on Agent Theories, Architectures, and Languages, eds. M. J. Wooldridge & N. R. Jennings, 1–39.* Berlin: Springer-Verlag.

Chapter V
Probabilistic Models for the Semantic Web:
A Survey

Livia Predoiu
University of Mannheim, Germany

Heiner Stuckenschmidt
University of Mannheim, Germany

ABSTRACT

Recently, there has been an increasing interest in formalisms for representing uncertain information on the Semantic Web. This interest is triggered by the observation that knowledge on the web is not always crisp and we have to be able to deal with incomplete, inconsistent and vague information. The treatment of this kind of information requires new approaches for knowledge representation and reasoning on the web as existing Semantic Web languages are based on classical logic which is known to be inadequate for representing uncertainty in many cases. While different general approaches for extending Semantic Web languages with the ability to represent uncertainty are explored, we focus our attention on probabilistic approaches. We survey existing proposals for extending semantic web languages or formalisms underlying Semantic Web languages in terms of their expressive power, reasoning capabilities as well as their suitability for supporting typical tasks associated with the Semantic Web.

INTRODUCTION

The Semantic Web is an extension of the World Wide Web that allows for expressing the semantics and not only the markup of data. By means of the representation of the semantics of data, new and not explicitly stated information can be derived by means of reasoners. In this way, software agents can use and integrate information automatically. As common web languages like (X)HTML and XML are not enough for this purpose (Decker et al., 2000), Semantic

Web languages have been standardised (RDF, RDF Schema and OWL), proposed (e.g. WRL, SWRL) and new ones are still being devised. However, most languages that are intended for usage on the Semantic Web are deterministic and cannot represent uncertainty. Currently, there is a growing interest in probabilistic extensions of Semantic Web languages. People start to realize that there is inherently probabilistic knowledge that needs to be represented on the Semantic Web. In the following, we briefly describe five areas where probabilistic information plays a role in the context of the Semantic Web:

- **Representing inherently uncertain information:** Not all of the information that needs to be represented on the Semantic Web is given in terms of definite statements. E.g. statistical information can provide insights to data to be shared on the Semantic Web. Ontological information attached with statistical values like the percentage of people in a population that are of a certain age can help answer queries about the correlation between this age and a certain chronic disease. There are many situations in which the use of this statistical information could be used to improve the behaviour of intelligent systems. An example would be a recommender System that points the user to certain information based on information about the age group.
- **Ontology Learning:** The manual creation of ontologies has been identified as one of the main bottlenecks on the Semantic Web. In order to overcome this problem several researchers are investigating methods for automatically learning ontologies from texts. Existing approach normally use a combination of NLP and text mining techniques (Maedche & Staab, 2004). Typical tasks are the detection of synonyms and of subclass relations using clustering techniques and association rule mining. In both fields, the result of the mining process can be interpreted in terms of a probabilistic judgement of the correctness of the learned relation.
- **Document Classification:** Document Classification can be seen as a special case of ontology learning called Ontology population. Today a major part of the information on the web is present in terms of documents (Web Pages, PDF Documents etc.). A common way of linking documents to knowledge encoded in ontologies is to assign individual documents to one or more concepts representing its content. Different machine learning techniques have been applied to this problem (Sebastiani, 2002). The most commonly used is the use of naïve Bayes classifiers that estimate the probability of a document belonging to a topic based on the occurrence of terms in sample documents.
- **Ontology Matching:** Different sources often use different ontologies to organize their information. In the case of documents, these are often classified according to different topic hierarchies. In order to be able to access information across these different sources, semantic correspondences between the classes in the corresponding ontologies have to be determined and encoded in mappings that can be used to access information across the sources. Recently, a number of approaches for automatically determining such mappings have been proposed (Euzenat & Shvaiko, 2007). Some of the most successful ones use machine learning techniques to compute the probability that two classes represent the same information.
- **Ontology mapping usage for information integration:** The usage of the mappings that have been found by matchers as explained in the paragraph above is currently mainly deterministic. Although the mappings are attached with a confidence that expresses how sure the matcher is that the mapping holds, the usage of those mappings consists

of a preprocessing step: All mappings that have a confidence value above that threshold are considered deterministically true and all mappings that have a confidence value below that threshold are considered deterministically false. However, there is evidence that this kind of usage is error prone, especially when mappings are composed over several ontologies.

The five examples above clearly demonstrate the importance of probabilistic information in the context of the Semantic Web. For example, in order to use the learned structures effectively, we need ways to represent and reason about the probabilities assigned to them. Most existing Semantic Web languages are mainly based on classical, deterministic logic and do not support this aspect. In the following, we review a number of general approaches for combining logical languages with probabilistic models and discuss existing proposals for extending semantic web languages with probabilistic information in more details.

Aim and Scope

In this paper, we review existing proposals to extend Semantic Web languages with the capability to handle uncertain information to better deal with the situations mentioned above. There are many ways of representing and dealing with uncertainty. In this paper, we restrict our attention to approaches that use probabilistic methods for representing uncertain information. In particular, we will not cover recent proposals for fuzzy-logic based extensions of semantic web languages. We will also not discuss nonmonotonic and non-standard logics for representing uncertainty unless they are based on a probabilistic semantics. We focus on these approaches, because we believe that probabilistic methods are a natural choice for representing the kinds of uncertainty we often find on the web. A strong motivation is the awareness that Semantic Web technology could greatly benefit from a tighter integration with machine learning and information retrieval techniques which are mostly based on probabilistic models. Probabilities have been criticised mostly due to the fact that people are very bad in providing correct judgements of the probability of events. We think that on the Semantic Web, this argument does not apply, because the aim here is not to use subjective judgements of probability but to provide mechanisms to represent inherently statistical information found on the web or produced by machine learning and matchers. The five examples above clearly demonstrate the importance of probabilistic information in the context of the Semantic Web. In this paper, we review a number of proposals for extending logical languages with probabilistic information in more details. We focus on:

1. Approaches that directly extend Semantic Web languages, in particular RDF and OWL.
2. Approaches that extend formalisms that have a very close connection to Semantic Web languages or that have explicitly designed to be used on the Semantic Web by the authors.

In the latter category, on the one hand, we cover probabilistic extensions of Description Logics which are commonly accepted as being the formal basis of OWL. Even though most approaches only cover logics that are much weaker than OWL, the methods proposed can directly be applied to the corresponding subset of OWL. The second kind of languages we consider are rule languages. Although there is not yet an official rule language for the Semantic Web, it is clear, however that rule languages have an important role to play on the Semantic Web. As the area of rule languages is also very broad, we focussed on approaches that have been developed for the Semantic Web. Due to the fact that ontologies and thus Description Logics play a very important role in the Semantic Web, all approaches that extend are that combine rules and ontologies in some way. We restrict ourselves to probabilistic logics that allow combinations of rule and ontologies also with our application example in the area of ontology matching and ontology mapping usage in mind. This application example is presented below.

When talking about the different approaches, we will distinguish between the logical language which is used to describe knowledge and the probabilistic model used to assign probabilities to certain assertions of the logical language. Based on this distinction, we discuss the following issues of the different approaches:

- The general probabilistic model used
- Expressiveness of the logical language
- Kind of logical sentences that can be assigned a probability
- Reasoning support and expected efficiency for large scale models

In order to evaluate the applicability of the respective approaches, we also consider an example scenario from the area of ontology matching and ontology mapping usage. This example illustrates also the inherent uncertainty of mappings and why this uncertainty needs to be taken into account for reasoning. Our example is based on two ontologies used in the Ontology Alignment Evaluation Challenge.[1] Assume a situation where a user is looking for publications about AI based on two ontologies O_1 and O_2.

Let O_1 be specified by the following axiom which specify that for each publication there is a keyword which is a subject. Furthermore, there is a publication about the Semantic Web which has the keyword Artificial Intelligence.

1. Publication v 8keyword.Subject
2. (SW, AI): keyword
3. SW: Publication

Let O_2 be specified by the following axioms which specify that reports are always publications and every concept in the knowledge base is about some topic. Furthermore, there is one report about Logic Programming and a publication about Description Logics. Both are about Logics.

4. Report v Publication
5. > v 8about.Topic
6. BN:Report
7. DL: Publication
8. (BN, Probability): about
9. (DL, Logics): about

Without loss of generality, we can assume that O_1 is the local ontology, i.e. the ontology being queried explicitly by the user. In order to integrate the information which is stored in both ontologies, mappings are needed. With a probabilistic matcher like GLUE (Doan et al., 2003) mappings can be found which map the second ontology O_2 to our local ontology O_1.

10. O1: Publication(x) ← O2: Publication(x) with probability 0.8
11. O1: Publication(x) ← O2: Report(x) with probability 0.9
12. O1: Subject(x) ← O2: Topic(x) with probability 0.9
13. O1: keyword(x, y) ← O2: about(x, y) with probability 0.8

The mapping (10) basically says that all instances that are belonging to the concept Publication in O_2 are also belonging to the concept publication of O_1 with the probability 0,9. Due to the Kolmogorov axioms of probability theory, the probability that instances belonging to O_2: Publication do not belong to O_1:Publication is 0,1. For completeness, the probability instances that do not belong to O_2:Publication belong to O_1: Publication need to be derived by a matcher as well. GLUE can be modified such that it conforms to this requirement. Let's assume that for (10) this probability is 0.2, for (11) it is 0.4, for (12) it is 0.3 and for (13) it is 0.4.

If we pose a query, we want to get an answer that integrates the information of both ontologies. So, in our example, if we query our local ontology for all publications:

Publication(x) $\wedge$ keyword(x, AI)

we want to get also all relevant publications mentioned only in the second ontology. The answer here is:

- The publication about Semantic Web with probability 1.0 because it is mentioned in the local ontology and no mapping has been used for deriving it.
- The publication about Logic Programming in the second ontology which was derived by two mappings (10) and (11) and thus gets an accumulated probability of 0,75.
- The publication about Description Logics which was derived by only one mapping (10) and has only the probability 0,44.

The computation is based on the semantics of the Bayesian Description Logic Programming formalism and shows nicely the importance of the consideration of uncertainty in the area of information integration in the Semantic Web. Without the consideration of the uncertainty each mapping is associated with, all 3 answers would be needed to be treated in the same way although the publication about the Semantic Web is much more relevant than the one about Description Logics. Furthermore, if mapping composition is considered with mapping chains over several ontologies, mappings with rather low probabilities can contribute to an answer with a rather high probability.

Another requirement for a mapping language is the possibility to express mappings between individuals. In our example, publications of O_2 that are about probabilities are less probable to be publications in O_1 that deal with AI than publications of O1 that are about logics:

14. O1:keyword(x, AI) $\leftarrow$ O2: about(x, Probability)
    e.g. with probability 0.7
15. O1:keyword(x, AI) $\leftarrow$ O2: about(x, Logics)
    e.g. with probability 0.9

It is immediately clear that such mappings need to be expressed for a comprehensive handling of mappings in the Semantic Web area. Mappings that do not involve any variables might also be necessary to be expressed in certain scenarios. When we investigate the different probabilistic extensions of Semantic Web languages, we also have a look at the applicability of the formalisms for the area of Information Integration as presented in this example.

This chapter is structured as follows. In the next section, we present an overview of current Semantic Web languages and related formalisms that are the basis for the logical languages used in the different approaches discussed later in the paper. We also provide a brief introduction to some basic probabilistic models that are used in the different approaches. Based on these basic methods, we discuss proposals for probabilistic languages for the Semantic Web, in the section "probabilistic extensions of Semantic Web languages" below in this chapter. We start with proposals for extending RDF and OWL. Afterwards, we discuss approaches for extending related formalisms with notions of probability, namely Description Logics and different Rule Languages. We conclude the chapter with a critical review of the state of the art and an analysis of directions for future research.

PRELIMINARIES AND BACKGROUND

In this section, we introduce the reader to the state of the art in current Semantic Web languages and the background on the probabilistic models used in the probabilistic extensions surveyed below in the section "probabilistic extensions of Semantic Web languages" below in this chapter.

Current Semantic Web Languages

So far, the development of languages for the Semantic Web was dominated by traditional views on metadata models and logic-based knowledge representation. The major languages that have been developed are RDF/RDF Schema (Lassila & Swick, 1999; Manola & Miller, 2004) for representing metadata and the Web Ontology language OWL (Bechhofer et al., 2004) for representing terminological knowledge in terms of ontologies. The Web Ontology language OWL has its root in the formalism of Description Logics, a decidable subset of first-order logic that contains special constructs for defining classes in terms of necessary and sufficient conditions based on predicates representing binary relations between instances of different classes. More specifically, OWL corresponds to particular Description Logic variants (OWL Lite corresponds to SHIF(D) and OWL DL corresponds to SHOIN(D) (Horrocks et al., 2003)) in the sense that reasoning in OWL can be reduced to checking satisfiability in this logic (Horrocks & Patel-Schneider, 2004). Similarly, the semantics of RDF can be modelled with First-Order Logics, Description Logics and Datalog (Fikes & Guiness, 2001), (de Bruijn & Heymans, 2007).

Recently the need for rule languages on the Semantic Web has been recognized. Rule languages complement Description Logics as they allow to represent kinds of axioms not expressible in SHIF and SHOIN (e.g. property chaining, Horrocks, 2005). Thus, several rule language proposals for the Semantic Web have emerged, examples being the Semantic Web Rule Language SWRL (Horrocks et al., 2005) and the Web Rule Language WRL (Angele et al., 2005) for describing domain-dependent inference rules. The Semantic Web Rule language allows the definition of conjunctive rules over the concepts and binary relations or roles, respectively, which are contained in an OWL ontology (Horrocks et al., 2005). Finally, similar to OWL, WRL is a layered language consisting of three languages, one being a superset of the other. WRL-Core which is the least subset of the WRL language family corresponds to a subset of OWL which lies in the language of Logic Programming (also known as the DLP fragment, Grosof et al., 2003). WRL-Flight contains WRL-Core and is a Datalog-based rule language. WRL-Full contains WRL-Flight and is a rule language with function symbols and negation under the Well-Founded Semantics (Angele et al., 2005).

Description Logics which is represented by OWL in the Semantic Web and Logic Programming which is represented by a couple of W3C rule language proposals have both nice orthogonal properties and expressivity. Ways for combing both have been and still are investigated. Description Logics and Logic Programming have been found to have a common subset called Description Logic Programs (Grosof et al., 2003). Therefore, Description Logic Programs have a Logic Programming and a Description Logic syntax and wrappers can be used to translate them. Another subset of Description Logics and Logic Programming has been recently proposed that is called Horn-SHIQ (Hustadt et al., 2005) and is a strict superset of Description Logic Programs. Besides the investigation of the intersection of Description Logics and Logic Programming, a lot of research aims at a more comprehensive integration of both formalisms. Several approaches for enabling an interaction between logic programs and description logics exist. Usually, they consist of a Description Logics knowledge base and a Logic Program and the latter is equipped with special features for interacting with the Description Logics knowledge base. An example of such an approach where the Description Logic knowledge is an OWL Lite or OWL DL knowledge base is the formalism of

Description Logic Programs under the answer set semantics by (Eiter et. al, 2004).

All of the languages mentioned above are logical languages with a classic model-theoretic semantics that makes a statement either true or false and have no means to represent uncertainty in any way.

Probabilistic Languages and Models

In the following, a short overview of the probabilistic models used for the languages in the sections below is presented. Those models are *Bayesian Networks, Bayesian Logic Programs, Independent Choice Logic, Probabilistic Datalog* and *Multi-Entity Bayesian Networks.* Some of these models are related to each other, e.g. Bayesian Networks can be considered as a subset of Bayesian Logic Programs because the latter provide a compact representation of the former in the same way like first-order logic does with sentential logic. Independent Choice Logic is a generalization and a superset of the formalism of Bayesian Logic Programs. The relationship of Bayesian Networks, Bayesian Logic Programs and Independent choice Logic with probabilistic Datalog is unclear. Multi Entity Bayesian Networks are comprising Bayesian Networks in the same way like Bayesian Logic Programs do. Multi Entity Bayesian Networks are more expressive than Bayesian Logic Programs, but it is unclear whether there is a semantical subset relationship. The relationship between Multi Entity Relationship Programs and Independent Choice Logic has not been investigated yet either. Multi Entity Relationship Programs differ from Probabilistic Datalog by the usage of negation. Probabilistic Datalog uses well-founded negation and the closed world assumption while Multi Entity Relationship Programs model probabilistic First-Order Logic knowledge bases and employ classical negation as well as the open world assumption.

Bayesian Networks (BNs)

One of the best understood models for representing the joint probability distribution of a domain of interest is the model of Bayesian Networks (BNs) (Jensen, 2001). A BN is a compact representation of the joint probability distribution among a set of random variables in a domain under consideration. More precisely, a BN is a directed, acyclic graph with the random variables as nodes and direct influence relationships as arcs. Several exact or approximate algorithms for reasoning in Bayesian Networks exist. Exact inference has been proven to be NP-complete in the maximal number of parents of nodes in the network. A considerable amount of research effort has been spent on different issues like learning of the conditional probability tables/distributions of the nodes in the BN, learning the structure of a BN, etc. (Castillo et al., 1997; Cowell et al., 1999; Jensen, 2001). A BN has been found to correspond to a probabilistic extension of sentential definite clauses.

In the area of the Semantic Web where the same or similar knowledge can happen to be represented on different and independent peers and integrated reasoning and information usage requires mappings, cycles in the complete representation may occur. Unfortunately, BNs are not allowed to have directed cycles. For reasoning with BNs, a huge amount of free and commercial software tools and implementations exist.

Bayesian Logic Programs (BLPs)

Bayesian Logic Programs (Kersting & De Raedt, 2001) are an extension of Bayesian Networks to first-order definite clause logic and a probabilistic extension of definite first-order logic at the same time. A BLP consists of a set of rules and facts, i.e. a definite clause logic program. Each fact is associated with an a-priori probability and each rule with a conditional probability where the probability of the head atom is conditioned on the states of the body atoms. Each ground atom of the Herbrand Model of the definite clause logic program corresponds to a node in a corresponding Bayesian Network. The arcs are defined through the rules. For each valid ground rule, an arc from each node representing a body atom to the node representing the head atom exists in the corresponding Bayesian Network. Additionally, combining rules are defined in order to enable the combination of conditional probabilities of different valid ground rules with the same head atom. BLPs are defined to be acyclic. Therefore, the corresponding Bayesian Networks are acyclic as well. Reasoning with BLPs corresponds to deriving the Herbrand Model or the part of it which is relevant to the query and building the corresponding Bayesian Network. For BLPs, no complexity results have been published, yet. Currently, only one tool for reasoning with BLPs exists: the Balios engine (Kersting & Dick, 2004).

Independent Choice Logic (ICL)

Independent Choice Logic (Poole, 1997) is a logic that is built upon a given base logic that conforms to some restrictions and determines truth in the possible worlds defined by choice spaces. Possible worlds are built by choosing propositions from sets of independent choice alternatives. As base logic, Poole suggests acyclic logic programs under the stable model semantics. However, as we will see later in the subsections on probabilistic (disjunctive) description logic programs below, the approach works for other base logics as well.

An independent choice logic theory on a base logic is a pair (C, F) where C is a so-called choice space and F is a knowledge base in the base logic. C is a set of sets of ground atomic formulae from the language of the base logic such that for two choices $c_1, c_2 \in C$, if $c_1 \neq c_2$ then $c_1 \cap c_2 = \emptyset$. The elements of C are called alternatives and are basically random variables. The elements of an alternative *c* are called atomic choices and are basically possible values for the random variable *c*. The semantics of ICL is defined in terms of possible worlds. A possible world corresponds to the selection of one element from each alternative. Such a selection is called total choice. The atoms that follow using the consequence relation of the base logic from these selected atoms together with the knowledge base of the base logic are true in this possible world. Reasoners for ICL are conceivable but depend on the base logic used. Also, the complexity for deciding consistency and query answering depends on the base logic used.

Multi-Entity Bayesian Networks (MEBNs)

Multi-entity Bayesian Networks (Laskey & Costa, 2005) extend the Bayesian Network model to full First-Order logic. In this way, graphical models with repeated sub-structures can be represented and a probability distribution over models of any consistent, finitely axiomatizable first-order theory can be expressed. With MEBN logic, entities that have attributes and are related to other entities can be represented. Features of entities and relationships among entities are random variables. The knowledge about attributes and relationships is expressed as a collection of MEBN fragments (MFrags) organized into MEBN theories (MTheories). An MFrag represents a conditional probability distribution and an MTheory is a set of MFrags that collectively satisfies consistency constraints ensuring the existence of a unique joint probability distribution over instances of the random variables represented in the MTheory. Possible queries are queries for the degree of belief in specific random variables given evidence random variables. The response to a query is computed by constructing a so-called situation-specific Bayesian Network that can be processed by a usual tool for Bayesian Networks. We are not aware of the existence of general complexity results for reasoning with the MEBN formalism. There are proposals for reasoning algorithms (Laskey, 2006) but no direct implementation of a reasoner for MEBN logic. But there is a translation of a subset of the

MEBN formalism into probabilistic relational models implemented in the Quiddity*Suite (cf. http://www.iet.com/quiddity).

Probabilistic Datalog (pDatalog)

Probabilistic Datalog (Fuhr, 2000) is Datalog where each fact and each rule is extended with a probability which states the certainty of it being true. An important underlying assumption is that each element of the probabilistic Datalog program (i.e. every fact and every rule) is probabilistically independent from the other elements. Probabilistic Datalog has been equipped with a well-founded semantics. According to Nottelmann (2005), the probability of a rule can be seen as a conditional probability like with Bayesian Logic Programs. However, while Bayesian Logic Programs allow an arbitrary set of states for the ground atoms in the Herbrand Base, probabilistic Datalog envisions just Boolean states for the atoms. Bayesian Logic Programs do not allow any negation while probabilistic Datalog allows negation under the well-founded semantics. As yet, it is unclear whether probabilistic Datalog programs can be represented as Bayesian Networks. Probabilistic Datalog has been implemented in the HySpirit system (Roellecke et al, 2001) and query answering and the computation of probabilities is a two step process. First, the answers to the Datalog component of the query are computed by means of bottom-up evaluation that employs magic sets. Afterwards, the inclusion-exclusion principle is used to compute the probability of the resulting expressions in Disjunctive Normal Form. (Fuhr, 2000) states "Practical experimentation with HySpirit has shown that the evaluation of about 10 or more conjuncts is not feasible". However, recently, in (De Raedt et. al, 2007) an algorithm has been proposed that is able to perform approximate probabilistic reasoning by combining iterative deepening with binary decision diagrams and is very efficient. (De Raedt et. al, 2007) claims that "one can deal with up to 100000 conjuncts".

PROBABILISTIC EXTENSIONS OF SEMANTIC WEB LANGUAGES

In this section, we survey probabilistic extensions of RDF, RDF Schema and OWL which are W3C recommendations and thus correspond to a standard. We also have a look at probabilistic extensions of subsets of the Description Logics corresponding to OWL, i.e. SHIF(D) and SHOIN(D), and RDF (Schema).

Extensions of RDF

RDF can be considered as the most widely accepted Semantic Web language as it provides the syntactic basis for other Semantic Web languages. A proof for its success is the huge amount of software for processing RDF data that has been implemented up to now. Quite naturally, also some approaches for combining probabilities with RDF have been proposed. Fukushige (2005) proposes an RDF vocabulary for representing Bayesian Networks. In (Udrea et al., 2006), a probabilistic extension of acyclic RDF statements with a model-theoretic semantics and a fixpoint semantics has been proposed. While the first work concentrates on representation issues, the second work can be considered as probabilistic logic on its own.

Representing Probabilistic Information in RDF

In (Fukushige, 2005), a vocabulary extension of RDF has been proposed that is capable of representing the different elements of a Bayesian Network and link them to regular RDF statements. The vocabulary consists of a set of classes (*prob:Partition*, *prob:ProbabilisticStatement*, *prob:Clause*, *prob:Probability*,) and a set of predicates (e.g. *prob:predicate*, *prob:condition*, *prob:case*, *prob:about*) that can represent a Bayesian Network. This vocabulary allows to link statements to their probabilities, express conditional probabilities and more complex probabilistic statements.

Expressiveness

The vocabulary can solely represent Bayesian Networks and can basically be considered as a syntactical interchange format for Bayesian Networks. Thus, as with Bayesian Networks, cyclic probabilistic descriptions cannot be represented. We deem this as a clear disadvantage, because we think that cyclic descriptions cannot be forbidden or avoided in such an open and unstructured environment like the web.

Reasoning and Efficiency

As yet no reasoning support has been implemented. However, after having implemented a parser and wrapper for this vocabulary, in principle any tool for reasoning with Bayesian Networks can be used for reasoning.

Applicability to Information Integration

In principle, the vocabulary can be used for representing mappings between ontologies in a similar way as done with Bayesian Description Logic Programs (see a more detailed presentation on Bayesian Description Logic Programs in the subsection entitled likewise below in this chapter). A huge disadvantage, however, is that Bayesian Networks are not properly integrated with RDF on the meta level: the vocabulary for representing Bayesian Networks uses RDF for its syntax without a tight coupling to the logical model of RDF. Therefore, RDF ontologies cannot be integrated with mappings expressed in this vocabulary properly. Clearly, with OWL ontologies, it is not possible either.

pRDF

In contrast to the former formalism that is intended to just provide a vocabulary for representing Bayesian Networks, pRDF is a formal probabilistic extension of RDF which corresponds to a of probabilistic logic on its own.

Expressiveness

pRDF is a probabilistic extension of a subset of RDF and consists of a pair (S, I) with S being a pRDF schema and I being a pRDF instance base. A pRDF schema S is defined as a finite set consisting of probabilistic quadruples extending the RDF Schema built-in predicate *rdfs:subClassOf* and non-probabilistic triples using the RDF Schema built-in predicates *rdfs:subPropertyOf*, *rdfs:range* and *rdfs:domain*. This means that in pRDF neither the subproperty relationship nor domain and range restrictions can be defined probabilistically. A pRDF instance base I is a finite set of quadruples extending the RDF built-in *rdf:type* and arbitrary properties $p \in P$.

More precisely, pRDF allows the following kinds of probabilistic definitions:

- A sequel of axioms: $C(x) \to D_1(x), \ldots, C(x) \to D_n(x)$ and a probability distribution over the axioms in the sequel where $C \neq D_1 \neq \ldots \neq D_n$.
- A sequel of axioms : $P(inst, inst_1), \ldots, P(inst, inst_n)$ and a probability distribution over the axioms in this sequel, where $inst \neq inst_1 \neq \ldots \neq inst_n$ and P being either the RDF built-in ***rdf:type*** or an arbitrary user-defined property.

Furthermore, the following deterministic expressions are allowed:

- $R(x, y) \to R_2(x, y)$
- $R(x, y) \to C(x)$
- $R(x, y) \to C(y)$

A disadvantage of this approach is that only a very small subset of RDF/S is supported by pRDF yielding a very low expressivity. Furthermore, pRDF instances are required to be acyclic, which again can only be realized in small and closed environments, but not on the Web as it is.

Reasoning and Efficiency

A model theoretic semantics and a fixpoint operator has been defined basing on a t-norm (Fagin, 1999). Furthermore, a reasoner has been implemented that evaluates the fixpoint operator until the least fixpoint has been reached. The properties of a t-norm allow certain pruning strategies that are employed in the reasoning algorithms. Queries to pRDF instances are atomic, i.e. conjunctions cannot be dealt with. A query is a quadruple (*i*, *p*, *S*, *P*) where *i* can be an instance, *p* can be a property, *S* can be a set of instances *i* is related to via *p* and *P* can be a probability distribution for this sequel of property axioms. At most one of the elements of the quadruple is allowed to be a variable.

Unfortunately, for pRDF schema no query answering facility has been defined yet. The reasoning engine supports only reasoning with pRDF instances.

Applicability to Information Integration

This formalism can be used for information integration with mappings. Mappings that map classes from one ontology to classes of the other ontology can be expressed. Also, mappings that map instances from one ontology to instances of another ontology can be expressed. But no mappings can be expressed that capture partly uninstancialized axioms like the ones in (14) and (15). However, the uncertainty attached to each mapping can be used for integrated reasoning with the mappings and the ontologies. But, due to the limited RDF support, not only the mappings but especially also the RDF ontologies which are to be mapped have a very limited expressivity.

Extensions of OWL

Quite naturally a number of proposals for using probabilistic knowledge on the Semantic Web focus on the extension of the Web Ontology Language as the central mechanism of representing complex knowledge in semantic web applications. When looking at the existing proposals, we see two fundamentally different approaches for combining OWL with probabilistic information.

The first kind of approach implements a loose coupling of the underlying semantics of OWL and probabilistic models. In particular these approaches use OWL as a language for talking about probabilistic models. An example of this approach is the work of Yang and Calmet (2006) that propose a minimal OWL ontology for representing random variables and dependencies between random variables with the corresponding conditional probabilities (Yang & Calmet, 2006). This allows the user to write down probabilistic models that correspond to Bayesian networks as instances of the OntoBayes Ontology. The encoding of the model in OWL makes it possible to explicitly link random variables to elements of an OWL ontology, a tighter integration on the formal level, however, is missing. A similar approach is proposed by Costa and Laskey (2006). They propose the PR-OWL model which is an OWL ontology for describing first order probabilistic models (Costa & Laskey, 2006). More specifically, the corresponding ontology models Multi-Entity Bayesian networks (Laskey & Costa, 2005) that define probability distributions over first-order theories in a modular way. Similar to OntoBayes, there is no formal integration of the two representation paradigms as OWL is used for encoding the general structure of Multi-entity Bayesian networks on the meta-level.

The second kind of approaches actually aims at enriching OWL ontologies with probabilistic information to support uncertain reasoning inside OWL ontologies. These approaches are comparable with the work on probabilistic extensions of Description Logics also presented in this section. A survey of the existing work reveals, however, that approaches that directly address OWL as an ontology language are less ambitious with respect to combining logical and probabilistic semantics that the work in the DL area. An example is the work of Holi and Hyvönnen (2006) that describe a framework for representing uncertainty in simple classification hierarchies using Bayesian networks. A slightly more expressive approach called BayesOWL is proposed by Ding and others (Ding et. al, 2006). They also consider Boolean operators as well as disjointedness and equivalence of OWL classes and present an approach for constructing a Bayesian network from class expressions over these constructs. An interesting feature of BayesOWL is some existing work on learning and representing uncertain mappings between different BayesOWL ontologies reported in (Pan et al., 2005) which is an interesting alternative to existing matching tools.

In the following, we discuss PR-OWL and BayesOWL which are the most interesting representatives of the two general approaches to combining OWL and probabilistic models in more details.

PR-OWL

Expressiveness

As mentioned above PR-OWL is an OWL Ontology that describes Multi-Entity Bayesian Networks. OWL is mainly used as a basis for a Protégé plugin for modelling MEBNs and as a language for representing MEBNs and linking them to domain ontologies encoded in OWL. On the other hand, MEBNs can be translated into Bayesian networks. This means that PR-OWL can be used to link OWL ontologies to Bayesian networks through the MEBN formalism. The Question about the expressiveness of PR-OWL therefore boils down to an analysis of the expressiveness of MEBNs as the actual representation model for uncertainty provided by the approach. According to the authors, MEBNs are capable of representing and reasoning about probabilistic information about any sentence in first-order logic by compiling it into a Bayesian network[2] but they define some restrictions on the nature of the theory, especially on the use of quantifiers. MEBNs specify random variables representing terms and organize them in so-called fragments that describe a certain aspect of the world. Fragments have an interface that defines the terms covered by the fragment. Each fragment defines the joint distribution over the random variables in terms of conditional probabilities encoded as part of a Bayesian network. Variables in terms can be instantiated with multiple constants each instantiation leading to a unique node in the resulting network. Logical formulas are modelled by special fragments that encode the semantics of Boolean operators, quantifiers and instantiation. Fragments are linked via shared terms and additional constraints ensure that only wanted instantiations take place.

It is quite hard to say whether MEBNs are expressive enough to capture probabilistic information about OWL ontologies. In principle it should be possible to translate each OWL ontology into first order logic and assign probabilities to conditional probabilities of the resulting model by encoding it as an MEBN. So far, it has not been investigated whether the restrictions on the use of quantifiers in MEBNs affect the representation of Ontologies. The language should be expressive enough top represent mappings between terms from different ontologies that go beyond simple concept-to concept mappings because it allows to combine terms from different ontologies using arbitrary logical operators as well as the conditional probability of one given the other. It is less clear whether the representation of the mappings can be integrated with the definitions in the semantically consistent way that goes beyond simple reference to parts of the ontologies. In the same way, we could also represent the result of ontology learning methods in terms of conditional probabilities between terms. As fragments in MEBN need input in terms of instantiations of the interface, probabilistic information about instances (e.g. the probability that a paper is about a certain topic) cannot directly be encoded in MEBNs, we could, however find a workaround by explicitly representing a Bayesian classifier as a fragment.

Reasoning and Efficiency

Reasoning in MEBNs is performed by constructing a Bayesian network from the instantiations of fragments. Inside each fragment, a network fragment is created that includes random variables and conditional probabilities for all input objects based on the network pattern specified in the fragment. Here, the actual conditional probability values depend on the number of input objects. The independent network fragments are then combined into a so-called situation-specific network, a Bayesian network that is customized to the given situation in terms of fragments actually instantiated and input objects. The basic reasoning task supported by this network is to compute the probability of one or more random variables given some evidence in terms of instantiations of some input random variables. This means that we can ask for the probability that certain terms are true or false given some knowledge about the truth or falseness of some other terms.

The basic problem of MEBNs when it comes to efficiency is the complexity of the logical language supported. In particular, this has an impact on the size of the situation specific network created as this network represents probabilistic information about all instances simultaneously instead of re-evaluating a standard network multiple times. In information retrieval applications, we often assume that information objects are independent of each other and do not have to be treated in parallel. Although, the bottom-up creation of this network ensures that only the part of the network that is actually needed to answer the query is constructed, this network can still have an infinite size. It would be interesting to identify tractable subsets of MEBNs that correspond to more tractable fragments of first order logic.

Applicability to Information Integration

Again, as with the formalism of Fukushige (2005) presented above, the vocabulary can be used for representing very expressive mappings between ontologies in the MEBN formalism. However, as PR-OWL does not provide a proper integration of the formalism of MEBN and the logical basis of OWL on the meta level, OWL ontologies cannot be integrated with mappings expressed in this vocabulary properly. More specifically, as the connection between a statement in PR-OWL and a statement in OWL is not formalized, it is unclear how to perform the integration of ontologies that contain statements of both formalisms.

BayesOWL

Expressiveness

BayesOWL is an approach for representing probabilistic information about class membership within OWL ontologies. The approach can be seen as an extension of Holi & Hyvönnen (2006). Both approaches support the representation of degrees of overlap between classes in terms of conditional probabilities of the form P(C|D) where C and D are class names. These statements denote the probability that an instance that is a member of D is also a member of C. The main feature of BayesOWL is that it does not only support simple class hierarchies but also class definitions of the following form:

- Equivalence: $C(x) \leftrightarrow D(x)$
- Complement: $C(x) \leftrightarrow \neg D(x)$
- Disjointness: $C(x) \rightarrow \neg D(x)$
- Intersection: $C(x) \leftrightarrow D(x) \wedge E(x)$
- Union: $C(x) \leftrightarrow D(x) \vee E(x)$

This means that BayesOWL is actually a probabilistic extension of propositional logic rather than more expressive description logics. This is a quite a strong restriction as it means that we cannot represent probabilistic information about any relations except the subsumption relation. This limits the applicability to scenarios where we are only interested in the classification of information objects and not in relations between them. This means that the approach is not suitable to support the reasoning about structured information which plays an important role in many semantic web applications.

Reasoning and Efficiency

The basic reasoning task associated to BayesOWL is given some evidence for an object in terms of its classification to determine membership probabilities for all the classes in the ontology. For this purpose a Bayesian network is constructed from the definitions in the model. As in PR-OWL network nodes with a predefined conditional probability table are used to represent Boolean Operators. This computation is done using iterative proportional fitting, a special technique from statistics that selects a probability distribution that best fits the conditional probabilities given in the network. This approach is quite different from the other approaches presented in this survey as the inference is not guided by a specific query. This can be an advantage if many queries about different aspects of the model are issued; we can expect it to be unnecessarily complex if we are only interested in very specific aspects of the model as the method will also compute probabilities that do not have an influence on the variable. Despite this fact, the use of Bayesian networks for implanting probabilistic reasoning can be expected to be relatively efficient. A special feature of BayesOWL is that it allows including probabilistic mappings between different ontologies into the inference procedure (Pan et al., 2005). Mappings are represented in terms of conditional probability statements that include concepts from different ontologies. The probabilistic influence of these statements on the distributions is used to update the distribution in the mapped ontologies. The conditional probabilities used in the mappings can be created using statistical learning methods.

In summary, the approach is well suited for applications that use rather simple classifications of information items such as documents that are classified according to a topic hierarchy. It supports the representation and semi-automated mapping of such hierarchies. As soon as the application demands for more structural information such as document metadata, the approach reaches it limits in terms of the inability to represent information about relations.

Applicability to Information Integration

This formalism provides an integration between Bayesian Networks and OWL and thus it can be used for expressing uncertain mappings between OWL ontologies and for using those mappings for integrating the information distributed over the ontologies. As only class definitions are supported, however, neither the mappings nor the ontologies themselves can contain instances which is a severe drawback of this approach. Also, the expressivity on the schema level is very low in general and thus only a very small subset of OWL can be used for expressing ontologies to be mapped (and mappings).

Extensions of Description Logics

There have been a number of approaches for extending description logics with probabilistic information in the earlier days of description logics. Heinsohn (Heinsohn, 1991) was one of the first to propose a probabilistic notion of subsumption for the logic ALC. Jaeger (Jaeger, 1994) investigated some general problems connected with the extension of T-Boxes and A-Boxes with objective and subjective probabilities and proposed a general method for reasoning with probabilistic information in terms of probability intervals attached to Description logic axioms. Recently, Giugno and Lukasiewicz proposed a probabilistic extension of the logic SHOQ along the lines sketched by Jäger (Giugno & Lukasiewicz, 2002). A major advantage of this approach is the integrated treatment of probabilistic information about Conceptual and Instance knowledge based on the use of nominals in terminological axioms that can be used to model uncertain information about instances and relations. An alternative way of combining description logics with probabilistic information has been proposed by Koller et al. (1997). In contrast to the approaches mentioned above, the P-CLASSIC approach is not based on probability intervals. Instead it uses a complete specification of the probability distribution in terms of a Bayesian network which nodes correspond to concept expressions in the CLASSIC description logic. Bayesian networks have also been used in connection with less expressive logics such as TDL (Yelland, 2000). The approaches for encoding probabilities in concept hierarchies using Bayesian networks described in the section "preliminaries and background" can be seen as a simple special case of these approaches.

We can see two general approaches for extending description logics with probabilistic information. The first is based on probability intervals describing the validity of concept inclusion axioms, the other one is based on the use of Bayesian networks for assessing and relating the probability of different features of the terminological model. In the following, we will restrict our discussion to representative approaches of these different strategies, namely P-SHOQ and P-CLASSIC.

P-SHOQ(D)

Expressiveness

P-SHOQ(D) is based on the description logics SHOQ(D) which is very close to the description logic which provides the semantics of OWL. The only feature of OWL that is not contained in the language is the use of inverse roles. In particular, the language also supports datatypes in the same way as OWL does. Probabilistic information is represented by statements of the form (C|D)[l,u] where C and D are concept expressions in SHOQ(D) and l and u are the maximal and the minimal probability that an instance of D is also an instance of C. Using this general scheme, different kinds of knowledge can be represented, for instance:

1. The probability that C is subsumed by D P(C(x)|D(x))
2. The probability that a particular individual o is a member of a concept C P(C(o))
3. The probability that an individual o is related to an instance of a concept C P(R(o,x)|C(x))
4. The probability that two individuals o and o' are related P(R(o,o'))

From a representational point of view, P-SHOQ(D) offers a lot of possibilities for supporting the task mentioned in the motivation. For the case of overlapping ontologies uncertain mappings between concepts in different ontologies can be represented using probabilistic subsumption statements of the form P(i:C(x)| j:D(x)) where C is a concept from ontology i and D a concept from ontology j. Concerning the task of ontology learning, the language is expressive enough to capture typical information that is determined in the learning process such as the concept hierarchy. We can also represent uncertain information about the range of concepts. The lack of inverse relations in the language, however, makes it impossible to represent domain restrictions. The use of nominals allows us to represent the results of instance learning both for concept and relation instances using statement 3 and 4 mentioned above.

Reasoning and Efficiency

Reasoning in P-SHOQ is based on a function μ that maps every instance of the interpretation domain Δ on a number in [0,1] such that the value of this function for all elements in Δ sum up to 1. The Probability Pr(C) of a concept expression C is defined as the sum of all μ values of the instances of C. Based on this semantics a number of reasoning task have been defined that can be solved using appropriate inference procedures. At the most basic level, the tasks supported by the language are to determine whether a given knowledge base is consistent and to compute the upper and lower bounds l and u of a conditional probability statement P(C(x)|D(x))∈[l,u]. Computing these bounds in based on independent choice logic. Different choices are specified by the possible semantic relations that could hold between any pair of concepts. This definition of choices leads to two linear equation systems whose solutions are the upper and the lower bound of the probability. Solving the equation system involves reasoning in SHOQ(D) for determining the possible choices.

Based on this general method for computing upper and lower bounds a number of reasoning tasks that generalize standard reasoning tasks in Description Logics can be defined. In particular, the approach supports the following tasks

- **Concept satisfiability:** In particular decide whether P(∃x:C(x))∈[0,0] does not follow.
- **Concept Subsumption:** Given two concepts C and D compute l and u such that P(C|D)∈[l,u] follows from the knowledge base.
- **Concept Membership:** Given an instance o and a concept C compute l and u such that P(C(o))∈ [l,u] follows from the knowledge base.
- **Role Membership:** Given two instances o and o' and a relation R compute l and u such that P(R(o,o'))∈[l,u] follows from the knowledge base.

These reasoning tasks provide a suitable basis for supporting tasks such as probabilistic data retrieval across different ontologies. In particular, we can formulate queries as concept expressions in SHOQ(D) and compute the probabilities that certain instances are members of this query concept. Probabilistic information originating from uncertain mappings and classifications provide background constraints for this reasoning task. A potential problem of the approach with respect to the retrieval scenario is the ability to use the probabilities as a basis for ranking. As the approach is based on intervals rather than exact probabilities, there is no total order on the results that could be used for this purpose. Another potential problem is the complexity of the approach which has not been investigated in detailed. It is clear however, that reasoning in SHOQ(D) is likely to be highly intractable.

Applicability to Information Integration

P-SHOQ can be used for expressing all the mappings mentioned in the introduction. The ontologies, however, are not allowed to contain inverse roles. Furthermore, RDF ontologies whose semantics cannot be described solely with the Description Logics paradigm cannot be integrated, because the Logic Programming paradigm which is needed for describing the RDF semantics as well, is not covered by P-SHOQ.

P-CLASSIC

Expressiveness

P-CLASSIC is a probabilistic extension of the CLASSIC Description Logics. Different from SHOQ, the CLASSIC description logics is designed for efficiency of reasoning rather that for expressive power. In particular, CLASSIC does only contain conjunction, negation on atomic concepts, universal and number restrictions as well as role fillers. As a result, deciding subsumption in CLASSIC can be computed in polynomial time based on structural comparison of concept expressions. P-CLASSIC extends the language with probabilistic information about properties of typical instances in terms of a Bayesian network. The corresponding network contains random variables indicating the following information:

- Membership in atomic concepts A
- For each Property R:
  - A distribution over possible fillers o in expressions of the form P(R(x,o))
  - A distribution over possible ranges C in expressions of the form (R(x,y)→

C(y)) where C is specified in terms of a separate Bayesian network.
- A distribution over the number of fillers n in equations of the from ($\exists^{=n}y$: R(x,y))

Additionally, the network represents an efficient encoding of the joint probability over these random variables in terms of conditional probabilities between kinds of assertions mentioned above. This means that P-CLASSIC can be used to represent probabilistic information about terminological knowledge. In particular, we can represent probabilistic subsumption relations between atomic concepts that can be used to represent uncertain mappings and the results of learning subsumption relations. The other features of the language can also be used to represent the result of ontology learning especially distributions over property fillers and ranges are useful for this purpose.

Reasoning and Efficiency

The basic reasoning service in P-CLASSIC is to compute the probability of a complex concept expression based on the definition of the joint probability distribution over atomic classes and features of relations. The inference algorithm given in (Koller et al., 1997) takes a concept expression and a P-CLASSIC knowledge base as input and returns the probability of the concept expression. This probability is computed by bottom-up construction of a Bayesian network that represents the concept and using it to infer the probability that an arbitrary object is member of this concept expression. This method can be used to implement probabilistic data retrieval by computing the probability of a class description using a Bayesian network that has been initialized with evidence that corresponds to the properties of the individual we want to test. The fact that P-CLASSIC is based on exact probabilities rather than probability intervals means that the probability defines a natural ranking function for answers.

The major advantage of P-CLASSIC is the fact that reasoning is relatively efficient compared to other formalisms. This is due to the fact that both, the logical and probabilistic formalism have been chosen with efficiency in mind. The algorithm for constructing the Bayesian Network of a class description is defined as a direct extension of the structural subsumption algorithm of P-CLASSIC that is known to be polynomial. Additional complexity is added by the need to evaluate the network. This problem is known to have an exponential complexity, but only in the maximal the number of parents of a node. Further, the reuse of results for certain class expressions improve the time needed for actually compute the probability. This means that P-CLASSIC has relatively nice properties with respect to the computational complexity.

Applicability to Information Integration

When P-CLASSIC was devised, its application in the area of information integration was not intended. Mainly, it was intended to express and reason about the degree of overlap between concepts of an ontology. P-CLASSIC works with probabilistic formalizations of so-called p-classes each of which describes a certain class of individuals. Except of the expressibility of a the probability distribution over the role fillers of a role, the probabilistic expressions formalize concepts. The possibility to express a probability distribution over the role fillers of a role is not enough for the area of information integration. Therefore, this formalism is too restricted for being used in the area of information integration.

Extensions of Logic Programming Formalisms

Several approaches for extending Logic Programming formalisms with probabilities have been proposed. However, most of them have not been designed with the Semantic Web in mind. In the following, we discuss only those probabilistic logic programming approaches that have been designed for the Semantic Web and involve ideas about how to connect rule bases with ontologies represented in OWL or related formalisms. Two kinds of such approaches can be distinguished. The first kind integrates OWL with Logic Programming by allowing to specify a logic program and a description logics knowledge base at the same time and allowing them to interact in some way. In general, the logic program is used for querying both knowledge bases. For this purpose, the logic program can contain atoms that query the Description Logics knowledge base. We survey two approaches of this kind, (Lukasiewicz, 2005) (and a restricted version thereof by Lukasiewicz (2006)) and (Cali et al, 2008). The other kind of approaches base on a subset OWL and Logic Programming have in common and on a translation from OWL to Logic Programming formalisms that have been extended with probabilities. The subset of OWL and Logic Programming, that these approaches consider is Description Logic Programs (DLP) which is very close to Datalog (Grosof et al., 2003). (Predoiu, 2006; Predoiu & Stuckenschmidt, 2007) translates OWL ontologies that lie in the DLP fragment to a probabilistic Datalog formalism that is close to Bayesian Logic Programs (Kersting & De Raedt, 2001) while (Nottelmann & Fuhr, 2005) translate a slight extension of the DLP fragment, namely DLP with equality, to probabilistic Datalog (Fuhr, 2000).

In the following, we present a short overview on Description Logic Programs: As they are a subset of the Description Logics underlying OWL and the Logic Programming paradigm and thus have a Description Logics and a Logic Programming syntax. In the logic programming syntax, they correspond to pure Datalog without negation, equality and integrity constraints. I.e. as with Datalog, a Description Logic Program consists of facts and rules. Each rule has the form $H \leftarrow B_1, ..., B_n$, where H and the B_i are atomic formulae and $n \geq 1$. An atomic formula consists of a predicate symbol p followed by a bracketed n-tuple of terms ti, $p(t_1, \ldots, t_n)$ with $n \geq i \geq 0$. A term can be either a constant (i.e. an instance) or a variable (i.e., a placeholder for an instance). If all terms in an atomic formula are constants, the atomic formula is called a ground atom. The left hand side of a rule, H, is called head and the right-hand side of a rule, $B_1 \wedge \ldots \wedge B_m$, is called body. All variables in rules are universally quantified, although this is not explicitly written. For i = 0, the rule is called a fact. Only ground atoms are allowed in facts.

In the DLP language, the predicates are only allowed to be 2-ary and the variable graph of the body of each rule is connected and acyclic. Semantically, Description Logic Programs in the logic programming syntax do not differ from them having been specified in the description logics syntax. As reasoning is concerned with syntactical manipulations, however, Description Logic Programs in the logic programming syntax are restricted to fact-form inference with logic programming reasoners, i.e. only facts can be derived and no axioms like with description logics reasoners that reason with the description logics syntax of Description Logic Programs.

In the following we compare two formalisms that are based on the Description Logic Programming fragment and 2 formalisms that are more expressive.

Bayesian Description Logic Programs

In (Predoiu, 2006), Description Logic Programs have been embedded into the Bayesian Logic Programming formalism (Kersting & De Raedt, 2001). In this approach, the probabilistic extension has the purpose of information integration and has been proposed in order to represent uncertain mappings between ontologies and rules. Also, a means to reason with the mappings and the ontologies and rules having been mapped in an integrated way has been proposed.

Expressiveness

Bayesian Description Logic Programs (BDLPs) are a probabilistic extension of the logic programming syntax (and semantics) of Description Logic Programs (Grosof et al., 2003). In Bayesian Description Logic Programs, facts are attached with an apriori probability and rules are attached with a conditional probability where the states of the head atom are conditioned on the states of the body atoms. Like a Bayesian Logic Program, a Bayesian Description Logic Program encodes a Bayesian Network.

Reasoning and Efficiency

The basic reasoning task associated with Bayesian Description Programs is querying for the probability density of a conjunction of ground atoms given a conjunction of ground evidence atoms. In Predoiu & Stuckenschmidt (2007), the semantics has been extended to allow non-ground query atoms in order to enable information retrieval by deriving all ground atoms that satisfy the query and rank them by means of their probabilities. There are no complexity results known yet for Bayesian Description Logic Programs and no inference engine is available yet. However, the inference engine for Bayesian Logic Programs, Balios (Kersting & Dick, 2004) which calls Sicstus Prolog for deriving the least Herbrand Model, can be used for reasoning with Bayesian Description Logic programs as well, because Bayesian Description Logic Programs are a subset of Bayesian Logic Programs.

Applicability for Information Integration

Bayesian Description Logic Programs have been devised in order to enable Information Integration and they are able to cover all representational issues mentioned in the introduction. However, the ontologies to be mapped are restricted to the Description Logic Programming fragment and this is often a too severe expressivity restriction.

pOWL Lite^{-} and pOWL Lite^{EQ}

Nottelmann & Fuhr (2005) have presented probabilistic extensions of two OWL Lite subsets. One of these subsets corresponds to Description Logic Programs and the other one to Description Logic Programs with equality. The probabilistic extensions are both based on probabilistic Datalog (c.f. the section on probabilistic models above in this chapter). OWL formulae that can be translated to Datalog can each be provided with probabilities and processed afterwards by a pDatalog system.

Expressiveness

As mentioned above, two OWL Lite subsets have been extended with probabilities. One corresponds to Description Logic Programs, its probabilistic extension being called pOWL Lite^{-}.[3] The other one corresponds to Description Logic Programs extended with equality, its probabilistic extension being called pOWL Lite^{EQ}. A translation of OWL formulae in the Description Logic Programming fragment (possibly with equality) into the Logic Programming syntax is provided and these can be attached with probabilities in the way that pDatalog allows. These probabilistic Datalog rules are processed afterwards by a pDatalog system.

Possible pOWL Lite^{-} expressions are listed below. Note that α ($\alpha \in [0, 1]$) which is written in front of each uncertain expression is the probability for the complete expression which is written behind it.

- **Class membership axioms:** α C(a) with $\alpha \in [0, 1]$. This expression corresponds to the statement that a is an instance of class C with probability α.
- **Complex class membership assertions:** α C(y) $\leftarrow$ R(a, y)
- **Role assertions:** α R(a, b)
- **Class inclusions:** α_1 B_1(x) $\leftarrow$ A(x). And ... and α_n B_n(x) $\leftarrow$ A(x). with $n \geq 1$. This expression corresponds to the OWL expression

Class(A partial $B_1 \ldots B_n$) and its probabilistic extension allows to express for each B_i a certainty with which A is a subclass of B_i.

- **Class inclusions with a restriction:** α B(y) $\leftarrow$ A(x), R(x, y). This expression corresponds to the OWL expression Class(A partial restriction(R allValuesFrom B)) and its probabilistic extension allows to express the probability for A being a subclass of the class of elements that have a relation with elements of B.
- **Role inclusions:** α R(x, y) $\leftarrow$ S(x, y)
- **Symmetric role axioms:** α R(x, y) $\leftarrow$ R(y, x)
- **Transitive role axioms:** α R(x, z) $\leftarrow$ R(x, y), R(y, z)
- **Domain restrictions:** α B(x) $\leftarrow$ R(x, y)
- **Range restrictions:** α B(y) $\leftarrow$ R(x, y)

Additionally, OWL Lite^{EQ} allows the expression of the following axioms:

- **Individual equivalence expressions:** α a = b $\leftarrow$ Y(a), Y(b)
- **Maximal Cardinality of 1 expressions:** α y = z $\leftarrow$ A(x), R(x, y), R(x, z)
- **Functional role axioms:** α y = z $\leftarrow$ R(x, y), R(x, z)
- **Inverse functional role axioms:** α x = y $\leftarrow$ R(x, z), R(y, z)

Y is a predicate which contains all individuals that are available in the pOWL Lite^{-} or pOWL Lite^{EQ} knowledge base.

Additionally, in order to deal with pOWL Lite^{-} /pOWL Lite^{EQ} more easily, a language for stating probabilistic horn rules basing on the SWRL syntax has been added. For the purpose of reasoning, however, this language is translated to pDatalog as well. Clearly, with this addition, the expressivity goes beyond Description Logic Programs. Although the supported fragment of OWL is not extended, much more of the Logic Programming fragment is covered. It is unclear whether full pDatalog or only a subset is supported.

Reasoning and Efficiency

In (Nottelmann & Fuhr, 2005), an implementation, i.e. a wrapper for a pDatalog reasoner like HySpirit, has not been provided. Efficiency for reasoning with pOWLLite^{-} and pOWLLite^{EQ} can be considered promising due to its limited expressivity. However, with the addition of the capability for stating horn rules basing of the SWRL syntax, one might end up with the full expressivity of pDatalog. Then, the general empirical complexity results of pDatalog mentioned in the section "probabilistic languages and models" above in this chapter is carried forward to pOWLLite^{-} and pOWLLite^{EQ} with the addition of probabilistic horn rules in the SWRL syntax.

Applicability for Information Integration

This formalism is applicable for information integration and can express all kinds of mappings suggested in the introduction. But again, the restriction of the ontologies to the Description Logic Programming fragment is often too severe. Note that, although the formalism has been additionally equipped with horn rules basing on the SWRL syntax, the integration with the translation of the OWL ontologies in the DLP fragment has not been formalized explicitly and thus cannot be considered concerning the expressivity of the ontologies.

Probabilistic Description Logic Programs with Special DL-Atoms

In (Lukasiewicz, 2005) and (Lukasiewicz, 2006), probabilistic description logic programs[4] (pdl programs) are presented that base on a loose query-based coupling of a Logic Program and a Description Logic knowledge base. The non-probabilistic formalism that pdl programs are based on has been published in (Eiter et al., 2004) as a combination of answer set programming with Description Logics. This non-probabilistic formalism has been combined with independent choice logic yielding a probabilistic extension of the base formalism.

Expressiveness

By means of the non-probabilistic base logic, a knowledge base KB = (*L*, *P*) can be specified. *L* corresponds to a classical SHIF(D) or SHOIN(D) knowledge base and *P* corresponds to a Logic Program which may contain queries to *L*. While *L* can be specified in the typical Description Logics syntax and has the typical Description Logics semantics, the Logic Program consists of a finite set of rules of the form:

$a \leftarrow b_1, ..., b_k$, not $b_{k+1}, ...,$ not b_m
with $m \geq k \geq 0$.

Here, a and the b_i are atomic formulae. An atomic formula consists of a predicate symbol *p* followed by a bracketed n-tuple of terms ti, $p(t_1, \ldots, t_n)$ with $n \geq i \geq 0$. A term can be either a constant (i.e. an instance) or a variable (i.e. a placeholder for an instance). Two kinds of negated atoms are distinguished: classically negated atoms $\neg a$ and default-negated atoms *not a*. Furthermore, there are special kinds of atoms called dl-atoms that are allowed to be one of the $_{bi}$ with $k \geq i$. That is, the dl-atoms are only allowed to occur in the positive, unnegated part of the body. Such dl-atoms form a query to *L* with additional constraints that extend or shrink the instance set associated with concepts and roles occurring in L. The logic program *P* has been given a well-founded and an answer-set semantics in (Eiter et. al, 2004).

Basing on this formalism, in (Lukasiewicz, 2005) and (Lukasiewicz, 2006), a probabilistic extension has been proposed that combines this formalism with independent choice logic. A probabilistic description logic program is a knowledge base KB = (*L*, *P*, *C*, μ) where:

- (*L*, *P*) is a dl program as explained above. Note that in (Lukasiewicz, 2005), a well-founded and an answer-set semantics have been defined for *P*.
- *C* is a choice space that corresponds to a set of sets whose union is a subset of the Herbrand Base HB_P of *P*. Alternatives, atomic choices and total choices are defined analogously to independent choice logic (c.f. the section "probabilistic languages and models" above in this chapter). No atomic choice is allowed to occur in the head of rule in *P*, but in anywhere in the body.
- μ is a probability distribution on the choice space C, i.e. μ: $\cup C \rightarrow [0, 1]$ such that $\Sigma_{a \in A}$ $\mu(a) = 1$ for all alternatives $A \in C$ and $\mu(B) = \Pi_{b \in B}\, \mu(b)$ for all total choices B of C. Note that the probability of total choices imposes probabilistic independence between the alternatives of C or, differently worded, the random variables specified by C.

Reasoning and Efficiency

Probabilistic queries to a pulp knowledge base as specified above can be either atomic or complex:

- An atomic probabilistic query queries for the probability of a formula ψ given another formula ϕ: $(\psi \mid \phi)[l, u]$. Here, l, u are placeholders for reels in the interval [0, 1] and stand for the lower bound and the upper bound of the probability. Formulas can be arbitrary contain of negation and conjunction.
- (Complex) probabilistic queries F are inductively defined as follows: each atomic probabilistic query A (with l, u being instatiated, however) is a probabilistic query. If G and H are probabilistic queries, then so are $\neg G$ and $G \wedge H$.

The correct answer to a complex probabilistic query F is defined to be the set of all substitutions

θ such that $F\theta$ is a consequence of the knowledge base. With the answer set semantics, it is distinguished between answer set consequences and tight answer set consequences. For answer set consequences, every model of the knowledge base has to be a model of $F\theta$ as well. For tight answer set consequences, furthermore, *l* (resp. *u*) have to be the infimum (resp. supremum) of $Pr(\psi\theta \mid \phi\theta)$ subject to all models of KB given that $Pr(\phi\theta) > 0$.

With the well-founded semantics, $F\theta$ is a consequence of KB if $F\theta$ is true in the well-founded model. Again, a query $(\psi \mid \phi)[l, u]\theta$ is a tight well-founded answer, is *l* (resp. *u*) are the infimum (resp. supremum) of $Pr(\psi\theta \mid \phi\theta)$ given that $pr(\phi\theta) > 0$. Note that $Pr(\psi\theta \mid \phi\theta)$ is a probabilistic interpretation either under the answer-set semantics or under the well-founded semantics as defined in (Lukasiewicz, 2005), depending on the context. More specifically, Pr is a probabilistic distribution over all models.

The computation of tight answers to queries $(\psi \mid \phi)[L, U]\theta$ under the answer-set semantics involves classical logical deduction (according to the semantics used) and solving two linear optimization problems. The complexity of solving these linear optimization problems has not been discussed, yet. However, deduction under the answer set semantics has a very high complexity. More specifically, for *L* being a SHIF(D) knowledge base (resp. a SHOIN(D) knowledge base) query answering is in the complexity class co-NEXP (resp. co-NP^{NEXP}) (Eiter et. al, 2004). Query answering under the well-founded semantics is for L being a SHIF(D) knowledge base (resp. SHOIN(D) knowledge base) complete for EXP (resp. P^{NEXP}) (Eiter et. al, 2004). In (Lukasiewicz, 2006), for the same syntax as shown above for both, knowledge bases and queries, a stratified semantics based on a (local) stratification of the knowledge base has been defined. Complexity for this semantics has not been considered at all. However, query answering in stratified logic programs in general, i.e. without integrating Description Logic knowledge bases, has a much lower complexity than in those that go beyond stratification and lie in the well-founded semantics, but is still intractable in the worst case.

Applicability to Information Integration

This formalism is the first one mentioned in this chapter that is able to fully integrate full OWL and a huge part of RDF. Concerning the expressivity, this formalism is therefore very suitable for the representation of OWL (i.e. the OWL-Lite and OWL-DL fragments) and a huge part of RDF in the same syntax. However, as dl-atoms are not allowed to occur in the head of the rules, only a Logic Program can be the target of a mapping. Therefore, it cannot be used for information integration on the Semantic Web where OWL ontologies can be the target of mappings.

Probabilistic Disjunctive Description Logic Programs

In (Cali et al., 2008), a tighter integration of Logic Programs and the Description Logics underlying OWL has been combined with independent choice logic. This approach is called probabilistic disjunctive description logic programs (pddl programs) and differs from the formalism mentioned above in the fact that there are no special dl-atoms necessary for the flow of information between *L* and *P*. In fact, concepts and roles of L can occur as unary or binary predicates in P as well. Furthermore, the logic programming component *P* is allowed to have rules with disjunction in the head while with probabilistic description logic programs with special DL-atoms mentioned above, *P* was only allowed to consist of rules with a single, positive atom in the head.[5] Note also that classical negation is not allowed to occur in probabilistic disjunctive description logic programs in contrast to probabilistic description logic programs with special dl-atoms described above.

Expressiveness

As before, in the section above, a non-probabilistic base logic is combined with independent choice logic yielding probabilistic disjunctive description logic programs. The non-probabilistic logic used is disjunctive description logic programs (Lukasiewicz, 2007). It allows to specify a knowledge base KB = (L, P) with L being either a SHIQ(D) or a SHOIN(D) knowledge base and P being a logic program. P is a finite set of disjunctive rules of the form:

$$\alpha_1 \vee \ldots \vee \alpha_k \leftarrow \beta_1, \ldots, \beta_n, \text{not } \beta_{n+1}, \ldots, \text{not } \beta_{n+m}$$

with $\alpha_1, \ldots, \alpha_k, \beta_1, \ldots, \beta_{n+m}$ being atoms built with the predicate, role and concept symbols of P an L in the usual way. The logic program P has been given an answer set semantics in (Lukasiewicz, 2007).

Basing on this formalism, in (Cali et. al, 2008), a probabilistic extension has been proposed that combines this formalism with independent choice logic. A pddl program is a knowledge base KB = (L, P, C, μ) where

- (L, P) is a ddl program as explained above
- C is a choice space that corresponds to a set of sets whose union of its elements A $\in$ C corresponds to a subset of the set $HB_P \setminus DL_P$. Here, HB_P is the Herbrand base of P and DL_P is the subset of the Herbrand base of P that is built with predicates that occur in L as concepts or roles, too. Alternatives, atomic choices and total choices are defined analogously to independent choice logic (c.f. the section "probabilistic languages and models" above in this chapter).
- μ is a probability distribution on the choice space C as defined in the section above.

Reasoning and Efficiency

A probabilistic query to a pddl knowledge base has the form $\exists (c_1(\mathbf{x}) \vee \ldots \vee c_n(\mathbf{x}))[r, s]$ where $\mathbf{x}$, r, s are tuples of variables, $n \geq 1$, and each $c_i(\mathbf{x})$ is a conjunction of atoms constructed from predicate and constant symbols in P and variables in $\mathbf{x}$. Similarly to probabilistic description logic programs with special dl-atoms, it is distinguished between correct and tight answers to such a query. Given a probabilistic query $\exists (q(\mathbf{x}))[r, s]$, a formula $(q(\mathbf{x}))[l, u]$ with $l, u \in [0, 1]$ is a *correct consequence* of the knowledge base iff the probability of it lies always in the interval [0, 1] for every answer set of KB and every variable assignment σ. A formula $(q(\mathbf{x}))[l, u]$ with $l, u \in [0, 1]$ is a *tight consequence* of the knowledge base iff l (resp. u) is the infimum (resp. supremum) of the probability of the formula subject to all answer sets of the knowledge base and all variable assignments σ.

The consistency and the query processing problem are decidable in pddl programs. For a pddl knowledge base KB = (L, P, C, μ) with L being either a SHIF(D) or a SHOIN(D) knowledge base, deciding whether KB is consistent is complete for $NEXP^{NP}$ given that the size of C is bounded by a constant. For a pddl knowledge base KB = (L, P, C, μ) with L being either a SHIF(D) or SHOIN(D) knowledge base, deciding whether $(q)[l, u]$ with q being a ground atom from HB_P and $l, u \in [0, 1]$ is a consequence of KB is complete for co-$NEXP^{NP}$.

In (Cali et al, 2008), a subset of pddl knowledge bases with strictly limited expressivity has been presented which allows for deciding consistency and query processing in polynomial time. However, for this purpose, the Description Logics part L must be in DL-Lite (Calvanese et. al, 2005) and the logic programming part P extended with additional rules modelling basic inclusion in L must be normal, i.e. only one non-negated atom in the head is allowed, and locally stratified.

Applicability to Information Integration

This formalism is capable of representing full OWL (i.e. full OWL-Lite and OWL-DL ontologies) and a huge part of RDF in the same syntax and is therefore capable for integrated query answering and reasoning with both formalisms.

Furthermore, as predicates representing concepts and roles in the ontology can occur freely in the rule, i.e. also in the head, mappings can be represented with the formalism straightforwardly. Furthermore, as disjunction in the head is allowed, inconsistent mappings can be dealt with more easily that with pure horn rules that allow only one atom in the head of a rule. The representation of mappings with this formalism has been investigated and described in detail by Cali & Lukasiewicz (2007).

DISCUSSION AND CONCLUSION

We conclude the chapter with a discussion of the benefits and drawbacks of the different approaches for extending Semantic Web languages with probabilistic information that we have surveyed above. It turns out that there exist *two different kinds of probabilistic extensions*. The first kind of extensions is a rather loose coupling between an existing Semantic Web language and a probabilistic model. There, the Semantic Web Language is just used syntactically as a vocabulary for exchanging knowledge bases specified in the probabilistic model. The second kind of extensions provides a tight integration on the formal level between a Semantic Web Language or a subset of it and a probabilistic model. The second kind of extensions encompasses as well the formalisms that integrate a Semantic Web language with logic programming and combine the resulting formalisms with a probabilistic model. These extensions provide also a tight formal integration of a Semantic Web language which usually is OWL-Lite/OWL-DL or the Description Logic which underlies these OWL fragments with a logic programming formalism and a probabilistic model.

Extensions of the first kind that are mentioned in this survey are the approaches of:

- (Fukushige, 2005) which proposes a vocabulary for encoding Bayesian Networks with RDF.
- (Yang & Calmet, 2006) which proposes a vocabulary for encoding Bayesian Networks with OWL.
- (Costa & Laskey, 2006) which proposes a vocabulary for encoding Multi-Entity Bayesian Networks with OWL.

These approaches are rather unsatisfying because they do not consider the semantics of Semantic Web languages but rather focus at a special kind of probabilistic model, i.e. Bayesian Networks or Multi-Entity Bayesian Networks, and provide a Semantic Web based syntactical interchange format for these probabilistic models and their semantics. By means of these approaches uncertainty can only be represented on the Semantic Web but no Semantic Web statement is extended by some kind of uncertainty. Thus, from the five areas mentioned in the introduction where a consideration of uncertainty is needed on the Semantic Web, only the needs of the first area are met. I.e. only the requirements for representing statistical information are met. The area of the Semantic Web itself does not benefit substantially from these extensions. It is even arguable whether the probabilistic models represented benefit from using a vocabulary basing on a Semantic Web language without any formal integration. Note that currently no reasoning support for these vocabularies has been implemented yet, i.e. no wrappers exist that is able to parse the Semantic Web language vocabulary defined for the particular probabilistic models and feed it to a reasoner that is capable to deal with them. However, for PR-OWL, a reasoner implementation effort has recently been started.

Extensions of the second kind naturally fulfill the requirements for representing statistical information. Additionally, because of the much tighter integration on the formal level, they are also much more appropriate for Ontology matching and aligning and also for ontology learning by means of Bayesian machine learning methods. The same holds for ontology population or document classification, respectively. E.g. (Straccia & Troncy, 2006) have proposed methods for learning probabilistic mappings between OWL ontologies that are represented as very simple pDatalog rules. These methods have been implemented in the oMAP framework. The pDatalog rules that can be learned in the oMAP framework are contained in pOWLLite^{-} as well. Thus, those mappings are very much related to POWLLite^{-} and pOWLLite^{EQ}. Probabilistic disjunctive description logic programming as described above has also been proposed for usage in the area of the usage of ontology mappings and information integration. These considerations have been theoretical and no implementation has been provided, yet, but is considered as future work. In (Predoiu, 2006), Bayesian Description Logic Programs have been proposed solely for the representation of mappings and the uncertainty inherently associated with any automatically discovered mapping. An implementation, however, is not yet provided, but under development. The only further formalism for which a mapping scenario has been considered is BayesOWL. As each BayesOWL ontology corresponds to a Bayesian Network, in the mapping scenario, Bayesian Networks are mapped to each other. Hence, this scenario is computationally very expensive. The formalism which has been identified as being the most appropriate for information integration is probabilistic disjunctive description logic programming because of its expressivity concerning the ontologies to be mapped and the mappings and the possibility to deal with inconsistencies introduced by mappings to a certain extent which needs to be further investigated. For the other probabilistic extensions surveyed in this paper, no mapping scenario has been considered. Most of them have been proposed without the area of ontology mapping and information integration in mind and therefore they all have drawbacks concerning their usage in this area. Furthermore, no research on learning or using mappings has been performed yet in any of the formalisms except of pOWLLite^{-}.

The probabilistic extensions that integrate Semantic Web languages or subsets thereof tightly with a probabilistic model, can be distinguished as follows:

- Extensions that consider not only the semantics but also the syntax of established Semantic Web languages, examples being pRDF and BayesOWL. Both support only a small subset of the languages they extend probabilistically. pRDF extends basically only the three RDF built-in predicates for specifying subclass relations, instance and role membership with probabilities. Furthermore, RDF built-in predicates around properties (the subproperty relation, the definition of the range and the domain of properties) are allowed to be used classically in deterministic triples. BayesOWL has an even more limited expressivity than pRDF because it does not even allow to express uncertainty of properties and instances.
- Extensions that consider subsets of the Description Logics underlying OWL, examples being P-SHOQ(D) and P-CLASSIC. P-CLASSIC has a rather limited expressivity as it combines the description logic CLASSIC that has been designed for efficiency of reasoning and suffers thus of a limited expressivity with the probabilistic model of Bayesian Networks. CLASSIC is a very small subset of SHOQ(D). For P-CLASSIC no reasoning tools have been devised. P-SHOQ(D) has the full expressivity of SHOQ(D) and is very near to OWL-DL which corresponds to SHOIN(D). The only difference is that inverse roles cannot be specified. However, for P-SHOQ(D) no reasoning tools exist either. Furthermore, the proposed reasoning algorithm can be expected to have a very high complexity

because it involves solving a linear equation system.

- Extensions that consider integrations of a Logic Programming variant and a Description Logic underlying OWL. Such extensions are Bayesian Description Logic Programs, pOWLLite^{-} and pOWLLite^{EQ}, probabilistic Description Logic Programs and probabilistic Disjunctive Description Logic Programs. We think that probabilistic extensions of integration formalisms that integrate Description Logics and Logic Programs are very important also because Logic Programming is a very important paradigm especially present in the database area. Furthermore, as shown by the Rule-Interchange-Format working group at the W3C[6] that intends to carry over the Logic Programming paradigm into the Semantic Web, there is a huge interest in representing rules on the Web. In the next paragraph we will shortly summarize a comparison of the form of integration between DL and LP, the expressivity of the formalisms and the tightness of the combination between the deterministic logical model and the probabilistic model.

Two of the probabilistic approaches that integrate Logic Programming with Description Logics, integrate only a subset of OWL. These approaches are Bayesian Description Logic Programs and pOWLLite^{-}/pOWLLite^{EQ}. Bayesian Description Logic Programs combine pure Description Logic Programs, i.e. Datalog without equality and negation, a common subset that is shared by the Description Logics underlying OWL and the Logic programming paradigm, with Bayesian Logic Programs. The integration of the deterministic and the probabilistic model is very tight and yields even a subset of the probabilistic model. pOWLLite^{-} and pOWLLite^{EQ} are intended to be a probabilistic extension of Description Logic Programs as well (the latter extends them also with equality). Besides a probabilistic extension of Description Logic Programs (possibly extended with equality) also probabilistic Horn rules are supported that increase the expressivity and it is unclear whether the expressivity ends up in full pDatalog. However, as negation is allowed and also equality, pOWLLite$^{-/EQ}$ seems to support a larger expressivity of the deterministic model. The probabilistic models used in Bayesian Description Logic Programs and pOWLLite^{-}/^{EQ} differ as well. Bayesian Logic Programs do not support negation and are a compact representation of a Bayesian Network. pDatalog supports negation under the well-founded semantics and until now no relation to Bayesian Networks has been found.

Differently from Bayesian Logic Programs and pOWLLite^{-}/^{EQ}, probabilistic Description Logic Programs and probabilistic Disjunctive Description Logic Programs support full OWL-Lite and OWL-DL and integrate them with stratified logic programs, logic programs under the well-founded and under the answer set semantics. These approaches have a strong theoretical basis and all of them combine the deterministic model with independent choice logic as probabilistic model. The query language supports differently form Bayesian Logic Programs and pOWLLite^{-}/pOWLLite^{EQ} queries for probabilistic intervals. The query language is very expressive and reasoning is very complex because it involves solving a linear equation system like with P-SHOQ. However, for a restricted subset of probabilistic Disjunctive Description Logic programs, a polynomial complexity has been shown. This subset consists of a Description Logics knowledge base lying in a subset of the Description Logic programming fragment and of a Logic Program that corresponds to Datalog with negation that is locally stratified.

Most of the approaches that probabilistically integrate the Logic Programming paradigm with the Description Logics paradigm, provide own reasoners. For Bayesian Description Logic Programs, the reasoner Balios (Kerstin & Dick, 2004) that has been implemented for its probabilistic model which is a superset of itself can be used. For pOWLLite$^{-/EQ}$, HySpirit or Pire which are reasoners for full pDatalog which is their underlying probabilistic model can be used. In fact, an implementation for pOWLLite$^{-/EQ}$ basing on PIRE exists. For probabilistic Description Logic Programs and probabilistic Disjunctive Description Logic Programs no reasoners exist yet.

FUTURE RESEARCH DIRECTIONS

As overall conclusion, we can summarize that until recently, research has not paid much attention to uncertainty in the area of the Semantic Web. However, it gains more and more interest and new approaches considering uncertainty tend to emerge. Still, many of these approaches are rather half-baked and a lot of things are missing:

- **Reflections on gathering probabilities.** *Where do the probabilities used in the web come from? What kinds of probabilities exist?* Cali & Lukasiewicz (2007) make the first proposal to distinguish between mapping trust, mapping error or plain mapping probabilities. However, we think that this is just a very first step and might be a beginning for new insights into the types and usages of probability usage, depending on the event space and intended semantics. *How can those probabilities be gathered?* (Straccia & Troncy, 2006) make proposals for learning very simple pDatalog rules. Investigations of methods for learning more complex structures of different probabilistic models would enable the Semantic Web community to anticipate in which forms a Semantic Web where automatic information integration would be possible.
- **Reflections on which probabilistic models are suitable for which subareas of the Semantic Web.** That is, investigations of the applicability and usefulness of probabilistic extensions of Semantic Web languages in the different areas that need to consider uncertainty have to be done. For example, it has to be seen whether a probabilistic Logic Programming approach is better suited for discovering and representing mappings than a purely probabilistic Description Logic one when only OWL ontologies and no rules are involved. This requirement is interweaved with the requirement above because the investigations on the different kinds of probabilities might lead to usefulness results. Furthermore, investigations on methods for learning those different probabilistic Semantic Web extensions, might naturally lead to further insights of the usability of the different formalisms in the different areas by means of complexity results and learnability results.
- **Reflections on cyclic probabilistic representations:** None of the above mentioned probabilistic extensions of Semantic Web languages can deal with cyclic representations. We deem this as a severe drawback because of the open and free nature of the Semantic Web. If ontologies, logic programs and mappings between them are considered as a whole, cyclic descriptions are very likely to occur and are not avoidable. Only in small toy worlds, cycles can be avoided. It has to be investigated in which ways cyclic probabilistic representations can be dealt with.
- **Reasoning methods and implementations:** Reasoning tools in general are not provided for the languages themselves, only for related logical formalisms which can used by means of wrappers but are not optimized for the languages at hand. If there are reasoning tools that are specialized for the languages themselves, then they support only a part of the language like in the case of pRDF. Research needs to focus on the development

of optimized reasoning methods and reasoning tools need to be implemented in order to enable the usage of uncertain statements in the Semantic Web and in order to make reasoning feasible facing the huge amount of ontologies and data that can be expected to be present in the future of the Semantic Web. For example research on approximate and distributed reasoning would enable feasible query answering with large-scale knowledge bases and instance bases like imposed by the Semantic Web. None of the approaches above employ or consider currently any form of approximate or distributed reasoning.

REFERENCES

Angele, J., Boley, H., de Bruijn, J., Fensel, D., Hitzler, P., Kifer, M., Krummenacher, R., Lausen, H., Polleres, A. & Studer, R. (2005). *Web Rule language (WRL).* W3C Member Submission, from http://www.w3.org/Submission/WRL/

Bechhofer, S., van Harmelen, F., Hendler, J., Horrocks, I., McGuinness, D. L., Patel-Schneider, P. F. & Stein, L. A. (2004). *OWL Web Ontology Language Reference.* W3C Recommendation, from http://www.w3.org/TR/2004/REC-owl-ref-20040210

Cali, A., Lukasiewicz, T., Predoiu, L. & Stuckenschmidt, H. (2008). Tightly Integrated Probabilistic Description Logic Programs for Representing Ontology Mappings. In *Proceedings of the International Symposium on Foundations of Information and Knowledge Systems (FOIKS).*

Cali, A. & Lukasiewicz, T. (2007). *Tightly Integrated Probabilistic Description Logic Programs.* Technical Report, Institut für Informationssysteme, TU Wien.

Calvanese, D., de Giacomo, G., Lembo, D., Lenzerini, M., & Rosati, R. (2005). DL-Lite: Tractable description logics for ontologies. In *Proceedings 20th AAAI conference on Artificial Intelligence.*

Castillo, E., Gutierrez, J. M. & Hadi. A. S. (1997). *Expert systems and probabilistic network models.* Springer-Verlag

Costa, P. C. G. & Laskey, K. B. (2006). *PR-OWL:* A Framework for Probabilistic Ontologies. In *Proceedings of the International Conference on Formal Ontology in Information Systems (FOIS).*

Cowell, R. G., Dawid, A. P., Lauritzen, S. L. & Spiegelhalter, D. J. (1999). *Probabilistic Networks and Expert Systems.* Springer-Verlag.

de Bruijn & J., Heymans, S. (2007). Logical Foundations of (e)RDF(S): Complexity and Reasoning. In *Proceedings of the International Semantic Web Conference (ISWC).*

De Raedt, L., Kimmig, A. & Toivonen, H. (2007). ProbLog: A Probabilistic Prolog and Its Application in Link Discovery. In *Proceedings of the 20th International Joint Conference on Artificial Intelligence.*

Decker, S., Melnik, S., van Harmelen, F., Fensel, D., Klein, M., Broekstra, J., et al. (2000). The Semantic Web: The roles of XML and RDF. *IEEE Internet Computing,* 4(5), 63-67.

Ding, L., Kolari, P., Ding, Z. & Avancha, S. (2006). BayesOWL: Uncertainty Modeling in Semantic Web Ontologies. In *Soft Computing in Ontologies and Semantic Web.* Springer Verlag..

Doan, A., Madhavan, J., Domingos, P. & Halevy, A. (2003). Ontology Matching: A Machine Learning Approach. In *Handbook on Ontologies in Information Systems* (pp 397-416), Springer-Verlag.

Eiter, T., Lukasiewicz, T., Schindlauer, R. & Tompits, H. (2004). Combining answer set programming with description logics for the Semantic Web. In *Proceedings of the 9th international conference on the Principles of Knowledge Representation and Reasoning* (KR-2004).

Euzenat, J. & Shvaiko, P. (2007). *Ontology Matching.* Springer Verlag.

Fagin, R. (1999). Combining fuzzy information from multiple systems. *Journal of Computer and Systems Sciences*, 58:83-99.

Fikes, R. & McGuinness, D. (2001). *An Axiomatic Semantics for RDF, RDF-S and DAML+OIL.* W3C Note from http://www.w3.org/TR/daml+oil-axioms

Fuhr, N. (2000). Probabilistic Datalog: Implementing Logical Information Retrieval for Advanced Applications. *Journal of the American Society for Information Science*, 51(2): 95-110.

Fukushige, Y. (2005). *Representing Probabilistic Knowledge in the Semantic Web.* From http://www.w3.org/2004/09/13-Yoshio/PositionPaper.html

Fukushige, Y. (2005). Representing Probabilistic Relations in RDF. In *Proceedings of Workshop on Uncertainty Reasoning for the Semantic Web (URSW).*

Giugno, R. & Lukasiewicz, T. (2002). P-SHOQ(D): A Probabilistic Extension of SHOQ(D) for Probabilistic Ontologies in the Semantic Web. In *Proceedings Logics in Artificial Intelligence, European Conference, JELIA.*

Grosof, B., Horrocks, I., Volz, R. & Decker, S. (2003). Description Logic Programs: Combining Logic Programs with Description Logic. In *Proceedings of 12th International Conference on the World Wide Web.*

Heinsohn, J. (1991). A Hybrid Approach for Modeling Uncertainty in Terminological Logics. In *Proceedings of the European Conference on Symbolic and Qualitative Approaches to Reasoning with Uncertainty.*

Holi, M. & Hyvönen, E. (2006). Modeling Uncertainty in Semantic Web Taxonomies. In Z. Ma (Ed.), *Soft Computing in Ontologies and Semantic Web.* Springer-Verlag.

Horrocks, I. (2005). OWL Rules, OK? In *Proceedings of W3C Workshop on Rule Languages for Interoperability.*

Horrocks, I. & Patel-Schneider, P. F. (2004). Reducing OWL entailment to description logic satisfiability. *Journal of Web Semantics*, 1(4):345-357.

Horrocks, I. & Patel-Schneider, P. F., van Harmelen, F. (2003). From SHIQ and RDF to OWL: The making of a web ontology language. *Journal of Web Semantics*, 1(1):7-26.

Horrocks, I., Patel-Schneider, P. F., Bechhofer, S. & Tsarkov, D. (2005). OWL rules: A proposal and prototype implementation. *Journal of Web Semantics*, 3(1):23-40.

Hustadt, U., Motik, B. & Sattler, U. (2005). Data complexity of reasoning in very expressive description logics. In *Proceedings of the 19th International Joint Conference on Artificial Intelligence.*

Jaeger, M. (1994). Probabilistic Reasoning in Terminological Logics. In *Proceedings of the 4th international Conference on Principles of Knowledge Representation and Reasoning.*

Jensen, F. V. (2001). *Bayesian Networks and Decision Graphs.* Springer-Verlag.

Kersting, K. & De Raedt, L. (2001). *Bayesian Logic Programs.* Technical Report No. 151, Institute for Computer Science, University of Freiburg, Germany.

Kersting, K. & Dick, U. (2004). Balios – The Engine for Bayesian Logic Programs. In *Proceedings of Knowledge Discovery in Databases (PKDD).*

Koller, D., Levy, A. & Pfeffer, A. (1997). P-CLASSIC: A tractable probabilistic description logic. In *Proceedings of the 14th AAAI Conference on Artificial Intelligence (AAAI-97).*

Laskey, K. B. (2006). *MEBN: A Logic for Open-World Probabilistic Reasoning.* Technical Report C4I06-01, George Mason University, USA.

Laskey, K. B & Costa, P. C. G. (2005). Of Klingons and Starships: Bayesian Logic for the 23rd Century. In *Proceedings of the 21st Conference of Uncertainty in AI (UAI).*

Lassila, O. & Swick, R. (1999). *Resource Description Framework (RDF) Model and Syntax Specification.* W3C Recommendation, from http://www.w3.org/TR/REC-rdf-syntax/

Lloyd, J. W. & Topor, R. W. (1984). Making Prolog more Expressive. *Journal of Logic Programming,* 3:225-240.

Lukasiewicz, T. (2005a). Probabilistic Description Logic Programs. In *Proceedings of the 8th European Conference on Symbolic and Quantitative Approaches to Reasoning with Uncertainty.*

Lukasiewicz, T. (2005b). Stratified Probabilistic Description Logic Programs. In *Proceedings of the ISWC-2005 Workshop on Uncertainty Reasoning for the Semantic Web (URSW).*

Lukasiewicz, T. (2007). A Novel Combination of Answer Set Programming with Description Logics for the Semantic Web. In *Proceedings of the 4th European Semantic Web Conference (ESWC 2007).*

Maedche, A. & Staab, S. (2004). Ontology Learning. In Staab, S. & Studer, R. (Eds.) *Handbook on Ontologies.* Springer 2004.

Manola, F. & Miller, E. (2004). *RDF Primer.* W3C Recommendation, from http://www.w3.org/TR/rdf-primer/

Nottelmann, H. (2005). *Inside PIRE: An extensible, open-source IR engine based on probabilistic logics.* Technical Report, University of Duisburg-Essen, Germany.

Nottelmann, H. & Fuhr, N. (2006). Adding Probabilities and Rules to OWL Lite Subsets based on Probabilistic Datalog. *International Journal of Uncertainty, Fuzziness and Knowledge-Based Systems,* 14(1):17-41.

Pan, R., Ding, Z., Yu, Y. & Pen, Y. A. (2005). *A* Bayesian Network Approach to Ontology Mapping. In *Proceedings of the Fourth International Semantic Web Conference (ISWC).*

Poole, D. (1997). The independent choice logic for modelling multiple agents under uncertainty. *Artificial Intelligence,* 94(1-2):7-56.

Predoiu, L. (2006). Information Integration with Bayesian Description Logic Programs. In *3rd IIWeb Interdisciplinary Workshop for Information Integration on the Web.*

Predoiu, L. & Stuckenschmidt, H. (2007). A probabilistic Framework for Information Integration and Retrieval on the Semantic Web. In *Proceedings of the 3rd International Workshop on Database interoperability (InderDB).*

Roelleke, T., Lübeck, R., Kazai, G. (2001). The HySpirit Retrieval Platform. In *Proc. of the 24th International ACM SIGIR Conference on Research and Development in Information Retrieval, SIGIR.*

Sebastiani, F. (2002). Machine learning in automated text categorization. *ACM Computing Surveys,* 34(1):1-47.

Straccia, U. & Troncy, R. (2006). Towards Distributed Information Retrieval in the Semantic Web: Query Reformulation Using the oMAP Framework. In *Proceedings of the 3rd European Semantic Web Conference (ESWC).*

Udrea, O., Subrahmanian, V. S., & Maijkic, Z. (2006). Probabilistic RDF. In *Proceedings of the Conference on Information reuse and integration.*

Yang, Y. & Calmet, J. (2006). OntoBayes: An Ontology-Driven Uncertainty Model. In *Proceedings of the International Conference on Computational*

Intelligence for Modelling, Control and Automation and International Conference on Intelligent Agents, Web Technologies and Internet Commerce (CIMCA-IAWTIC'06).

Yelland, P.M. (2000). An Alternative Combination of Bayesian Networks and Description Logics. In *Proceedings of the 7th international Conference on Knowledge Representation (KR).*

ADDITIONAL READING

General Logic

Ben-Ari, M. (2001). *Mathematical Logic for Computer Scientists.* Springer-Verlag.

Ebbinghaus, H.-D., Flum, J. & Thomas, W. (2007) *Mathematical Logic.* Springer-Verlag.

Enderton, H. B. (2002). *A mathematical Introduction to Logic*, 2nd edition, Academic Press.

Schoening, U. (1994). *Logic for Computer Scientists.* Birkhaeuser Verlag.

Logic Programming

Abiteboul, S., Hull, R. & Vianu, V. (1995) *Foundations of Databases: The Logical Level.* Addison Wesley.

Baral, C. (2003). *Knowledge Representation, Reasoning and Declarative Problem Solving.* Cambridge University Press.

Lloyd, J. W. (1987). *Foundations of Logic Programming.* Springer-Verlag.

Ullman, J. D. (1988). *Principles of Database and Knowledge-Base Systems, Volume I.* Computer Science Press.

Ullman, J. D. (1989). *Principles of Database and Knowledge-Base Systems, Volume II.* Computer Science Press.

Zaniolo, C., Ceri, S., Faloutsos, C., Snodgrass, R. T., Subrahmanian, V. S. & Zicari, R. (1997). *Advanced Database Systems.* Morgan Kaufmann.

General Probability Theory

Georgii, H.-O. (2008). *Stochastics.* de Gruyter Verlag.

Ross, S. M. (2005). *A first course in Probability.* Prentice Hall.

Bayesian Networks and Graphical Models

Castillo, E., Gutierrez, J. M. & Hadi. A. S. (1997). *Expert systems and probabilistic network models.* Springer-Verlag

Cowell, R. G., Dawid, A. P., Lauritzen, S. L. & Spiegelhalter, D. J. (1999). *Probabilistic Networks and Expert Systems.* Springer-Verlag.

Edwards, D. (2000). *Introduction to Graphical Modelling*, 2nd ed. Springer-Verlag.

Pearl, J. (1988). *Probabilistic Reasoning in Intelligent Systems: Networks of Plausible Inference.* Morgan Kaufmann.

Jensen, F. V. (2001). *Bayesian Networks and Decision Graphs.* Springer-Verlag.

Bayesian Logic Programming

Kersting, K. (2006). An Inductive Logic Programming Approach to Statistical Relational Learning. In *Frontiers in Artificial Intelligence*, Volume 148, IOS Press, Amsterdam, The Netherlands.

Kersting, K. & De Raedt, L. (2001). *Bayesian Logic Programs.* Technical Report No. 151, Institute for Computer Science, University of Freiburg, Germany.

Kersting, K. & De Raedt, L. (2007). Bayesian Logic Programs: Theory and Tool. In Getoor, L. & Taskar, B. (Ed.), *Introduction to Statistical Relational Learning*. MIT Press.

Independent Choice Logic

Poole, D. (1997). The independent choice logic for modelling multiple agents under uncertainty. *Artificial Intelligence*, 94(1-2):7-56.

Multi-Entity Bayesian Networks

Laskey, K. B & Costa, P. C. G. (2005). Of Klingons and Starships: Bayesian Logic for the 23rd Century. In *Proceedings of the 21st Conference of Uncertainty in AI (UAI)*.

Laskey, K. B. (2006). *MEBN: A Logic for Open-World Probabilistic Reasoning*. Technical Report C4I06-01, George Mason University, USA.

Probabilistic Datalog

Fuhr, N. (2000). Probabilistic Datalog: Implementing Logical Information Retrieval for Advanced Applications. *Journal of the American Society for Information Science*, 51(2): 95-110.

RDF and RDF Schema

A selection of documents on RDF and RDF Schema (Specification, Use Cases, Recommended Readings, Tools, Related Technologies, etc.) can be found at this url: http://www.w3.org/RDF/

de Bruijn & J., Heymans, S. (2007). Logical Foundations of (e)RDF(S): Complexity and Reasoning. In *Proceedings of the International Semantic Web Conference (ISWC)*.

OWL

Smith, M. K., Welty, C. & McGuiness, D. L. (2004). *OWL Web Ontology Language Guide*. W3C Recommendation, from http://www.w3.org/TR/2004/REC-owl-ref-20040210/

Horrocks, I. & Patel-Schneider, P. F., van Harmelen, F. (2003). From SHIQ and RDF to OWL: The making of a web ontology language. *Journal of Web Semantics*, 1(1):7-26.

ENDNOTES

1. For the sake of simplicity we are considering here only a part of the ontologies. The complete ontologies can be found at http://oaei.ontologymatching.org/.
2. Due to the semi-decidability of First-order logic this can only be true if the translation allows for networks of infinite size.
3. Note that Description Logic Programs are called OWL Lite$^-$ in (Nottelmann & Fuhr, 2005). This is the reason for calling its probabilistic extension pOWL Lite$^-$.
4. Note that although the formalism is called description logic programs like the formalism in (Grosof et al., 2003), it is a completely different language as it goes beyond the common subset of Description Logics and Logic Programming. In order to hint the difference, we are using lower case letters for this formalism while we call the formalism from Grosof et al. (2003) Description Logic Programs.
5. Note that conjunction in the head is allowed with probabilistic description logic programs with special DL-atoms as well, because rules with conjunction in the head can be split to regular horn rules by means of the Lloyd-Topor-Transformation (Lloyd & Topor, 1984).
6. http://www.w3.org/2005/rules

Chapter VI
Automatic Semantic Annotation Using Machine Learning

Jie Tang
Tsinghua University, Beijing, China

Duo Zhang
University of Illinois, Urbana-Champaign, USA

Limin Yao
Tsinghua University, Beijing, China

Yi Li
Tsinghua University, Beijing, China

ABSTRACT

This chapter aims to give a thorough investigation of the techniques for automatic semantic annotation. The Semantic Web provides a common framework that allows data to be shared and reused across applications, enterprises, and community boundaries. However, lack of annotated semantic data is a bottleneck to make the Semantic Web vision a reality. Therefore, it is indeed necessary to automate the process of semantic annotation. In the past few years, there was a rapid expansion of activities in the semantic annotation area. Many methods have been proposed for automating the annotation process. However, due to the heterogeneity and the lack of structure of the Web data, automated discovery of the targeted or unexpected knowledge information still present many challenging research problems. In this chapter, we study the problems of semantic annotation and introduce the state-of-the-art methods for dealing with the problems. We will also give a brief survey of the developed systems based on the methods. Several real-world applications of semantic annotation will be introduced as well. Finally, some emerging challenges in semantic annotation will be discussed.

INTRODUCTION

Semantic annotation of the web documents is the only way to make the Semantic Web vision a reality. The current Semantic Web meets a bottleneck that there is not much of a Semantic Web due to the lack of annotated web pages. There is such a lack that the Semantic Web is still submerged in the sea of the un-meaningful (un-annotated) web pages.

Semantic annotations are to tag ontology class instance data and map it onto ontology classes. Manual annotation is more easily accomplished today, using authoring tools such as OntoMat (Handschuh, Staab, and Ciravegna, 2002) and SHOE (Heflin, Hendler, and Luke, 2003). However, the use of human annotators is often fraught with errors due to factors such as annotator familiarity with the domain, amount of training, and complex schemas. Manual annotation is also expensive and cannot be used to deal with the large volume of the existing documents on the Web. Automatic semantic annotation is an ideal solution to the problem. However, the fully automatic creation of semantic annotations is also an unsolved problem. Hence, semi-automatic creation of annotations is the method mostly used in current systems.

There are many automatic annotation methods have been proposed, including: (A) supervised machine learning based method, (B) unsupervised machine learning based method, and (C) ontology based method.

(A) The supervised machine learning based method consists of two stages: annotation and training. In annotation, we are given a document in either plain text or semi-structured (e.g. emails, web pages, forums, etc.), and the objective is to identify the entities and the semantic relations between the entities. In training, the task is to learn the model(s) that are used in the annotation stage. For learning the models, the input data is often viewed as a sequence of units, for example, a document can be viewed as a sequence of either words or text lines (depending on the specific applications). In the supervised machine learning based method, labeled data for training the model is required.

(B) The unsupervised machine learning based method tries to create the annotation without labeled data. For example, Crescenzi, Mecca, and Merialdo (2001) propose a method for automatically generalizing the extraction patterns from the web pages. The generalized patterns can then be used to extract the data from the Web.

(C) The ontology based method employs the other knowledge sources like thesaurus, ontology, etc. The basic idea is to first construct a pattern-based ontology, and then use the ontology to extract the needed information from the web page. Some systems also utilize the human general knowledge from common sense ontologies such as Cyc (Lenat and Guha, 1990) and WordNet (Fellbaum, 1998).

In this chapter, we will focus on the first topic: how to create semantic annotation by using supervised machine learning. Figure 1 shows our perspective on semantic annotation. It consists of three layers: Theoretical layer, Annotation layer, and Advanced application layer. The bottom layer is the basic theories including machine learning, statistical learning, and natural language processing; based on these theories, the annotation layer (the middle layer) is mainly comprised of four subtasks: entity extraction, relation extraction, relation discovery, and annotation; based on the annotated results (i.e. semantic data), different advanced applications can be developed (the top layer), for example: semantic integration, semantic search, semantic mining, and reasoning. In semantic annotation, by entity extraction, we aim at identifying and pulling out a sub-sequence that we are interested in from a web page. The identified sub-sequence is viewed as an instance (Appelt, 1999; MUC, 1999). By relation extraction, given a pair of entities, the objective is to decide whether a particular relation holds between the entities (ACE, 2003; Culotta and Sorensen, 2004).

Figure 1. Overview of semantic annotation

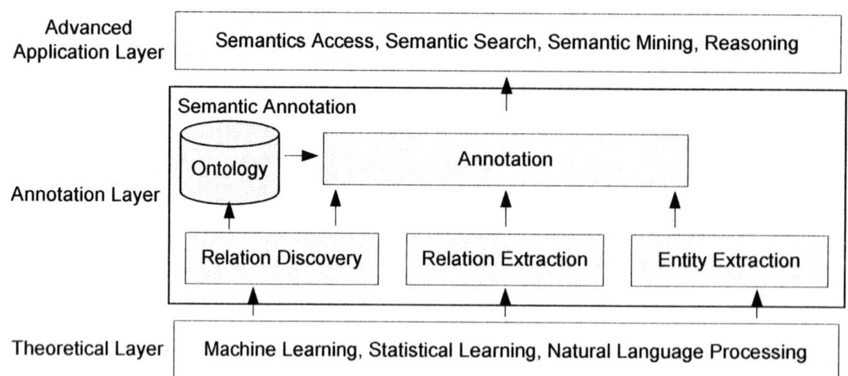

By relation discovery, we aim at discovering unknown relations between instances (Grefenstette, 1994; Maedche and Staab, 2000). The discovered relations can again be used to populate the ontology. The task of annotation is to describe the identified entities and relations according to the ontology.

There are still many challenges in this research area. Web pages of different characteristics (its size, redundancy and the lack of semantics in most plain texts) require different kinds of methods (sometimes even vary largely) to deal with. For example, for a template-based web page in which the data may be generated from a database, one may achieve good results using a rule based method; however for a web page containing a large portion of free text, the rule based method might not work well while a classification based method can be more appropriate. The previous methods to entity extraction, such as those applied to the Message Understanding Conferences (MUC) during the 1990s, usually induce extraction rules on small collections of documents. However, the characteristics of the web require more *effective* algorithms being able to learn more *efficiently*. Furthermore, new types of web content such as web forums, blogs and wikis (some of them included in the so-called Web 2.0), provide rich data sources for conducting semantic annotation, at the same time, bring big challenges to the field. The existing machine-learning based approaches rely on the assumption that documents have either the similar structure or the similar content, an assumption which seems unrealistic due to the heterogeneity of the Web.

This chapter tries to give a comprehensive investigation of the methods of automatic entity extraction and relation extraction using supervised machine learning. Specifically, for entity extraction we classify the methods into four categories: rule learning based extraction, classification based extraction, sequential learning based extraction, and non-linear Markov random fields based extraction. For relation extraction, we also classify the methods into four categories: classification based method, kernel based method, sequential labeling based method, and the other methods. All these methods have immediate real-life applications. Semantic annotation has been applied to, for example, social networking data annotation (Dingli, Ciravegna, and Wilks, 2003), researcher profile annotation (Mika, 2005; Tang, Zhang, and Yao, 2007c), Knowledge and Information Management (KIM) (Popov *et al.*, 2003), image annotation (Bloehdorn *et al.*, 2005), and company reports annotation (Tang, Li, Lu, Liang, and Wang, 2005).

In the rest of the chapter, we will describe the state-of-the-art methods for entity extraction and relation extraction. This is followed by a brief introduction of existing systems based on the methods. We then present several applications to better understand how the methods can be utilized to help businesses. The chapter will have a mix of research and industry flavor, addressing research concepts and looking at the technologies from an industry perspective. After that, we will discuss future research directions on semantic annotation. Finally, we will give the concluding remarks.

METHODOLOGIES

The Semantic Web promises to make web content machine understandable. In this context, one of the most important things is the annotation of the existing Web, called semantic annotation.

In the past years, several conferences, for example Message Understanding Conferences (MUC) and Automatic Content Extraction (ACE) provided a benchmark for evaluating the effectiveness of different automatic content extraction technologies developed to support automatic processing of human language in text form. Recently, Pattern Analysis Statistical Modeling and Computational Learning (PASCAL) Challenge also provides a rigorous evaluation of various machine learning techniques for extracting the information from documents. In both of the contests, the situations can be described as: given a standardized corpus of annotated and pre-processed documents, the participants are expected to perform a number of subtasks, with each examining a different aspect of the learning process (in addition, subtasks will look at the effect of limiting the availability of training data, the ability to select the most appropriate training data (i.e. active learning) and the use of un-annotated data to aid learning).

In this section, we present a survey of the current techniques that can be used to perform automatic entity extraction and relation extraction.

Entity Extraction

Entity extraction, as one of the most important problems in semantic annotation, is aimed at identifying a sub-sequence that we are interested in from the documents like web pages, emails, and PDF files and giving meaning to the identified text. Considerable research work has been conducted for entity extraction. Among these work, rule learning based method, classification based method, and sequential labeling based method are the three state-of-the-art methods. Recently, non-linear Markov random fields also attract much attention, aiming at improving the performance of semantic annotation by incorporating different types of dependencies (e.g. hierarchical laid-out) rather than traditional linear-chain dependencies.

Rule Based Entity Extraction

In this section, we review the rule based algorithms for entity extraction. Numerous extraction systems have been developed based on the method, for instance: AutoSlog (Riloff, 1993), Crystal (Soderland, Fisher, Aseltine, and Lehnert, 1995), $(LP)^2$ (Ciravegna, 2001), iASA (Tang *et al.*, 2005), Whisk (Soderland, 1999), Rapier (Califf and Mooney, 1998), SRV (Freitag, 1998), WIEN (Kushmerick, Weld, and Doorenbos, 1997), Stalker (Muslea, Minton, and Knoblock, 1998; Muslea, 1999a), and BWI (Freitag and Kushmerick, 2000). See (Muslea, 1999b; Peng, 2001; Siefkes and Siniakov, 2005) for an overview. In general, the methods can again be grouped into two categories: dictionary based method and wrapper induction. We give a detailed introduction in (Tang, Hong, Zhang, Liang, and Li, 2007a). Here we use $(LP)^2$ (Ciravegna, 2001) as an example to introduce the methods.

$(LP)^2$ is one of the typical rule based extraction methods, which conducts rule learning in a bottom-up fashion (Ciravegna, 2001). It learns two types of rules that respectively identify the start boundary and the end boundary of an entity to be extracted. The learning is performed in two steps: initially a set of tagging rules is learned from a user-defined corpus (training data set); then additional rules are induced to correct mistakes in extraction.

Three types of rules are defined in (LP)[2]: tagging rules, contextual rules, and correction rules. A tagging rule is composed of a pattern of conditions on a sequence of words and an action of determining whether or not the current position is a boundary of an instance. Table 1 shows an example of the tagging rule. The first column represents a sequence of words. The second to the fifth columns represent Part-Of-Speech, Word type, Lookup results in a dictionary, and Name Entity Recognition results of the word sequence respectively. The last column represents the action. In Table 1, the action "<Speaker>" indicates that if the text match the pattern, the word "Patrick" will be identified as the start boundary of a speaker.

The tagging rules are induced as follows: (1) First, a tag in the training corpus is selected, and a window of *w* words to the left and *w* words to the right is used as constraints in the initial rule pattern. (2) Then all the initial rules are generalized. The generalization algorithm could be various. For example, based on NLP knowledge, the two rules "at 4 pm" and "at 5 pm" can be generalized to be "at DIGIT pm". Each generalized rule is tested on the training corpus and an error score *E=wrong/matched* is calculated. (3) Finally, the *k* best generalizations for each initial rule are kept in a so called best rule pool. This induction algorithm is also used for the other two types of rules discussed below. Table 2 indicates

Table 1. Example of initial tagging rule

Pattern					Action
Word	**POS**	**Kind**	**Lookup**	**Name Entity**	
;	:	Punctuation			
Patrick	NNP	Word	Person's first name	Person	<Speaker>
Stroh	NNP	Word			
,	,	Punctuation			
assistant	NN	Word	Job title		
professor	NN	Word			
,	,	Punctuation			
SDS	NNP	Word			

Table 2. Example of generalized tagging rule

Pattern					Action
Word	**POS**	**Kind**	**Lookup**	**Name Entity**	
;	:	Punctuation			
		Word	Person's first name	Person	<Speaker>
		Word			
		Punctuation			
assistant	NN	Word	Jobtitle		
professor	NN	Word			

a generalized tagging rule for the start boundary identification of the Speaker.

Another type of rules, contextual rules, is applied to improve the effectiveness of the system. The basic idea is that <tag_x> can be used as an indicator of the occurrence of <tag_y>. For example, consider a rule recognizing an end boundary between a capitalized word and a lowercase word. This rule does not belong to the best rule pool as its low precision on the corpus, but it is reliable if used only when closing to a tag <speaker>. Consequently, some non-best rules are recovered, and the ones which result in acceptable error rate will be preserved as the contextual rules.

The correction rules are used to reduce the imprecision of the tagging rules. For example, a correction rule shown in Table 3 is used to correct the tagging mistake "at <time> 4 </time> pm" since "pm" should have been part of the time expression. So, correction rules are actions that shift misplaced tags rather than adding new tags.

After all types of rules are induced, information extraction is carried out in the following steps:

- The learned tagging rules are used to tag the texts.
- Contextual rules are applied in the context of introduced tags in the first step.
- Correction rules are used to correct mistaken extractions.
- All the identified boundaries are to be validated, e.g. a start tag (e.g. <time>) without its corresponding close tag will be removed, and vice versa.

Table 3. Example of correction rule

Pattern		Action
Word	**Wrong tag**	**Move tag to**
At		
4	</stime>	
pm		</stime>

Stalker (Muslea *et al.*, 1998; Muslea, Minton, and Knoblock, 1999a) is another wrapper induction system that performs hierarchical information extraction. It can be used to extract data from documents with multiple levels. See (Muslea, Minton, and Knoblock, 2003) for details. The Boosted Wrapper Induction (BWI) system (Freitag and Kushmerick, 2000; Kauchak, Smarr, and Elkan, 2004) aims at making wrapper induction techniques suitable for free text. It uses boosting to generate and combine the predictions from extraction patterns. See also WIEN (Kushmerick *et al.*, 1997) and (Kushmerick, 2000) for variant wrapper classes.

In learning of annotation rules, some methods, such as $(LP)^2$ (Ciravegna, 2001), SRV (Freitag, 1998), Whisk (Soderland, 1999), and iASA (Tang et al., 2005), use the top-down fashion by starting with the most generalized patterns and then gradually add constraints into the patterns in the learning processing. Some other methods, such as Rapier (Califf and Mooney, 1998; Califf and Mooney, 2003), adopt the bottom-up learning strategy.

Classification Based Entity Extraction

In this section, we introduce another principled approach to entity extraction using supervised machine learning. The basic idea is to cast the extraction problem as that of classification. We will first introduce briefly the classification model and then explain the method for entity extraction based on the classification model. The classification based methods can be enhanced from several dimensions, for example from the classification model itself or from the extraction process. Interested readers are referred to (Tang *et al.*, 2007a).

Classification Model

Let us first consider a two class classification problem. Let $\{(x_1, y_1), \ldots, (x_n, y_n)\}$ be a training data set, in which x_i denotes an instance (represented as a feature vector) and $y_i \in \{-1,+1\}$ denotes a classification label. In learning, one attempts to find a model from the labeled data that can separate the training data, while in prediction the learned model is used to identify whether an unlabeled instance should be classified as +1 or -1.

Support Vector Machines (SVMs) is one of the most popular methods for classification (Vapnik, 1998). Now, we use SVM as example to introduce the classification model.

Support vector machines (SVMs) are linear functions of the form $f(x) = w^T x + b$, where $w^T x$ is the inner product between the weight vector w and the input vector x. The main idea of SVM is to find an optimal separating hyper-plane that maximally separates the two classes of training instances (more precisely, maximizes the margin between the two classes of instances). The hyper-plane then corresponds to a classifier (linear SVM). The problem of finding the hyper-plane can be stated as the following optimization problem:

$$Minimize: \frac{1}{2} w^T w$$
$$s.t.: y_i(w^T x_i + b) \geq 1, i = 1, 2, \ldots, n \quad (1)$$

To deal with cases where there may be no separating hyper-plan due to noisy labels of both positive and negative training instances, the soft margin SVM is proposed, which is formulated as:

$$Minimize: \frac{1}{2} w^T w + C\sum_{i=1}^{n} \xi_i$$
$$s.t.: y_i(w^T x_i + b) \geq 1 - \xi_i, i = 1, 2, \ldots, n \quad (2)$$

where $C \geq 0$ is the cost parameter that controls the amount of training errors allowed.

It is theoretically guaranteed that the linear classifier obtained in this way has small generalization errors. Linear SVM can be further extended into non-linear SVMs by using kernel functions such as Gaussian and polynomial kernels (Boser, Guyon, and Vapnik, 1992; Schölkopf, Burges, and Smola, 1999; Vapnik, 1999). When there are more than two classes, we can adopt the "one class versus all others" approach, i.e., take one class as positive and the other classes as negative.

Boundary Detection Using Classification Model

We are using a supervised machine learning approach to entity extraction, so our system consists of two distinct phases: learning and extracting. In the learning phase the system uses a set of labeled documents to generate models which we can use for future predictions. The extraction phase takes the learned models and applies them to new unlabelled documents using the learned models to generate extractions.

The method aims at detecting the boundaries (start boundary and end boundary) of an instance. For entity extraction from text, the basic unit that we are dealing with can be a token or a text-line. (Hereafter, we will use token as the basic unit in our explanation.) We try to learn two classifiers that are respectively used to identify the boundaries. The instances are all tokens in the document. All tokens that begin with a start-label are positive instances for the start classifier, while all the other tokens become negative instances for this classifier. Similarly, the positive instances for the end classifier are the last tokens of each end-label, and the other tokens are negative instances.

Figure 2 gives an example of entity extraction as classification. There are two classifiers – one to identify starts of target text fragments and the other to identify ends of text fragments. Here, the classifiers are based on token only (however other patterns, e.g. syntax, can also be incorporated into). Each token is classified as being a start or non-start and an end or non-end. When we classify a token as a start, and also classify one of the closely following token as an end, we view the tokens between these two tokens as a target instance.

Figure 2. Example of information extraction as classification

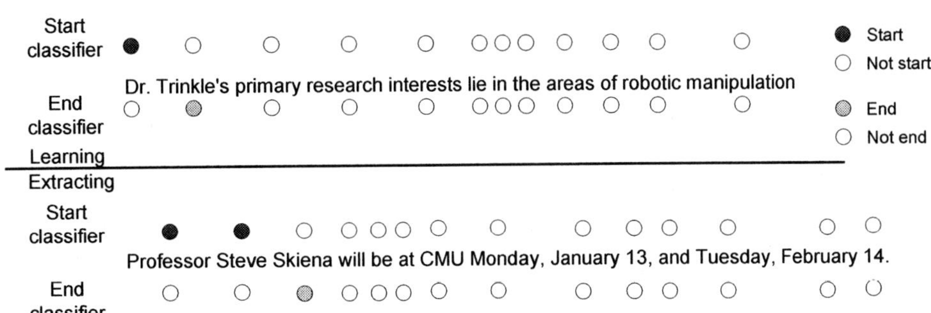

In the example, the tokens "Dr. Trinkle's" is annotated as a "speaker" and thus the token "Dr." is a positive instance and the other tokens are as negative instances in the speaker-start classifier. Similarly, the token "Trinkle's" is a positive instance and the other tokens are negative instances in the speaker-end classifier. The annotated data is used to train the two classifiers in advance. In the extracting stage, the two classifiers are applied to identify the start token and the end token of the speaker. In the example, the tokens "Professor", "Steve", and "Skiena" are identified as two start tokens by the start classifier and one end token by the end classifier. Then, we combine the identified results and view tokens between the start token and the end token as a speaker. (i.e. "Professor Steve Skiena" is outputted as a speaker)

In the extracting stage, we apply the two classifiers to each token to identify whether the token is a "start", "end", neither, or both. After the extracting stage, we need to combine the starts and the ends predicted by the two classifiers. We need to decide which of the starts (if there exist more than one starts) to match with which of the ends (if there exist more than one ends). For the combination, a simple method is to search for an end from a start and then view the tokens between the two tokens as the target. If there exist two consecutive starts and only one end (as the example in Figure 2), then we start the search progress from the first start and view the tokens between the first token and the end token (i.e. "Professor Steve Skiena") as the target. However, in some applications, the simple combination may not yield good results.

Several works have been conducted to enhance the combination. For example, Finn *et al.* propose a histogram model (Finn and Kushmerick, 2004; Finn, 2006). In Figure 2, there are two possible extractions: "Professor Steve Skiena" and "Steve Skiena". The histogram model estimates confidence as $C_s * C_e * P(|e - s|)$. Here C_s is the confidence of the start prediction and C_e is the confidence of the end prediction. (For example, in Naïve Bayes, we can use the posterior probability as the confidence; in SVM, we can use the distance of the instance to the hyper-plane as the confidence.) $P(|e - s|)$ is the probability of a text fragment of that length which we estimate from the training data. Finally, we select the text with the highest confidence as the output.

To summarize, this classification approach simply learns to detect the start and the end of text fragments to be extracted. It treats entity extraction as a standard classification task, augmented with a simple mechanism to combine the predicted start and end tags. Experiments indicate that this approach generally has high precision but low recall. This approach can be viewed as that of one-level boundary classification (Finn and Kushmerick, 2004).

Many approaches can be used to training the classification models, for example, Support Vector Machines (Vapnik, 1998), Maximum Entropy (Berger, Pietra, and Pietra, 1996), Adaboost (Shapire, 1999), and Voted Perceptron (Collins, 2002).

Sequential Labeling Based Entity Extraction

Entity extraction can be cast as a task of sequential labeling. In sequential labeling, a document is viewed as a sequence of tokens, and a label is assigned to each token to indicate the *property* of the token. For example, consider the researcher profiling problem, the task is to label a sequence of tokens with their corresponding profile attributes (e.g. position, affiliation, etc.), called tags. Thus the inputting sentence "Lars Arge, Associate Professor, Department of Computer Science Duke University" will result in an output as:

[Lars / *Firstname*] [Arge / *Lastname*] [, / *Other*] [Associate / *Position*]

[Professor / *Position*] [, / *Other*] [Department / *Affiliation*] [of / *Affiliation*]

[Computer Affiliation] [Science Affiliation] [Duke Affiliation] [University Affiliation]

Formally, given an observation sequence $\boldsymbol{x} = (x_1, x_2, \ldots, x_n)$, the entity extraction task as sequential labeling is to find a label sequence $\boldsymbol{y}^*$ $= (y_1, y_2, \ldots, y_n)$ that maximizes the conditional probability $p(\boldsymbol{y}|\boldsymbol{x})$, that is:

$$\boldsymbol{y}^* = \text{argmax}_y\, p(\boldsymbol{y}|\boldsymbol{x}) \qquad (3)$$

Different from the rule learning and the classification based methods, sequential labeling enables describing the dependencies between target information. The dependencies can be utilized to improve the accuracy of the extraction. Hidden Markov Model (Ghahramani and Jordan, 1997), Maximum Entropy Markov Model (McCallum, Freitag, and Pereira, 2000), and Conditional Random Field (Lafferty, McCallum, and Pereira, 2001) are widely used sequential labeling models. In this section, we will briefly introduce the linear sequential labeling based models (for details, please refer to Tang *et al.*, 2007a).

Generative Model

Generative models define a joint probability distribution $p(\mathbf{X}, \mathbf{Y})$ where $\mathbf{X}$ and $\mathbf{Y}$ are random variables respectively ranging over observation sequences and their corresponding label sequences. In order to calculate the conditional probability $p(y|x)$, Bayesian rule is employed:

$$y^* = \arg\max_y p(y \mid x) = \arg\max_y \frac{p(x, y)}{p(x)} \qquad (4)$$

Hidden Markov Models (HMMs) (Ghahramani and Jordan, 1997) are one of the most common generative models. In HMMs, each observation sequence is considered to be generated by a sequence of state transitions, beginning in some start state and ending when some pre-designated final state is reached. At each state an element of the observation sequence is stochastically generated, before moving to the next state. In the case of researcher profile annotation, each state of the HMM is associated with a profile attribute or "Other". Although profile attributes do not generate words, the attribute tag associated with any given word can be considered to account for that word in some fashion. It is, therefore, possible to find the sequence of attribute tags that best accounts for any given sentence by identifying the sequence of states most likely to have been traversed when "generating" that sequence of words. Figure 3 shows the structure of a HMM.

These conditional independence relations, combined with the probability chain rule, can be used to factorize the joint distribution over a state sequence y and observation sequence x into the product of a set of conditional probabilities:

Figure 3. Graphic structure of first-order HMMs

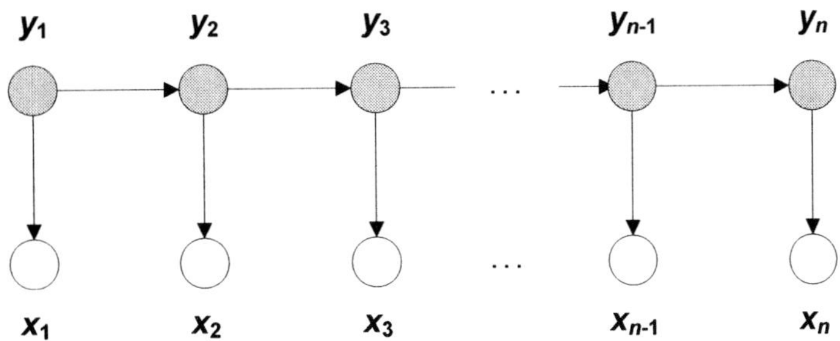

$$p(y,x) = p(y_1)p(x_1 \mid y_1)\prod_{t=2}^{n} p(y_t \mid y_{t-1})p(x_t \mid y_t) \quad (5)$$

In supervised learning, the conditional probability distribution $p(y_t|y_{t-1})$ and observation probability distribution $p(x|y)$ can be gained with maximum likelihood. While in unsupervised learning, there is no analytic method to gain the distributions directly. Instead, Expectation Maximization (EM) algorithm is employed to estimate the distributions.

Finding the optimal state sequence can be efficiently performed using a dynamic programming such as Viterbi algorithm.

Generative models define a joint probability distribution $p(\mathbf{X}, \mathbf{Y})$ over observations and label sequences. This is useful if the trained model is used to generate data. However, for defining a joint probability over observations and label sequences, a generative model needs to enumerate all possible observation sequences, usually resulting into highly expensive cost. Therefore, generative models must make strict independence assumptions in order to make inference tractable. Consequently, it is not practical to represent complicated interacting features or long-range dependencies of the observations, since the inference problem for such models is intractable.

Discriminative models provide a convenient way to overcome the strong independence assumption of generative models.

Discriminative Models

Instead of modeling joint probability distribution over observation and label sequences, discriminative models define a conditional distribution $p(y|x)$ over observation and label sequences. This means that when identifying the most likely label sequence for a given observation sequence, discriminative models use the conditional distribution directly, without bothering to make any dependence assumption on observations or enumerate all the possible observation sequences to calculate the marginal probability $p(x)$.

MEMMs (McCallum *et al.*, 2000) are a form of discriminative models for labeling sequential data. MEMMs consider observation sequences to be conditioned upon rather than generated by the label sequence. Therefore, a MEMM has only a single set of separately trained distributions of the form:

$$p(y_{t+1} \mid y_t, x) \quad (6)$$

which represent the probability of transition from state y_t to y_{t+1} on observation x. The fact that each of these functions is specific to a given state means that the choice of possible states at any given instant in time t+1 depends only on the state of the model at time t. Figure 4 show the graphic structure of MEMMs.

Given an observation sequence x, the conditional probability over label sequence y is given by:

Figure 4. Graphic structure of first-order MEMMs

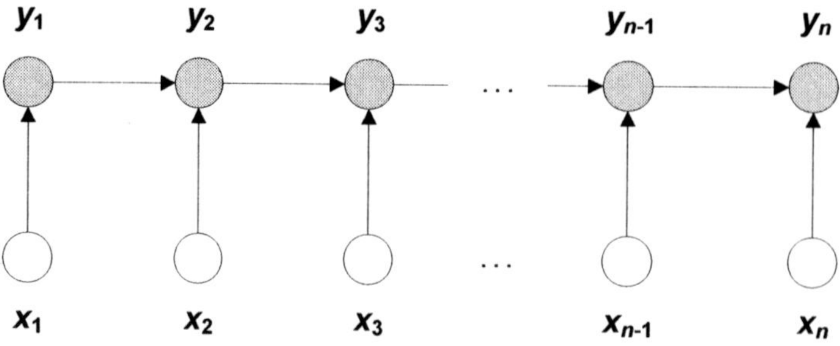

Figure 5. MEMM designed for shallow parsing

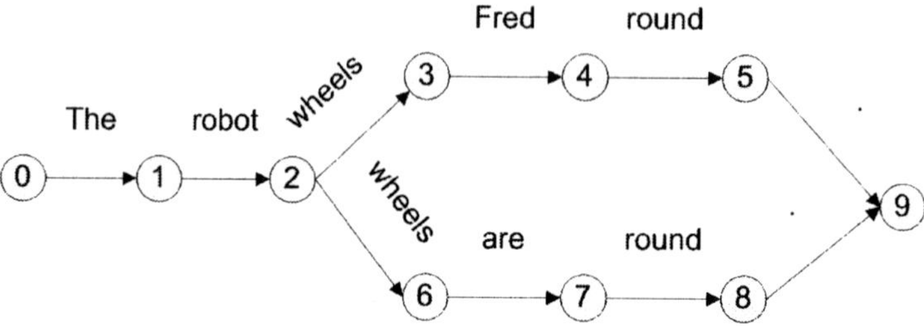

$$p(y \mid x) = p(y_1 \mid x_1) \prod_{t=2}^{n} p(y_t \mid y_{t-1}, x_{t-1}) \qquad (7)$$

Treating observations to be conditioned upon states rather than generated by means that the probability of each transition may depend on non-independent, interacting features of the observation sequence. Making use of maximum entropy framework and defining each state-observation transition function to be a log-linear model, equation (6) can be calculated as:

$$p(y_{t+1} \mid y_t, x) = \frac{1}{Z(y_t, x)} \exp\left(\sum_k \lambda_k f_k(y_{t+1}, y_t, x)\right) \qquad (8)$$

where $Z(y_t, x) = \sum_{y_{t+1}} \exp(\sum_k \lambda_k f_k(y_{t+1}, y_t, x))$ is a normalization factor; λ_k are parameters to be estimated and f_k is a feature function. The parameters can be estimated using Generalized Iterative Scaling (GIS) (McCallum *et al.*, 2000). Each feature function is a binary feature. For example, feature $f(y', y, x_t)$ implies that if the current and the previous tags are y and y', and the observation is x_t, then the feature value is 1; otherwise 0. Identifying the most likely label sequence given an observation sequence can be done efficiently by dynamic programming (McCallum *et al.*, 2000).

Maximum Entropy Markov Models suffer from the *Label Bias Problem* (Lafferty *et al.*, 2001), because MEMMs define a set of separately trained per-state probability distributions. Here we use an example to describe the label bias problem. The MEMM in Figure 5 is designed to shallow parse the sentences:

1. The robot wheels Fred round.
2. The robot wheels are round.

Consider when shallow parsing the sentence (1). Because there is only one outgoing transition from state 3 and 6, the per-state normalization requires that $p(4|3, \text{Fred}) = p(7|6, \text{are}) = 1$. Also it's easy to obtain that $p(8|7, \text{round}) = p(5|4, \text{round}) = p(2|1, \text{robot}) = p(1|0, \text{The}) = 1$, etc. Now, given

p(3|2, wheels) = p(6|2, wheels) = 0.5, by combining all these factors, we obtain:

p(0123459|The robot wheels Fred round.) = 0.5,
p(0126789|The robot wheels Fred round.) = 0.5.

Thus the MEMM ends up with two possible state sequences 0123459 and 0126789 with the same probability independently of the observation sequence. It's impossible for the MEMM to tell which one is the more likely state sequence over the given sentence. Likewise, given p(3|2, wheels) < p(6|2, wheels), MEMM will always choose the bottom path despite what the preceding words and the following words are in the observation sequence.

The label bias problem occurs because a MEMM uses per-state exponential model for the conditional probability of the next states given the current state.

People, therefore, propose Conditional Random Fields (CRFs) to benefit the advantages from modeling conditional probability, at the same time to avoid the label bias problem. CRFs are undirected graphical model trained to maximize a conditional probability. CRFs can be defined as follows:

A CRF is a random field globally conditioned on the observation. Linear-chain CRFs were first introduced by Lafferty *et al.* (2001). Figure 6 shows the graphical structure of the linear-chain CRFs.

By the fundamental theorem of random fields (Hammersley and Clifford, 1971), the conditional distribution of the labels y given the observations data x has the form:

$$p(y \mid x) = \frac{1}{Z(x)} \exp(\sum_{t=1}^{T} \sum_{k} \lambda_k \cdot f_k(y_{t-1}, y_t, x, t)) \quad (9)$$

where $Z(x)$ is a normalization factor, also known as partition function, which has the form:

$$Z(x) = \sum_{y} \exp(\sum_{t=1}^{T} \sum_{k} \lambda_k \cdot f_k(y_{t-1}, y_t, x, t)) \quad (10)$$

where $f_k(y_{t-1}, y_t, x, t)$ is a feature function which can be either real-valued or binary-valued. The feature functions can measure any aspect of a state transition, $y_{t-1} \rightarrow y_t$, and the observation sequence, x, centered at the current time step t. λ_k corresponds to the weight of the feature f_k.

The most probable labeling sequence for an input x:

$$y^* = \arg\max_y p_\lambda(y \mid x) \quad (11)$$

can be efficiently calculated by dynamic programming using Viterbi algorithm.

We can train the parameters $\lambda=(\lambda_1, \lambda_2, \ldots)$ by maximizing the likelihood of a given training set $T = \{(x^{(k)}, y^{(k)})\}_{k=1}^{N}$:

Figure 6. Graphic structure of linear-chain CRFs

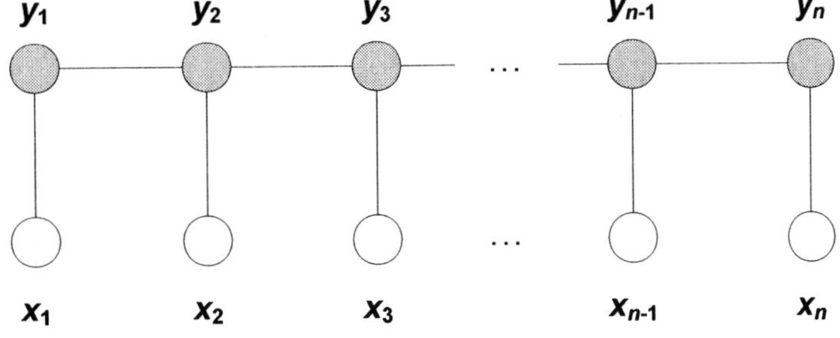

$$L_\lambda = \sum_{i=1}^{N}(\sum_{t=1}^{T}\sum_{k}\lambda_k \cdot f_k(y_{t-1}, y_t, x^{(i)}, t) - \log Z(x^{(i)})) \quad (12)$$

Many methods can be used to do the parameter estimation. The traditional maximum entropy learning algorithms, such as GIS, IIS can be used to train CRFs (Darroch and Ratcliff, 1972). In addition, preconditioned conjugate-gradient (CG) (Shewchuk, 1994) or limited-memory quasi-Newton (L-BFGS) (Nocedal and Wright, 1999) have been found to perform better than the traditional methods (Sha and Pereira, 2003). The voted perceptron algorithm (Collins, 2002) can also be utilized to train the models efficiently and effectively.

To avoid overfitting, log-likelihood is often penalized by some prior distribution over the parameters. Empirical distributions such as Gaussian prior, exponential prior, and hyperbolic-L_1 prior can be used, and empirical experiments suggest that Gaussian prior is a safer prior to use in practice (Chen and Rosenfeld, 1999).

CRFs avoid the label bias problem because it has a single exponential model for the conditional probability of labels of the entire sequence given the observation. Therefore, weights of different features at different states can be traded off against each other.

Alternative Conditional Random Fields

Lafferty, Zhu, and Liu (2004) investigated employing kernel in conditional random fields. Kernel can be considered as a function comparing the cliques of different graphs. The dual parameters (like those in SVM) depend on all potential assignments of the cliques in the graph. Therefore, clique selection becomes important. They also argued that kernel enables semi-supervised learning.

Taskar, Guestrin, and Koller (2003) employed the idea of large margin under the framework of Markov random fields for assigning labels to structured data.

Jiao, Wang, and Lee (2006) proposed an alternative objective function for linear-chain CRFs using labeled and unlabeled data. The experiments on protein prediction showed the model taking advantage of unlabeled data gained accuracy compared with the model without unlabeled data.

Using Sequential Labeling for Entity Extraction

By casting entity extraction as sequential labeling, a set of labels need to be predefined based on the extraction task. For example, in the annotation of researcher profile (Tang *et al.*, 2007c), labels such as "Researcher Name", "Position", "Affiliation", "Email", "Address", and "Telephone" were defined. Then a document is viewed as a sequence x of observation unit. The observation unit can be a word, a text line, or any other granularity of linguistic information. Then the task is to find a label sequence y that maximizes the conditional probability $p(y|x)$ using the models described above.

In generative models, only features on the current observation unit can be defined. Due to the conditional nature, discriminative models provide the flexibility of incorporating non-independent or even arbitrary features of input to improve the performance. For example, in the task of researcher profile annotation, with CRFs we can use as features not only text content, but also layout and external lexicon. Empirical experiments show that incorporating non-independent and arbitrary features can significantly improve the performance.

On the other hand, incorporation of non-independent and arbitrary features of discriminative models may also lead to too many features and some of the features are of little contributions to the model. The method of feature induction can be used to obtain the most useful features for efficiently performing training the model (McCallum, 2003).

Non-Linear Markov Random Fields Based Semantic Annotation

Markov random field models, for instance HMMs (Ghahramani and Jordan, 1997), MEMMs (McCallum *et al.*, 2000), and CRFs (Lafferty *et al.*, 2004) are widely used for semantic annotation including both entity extraction and relation extraction (we will introduce the methods for relation extraction in the next sub section). However, most of the previous methods based on the three models are linear-chain models, which can only describe the linear-dependencies, and cannot describe non-linear dependencies (Lafferty *et al.*, 2001; Zhu, Nie, Wen, Zhang, and Ma, 2005; Tang, Hong, Li, and Liang, 2006). In this section, we will discuss several non-linear Markov random fields for semantic annotation. We will also introduce the inference on the non-linear Markov model.

Hierarchical Hidden Markov Models

A Hierarchical Hidden Markov Model (HHMM) is a structured multi-level discrete stochastic process. The HHMM generalizes the familiar HMM by making each of its hidden node states a similar stochastic model on its own, i.e. each state is an HMM as well (Skounakis, Craven, and Ray, 2003). The graphical structure of a two-level HHMM can be represented as Figure 7.

In the figure, we use the white circle to denote the observation x_i and the gray circle the hidden variable y_i. The HMMM model has two levels. In the inner level, each node y_{ij} represents a unit of fine granularity, for example a unique token. Each node y_{ij} generates an observation node. In the outer level, each node y_i' represent a unit of coarse granularity, for example a text line or several tokens. Each node y_i' generates a state sequence rather than a single observation. The two-level HHMM can be easily extended to a multi-level model (c.f., e.g., (Fine, Singer, and Tishby, 1998)).

Hierarchical Conditional Random Fields

A Hierarchical Conditional Random Field (HCRF) model is a tree structured version of the Conditional Random Fields. Information on web pages is usually organized as hierarchy. The conventional linear-chain CRF model cannot describe dependencies across the hierarchically laid-out information. To better incorporate dependencies across the hierarchically laid-out information, proposal of new CRF models is necessary.

For example, Zhu *et al.* (2007) propose a Hierarchical Conditional Random Field for simultaneous record detection and attribute labeling in web data. The task is to extract product information from web pages. A data record, describing a product, is a block in the web page and product attributes are information in the data record and are used to describe different aspects of the product. Instead of using traditional methods that attempt to do data record detection and attribute labeling in two separate phases the authors propose using a Hierarchical Conditional Random Field Model (HCRF) to conduct record extraction and attribute labeling simultaneously. The basic idea

Figure 7. Graphic structure of a two-level HHMM

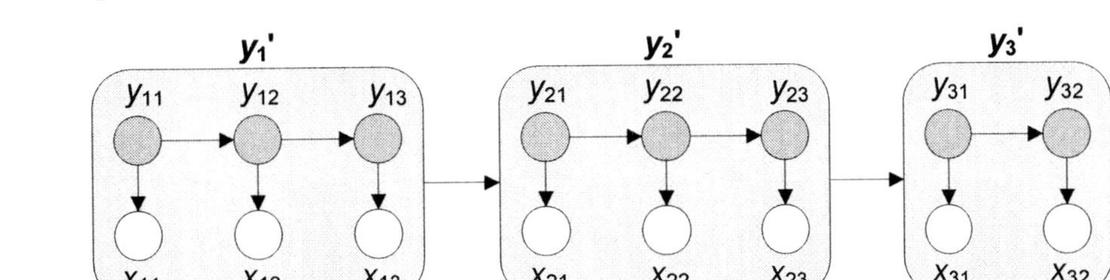

of using HCRF is that record detection and attribute labeling from web pages can benefit from each other. The structure of the proposed HCRF model is shown in Figure 8. The hidden variables (indicated as gray nodes) represent a product record or an attribute of the product record and the observations (indicated as white nodes) represent an observation unit on the web page. The hidden variables are organized hierarchically. In the bottom level the hidden variables represent the label of attributes (for example, product image, product name) and in the upper level the hidden variables represent the label of product records or part of product records (for example, a product name-image block that contains the product name and the product image).

We also propose Tree-structured Conditional Random Fields (TCRFs), which can incorporate dependencies across the hierarchically laid-out information (Tang *et al.*, 2006). Here we use an example to introduce the problem of hierarchical semantic annotation. Figure 9 (a) give an example document, in which the underlined text are what we want to extract including two telephone numbers and two addresses. The information can be organized as a tree structure (cf. Figure 9 (b)). In this case, the linear-chain CRFs cannot model the hierarchical dependencies and thus cannot distinguish the office telephone number and the home telephone number from each other. Likewise for the office address and the home address.

We present the graphical structure of the TCRF model as a tree and reformulate the conditional distribution by defining three kinds of transition features respectively representing the parent-child dependency, child-parent dependency, and sibling dependency. As the tree structure can be cyclable, exact inference is expensive. We propose using the Tree-based Reparameterization (TRP) algorithm (Wainwright, Jaakkola, and Willsky, 2001) to compute the approximate marginal probabilities for edges and vertices. We conducted experiments on company annual reports collected from Shang Stock Exchange. Experimental results indicate that the TCRFs can significantly outperform the existing linear-chain CRF model (+7.67% in terms of F1-measure). See (Tang *et al.*, 2007a) for details.

Skip-Chain Conditional Random Fields

In some specific application, it might be helpful to incorporate long-distant dependencies. Skip-

Figure 8. Graphic structure of HCRF Model

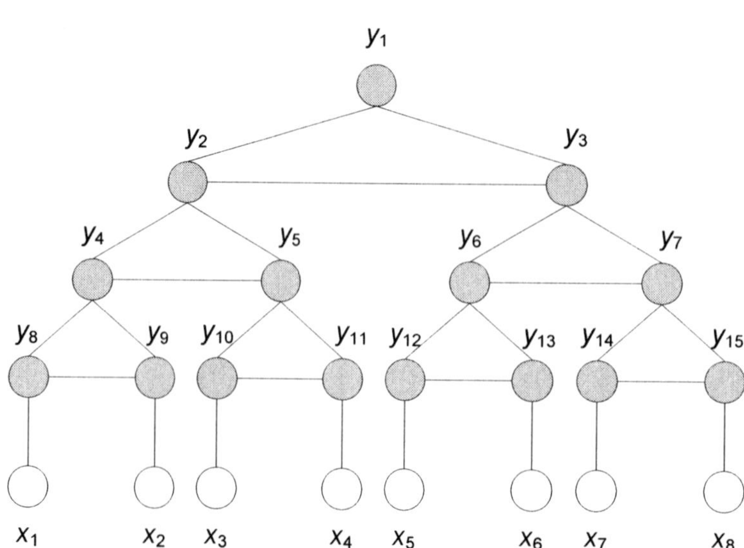

Figure 9. Example of tree-structured laid-out information

Contact Information:
John Booth
Office:
Tel: 8765-4321
Addr: F2, A building
Home:
Tel: 1234-5678
Addr: No. 123, B St.

(a) Example document

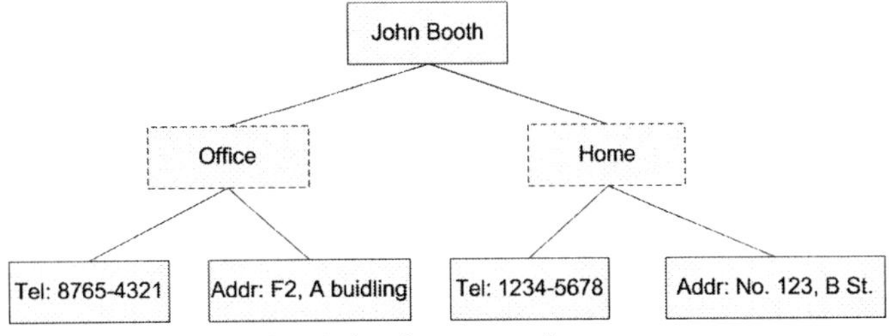

(b) Organized the document in tree-structure

chain Conditional Random Fields are proposed to address this problem (Sutton and McCallum, 2006; Bunescu and Mooney, 2005b).

Skip-chain Conditional Random Fields can incorporate long-distant dependencies. For example, in entity extraction, a person name (e.g. *Robert Booth*) is mentioned more than one time in a document. All mentions might have the same label, such as SEMINAR-SPEAKER. An IE system can take advantage of this fact by labeling repeated words identically. Furthermore, identifying all mentions of an entity can be useful in itself, because each mention might contain different useful information. The skip-chain CRF, by identifying all mentions identically, combine features from all occurrences so that the extraction can be made based on global information. The skip-chain CRF is proposed to address this (Sutton and McCallum, 2006; Bunescu and Mooney, 2005b).

The skip-chain CRF is essentially a linear-chain CRF with additional long-distance edges between similar words. These additional edges are called *skip edges*. The features on skip edges can incorporate information from the context of both endpoints, so that strong evidence at one endpoint can influence the label at the other endpoint.

Formally, the skip-chain CRF is defined as a general CRF with two clique templates: one for the linear-chain portion, and one for the skip edges. For an input $\boldsymbol{x}$, let $C = \{(u,v)\}$ be the set of all pairs of sequence positions for which there are skip edges. The probability of a label sequence $\boldsymbol{y}$ given an $\boldsymbol{x}$ is modeled as:

$$p(y \mid x) = \frac{1}{Z(x)} \exp\Big(\sum_{t=1}^{T} \sum_{k} \lambda_k \cdot f_k(y_{t-1}, y_t, x, t) + \sum_{(u,v)\in C} \sum_{l} \lambda_l \cdot f_l(y_u, y_v, x, u, v)\Big) \tag{13}$$

where $Z(x)$ is a normalization factor, f_k is the feature function similar to that in the linear-chain CRF model and f_l is the feature function on a skip edge. λ_k and λ_l are weights of the features.

Because there might have a loop in the skip-chain CRF, exact inference is intractable. The running time required by exact inference is exponential in the size of the largest clique in the graph's junction tree. Instead, approximate inference using loopy belief propagation is performed, such as TRP (Wainwright *et al.*, 2001).

Richer kinds of long-distance factor than just over pairs of words can be considered to augment the skip-chain model. These factors are useful for modeling exceptions to the assumption that similar words tend to have similar labels. For example, in Named Entity Recognition, the word "*China*" is as a location name when it appears alone, but when it occurs within the phrase *The China Daily*, it should be labeled as an organization (Finkel, Grenager, and Manning, 2005).

Dynamic Conditional Random Fields

Sutton, Rohanimanesh, and McCallum (2004) proposed Dynamic Conditional Random Fields (DCRFs). It generalizes the linear-chain conditional random fields, in which each slice is a Bayesian network, the interaction between slices can be seen as chain conditional random fields. Figure 10 shows the graph structure of a two-dimensional grid CRF model, which can be regarded as a special kind of DCRF.

The two-dimensional CRF has practical applications. For example, it can perform POS (Part-Of-Speech) tagging and NER (Named Entity Recognition), two typical tasks in NLP, simultaneously. The model can describe dependencies between the two subtasks.

Some other CRF models or Markov models are also proposed for addressing different types of special cases. For example 2D Conditional Random Fields (2D CRFs) (Zhu *et al.*, 2005).

Inference on the Non-Linear CRFs

Non-linear graphical models can capture the long-range interaction between different labels. However, the difficulty of this kind of model lies in inference.

Given a set of observations, inference in graphical model has two tasks: (a) to estimate the marginal distribution of each random hidden variable or to estimate the most likely configuration of the hidden variables, that is maximum a posteriori (MAP) estimation. Both tasks can be solved under the framework of belief propagation (BP) (Yedidia, Freeman, and Weiss, 2003). The basic process is to set a root node and then collect messages from all nodes until root node by starting from leave nodes and send back the messages to the leave nodes from the root node. The process continues in the whole graph until convergence. BP generates correct results if the graph has no loops. If the graph contains loops, we can carry out approximate inference. The proposed algorithms include Tree-based reparameterization (TRP) (Wainwright *et al.*, 2001) and Junction tree based inference, also called Generalized Belief Propagation (GBP) (Yedidia *et al.*, 2003).

Figure 10. Graphic structure of two-dimensional grid CRFs

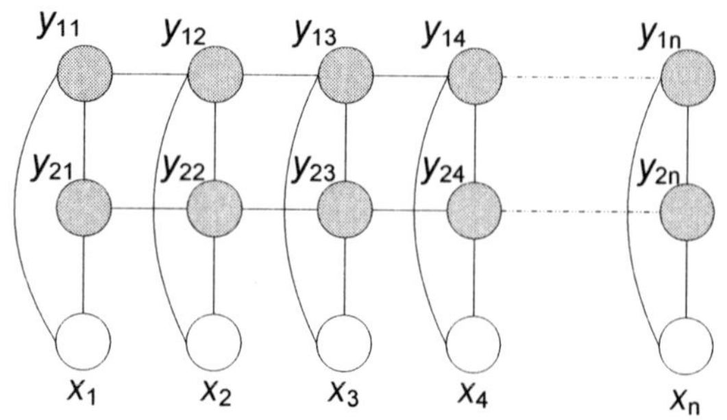

Here we would like to give some definitions of belief at node and edge, and message between nodes. The belief at a node is proportional to the product of the local potential of that node ($\phi(y_i) \leftarrow \exp(f_i(x_i, y_i))$), and all the messages coming into node i is:

$$b_i(y_i) = k\phi(y_i) \prod_{j \in N(i)} m_{ji}(y_i) \tag{14}$$

In the formula, k is a normalization factor, and $N(i)$ denotes the neighboring nodes of i. In fact, the belief at a node i is the marginal probability of that corresponding variable (y_i). The message can be computed using the following formula:

$$m_{ij}(y_j) \leftarrow \sum_{y_i} \phi_i(y_i)\psi_{ij}(y_i, y_j) \prod_{k \in N(i)\backslash j} m_{ki}(y_i) \tag{15}$$

Considering we also need the belief at an edge in solving the Markov random field, we define:

$$b_{ij}(y_i, y_j) = k\phi(y_i)\phi(y_j) \prod_{k \in N(i)\backslash j} m_{ki}(y_i) \prod_{l \in N(j)\backslash i} m_{lj}(y_j) \tag{16}$$

We will take the tree structure as an example to explain the message passing process. In Figure 11, we omit observation nodes since we concentrate on message passing through hidden nodes), $m_{ij}(y_j)$

is a "message" from a hidden node i to the hidden node j about what state node j should be in, just as we defined above. We schedule message passing in two stages by choosing one node as root, collecting message from all nodes at leaves and sending message to all nodes from root. In the figure, suppose we choose y_1 as root, collecting messages in orders: m_{43}, m_{53}, m_{32} and m_{21}, then sending messages in orders: m_{12}, m_{23}, m_{35}, m_{34}. After these two stages, we can get the belief at one node and at one edge, as well as marginal probabilities of a variable and two joint variables.

For structures with loops, we can convert the graph to a tree, through pruning some edges randomly (TRP) or through triangulating the graph and generating junction tree (Junction tree inference), see (Wainwright *et al.*, 2001) and (Yedidia *et al.*, 2003) for details.

Relation Extraction

Relation extraction is another important issue in semantic annotation. It is aimed at finding semantic relations between entities. That is to say, given a pair of entities, the objective is to decide whether a particular relation holds between the entities. It can be also viewed as a step following the entity extraction. For example, consider the following sentence:

"Andrew McCallum is an Associate Professor at University of Massachusetts, Amherst."

An entity extraction system should recognize that "Andrew McCallum" is a person, "University of Massachusetts" is an organization, and "Amherst" is a location. In the above example, relations between these entities, such as the relation "work-for" ("Andrew McCallum" works for "University of Massachusetts") and the relation "located-in" ("University of Massachusetts" is located in "Amherst"), will be found in an ideal relation extraction system. Table 4 shows the extracted relations from the sentence.

Let us start from some background knowledge of relation extraction. The problem of relation extraction was formulated as a part of Message Understanding Conferences (MUC). Systems attending the conference were tested and evaluated on New York Times News Service data and the task is limited to relations with organizations: "employee_of", "product_of", "location_in".

In another program, the NIST Automatic Content Extraction (ACE) program, this task is defined as Relation Detection and Characterization (RDC). ACE program defines three main objectives for information extraction: Entity Detection and Tracking (EDT), Relation Detection and Characterization (RDC), and Event Detection and Characterization (EDC). The EDT task entails the detection of entity mentions and chain them together by identifying their coreference. In ACE vocabulary, entities are objects, mentions references to them, and relations are semantic relationships between entities. The RDC task detects and classifies implicit and explicit relations between entities identified by the EDT task. RDC is broadly comparable with the relation extraction task in MUC. In ACE 2004 a type and sub-type hierarchy for both entities and

Figure 11. Illustration of message passing

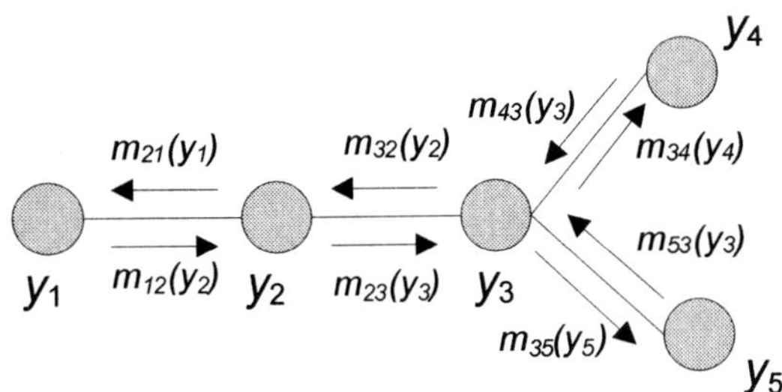

Table 4. Example of relation extraction

Relation	Instance
Employee_of	Andrew McCallum is employee of University of Massachusetts
Located_in	University of Massachusetts is located in Amherst

relations was introduced, which is regarded as an important step towards ontology-based Semantic Annotation. ACE continues the competition from 1999 up to now.

The benefit of relation extraction technology is obvious. With this technology, we can integrate large databases of relational information and generate new information for data mining, question answering systems, and information retrieval. Therefore, numerous studies on relation extraction have been conducted. In this section, we will introduce four typical methods for relation extraction: classification based approach, kernel based approach, sequential labeling based approach, and unsupervised approach.

Classification Based Methods

The classification based method is one of the most popular methods for relation extraction. It formalizes the problem as classification, i.e. identifying whether an entity pair has a specific relation using a classifier.

For example, Kambhatla (2004) proposes combining diverse lexical, syntactic, and semantic features for each entity pairs. Then, they use Maximum Entropy models as classification models and apply their method to the dataset of ACE RDC task. Here is an example:

The *American Medical Association* voted yesterday to install the *heir* apparent as *its president-elect*, rejecting a strong, upstart challenge by a District doctor who argued that the nation's largest physicians' *group* needs stronger ethics and new leadership.

In electing *Thomas R. Reardon*, an Oregon general *practitioner* who had been the *chairman* of *its board*, ...

...

For each pair of mentions (references to entities), we can define the following features:

- **Words.** The features represent the words of both the mentions and all the words in between.
- **Entity Type.** The feature represents the entity type (including PERSON, ORGANIZATION, LOCATION, FACILITY, Geo-Political Entity or GPE) of both the mentions.
- **Mention Level.** The feature represents the mention level (one of NAME, NOMINAL, or PRONOUN) of both the mentions.
- **Overlap.** The features represent the number of words (if any) separating the two mentions, the number of other mentions in between, flags indicating whether the two mentions are in the same noun phrase, verb phrase or prepositional phrase.
- **Dependency.** The features represent the words and part-of-speech and chunk labels of the words on which the mentions are dependent in the dependency tree derived from the syntactic parse tree.
- **Parse Tree.** The feature represents the path of non-terminals (removing duplicates) connecting the two mentions in the parse tree, and the path annotated with head words.

Compared with (Kambhatla, 2004), Zhou, Su, Zhang, and Zhang (2005) separately incorporate the base phrase chunking information, which contributes to most of the performance improvement from syntactic aspect. See also (Jiang and Zhai, 2007)

Kernel Based Methods

Kernel based method is an emerging method in these years for relation extraction. In many cases, it is used as an alternative to feature vector based method, especially when it is infeasible to create a feature vector for an instance due to the high dimensionality of the feature space. Generally, kernel methods are non-parametric density estimation techniques that compute a kernel function between data instances, where a kernel function can be thought of as a similarity measure. Given a set of labeled instances, a kernel based method determines the label of a novel instance by comparing it to the labeled training instances using this kernel function. Formally, a kernel function K is a mapping $K: \mathrm{X} \times \mathrm{X} \rightarrow [0, \infty]$ from instance space X to a similarity score:

$$K(x,y) = \sum_i \phi_i(x)\phi_i(y) = \phi(x)\cdot\phi(y) \qquad (17)$$

Here, $\phi_i(x)$ is a feature function over the instance x. The kernel function must be symmetric and positive semi-definite, which means the $n \times n$ Gram matrix G defined by $G_{ij} = K(x_i, x_j)$ is positive semi-definite. Given a training set $S = \{x_1, \ldots, x_N\}$, Gram matrix G will be computed. Then, the classifier finds a hyperplane which separates instances of different classes. To classify an unseen instance x, the classifier first projects x into the feature space defined by the kernel function and then determine which side of the separating hyperplane x lies.

Culotta and Sorensen (2004) investigate a rich sentence representation and propose a general framework to allow feature weighting, as well as the use of composite kernels to reduce kernel scarcity. In (Culotta and Sorensen, 2004), the task is defined to generate potential relation instances by iterating over all pairs of entities occurring in the same sentence. For each entity pair, they create an augmented dependency tree to represent this instance. A dependency tree is a representation that denotes grammatical relations between words in a sentence. A set of rules are used to map a parse tree to a dependency tree. For example, subjects are dependent on their verbs and adjectives are dependent on the nouns they modify. Then, they define a tree kernel function $K(T_1, T_2)$ which returns a normalized, symmetric similarity score in the range (0, 1) for two trees T_1 and T_2.

Formally, a relation instance is a dependency tree T with nodes $\{t_0 \ldots t_n\}$. The features of node t_i are given by $\phi(t_i) = \{v_1 \ldots v_d\}$. Also, $t_i[j]$ denotes the j-th child of node t_i, $t_i[c]$ denotes the set of all children of node t_i, $t_i[j] \subseteq t_i[c]$ denotes a subset j of children of t_i, and $t_i.p$ denotes the parent of t_i.

First, two functions over the features of tree nodes are defined: a matching function $m(t_i, t_j) \in \{0,1\}$ and a similarity function $s(t_i, t_j) \in (0, \infty]$:

$$m(t_i,t_j) = \begin{cases} 1 & \text{if } \phi_m(t_i) = \phi_m(t_j) \\ 0 & \text{otherwise} \end{cases} \qquad (18)$$

$$s(t_i,t_j) = \sum_{v_q \in \phi_s(t_i)} \sum_{v_r \in \phi_s(t_j)} C(v_q, v_r) \qquad (19)$$

where $C(v_q, v_r)$ is a compatibility function between two feature values. For example, in the simplest case where:

$$C(v_q,v_r) = \begin{cases} 1 & \text{if } v_q = v_r \\ 0 & \text{otherwise} \end{cases}$$

$s(t_i,t_j)$ returns the number of feature values in common between feature vectors $\phi_s(t_i)$ and $\phi_s(t_j)$.

For two dependency trees T_1, T_2, with root nodes r_1 and r_2, we define the tree kernel $K(T_1,T_2)$ as follows:

$$K(T_1,T_2) = \begin{cases} 0 & \text{if } m(r_1,r_2) = 0 \\ s(r_1,r_2) + K_c(r_1[c], r_2[c]) & \text{otherwise} \end{cases} \qquad (20)$$

where K_c is a kernel function over children. Let **a** and **b** be sequences of indices such that **a** is a sequence $a_1 \leq a_2 \leq \ldots \leq a_n$, and likewise for **b**. Let $d(\mathbf{a}) = a_n - a_1 + 1$ and $l(\mathbf{a})$ be the length of **a**. Then we have:

$$K_c(t_i[\mathbf{c}], t_j[\mathbf{c}]) = \sum_{\mathbf{a},\mathbf{b}, l(\mathbf{a})=l(\mathbf{b})} \lambda^{d(\mathbf{a})} \lambda^{d(\mathbf{b})} K(t_i[\mathbf{a}], t_j[\mathbf{b}]) \qquad (21)$$

The constant $0 < \lambda < 1$ is a decay factor that penalizes matching subsequences that are spread out within the child sequences.

Intuitively, in formula (18) and (19), $m(t_i,t_j)$ and $s(t_i,t_j)$ provide a way to discretize the similarity between two nodes. If $\phi_m(t_i) \neq \phi_m(t_j)$, then two nodes are completely dissimilar. On the other hand, if $\phi_m(t_i) = \phi_m(t_j)$, then $s(t_i,t_j)$ is computed. Thus, restring nodes by $m(t_i,t_j)$ is a way to prune the search space of matching subtrees, as shown in formula (20). In formula (21), the function means, whenever we want to find a pair of matching nodes, we search for all matching subsequences of the children of each node. A matching subsequence of children is a sequence of children **a** and **b** such that $m(a_i,b_i) = 1(\forall i < n)$. For each matching pair of nodes (a_i, b_i) in a matching subsequence, we accumulate the result of the similarity function $s(a_i,b_j)$ and then recursively search for matching subsequences of their children a_i[**c**], b_j[**c**].

Zelenko, Aone, and Richardella (2003) investigate identifying relations like *person-affiliation* and *organization-location* from text. They define kernels over shallow parse representations of text and design efficient algorithms for computing the kernels. Bunescu and Mooney (2005a) also present a new kernel method based on a generalization of subsequence kernels. This kernel uses three types of subsequence patterns that are typically employed in natural language to assert relationships between two entities. For more details, please refer (Zelenko *et al.*, 2003; Bunescu and Mooney, 2005a; Zhang, Zhang, and Su, 2006; Zhao and Grishman, 2005)

Sequential Labeling Based Methods

Although classification based methods have been proved successful in various kinds of applications, there are still some disadvantages. First, for any two entities, the candidate relations might be numerous. This makes it inconvenient, even impossible, to train different models for each relation. Second, classification based methods build local classifier from labeled relations and context around them. They cannot model correlations between different entity-pairs, therefore cannot take advantage of dependencies between them.

In order to address the problem, sequential labeling based methods for relation extraction have been studied. Sequential Labeling methods, for example Conditional Random Fields (Lafferty *et al.*, 2001) have been proved to be successful in entity extraction tasks such as Named Entity Recognition and Part-Of-Speech tagging. Culotta, McCallum, and Betz (2006) introduce CRFs into relation extraction. They propose formalizing relation extraction as a sequential labeling task and using a Conditional Random Field model to identify relations from entities.

The proposed method supposes that there is an identified principal entity and the task is to identify the relations between the secondary entities (defined below) and the principal entity. The authors concentrate their investigation on biographical text, e.g. encyclopedia articles. A biographical text mostly discusses one entity, which is referred as the principal entity. Other entities mentioned in the text are referred as secondary entities. Therefore, the problem is viewed as a tagging problem, that is, assigning a label to each observation unit in the sequence. The label indicates a relation between the principal entity and the current unit. For example, as shown in Figure 12, the principal entity in this biographical text is George W. Bush. Two secondary entities, "George H. W. Bush" and "Barbara Bush", are labeled with their relation with George W. Bush.

Figure 12. An example of sequence labeling for relation extraction

George W. Bush
George is the son of George H. W. Bush and Barbara Bush.
father mother

A linear-chain Conditional Random Field model is employed to find relation from a biographical data. See Section 2.1.3 for details of the CRFs.

Roth and Wen (2002) propose another sequential labeling based method for relation extraction. They first train different local classifiers for identifying entities and relations. Then, they perform global inference that accounts for the mutual dependencies across entities. They construct a belief network along with constraints induced among entity types and relations. At last, the most probable assignment for entities and relations are discovered by an efficient Viterbi-like algorithm. See (Roth and Wen, 2002) for details.

Other Methods

Besides the methods discussed above, other unsupervised approaches have also been studied, including clustering, semi-supervised learning, and rule based methods.

Clustering is one of the important methods for relation extraction. For instance, (Brody, 2007) created a simplified and generalized grammatical clause representation which utilized information-based clustering and inter-sentence dependencies to extract high level semantic relations. (Davidov, Rappoport, and Koppel, 2007) discovered and enhanced concept specific relations other than general relations by web mining. They utilized clustering patterns which contain concept words and words related to them to implement their methods. Their approach can be used to discover unknown relations.

As supervised learning requires a large number of training data which leads to expensive labor cost, many research works have been made to minimize the labeling cost. For example, (Bunescu and Mooney, 2007) presented a new approach requiring only handful training examples to extract relations between entities. They used web as the corpus. First, pairs of entities which exhibit relations or no relations are found. Then searching all the sentences which describe these entities and creating positive and negative bags (weak form of multiple instances learning), they extended an existing approach using Support Vector Machines and string kernel to handle this weak form of multiple instances learning. As many errors generated in unsupervised and semi-supervised learning for relation extraction were attributed to the entities in the relations were not extracted correctly. (Rosenfeld and Feldman, 2007) proposed incorporating corpus statistics to validate and correct the arguments of the extracted relation instances.

Rule based methods are also studied and implemented in several systems including DIPRE (Brin, 1998), Snowball (Agichtein and Gravano, 2000), and Espresso (Pennacchiotti and Pantel, 2006). All these systems use bootstrapping techniques which have been proved as a successful automatic text processing methods. Here, we use the Snowball system, which is based on the DIPRE algorithm, as an example to illustrate the rule based approach.

Given a handful of training examples from users, the Snowball system uses these examples to generate extraction patterns, which in turn result in new tuples (i.e. train examples) extracted from the document collection.

The main processing flow includes:

1. Start with a few certain relationship (e.g. <Microsoft, Redmond> for location relationship)
2. Locate occurrences of these examples (e.g. "Microsoft is at Redmond.")
3. Generalize patterns of the relationship from these occurrences
4. Repeat (2) until no more examples can be extracted

The advantage of the method is that it does not need a large number of manually labeled training data. However, a strong limitation of the mutual bootstrapping based method is that a minor error can introduce a large amount of errors during the following iteration s. Therefore, in each iteration, the confidence of the extracted patterns and examples are estimated and the most reliable ones are selected for further consideration.

Another problem of this method is the low extraction recall, because the relation patterns produced by the bootstrapping based method may be specific to some examples. In order to improve recall, Snowball patterns are generalized by clustering similar examples using a simple single-pass clustering algorithm. After generalizing patterns, the system discovers new tuples that match the patterns in a certain degree. Each candidate tuple will then have a number of patterns that help generate it associated with a degree of match. This information helps Snowball to decide what candidate tuples to add to the final template.

Some other relation extraction systems also perform relation extraction by combining the linguistic patterns and statistical processing. For example, RelExt (Schutz and Buitelaar, 2005) is a system intending to automatically identify relations between concepts from an existing domain-specific ontology. RelExt works by extracting relevant verbs and their grammatical arguments (i.e. terms) from a domain-specific text collection and computing corresponding relations through a combination of linguistic and statistical processing. LEIL (Suchanek, Ifrim, and Weikum, 2006) argues that relation extraction can benefit significantly from deep natural language processing. Their strategy is to discover text patterns that express the semantic relation, generalize these patterns, and then apply them to the new text. They utilized parsing and statistical learning to discover and generalize the patterns. (Maedche and Staab, 2000) utilizes shallow text processing to discover non-taxonomic conceptual relations. They introduced association rule learning to discover more relations based on texts building on shallow parsing techniques.

SEMANTIC ANNOTATION SYSTEMS

There are a number of available systems that address semantic annotation from different aspects. A complete review of this subject is outside the scope of this chapter. We present some of them through their principles and availabilities. Many systems support manual annotation, for example: Protégé-2000 (Eriksson, Fergerson, Shahar, and Musen, 1999), WebKB (Martin and Eklund, 1999), SHOE (Heflin and Hendler, 2000), Artequakt (Alani *et al.*, 2003), Annotea (Kahan and Koivunen, 2001), Ontobroker (Fensel, Decker, Erdmann, and Studer, 1998), and SEAN (Mukherjee, Yang, and Ramakrishnan, 2003). As manual annotation is not our focus here, we will concentrate on (semi-) automatic annotation systems.

CREAM

CREAM is a comprehensive framework for creating annotations, relational metadata in the Semantic Web, including tools for both manual and semi-automatic annotation of pages (Handschuh, Staab, and Ciravegna, 2001). Figure 13 shows the architecture of CREAM. The complete design of CREAM comprises a plug-in structure, which is flexible with regard to adding or replacing modules. We give a brief introduction of the main modules in the system as follows:

- **Document Viewer:** The document viewer visualizes the web page contents. The annotator may easily provide annotations by highlighting text.
- **Ontology Guidance:** The newly created annotations must be consistent with a community's ontology. The ontology is used to guide annotators towards creating relational metadata.
- **Crawler:** The crawler collects the availably relevant entities so that annotators can look for proper reference or recognize whether properties have already been instantiated.

- **Annotation Inference Server:** Relational metadata, proper reference and avoidance of redundant annotation require querying for instances. The annotation inference server reasons on crawled and newly annotated instances.
- **Document Management:** It stores annotated web pages together with their annotations. When the web page changes, the old annotations may still be valid or they may become invalid. The annotator can decide based on the old annotations and the changes of the web page.
- **Information Extraction:** CREAM uses two major techniques: First, "wrappers" can be learned from given markup in order to annotate similarly pages (cf., e.g., Kushmerick, 2000). Second, named entities, propose coreferences, and relations are recognized from texts (cf., e.g., MUC).
- **Storage and Replication:** CREAM stores annotations both inside the document in the document management and in the annotation inference server.

Based on CREAM framework, Handschuh, Staab, and Maedche (2001) have implemented a semantic annotation tool called OntoMat.

KNOWITALL

KNOWITALL system aims to automate the process of extracting large collections of facts, concepts, and relationships from the Web in an unsupervised, domain-independent, and scalable manner. KNOWITALL uses a generate-and-test architecture that extracts information in two stages. Inspired by Hearst (Etzioni *et al.*, 2004), KNOWITALL is seeded with an extensible ontology and a small set of domain-independent extraction patterns from which it creates text extraction rules for each class and relation in its ontology. Next, KNOWITALL automatically tests the plausibility of the candidate facts it extracts using point-wise mutual information (PMI) statistics computed by treating the Web as a massive corpus of text. KNOWITALL leverages existing Web search engines to compute these statistics efficiently. Based on these PMI statistics, KNOWITALL associates a probability with every fact it extracts, enabling it to automatically manage the tradeoff between precision and recall.

TEXTRUNNER

Banko, Cafarella, Soderland, Broadhead, and Etzioni (2007) introduce Open Information Extraction (OIE) which is a novel extraction

Figure 13. Architecture of CREAM

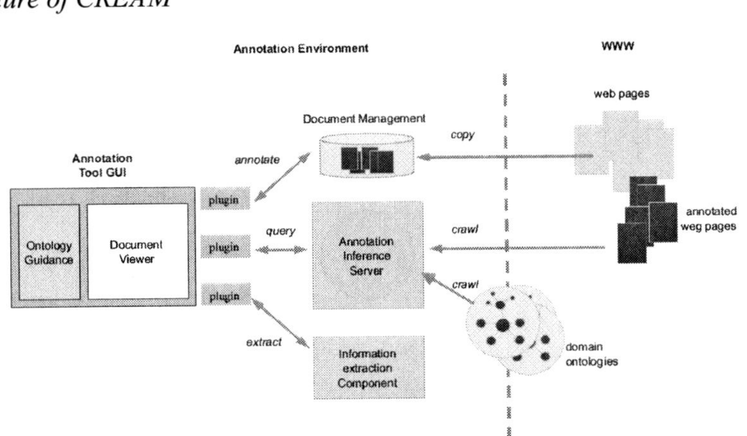

paradigm that facilitates domain-independent discovery of relations extracted from text and readily scales to the diversity and size of the Web corpus. The sole input to an OIE system is a corpus, and its output is a set of extracted relations. An OIE system makes a single pass over its corpus guaranteeing scalability with the size of the corpus.

It also introduces TEXTRUNNER, a fully implemented, highly scalable OIE system where the tuples are assigned a probability and indexed to support efficient extraction and exploration via user queries. TEXTRUNNER consists of three key modules:

1. **Self-Supervised Learner:** Given a small corpus sample as input, the Learner outputs a classifier that labels candidate extractions as "trustworthy" or not. The Learner requires no hand-tagged data.
2. **Single-Pass Extractor:** The Extractor makes a single pass over the entire corpus to extract tuples for all possible relations. The Extractor does not utilize a parser. The Extractor generates one or more candidate tuples from each sentence, sends each candidate to the classifier, and retains the ones labeled as trustworthy.
3. **Redundancy-Based Assessor:** The Assessor assigns a probability to each retained tuple based on a probabilistic model of redundancy in text (Downey, Etzioni, and Soderland, 2005).

KIM

The Knowledge and Information Management (KIM) platform (Popov *et al.*, 2003) contains an ontology, a knowledgebase, a semantic annotation, an indexing and retrieval server, as well as front-ends for interfacing with the server. For ontology and knowledgebase storage it uses the SESAME RDF repository (Broekstra, Kampman, and Harmelen, 2002), and for search it uses a modified version of Lucene, a keyword-based search engine. The semantic annotation process relies on a pre-built lightweight ontology called KIMO as well as an inter-domain knowledgebase. KIMO defines a base set of entity classes, relationships, and attribute restrictions. The knowledgebase is populated with 80,000 entities consisting of locations and organizations, gathered from a general News corpus. Named-entities found during the annotation process are matched to their type in the ontology and also to a reference in the knowledgebase. The dual mapping allows the information extraction process to be improved by providing disambiguation clues based on attributes and relations (Popov *et al.*, 2003).

The information extraction component of semantic annotation is performed using components of the GATE toolkit (Cunningham, Maynard, Bontcheva, and Tablan, 2002). Some components of GATE have been modified to support the KIM server. Some other components of semantic annotation have been custom developed.

MUSE

MUSE (Maynard, 2003) was designed to perform named entity recognition and coreferencing. It has been implemented using the GATE framework. The IE components, called processing resources (PRs), form a processing pipeline used to discover named entities. MUSE executes PRs conditionally based on text attributes. Conditional processing is handled using a Switching Controller, which calls the appropriate PRs in the specified order. The use of conditional processing allows MUSE to obtain accuracies similar to machine learning systems. Semantic tagging is accomplished using the Java Annotations Pattern Engine (JAPE) (Cunningham, Maynard, and Tablen, 2000). Rules using the JAPE grammar are constructed to generate annotations. The Semantic Tagger can use tags generated by processing resources run earlier in the pipeline. For example, if the gazetteer recognizes a first name and the part-of-speech tagger recognizes a proper noun, a JAPE rule can use both tags to annotate an entity of type Person. The MUSE system is more sophisticated than a gazetteer because a gazetteer cannot provide an exhaustive list of all potential named-entities, and cannot resolve entity ambiguities.

AeroDAML

AeroDAML (Kogut and Holmes, 2001) is a knowledge markup tool that applies information extraction techniques to automatically generate DAML annotations from web pages. AeroDAML uses a pattern-based approach to link the most proper nouns and common relationships with classes and properties in DAML (DARPA Agent Markup Language) ontologies (Hendler and McGuinness, 2000). AeroDAML consists of an information extraction module called AeroText™ and components for DAML generation. AeroText™ (Kogut and Holmes, 2001) is designed to support various text processing tasks, and is comprised of four major components: 1) Knowledge Base Compiler for converting linguistic data files into an efficient runtime knowledge base; 2) Knowledge Base Engine for applying the knowledge base to input documents; 3) an IDE for building, testing, and analyzing linguistic knowledge base; and 4) Common Knowledge Base containing general rules for extracting proper nouns and frequently occurring relations.

Armadillo and MnM

Armadillo (Dingli, Ciravegna, and Wilks, 2003) and MnM (Vargas-Vera *et al.*, 2002) utilize the Amilcare IE system (Ciravegna, 2001) to perform wrapper induction on web pages. We use Armadillo as the example here. Armadillo uses a pattern-based approach to find entities. It finds its own initial set of seed-patterns rather than requiring an initial set of seeds (Brin, 1998). Manual patterns are used for the named entity recognizer. No manual annotation of corpus documents is required. Once the seeds are found, pattern expansion is then used to discover additional entities. Information redundancy, via queries to Web services such as Google and CiteSeer, is used to verify discovered entities by analyzing query results to confirm or deny the existence of an entity. The use-case implemented in Armadillo is extracting worker details from a university computer science department web site in order to find personal data, such as name, position, home page, email address, and other contact information. The seed-discovery and expansion finds worker names in the web pages. Since many names may be discovered, the Web services are queried to confirm whether a person actually works in the department. The names are then used to discover home pages, where detailed information about a person can often be found and extracted. Armadillo is also interesting in that it attempts to discover citations for each person discovered. The information redundancy approach was also applied to bibliographic entries, but with a lower success rate than discovering and extracting information about people from home pages.

DIPRE

Dual Iterative Pattern Expansion (DIPRE) (Brin, 1998) was proposed as an approach for extracting a structured relation (or table) from a collection of HTML documents. The method works well in an environment like the World-Wide-Web, where the table tuples to be extracted will tend to appear in uniform contexts repeatedly in the collection documents (i.e., in the available HTML pages). DIPRE exploits this redundancy and inherent structure in the collection to extract the target relation with minimal training from a user.

Snowball

The techniques of Snowball build on the idea of DIPRE. Snowball (Agichtein and Gravano, 2000) is a bootstrapping-based system that requires only a handful of training examples of interest. These examples are used to generate extraction patterns, which in turn results in new tuples being extracted from the document collection. During each iteration of the extraction process, Snowball evaluates the quality of these patterns and tuples without human intervention, and keeps only the most reliable ones for the next iteration.

SemTag

SemTag (Dill *et al.*, 2003) is the semantic annotation component of a comprehensive platform, called Seeker, for performing large-scale annotation of web pages. SemTag performs annotation in three passes: Spotting, Learning, and Tagging. The Spotting examines tokenized words from source documents and finds label matches from the taxonomy. If a label match is found, a window of ten words to either side of the source match is kept. In the Learning pass, a sample of the corpus is examined to find the corpus-wide distribution of terms at each node of the taxonomy. The Tagging pass is then executed, scanning all of the windows from the Spotting pass and disambiguating the matches. Once a match is confirmed, the URL, text reference, and other metadata are stored. SemTag/Seeker is an extensible system, so new annotation implementations can replace the existing Taxonomy-based Disambiguation algorithm (TBD). The taxonomy used by SemTag is TAP. TAP is shallow and covers a range of lexical and taxonomic information about popular items such as music, movies, authors, sports, health and so forth. The annotations generated by SemTag are stored separately from the source document.

C-PANKOW

PANKOW (Pattern-based Annotation through Knowledge On the Web) (Cimiano, Handschuh, and Staab, 2004) uses globally available knowledge to annotate resources such as web pages. The core of PANKOW is a pattern generation mechanism which creates pattern strings out of a certain pattern schema conveying a specific semantic relation, an instance to be annotated and all the concepts from a given ontology. It counts the occurrences of these pattern strings on the Web using the Google API. The ontological instance in question is then annotated semantically according to a principle of maximal evidence, i.e. with the concept having the largest number of hits.

C-PANKOW (Context-driven PANKOW) (Cimiano, Ladwig, and Staab, 2005) alleviates several shortcomings of PANKOW. First, by downloading abstracts and processing them off-line, it avoids the generation of large number of linguistic patterns and correspondingly large number of Google queries. Second, by linguistically analyzing and normalizing the downloaded abstracts, it increases the coverage of pattern matching mechanism and overcome several limitations of the earlier pattern generation process. Third, it uses the annotation context in order to distinguish the significance of a pattern match for the given annotation task. C-PANKOW is implemented as a plug-in for OntOMat.

Summary

Table 5 gives the comparison of the semantic annotation systems. It shows the methods and the algorithms employed in the systems. We can see from the table that most of the annotation systems focus on dealing with one specific genre of documents or a specific application. For example, SEAN (Mukherjee, Yang, and Ramakrishnan, 2003) aims at annotating documents generated based on a specific template; AeroDAML (Kogut and Holmes, 2001) only supports annotation with the ontology description language DAML; systems like ALPHA (Li and Yu, 2001) and MUMIS (Buitelaar and Declerck, 2003) support annotation of only natural language text.

Based on methods employed in the system, we can see some system only support manual

Table 5. Comparison of annotation systems

System	Method	Algorithm
AeroDAML	Manual Rules	AeroText, NLP
ALPHA	NLP	Linker grammar parser
Annotea	Manual	Manual
Armadillo	Pattern Discovery	LP^2
Artequakt	Manual Rules + NLP	GATE+ Apple Pie Parser
CREAM/OntoMat	Multiple	Multiple
Dome	Manual Rules	Remember User Operation
Esperonto	Rules Learning	Wrapper Induction
KIM	Manual Rules	GATE
Melita	Rules Learning	LP^2
MnM	Rules Learning	LP^2, Badger, Marmot, Crystal
MUMIS	NLP	ShProT
MUSE	Manual Rule	GATE
Ontobroker	Manual	Manual
C-PANKOW	NLP + Unsupervised Pattern Discovery	Pattern Discovery + Statistical Learning
SCORE	Classification Model + Statistical Learning	Name entity and relation learning
S-CREAM	Manual Rules + Learning	LP^2
SEAN	Rules + Webpage Template Analysis	Template Discovery + Semantic Analysis
SemTag	Manual Rules + Statistical Learning	TBD
SHOE	Manual	Manual
WebKB-1	Rules Learning	SRV
WebKB-2	Rules Learning	Unknown
KnowItAll	Rules Learning	Bootstrapping + PMI-IR
KnowItNow	Rules Learning	Binding Engine + URNS
TextRunner	Rules Learning	Statistical Learning Algorithm
Snowball	Pattern Discovery	Based on DIPRE
Gate	Rule Learning	Annie
ESpotter	Manual Rules + Pattern Discovery	Named Entity Recognition
T-Rex	Framework	Multiple

annotation or rule based annotation (for example $(LP)^2$ (Ciravegna, 2001) and GATE (Cunningham *et al.*, 2002)); some systems can take advantage of natural language analysis techniques (e.g. ALPHA (Li and Yu, 2001) and MUMIS (Buitelaar and Declerck, 2003)) and statistical learning methods (e.g., SemTag (Dill *et al.*, 2003) and SCORE (Hammond, Sheth, and Kochut, 2002)); and some other systems enable learning from users' feedbacks or domain knowledge to improve the performance of annotation (e.g., KIM (Popov *et al.*, 2003)).

We can also see from Table 5 that few systems utilize the dependencies between the annotated instances. Although Reeve has investigated the Hidden Markov Model for semantic annotation, the annotation systems have not employed the dependent models in practical applications.

Generally speaking, it is still necessary to conduct a thorough investigation of the semantic annotation issue. Many real-world problems require to be solved as the first step for automatic semantic annotation. The major problems include:

1. Lack of analysis of the characteristics of the emerging Web documents. There are a lot of new types of documents, especially with the development of the Web 2.0. The traditional annotation method often focuses on one type of document or application in a specific domain. A comprehensive analysis of characteristics of the documents is thus necessary.
2. The current annotation methods still need improvements. Existing systems usually make use of the rule learning based annotation method. However, the proposed rule learning methods (e.g., LP^2; Ciravegna, 2001) still have some problems such as low efficiency and too many parameters needed to tune.
3. Lack of a theoretical model that can efficiently take advantage of dependencies between the annotated instances. The dependencies between the annotated instances can be used to improve the annotation performance. However, dependencies in different types of documents are different (sometimes even vary largely). For example, sometimes the dependencies are linear and sometimes are hierarchical. Therefore, a theoretical model is required for efficiently and effectively incorporating the dependencies.

APPLICATIONS

In this section, we introduce several semantic annotation applications that we experienced. We will also introduce some well-known applications in this area.

Semantic Annotation in Digital Libraries

In digital libraries (DL), "metadata" is structured data for helping users find and process documents and images. With the metadata information, search engines can retrieve required documents more accurately. Scientists and librarians need use great manual efforts and lots of time to create metadata for the documents. To alleviate the hard labor, many efforts have been made toward the automatic metadata generation, based on the techniques of information extraction. Here we take Citeseer, a popular scientific literature digital library, as an example in our explanation.

Citeseer is a public specialty scientific and academic DL that was created in NEC Labs, which is hosted on the World Wide Web at the College of Information Sciences and Technology, The Pennsylvania State University, and has over 800,000 documents, primarily in the fields of computer and information science and engineering (Lawrence, Giles, and Bollacker, 1999; Han *et al.*, 2003). Citeseer crawls and harvests documents on the web, extracts documents metadata automatically, and indexes the metadata to permit querying by metadata.

By extending Dublin Core metadata standard, Citeseer defines 15 different meta-tags for the document header, including Title, Author, Affiliation, and so on. They view the task of automatic document metadata generation as that of labeling the text with the corresponding meta-tags. Each meta-tag corresponds to a metadata class. The annotation task is cast as a classification problem and SVM is employed to perform the classification. They show that classifying each text line into one or more classes is more efficient for meta-tagging than classifying each word, and decompose the metadata extraction problem into two sub-problems: (1) line classification and (2) chunk identification of multi-class lines.

In line classification, both word-level and line-level features are used. Each line is represented by a set of words and line-specific features. A rule-based, context-dependent word clustering method is developed to overcome the problem of word sparseness. For example, an author line "Chungki Lee James E. Burns" is represented as "CapNonDictWord: :MayName: :MayName: : SingleCap: :MayName", after word clustering. The weight of a word-specific feature is the number of times this feature appears in the line. And line-specific features are features such as "Number of the words in the line", "The position of the line", "The percentage of dictionary words in the line", and so on. The classification process is performed in two steps, an independent line classification followed by an iterative contextual line classification. Independent line classification use the features described above to assign one or more classes to each text line. After that, by making use of the sequential information among lines output by the first step, an iterative contextual line classification is performed. In each iteration, each line uses the previous *N* and next *N* lines' class information as features, concatenates them to the feature vector used in step one, and updates its class label. The procedure converges when the percentage of line with new class labels is lower than a threshold. The principle of the classification based method is the Two-level boundary classification approach as described in Section 2.2.3.

After classifying each line into one or more classes, meta-tag can be assigned to lines that have only one class label. For those that have more than one class label, a further identification is employed to extract metadata from each line. The task is cast as a chunk identification task. Punctuation marks and spaces between words are considered candidate chunk boundaries. A two-class chunk identification algorithm for this task was developed and it yields an accuracy of 75.5%. For lines that have more than two class labels, they are simplified to two-class chunk identification tasks by detecting natural chunk boundary. For instance, using the positions of email and URL in the line, the three-class chunk identification can be simplified as two-class chunk identification task. The position of the email address in the following three-class line "International Computer Science Institute, Berkeley, CA94704. Email: aberer@icsi.berkeley.edu." is a natural chunk boundary between the other two classes. The method reaches an overall accuracy of 92.9%. See also (Lawrence *et al.*, 1999; Han *et al.*, 2003) for details.

Researcher Profile Extraction

We present a novel expertise oriented search system for web community, which is available at http://www.arnetminer.org (Tang, Zhang, Zhang, Yao, and Zhu, 2007b). Our objective in this system is to provide services for searching and mining the semantic-based web community.

We define a researcher profile ontology, which include basic information (e.g. photo, affiliation, and position), contact information (e.g. address, email, and telephone), educational history (e.g. graduated university and major), and publications. For each researcher, we intend to create a profile based on the ontology by extracting the profile information from his/her homepage or Web pages introducing him/her. Figure 14 shows a researcher's homepage. It includes typical information in a researcher profile. The top section includes a photo, two addresses, and an email address; the middle section describes the educational history of the researcher; the bottom section provides the position and affiliation information. The ideal annotation result is shown in the right part of Figure 14.

We formalize the problem as that of sequential labeling. Next, we propose a unified approach on the basis of tagging. We view the problem as assigning tags to the input texts, with each tag representing one profile property. As the tagging model, we employ Conditional Random Fields (CRFs). The unified approach can achieve better performance in researcher profiling than the separated methods, because the approach can take advantage of the interdependencies between the

Figure 14. An example of researcher homepage and the ideal annotated results

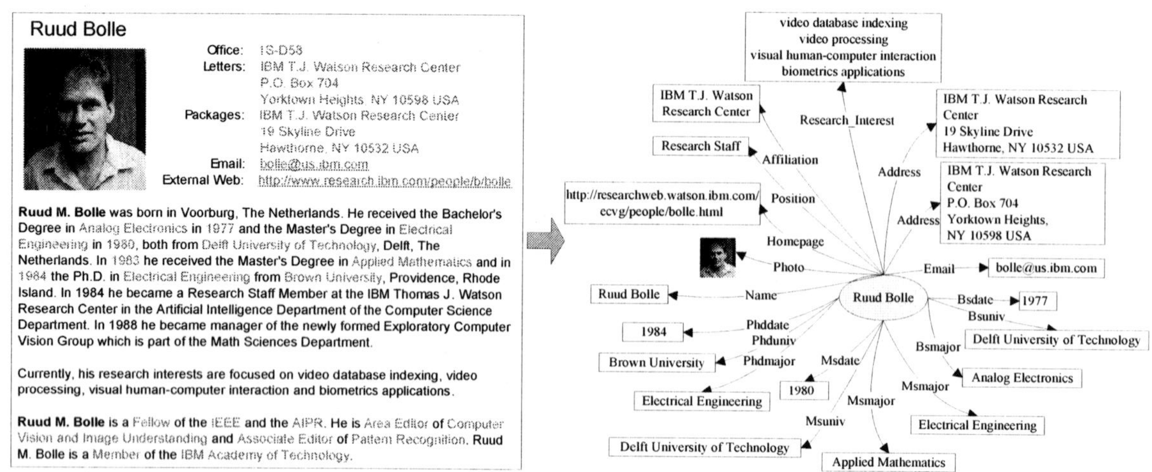

subtasks of profiling. Furthermore, there is no need to define specialized models to annotate different types of properties; all the properties can be extracted in one unified model.

There are three steps in our approach: relevant page finding, preprocessing, and tagging. In relevant page finding, given a researcher name, we first get a list of web pages by a web search engine (i.e. Google) and then identify the homepage or introducing page using a classifier. We view the URL of the identified web page as the value of the *Homepage* property in the profile.

In preprocessing, (A) we segment the text into tokens and (B) we assign possible tags to each token. The tokens form the basic units and the pages form the sequences of units in the tagging problem. In tagging, given a sequence of units, we determine the most likely corresponding sequence of tags using a trained tagging model. (The tags correspond to the properties defined in the ontology.)

(A). We identify tokens in the Web page heuristically. We define five types of tokens: 'standard word', 'special word', '<image>' token, term, and punctuation mark. Standard words are unigram words in natural language. Special words (Sproat, Black, Chen, Kumar, Ostendorf, and Richards, 1999) include email address, IP address, URL, date, number, percentage, words containing special symbols (e.g. 'Ph.D.', 'Prof.'), unnecessary tokens (e.g. '===' and '###'), etc. We identify special words using regular expressions. '<image>' tokens are '<image>' tags in the HTML file. We identify them by parsing the HTML file. Terms are base noun phrases extracted from the Web pages. We employed the methods proposed in (Xun, Huang, and Zhou, 2000). Punctuation marks include period, question, and exclamation mark.

(B). We assign tags to each token based on their corresponding type. For standard word, we assign all possible tags. For special word, we assign tags: *Position*, *Affiliation*, *Email*, *Address*, *Phone*, *Fax*, and *Bsdate*, *Msdate*, and *Phddate*. For '<image>' token, we assign two tags: *Photo* and *Email* (it is likely that an email address is shown as an image). For term token, we assign *Position*, *Affiliation*, *Address*, *Bsmajor*, *Msmajor*, *Phdmajor*, *Bsuniv*, *Msuniv*, and *Phduniv*. In this way, each token can be assigned several possible tags. Using the tags, we can perform most of the profiling processing.

Experimental results show that our method can obtain high performance (83.37% in terms of F1-measuer) and outperforms the separated classification based and rule-learning based methods on profiling significantly (+9.8%).

Semantic Annotation for Biomedical Information

Biomedical information, such as the protein or gene name and the biological relations between biomolecules, is presented in unstructured text of biomedical journal articles. Manual annotation requires lots of human efforts for interpreting molecules and the interactions between them. Thus, automatic annotation of entities and relations is extremely useful for biomedical information.

Identifying the names of proteins and genes is a Named Entity Recognition task. Rule-based, classification based, and sequential labeling based methods can all be applied to this task. For example, ABNER is a tool for automatic annotation of genes, proteins, and other entity names from text, which utilizes the Conditional Random Field model.

Extracting the biomedical relationship between proteins (i.e. interaction) is another important step toward understanding the biological organism. Uncovering the complex network of protein interactions is the key aspect of proteomic effort, which is also called PPI. The interactions are always presented in the abstracts of biomedical articles. Researchers have proposed different kinds of methods to solve the problem. Early solutions are rule-based methods, discovering useful patterns. Blaschke, Andrade, Ouzounis, and Valencia (1999) propose to extract patterns with restricted protein names and some verbs describing the interaction to detect protein-protein interaction. Rule-based method can only discover the subset of the interactions. Statistical method can solve the task more efficiently. (Donaldson *et al.*, 2003) designed a system, PreBIND and Textomy for mining the biomedical literature for protein-protein interactions using Support Vector Machines. The abstracts of scientific articles which contain interactions are positive examples, and the abstracts without interactions are negative examples. Then the classifier detects abstracts containing the interactions. This will help reduce human efforts for building the database of protein-protein interactions. Soni (2006) utilized Conditional Random Fields for detecting protein-protein interactions. The interaction detection is cast as sequential labeling – assigning labels to each word. The labels include PAIR-1, PAIR-2 (the two proteins), PAIR-1-2 (the protein involved in two interactions) and the FILTER (the language between the protein pairs. In theory, it should be a phrase which describe the real interaction between the pairs).

FUTURE RESEARCH DIRECTIONS

There are varieties of promising directions for future research in semantic annotation using machine learning.

On the machine-learning side, it would be interesting to generalize the idea of large-margin classification to sequential labeling models, strengthening the extraction results and leading to new optimal learning algorithms with stronger guarantees against overfitting. For example, Taskar (2003) proposes a maximal Markov model for sequential labeling task using the maximal margin theory. It is also attractive to study the new model for annotating the multimedia documents. As the video and audio becomes more and more popular, it would be very useful to study a new model with higher accuracy by considering the text, audio, and video documents simultaneously.

Although much research work has been conducted for automating semantic annotation, there is still a long way before making the dream of "automatic" reality. Many problems needed to be investigated and solved. We here list several challenging problems:

- The traditional supervised machine learning based annotation methods require a large number of annotated data to train the annotation model. Manually labeling the training data is expensive. How to learn a good annotation model from limited data is a challenging problem. Methods, such as active learning, bootstrapping, and semi-supervised learning, have been proposed. However, the problem is unsolved and still needs further investigation.

- How to deal with the problem of "domain adaptation" is another challenging problem. Many semantic annotation methods can learn good annotation models for a specific domain. However, the annotation models cannot be applied to the other domains. How to solve this problem is a key factor to the development of a real-world semantic annotation system.
- How to learn annotation models in some special cases is also a challenging problem. For example, in researcher profile annotation, a general method is to identify a person homepage first and conduct entity extraction from the identified pages, and then identify relations between the identified entities. The challenge is: Can we propose a unified approach that performs the three separated steps simultaneously? For example, sometimes one kind of entity (e.g. Time) may be easy to be identified while the other entities may be difficult (e.g. Address). How can we use the former one to help identify the annotation of the later ones?
- How to conduct complex semantic annotation is a critical problem for Semantic Web community as well. Conventional semantic annotation tasks are usually aimed at annotating specific type of web pages by a simple metadata or ontology. However, the ontology would be complex in practical applications. In such cases, how to conduct the annotation, especially, relation annotation is really a challenge.
- How to enrich the representation of the text needs to be considered as well. Exiting methods often view a document as a "bag of words", which is obviously limited. The effectiveness of several attempts by making use of domain knowledge or background knowledge to represent the document is not satisfactory. Furthermore, how to represent the document so as to improve the performance of semantic annotation also need further studies.
- How to develop multimodal techniques for conducting semantic annotation from information encoded in different modalities (text, images, audio, video, and background knowledge. By integrating the processes on all kinds of modalities and conduct the annotations simultaneously can be more accurate and more efficient.

Another interesting also important issue is how to make use of the prior knowledge in semantic annotation. So far, a common method for incorporating the prior knowledge is to use some domain-specific dictionaries (e.g. ontology) in the extraction. The question is whether the simple method still works well when dealing with more complex extraction tasks. A further question is if we can incorporate the different types of prior knowledge into a unified model for extraction.

As another future work, more applications, especially practical applications, need to be investigated. The new applications can provide rich data sources for conducting semantic annotation, as well as bring new challenges to the field. This is because various applications have various characteristics, requiring different methods to deal with.

CONCLUSION

Aiming to provide Semantic Web with fundamental semantics, semantic annotation has become an important sub-discipline of artificial intelligence, language processing, text mining, and Semantic Web. Nowadays, the significance of Semantic Annotation is promoted by the fast growing amount of information available in the unstructured form, for example on the Web.

In this chapter, we have reviewed the existing principled methods for semantic annotation. Specifically, we focus on two most important issues in semantic annotation: entity extraction and relation extraction. For entity extraction, we introduce four state-of-the-art methods: rule based methods, classification based methods, sequential labeling based methods, and non-linear based Markov random fields based methods. For relation extraction, we also introduce four typical methods: classification based methods, kernel based method, sequential labeling based methods, and other methods. We have explained the principle of these methods by using several approaches as examples. We have described several annotation systems and compared the main features and the algorithms employed in the systems. Moreover, we have introduced several practical application of semantic annotation.

ACKNOWLEDGMENT

The work is supported by the National Natural Science Foundation of China (90604025, 60703059), Chinese National Key Foundation Research and Development Plan (2007CB310803), and Chinese Young Faculty Funding (20070003093).

Thanks to the anonymous reviewers for their constructive suggestions.

REFERENCES

Agichtein, E. & Gravano, L. (2000). Snowball: Extracting Relations from Large Plain-Text Collections. In *Proceedings of the 5th ACM International Conference on Digital Libraries (JCDL'00).*

Alani, H., Kim, S., Millard, D., Weal, M., Hall, W., Lewis, P., & Shadbolt, N. (2003). Automatic Ontology-Based Knowledge Extraction from Web Documents. *IEEE Intelligent Systems, 18*(1): 14-21.

Appelt, D. E. (1999). Introduction to Information Extraction Technology. Tutorial. In *Proceedings of the International Joint Conference on Artificial Intelligence* (*IJCAI'1999*). August 2, 1999, Stockholm, Sweden.

Banko, M., Cafarella, M. J., Soderland, S., Broadhead, M., & Etzioni, O. (2007). Open information extraction from the web. In *Proceedings of the 20th International Joint Conference on Artificial Intelligence*

Berger, A., Pietra, S. D., & Pietra, V. D. (1996). A maximum entropy approach to natural language processing. In *Computational Linguistics, Vol.22*, 39-71. MA: MIT Press.

Blaschke, C., Andrade, M. A., Ouzounis, C., & Valencia, A. (1999). Automatic extraction of biological information from scientific text: protein-protein interactions. In *Proceedings of International Conference on Intelligent Systems for Molecular Biology.*

Bloehdorn, S., Petridis, K., Saathoff, C., Simou, N., Tzouvaras, V., Avrithis, Y., Handschuh, S., Kompatsiaris, I., Staab, S., & Strintzis, M. G. (2005). Semantic Annotation of Images and Videos for Multimedia Analysis. In *Proceedings of the 2nd European Semantic Web Conference (ESWC 2005).*

Boser, B. E., Guyon, I. M., & Vapnik, V. N. (1992). A training algorithm for optimal margin classifiers. In D. Haussler (Eds.), *5th Annual ACM Workshop on COLT* (pp. 144-152). Pittsburgh, PA: ACM Press.

Brin, S. (1998). Extracting Patterns and Relations from the World Wide Web. In *Proceedings of the 1998 International Workshop on the Web and Databases (WebDB'98)*

Brody, S. (2007). Clustering Clauses for High-Level Relation Detection: An Information-theoretic Approach. In *Proceedings of the 45th Annual Meeting of the Association of Computational Linguistics* (*ACL'2007*), pp. 448–455.

Broekstra, J., Kampman, A., & Harmelen, F. (2002). Sesame: A generic architecture for Storing and Querying RDF and RDF Schema. In *Proceedings of International Semantic Web Conference.* Sardinia, Italy

Buitelaar, P. & Declerck, T. (2003). Linguistic annotation for the semantic web. In *Annotation for the Semantic Web, Frontiers in Artificial Intelligence and Applications Series, Vol. 96.* IOS Press.

Bunescu, R. C. & Mooney, R. J. (2005a). Subsequence Kernels for Relation Extraction. In *Proceedings of the 19th Annual Conference on Neural Information Processing Systems*, Vancouver, British Columbia

Bunescu, R. & Mooney, R. J. (2005b). Statistical relational learning for natural language information extraction. In Getoor, L., & Taskar, B. (Eds.), *Statistical Relational Learning*, forthcoming book

Bunescu, R.C. & Mooney, R.J. (2007). Learning to Extract Relations from the Web using Minimal Supervision. In *Proceedings of the 45th Annual Meeting of the Association of Computational Linguistics* (ACL2007), pp. 576-583.

Califf, M. E., & Mooney, R. J. (1998). Relational learning of pattern-match rules for information extraction. In *Working Notes of AAAI Spring Symposium on Applying Machine Learning to Discourse Processing.* pp. 6-11.

Califf, M. E., & Mooney, R. J. (2003). Bottom-up relational learning of pattern matching rules for information extraction. *Journal of Machine Learning Research, Vol.4*, pp.177-210.

Chen, S. F. & Rosenfeld, R. (1999). A Gaussian prior for smoothing maximum entropy models. *Technical Report CMU-CS-99-108*, Carnegie Mellon University.

Cimiano, P., Handschuh, S., & Staab, S. (2004). Towards the self-annotating web. In *Proceedings of the Thirteenth International Conference on World Wide Web.* pp. 462-471.

Cimiano, P., Ladwig, G., & Staab, S. (2005). Gimme' the context: context-driven automatic semantic annotation with C-PANKOW. In *Proceedings of the 14th World Wide Web Conference.*

Ciravegna, F. (2001). $(LP)^2$, an adaptive algorithm for information extraction from Web-related texts. In *Proceedings of the IJCAI-2001 Workshop on Adaptive Text Extraction and Mining held in conjunction with 17th International Joint Conference on Artificial Intelligence (IJCAI)*, Seattle, USA.

Collins, M. (2002). Discriminative training methods for Hidden Markov models: theory and experiments with Perceptron algorithms. In *Proceedings of the Conference on Empirical Methods in NLP (EMNLP'02).*

Crescenzi, V, Mecca, G., & Merialdo, P. (2001). RoadRunner: Towards Automatic Data Extraction from Large Web Sites. In *Proceedings of the 27th International Conference on Very Large Data Bases* (VLDB'2001). pp. 109-118.

Culotta, A. & Sorensen, J. (2004). Dependency tree kernels for relation extraction. In *Proceedings of the 42nd Annual Meeting of the Association for Computational Linguistics* (pp. 423-429). Barcelona, Spain

Culotta, A., McCallum, A., & Betz, J. (2006). Integrating Probabilistic Extraction Models and Data Mining to Discovering Relations and Patterns in Text. In *Proceedings of the Human Language Technology Conference of the North American Chapter of the ACL* (pp. 296-303). New York.

Cunningham, H., Maynard, D. & Tablan, V. (2000). JAPE: A Java annotation patterns engine. Department of Computer Science, University of Sheffield

Cunningham, H., Maynard, D., Bontcheva, K., & Tablan, V. (2002). GATE: a framework and graphical development environment for robust NLP tools and applications. In *Proceedings of the 40th Anniversary Meeting of the Association for Computational Linguistics (ACL'02)*

Davidov, D., Rappoport, A., & Koppel, M. (2007). Fully Unsupervised Discovery of Concept-Specific Relationships by Web Mining. In *Proceedings of the 45th Annual Meeting of the Association of Computational Linguistics* (ACL2007), pp. 232–239.

Darroch, J. N., & Ratcliff, D. (1972). Generalized iterative scaling for log-linear models. *The Annals of Mathematical Statistics, 43 (5)*, 1470-1480.

Dill, S., Gibson, N., Gruhl, D., Guha, R., Jhingran, A., Kanungo, T., Rajagopalan, S., Tomkins, A., Tomlin, J. A., & Zien, J.Y. (2003). SemTag and Seeker: bootstrapping the semantic web via automated semantic annotation. In *Proceedings of the Twelfth International World Wide Web Conference*. pp. 178-186.

Dingli, A., Ciravegna, F., & Wilks, Y. (2003). Automatic semantic annotation using unsupervised information extraction and integration. In *Proceedings of K-CAP 2003 Workshop on Knowledge Markup and Semantic Annotation.*

Donaldson, I., Martin, J., Bruijn, B., Wolting, C., Lay, V., Tuekam, B., Zhang, S., Baskin, B., Bader, G., Michalickova, K., Pawson, T., & Hogue, C. W. (2003). PreBIND and Textomy – mining the biomedical literature for protein-protein interactions using a support vector machine. *BMC Bioinformatics*, 4:11.

Downey, D., Etzioni, O., & Soderland, S. (2005). A probabilistic model of redundancy in information extraction. In *Proceedings of the 19th International Joint Conference on Artificial Intelligence.* Edinburgh, Scotland.

Eriksson, H., Fergerson, R., Shahar, Y., & Musen, M. (1999). Automatic Generation of Ontology Editors. In *Proceedings of the 12th Banff Knowledge Acquisition Workshop.* Banff Alberta, Canada

Etzioni, O., Cafarella, M., Downey, D., Kok, S., Popescu, A., Shaked, T., Soderland, S., Weld, D., & Yates, A. (2004). Web-scale information extraction in KnowItAll. In *Proceedings of the 13th International World Wide Web Conference* (pp. 100-110). New York City, New York

Fellbaum, C. (Ed.). (1998). *Wordnet: An Electronic Lexical Database.* MA: MIT Press.

Fensel, D., Decker, S., Erdmann, M., & Studer, R. (1998). Ontobroker: Or how to enable intelligent access to the WWW. In *Proceedings of 11th Banff Knowledge Acquisition for Knowledge-Based SystemsWorkshop.* Banff, Canada, 1998.

Fine, S., Singer, Y., & Tishby, N. (1998). The Hierarchical Hidden Markov Model: Analysis and Applications. In *Machine Learning, Vol.32, Issue 1*, 41-62

Finkel, J. R., Grenager, T., & Manning, C. D. (2005). Incorporating non-local information into information extraction systems by gibbs sampling. In *Proceedings of the 43rd Annual Meeting of the Association for Computational Linguistics (ACL-2005).* pp. 363-370.

Finn, A., & Kushmerick, N. (2004). Information extraction by convergent boundary classification. In *AAAI-04 Workshop on Adaptive Text Extraction and Mining.* San Jose, USA.

Finn, A. (2006). *A multi-level boundary classification approach to information extraction.* Phd thesis, University College Dublin.

Freitag, D. (1998). Information extraction from HTML: Application of a general machine learning approach. In *Proceedings of the 15th Conference on Artificial Intelligence (AAAI'98)*. pp. 517-523.

Freitag, D., & Kushmerick, N. (2000). Boosted wrapper induction. In *Proceedings of 17th National Conference on Artificial Intelligence*. pp. 577-583.

Ghahramani, Z. & Jordan, M. I. (1997). Factorial Hidden Markov Models. *Machine Learning, Vol.29*, 245-273

Grefenstette, G. (1994). Explorations in Automatic Thesaurus Discovery. Kluwer Academic Publishers, Norwell, MA, USA.

Hammersley, J. & Clifford, P. (1971). *Markov fields on finite graphs and lattices*. Unpublished manuscript.

Hammond, B., Sheth, A., & Kochut, K. (2002). Semantic enhancement engine: a modular document enhancement platform for semantic applications over heterogeneous content. In: V. Kashyap & L. Shklar (Eds.), *Real World Semantic Web Applications*, 29-49. IOS Press

Han, H., Giles, L., Manavoglu, E., Zha, H., Zhang, Z., & Fox, E. A. (2003). Automatic document metadata extraction using support vector machines. In *Proceedings of 2003 Joint Conference on Digital Libraries (JCDL'03)*. pp. 37-48

Handschuh, S., Staab, S., & Maedche, A. (2001). CREAM—Creating relational metadata with a component-based, ontology driven framework. In *Proceedings of K-Cap 2001*, Victoria, BC, Canada

Handschuh, S., Staab, S., & Ciravegna, F. (2002). S-CREAM — semi-automatic creation of metadata. In *Proceedings of the 13th International Conference on Knowledge Engineering and Management*. pp. 358-372

Heflin, J. & Hendler, J. (2000). Searching the Web with SHOE. In *Proceedings of AAAI-2000 Workshop on AI for Web Search*. Austin, Texas.

Heflin, J., Hendler, J. A., & Luke, S. (2003). SHOE: a blueprint for the semantic web. In: D. Fensel, J. A. Hendler, H. Lieberman, & W. Wahlster (Eds.), *Spinning the Semantic Web* (pp. 29-63). MA: MIT Press.

Hendler, J. & McGuinness, D. (2000). The DARPA Agent Markup Language. *IEEE Intelligent Systems, 15*, No. 6:67-73.

Jiang, J. & Zhai. C. (2007). A Systematic Exploration of the Feature Space for Relation Extraction. In *Proceedings of the Human Language Technology Conference of the North American Chapter of the ACL*.

Jiao, F., Wang, S., & Lee, C. (2006). Semi-supervised conditional random fields for improved sequence segmentation and labeling. In *Proceedings of the 21st International Conference on Computational Linguistics and the 44th annual meeting of the ACL*. pp. 209-216

Kahan, J. & Koivunen, M. R. (2001). Annotea: an open RDF infrastructure for shared web annotations. In *Proceedings of the 10th International World Wide Web Conference (WWW 2005)*. pp. 623-632

Kambhatla, N. (2004). Combining Lexical, Syntactic, and Semantic Features with Maximum Entropy Models for Extracting Relations. In *Proceedings of the 42nd Annual Meeting of the Association for Computational Linguistics*.

Kauchak, D., Smarr, J., & Elkan, C. (2004). Sources of success for boosted wrapper induction. *The Journal of Machine Learning Research, Vol.5*, 499-527. MA: MIT Press.

Kogut, P. & Holmes, W. (2001). AeroDAML: Applying Information Extraction to Generate DAML Annotations from Web Pages. In *Proceedings of the First International Conference on Knowledge Capture*.

Kushmerick, N., Weld, D. S., & Doorenbos, R. (1997). Wrapper induction for information extraction. In *Proceedings of the International Joint Conference on Artificial Intelligence (IJCAI'97)*. pp. 729-737.

Kushmerick, N. (2000). Wrapper induction: Efficiency and expressiveness. *Artificial Intelligence, Vol.118*, 15-68.

Lafferty, J., McCallum, A., & Pereira, F. (2001). Conditional Random Fields: Probabilistic models for segmenting and labeling sequence data. In *Proceedings of the 18th International Conference on Machine Learning (ICML'01)*. pp. 282-289.

Lafferty, J., Zhu, X., & Liu, Y. (2004). Kernel conditional random fields: representation and clique selection. In *Proceedings of the 21st International Conference on Machine Learning.*

Lawrence, S., Giles, C.L., & Bollacker K. (1999). Digital libraries and autonomous citation indexing. *IEEE Computer, Vol.32(6)*, 67-71.

Lenat, D.B. & Guha, R.V. (1990). Building Large Knowledge Based Systems Reading, Massachusetts: Addison Wesley.

Li, J. & Yu, Y. (2001). Learning to generate semantic annotation for domain specific sentences. In *Proceedings of the Knowledge Markup and Semantic Annotation Workshop in K-CAP'2001.* Victoria, BC.

Maedche, A. & Staab, S. (2000). Discovering Conceptual Relations from Text. In *Proceedings of European Conference on Artificial Intelligence (ECAI'2000).*

Martin, P. & Eklund, P. (1999). Embedding knowledge in web documents. In *Proceedings of the 8th International World Wide Web Conference* (pp. 1403-1419). Toronto

Maynard, D. (2003). Multi-Source and Multilingual Information Extraction. In *BCS-SIGAI Workshop.* Nottingham Trent University, Sep. 12th

McCallum, A., Freitag, D., & Pereira, F. (2000). Maximum Entropy Markov Models for information extraction and segmentation. In *Proceedings of the 17th International Conference on Machine Learning (ICML'00)*. pp. 591-598.

McCallum, A. (2003). Efficiently inducing features of Conditional Random Fields. In *Proceedings of the 19th Conference in Uncertainty in Artificial Intelligence.* pp. 403-410.

Mika, P. (2005) Flink: Semantic Web Technology for the Extraction and Analysis of Social Networks. *Web Semantics: Science, Services and Agents on the World Wide Web. Vol.3*, 211-223. October 2005.

Mukherjee, S., Yang, G., & Ramakrishnan, I. (2003). Automatic annotation of content-rich HTML documents: structural and semantic analysis. In *Proceedings of the Second International Semantic Web Conference* (pp. 533-549). Sanibel Island, Florida

Muslea, I., Minton, S., & Knoblock, C. (1998). STALKER: Learning extraction rules for semistructured, web-based information sources. In *AAAI Workshop on AI and Information Integration.* pp. 74-81.

Muslea, I., Minton, S., & Knoblock, C. (1999a). Hierarchical wrapper induction for semistructured information sources. *Autonomous Agents and Multi-Agent Systems, Vol.4*, pp. 93-114.

Muslea, I. (1999b). Extraction patterns for information extraction tasks: A survey. In *Proceedings of AAAI-99: Workshop on Machine Learning for Information Extraction.* Orlando.

Muslea, I., Minton, S., & Knoblock, C. A. (2003). Active learning with strong and weak views: A case study on wrapper induction. In *Proceedings of the International Joint Conference on Artificial Intelligence (IJCAI).* Acapulco, Mexico.

Nocedal, J. & Wright, S. J. (1999). *Numerical optimization.* New York: Springer press.

Peng, F. (2001). *Models for Information Extraction*. Technique Report.

Pennacchiotti, M. & Pantel, P. (2006). A Bootstrapping Algorithm for Automatically Harvesting Semantic Relations. In *Proceedings of Inference in Computational Semantics (ICoS-06)*, Buxton (England)

Popov, B., Kiryakov, A., Kirilov, A., Manov, D., Ognyanoff, D., & Goranov, M. (2003). KIM – semantic annotation platform. In *Proceedings of 2nd International Semantic Web Conference* (pp. 834-849). Florida, USA.

Riloff, E. (1993). Automatically Constructing a Dictionary for Information Extraction Tasks. In *Proceedings of the Eleventh National Conference on Artificial Intelligence*. pp. 811-816.

Rosenfeld, B. & Feldman, R. (2007). Using Corpus Statistics on Entities to Improve Semi-supervised Relation Extraction from the Web. In *Proceedings of the 45th Annual Meeting of the Association of Computational Linguistics (ACL2007)*, pp. 600-607.

Roth, D. & Wen, T. Y. (2002). Probabilistic Reasoning for Entity & Relation Recognition. In *Proceedings of the 19th International Conference on Computational linguistics, Vol.1.* 1-7. Taipei, Taiwan

Schölkopf, B., Burges, C. JC, & Smola, A. J. (1999). *Advances in kernel methods: Support vector learning.* MA: MIT Press.

Schutz, A. & Buitelaar, P. (2005). RelExt: A Tool for Relation Extraction from Text in Ontology Extension. In *Proceedings of International Semantic Web Conference* (*ISWC'05*). pp. 593-606.

Sha, F. & Pereira, F. (2003). Shallow parsing with Conditional Random Fields. In *Proceedings of Human Language Technology, NAACL*. pp. 188-191.

Shapire, R. E. (1999). A brief introduction to Boosting. In *Proceedings of the 16th International Joint Conference on Artificial Intelligence (IJCAI-1999)*. pp. 1401-1405.

Shewchuk, J. R. (1994). *An introduction to the conjugate gradient method without the agonizing pain*, from http://www-2.cs.cmu.edu/.jrs/jrspapers.html#cg.

Siefkes, C., & Siniakov, P. (2005). An overview and classification of adaptive approaches to information extraction. *Journal on Data Semantics IV.* Berlin, Germany: Springer.

Skounakis, M., Craven, M., & Ray, S. (2003). Hierarchical Hidden Markov Models for Information Extraction. In *Proceedings of the 18th International Joint Conference on Artificial Intelligence.* Acapulco, Mexico.

Soderland, S., Fisher, D., Aseltine, J., & Lehnert, W. (1995). CRYSTAL: Inducing a conceptual dictionary. In *Proceedings of the Fourteenth International Joint Conference on Artificial Intelligence (IJCAI'95).* pp. 1314-1319.

Soderland, S. (1999). Learning information extraction rules for semi-structured and free text. *Machine Learning.* Boston: Kluwer Academic Publishers

Soni, A. (2006) Protein Interaction Extraction from Medline Abstracts Using Conditional Random Fields. Technical Report, from http://www.cs.wisc.edu/~apirak/cs/cs838/soni_report.pdf

Sproat, R., Black, A., Chen, S., Kumar, S., Ostendorf, M., & Richards, C. (1999). Normalization of Non-Standard Words, WS'99 Final Report.

Suchanek, F.M., Ifrim, G., & Weikum, G. (2006). Combining Linguistic and Statistical Analysis to Extract Relations from Web Documents. In *Proceedings of the 12th ACM SIGKDD.* pp.712-717.

Sutton, C., Rohanimanesh, K., & McCallum, A. (2004). Dynamic conditional random fields:

factorized probabilistic models for labeling and segmenting sequence data. In *Proceedings of ICML'2004*. pp. 783-790.

Sutton, C. & McCallum, A. (2006). An introduction to Conditional Random Fields for relational learning. In L. Getoor & B. Taskar (Eds.), *Statistical Relational Learning*, forthcoming book.

Tang, J., Li, J., Lu, H., Liang, B., & Wang, K. (2005). iASA: learning to annotate the semantic web. *Journal on Data Semantic, IV*, 110-145. Springer Press.

Tang, J., Hong, M., Li, J., & Liang, B. (2006). Tree-structured conditional random fields for semantic annotation. In *Proceedings of 5th International Conference of Semantic Web* (*ISWC'2006*), pp. 640-653.

Tang, J., Hong, M., Zhang, D., Liang, B., & Li, J. (2007a). Information extraction: methodologies and applications. In: H. A. Prado & E. Ferneda (Eds.), *The Book of Emerging Technologies of Text Mining: Techniques and Applications*. Hershey, USA: Idea Group Inc, pp. 1-33.

Tang, J., Zhang, D., Zhang, D., Yao, L., & Zhu, C. (2007b). ArnetMiner: An Expertise Oriented Search System for Web Community. Semantic Web Challenge. In *Proceedings of the 6th International Conference of Semantic Web* (*ISWC'2007*).

Tang, J., Zhang, D., & Yao, L. (2007c). Social Network Extraction of Academic Researchers. In *Proceedings of 2007 IEEE International Conference on Data Mining (ICDM'2007).*

Taskar, B., Guestrin, C., & Koller, D. (2003) Max-Margin Markov Networks. In *Proceedings of Annual Conference on Neural Information Processing Systems*. Vancouver, Canada

Vapnik, V. (1998). Statistical Learning Theory. New York: Springer Verlag

Vapnik V. (1999). *The Nature of Statistical Learning Theory*. New York: Springer Verlag

Vargas-Vera, M., Motta, E., Domingue, J., Lanzoni, M., Stutt, A., & Ciravegna, F. (2002). MnM: ontology driven semi-automatic and automatic support for semantic markup. In *Proceedings of the 13th International Conference on Knowledge Engineering and Management*. pp. 379-391.

Wainwright, M., Jaakkola, T., & Willsky, A. (2001). Tree-based reparameterization for approximate estimation on loopy graphs. In *Proceedings of Advances in Neural Information Processing Systems (NIPS'2001)*. pp. 1001-1008.

Xun, E., Huang, C., and Zhou M. (2000). A Unified Statistical Model for the Identification of English baseNP. In *Proceedings of the 38rd Annual Meeting of the Association for Computational Linguistics* (*ACL'2000*).

Yedidia, J. S., Freeman, W. T., & Weiss, Y. (2003). Understanding Belief Propagation and its Generalization. In: G. Lakemeyer & B. Nebel (Eds.), Exploring Artificial intelligence in the new millennium (pp. 239-269). San Francisco: Morgan Kaufmann Publishers Inc.

Zelenko, D., Aone, C., & Richardella, A. (2003). Kernel Methods for Relation Extraction. *Journal of Machine Learning Research. Vol. 3*, 1083-1106.

Zhang, M., Zhang, J., & Su, J. (2006). Exploring Syntactic Features for Relation Extraction using a Convolution Tree Kernel. In *Proceedings of the Human Language Technology Conference of the North American Chapter of the ACL* (*HLT-NAACL'2006*). pp. 288-295. New York.

Zhao, S. & Grishman, R. (2005). Extracting relations with integrated information using kernel methods. In *Proceedings of the 43rd Annual Meeting of the Association for Computational Linguistics* (*ACL'2005*).

Zhou, G., Su, J., Zhang, J., & Zhang, M. (2005). Exploring Various Knowledge in Relation Extraction. In *Proceedings of the 43rd Annual Meeting of the Association for Computational Linguistics.*

Zhu, J., Nie, Z., Wen, J., Zhang, B., & Ma, W. (2005). 2D Conditional Random Fields for Web information extraction. In *Proceedings of 22nd International Conference on Machine Learning.* pp. 1044-1051.

Zhu, J., Nie, Z., Zhang B., & Wen J. (2007). Dynamic Hierarchical Markov Random Fields and their Application to Web Data Extraction. In *Proceedings of ICML2007.*

ACE: NIST, 2003, Automatic Content Extraction. www.nist.gove/speech/tests/ace

MUC: NIST, 1999, Message Understanding Conference. http://www.itl.nist.gov/iaui/894.02/related_projects/muc/proceedings/ie_task.html

ADDITIONAL READING

Adwait, R. (1996). Maximum Entropy Model for POS tagging. In *Proceedings of the Conference on Empirical Methods in Natural Language Processing.* pp.133-142. Somerset, New Jersey, 1996.

Ahn, D. (2006). The Stages of Event Extraction. *In Proceedings of the Workshop on Annotating and Reasoning about Time and Events.* pp. 1–8. Sydney, July 2006.

Allen, J. (1994). Natural Language Understanding (2nd Edition). Addison Wesley. 1994

Altun, Y., Tsochantaridis, I., & Hofmann, T. (2003). Hidden Markov Support Vector Machines. *In Proceedings of the 20th International Conference on Machine Learning (ICML 2003).*

Appelt, D. & Israel, D. (1999). Introduction to Information Extraction Technology. *In Proceedings of International Joint Conference on Artificial Intelligence (IJCAI'99) Tutorial.*

Baeza-Yates, R. & Tiberi, A. (2007). Extracting Semantic Relations from Query Logs. In *Proceedings of KDD2007.*

Baum, L. E. & Petrie, T. (1966). Statistical Inference for Probabilistic Functions of Finite State Markov Chains. *Annual of Mathematical statistics*, 37:1554-1563, 1966.

Borthwick, A., Sterling, J., Agichtein, E., & Grishman, R. (1998). Exploiting Diverse Knowledge Sources via Maximum Entropy in Named Entity Recognition. *In Proceedings of the Sixth Workshop on Very Large Corpora New Brunswick*, New Jersey.

Branavan, S.R.K., Deshpande, P. & Barzilay, R. (2007). Generating a Table-of-Contents. In *Proceedings of the 45th Annual Meeting of the Association of Computational Linguistics*, pages 544–551, ACL2007

Bunescu, R.C. & Mooney, R.J. (2004). Collective Information Extraction with Relational Markov Networks. *In Proceedings of Association of Computing Linguistics (ACL'2004).*

Cafarella, M.J., Downey, D., Soderland, S., & Etzioni, O. (2005). KnowItNow: Fast, Scalable Information Extraction from the Web. In *Proceedings of Human Language Technology Empirical Methods in Natural Language Processing (HLT/EMNLP'2005).*

Chang, M., Ratinov, L., & Roth D. (2007). Guiding Semi-Supervision with Constraint-Driven Learning. In *Proceedings of the 45th Annual Meeting of the Association of Computational Linguistics (ACL2007)*, pages 280–287

Chieu, H.L. (2002). A Maximum Entropy Approach to Information Extraction from Semi-Structured and Free Text. *In Proceedings of the Eighteenth National Conference on Artificial Intelligence (AAAI'2002).* pp.786-791.

Chu-Carroll, J. & Prager, J. An Experimental Study of the Impact of Information Extraction Accuracy on Semantic Search Performance. In *Proceedings of Conference on Information and Knowledge Management (CIKM2007).*

Collins, M. (2002). Discriminative Training Methods for Hidden Markov Models: Theory and Experiments with Perceptron Algorithms. In *Proceedings of the Conference on Empirical Methods in Natural Language Processing (EMNLP'2002).* pp.1-8, July 06, 2002.

Dietterich, T. (2002). Machine Learning for Sequential Data: A Review. In *Proceedings of the Joint IAPR International Workshop on Structural, Syntactic, and Statistical Pattern Recognition.* pp. 15–30. 2002. Springer-Verlag.

Downey, D., Etzioni, O., & Soderland, S. (2005). A Probabilistic Model of Redundancy in Information Extraction. In *Proceedings of 22th International Joint Conference on Artificial Intelligence (IJCAI'2005).* pp. 1034-1041.

Duchi, J., Tarlow, D., Elidan, G. & Koller, D. (2006) Using Combinatorial Optimization within Max-Product Belief Propagation. In *Proceedings of Advances in Neural Information Processing Systems (NIPS2006)*

Durbin, R., Eddy, S., Krogh, A., & Mitchison, G. (1998). Biological sequence analysis: Probabilistic models of proteins and nucleic acids. Cambridge University Press, 1998.

Eikvil, L. (1999). Information Extraction from World Wide Web - A Survey. Rapport Nr. 945, July, 1999.

Embley, D.W. (2004). Toward Semantic Understanding - An Approach Based on Information Extraction. In *Proceedings of the Fifteenth Australasian Database Conference*, 2004.

Felzenszwalb, P. F., & Huttenlocher, D. P. (2006). Efficient Belief Propagation for Early Vision. *International Journal of Computer Vision*, Vol. 70, No. 1, October 2006.

Gatterbauer, W., Bohunsky, P., Herzog, M., Kr¨upl, B. & Pollak B. (2007). Towards Domain Independent Information Extraction from Web Tables. In *Proceedings of World Wide Web Conference (WWW2007).*

Grishman, R. & Sundheim, B. (1996). Message Understanding Conference –6: A Brief History. In *Proceedings of the 16th International Conference on Computational Linguistics*, Copenhagen, June 1996.

Haghighi, A. & Klein, D. (2007). Unsupervised Coreference Resolution in a Nonparametric Bayesian Model. In *Proceedings of Association of Computing Linguistics (ACL2007).*

Hu, Y., Li, H., Cao, Y., Meyerzon, D., Teng, L., & Zheng, Q. (2006). Automatic Extraction of Titles from General Documents using Machine Learning. *Information Processing and Management.* pp.1276-1293, 2006

Huffman, S.B. (1995). Learning Information Extraction Patterns from Examples. In *Proceedings of Learning for Natural Language Processing'1995.* pp. 246-260.

Jackson, P. & Moulinier, I. (2002). Natural Language Processing for Online Applications. John Benjamins, 2002.

Janssens, F., Glänzel, W. & Moor, B. D. (2007). Dynamic Hybrid Clustering of Bioinformatics by Incorporating Text Mining and Citation Analysis. In *Proceedings of ACM SIGKDD2007.*

Jin, W., Ho, H., & Wu, X. (2007). Improving Knowledge Discovery by Combining Text Mining and Link Analysis Techniques. In *Proceedings of International Conference on Data Mining (ICDM2007).*

Jordan, M. I. & Weiss, Y. (2002). Graphical Models: Probabilistic Inference. In M. Arbib (Eds.),

The Handbook of Brain Theory and Neural Networks, 2nd edition. Cambridge, MA: MIT Press, 2002.

Klein, D. & Manning, C. (2002). Conditional Structure Versus Conditional Estimation in NLP Models. In *Proceedings of the Conference on Empirical Methods in Natural Language Processing (EMNLP'2002)*, Philadelphia.

Kou, Z. & Cohen, W. W. (2007). Stacked Graphical Models for Efficient Inference in Markov Random Fields. In *Proceedings of SIAM Conference on Data Mining (SDM2007).*

Krishnan, V. & Manning, C. D. (2006). An Effective Two-Stage Model for Exploiting Non-Local Dependencies in Named Entity Recognition *Proceedings of the 21st International Conference on Computational Linguistics and 44th Annual Meeting of the ACL*, pages 1121–1128, ACL2006

Kschischang, F. R., Frey, B. J., & Loeliger, H. (2001). Factor Graphs and the Sum-Product Algorithm. *IEEE Transitions on Information Theory,* VOL. 47, No. 2, February, 2001.

Laender, A.H.F., Ribeiro-Neto, B.A., da Silva, A.S., & Teixeira, J.S. (2002). A Brief Survey of Web Data Extraction Tools. *Journal of ACM SIGMOD Record*, 2002.

Leek, T.B. (1997). Information Extraction Using Hidden Markov Models. M.S. thesis.

Moens, M. (2006). Information Extraction: Algorithms and Prospects in a Retrieval Context. Springer press

Li, Y. & Bontcheva K. (2007). Hierarchical, Perceptron like Learning for Ontology Based Information Extraction In *Proceedings of World Wide Web (WWW2007).*

Li, Y., Bontcheva, K., & Cunningham, H. (2005). Using Uneven-Margins SVM and Perceptron for Information Extraction. In *Proceedings of Ninth Conference on Computational Natural Language Learning (CoNLL-2005).* pp.72-79

Manning, C., & Schutze, H. (1999). Markov Models. In Book: Foundations of Statistical Natural Language Processing. The MIT Press. 1999.

Nie, Z., Ma, Y., Shi, S., Wen, J., & Ma., W. (2007). Web Object Retrieval. In *Proceedings of World Wide Web (WWW2007).*

Pazienza, M.T. (1999). Information Extraction: Towards Scalable, Adaptable Systems. Springer press.

Pham, T. T, Maillot, N., Lim, J. H., & Chevallet, J. P. (2007). Latent Semantic Fusion Model for Image Retrieval and Annotation. In *Proceedings of Conference on Information and Knowledge Management (CIKM2007)*

Punyakanok, V. & Roth, D. (2001). The Use of Classifiers in Sequential Inference. In *Proceedings of NIPS'01.* pp.995-1001.

Rabiner, L. A. (1989). Tutorial on Hidden Markov Models and Selected Applications in Speech Recognition. In *Proceedings of the IEEE'1989.*

Shawe-Taylor, J. & Cristianini, N. (2000). Introduction to Support Vector Machines. Cambridge University Press, 2000

Sutton, C. & McCallum A. (2005). Composition of Conditional Random Fields for Transfer Learning. In *Proceedings of Human Language Technology Empirical Methods in Natural Language Processing (HLT/EMNLP2005).*

Sutton, C. & McCallum, A. (2007). Piecewise Pseudolikelihood for Efficient Training of Conditional Random Fields. In *Proceedings of International Conference on Machine Learning (ICML2007).*

Vishwanathan, S.V. N., Schraudolph, N. N., Schmidt, M. W., & Murphy, K. P. (2006). Accelerated Training of Conditional Random Fields with Stochastic Gradient Methods. In *Proceedings of the 23 rd International Conference on Machine Learning (ICML2006)*

Wainwright, M. J., Jaakkola, T. S., & Willsky, A. S. (2003). Tree-based reparameterization framework for analysis of sum-product and related algorithms. *IEEE transaction on Information Theory*, 49:1120-1146

Wainwright, M. J., & Jordan, M. I. (2005). A Variational Principle for Graphical Models. Chapter 11 in New Directions in Statistical Signal Processing. In Haykin, S., Principe, J., Sejnowski, T., & McWhirter, J. (Eds.). MIT Press.

Wang, X. (2007). SHINE: Search Heterogeneous Interrelated Entities. In *Proceedings of Conference on Information and Knowledge Management (CIKM2007).*

Wang, R. C. & Cohen, W. W. (2007). Language-Independent Set Expansion of Named Entities using the Web. In *Proceedings of International Conference on Data Mining (ICDM2007).*

Zhang, Z. (2004). Weakly-Supervised Relation Classification for Information Extraction. In *Proceedings of the Thirteenth ACM International Conference on Information and Knowledge Management (CIKM'2004).* pp581-588.

Zhang, W., Liu, S., Sun, C., Liu, F., Meng, W., & Yu. C. T. (2007). Recognition and Classification of Noun Phrases in Queries for Effective Retrieval. In *Proceedings of Conference on Information and Knowledge Management (CIKM2007).*

Section II

Chapter VII
Paving the Way to an Effective and Efficient Retrieval of Data over Semantic Overlay Networks

Federica Mandreoli
University of Modena and Reggio Emilia, Italy

Riccardo Martoglia
University of Modena and Reggio Emilia, Italy

Wilma Penzo
University of Bologna, Italy

Simona Sassatelli
University of Modena and Reggio Emilia, Italy

Giorgio Villani
University of Modena and Reggio Emilia, Italy

ABSTRACT

In a Peer-to-Peer (P2P) system, a Semantic Overlay Network (SON) models a network of peers whose connections are influenced by the peers' content, so that semantically related peers connect with each other. This is very common in P2P communities, where peers share common interests, and a peer can belong to more than one SON, depending on its own interests. Querying such a kind of systems is not an easy task: The retrieval of relevant data can not rely on flooding approaches which forward a query to the overall network. A way of selecting which peers are more likely to provide relevant answers is necessary to support more efficient and effective query processing strategies. This chapter presents a semantic infrastructure for routing queries effectively in a network of SONs. Peers are semantically rich, in that peers' content is modelled with a schema on their local data, and peers are related each other through semantic mappings defined between their own schemas. A query is routed through the network by means of a sequence of reformulations, according to the semantic mappings encountered in the routing path. As reformulations may lead to semantic approximations, we define a fully distributed indexing mechanism which summarizes the semantics underlying whole subnetworks, in order to be able to locate the semantically best directions to forward a query to. In support of our proposal, we demonstrate through a rich set of experiments that our routing mechanism overtakes algorithms which are usually limited to the only knowledge of the peers directly connected to the querying peer, and that our approach is particularly successful in a SONs scenario.

OVERVIEW AND MOTIVATION

In recent years, Peer-to-Peer (P2P) systems have known an enormous success among Internet users. In these systems, each user, called peer, connects to other users (peers) for data sharing purposes. Notable examples are (*Napster*), (*Kazaa*), and (*Gnutella*), just to mention a few. The large diffusion of this phenomenon emphasized the need of efficient algorithms for the retrieval of relevant information. In fact, a P2P system usually involves a high number of peers, and approaches which flood the network with a huge amount of messages are not adequate as to efficiency as well as to effectiveness purposes. Thus, a key challenge when querying a large set of peers is *query routing* (Crespo and Garcia-Molina, 2002), i.e., the capability of selecting a small subset of relevant peers to forward a query to.

On the other hand, as envisioned by the Semantic Web (Berners-Lee, Hendler, and Lassila, 2001), the need of complementing the Web with more semantics has spurred much efforts towards a rich representation of data. Thus, being peers given more semantics, new potentialities are available as to query formulation, and, consequently, new challenges arise for query processing.

In this view, Peer Data Management Systems (PDMSs) have been introduced as a solution to the problem of large-scale sharing of semantically rich data (Halevy *et al.*, 2004). Peers are semantically rich, in that peers' content is modelled with a schema on their local data, and peers are related each other through semantic mappings defined between their own schemas. In such a scenario, queries can be semantically richer than keyword-based search, rather they can be complex queries on ontologies, XML schemas, RDF schemas, aso. However, the key problem is that peers do not know *where* to find information, and in some sense a P2P network resembles a social network to a large extent, in that a question is asked to the person who one assumes that she best answers the question (Tempich, Staab, and Wranik, 2004).

Similar motivations underlie the concept of Semantic Overlay Networks (SONs) (Crespo and Garcia-Molina, 2004), where peers connects to other peers on the basis of the similarity of their semantic content. SONs cut down the inefficiencies due to random connections among peers, where queries are blindly forwarded from node to node. Then, despite of several P2P systems that require a rigid placement of content in specific nodes for efficient query processing purposes (e.g. Stoica, Morris, Karger, Kaashoek, and Balakrishnan, 2001), SONs allow peers to be autonomous as to the content they store locally, and to the connections they establish with other peers.

In such a semantically rich scenario, a query on the network is routed through semantic paths, i.e. sequences of semantic mappings between pairs of peers. In this process, a query undergoes a multi-step reformulation which may involve a chain of semantic approximations, and, consequently, the returned data may not exactly fit with the query conditions.

Our proposal is to exploit such approximations for selecting the directions which are *more likely* to provide the best results to a given query. To this purpose, semantic mappings can be conveniently extended with a score to reflect the relevance of peer's data to a query. Then, an important aspect to be considered is that a PDMS underlies a potentially very large network able to handle huge amounts of data. In this context, any relevant peer may add new answers to a given query and different paths to the same peer may yield different answers (Tatarinov and Halevy, 2004). Also for this reason, query routing is a fundamental issue for querying distributed resources. In particular, in a Semantic Web perspective, a query posed over a given peer should be forwarded to the most relevant peers that offer semantically related results among its immediate neighbors first, then among their immediate neighbors, and so on.

Our perspective is knowledge-based, in that the routing of a query is guided by the semantic mappings between the peers. To this end, each peer locally maintains a *Semantic Routing Index (SRI)* which summarizes, for each concept of the peer's schema, the semantic approximation "skills" of each subnetwork reachable from its immediate neighbors, and thus gives a hint of the relevance of the data which can be reached in each path. Broadly speaking, some kind of information about the relevance of the whole semantic paths should be available in the network, maintained up-to-date, and easily accessible for query routing purposes.

In this chapter, we present SRIs as a fully distributed indexing mechanism for routing queries effectively and efficiently in such a context. The semantic knowledge stored in a SRI is summarized on the available directions in order to maintain the size of the semantic index proportional to the number of neighbors, thus scaling well in a network of semantic peers.

Our framework easily applies to a distributed scenario like a PDMS environment, yet well fitting into other application areas, for instance into any query answering setting where semantic heterogeneity is pervasive, such as Dataspaces or into Personal Information Management platforms (Halevy, Franklin, and Maier, 2006).

Leveraging on our previous work on PDMSs (Mandreoli, Martoglia, Penzo, and Sassatelli, 2006), we present the peculiarities of our proposal and we consider a more general scenario according to several directions:

- We extend the notion of semantic mapping and semantic paths with a score, expressing the grade of uncertainty which naturally arises from establishing a correspondence between semantic concepts. To this purpose we rely on the fuzzy set theory (Klir and Yuan, 1995).
- We consider complex queries as conjunctions and disjunctions of conditions on the concepts of a peer's schema.
- With the aim of evaluating the effectiveness of SRIs, we investigate different navigation strategies for query routing purposes.
- We conduct an extensive set of experiments on SONs, and we prove the successfulness of SRIs in clustered networks.

We start introducing the basics of P2P systems, PDMSs, and SONs, by taking advantage of a reference example that will be used throughout the chapter, and we discuss related work. We then present SRIs and we show how they are built and used for query processing purposes. SRIs evolution in response to network changes is also considered. Afterwards, we go into details for the query answering process, by specifying how semantic approximation is computed for complex queries, and how these are executed. Then, we demonstrate through a rich set of experiments the effectiveness of our routing mechanism, and we prove that our approach is particularly successful in a SONs scenario. We finally conclude and discuss future research directions we intend to follow.

P2P SYSTEMS AND SEMANTIC OVERLAY NETWORKS

Basic P2P computing is simply defined as the sharing of computer resources and services by direct exchange (Barkai, 2000). Each participating computer, referred to as a peer, acts both as a client and as a server in the application perspective, i.e. in sharing resources such as, for instance, music, images, bibliographic data, and so on. No centralized architecture is present, while the focus is on self-organized systems allowing a dynamic network behavior. This flexibility is possible thanks to the multiple layers on which a P2P system is based: Along with the *physical layer*, an *overlay layer* allows the connection and organization of the nodes following various strategies. Different kinds of overlay networks have been proposed over the years: *Unstructured networks*, e.g. (*Gnutella*), which allow complete autonomy as to the network organization as well as to the content of the data sources (peers), whereas often being less efficient in the information searching phase which usually floods the network (Ng, Ooi, Tan, and Zhou, 2003); *Structured networks*, where data retrieval is indeed more efficient, at the expense of constraining data location to be totally controlled by the system, e.g. CAN (Ratnasamy, Francis, Handley, Karp, & Schenker, 2001), Chord (Stoica *et al.*, 2001), Pastry (Rowstron and Druschel, 2001), Tapestry (Zhao, Kubiatowicz, and Joseph, 2001), Freenet (Clarke, Sandberg, Wiley, and Hong, 2000), P-Grid (Aberer 2001), and Maan (Cai, Frank, Chen, and Szekely, 2004); *Hierarchical networks*, e.g. (*Napster, Kazaa*), where peers are organized in a hierarchical fashion, so that a subset of peers, called super-peers, is identified, where each super-peer is responsible for a subnetwork of peers (Kleis, Lua, and Zhou 2005; Renda, and Callan, 2004; Nejdl *et al.*, 2003).

In such distributed scenarios the problem of effective and efficient retrieval of data is a particularly complex issue that has been tackled by researchers in past few years. While all these systems can be usefully adopted for "simple" applications such as file sharing, they provide only very basic data management capabilities, and rarely offer mechanisms to represent and exploit truly heterogeneous data and their semantics, with negative consequences as to the effective localization and retrieval of complex information. Most of these systems base their search capabilities on distributed hash table lookups to locate information, and only standard Information Retrieval-style keyword search is provided. Actually, in these systems efficiency of query answering is often achieved at the expense of both network flexibility and peer autonomy. Furthermore, peers' query capabilities are limited to exact match of data, thus being lacking in any support to deal with data heterogeneity, which is a crucial issue in an open environment, as P2P systems are. A further step is then needed in order to be able to effectively manage and query heterogeneous but semantically related data in the network. This step is represented by Peer Data Management Systems (PDMSs).

Peer Data Management Systems' Basics

PDMSs are a recent evolution of original P2P systems, synthesizing database world semantic expressiveness and P2P network flexibility. They intend to offer a decentralized and easily extensible architecture for advanced data management, in which anytime every node can act freely on its data, while in the meantime accessing data stored by other participants. The core idea is to allow peers to use different *schemas* to represent their own data, and to manage this heterogeneity by means of a *semantic mediation layer* which is used to relate data above the actual overlay network. The most successful PDMSs, such as Hyperion (Arenas *et al.*, 2003) or Piazza (Halevy *et al.*, 2003; Halevy *et al.*, 2004), base their data interoperability on the concept of *semantic mappings*, where the correspondences between semantically equivalent schema portions are represented. This is crucial for the querying operation: A query posed at a given peer is usually answered presenting the local data but, most importantly, it might be propagated through the network to retrieve further useful information possibly owned by other peers. In this context, semantic mappings allow the query to be appropriately *reformulated* in order to be compatible with the different schemas.

Figure 1 depicts a very small portion of a PDMS managing bibliographic data. Each peer composing the network is enriched with a schema (in this case, represented by a fragment of an OWL ontology) representing its domain of interests. Semantic mappings are locally established between the peers' schemas, and are depicted as bold lines. In Figure 1, classes (such as "Paper") start with a capital letter and are shown with a dark circle in order to differentiate them from properties (such as "title"). A query can be posed, for instance, on Peerl, by asking to "Retrieve the titles of the scientific papers written by author Alon Halevy". Peerl will directly provide the answers based on its local information. However many other peers in the network, such as Peer2, Peer 3 or Peer4 in Figure, could contribute to provide useful related results. Thus, the query needs to be appropriately *reformulated* and then forwarded in the network by following suitable *semantic paths*: "Paper" could become "Article" for Peer2 and Peer4, and so on.

Because it is not desirable to flood the network with queries to all peers, some kind of query routing mechanism should be supported. *Query routing* is the process of selecting a small subset of relevant peers to forward a query to. In a PDMS, we can take advantage of the semantic layer to select the most semantically relevant peers. Consider again Figure 1: Peerl's neighbors Peer2 and Peer4 are very similar as to the portion of the schemas involved in the query; however, as to the second step of query reformulation,

Figure 1. A sample portion of a bibliographic PDMS

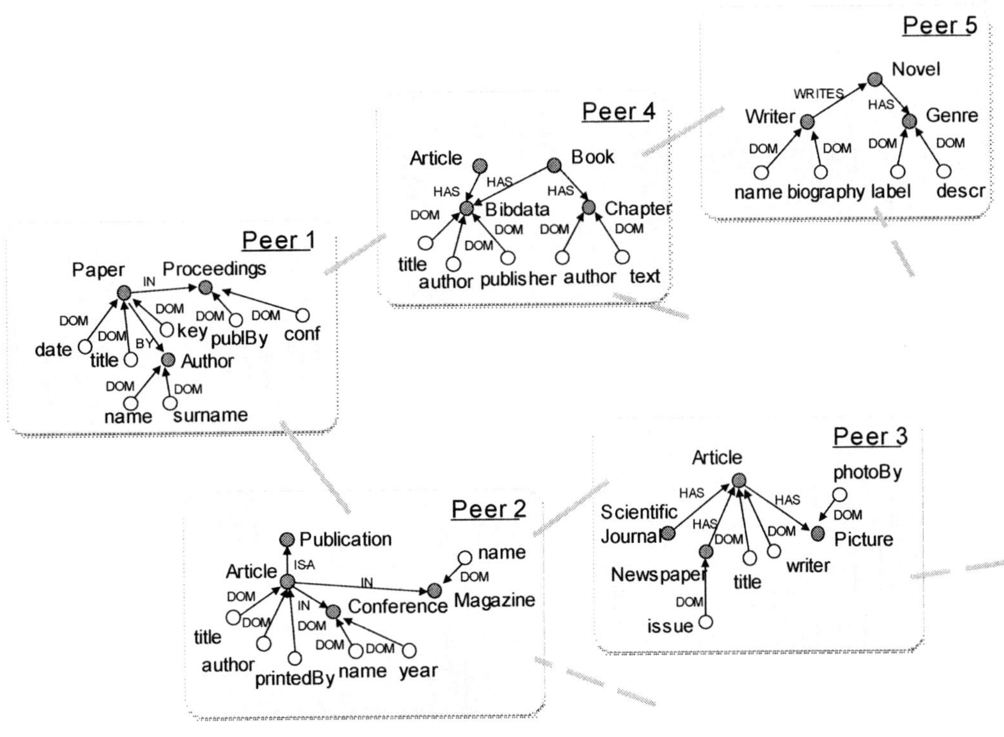

Peer3 is more relevant than Peer5, since, besides newspapers ones, it deals with scientific articles, whereas Peer5 is about novels. Therefore, it can be supposed that forwarding the query through the path Peer1-Peer2-Peer3 would deliver better results than path Peer1-Peer4-Peer5.

In the next section we will deepen our understanding of the importance of exploiting semantic information for an optimal organization of the network overlay structure (by introducing the concept of Semantic Overlay Network) and, ultimately, for query routing purposes in such environments.

Routing Queries over Semantic Overlay Networks

From the considerations outlined above, it is clear that the ability to obtain relevant data from other nodes in a PDMS network is heavily dependent on the existence of "good" semantic paths to those nodes. These paths relate the terms used in the query with the terms used by the node providing the data. Because long paths inevitably bring to information losses, due to missing or incomplete mappings, the network of mappings in a PDMS should be boosted such that peers containing similar concepts are close, thus giving rise to "short" paths (Halevy, Ives, Suciu, and Tatarinov, 2005).

Being able to improve the retrieval of the required data, while maintaining a high degree of node autonomy, is exactly the main goal pursued by one of the most recent evolutions in network organization strategies: *Semantic Overlay Networks* (SONs).

SONs present a further evolution in the semantic mediation layer management: The key idea is to exploit self-organization principles in order to "cluster" together semantically similar nodes and, thus, similar contents. There are several proposals dealing with different aspects of SONs. Crespo and Garcia-Molina (2004) propose the original SON idea, which is based on a classification method for assigning peers to SONs through hierarchies which are shared in the network. Other works address the problem of building SONs. The papers (Aberer, Cudré-Mauroux, Hauswirth, and van Pelt, 2004; Comito, Patarin, and Talia, 2005; Linari and Weikum, 2006) adopt gossip-based membership protocols to derive neighborhoods and, then, SONs translate to the sets of those peers which are logically interconnected. In the schema-based P2P scenario considered in (Aberer *et al.*, 2004), semantic gossiping is applied to derive as neighbors the peers that have annotated their data according to the same schema. A similar approach is also adopted in (Comito *et al.*, 2005) where the resulting unstructured network coexists with a DHT-based structured one in a hybrid topology. In (Linari and Weikum, 2006), a metric distance for Language Models is adopted to compare the peer's local collections of documents to decide whether two peers should become neighbors.

Other works (Bawa, Manku, and Raghavan, 2003; Doulkeridis, Nørvåg, and Vazirgiannis, 2007; Li, Lee, and Sivasubramaniam, 2004; Triantafillou, Xiruhaki, Koubarakis, and Ntarmos, 2003) found on principles of clustering in order to provide answers to the issue of how to actually create SONs of autonomous peers for efficient IR search. In (Doulkeridis *et al.*, 2007) the clustering method is guided by description of peers in terms of processing power, storage capacity, etc., and the network of peers results in a hierarchical organization. Instead, (Bawa *et al.*, 2003; Li *et al.*, 2004) propose to cluster together peers sharing objects with similar representations and maintains intra- and inter-cluster connections. In (Triantafillou *et al.*, 2003), the main focus is to ensure load balancing in a network where nodes are logically organized into a set of clusters and where a set of super-peer nodes maintains information about which documents are stored by which cluster nodes.

In (Parreira, Michel, and Weikum, 2007) a different perspective is considered. The approach relies on caching high quality peers to be remembered as "friends" to be connected to. Semantic similarity between peers is measured following an IR-style approach based on term frequency distributions. Querying histories and levels of trust of each participant are also considered when establishing peer connections.

In a SON organization, each peer belongs to one or more SONs. Figure 2 shows a possible SON organization of a larger portion of the previously considered bibliographic PDMS, where SONs boundaries are represented as rectangles: For instance, Peers 1 to 4 deal with scientific publications data and thus belong to the "scientific bibliography SON" (SON1 in Figure), and Peer4 also belongs to the "books bibliography SON" (SON3), since it mainly deals with book data. All peers belong to a general bibliography SON (SON4).

In a SON organization, queries are processed by identifying which SONs are best suited to answer it, then the query is forwarded mainly to the members of that SON, thus allowing an optimal allocation of resources and a performance improvement in query management. For instance, thanks to the SONs organization, our sample query on Peer1 would be primarily managed by the nodes in SON1.

For the sake of simplicity, the SON presented above is a "toy" network; however, in the real world, SONs could include several peers having different query answering capabilities. Thus, as to efficiency, a key challenge is query routing, so as to select only a subset of (the most) relevant peers to be contacted for answers.

While simple P2P systems basically make use of inefficient flooding techniques (e.g. *Gnutella*), much research work in the P2P area has focused on this issue (Stoica *et al.*, 2001; Crespo and Garcia-Molina, 2002; Cooper, 2004; Cuenca-Acuna, Peery, Martin, and Nguyen, 2003; Haase, Siebes, and van Harmelen, 2004; Koloniari and Pitoura 2004; Michel, Bender, Triantafillou, and Weikum,

Figure 2. SON organization example: Bibliography SONs

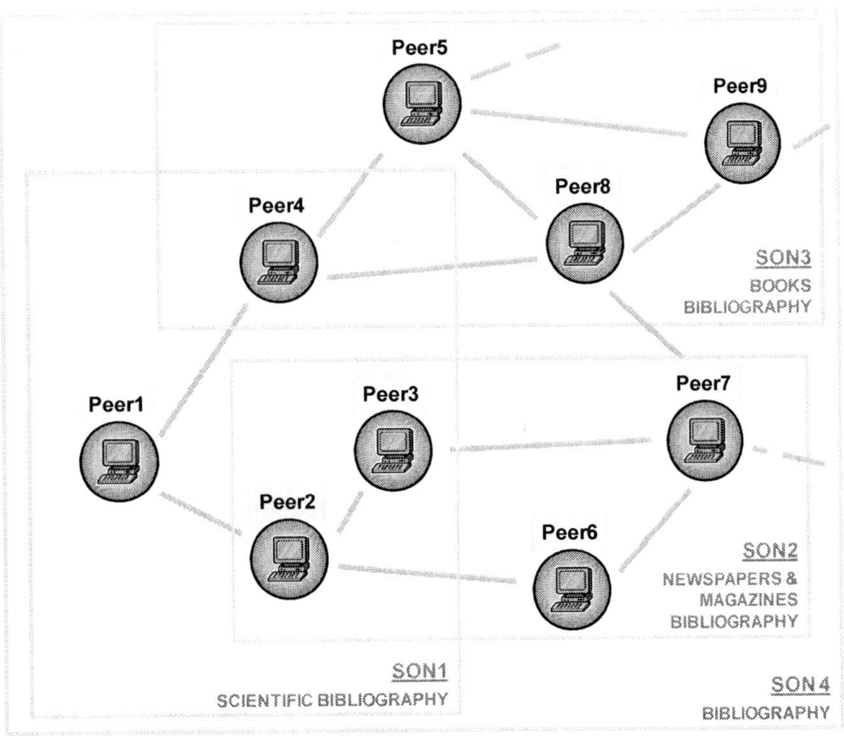

2006; Nejdl *et al.*, 2003; Joseph, 2002; Tempich *et al.*, 2004).

Some of these works discuss id/keyword-based search of documents (Stoica *et al.*, 2001; Cooper, 2004; Michel *et al.*, 2006), some assume a common vocabulary/ontology is shared by peers in the network (Crespo and Garcia-Molina, 2002; Cuenca-Acuna, Peery, Martin, and Nguyen, 2003; Haase *et al.*, 2004), some address scalability of query routing by means of a properly tailored super-peer topology for the network (Nejdl *et al.*,2003), or by adapting their own semantic topology according to the observation of query answering (Tempich *et al.*, 2004). Most of these proposals are based on IR-style and machine-learning techniques exploiting quantitative information about the retrieved results (Crespo and Garcia-Molina, 2002; Cooper, 2004; Koloniari and Pitoura 2004; Michel *et al.*, 2006; Joseph, 2002; Tempich *et al.*, 2004). Basically, they utilize measures that rely on keyword statistics, on the probability of keywords to appear into documents, on the number of documents that can be found along a path of peers, on caching/learning from the number of results returned for a query. However, all these methods do not take into account effectively the presence of heterogeneous semantic knowledge about the contents of the peers in the network: For instance, in (Joseph, 2002) peers are assumed to share the same set of keywords they store data about, whereas in (Tempich *et al.*, 2004) each peer approximates the query concepts with any concept (through the use of wildcards), thus disregarding the semantic similarity between them.

Other approaches (such as Haase *et al.*, 2004) exploit such semantic information. However, all these works (but Crespo and Garcia-Molina's one) provide routing techniques which either assume distributed indices which are indeed conceptually global (Stoica *et al.*, 2001; Michel *et al.*, 2006), or support completely decentralized search algorithms which, nevertheless, exploit information about neighboring peers only. More precisely, the only work (Crespo and Garcia-Molina, 2002) proposes a routing mechanism which does not limit the peer's capability of selecting peers to the information available at a 1-hop horizon. However, the specific data structures proposed by Crespo and Garcia-Molina, although providing a summary of subnetworks' content to provide a *direction* to send a query to, yet are limited to answering only IR-style queries.

In order to provide an effective and efficient query answering mechanism, our proposal is to take full advantage of the semantic layer to forward the query towards the most relevant peers in the network. In particular, due to the heterogeneity of the schemas, the reformulation of a query may lead to some semantic approximation and, consequently, the returned data may not exactly fit with the query conditions. For this purpose, semantic mappings can be conveniently extended with a score, thus giving a measure of the semantic compatibility occurring between the involved portions of schemas. As such scores reflect the relevance of peer's data to a query, we deem that semantic mappings can be exploited in the searching phase to suggest a direction towards the semantic paths which *better* satisfy the query conditions. As a consequence, query execution is improved under the following aspects:

- *Effectiveness* of retrieval, since the search would primarily be directed towards peers belonging to the SONs of interest.
- *Efficiency* of the process, since only the most relevant paths would be selected.

SEMANTIC ROUTING INDICES

Summing up, our reference scenario is represented by a PDMS where each peer stores local data, modelled upon a local schema, and it is connected through semantic mappings to some other peers (named neighbors). Let us denote with P the set of peers of the PDMS. Each peer $p_i \in P$ is a *semantic* peer, as its schema S_i, which can be for instance an ontology, a relational, or an XML schema, describes the semantic contents of the underlying data. Without loss of generality, we consider a peer schema S_i as a set of semantic concepts $\{C_{i_1},...,C_{i_{m_i}}\}$, each one understanding for instance an ontology class, or a relational table, or an XML schema element. Peers are pairwise connected in a semantic network through semantic mappings established between their schemas. In this chapter we abstract from the specific format that semantic mappings may have. For the sake of clarity we consider a simplified scenario, assuming directional, pairwise and one-to-one semantic mappings. Nevertheless, the described approach can be straightforwardly applied to more complex mappings relying on query expressions as proposed in (Arenas *et al.*, 2003; Halevy *et al.*, 2004; Nejdl, Wolf, Staab, and Tane, 2002).

Semantic Mappings

A semantic mapping $M(S_i, S_j)$, established from a source schema S_j to a target schema S_i, defines how to represent S_i in term of S_j's vocabulary. In particular, it associates each concept in S_i to a corresponding concept in S_j, according to a score, denoting the degree of semantic similarity between the two concepts. A formal definition of semantic mappings can be given according to a fuzzy interpretation, relying on the concept of fuzzy relation (Klir and Yuan, 1995). Following this interpretation, a semantic mapping from a source schema S_j to a target schema S_i, not necessarily distinct, is defined as a fuzzy relation $M(S_i,S_j) \subseteq S_i \times S_j$ where each instance (C,C') has a membership grade, $\mu(C,C') \in [0,1]$, denoting the strength of the relation between C and C'. Without loss of generality, we assume that the self mapping $M(S_i, S_i)$ is the identity relation. Notice that a non-mapped concept has membership grade 0. A sample tuple of the semantic mapping between the schemas S_1 and S_2 of the reference example is $M(S_1, S_2)(Paper, Article)=0.8$.

Routing Indices

Whenever a peer joins a PDMS, it selects a small subsets of peers as its neighboring peers, computes the corresponding mappings, and stores them in its local repository. Semantic mappings are then used for query reformulation: When a querying peer p_i forwards the query q to one of its neighbors, say p_j, q must be reformulated into q' so that it refers to concepts of the p_j's schema.

In order to effectively and efficiently answer queries in such a context, semantic query routing is a key issue. In particular, as seen in the previous section, it is fundamental to select the direction which is *more likely* to provide the best results to a given query. To this end, our approach relies on the idea that each peer p associates each concept in its schema to cumulative information summarizing the semantic approximation capabilities of each subnetwork reachable from its neighbors, and thus giving a hint of the relevance of the data which can be reached in each path.

Such information is stored in a local data structure called *Semantic Routing Index (SRI)*. More precisely, the SRI stored at a peer p having n neighbors and m concepts in its schema is a matrix with m columns and n+1 rows, where the first row refers to the knowledge on the local schema of peer p. Each entry *SRI[i][j]* contains a score expressing how the j-th concept is semantically approximated by the subnetwork rooted at the i-th neighbor, i.e. by all paths in the p_i's subnetwork.

Notice that, being SRIs completely distributed indices, the autonomy and dynamicity features of a SON network are fully preserved. Further, scalability is ensured in large SON scenarios, since

Figure 3. Sample SRI

SRI_{Peer1}	Paper	title	Author	...
Peer1	1.0	1.0	1.0	...
Peer2	0.7	0.73	0.7	...
Peer4	0.3	0.2	0.6	...

the amount of semantic knowledge maintained in an SRI is proportional to the available directions, and thus the space required for storing an SRI at a peer is proportional to the number of the peer's neighbors, which is usually quite modest w.r.t. the number of peers which join a PDMS.

A sample of a portion of Peer1's SRI of the reference scenario is shown in Figure 3. For example, the number 0.7 in the cell corresponding to the second row and the first column of the matrix, means that the concept "Paper" is approximated with a score of 0.7 in the subnetwork rooted at Peer2. Notice that scores in the first row are those associated with the self mapping, which we assume to be the identity relation.

Building a SRI

In an SRI, each score *SRI[i][j]* summarizes the semantic approximation capabilities of all the semantic paths that are available for the *j*-th concept starting from the *i*-th neighbor, and should consequently be a sort of summary of the scores that are associated to these paths. Let us now understand how these scores are computed.

Because a semantic path is a chain of semantic mappings connecting a pair of peers, the semantic approximation given by a semantic path can be obtained by *composing* the fuzzy relations understood by the involved mappings. This relies on the notion of generalized composition of binary fuzzy relations (Klir and Yuan, 1995). In particular, we are not properly interested in the instances of the resulting semantic mapping, but rather on their membership grades. Further, the composition function *compose* should capture the intuition that the longer the chain of mappings, the lower the grades, thus denoting the accumulation of semantic approximations given by a sequence of connected peers.

In order to obtain such an effect of semantic attenuation, several alternatives exist for the choice of the specific mathematical function to adopt for the composition of the involved semantic grades (Mandreoli *et al.*, 2006). A possible choice is, for instance, the *algebraic product*: Given that the arguments are grades in [0,1], it is indeed easy to show that their algebraic product is still in [0,1] and it is lower than or at most equal to its arguments. For instance, given the semantic mappings $M(S_1, S_2)(Paper, Article)=0.8$ and $M(S_2, S_3)(Article, Article)= 0.9$ in the reference example, their composition based on the algebraic product yields to the following instance of the semantic path Peer1-Peer2-Peer3: $Path_{Peer1-Peer2-Peer3} \subseteq S_1 \times S_3$: *(Paper, Article)*, with an associated composed score of $compose(M(S_1, S_2)(Paper, Article), M(S_2, S_3)(Article, Article))= 0.8 * 0.9=0.72$.

As to the semantic approximation of an entire subnetwork made of several semantic paths, the scores of the components semantic paths have to be *aggregated* so as to provide a single value reflecting the relevance of the subnetwork as a whole. More formally, giver two peers p_i and p_j, in order to model the semantic approximation of p_j's subnetwork w.r.t. p_i's schema, the values μ_j^k, $k=1,2...K$, which express the semantic approximations given by each path P_j^k in p_j's subnetwork, are aggregated according to an aggregation function *g*. *g* should be chosen conveniently to model the semantic aggregation of semantic grades. In fact, each resulting grade for a given concept should be representative of the semantic approximation given by the peer and its own subnetwork.

Several choices are possible for *g*, for instance functions such as *min()*, *max()*, any generalized mean (e.g. harmonic and arithmetic means), or any ordered weighted averaging (OWA) function (e.g. a weighted sum) (Klir and Yuan, 1995). For instance, with reference to Figure 1, the semantic approximation given by the subnetwork rooted at Peer2 with respect to the concept *Paper* in Peer1's schema is given by the aggregation of the semantic paths: $P_1^1 = Path_{Peer1-Peer2}$: *(Paper, Article)* with $\mu_1^1=0.8$ and $P_1^2 = Path_{Peer1-Peer2-Peer3}$: *(Paper, Article)* with $\mu_1^2=0.72$. The result of the their aggregation computed as the arithmetic mean is $g(\mu_1^1, \mu_1^2) = (0.8+0.72)/2=0.76$. As a further choice, a modified version of a function commonly used in the field of discrete choice analysis with application to travel demand (Ben-Akiva and Lerman, 1985) can also be successfully exploited (Mandreoli *et al.*, 2006). In travel demand applications, it is often the case that the actual alternatives from which a decision maker chooses are unidentifiable, and aggregated geographical zones are used as the alternatives (Ben-Akiva and Lerman, 1985). This is very close to the considered scenario, in that a peer should be able to choose a direction on the basis of the aggregated information about the paths which can be explored by following that direction.

The proposal is thus to adapt the function used in travel demand applications, which relies on the concept of *utility*, i.e. the amount of advantages in making a choice among several alternatives, for modelling the aggregation of the membership grades μ_j^k associated to the different paths P_j^k. The proposed function U satisfies the properties of an aggregation function:

$$U = \bar{\mu} + \frac{1}{\nu}\ln\left[\frac{1}{K}\sum_k e^{\nu(\mu_j^k - \bar{\mu})}\right]$$

where $\bar{\mu} = 1/K\sum_k \mu_j^k$, K is the number of membership grades to be aggregated, and ν is a positive scale parameter. As shown by the experiments, U proved to be a good function for aggregation as it adjusts the average value $\bar{\mu}$ with a measure of the variance among the elemental alternatives, in that it is particularly sensitive to the presence of elemental alternatives having high grades. For instance, it is able to distinguish the case [0.9,0.5,0.1] from the case [0.6,0.5,0.4] which have the same mean, but have values U=0.552 and U=0.503, respectively.

SRI Evolution

Since SRIs summarize the semantic information offered by the network, they change whenever the network itself changes. This may occur in response to either the joining/leaving of peers, or to changes in peers' schemas. We first focus our attention on the evolution of the PDMS's topology.

SRIs evolution is managed in an incremental fashion as follows. As a base case, the SRI of an isolated peer p having schema S is made of the single row [1,…,1], i.e. it contains the membership grades of the concepts in S in the self mapping. This row expresses the semantic approximation offered by the subnetwork rooted at p, yet made of the only peer p. A simplification of the actions required for the SRIs update after Peer1 connects

Figure 4. SRI evolution

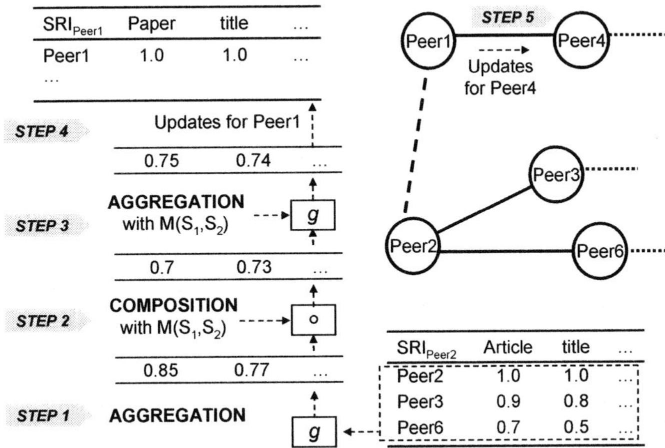

to Peer2 is shown in Figure 4. Notice that, for the sake of clarity, the figure only shows the steps involving Peerl, while the same process applies to Peer2.

When a peer connects to another peer, each one *aggregates* its own SRI by rows, according to an appropriate aggregation function g (stepl in figure). The result of this aggregation operation and the schema S are then sent to the other peer. After a peer, say p_i (Peerl in figure), receives such knowledge from the other peer, say p_j (Peer2 in figure), a semantic mapping $M(S_i, S_j)$ is established between S_i and S_j. Then, p_i needs to extend its SRI with a new row for p_j. The membership grades of this new row are obtained in two steps: Firstly, $M(S_i, S_j)$ is *composed*, according to an appropriate composition function, with the aggregated SRI provided by p_j to obtain the extension of the semantic paths originating from p_j (represented by the aggregated SRI) with the connection between p_i and p_j (step2 in figure); Then, the so obtained result is aggregated with $M(S_i, S_j)$ to include the semantic path connecting p_i to p_j (step3 in figure). At this point the new row is inserted in p_i's SRI (step 4 in figure). Afterwards, both peers p_i and p_j need to inform their own reverse neighbors that a change occurred in the network and thus they have to update their SRIs accordingly. To this end, each peer, say p_i, sends to each reverse neighbor p_{i_k} (Peer4 in figure) an aggregate of its SRI, excluding the p_{i_k}'s row (step5 in figure). When p_{i_k} receives such aggregated information, it updates the i-th row of its SRI by recomputing the membership values as discussed above.

Disconnections are treated in a similar way as connections. When a node disconnects from the network, each of its neighbors must delete the row of the disconnected peer from its own SRI and then inform the remaining neighbors that a change on its own subnetwork has occurred by sending new aggregates of its SRI to them. A similar procedure applies in case of modifications to the semantic knowledge maintained at each peer, for instance when a new concept is added to the peer's schema.

When many changes occur in the PDMS, a careful policy of updates propagation may be adopted. For instance, when changes have a little impact on its SRI, a peer may also decide not to notify the network. This would reduce the amount of exchanged messages as well as the computational costs due to SRI manipulation.

ROUTING QUERIES WITH SRIs

Users send requests consisting of a query formula f, an optional threshold t of peer semantic relevance, and a stopping condition (see Section "Experiments" for possible stopping conditions). Starting from the queried peers, the objective of the query execution mechanism is to answer those requests over the network by avoiding querying those peers whose semantic relevance is under the threshold t and by stopping the process when the stopping condition is reached. A query is posed on the schema of the queried peer. Query conditions are expressed using predicates that can be combined in logical formulas through logical connectives, according to the syntax: $f ::= p \mid f \wedge f \mid f \vee f \mid (f)$. Predicates can be of three types: 1) *schema concepts*, which represent output data, 2) *relational predicates*, where relational operators (=, <, >, <=, >=, !=) compare concept values to constants, or 3) *relationship-type predicates*, which express relationship conditions between schema concepts. As an example, the query: "Retrieve the title of articles published by Halevy either at the 2006 VLDB Conference or in the Computer Magazine" posed on Peer2 of Figure 1 can be expressed as shown in Box 1, where `Article.title` is the query output, `Article.author = 'Halevy'` is a relational predicate, and `Article.IN(Conference)` is a relationship-type predicate which relates concepts `Article` and `Conference` with the relationship `IN` in the queried peer's schema.

In order to deal with semantic approximations, we represent a query as a tuple $q = (id, f, sim, t)$ where:

Box 1.

```
q   ::=   Article.title ∧ Article.author = 'Halevy'∧ ((Article.IN(Conference) ∧
          Conference.name = 'VLDB' ∧ Conference.year = '2006') ∨ (Article.IN(Magazine)
          ∧ Magazine.name = 'Computer')
```

- *id* is a unique identifier for the query
- *f* is the formula of predicates specifying the query conditions
- *sim* is the semantic approximation associated with the semantic path the query is following, that is the approximations given by the traversal of semantic mappings between peers' schemas
- *t* is the optional relevance threshold

Query Execution

Query execution is performed by following a *depth-first traversal* (DFT) policy. Starting from the queried node, each peer receiving the query *q*:

1. Accesses its local repository for query results
2. Decides a neighbor *Next* which forward the query to, among the unvisited ones
3. Reformulates the query q into q_{Next} for the chosen peer
4. Forwards the query q_{Next} to the neighbor *Next* and waits for a finite response from it

In order to accomplish the forwarding step, the semantic information stored at the peer's SRI is used to *rank* the neighbors, according to the semantic relevance of results which are likely to be retrieved from their own subnetworks. The evaluation of such semantic relevance is performed by assigning to each concept *c* in the formula *q.f* its corresponding similarity value in the SRI's row associated to the current neighbor, i.e. SRI[*Next*][*c*]. For ease of reference, here and in the following we will use the notation SRI[p][c] to denote the SRI's cell corresponding to the p's row and the c's column. The same applies for rows and columns. Recall that this value represents the semantic approximation provided by the neighbor's subnetwork w.r.t. the queried concept. Then, all values assigned to the concepts in *q.f* are combined according to a fuzzy logic approach, by using a triangular norm (T-norm) to express conjunction of predicates, whereas using a triangular conorm (T-conorm) to represent disjunction (Klir and Yuan, 1995). Examples of T-norms and T-conorms are the *min* and *max* operators, respectively. This combined value thus represents the semantic relevance of the current neighbor w.r.t. the query *q*.

Once the more promising neighbor has been chosen, the query q is reformulated into q_{Next}, according to the semantic mapping established between the peer and the chosen neighbor. In particular, query reformulation refers to unfolding (Tatarinov and Halevy, 2004). Then, q_{Next} is assigned the semantic approximation value obtained by composing the semantic approximation obtained so far, i.e. *q.sim*, and the approximation for *q.f* given by the semantic mapping M_{Next} between the current peer and the neighbor *Next*, thus instantiating $q_{\text{Next}}.sim$. As to the composition function to be used, several alternatives exist, as discussed in Section "Building a SRI".

The forwarding process starts backtracking when a "blind alley" is reached, that is when the list of unvisited neighbors for the current peer is empty. Thus, DFT progresses by going deeper and deeper until the stopping condition is verified. Because each node processes the query sequentially, searches can be terminated as soon as the query is satisfied, thereby minimizing cost.

We implemented the above visiting criteria in a distributed manner through a protocol of message exchange, thus trying to minimize the information spanning over the network. In particular, only the list of the visited peers "surfs" the network along with the query which, at each step, is locally instantiated on the peer's dictionary, whereas a *query navigation state* s is maintained at each node. The former is used for cycle detection, which is in order to avoid querying the same peer more times. The latter keeps track of the information needed to re-activate the local query execution flow when the control comes back to the peer during backtracking, that is $s = (q, PQ, C)$ where:

- q is the received query which refers to the local schema, with the approximation obtained so far
- PQ is a priority queue of neighbors to be selected
- C is the calling peer to be used for backtracking

The query navigation state is created in the forwarding phase, that is when a peer p receives the message `Execute(q,C,L)`. The peer p, univocally identified as *p*.ID, follows the algorithm shown in Figure 5, for the query q, received from the calling peer C, and according to the list L of already visited nodes. S, M, and SRI are the schema, the set of semantic mappings towards neighbors, and the SRI matrix of p, respectively. NS is an array of navigation states, one for each query processed by p.

First, the peer p includes itself in the list of visited peers, and then it executes q on its local repository to retrieve results. If the stopping condition has not been satisfied yet, it uses its own SRI for ranking its neighbors thus producing the list `NeighborList` (steps 04-07). Such a list is then ordered on the basis of the peers' relevance such

Figure 5. Query execution algorithm

```
Execute(q,C,L):   00   add p.ID to L;
                  01   execute q on local repository;
                  02   if(stopping condition is reached)
                  03     stop execution
                  04   NeighborList = Ø;
                  05   for each neighbor N of p except C
                  06     relevance = combine(q.f,SRI[N]);
                  07     add (N,relevance) to NeighborList;
                  08   PQ = order NeighborList in descending order
                            of relevance;
Restore(id,L):    09   do
                  10     (Next,relevance) = pop(PQ);
                  11     q_Next.id = q.id;
                  12     q_Next.f = reformulate(q.f,M_Next);
                  13     q_Next.sim = compose(q.sim,combine(q.f, M_Next));
                  14     q_Next.t = q.t;
                  15   while (Next not NULL and
                              (Next ∈ L OR q_Next.sim < q.t));
                  16   if (Next is NULL)
                  17     delete NS[q.id];
                  18     send message Restore(q.id,L) to peer C;
                  19   else
                  20     NS[q.id] = (q,PQ,C);
                  21     send message Execute(q_Next,p.ID,L) to Next;
```

that the top neighbor roots the subnetwork with the best approximation skills. Then, the query is reformulated over the chosen peer `Next` (step 12) using the semantic mapping $M_{\mathtt{Next}}$ established between *p*'s and `Next`'s schemas, and a new semantic approximation value is assigned to $q_{\mathtt{Next}}$, accordingly (step 13). The query identifier and the threshold value do not change.

However, peer *Next* could have already been visited (and thus belong to *L*) or the reformulated query approximation could be under the optional threshold *q.t*. In both cases, the neighbor selection process is reiterated on the next top peer.

Because at each iteration the algorithm pops the peer off the top of the stack, the stack could also become empty. In this case, the algorithm starts backtracking by returning the control to the calling peer (steps 16-18). Otherwise, it generates a navigation state for the query and then it forwards $q_{\mathtt{Next}}$ to the selected peer (steps 20-21).

During backtracking, each peer in the backward path has already processed the received query. When a peer receives the message `Restore(id,L)`, it reactivates the navigation state $s = (q, \mathtt{PQ}, C)$ for the query identifier `id` and then follows steps 09-21 of Figure 5 either to select the next peer which to forward the query to, or to continue backtracking.

The overall query execution process stops when the stopping condition is reached.

EXPERIMENTS

Data Sets and Network Organization

For our experiments we used SimJava 2.0, a discrete, event based, general purpose simulation framework (Howell, 1997). We reproduced a small scale PDMS as a network of 27 semantic peers connected as in Figure 6.

Each peer has been assigned a schema and the schemas distributed among peers are about three different topics: Sport, music, and publications. Each schema deals with only one topic and is derived from real world data sets. The schemas about the same topic differ from each other, in that they present different points of view of a topic. For

Figure 6. Network topology: Dashed lines denote clusters of peers sharing similar information, i.e. SONs

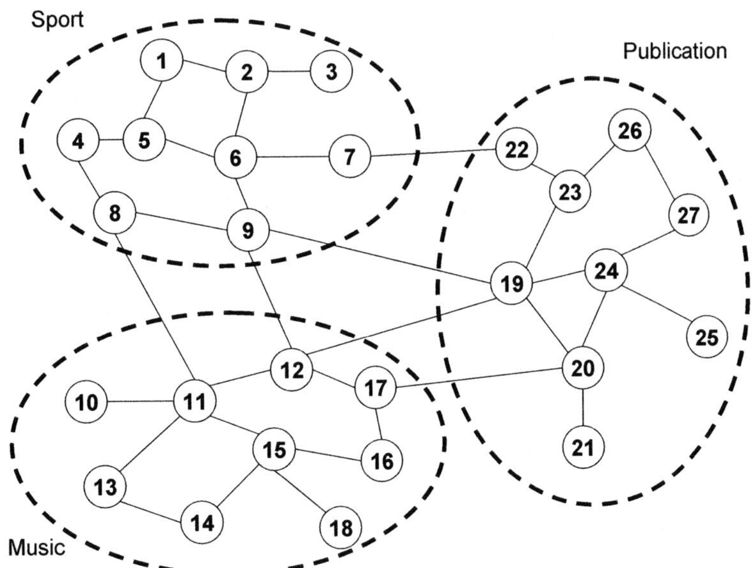

instance, in the sport domain, one schema might deal with players and teams, whereas another might focus on teams and championships.

In our experiments, we compared two different network semantic organizations: A network where schemas are randomly distributed among peers (*Random Network*), and a network where schemas about the same topic are assigned to a set of neighboring peers, in order to form semantic clusters. The latter configuration has been used to represent a set of Semantic Overlay Networks (*SON Network*). Figure 6 shows three SONs, one for each topic: Dashed lines denote clusters of peers sharing similar information.

Evaluation Methodology

We simulated several hundreds of queries over both the Random Network and the SON Network. All queries were about concepts randomly extracted from the schema of the querying peer. A query has been propagated among peers until a stopping condition has been reached. We set two alternative stopping conditions: (a) the maximum number of hops for query forwarding; (b) a satisfaction goal that queries should reach. The former condition is a constraint on the number of edges a query can go through. The latter is based on a semantic metric, that is, satisfaction, which is a specific quantity that grows proportionally to the goodness of the results returned by each queried peer. In particular, it is computed as the sum of *q.sim* values of the traversed peers.

The performance metrics we evaluated are: (i) the satisfaction goal a query reaches when a maximum number of hops is set for query propagation, and (ii), dually, the average number of hops needed to reach a given satisfaction goal. These metrics allow us to evaluate the effectiveness and the efficiency of different query forwarding policies. Policy's capability to forward the queries towards the best directions, that is, policy's effectiveness, can be measured by considering the satisfaction goal a policy gets when a constraint on the maximum distance a query can go through is set. Dually, if a satisfaction goal is set, policy's efficiency can be measured by considering the number of hops needed to reach the given satisfaction goal.

We compared the query forwarding strategy that uses SRIs to other two query forwarding policies, *Random* and *Semantic Mapping*–based forwarding. In the former case, a query is forwarded to a peer randomly selected among the neighbors of the querying peer; in the latter, forwarding is performed according to the best query approximation given by the semantic mappings between the querying peer and each neighbor of its.

Figure 7. Query forwarding policies' effectiveness on the SON Network

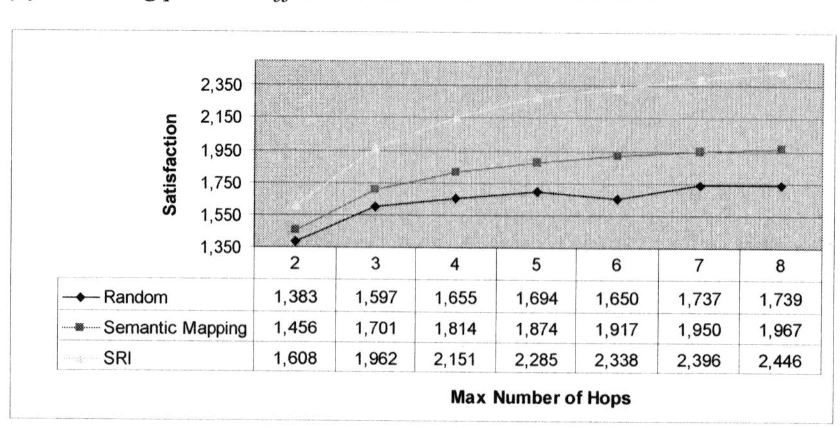

	2	3	4	5	6	7	8
Random	1,383	1,597	1,655	1,694	1,650	1,737	1,739
Semantic Mapping	1,456	1,701	1,814	1,874	1,917	1,950	1,967
SRI	1,608	1,962	2,151	2,285	2,338	2,396	2,446

Our experiments show that, in a network of SONs, the *SRI*-based policy allows to reach better results than both other query forwarding policies. This is because SRIs extend the semantic scope of a peer beyond its neighbors and prove to address the queries towards peers belonging to the same SON, thus improving effectiveness and efficiency of retrieval.

Comparison of Forwarding Policies

We start showing the results obtained by the comparison of the SRI-based policy with both Random and Semantic Mapping–based policies according to two different stopping conditions. Figure 7 proves the increase of satisfaction, i.e. the effectiveness, when using SRIs under the constraint of a maximum number of hops for query propagation. As expected, the semantic information stored at the SRIs allows to reach better results than forwarding queries at random. Also, the Semantic Mapping–based policy is less effective than using SRIs: This is due to its semantic scope which is limited to the only neighbors, and which may forward queries towards the borders of a SON, thus possibly going beyond it and entering a different SON.

For instance, considering a maximum of 6 hops, the SRI-based policy improves the satisfaction goal by the 29% w.r.t. the Random approach, and by the 18% w.r.t. the Semantic Mapping–based policy. Figure 8 shows the efficiency of using SRIs. In particular, when a satisfaction goal is set, the SRI-based policy reduces the average number of hops by about the 60% w.r.t. the Random approach, and by about the 40% w.r.t. the Semantic Mapping–based policy. As in the case of Figure 7, this efficiency is the result of the intuition that forwarding a query to a highly promising peer surrounded by no interesting neighbors, i.e. towards a peer in a SON's border, is probably a worse choice than forwarding it towards a peer underlying a subnetwork of many promising peers.

Changing the Network Type

We also compared the use of SRIs over the Random Network w.r.t. the SON Network. We first considered the satisfaction goal values under the constraint of a maximum number of hops. Intuitively, the presence of clusters of peers with similar information allows queries to reach a higher satisfaction. In particular, Figure 9 shows an increase of satisfaction by 40% under the constraint of 8 hops. If we consider the number of hops needed to reach a given satisfaction goal, as shown in Figure 10, the SRI-based policy provides a reduction of messages by about the 60% over a network of SONs, w.r.t. the results obtained over the Random Network. The increase of the

Figure 8. Query forwarding policies' efficiency on the SON Network

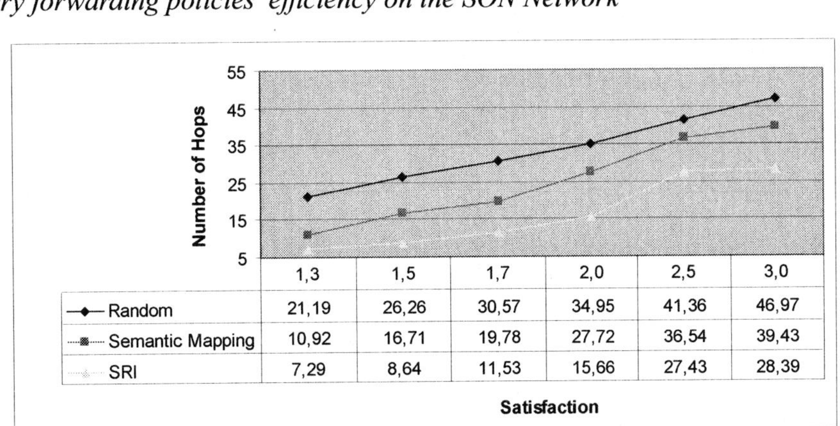

	1,3	1,5	1,7	2,0	2,5	3,0
Random	21,19	26,26	30,57	34,95	41,36	46,97
Semantic Mapping	10,92	16,71	19,78	27,72	36,54	39,43
SRI	7,29	8,64	11,53	15,66	27,43	28,39

Figure 9. Comparison of the SRI-based policy under a maximum number of hops constraint over the Random Network and over the SON Network

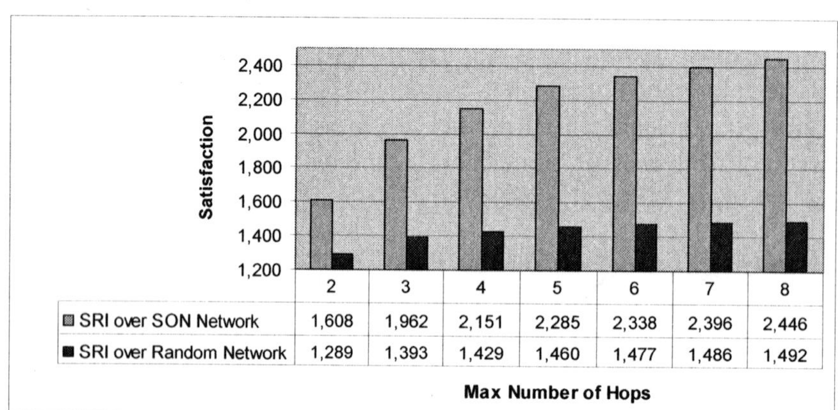

	2	3	4	5	6	7	8
SRI over SON Network	1,608	1,962	2,151	2,285	2,338	2,396	2,446
SRI over Random Network	1,289	1,393	1,429	1,460	1,477	1,486	1,492

Figure 10. Comparison of the SRI-based policy, given a satisfaction goal constraint, over the Random Network and over the SON Network

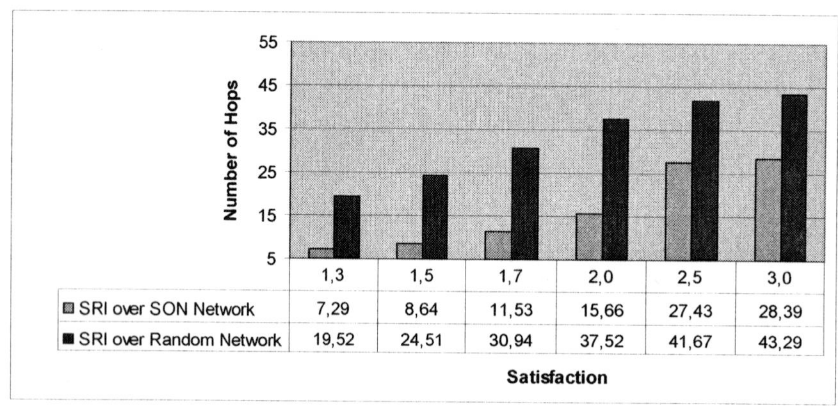

	1,3	1,5	1,7	2,0	2,5	3,0
SRI over SON Network	7,29	8,64	11,53	15,66	27,43	28,39
SRI over Random Network	19,52	24,51	30,94	37,52	41,67	43,29

efficiency of the SRI-based policy depends on the capability to reach relevant peers without wasting efforts due to the traversal of paths outside the SON the query was originated from.

Additional Tests

We also considered the number of queries that reach the requested level of satisfaction, since the approximations introduced by long paths and the small size of SONs in our scenario do not allow all queries to reach high satisfaction goals.

We first show in Figure 11 the number of queries that reach a given satisfaction goal over a network of SONs, according to the three query forwarding policies we considered. The SRI-based policy presents a constantly higher number of queries satisfying the constraint w.r.t. both Random and Semantic Mapping–based policies.

Then, Figure 12 shows that in a network of SONs, although the required satisfaction goal increases, the number of queries that satisfy the constraint condition is clearly higher than that in the Random Network, and it maintains high values also when the Random case rapidly decreases to the zero value. This is because, when a network presents clusters of peers with similar information, the chance that a query could reach the satisfaction

Figure 11. Number of queries that reach a given satisfaction goal using different query forwarding policies over the SON Network

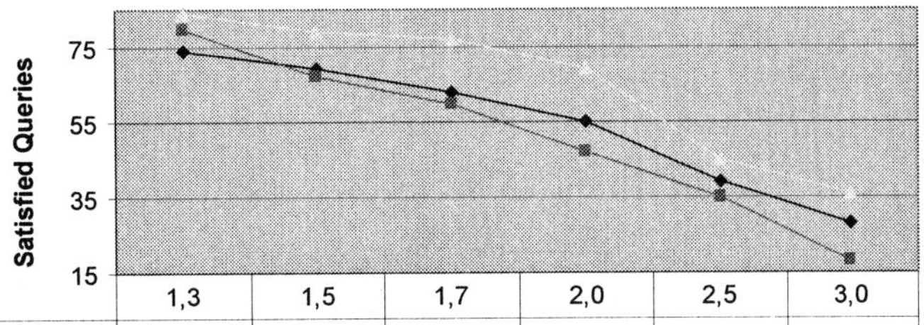

Satisfaction	1,3	1,5	1,7	2,0	2,5	3,0
Random	74	69	63	55	39	28
Semantic Mapping	80	67	60	47	35	18
SRI	84	79	77	69	45	36

Figure 12. Number of queries that reach a given satisfaction goal using the SRI-based query forwarding policy over the Random Network and over the SON Network

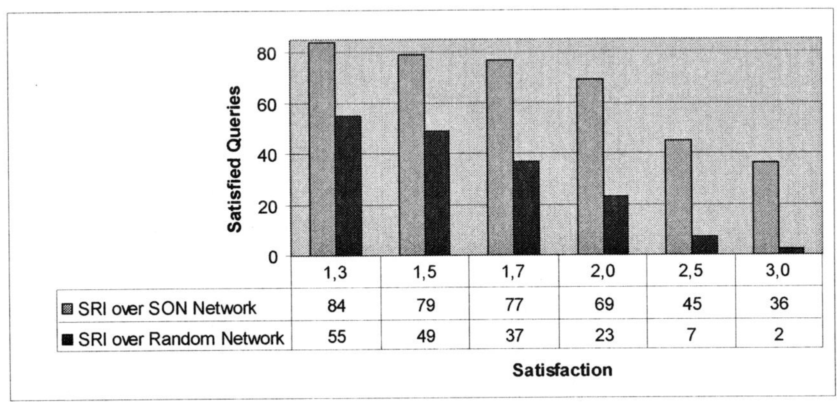

Satisfaction	1,3	1,5	1,7	2,0	2,5	3,0
SRI over SON Network	84	79	77	69	45	36
SRI over Random Network	55	49	37	23	7	2

goal becomes significantly higher, rather than the case of relevant information randomly distributed among all peers.

CONCLUSION

The advent of peer-to-peer computing has represented a revolution for the Internet community, since it provides a new paradigm that goes beyond traditional client/server architectures. In particular, it offers new potentialities as to data sharing capabilities, while being characterized by high network dynamicity. However, as envisioned by the Semantic Web, the need of complementing the Web with more semantics has spurred much effort towards a rich representation of data. In this view, Peer Data Management Systems (PDMSs) have been introduced as a solution to the problem of large-scale sharing of semantically rich data (Halevy *et al.*, 2004). Nevertheless, querying a PDMS is different than querying a P2P system, primarily because of the presence of heterogeneous schemas at the peers. Then, a recent evolution in network organization strategies has introduced the concept of Semantic Overlay Networks (SONs), where semantically similar nodes are clustered together.

In this chapter we presented a semantics-based query routing mechanism which, as shown by our experiments, proved to be successfully exploited in a complex SON scenario. The main differences of our proposal w.r.t. other approaches are:

- We do not assume any global characterization of data in the network.
- We assume the presence of heterogeneous schemas describing the content of peers' data, as well as pairwise semantic relationships between the peers' schemas, in a PDMS fashion.
- Schema-based, rather than a keyword-based, search is fully supported.
- Semantic Routing Indices summarize the *semantics* of the data that can be retrieved following a given direction in the network.
- SRIs are fully distributed structures, thus scaling well in very large SON networks.

FUTURE RESEARCH DIRECTIONS

As a future work, SRIs could be integrated in a more general framework, together with other approaches such as (Crespo and Garcia-Molina, 2002; Michel *et al.*, 2006) which are orthogonal to ours, and which cover complementary aspects such as knowledge on quantitative information, as well as on novelty of results, so as to blend different dimensions a peer can be queried on. Then, as also stated in (Tempich *et al.*, 2004), the *best* peer has been understood as a peer that has the most knowledge. Other aspects one might include in the evaluation of peers are properties like latency, costs, etc.

As to query processing on PDMSs, a variety of routing policies could be tested in order to identify the best trade-off between effectiveness and efficiency of data retrieval according to different users' needs. A preliminary work on this issue, based on a SRI-enhanced PDMS, has been presented in (Mandreoli, Martoglia, Penzo, Sassatelli, and Villani, 2007). SRI-based query processing strategies are also planned to be explored in a scenario like the one presented in (Lodi, Mandreoli, Martoglia, Penzo, and Sassatelli, 2008), where Semantic Overlay Networks are constructed incrementally through an indexing paradigm which arrange peers in semantic clusters.

A further research direction to be explored is concerned with the well-known object fusion problem. Peers in the network might be able to answer the query only partially, thus returning pieces of information to be consistently collected in an integrated result on the basis of the different contributions of the answering peers. A similar situation might occur also in case of optimization policies which intentionally split a complex query in subqueries to be answered by different peers, depending on the competences of each peer with respect to the conditions expressed by each specific subquery. Among the several aspects that need to be investigated in this context, it is particularly challenging to find appropriate strategies about: (1) finding an optimal partition of a query in a set of subqueries; (2) identifying the best choice of peers to send subqueries to; (3) collecting partial results in an integrated form, namely performing object fusion; (4) ranking the final results by means of an appropriate combination of the ranking scores returned by the answering peers for their partial results. For the last purpose, it could conveniently be used a scoring rule which incorporate weights to rate differently the contributing peers according to parameters like, for instance, trustworthiness and domain specificity.

REFERENCES

Aberer, K. (2001). P-Grid: A Self-Organizing Access Structure for P2P Information Systems. In Proc. of the 9th International Conference on Cooperative Information Systems (CoopIS), 179-194.

Aberer, K., Cudré-Mauroux, P., Hauswirth, M., & van Pelt, T. (2004). GridVine: Building Internet-Scale Semantic Overlay Networks. In Proc. of the 3rd International Semantic Web Conferenc (ISWC), 107-121.

Arenas, M., Kantere, V., Kementsietsidis, A., Kiringa, I., Miller, R.J., & Mylopoulos, J. (2003). The Hyperion Project: From Data Integration to Data Coordination. SIGMOD Record, 32(3), 53-58.

Barkai, D. (2000). An Introduction to Peer-to-Peer Computing. Intel Developer Update Magazine, February 2000, 1-7.

Bawa, M., Manku, G., & Raghavan, P. (2003). SETS: Search Enhanced by Topic Segmentation. In Proc. of the 26th ACM SIGIR Conference, 306-313.

Ben-Akiva, M., & Lerman, S. (1985). Discrete Choice Analysis: Theory and Application to Travel Demand. Cambridge: MIT Press.

Berners-Lee, T., Hendler, J., & Lassila, O. (2001, May). The Semantic Web. Scientific American.

Cai, M., Frank, M., Chen, J., & Szekely, P. (2004). Maan: a Multi-Attribute Addressable Network for Grid Information Services. Journal of Grid Computing, 2(1), 3-14.

Clarke, I., Sandberg, O., Wiley, B., & Hong, T.W. (2000). Freenet: A Distributed Anonymous Information Storage and Retrieval System. In Proc. of the International Workshop on Design Issues in Anonymity and Unobservability, 46-66.

Comito, C., Patarin, S., & Talia, D. (2005). PARIS: A Peer-to-Peer Architecture for Large-Scale Semantic Data Integration. In Proc. of the International Workshop on Databases, Information Systems, and Peer-to-Peer Computing (DBISP2P), 163-170.

Cooper, B. (2004). Using Information Retrieval Techniques to Route Queries in an InfoBeacons Network. In Proc. of the International Workshop on Databases, Information Systems, and Peer-to-Peer Computing (DBISP2P), 46-60.

Crespo, A., & Garcia-Molina, H. (2002). Routing Indices for Peer-to-Peer Systems. In Proc. of the 22nd IEEE International Conference on Distributed Computing Systems (ICDCS), 23-34.

Crespo, A., & Garcia-Molina, H. (2004). Semantic Overlay Networks for P2P Systems. In Proc. of the 3rd International Workshop on Agents and Peer-to-Peer Computing (AP2PC), 1-13.

Cuenca-Acuna, F.M., Peery, C., Martin, R.P., & Nguyen, T.D. (2003). PlanetP: Using Gossiping to Build Content Addressable Peer-to-Peer Information Sharing Communities. In Proc. of the 12th International Symposium on High-Performance Distributed Computing (HPDC), 236-249.

Doulkeridis, C., Nørvåg, K., & Vazirgiannis, M. (2007). DESENT: Decentralized and Distributed Semantic Overlay Generation in P2P Networks. IEEE Journal on Selected Areas in Communications, 25(1), 25-34.

Gnutella. [Online]. Available: http://www.gnutella.com.

Haase, P., Siebes, R., & van Harmelen, F. (2004). Peer Selection in Peer-to-Peer Networks with Semantic Topologies. In Proc. of the 1st International Conference on Semantics of a Networked World: Semantics for Grid Databases (ICSNW), 108-125.

Halevy, A., Franklin, M.J., & Maier, D. (2006). Principles of Dataspace Systems. In Proc of the 25th ACM SIGACT-SIGMOD-SIGART Symposium on Principles of Database Systems (PODS), 1-9.

Halevy, A.Y., Ives, Z., Madhavan, J., Mork, P., Suciu, D., & Tatarinov, I. (2004). The Piazza Peer Data Management System. IEEE Transactions on Knowledge and Data Engineering. 16(7), 787-798.

Halevy, A.Y., Ives, Z., Suciu, D., & Tatarinov, I. (2005). Schema Mediation for Large-Scale Semantic Data Sharing. VLDB Journal. 14(1), 68-83.

Halevy, A.Y., Tatarinov, I., Ives, Z., Madhavan, J., Suciu, D., Dalvi, N., Dong, X., Kadiyska, Y., Miklau, G., & Mork, P. (2003). The Piazza Peer Data Management Project. SIGMOD Record, 32(3), 47-52.

Howell, F.W. (1997). The SimJava Home Page [Online]. Available: http://www.dcs.ed.ac.uk/home/hase/simjava.

Joseph, S. (2002). NeuroGrid: Semantically Routing Queries in Peer-to-Peer Networks. In Proc. of the International Workshop on Peer-to-Peer Computing (NETWORKING), 202-214.

Kazaa. [Online]. Available: http://www.kazaa.com.

Kleis, M., Lua, E.K., & Zhou, X. (2005). Hierarchical Peer-to-Peer Networks Using Lightweight SuperPeer Topologies. In Proc. of the 10th IEEE Symposium on Computers and Communications (ISCC), 143-148.

Klir, G. J., & Yuan, B. (1995). Fuzzy Sets and Fuzzy Logic: Theory and Applications. Upper Saddle River: Prentice Hall.

Koloniari, G., & Pitoura ,E. (2004). Content-Based Routing of Path Queries in Peer-to-Peer Systems. In Proc. of the 9th International Conference on Extending Database Technology (EDBT), 29-47.

Li, M., Lee, W. C., & Sivasubramaniam, A. (2004). Semantic Small World: An Overlay Network for Peer-to-Peer Search. In Proc. of the 12th IEEE International Conference on Network Protocols (ICNP), 228-238.

Linari, A., & Weikum, G. (2006). Efficient Peer-to-Peer Semantic Overlay Networks Based on Statistical Language Models. In Proc. of the ACM CIKM International Workshop on Peer-to-Peer Information Retrieval (P2PIR), 9-16.

Lodi, S., Mandreoli, F., Martoglia, R., Penzo, W., & Sassatelli, S. (2008). Semantic Peer, Here are the Neighbors You Want! In Proc. of the 11th International Conference on Extending Database Technology (EDBT), 26-37.

Mandreoli, F., Martoglia, R., Penzo, W., & Sassatelli, S. (2006). SRI: Exploiting Semantic Information for Effective Query Routing in a PDMS. In Proc. of the 8th ACM CIKM International Workshop on Web Information and Data Management (WIDM), 19-26.

Mandreoli, F., Martoglia, R., Penzo, W., Sassatelli, S., & Villani, G. (2007). SRI@work: Efficient and Effective Routing Strategies in a PDMS. In Proc. of the 8th International Conference on Web Information Systems Engineering (WISE), 285-297.

Michel, S., Bender, M., Triantafillou, P., & Weikum, G. (2006). IQN Routing: Integrating Quality and Novelty in P2P Querying and Ranking. In Proc. of the 10th International Conference on Extending Database Technology: Advances in Database Technology (EDBT), 149-166.

Napster. [Online]. Available: http://www.napster.com.

Nejdl, W., Wolf, B., Staab, S., & Tane, J. (2002). EDUTELLA: Searching and Annotating Resources within an RDF-based P2P Network. In Proc. of the WWW International Workshop on the Semantic Web, pp.19-26.

Nejdl, W., Wolpers, M., Siberski, W., Schmitz, C., Schlosser, M. T., Brunkhorst, I., & Löser, A. (2003). Super-peer-based Routing and Clustering Strategies for RDF-based Peer-to-Peer Networks. In Proc. of the 12th International World Wide Web Conference (WWW), 536-543.

Ng, W.S., Ooi, B.C., Tan, K., & Zhou, A. (2003). PeerDB: A P2P-based System for Distributed Data Sharing. In Proc. of the 19th International Conference on Data Engineering (ICDE), 633-644.

Parreira, J. X., Michel, S., & Weikum, G. (2007). P2PDating: Real life inspired semantic overlay networks for Web search. Information Processing & Management, 43(3), 643-664.

Ratnasamy, S., Francis, P., Handley, M., Karp, R., & Schenker, S. (2001). A Scalable Content-Addressable Network. In Proc of the 2001 Conference on Applications, Technologies, Architectures, and Protocols for Computer Communications (SIGCOMM), 161-172.

Renda, M.E., & Callan, J. (2004). The Robustness of Content-based Search in Hierarchical Peer to Peer Networks In Proc. of the 2004 ACM CIKM International Conference on Information and Knowledge Management, 562-570.

Rowstron, A., & Druschel, P. (2001). Pastry: Scalable, Decentralized Object Location, and Routing for Large-Scale Peer-to-Peer Systems. In Proc. of the IFIP/ACM International Conference on Distributed Systems Platforms (Middleware), 329-350.

Stoica, I., Morris, R., Karger, D., Kaashoek, F., & Balakrishnan, H. (2001). Chord: A Scalable Peer-To-Peer Lookup Service for Internet Applications. In Proc. of the ACM SIGCOMM Conference, 149-160.

Tatarinov, I., & Halevy, A. Y. (2004). Efficient Query Reformulation in Peer-Data Management Systems. In Proc. of the ACM SIGMOD International Conference on Management of Data, 539-550.

Tempich, C., Staab, S., & Wranik, A. (2004). REMINDIN': Semantic Query Routing in Peer-to-Peer Networks Based on Social Metaphors. In Proc. of the 13th World Wide Web Conference (WWW), 640-649.

Triantafillou, P., Xiruhaki, C., Koubarakis, M., & Ntarmos, N. (2003). Towards High Performance Peer-to-Peer Content and Resource Sharing Systems. In Proc. of the 1st Biennial Conference on Innovative Data Systems Research (CIDR), 2003. Online proceedings.

Zhao, B.Y., Kubiatowicz, J., & Joseph, A.D. (2001). Tapestry: An Infrastructure for Fault-tolerant Wide-area Location and Routing. Technical Report UCB/CSD-01-1141, UC Berkeley.

ADDITIONAL READING

Aberer, K., & Cudrè-Mauroux, P. (2005). Semantic Overlay Networks. In Proc. of the 31st International Conference on Very Large Data Bases (VLDB), Tutorial, 1367.

Aberer, K., Datta, A., Hauswirth, M., & Schmidt, R. (2005). Indexing Data-Oriented Overlay Networks. In Proc. of the 31st International Conference on Very Large Databases (VLDB), 685-696.

Aberer, K., Hauswirth, M., & Cudrè-Mauroux, P. (2002). A Framework for Semantic Gossiping. ACM SIGMOD Record, 31(4), 48–53.

Androutsellis-Theotokis, S., & Spinellis., D. (2004). A Survey of Peer-to-Peer Content Distribution Technologies. ACM Computing Surveys, 36(4), 335–371.

Beliakov, G., Pradera, A., & Calvo, T. (2007). Aggregation Functions: A Guide for Practitioners. Berlin: Springer.

Cooper, B. F., & Garcia-Molina, H. (2005). Ad Hoc, Self-Supervising Peer-to-Peer Search Networks. ACM Transactions on Information Systems, 23(2), 169-200.

Daswani, N., Garcia-Molina, H., & Yang, B. (2003). Open Problems in Data-Sharing Peer-to-Peer Systems. In Proc. of the 9th International Conference on Database Theory (ICDT), 1-15.

Decker, S., Melnik, S., van Harmelen, F., Fensel, D., Klein, M. C. A., Broekstra, J., Erdmann, M., & Horrocks, I. (2000). The Semantic Web: The

Roles of XML and RDF. IEEE Internet Computing, 4(5), 63-74.

Dubois, D., & Prade, H. (2004). On the use of aggregation operations in information fusion processes. Fuzzy Sets and Systems, 142(1), 143-161.

Euzenat, J., & Shvaiko, P. (2007). Ontology matching. Heidelberg: Springer-Verlag.

Fagin, R. (2002). Combining Fuzzy Information: an Overview. SIGMOD Record, 31(2), 109-118.

Fagin, R., & Wimmers, E. L. (2000). A formula for incorporating weights into scoring rules. Theorethical Computer Science, 239(2), 309-338.

Fuxman, A., Kolaitis, P. G., Miller, R. J., & Tan, W. C. (2006). Peer Data Exchange. ACM Transactions on Database Systems, 31(4), 1454-1498.

Gribble, S., Halevy, A., Ives, Z., Rodrig, M., & Suciu, D. (2001). What Can Databases Do for Peer-to-Peer? In Proc. of the 4th International Workshop on the Web and Databases (WebDB), in conjunction with ACM PODS/SIGMOD, 31-36.

Huebsch, R., Hellerstein, J.M., Lanham, N., Thau Loo, B., Shenker, S., & Stoica, I. (2003). Querying the Internet with PIER. In Proc. of the 29th International Conference on Very Large Data Bases (VLDB), 321-332.

Jagadish, H. V., Ooi, B. C., Tan, K. L., Vu, Q. H., & Zhang, R. (2006). Speeding Up Search in Peer-to-Peer Networks with a Multi-Way Tree Structure. In Proc. of the ACM SIGMOD International Conference on Management of Data (SIGMOD), 1-12.

Khambatti, M., Ryu, D. K., & Dasgupta, P. (2002). Efficient Discovery of Implicitly Formed Peer-to-Peer Communities. International Journal of Parallel and Distributed Systems and Networks, 5(4), 155-164.

Kossmann, D. (2000). The state of the art in distributed query processing. ACM Computing Surveys, 32(4), 422-469.

Madhavan, J., Bernstein, P. A., Doan, A., & Halevy, A. Y. (2005). Corpus-based Schema Matching. In Proc. of the 21st International Conference on Data Engineering (ICDE), 57-68.

Melnik, S., Bernstein, P. A., Halevy, A. Y., & Rahm, E. (2005). Supporting Executable Mappings in Model Management. In Proc. of the ACM SIGMOD International Conference on Management of Data, 167-178.

Melnik, S., Garcia-Molina, H., & Rahm E. (2002). Similarity Flooding: A Versatile Graph Matching Algorithm and Its Application to Schema Matching. In Proc. of the 18th International Conference on Data Engineering (ICDE), 117-128.

Meng, W., Yu, C., & Liu, K. (2002). Building efficient and effective metasearch engines. ACM Computing Surveys, 34(1), 48-89.

Mika, P. (2004). Social Networks and the Semantic Web. In Proc. of the IEEE/WIC/ACM International Conference on Web Intelligence (WI), 285-291.

Miller, R. J., Haas, Laura M., & Hernández, M. A. (2000). Schema Mapping as Query Discovery. In Proc. of the 26th International Conference on Very Large Data Bases (VLDB), 77-88.

Nejdl, W., Siberski, W., & Sintek, M. (2003). Design Issues and Challenges for RDF- and Schema-based Peer-to-Peer Systems. ACM SIGMOD Record, 32(3), 41-46.

Torra, V., & Narukawa, Y. (2007). Modeling Decisions. Information Fusion and Aggregation Operators. Berlin: Springer.

Yang, B., & Garcia-Molina, H. (2002). Improving Search in Peer-to-Peer Networks. In Proc. of the 22nd Int. Conference on Distributed Computing Systems (ICDCS), 5-14.

Zeinalipour-Yazti, D., Kalogeraki, V., & Gunopulos, D. (2005). Exploiting Locality for Scalable Information Retrieval in Peer-to-Peer Networks. Information Systems, 30(4), 277-298.

Chapter VIII
SWARMS: A Platform for Domain Knowledge Management and Applications

Jie Tang
Tsinghua University, Beijing, China

Bangyong Liang
NEC Labs, China

Juanzi Li
Tsinghua University, Beijing, China

ABSTRACT

This chapter describes the architecture and the main features of SWARMS, a platform for domain knowledge management. The platform aims at providing services for 1) efficiently storing and accessing the ontological information; 2) visualizing the networking structure in the ontological data; 3) searching and mining the semantic data. One advantage of the system is that it provides a suite of components for not only supporting efficient semantic data storage but also searching and mining the semantics. Another advantage is that the system supports visualization in the process of search and mining, which would greatly help a normal user to understand the knowledge inside the ontological data. SWARMS can be easily customized to adapt to different domains. The system has been applied to several domains, such as News, Software, and Social Network. In this chapter, we will also present the performance evaluations of the system.

INTRODUCTION

With the rapid growing interest in Semantic Web, more and more 'semantic' data becomes available. Semantic search can assistant users and applications to fetch relevant knowledge in the domain (Berendt *et al.*, 2003). Semantic mining is used to reveal the hidden facts in order to empower the 'semantics' in ontological data. For example, to answer the question "get all persons involved in the project of web spider", data semantic search may be sufficient to give the answer by using SPARQL (Prud'hommeaux and Seaborne, 2007). However, for the question "get all the persons who are experts on data mining in the project of web spider", the simple search based method cannot be sufficient. Instead, mining might be a better solution to answer this question. Unlike mining on the unstructured Web, the metadata on the Semantic Web might be complicated, the traditional search and mining methods cannot be directly adapted to this scenario. In addition, as the semantic data is often represented by a complex metadata and how to make it easy for a normal user to understand is also a challenging issue. Consequently, a comprehensive investigation including semantic data storage, indexing, search, and mining is required. Furthermore, a practical platform for supporting the management is also necessary. This is exactly the problem addressed in this chapter.

There have been many researching and industrial efforts on semantic data management in recent years. However, most of the works focus on specific problems. For example, Swoogle (Ding and Finin, 2005) focuses on semantic search (searching for ontologies that contain the input query terms); Flink (Mika, 2005) provides a graphical view for the researcher social network. Different from the existing works, we aim at integrating the semantic search and mining in a general platform in order to provide a comprehensive tool for semantic data management; we also try to visualize the processes of search and mining so as to facilitate the normal user to easily browse and understand the complicated ontological data. For several features in the system, e.g., semantic data caching, expert finding, and association search, we propose new approaches trying to overcome the drawbacks that exist in the conventional methods. For some other features, e.g., storage, searching, and visualization, we utilize the state-of-the-art methods. This is because, these issues have been intensively investigated previously and the conventional methods can result in good performances.

SWARMS (Semantic Web Aided Rich Mining System) is a general platform for semantic content management in Semantic Web. SWARMS provides various functions for domain semantic data management. SWARMS can be easily adapted to different domains by importing the ontological data of that domain (Liang, Tang, Li, and Wang, 2005b; Liang, Tang, Li, and Wang, 2006b)

The rest of the paper is organized as follows: Section 2 gives the whole architecture of SWARMS. Section 3 describes the knowledge access layer. Section 4 describes the search functions provided by SWARMS. Section 5 presents the association search algorithm in SWARMS. In Section 6, we introduce an application of the SWARMS platform to the researcher community domain. Finally, before concluding the chapter we give related work and future research directions.

ARCHITECTURE OF SWARMS

We start by giving a general overview of SWARMS. SWARMS includes (1) an indexing module that creates indexes for both semantic data and text-based data, (2) a knowledge access layer which provides a common API for accessing the knowledge data, which also includes a cache module to fast the search process, (2) a knowledge search engine that can search both semantic data and the text-based data, (4) an association search module that searches for the connections between instances, (5) a mining module that includes several basic mining algorithms including propagation and clustering, and (6) a visualization module that supports visualizing the process of search, association search, and mining.

Figure 1 shows the SWARMS architecture. Domain knowledge base stores the semantic data of a specific domain. The semantic data can be imported by domain experts or extracted from the existing Web automatically. There are main tools developed for manually inputting the semantic data for example OntoMat (Handschuh, Staab, and Ciravegna, 2002) and SHOE (Heflin, Hendler, and Luke, 2003). We have also developed several algorithms in SWARMS for automatic semantic annotation. The interested reader is referred to (Tang, Hong, Zhang, Liang, & Li, 2007) for a detailed introduction.

The indexing module creates an indexing file for the domain semantic data and stores it into a repository. The indexing module is critical for efficient access, especially when the number of instances in the knowledge base is scale up to millions (in many applications, it is the case).

Knowledge access layer provides the common API to store and fetch the data from the knowledge base. Knowledge annotator can use the API to store instances into the knowledge base. This layer is also the basic component for supporting advanced services such as knowledge search, association search, and knowledge mining to access the semantic data.

The search module provides metadata search and instance search in the knowledge base. By metadata search, one can search concepts and properties defined in the domain ontology. By

Figure 1. SWARMS Architecture

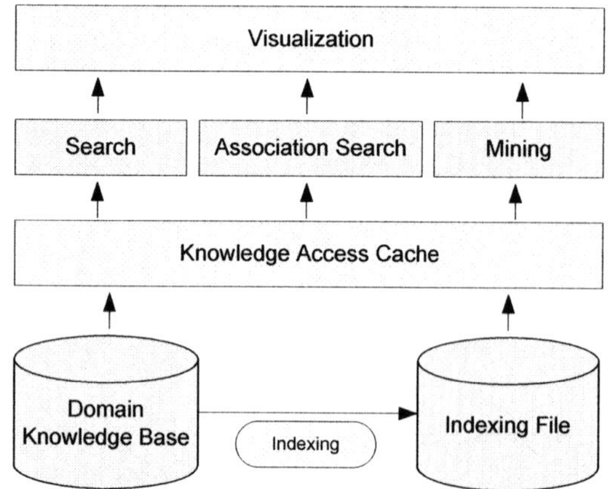

instance search, one can search instances of concepts or properties. The search module also supports keyword based search and constraint based search, as well as search with complex queries. As ontology can be complicated, sometimes it is important to allow users to specify explicit query conditions to search for more accurate results. For example, with the function, users can ask questions like "give me titles of all the publications written by 'Jing Zhang' in 2002".

Association search module is aimed at finding connection between instances. Ontology describes entities (concepts or instances) and relations (or properties) between them. The module supports finding explicit relations directly defined in the ontology and implicit relations hidden in the ontology.

The mining module provides several basic algorithms for mining the semantic data. Semantic mining includes considerable sub topics and a comprehensive investigation is beyond our objectives. We developed two basic algorithms for mining graph data: clustering and propagation. The clustering algorithm is an implementation of the Hierarchical Clustering algorithm (Zhao, Karypis, and Fayyad, 2005). It can be used in, for example, topic detection of News, sub-communities finding from researchers, and similar document grouping. The propagation algorithm is widely used to analyze graph data. Ontological data can be represented as a graph thus the propagation algorithm is really useful. We implemented the propagation algorithm based on (Kamvar, Schlosser, and Garcia-Molina, 2003; Guha, Kumar, Raghavan, and Tomkins, 2004). We will not explain the two algorithms in details, as the two issues have been investigated intensively. Instead, we would like to use examples of applications (cf. Section 6) to explain them.

We also provide an extension API to support integrating more mining algorithms in a specific domain.

The underlying data models in our process are ontologies. To facilitate further description, we briefly summarize the major primitives and introduce some shorthand notations. The main components of an ontology are concepts, relations, instances and axioms (Bechhofer *et al.*, 2004; Ting and Witten, 1999):

$$O = (C, R, I, A^O) \quad (1)$$

A concept $c_i \in C$ represents a set or class of entities or 'things' within a domain. The concepts can be organized into a hierarchy.

A relation $r_i \in R$ describes the interactions between concepts or properties of a concept. Relations fall into two broad types: *Taxonomies* that organize concepts into sub- or super-concept hierarchy, and *Associative relationships* that relate concepts beyond the hierarchy. The relations, like concepts, can also be organized into a hierarchy structure. Relations also have properties that can describe the characteristics of the properties. For example, the cardinality of the relationship, and whether the relationship is transitive.

Instances $\{i \mid i \in I\}$ are the "things" represented by a concept. Strictly speaking, an ontology should not contain any instances, because it is supposed to be a conceptualization of the domain. The combination of an ontology with associated instances is what is known as a knowledge base. However, deciding whether something is a concept or an instance is difficult, and often depends on the application. For example, "Course" is a concept and "Linguistics" is an instance of that concept. It could be argued that "Linguistics" is a concept representing different instances of Linguistics courses such as "French Linguistics Course" and "Spanish Linguistics Course". This is a well known and open question in knowledge management research.

Finally, axioms A^O are used to constrain values for classes or instances. In this sense the properties of relations are kinds of axioms. Axioms also, however, include more general rules, such as a course has at least one teacher.

KNOWLEDGE ACCESS LAYER

In this section, we describe the knowledge access layer. It is designed for efficiently storing and retrieving the semantic data from the knowledge base.

Knowledge Access API

The knowledge access component provides an ontological data access API for other components. The domain knowledge base stores the ontological data in a relational database. In the current implementation, the knowledge access API is implemented by Jena (Carroll *et al.*, 2004), a tool to store and retrieve ontological data. The API supports retrieving a unique instance/entity using a URI. It also supports retrieving a list of instances/concepts/properties using a complex query based on SPARQL. These two functions are the basic for supporting the knowledge search.

Basically, the knowledge access API has the following functions to allow other components to fetch ontological data:

1. Get concept information by a concept URI. The function receives the URI of the concept and return the concept's property values and context. The property values are all the literal property values like *rdfs:label* and *rdfs:comment*. The context is defined as the concept's super classes and sub classes.
2. Get property information by a property URI. The function receives the URI of the property and returns the property information including the properties' *rdfs:label* and *rdfs:comment*'s values and the properties' domain and range. Furthermore, sub and super properties of the current property can be also returned.
3. Get instance information by an instance URI. The function receives the URI of the instance and returns all values of the instance's prop-

erties. Furthermore, the concept which the instance belongs to is also returned.

4. Get ontological data by SPARQL query. The function receives a SPARQL query and returns all the triples satisfied with the query criteria.

In the module, we also design a caching strategy to support fast search. It is important for fast accessing the semantic data, especially for an online application.

Ontology Cache

In a Semantic Web application, there are often a large number of requests to the ontology base. The request may be accesses of concept, property or instance in the ontology. Frequently accesses to the ontology base would result in a heavy workload to the ontology server.

In order to achieve high efficient response of the ontology server, we propose caching the ontology data. In database community, the problem of data caching has been intensively investigated (Dar, Franklin, Jonsson, Srivastava, and Tan, 1996). The methodologies proposed can be used in ontology caching. However, they are not sufficient for dealing with all the problems. For database caching, usually the most frequently accessed data are cached and the recently less frequently accessed data in the cache are removed from it. Different from that, in ontology base, data are organized as objects and relations among objects. A user may request one object, and then request another object via a relation of that object. He may also request a similar object that has no any relations to the object. Ontology caching should consider more factors and thus is more difficult. Unfortunately, despite the importance of the problem, ontology caching has received little attention in the research community. No previous study has so far sufficiently investigated the problem, to the best of our knowledge.

We formalize ontology caching as that of classification. We propose to conduct ontology caching using machine learning methods. In the approach, when a user requests an object, we take its similar objects as candidates, and use a classification model to predict whether they should be cached or not.

Our Approach

We propose the SSOC (Semantic Similarity based Ontology Caching) for the task of ontology caching. Figure 3 shows the flow.

The "preprocess" takes the ontologies and the ontology access logs as its input and outputs the features of entities in ontologies. Then the features are used as input for similarity calculation and the entity similarities are generated. In the training process, a cache model is learned with machine learning methods. As the classification model, we use Genetic Algorithm (GA), an adaptive heuristic

Figure 3. Semantic similarity based ontology cache flow

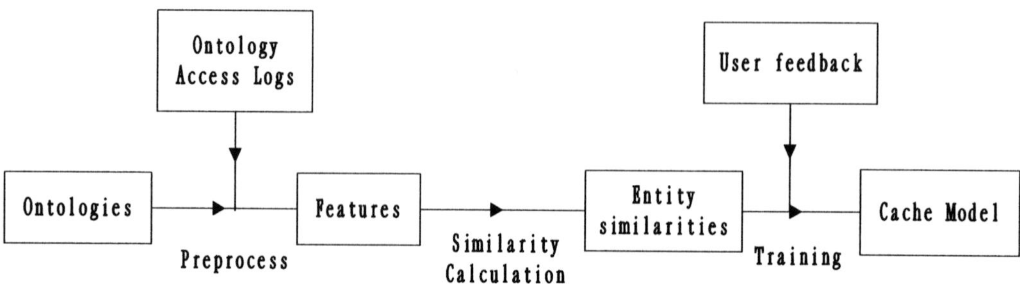

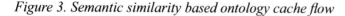

search algorithm based on the evolutionary ideas of natural selection and genetic. For details of GA, the interested reader is referred to (Zhu, 2001; De Jong, 1994). The key issue here is how to define features for effectively performing the predicting task. We use semantic similarity to define features in the classification model. Semantic similarity is the measurement of the similarity between two entities in an ontology. We define the similarity measure as a real-valued function:

$$Sim(x, y): S^2 -> [0,1] \quad (2)$$

where S is the set of entities in the ontology (including concepts, properties, and instances). Function $Sim(x, y)$ satisfies the reflexivity and symmetry:

$$Sim(x, x) = 1 \quad \text{(Reflexivity)}$$
$$Sim(x, y) = Sim(y, x) \quad \text{(Symmetry)} \quad (3)$$

Similarities between two concepts or two instances include hierarchy similarities, property similarities, label similarities, and access similarities.

Features

We use semantic similarity to define features.

Hierarchy Similarity

Hierarchy similarities between concepts and instances have different meanings. Let the hierarchy similarity of two entities as Sim_h.

Let all concept A's super concepts be $P(A)$ and concept B's super concepts be $P(B)$. For two concepts, the similarity can be calculated as follows (Resnik, 1999):

$$Sim_{ch}(A, B) = \frac{|P(A) \cap P(B)|}{|P(A) \cup P(B)|} \quad (4)$$

For two instances, the hierarchy similarity can be calculated by:

1. Denote the concept of instance A as $C(A)$ and concept of instance B as $C(B)$.
2. Use the concept hierarchy similarity to compute this similarity between instance A and B, which is as follows:

$$Sim_{ih}(A, B) = \frac{|P(C(A)) \cap P(C(B))|}{|P(C(A)) \cup P(C(B))|} \quad (5)$$

Property Similarity

A concept can have multiple properties each of which may have instances or relate to other concept. There are two kinds of properties. One is property with type constraint and the other is property with cardinality constraint. Let $P_d(A)$ be the type constraint of concept A; $P_c(A)$ be the cardinality constraint of concept A; and $P_{all}(A)$ be all the properties of concept A. The property similarity Sim_p of two concepts is defined as follows:

$$Sim_{cp} = \frac{|(P_d(A) \cap P_d(B)) \cup ((P_c(A) \cap P_c(B))|}{|P_{all}(A) \cup P_{all}(B)|} \quad (6)$$

The property similarity of two instances is different from concepts because the instances have values of their properties. The same typed properties with the same instances should be considered. Here we define the "same value" of two kinds of properties:

1. The same value of the properties instances is that the two values are the same. For example, the same of string values means that two strings are same in all characters.
2. The same value of the properties instances which points to another instance is that the two instances are the same. It means that they are the one instance or have the relation of "sameIndividualAs" between them.

Denote such same properties of instance A and B as $P_s(A, B)$. The property similarity of the two instances can be defined as follows (Resnik, 1999):

$$Sim_{ip} = \frac{|P_s(A,B)|}{|P(A) \cup P(B)|} \tag{7}$$

Label Similarity

Both concept and instance have labels representing the textual names of the entities. Let the label similarity of two entities as Sim_l. Although the textual name can be any symbols, for sharable and reusable purpose, people usually define the name of an entity in terms of natural language words. A usual name of an entity is made up by one or more words. WordNet (Fellbaum, 1998; Richardson, 1994), a popular electronic dictionary can be used to calculate the words' similarities. Let entity A's textual name as $name_l$ and entity B's textual name as $name_2$. For two words w_1 and w_2, the formula of the similarity is as follows:

$$Sense(s_1, s_2) = \frac{2 \times \log p(s)}{\log p(s_1) + \log p(s_2)} \tag{8}$$

where $p(s) = \frac{count(s)}{total}, w_1 \in s_1, w_2 \in s_2$. S is a sense node in WorldNet. It is the common hypernym for S_l and S_2. To sum up, entity name similarity can be defined as:

$$Sim_l(name_1, name_2) = \frac{\sum_{i=1}^{n}\sum_{j=1}^{m} Sense(w_{1i}, w_{2j})}{n \times m} \tag{9}$$

where n is the word count in $name_l$ and m is the word count in $name_2$.

Access Similarity

The access log is important information for caching. Let the access similarity of two entities as Sim_a. The access similarity can be obtained by the statistics on access log. The access similarity between two concepts or instances is thus defined as follows.

In a period of time, a client may access many concepts and instances. Let the set of entities as $S(client_1) = \{C_1, C_2, \ldots, C_n\}$. If the set S contains both entity A and entity B, then we say entity A and entity B have some kind of similarity. There are three kinds of clients with different access patterns about entity A and entity B. They are as follows:

$$\begin{cases} C_1(A,B)\ A \in S(C_1)\, and\ B \in S(C_1) \\ C_2(A,B)(A \in S(C_2)\, and\ B \notin S(C_2)) \\ \qquad or\ (A \notin S(C_2)\, and\ B \in S(C_2)) \\ C_3(A,B)\ A \notin S(C_3)\, and\ B \notin S(C_3) \end{cases} \tag{10}$$

The access similarity of entity A and entity B will be enhanced if the number of C_1 increases and will decrease if the number of C_2 increases. However, in most cases, it is hard to obtain the information for the number of C_3. Thus, in many practical applications, the access similarity of A and B is defined as follows:

$$Sim_a(A,B) = \frac{count(C_1)}{count(C_1) + count(C_2)} \tag{11}$$

where $count(C_x)$ is the number of C_x.

Semantic Similarity Calculation

By combining the four semantic similarities, we can obtain the final similarity. We use a linear function for the combination. Let $Sim_1 = Sim_h$, $Sim_2 = Sim_p$, $Sim_3 = Sim_l$, $Sim_4 = Sim_a$, and the formula of the similarity function is as follows:

$$Sim(x,y) = \sum_{i=1}^{4} x_k Sim_k(x,y) \tag{12}$$

Intuition of the final similarity is straightforward: if the similarity of x and y is higher (e.g., than a threshold), then x and y has high likelihood to be accessed together. Thus when one of them is accessed, the other will be loaded into the cache. The cache model then is defined formally:

x is accessed, y is loaded to the cache *iff* $Sim(x,y) > \lambda$.

Semantic Similarity Based Cached Model

The next task is to determine the parameters of $\{x_k \mid k= 1, 2, 3, 4\}$ and λ. A search algorithm can be applied to get the optimal values of these parameters. The search algorithm should have the following features:

1. The algorithm can get the approximate optimal solutions of the parameters.
2. The algorithm must be convergent in finite iteration steps.

We use Genetic Algorithms to learn the optimal parameters. After $\{x_k \mid k= 1, 2, 3, 4\}$ and λ are determined, the cache model is generated. The cache model is the final output of the approach.

Experimental Results

We use two evaluation measures to evaluate the cache approach.

The first one is how much time needed for processing n requests from clients, which is defined as:

$$TimeConsume(n) \tag{13}$$

where n represents the times of requests from clients.

The other measure is the cache hit rate. It defines how many hits in the cache for n requests from clients, which is defined as follows:

$$hitrate(n) = \frac{t}{n} \tag{14}$$

where t represents the times of hits in the n requests.

We created a test set containing 12,000 instances from an application of the system (cf. Liang *et al.*, 2006b for details). Among the 12,000 instances, 3,000 instances are used for training the model. In the model training, the genetic algorithm has the following parameters:

1. The number of individual in the Genetic Algorithm is 50
2. The probability of mutation: $p_{mutation}=0.2$
3. Stop conditions are as follows: $fitness_{expect}=0.9$ or $\varepsilon = 10^{-5}$ or $gen_{expect}=100$

Thus, Table 1 shows the parameters of the trained model.

We use eight clients to simulate the ontological data access to the server to test the effectiveness of the cache approach. In the simulation of the clients, we try to make it as real as possible. Thus we consider two problems:

1. Not all entities in an ontology have the same request probability. Some of them are likely to be requested than others.
2. Not all clients have the same period to visit the ontological data. Some of them may request ontological data more frequently than others.

We divide the ontological data into two regions. In one region, the entities' visit probability is p. In the other region, the entities' visit probabil-

Table 1. Parameters of the trained model

x_1	x_2	x_3	x_4	λ
0.41	0.11	0.18	0.30	0.80

ity is *1-p*. The client will randomly generate a number *d*. if $d<p$, the client will randomly select an entity in the region with the visit probability *p*. Otherwise the client will randomly select an entity in the region with the visit probability *1-p*. These two regions can be in different size. Here we use p_{ratio} to denote this parameter, p_{ratio} can be calculated as follows:

$$p_{ratio} = \frac{Number\ of\ entities\ in\ region\ p}{Total\ number\ of\ entities} \quad (15)$$

In the cache experiments, the cache size is another important factor, here we use how many entities can a cache size contain to measure the cache size, it is defined as:

$$ratio_{cache} = \frac{Number\ of\ entities\ cache\ can\ contain}{Total\ number\ of\ entities} \quad (16)$$

Thus, in an experiment, we need to have the following parameters:

1. Clients' request frequency
2. The region's probability *p* and the region's size p_{ratio}
3. Cache size: $ratio_{cache}$

We have used several experiments to test the cache approach.

The First Experiment
Client's request frequency is displayed in Box 1, with $p=0.5$, $p_{ratio}=0.5$, $ratio_{cache}=0.1$. Figure 4 shows the experimental results.

The Second Experiment
Client's request frequency is displayed in Box 2, with $p=0.8$, $p_{ratio}=0.5$, $ratio_{cache}=0.1$. Figure 5 shows the experimental results.

The Third Experiment
Client's request frequency is displayed in Box 3, with $p=0.8$, $p_{ratio}=0.2$, $ratio_{cache}=0.1$. Figure 6 shows the experimental results.

From the above experiments, we see that the cache algorithm works well with *p* increasing.

Box 1.

Client1,2	Client 3,4,5,6	Client 7,8
20 Second	60 Second	120 Second

Figure 4. Performance of ontology cache

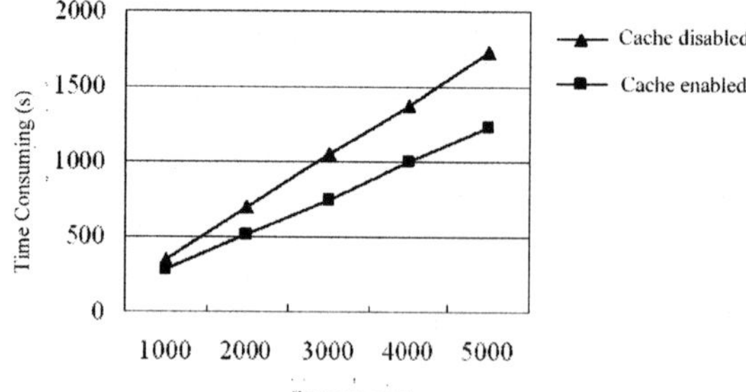

Performance of time consuming

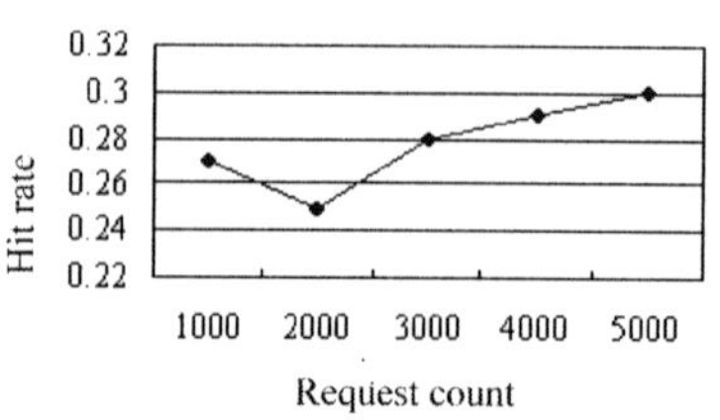

Performance of cache hit rate

Box 2.

Client1,2	Client 3,4,5,6	Client 7,8
20 Second	60 Second	120 Second

Figure 5. Performance of ontology cache

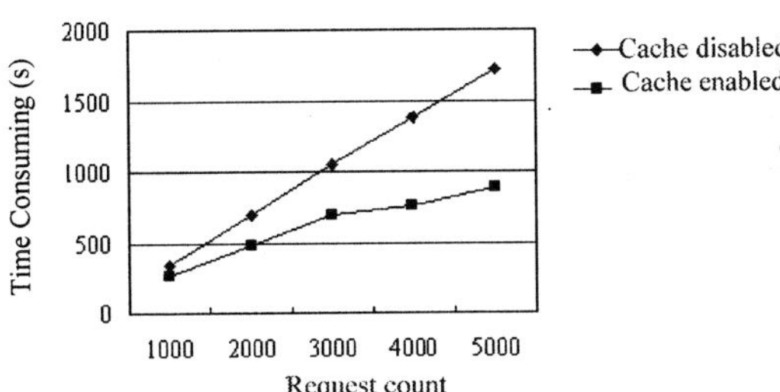

Performance of time consuming

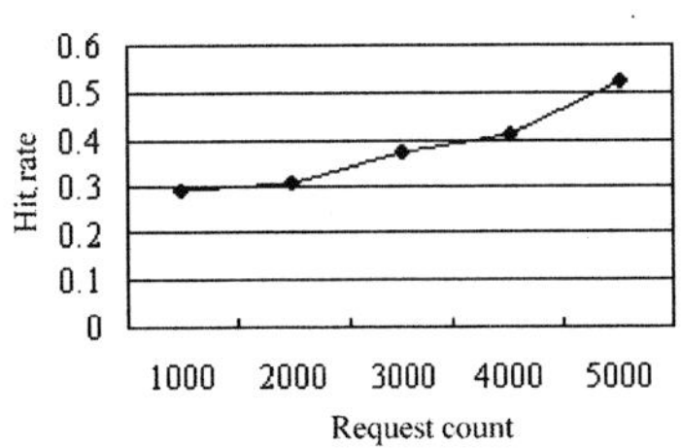

Performance of cache hit rate

Box 3.

Client1,2	Client 3,4,5,6	Client 7,8
20 Second	60 Second	120 Second

Figure 6. Performance of ontology cache

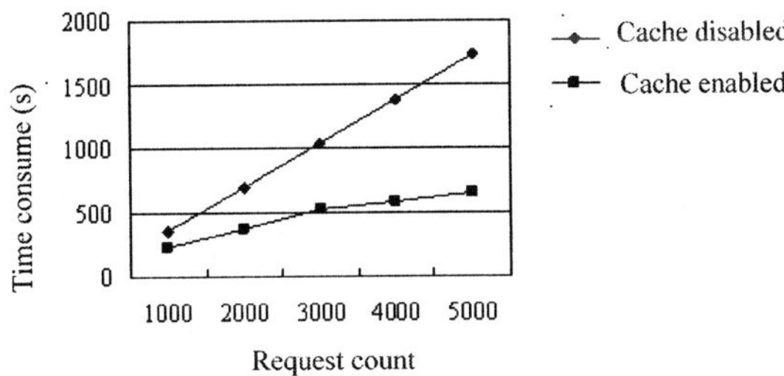

Performance of time consuming

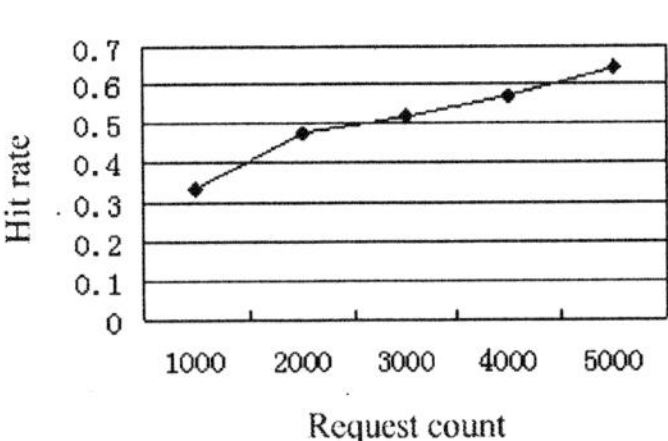

Performance of cache hit rate

When p keeps unchanged, the cache algorithm works well with p_{ratio} increasing. This indicates that the cache algorithm can improve the ontological data access efficiently.

KNOWLEDGE SEARCH

The knowledge search module includes keyword based search and complex knowledge search. In the former component, we implemented the keyword-matching based search and index based search. In the later component, we employed the typical RDF query language: SPARQL (Prud'hommeaux and Seaborne, 2007).

Knowledge Search

This component includes keyword-matching based search and index based search. In both modes, the user inputs keywords and the system returns instances or metadata or both (concepts *c* or properties *p*).

In the keyword-matching based method, keywords are matched with every property's value of each instance. For example, if the user inputs a keyword 'Jack', the keyword will be matched to every property and the system may return a Person's (a concept) instance with its property 'name' containing 'Jack'. Different from traditional search engines which return documents in free texts, SWARMS returns instances of an ontology and present a summary of each instance. For instance, for a Person's instance, the returned results contain the information about the person, including properties like phone number, homepage, etc. We also make a summary for the returned instance that is represented in natural language text. For a general keyword, e.g. "book", the system may return a number of instances.

The problem of match based method is the low efficiency. When the system contains a large number of instances, it is time consuming to match all the instances' properties with the keyword. In order to alleviate the problem, we employ the index technique. Index techniques are widely used in traditional information retrieval. In searching ontological data, an instance is viewed as a 'document'. The literal properties' values are used to construct the inverted index after segmentation, stop words removing, and stemming. The index based method has good performance in combination keyword based query like "AND", "OR" and "NOT" query criteria. We use the inverted index, which is a popular indexing method in Information Retrieval, as the index for instances. We view an instance as a search unit (document) in information retrieval. Properties of an instance are viewed as content of the document. Descriptions and comments of the instance are also viewed as content of the document. For example, in FOAF domain, users' search goal is to find relevant persons or relevant papers. So the persons' names and papers' title are indexed. The index structure is shown in Figure 2.

Figure 2. Index structure

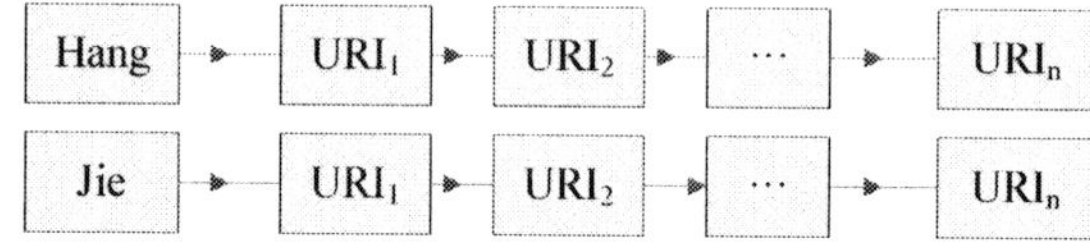

In Figure 2, "Hang" is a term. The URI_1, URI_2, …, URI_n are instances' URIs. When users input "Hang" as the search keyword, we can easily fetch the URI of the instance that contains the keyword "Hang". Then we use the URI to read the detailed information about the instance.

SWARMS's indexing method is to view concepts, properties and instances as a document first. And then, traditional indexing methods on documents can be used to index them. The approach to turn concepts, properties and instances to documents are different which is as follows:

1. **Viewing concepts as documents.** For a concept, we get the labels and descriptions of the concept. That is all the values of *rdfs:label* and *rdfs:comment*. These contents usually specify the concept's names and explanations in different languages. Thus, the contents are used to build the document for the concept.
2. **Viewing properties as documents.** This process is the same with viewing concepts to documents. The values of all the *rdfs:label* and *rdfs:comment* are taken to make the document for the property.
3. **Viewing instances as documents.** The difference of this process from the above process is that besides the values of all the *rdfs:label* and *rdfs:comment*, we should get all the literal properties' values of the instance. Thus, the values of the *rdfs:label* and *rdfs:comment* combined with all the literal properties' values are used to make the document for the instance.

The documents corresponding to the concepts, properties and instances are indexed using traditional document index approach. The URIs of the concepts, properties and instances are used in indexing to represent the search target instead of document id.

Complex Knowledge Search

To enable users to specify complex queries, a query language (like SQL for database) is needed. W3C, the leader of developing the common protocol, has proposed SPARQL (Simple Protocol And RDF Query Language) to query the complex ontological data. SPARQL is already in the status of candidate recommendation (cf. http://www.w3.org/TR/). We employed SPARQL as our query language in SWARMS. As SPARQL has complex syntax, it is not easy for a normal user to write a complete SPARQL query or understand the complex query syntax. We therefore design a simple editor to allow the user to specify constraints on concepts or properties and generate the SPARQL query automatically based on the constraints. Moreover, when a user visualizes an instance, she/he can also conduct the SPARQL query by several simple clicks. For example, when the user is browsing a "researcher" instance, she/he can see the publications, organization, and projects related to the researcher in a visualized graph with node indicating the instances and edge indicating the relations. If she/he wants to see the detail of an interested organization, she/he can simply double-click the organization node. Then system will switch to an organization-center graph. Such switch is actually conducted first by an automatic generated SPARQL query and then a graph generation process according to the query results.

Sometimes, a complex query cannot be efficiently accomplished by a SPARQL query, for example, "give me the publications related to 'semantic web' and written by 'Jing Zhang'". We need combine the index-based search and the complex knowledge search by: 1) querying all publications by 'Jing Zhang' using SPARQL; 2) retrieving all instances that contain the keyword 'semantic web'; 3) calculating the intersection of the two results. Actually, the combination of the two methods is used in many real-world queries.

ASSOCIATION SEARCH

Association search is to search for certain instances in semantic web and then make inferences from and about the instances we have found. This section proposes our solution to the problem.

Problem Statement

Now we formally define the association search problem that we are solving (Liang, Tang, and Li, 2005a).

Definition 1. Given a knowledge base *KB* and a user's query q represented by a set of keyword $q=\{k_i\}$, the task of association search is to:

1. Search for instances I_q related to q. Let $I_{ki}=\{i_{ki}\}$ denote the set of instances that contain keyword k_i. We have $I_q= I_{kl}\cup\cdots\cup I_{ki}\cup\cdots$.
2. Infer the association A between i_{ki} and i_{kj}, where $i_{ki}\in I_{ki}$ and $i_{kj}\in I_{ki}$.
   - If instance i contains both k_i and k_j, then we define the association between k_i and k_j as **Null Association** (also denoted as $A_{\emptyset}=(i, null, i)$) for the given instance i;
   - If instances i_{ki} and i_{kj} are related by a property p, then we define the association between k_i and k_j as **Direct Association** (also denoted as $A_D=(i_{ki},p, i_{kj})$) for the given instances i_{ki} and i_k;
   - If instances i_{ki} and i_{kj} do not have any direct relation, then our target is to find the **Indirect Association** between i_{ki} and i_{kj} (denoted as a set $A_{\Phi}=\{(i_{ki}, p_a, i_i), \{(i_i,p_m, i_j)\}, (i_j,p_b, i_{kj})\}$), which constructs

a relation path from i_{ki} to i_{kj} via **Intermediate Association** $A_I=\{(i_i, p_i, i_j)\}$.

3. Rank all possible associations for the query q. Given all possible associations (including Null Association, Direct Association, Indirect Association), represent them to the user by a ranked list according to their "relevance" to the query.

It has been carefully studied that the average number of keywords used in web search is 2.35 (Oyama, 2002). Thus, to facilitate the illustration, we focus on the scenario of two keywords (k_i, k_j) in association search in the rest of the paper. Generalizing our approach to multiple keywords is straightforward.

Given a large-scale graph (note: an ontology base can be directly converted into a graph model), to find all possible associations between two instances is obviously an NP-hard problem. In this paper, we concentrate ourselves on finding the most 'goodness' associations. More specifically, we use distance to represent the score of an association. We call the association with the smallest score as the *shortest association* and our goal is to find the *near-shortest associations*. By near-shortest associations, we mean associations whose scores are within a factor of $(1+\beta)$ of the score of the shortest association for some user-defined $\beta>0$.

Our Algorithm

In this work, we formalize the association search problem as that of near-shortest associations. We propose a two stage approach for finding the near-shortest associations.

The input is an association query (k_i, k_j). The objective is to find a ranked list of association $A_\Phi=\{(i_{ki}, p_a, i_i), \{(i_i, p_m, i_j)\}, (i_j, p_b, i_{kj})\}$. For facilitating the description, we will leave out i_i, i_j, and p_i from the notations hereafter when they are evident from the context and write it as $A=\{i_{ki}, i_{kj}\}$.

By combining the initialization step and the output step, our algorithm consists of four steps:

1. **Initialization.** We formalize a knowledge base as a directed graph. We specify a weight $w(e)$ to each relation e (i.e. object property) in the knowledge base. The weight can be computed in many different ways. For example, we can use the times of the two concepts connected by the relation as the weight of the relation. We view each instance of the concept as a node and each relation as an edge in the directed graph. We create an index for the directed graph and load the index into memory for the following steps. Then we use the keywords k_i and k_j to find related instances, i.e. two instance sets I_{ki} and I_{kj}. For any instance pair (with one from I_{ki} and the other from I_{kj}), perform Step 2 to Step 4.
2. **Shortest association finding.** It aims at finding shortest associations from all nodes $i\in I\backslash i_j$ in the graph to the target node i_j (including the shortest association from k_i to k_j with score L_{min}). In a graph, the shortest path between two nodes can be found using the state-of-the-art algorithms, for example, Dijkstra algorithm. However, we are dealing with a large-scale graph, the conventional Dijkstra algorithm results in a high time complexity of $O(n^2)$. We propose using a heap based Dijkstra algorithm to quickly find the shortest associations that can achieve a complexity of $O(n\log n)$.
3. **Near-shortest associations finding.** Based on the shortest association score $L_{min}>0$ found in Step 2 and a pre-defined parameter β, the algorithm requires enumeration of all associations that are less than $(1+\beta)L_{min}$ by a depth-first search. We constrain the length of an association to be less than a pre-defined threshold. This length restriction can reduce the computational cost.

4. **Ranking the found associations.** The association score is calculated by accumulating the weight of the relations involved in the association. And the associations found in Step 3 are ranked based on the scores according to the policy of 'the lower the best'.

The correctness of the approach follows from the obvious dynamic programming interpretation of Step 2 and Step 3. Figure 7 summarizes the proposed algorithm. In the rest of the section, we will explain the two main stages (Step 2 and Step 3) in details.

Experimental Results

We conducted experiments to test the effectiveness of our approach. We created an instance graph which contains 2,413,208 relations between instances with 5.38 relations for each instance on average.

We created 9 test sets, with each containing 369-1000 queries (i.e. keywords pairs).

In the experiments, we tried to find associations from the "source" instance to the "target" instance in each association query. We use the average running time on a test set to evaluate our approach and to compare with other methods. Running times do not include the time required to load the ontology model and that to output the associations.

It is not easy to find an appropriate baseline method. We here use the method of brute force enumeration as the baseline. In this method, we directly conducted depth-first search on the graph to find associations with length less than the threshold *max_length*. And we also defined a two-stage method as the baseline. In the first stage of the method, we make use of the conventional Dijkstra algorithm (Dijkstra, 1959) to find shortest paths and in the second stage we use depth-first search to find associations with length less than the threshold *max_length*. The method of depth-first search is similar to that in the second stage of our proposed approach.

Table 2 shows the results on the test set. In the table, Brute Force and Two-stage Baseline respectively represent the baseline method of brute force enumeration and the two-stage method with the conventional Dijkstra algorithm. The third and the fourth columns respectively represent the total running times and the average running times on the test sets.

We see that our approach achieve high performance in all of the association search tasks. In terms of the average time, our approach can find associations in less than 3 seconds on most of the test sets. The two-stage baseline uses nearly 400 times of the time cost of our approach on average. The Brute Force method uses nearly 164 times of the time cost of our approach on average.

APPLICATION IN RESEARCHER SOCIAL NETWORK

We have applied SWARMS to FOAF domain to manage the data of people in research community. Most components in SWARMS are domain independent. The knowledge extractor and domain

Table 2. Performances of association search (second)

Test Set	Method	Total Time	Avg. Time
Average	Brute Force	482708	482.71
	Two-stage Baseline	1161441	1161.44
	Our Approach	2941	2.94

Figure 7. The Association Search Algorithm

```
Input: a query (k_i, k_j) and a graph G = (V, E)
Output: a ranked list of associations A={(α_k , d(α_k))} with d(α_k)< (1+β)L_min, where L_min is the score of the shortest association and β is a user-defined parameter.
Algorithm: Our proposed algorithm
/*Step 1. Initialization*/
1.  foreach (e_ij∈E) {w(e_ij) ← w_ij, where w_ij is the weight of the relationship e_ij between instances i_i and i_j. }
2.  search for two instance sets I_ki and I_kj.
3.  for any instance pair denoted as v_i and v_j (one from I_ki and the other from I_kj), perform Step 2 to Step 4.
/*Step 2. Shortest association finding*/
 /*The following is resolved in a single heap-based */
4.  foreach (v∈V\v_j) {d'(v) ← shortest-association from v to k_j;}
5.  L_min ← d'(v_i);
/*Step 3. Near-shortest associations finding*/
6.  stack ← (v_i, NULL);
/*c(v) denotes the times v appears in the current association, used to avoid loops in the association*/
/*d(v) denotes the association score of the current association*/
7.  foreach (v∈V) {d(v) ← 0; c(v) ← 0;} c(v_i) ← 1;
8.  while (stack is not empty){
9.      (s, e) ← node at the top of stack;
10.     E(s) ← all edges pointing out from the node s;
11.     foreach (e_s∈E(s)){
12.      (s, u) ← the edge pointed to by e_s;
13.      if( c(u) = 0 && d(s) + w(e_s) + d'(u) < (1+β)L_min ){
14.        if( u is the target instance) {     /* find a new association */
15.          view all relations in the stack as the association; compute the
             score of the association
16.          add the association into A;
17.        } else {
18.          if( the length of the current association is less than a maximal
length){
19.             continue the depth-first search;
20.          }
21.        }
22.      } else {
23.        pop (s, e) from stack; c(s) ← c(s) - 1;
24.      }
25.   }
26. }
/*Step 4. Ranking the found associations */
/*to rank the found associations with the shortest on the top*/
27. A ← sort (A); return A;
```

data mining modules are domain dependent. In our FOAF domain, data sources are as follows:

1. **DBLP.** DBLP is a database for research community, storing researcher information and their publications. Knowledge extractor extracts the researchers' names. If two researchers are co-authors, a "*foaf:knows*" relation will be generated between them. From DBLP, we extract the following information to domain data repository:
   - o *foaf:knows*: This relation is annotated between two persons if they are co-authors;
   - o *foaf:publications*:This relation is annotated between a person and an instance of "*foaf:document*" if the person is one of the authors of the paper.
   - o *foaf:maker*: This relation is annotated between a paper and a person if the person is one of the authors of the paper.
   - o *foaf:topic*: This relation is annotated between a paper and a instance of "*foaf:topic*" if the paper is in the conference or journals that the topic instance presents.
   - o *foaf:name*: A person's instance has the "*foaf:name*" property whose value is his or her name.
2. **Personal homepages.** After a person's name is extracted from DBLP, we use Google to find web pages related to the person. A rule based classifier is used to determine if a web page is a person's homepage. Then we use a knowledge extractor to extract the researcher basic information from the identified homepage. The knowledge extractor's working process is shown in Figure 8. In both of the rule based classifier and the knowledge extractor, we use regex pattern to define the patterns and use the patterns to match the text. For example, in the rule based classifier for person's homepage identification, if a pattern matches a web page, then we say that the web page is the homepage of the person.

Domain data indexer and index-based search are implemented by Lucece (Hatcher and Gospodneti, 2004). Person's name and paper's title are indexed. The visualization and navigation is implemented on JUNG (O'Madadhain, 2003), a java visualization framework.

The data scale in our FOAF domain is more than 440,000 persons and 700,000 papers. The information we collect for persons are as follows: Person's name, person's homepage URL, person's phone number and fax number, person's email, person's title, person's friends(by *foaf:*

Figure 8. The processing flow in knowledge extractor

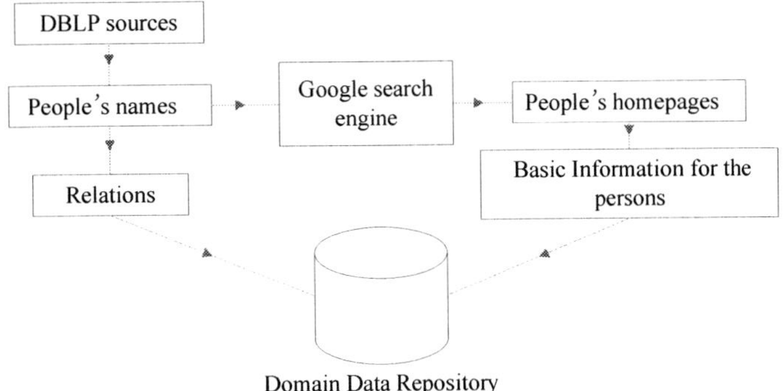

knows property), person's publications(by *foaf: publications* property).

The information we collect for documents are as follows: Publications' title, publications' authors (by *foaf:maker* property), and their published conferences or journals (by *foaf:topic* property).

We have developed a system based on the SWARMS platform, which is called ArnetMiner (available at http://www.arnetminer.org) (Tang, Zhang, Zhang, Yao, and Zhu, 2007a; Tang, Zhang, and Yao, 2007b; Li *et al.*, 2007). Our objective in this system is to provide services for managing semantic social networks. Specifically, we aim at answering three questions: (1) how to efficiently store and retrieve the data of a social network, (2) how to search in the social network, and (3) how to mine the social network. We use an academic researcher network as a case study. For the first question, we extend FOAF ontology as the metadata and employ a unified approach to extract, fuse, and create a person's profile from the existing Web. We store the extracted semantic data in a database using the knowledge access layer. For search in the social network, we aimed at person search and publication search. We also conduct association search by searching for connections between people. For mining the social network, we utilize the propagation based method for finding experts on a topic and people name disambiguation. We also employed a clustering algorithm to a person's communities and his/her sub communities. In the rest of the section, we will first briefly introduce the representation of the knowledge in the researcher social network. We then introduce the search and mining features in the system. Finally, we present several snapshots of the systems to explain the visualization supported by SWARMS.

Representation

We extend the FOAF ontology (Brickley and Miller, 2005) to define the researcher's profile in ArnetMiner. The profile includes four sections. Totally, 2 concepts and 24 properties are defined. Some details are listed in Figure 9.

We formalize profile extraction as a tagging problem and employ a unified approach to perform the whole task on the basis of tagging. Specifically, we take the problem as that of assigning tags to the input texts, with a tag representing one type of profile information. As tagging model, we employ Conditional Random Fields (CRF) (Lafferty, McCallum and Pereira, 2001). For details please refer to (Tang *et al.*, 2007).

Figure 9. Profile ontology

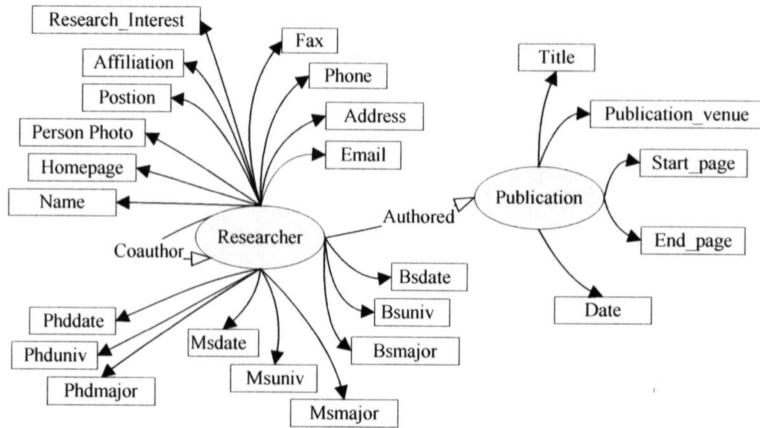

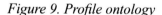

Search

In the researcher network, we provide four types of searches: person search, publication search, category based search, and association search.

The system has a simple user interface which allows users to select person search, publication search and association search. After select one kind of the search types, users input the search criteria to search the results. The search criteria for each search type are as follow

Person Search

The user inputs a person name, and the system returns the profile of the person. There are two kinds of search: offline search and online search. For offline search, we perform person search in the constructed researcher network. If a person can be found, the profile of the person stored in the local knowledge base will be displayed. For online search, we perform a real-time extraction of the person's profile as described in Section 6.1. The online process may last from 1 to 30 seconds depending on the network speed. The system also supports searching with constraints, for example, the user can input a query like "Jie Tang, uni:Tsinghua". With the query, the system searches for persons with the name "Jie Tang" and with its property "organization" containing "Tsinghua".

By default, users can input a text which separates with "," and each phases separated by "," specifies the search criteria. If there are no ":" in the search phase, we take the term as a search in the name field. Besides the name field, there are other fields in search which is represented as follows:

1. *uni*, which represents a search to the person's organization
2. *email*, which represents a search to the person's email
3. *phone*, which represents a search to the person's phone number
4. *title*, which represents a search to the person's title

Publication Search

The user inputs keywords, and the system returns publications with the most relevant publications on the top. We employ the conventional information retrieval model to do the publication search. Moreover, the system supports the user to read the publication content online. It achieves this by following steps. It first tries to find actual documents of the publications from the web. With a developed module, it converts the documents of any kinds of formats (e.g. PDF, WORD, HTML, etc.) into a unified vectorgraph format. The module is actually a print driver like PDF Distiller. It performs the conversion by printing the content onto a targeted graph. In this way, we are able to generate snapshots of every publication so that the user can view the publication online.

The search criteria of the publication search is relatively simple, users only need to input a set of keywords separated with a blank.

Category Based Search

We created a taxonomy containing 40 research topics. We use a classification model to categorize a person to research fields according to his/her profile information and his/her authored publications. Then the user can select the research field to view the research people classified to it.

The search criteria of the category based search is simple, users need to select a category in a list. All the categories are listed for users to select because users may not know which keywords are corresponding to a specific category.

Association Search

The associations between two persons may be direct (e.g. the two researchers coauthor a document) or indirect (e.g. one researcher coauthors a document with a friend of the other person). We formalize association search as a problem of near-shortest paths and propose an efficient algorithm to find near-shortest associations from a source person to a target person (see Section 5 for details).

The search criteria of the association search are made up by several steps. First, user inputs two names, and then systems returns two lists for each name. Each list represents the persons as the search result of the name. And then, user selects a person in the first name list and the other in the second name list, indicate that user wants to search associations between these two persons. Finally, the system gives the associations of these two persons.

Mining

For mining the researcher network, we currently focus on three subjects: expert finding, research sub communities, and people association finding. We make use of the clustering algorithm and the propagation algorithm developed in SWARMS to implement the mining components:

1. *Expert finding.* The user inputs a topic, and the system tries to answer who are experts on the topic. We use the graph-propagation based approach and make use of person's profile and his/her relationships in the researcher network to calculate an 'expertise degree' on the topic. One of the basic ideas behind this approach is that if a person has authored many documents on a topic, then it is very likely that he is an expert on the topic, or if the person's name co-occurs in many times with the topic, then it is likely that he is an expert on the topic. Another idea here is that if a person knows many experts on a topic, then it is very likely that he/she is also an expert on the topic, or if the person's name co-occurs in many times with another expert, then it is likely that he/she is also an expert on the topic. See (Zhang, Tang, and Li, 2007)
2. *Sub-community finding.* We employed a clustering method to find what communities a researcher might have been involved in. We conduct the process as follows. First, we collect all publications of the researcher. Then we construct a feature vector for each publication. The feature vector is constructed by using the terms occurred in the title and abstract of the publications. For each term, the term frequency value is used as the value in the feature vector for this term. Next, the clustering process is conducted on all the publications. The cluster algorithm is based on K-Means and the cosine similarity of two feature vectors are used as the distance between two publications. After that, we can obtain several clusters for each researcher. Each cluster represents a possible research interest of the researcher. Furthermore, we select representative keywords for each cluster and use it to name the research communities of the current researcher. In order to show the research interests of the author's friends, we use the coauthor relationship to find friends of the current researcher in each community and display them in the same graph. The found sub-communities for each researcher were stored into his/her profile.
3. *Name Disambiguation.* We also utilize the clustering method for name disambiguation. Name disambiguation is a critical problem in publication citations. For example, the mixture of publications, belonging to different people with the same name, exists in all current digital libraries like Citeseer and DBLP. Our strategy is to view the publications of different clusters as those of different persons.

Prototype System

SWARMS provide visualization of the process of search and mining. Figure 10 to Figure 13 show snapshots of the system applied to researcher social network mining.

Figure 10 shows an example search result of keyword based search. The user inputs keywords, and the system returns researchers that related to the keywords. In Figure 10, the top-left window shows the researchers related to the inputted keyword. The user can select to show the detailed ontological information of a researcher in the right window. When a researcher is selected, we also output a summary natural-language-based result in the bottom-left window. The summary would be very useful for a normal user who is not familiar with the ontology language.

Figure 11 shows the visualization view of a researcher. When the system returns a researcher list, the user can choose to show the visualization view of a researcher. In Figure 11, the main window shows the visualization result of the selected researcher (called focus instance). Around the selected researcher, we display his/her friends and published papers represented by different

Figure 10. Keyword based search user interface

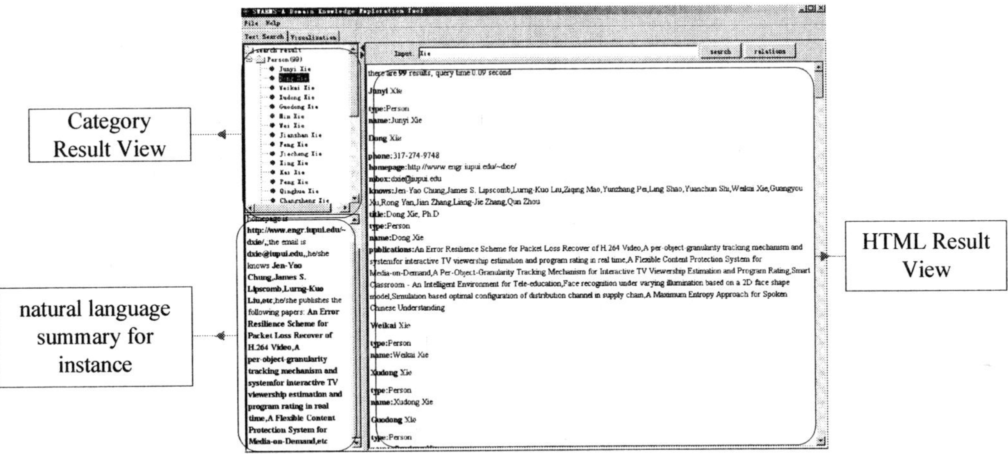

Figure 11. Sample visualization

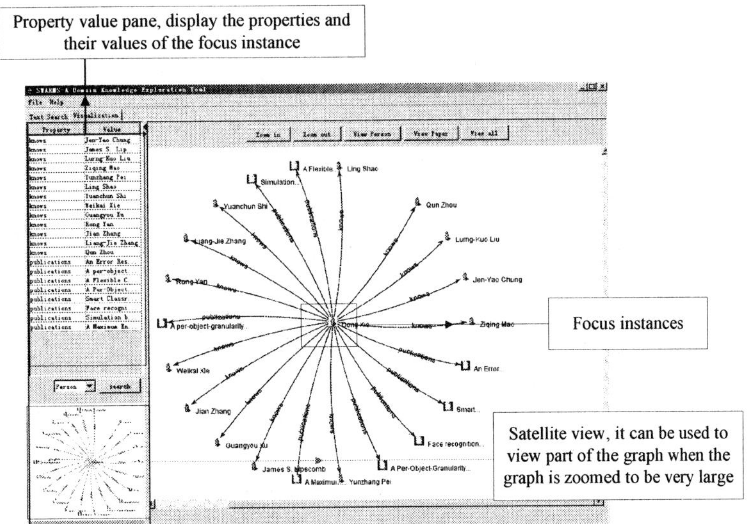

icons. Relations between the researchers are diagrammed as arrows. The top-left window shows the datatype properties of the selected instance in the right window. The bottom-left window is an eagle view window.

Figure 12 shows the results of sub-community mining by clustering. For each researcher, the system provides a function to discover his/her research communities. One researcher can be involved into several communities and his/her friends (i.e. coauthored researcher) would be classified into different communities. The function is useful to intuitively see research fields of a researcher and his/her research activities in each field. In Figure 12, the top-left and bottom-left windows still show the datatype properties and eagle view respectively (as explained above). The right window shows the mining results.

Figure 12. Sub-community Mining

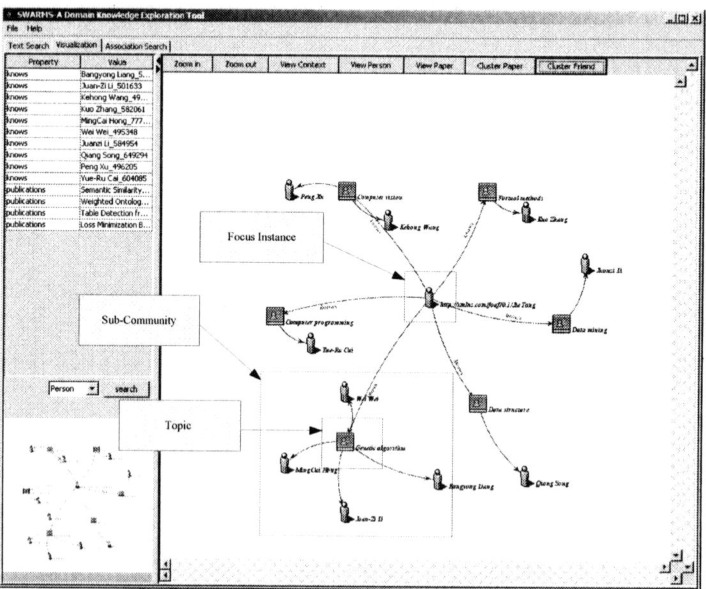

Figure 13. Association Search

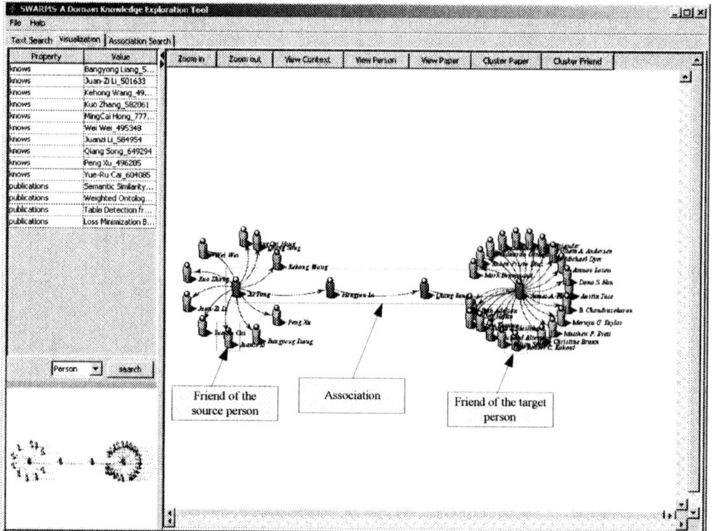

Figure 13 shows a sample association search. The left-most purple icon represents the source person and the right-most purple icon represents the target person. The other purple icons represent persons on the association. The yellow icons diagram friends of the source/target person.

The scope of this article does not allow us to provide a "User Manual" of the system — instead we try to provide a sense of the implementation, and some details that the reader can understand the architecture and the main features of the system.

Performance Evaluation

In such a large scale social network, SWARMS still has good performance. In speed analyzer, we use some keywords that will return many results and some keywords that will return few results to test the keyword based search's performance. The result of the speed analysis is shown in Table 3.

From Table 3, we can see that the time for a keyword with many results and a keyword with none results are almost the same.

We use twenty instances to test the speed for locating an instance in the repository. Some of the twenty instances only have few properties' values. For example, somebody only publishes few papers. Some of the twenty instances have hundreds of properties' values because the person publishes many papers and have many friends.

The max, min and average time consume in the twenty instances are shown in Table 4.

Table 3. Performance of search

Keyword	Number of Results	Time(seconds)
Li	921	0.11(s)
Zhang	759	0.11(s)
James	545	0.09(s)
Liang	180	0.09(s)
Tim	156	0.09(s)
Baul	0	0.09(s)

RELATED WORK

In this section, we present a survey of the current research work related to domain knowledge management.

Knowledge Management

Knowledge management aims at integrating and managing the information from the various sources so as to enable knowledge sharing and reuse. Considerable works have been conducted on knowledge management.

Noy, Sintek, and Decker, (2001) have developed a graphical tool, called Protégé, for ontology editing and knowledge acquisition. Protégé lets users think about domain models at a conceptual level without having to know the syntax of the knowledge language. Protege has various plugins to fulfill different requirements for knowledge management. Protege is a widely used ontology editing and maintenance tool currently.

KM Goodinator (Knowledge Management Group Coordinator) has been developed by (Kida and Shimazu, 2002). It's a knowledge management tool that runs with commercial schedule management groupware. The tool handles schedule data as knowledge repository. The repository contains multiple sources: A Human Relationship Database, a Who-Knows-What directory, and a Scheduling Knowledge Database.

Knowledge Search

Knowledge search can be seen as one part of knowledge management. Knowledge search is

Table 4. Time for loading an instance's information

Max(s)	Min(s)	Average(s)
0.02	0.01	0.014

concerned with finding the 'relevant' knowledge from the knowledge base.

For example, Swoogle uses the techniques from the information retrieval to build a search engine for the Semantic Web (Ding and Finin, 2005). The search results given by Swoogle can be ontology files, concepts, properties and instances. However, the results are not easily understandable for average users because it's represented in a HTML based way, which makes the relations among the entities hard to be observed by average users.

Semantic Search project extends the keyword based search (Guha, McCool and Miller 2003). It can find persons who are W3C members and display his or her personal information in a structured way. For the keywords that could not find matches in the W3C members repository, the system will forward the keywords to a traditional search engine, for example, google, to get the results from traditional search engine.

Semantic Web Mining

Semantic Web Mining aims at combining the two fast-developing research areas Semantic Web and Web Mining. Recently, an increasing number of researchers is working on improving the results of Web Mining by exploiting semantic structures in the Web, and they make use of Web Mining techniques for building the Semantic Web. Many researcher issues have been studied related to Semantic Web mining, for example ontology learning from text (e.g., Williams and Tsatsoulis, 2000; Maedche, 2002; Maedche, Staab, Studer, Sure, and Volz, 2002), building Semantic Web using information extraction techniques (e.g., Heflin and Hendler, 2000; Handschuh, Staab, and Ciravegna, 2001; Tang, *et al.*, 2007), and merging ontology bases by ontology alignment (e.g., Doan, Madhavan, Domingos, and Halevy, 2002; Melnik, Molina-Garcia, and Rahm, 2002; Do and Rahm, 2002; Jian, Hu, Cheng, and Qu, 2005; Tang *et al.*, 2006b). The first two problems aim at automatically learning ontology or extract instances from the existing Web so as to provide the Semantic Web with annotated data. The third problem is to integrate the semantic data described by different ontologies.

There are also some other work aiming at using semantics for web mining and mining the Semantic Web. For example, In (Hotho, Maedche, and Staab, 2001), ontologies are used as background knowledge during preprocessing, with the aim of improving clustering results; knowledge-rich approaches in automatic text summarization (cf. Mani and Maybury, 1999; Mani, 2001) aim at maximizing the information within a minimal amount of resulting text. And much research work investigates how to make use of web structure to improve the mining performance. A comprehensive survey of the knowledge mining is obviously beyond the purpose of the chapter. The interested reader is referred to a survey of Semantic Web Mining (Stumme, Hotho, and Berendt, 2006).

Association Search

Semantic Association Search

Semantic association represents the complex relationships between entities in the Semantic Web. Several research efforts have been made so far. The previous work focuses on how to represent the association in an ontology data model and how to enable processing the query of association in the ontology model. The problems addressed significantly differ in nature from that in this work.

For instance, Anyanwu et al. propose extending the existing RDF or OWL model to support representing the notion of a relationship in the RDF query and processing the association query on a knowledge base (Anyanwu and Sheth, 2003). They have implemented the approach by extending the existing RDF query system, e.g. RDFSuite (Alexaki, Karvounarakis, Christophides, Plexousakis, and Tolle, 2001) and Jena. In the approach, semantic association search is performed first on metadata of the ontology to find a RDF property sequence. Then instances of the RDF property sequence are viewed as associations in the knowledge base. Anyanwu proposes a method based on information gain to measure how much information is conveyed by a result of association in order to rank the found associations (Anyanwu, Maduko, and Sheth, 2005). See also (Aleman-Meza *et al*, 2006; Liang *et al.*, 2005; Sheth *et al*, 2005).

Association Search in Social Network

Many uses of recommender systems require finding associations between persons, not just providing "oracular" advice. Recently, a few methods have been proposed to solve the problem. For example, Kautz et al. have developed a recommender system called ReferralWeb (Kautz, Selman, and Shah, 1997). The ReferralWeb system helps people search and explore social networks that exist on the Web. They focus on expert recommendation rather than efficiently finding and ranking the associations.

Balog and Rijke formulate three sub tasks in people association finding: connection finding, collaboration finding, and reputation analysis (Balog and de Rijke, 2006). They focus on finding direct relationships between persons from Web documents using information retrieval models. They propose to model association finding as a mixture of a language modeling approach to snippet retrieval and a noisy channel approach to determine the likelihood that a retrieved snippet "generates" a relationship between persons.

Adamic and Adar have investigated the problem of association search in email networks (Adamic and Adar, 2005). They tested how three different properties (degree of relationships, position in the organizational hierarchy, and physical location) of the persons in the social network can be used to improve the performance of association search. They simulated an experiment based on a small network composed of 430 individuals with an average number of 10 acquaintances. Differing from their work, we focus on a large-scale social network. (The size of our network might be 1000 times of theirs.)

Knowledge Visualization

Knowledge visualization and navigation aims at helping users to understand the knowledge easier. 'focus+contex' is a method used in graph visualization. 'focus' means the object that satisfied current criteria which is usually specified by users. 'contex' means the related objects to the 'focus' object.

For example, Flink gives a graphical view of researcher social network (Mika, 2005). For a researcher, the view displays his interest fields and researchers that have the common research interests with him or her. The data of Flink is collected from the annotated web pages from the web site of ISWC conference.

Knowledge Visualization in Semantic Web aims at visualizing the entities and relations in domain ontology. RDF Gravity (http://semweb.salzburgresearch.at/apps/rdf-gravity/index.html) is a tool to visualize RDF data using node centric graph. FRODO RDFSViz (http://www.dfki.uni-kl.de/frodo/RDFSViz/) is a similar RDF visualization tool with RDF Gravity and it supports displaying the visualization of RDF data in the web browser.

Besides the graph based visualization, which is suitable for displaying the entities and relations in domain ontology, there are many other ways to visualize the ontology in Semantic Web. A careful survey of Semantic Web and information visualization (Albertoni 2004) points out the hierarchical view, map based view and other kinds of views can be applied to knowledge visualization in Semantic Web.

FUTURE RESEARCH DIRECTIONS

There are a variety of promising directions for future research on domain knowledge management.

Although much research work has been conducted for knowledge management, there are still many problems needed to be investigated and solved to make knowledge management system more practical. We here list several challenging problems related to knowledge indexing, efficiency on complex knowledge query, knowledge ranking and mining:

- Different knowledge management systems have different ways to index knowledge, for example to crawl the source data after a specific certain time. However, future systems may real-time data acquired from sources like sensor. Such data needs to be crawled and indexed immediately. How to keep index updated frequently and correctly is a challenging problem for a knowledge management system, especially for dealing with a large scale data.
- Knowledge efficient access is very important for making the system practical. Currently almost all Semantic Web based knowledge management systems have efficient problems in serving complex queries. Large scale knowledge is usually stored in database. Thus a complex SPARQL query can cause the execution of many SQL queries and sometimes cause SQL queries with "Like" Clause. Lots of efforts should be placed in this area to solve the efficient problems of complex query on ontological data.
- How to perform search ontological data represented by different distributed and heterogeneous ontologies? Another important aspect of the semantic search is that semantic content may come from different Web sites. The semantic content is distributed and heterogonous. At present, most semantic search research focus on the search in a specific domain or ontologies. For example, there are many kinds of ontologies about bibliographical data on the Web such as data from DBLP, ACM and Citeseer. Furthermore, some other sites can also publish data about same kinds of semantic data without getting permission from any centralized authority, i.e., they can all extend the cumulative knowledge on the Semantic Web about any resource in a distributed fashion. Semantic search in distributed and heterogamous semantic data is a very important aspect of the Semantic Web.
- How to perform efficient reasoning based semantic search? Semantic data are represented in the logic form. The semantic content which is inferred from existing semantic content on the Web also can meet the search requirement for users. Though reasoning based semantic search are studied, but much of the efforts focus on the semantic search on light weight ontological data. And the efficiency of reasoner and the control of reasoning process in semantic search constrain the development of reasoning based semantic search.
- Mining more information from the structured data other than associations. More mining targets should be considered and implemented in order to make use of the semantics in ontological data.
- How to implement the "question answering" in Semantic Web? Traditional keyword based search neither understands the user query requirement, nor returns the accurate search result. However, in Semantic web, ontology is the conceptualized description about the common interest of certain domains. It defines the concepts and relationships for certain domains, which provides the possibility for us to realize the "question answer". But how to understand user's query in natural language (most users cannot understand

ontological data), annotate the query by the ontology and find the answer about the query are still to be important issues in semantic search.

As another future work, more applications, especially commercial applications, which have impacts on taking advantages of knowledge management in doing successful business, need to be investigated. The commercial applications can provide rich real data, feedbacks and challenges for advising the research and industrial direction in this field.

Another interesting also important issue is how to make use of the prior knowledge in semantic search and mining. So far, a usual method for incorporating the prior knowledge is to use some domain-specific dictionaries (e.g. ontology) in the search process. The question is whether the simple method still works well when dealing with more complex search tasks.

In future work, research community has to face the rising challenges and focuses on how to enhance the practical usefulness of semantic search and mining methods.

CONCLUSION

In this chapter, we have introduced the architecture and the main features of SWARMS as a general platform for semantic content management in Semantic Web. SWARMS provides various functions over ontological data. Specifically, SWARMS includes an indexing module for creating indexes for semantic data, a knowledge search engine, a knowledge access layer, a cache module to fast the search, an association search module, a mining module, and a visualization module. We have explained in detail the design and implementation of each module. We have also presented the evaluation results of each module. The system is applied to the domain of researcher social network, in which we use SWARMS to store and access the semantic data. We have employed association search to find connection between researchers. We have utilized the mining module to develop expert finding, name disambiguation, and sub-community finding.

ACKNOWLEDGMENT

The work is supported by the National Natural Science Foundation of China (90604025, 60703059), Chinese National Key Foundation Research and Development Plan (2007CB310803), and Chinese Young Faculty Funding (20070003093).

Thanks to the anonymous reviewers for their constructive suggestions and also thanks to Limin Yao for helping format the chapter.

REFERENCES

Adamic, L. A. & Adar, E. (2005). How to Search a Social Network. *Social Networks,* 27 (3), 187-203.

Albertoni, R., Bertone, A., & Martino, M.D. (2004). Semantic Web and Information Visualization. *In Proceedings of Semantic Web Applications and Perspectives.* Italy, December 2004.

Aleman-Meza, B., Nagarajan, M., Ramakrishnan, C., Ding, L., Kolari P., Sheth, A.P., Arpinar, I. B., Joshi, A., & Finin, T. (2006). Semantic Analytics on Social Networks: Experiences in Addressing the Problem of Conflict of Interest Detection. *In Proceedings of the 15th International World Wide Web Conference.* pp.407-416. Edinburgh, UK, May 2006.

Alexaki, S., Karvounarakis, G., Christophides, V., Plexousakis, D., & Tolle, K. (2001). The ICS-FORTH RDFSuite: Managing Voluminous RDF Description Bases. *In Proceedings of 2nd International Workshop on the Semantic Web.* pp. 1-13. Hong Kong, May 2001.

Anyanwu, K. & Sheth, A.P. (2003). ρ-Queries: Enabling Querying for Semantic Associations on the Semantic Web. *In Proceedings of 12th International World Wide Web Conference.* pp.690-699. Budapest, Hungary, May 2003.

Anyanwu, K., Maduko, A., & Sheth, A.P. (2005). SemRank: Ranking Complex Relationship Search Results on the Semantic Web. *In Proceedings of 14th International World Wide Web Conference.* pp.117-127. Chiba, Japan, May 2005.

Balog, K. & de Rijke, M. (2006). Searching for People in the Personal Work Space. *In Proceedings of International Workshop on Intelligent Information Access.* pp.6-8. Helsinki, Finland, July 2006.

Bechhofer, S., Harmelen, F.V., Hendler, J., Horrocks I., McGuinness, D.L., Patel-Schneider, P.F., & Stein, L.A. (2004). OWL Web Ontology Language Reference. from http://www.w3.org/TR/owl-ref/

Berendt, B., Hotho, A., Mladenic, D., Someren, M.V., Spiliopoulou, M., & Stumme, G. (2003). A Roadmap for Web Mining: From Web to Semantic Web. *In Proceedings of First European Web Mining Forum.* pp.1-22. Croatia, September 2003.

Brickley, D., & Miller, L. (2005). FOAF Vocabulary Specification. from http://xmlns.com/foaf/0.1/

Dar, S., Franklin, M. J., Jónsson, B. T., Srivastava, D., & Tan, M. (1996). Semantic Data Caching and Replacement. *In Proceedings of 22nd International Conference on Very Large Data Bases.* pp.330-341. Bombay, India, September 1996.

De Jong, K.A. (1994). Genetic Algorithms: A 25 Year Perspective. *Computational Intelligence Life,* 68, 125-134.

Dijkstra, E. (1959). A Note on Two Problems in Connexion with Graphs. *Numerische Mathematik,* 1, 269-271.

Ding, L. & Finin, T.W. (2005). Boosting Semantic Web Data Access Using Swoogle. *In Proceedings of the 20th National Conference on Artificial Intelligence.* pp.1604-1605. Pittsburgh, Pennsylvania, July 2005.

Do, H. & Rahm, E. (2002). Coma: A System for Flexible Combination of Schema Matching Approaches. *In Proceedings of 28th International Conference on Very Large Data Bases.* pp.610-621. Hong Kong, August 2002.

Doan, A.H., Madhavan, J., Domingos, P., & Halevy, A. (2002). Learning to Map Between Ontologies on the Semantic Web. *In Proceedings of the 11th World Wide Web Conference.* pp.662–673. Hawaii, USA, May 2002.

Fellbaum, C. (1998). WordNet: *An Electronic Lexical Database.* Cambridge, MA: MIT Press. 1998

Guha, R.V., McCool, R., & Miller, E. (2003). Semantic Search. *In Proceedings of the 12th International World Wide Web Conference.* pp.700-709. Budapest, Hungry, May 2003.

Guha, R., Kumar, R., Raghavan, P., & Tomkins, A. (2004). Propagation of Trust and Distrust. *In Proceedings of the 13th international Conference on World Wide Web.* pp.403-412. NY, USA, May 2004.

Handschuh, S., Staab, S., & Maedche, A. (2001). CREAM—Creating Relational Metadata with a Component-based, Ontology Driven Framework. *In Proceedings of the First International Conference on Knowledge Capture.* pp.76-83. Victoria, BC, Canada, October 2001.

Hatcher, E., & Gospodneti, O. (2004). *Lucene in Action.* Manning Publications Corporation. 2004.

Heflin, J. & Hendler, J. (2000). Searching the Web with SHOE. *In Proceedings of the AAAI 2000 Workshop on Artificial Intelligence for Web Search.* pp.35-40. Austin, Texas, July 2000.

Hotho, A., Maedche, A., & Staab, S. (2001). Ontology-based Text Clustering. *In Proceedings of the IJCAI-2001 Workshop on Text Learning: Beyond Supervision.* Seattle, USA, August 2001.

Jeremy, J. Carroll, J.J., Dickinson, I., Dollin, C., Reynolds, D., Seaborne, A., & Wilkinson, K. (2004). Jena: Implementing the Semantic Web Recommendations. *In Proceedings of the 13th International World Wide Web Conference on Alternate Track Papers & Poster.* pp.74-83. NY, USA, May 2004.

Jian, N., Hu, W., Cheng, G., & Qu, Y. (2005). Falcon-AO: Aligning Ontologies with Falcon. *In Proceedings of the K-CAP Workshop on Integrating Ontologies.* Canada, October 2005.

Kamvar, S.D., Schlosser, M.T., & Garcia-Molina, H. (2003). The Eigen Trust Algorithm for Reputation Management in P2P Networks. *In Proceedings of the 12th International World Wide Web Conference.* pp.640–651. Budapest, Hungry, May 2003.

Kautz, H., Selman, B., & Shah, M. (1997). ReferralWeb: Combining Social Networks and Collaborative Filtering. *Communication of the ACM, 40* (3), 63-65.

Kida, K. & Shimazu, H. (2002). Ubiquitous Knowledge Management - Enabling an Office-work Scheduling Tool for Corporate Knowledge Sharing. *In Proceedings of Workshop on Knowledge Media Networking.* pp.99-104. Kyoto, Japan, Jul 2002.

Lafferty, J. McCallum, A., & Pereira, F. (2001). Conditional Random Fields: Probabilistic Models for Segmenting and Labeling Sequence Data, *In Proceedings of 18th International Conference on Machine Learning.* pp.282-289. Williamstown, MA, USA, June 2001.

Li, J., Tang, J, Zhang, J., Luo, Q., Liu, Y., & Hong, M. (2007). EOS: expertise oriented search using social networks. *In Proceedings of the 16th International Conference on World Wide Web.* pp.1271-1272. Alberta, Canada, May 2007.

Liang B., Tang J., & Li J. (2005a). Association search in Semantic Web: search + inference. (Poster Paper). *Proceedings of the 14th International World Wide Web Conference, Chiba, Japan, 10-14 May, 2005,* 992-993

Liang, B., Tang, J., Li, J., & Wang, K. (2005b). SWARMS: A Tool for Exploring Domain Knowledge on Semantic Web. *In Proceedings of the AAAI'05 workshop on Contexts and Ontologies: Theory, Practice and Applications.* pp.120-123. Pittsburgh, USA, July 2005.

Liang, B., Tang J., Li J., & Wang K. (2006a). Semantic Similarity Based Ontology Cache. *In Proceedings of the 8th Asia Pacific Web Conference.* pp.250-262. Harbin, China, January, 2006.

Liang, B., Tang, J., Li, J., & Wang, K. (2006b). SWARMS: A Tool for Domain Exploration in Semantic Web and its Application in FOAF Domain. *In Proceedings of the 1st Asia Semantic Web Conference on Demo Track.* Beijing, China, September 2006.

Maedche, A. (2002). *Ontology Learning for the Semantic Web.* Norwell, MA: Kluwer Academic Publishers. 2002.

Maedche, A., Staab, S., Studer, R., Sure, Y., & Volz, R. (2002). *SEAL – Tying up Information Integration and Web Site Management by Ontologies.* from http://lsdis.cs.uga.edu/SemNSF/Studer-SemWebPosition.pdf

Mani, I & Maybury, M. (1999). *Advances in Automatic Text Summarization.* Cambridge, MA: MIT Press. 1999.

Mani, I. (2001). *Automatic Summarization. Amsterdam.* AMSTERDAM, The Netherlands: John Benjamins Publishing Company. 2001.

Melnik, S., Molina-Garcia, H., & Rahm, E. (2002). Similarity Flooding: A Versatile Graph

Matching Algorithm. *In Proceedings of the 18th International Conference on Data Engineering.* pp.117-128. CA, USA, February 2002.

Mika, P. (2005). Flink: Semantic Web Technology for the Extraction and Analysis of Social Networks. *Journal of Web Semantics 3*(2), 211-223.

Noy, N.F., Sintek, M., & Decker, S. (2001). Creating Semantic Web Contents with Protégé-2000. *IEEE Intelligent Systems, 16*(2), 60-71.

O'Madadhain, J. (2003). *JUNG: A Brief Tour.* From http://jung.sourceforge.net/presentations/jung4.ppt

Oyama, S. (2002). *Query Refinement for Domain-Specific Web Search.* (Doctoral dissertation, Kyoto University, 2002). From http://www.lab7.kuis.kyoto-u.ac.jp/publications/02/oyama-kyotou-doctorthesis.pdf

Prud'hommeaux, E. & Seaborne, A. (2007). *SPARQL Query Language for RDF.* From W3C. http://www.w3.org/TR/rdf-sparql-query/

Resnik, P. (1999). Semantic Similarity in a Taxonomy: An Information-Based Measure and Its Application to Problems of Ambiguity in Natural Language. *Journal of Artificial Intelligence Research,* 11, 95-130.

Richardson, R., Smeaton, A.F., & Murphy, J. (1994). *Using WordNet as a Knowledge Base for Measuring Semantic Similarity.* From http://www.computing.dcu.ie/research/papers/1994/1294.ps

Sheth, A., Aleman-Meza, B., Arpinar, I.B., Halaschek, C., Ramakrishnan,C., Bertram, C., Warke,Y., Avant, D., Arpinar, F.S., Anyanwu, K., & Kochut, K. (2004). Semantic Association Identification and Knowledge Discovery for National Security Applications. *Journal of Database Management, 16*(1), 33-53.

Stumme, G., Hotho, A., & Berendt, B. (2006). Semantic Web Mining: State of the Art and Future Directions. *Web Semantics: Science, Services and Agents on the World Wide Web, 4*(2), 124-143.

Tang, J., Li, J., Liang, B., Huang, X., Li, Y., Wang K. (2006). Using Bayesian Decision for Ontology Mapping. *Web Semantics: Science, Services and Agents on the World Wide Web, 4* (4), 243-262.

Tang, J., Zhang, D., Zhang, D., Yao, L., & Zhu, C. (2007a). ArnetMiner: An Expertise Oriented Search System for Web Community. Semantic Web Challenge. In *Proceedings of the 6th International Conference of Semantic Web (ISWC'2007).*

Tang, J., Zhang, D., & Yao, L. (2007b). Social Network Extraction of Academic Researchers. In *Proceedings of 2007 IEEE International Conference on Data Mining (ICDM'2007).*

Tang, J., Hong, M., Zhang, D., Liang, B., & Li, J. (2007). Information extraction: methodologies and applications. In Hercules A. Prado & Edilson Ferneda (Ed.), *Emerging Technologies of Text Mining: Techniques and Applications,* (pp. 1-33). Hershey: Idea Group Inc.

Ting, K.M., & Witten, I.H. (1999). Issues in Stacked Generalization. *Journal of Artificial Intelligence Research,* 10, 271-289.

Williams, A.B. & Tsatsoulis, C. (2000). An Instance-based Approach for Identifying Candidate Ontology Relations within a Multiagent System. *In Proceedings of the First Workshop on Ontology Learning.* Berlin, Germany, August 2000.

Zhang, J., Tang, J., & Li, J. (2007). Expert Finding in a Social Network. *In Proceedings of Database Systems for Advanced Applications.* pp.1066-1069. Bangkok, Thailand, April 2007.

Zhao, Y., Karypis, G., & Fayyad U. M. (2005). Hierarchical Clustering Algorithms for Document Datasets. *Data Mining and Knowledge Discovery,* 10(2), 141-168.

Zhu, J. (2001). *Non-classical Mathematics for Intelligent Systems*. Wuhan: HUST Press. 2001.

ADDITIONAL READING

Balmin, A., Hristidis, V., Papakonstantinou, Y. (2004). ObjectRank: Authority-Based Keyword Search in Databases. In *Proceedings of VLDB*, 2004. 564-575.

Berners-Lee, T. (2006). Artificial Intelligence and the Semantic Web, July, 2006. [online] Available: http://www.w3.org/2006/Talks/0718-aaai-tbl/Overview.html

Chirita, P. A., Costache, S., Nejdl, W., & Paiu, R. (2006). Beagle++: Semantically Enhanced Searching and Ranking on the Desktop. Proceedings of The Semantic Web: Research and Applications. Springer Berlin / Heidelberg, 2006. 348–362.

Ding, L., Finin, T., Joshi, A., Cost, R. S., Peng, Y., Reddivari, P., Doshi, V., Sachs, J. (2004). Swoogle: a search and metadata engine for the semantic web. In *Proceedings of the thirteenth ACM international conference on Information and knowledge management*, New York, NY, USA: ACM Press, 2004. 652–659.

Ding, L., Pan, R., & Finin, T., Joshi, A., Peng, Y., & Kolari, P. (2005). Finding and Ranking Knowledge on the Semantic Web. In *Proceedings of ISWC*, 2005. 156–170.

Finin, T., Mayfield, J., Fink, C., Joshi, A. & Cost., R.S. (2005). Information Retrieval and the Semantic Web. In *Proceedings of the 38th Annual Hawaii International Conference on System Sciences* (HICSS'05) - Track 4, Washington, DC, USA: IEEE Computer Society, 2005. 113.1.

Furche, T., Linse, B., Bry, F., Plexousakis, D., & Gottlob, G. (2004). RDF Querying: Language Constructs and Evaluation Methods Compared. In *Proceedings of Reasoning Web*, 2006. 1-52.

Geerts F, Mannila H, Terzi E. (2004) Relational link-based ranking. In *Proceedings of VLDB*, 2004. 552-563.

Hayes, J. (2004). A Graph Model for RDF: [Master Thesis]. August, 2004.

Leighton, H. V. & Srivastava, J. (1999). First 20 precision among World Wide Web search services (search engines). *Journal of the American Society for Information Science*, 1999, 50(10):870–881.

Magkanaraki, A., Karvounarakis, G., Anh, T. T., Christophides, V., & Plexousakis, D. (2002). Ontology Storage and Querying. Technical Report 308, Foundation for Research and Technology Hellas, Institute of Computer Science, Information System Laboratory, April, 2002.

Nie, Z., Zhang, Y., Wen, J. R., & Ma, W. (2005). Object-level ranking: bringing order to Web objects. In *Proceedings of WWW*, 2005. 567-574.

Pan, Z. & Heflin, J. (2004). DLDB: Extending Relational Databases to Support Semantic Web Queries. Technical Report LU-CSE-04-006, Dept. of Computer Science and Engineering, Lehigh University, 2004.

Patel, C., Supekar, K., Lee, Y., & Park, E. K. (2003). OntoKhoj: a semantic web portal for ontology searching, ranking and classification. In *Proceedings of the 5th ACM international workshop on Web information and data management*, New York, NY, USA: ACM Press, 2003. 58–61.

Park, M. J., Lee, J., Lee, C. H., Lin, J., Serres, O., & Chung, C. (2007). An Efficient and Scalable Management of Ontology. In *Proceedings of DASFAA*, 2007. 975-980.

Sheykh, Esmaili, K. & Abolhassani, H. (2006). A Categorization Scheme for Semantic Web Search Engines. In *Proceedings of 4th ACS/IEEE International Conference on Computer Systems and Applications* (AICCSA-06), Sharjah, UAE, 2006. 171–178.

Stojanovic, N., Studer, R., & Stojanovic, L. (2007). An Approach for the Ranking of Query Results in the SemanticWeb. In *Proceedings of International Semantic Web Conference*, 2003. 500-516.

Vallet, D., Fern'andez, M., & Castells, P. (2005). An Ontology-Based Information Retrieval Model. In *Proceedings of ESWC*, 2005. 455-470.

W3C . SPARQL Query Language for RDF, 2007. [online] Available: http://www.w3.org/TR/rdf-sparql-query/.

W3C . RDF Semantics, 2004. [online] Available: http://www.w3.org/TR/rdf-mt/.

Zhang, L., Yu, Y., Zhou, J., Lin, C., & Yang, Y. (2005). An enhanced model for searching in semantic portals. In *Proceedings of the 14th international conference on World Wide Web*, New York, NY, USA: ACM Press, 2005. 453–462.

Zhang, Y., Vasconcelos. W., & Sleeman, D. (2004). OntoSearch: An Ontology Search Engine. In *Proceedings of Proceedings The Twenty-fourth SGAI International Conference on Innovative Techniques and Applications of Artificial Intelligence* (AI-2004), Cambridge, UK, 2004.

Zhou, Q., Wang, C., Xiong, M., Wang, H., & Yu, Y. (2007). SPARK: Adapting Keyword Query to Semantic Search. In *Proceedings of ISWC*, 2007.

Chapter IX
Modeling and Querying XML-Based P2P Information Systems: A Semantics-Based Approach

Alfredo Cuzzocrea
University of Calabria, Italy

ABSTRACT

Knowledge representation and management techniques can be efficiently used to improve data modeling and IR functionalities of P2P Information Systems, which have recently attracted a lot of attention from both industrial and academic research communities. These functionalities can be achieved by pushing semantics in both data and queries, and exploiting the derived expressiveness to improve file sharing primitives and lookup mechanisms made available by first-generation P2P systems. XML-based P2P Information Systems are a more specific instance of this class of systems, where the overall data domain is composed by very large, Internet-like distributed XML repositories from which users extract useful knowledge by means of IR methods implemented on top of XML join queries against the repositories. In this chapter, we first focus our attention on the definition and the formalization of the XML-based P2P Information Systems class, also deriving interesting properties on such systems, and then we present a knowledge-representation-and-management-based framework, enriched via semantics, that allows us to efficiently process knowledge and support advanced IR techniques in XML-based P2P Information Systems, thus achieving the definition of the so-called Semantically-Augmented XML-based P2P Information Systems. Also, we complete our analytical contribution with an experimental evaluation of our framework against state-of-the-art IR techniques for P2P networks, and its theoretical analysis in comparison with other similar semantics-based proposals.

INTRODUCTION

Motivations

During the last years, there has been a growing interest for *P2P Information Systems* (IS_{P2P}) (Aberer, 2001; Aberer & Despotovic, 2001), mainly because they fit a large number of real-life IT applications. Digital libraries over P2P networks are only a significant instance of IS_{P2P}, but it is very easy to foresee how large the impact of IS_{P2P} on innovative and emerging IT scenarios, such as *e*-government and *e*-procurement, will be in next years.

P2P networks are natively built on top of a very large repository of data objects (e.g., files), which is intrinsically distributed, fragmented, and partitioned among *participant* peers. P2P Users are usually interested in (*i*) retrieving data objects containing information of interest, like video and audio files, and (*ii*) sharing information with other (participant) users/peers. From the *Information Retrieval* (IR) perspective, P2P users (*i*) typically submit short, loose queries by means of keywords derived from natural-language-style questions (e.g., "*find all the music files containing Mozart's compositions*" is posed by means of the keywords "*compositions*" and "*Mozart*"), and, due to resource sharing purposes, (*ii*) are usually interested in retrieving as result a *set* of data objects rather than a specific one. As a consequence, well-founded IR methodologies (e.g., ranking), which have already reached a significant degree of maturity, can successfully be applied in the context of P2P systems in order to improve the capabilities of these systems in retrieving useful information (i.e., knowledge), and achieve performance better than that of more traditional database-like query schemes. On the other hand, the latter schemes are quite inadequate in the absence of fixed, rigorously structured data schemas, as happens in P2P networks.

Furthermore, the consolidate IR mechanism naturally supports the *self-alimenting* nature of P2P systems, as in such a mechanism intermediate results can then be (re-)used to share new information, or to set and specialize new search activities. As regards schemas, from the database perspective, P2P users typically adopt a semi-structured (data) model to query data objects rather than a structured (data) model. This feature also poses unrecognized problems concerning the issue of *integrating heterogeneous data sources* over P2P networks. In addition to this, efficiently access data in P2P systems, which is another interesting aspect directly related to our work, is still a research challenge (Aberer et al., 2002).

Basically, P2P IR techniques extend traditional functionalities of P2P systems (i.e., file sharing primitives and simple lookup mechanisms based on partial- or exact-match of strings), by enhancing the latter via useful (and more complex) knowledge extraction features. Accomplishment of the definition and development of innovative knowledge delivery paradigms over P2P networks is the goal that underlies the idea of integrating IR techniques inside core layers of P2P networks. In fact, P2P networks meaningfully marry with the IR philosophy, thus allowing us to (*i*) successfully exploit self-alimenting mechanisms of knowledge production, and (*ii*) take advantage from innovative knowledge representation and extraction models based on semantics, metadata management, probability etc. Therefore, without loss of generality, we can claim that IR techniques can be effectively used to support even complex processes like knowledge representation, discovery, and management over P2P networks, being the retrieval of information in the vest of appropriate sets of data objects the basic issue to be faced-off.

Nevertheless, several characteristics of P2P networks pose important limitations to the accomplishment of this goal. Among these, we recall: (*i*) the completely decentralized nature of P2P networks, which enable peers and data objects to come and go at will; (*ii*) the absence of global or mediate schemas of data sources, which is very common in real-life P2P networks; (*iii*) excessive computational overheads that could be introduced when traditional IR methodologies (such as those developed in the context of distribute databases) are applied as-they-are to the context of P2P systems. To overcome these limitations, P2P IR research is devoted to design innovative search strategies over P2P networks, whit the goal of making these strategies as more efficient and sophisticated as possible. A possible solution consists in looking at semantics-based techniques, which is the goal of this chapter.

Contribution of the Chapter

In this chapter, we formalize the classes of *XML-based P2P Information Systems* (IS_{P2P}^{XML}) and *Semantically-Augmented XML-based P2P Information Systems* ($IS_{P2P}^{\langle XML,S\rangle}$), which are an extension of IS_{P2P}^{XML} allowing functionalities of the latter systems to be improved via semantics. Furthermore, we propose a formal framework for supporting knowledge representation, discovery, and management on $IS_{P2P}^{\langle XML,S\rangle}$, thus extending traditional modeling and query functionalities of P2P systems. We also formally provide several definitions and properties about $IS_{P2P}^{\langle XML,S\rangle}$, from both a framework-oriented perspective and a theoretical point of view. Providing a comprehensive overview of IR models and techniques for P2P networks, along with a *taxonomy* which emphasizes the query mechanism used to retrieve information and knowledge from peers, is a secondary contribution of the chapter. Also, we provide formal knowledge representation and extraction models, along with their analysis on both an experimental and theoretical plan, and in comparison with other similar semantics-based proposals.

Chapter Outline

The chapter is organized as follows. In the second Section, we present related work, by also devising a taxonomy of IR models and techniques for P2P networks. In the third Section, we introduce concepts and principles of IS_{P2P}^{XML}. The fourth Section provides foundations and definitions of $IS_{P2P}^{\langle XML,S\rangle}$. The fifth Section illustrates our reference architecture for $IS_{P2P}^{\langle XML,S\rangle}$. In the sixth Section, we present the XML-based data model underlying our framework, and we describe how queries are modeled and evaluated in our framework. In the seventh Section, we formally describe models for supporting knowledge representation and management tasks in our framework, along with a cost-based algorithm for efficiently extracting knowledge from P2P XML repositories. The eighth Section contains the experimental evaluation of our proposed framework in comparison with well-known similar IR solutions for P2P networks. In the ninth Section, we provide a theoretical analysis of our proposed framework focusing on advanced aspects such as semantic expressiveness and related scalability-and-maintenance issues. Finally, in the last Section, we draw conclusions and illustrate future work.

BACKGROUND

Unstructured vs. Structured P2P Systems

First experiences of P2P systems, such as *Napster* (Napster, 2005), *Gnutella* (Gnutella, 2005) and *KaZaA* (KaZaA, 2005), which are mainly focused on data management issues on P2P networks, have been oriented towards designing techniques for which sharing data objects, and generating large communities of participant peers are the main goals. Under these assumptions, two reference architectures have gained a leading role for P2P systems, each of them addressing two different ways of retrieving data objects: *unstructured P2P systems*, and *structured P2P systems*.

Unstructured P2P systems appear in three main variants. In the first one (e.g., Napster

(Napster, 2005)), a centralized index storing a directory of all data objects currently available on the P2P network is located in a certain peer, whose identity is known to *all* the peers. When a participant peer p_i receives a request for a missing data object, it (*i*) performs a query against the peer containing the centralized index in order to retrieve the name of the (participant) peer p_j where the required data object is stored, and (*ii*) re-directs the request towards p_j. In the second variant (e.g., Gnutella (Gnutella, 2005)), there not exists any centralized index, as the latter can be source of failures, and each participant peer needs to maintain only (*i*) information about its own data for supporting data object lookups, and (*ii*) information about its *neighboring peers* for request routing. Given such a scheme, a request for a missing data object is flooded from a peer p_i towards other peers via the neighboring peers of p_i. In the last variant (e.g., KaZaA (KaZaA, 2005)), peers connect to a *super-peer* that builds an index over the data objects shared by its set of peers. In addition to this, each super-peer keeps information about neighboring super-peers in the system, and queries are routed among the super-peers. Scalability is the most important drawback for unstructured P2P systems. In fact, when the number of participant peers grows, the described query mechanism can become very inefficient, as flooding the P2P network for each data object lookup can became (very) resource-intensive.

In structured P2P systems, all the available data objects are indexed by a high-performance indexing data structure that is distributed among the participant peers (e.g., *Distributed Hash Tables* (DHTs)). Compared with the previous class of P2P systems, structured P2P systems introduce the important advantage that, at query time, they do not flood requests across the P2P network, but, indeed, required data objects are quickly localized thanks to the distributed index. As a consequence, structured P2P systems are highly scalable. Nevertheless, an important limitation is represented by the issue of updating the distributed index, particularly when highly dynamic P2P networks are considered, as dynamics of peers can modify the network topology with a very high *churn rate* (which refers to the tendency for peers to join and leave the network (Gummadi et al., 2003).

A Taxonomy of Information Retrieval Techniques for P2P Networks

It is well established (e.g., Tsoumakos & Roussopoulos, 2003a; Zeinalipour-Yazti et al., 2004) that P2P systems are mainly characterized by their proper query strategy allowing us to retrieve useful information from data. Also, performance of the query strategy gives us a *quality indicator* to decide about the goodness of the IR technique implementing such strategy. According to this vision, in this Section we propose a query-strategy-focused taxonomy of state-of-the-art P2P IR techniques (summarized results are shown in Table 1), which represent the background of our work.

The first general classification distinguishes between *Keyword-based P2P* (KbP2PS) and *Object Identifier-based P2P* (OIDbP2PS) *Systems*, by looking at the atomic construct they use to implement the search mechanism. In KbP2PS, traditional keywords are used to drive the search across peers, whereas, in OIDbP2PS, object identifiers are implemented on peers to enhance IR performance by biasing the search towards specific sub-sets of peers. Specifically, in the latter case, due to the decentralized nature of P2P systems, object identifiers are usually embedded into distributed indexing data structures such as DHTs. It should be noted that both KbP2PS and OIDbP2PS can be implemented on top of either unstructured or structured P2P networks, meaning that the search mechanism is independent by the specific network topology, even if different performance are achieved. Secondly, state-of-the-art proposals are classified according to their query strategies that concern with how to route across peers the messages needed to answer queries, being the latter the basic task to be accomplished in order to retrieve useful information from peers.

In the following, we provide an overview of IR models and techniques for P2P networks according to the above theoretical viewpoint.

Basic Search Techniques

Among the *Basic Search Techniques* (BST), the *Breadth First Search* (BFS) is one of the most popular ways of supporting IR over P2P networks. In BFS, a peer p_i receiving a query message q from a sender peer p_j first forwards q to all its neighboring peers, other than p_j, and then searches its local repository for relevant matches. Furthermore, if a peer p_k reached by q finds a match in its repository, it sends across the network the *hit message* along with (*i*) the identifiers needed to download the data objects of interest it stores, and (*ii*) the state of its network connectivity. Finally, if p_j receives hit messages from more than one peer, it may decide to download the retrieved documents from peers on the basis of their network connectivity states. BFS, which has been one of the first query strategies implemented in P2P networks, such as in Gnutella (Gnutella, 2005), KaZaA (KaZaA, 2005) and Napster (Napster, 2005), presents the advantage of being very simple so that no excessive computational overheads are introduced in the middleware software. Contrarily to this, BFS performance is usually very poor due to an inefficient network resource utilization that generates a lot of service messages across the P2P network, and peers with low bandwidth can become serious bottlenecks for such search mechanism. However, equipping query messages with the *Time-To-Live* (TTL) parameter, which determines the maximum number of hops allowed for any query message, can limit network flooding and sensitively increase performance.

Random Search Techniques

Random Search Techniques (RST) represent a simple yet effective derivation from BST. Kalogeraki *et al.* (Kalogeraki et al., 2002) propose a significant extension to the naïve version of BFS, called *Random Breadth First Search* (RBFS),

Table 1. A query-strategy-focused taxonomy of IR techniques for P2P networks

Class	*Search Kind*	*P2P IR Techniques*
BST	KbP2PS	(Gnutella, 2005), (KaZaA, 2005), (Napster, 2005)
RST	KbP2PS	(Kalogeraki et al., 2002), (Lv et al., 2002), (Tsoumakos & Roussopoulos, 2003b)
IST	KbP2PS	(Gen Yee & Frieder, 2005), (Meng et al., 2002), (Sripanidkulchai et al., 2003), (Zeinalipour-Yazti et al., 2005)
SST	KbP2PS	(Galanis et al., 2003), (Gong et al., 2005), (Koloniari & Pitoura, 2004), (Yang & Garcia-Molina, 2002)
IndST	OIDbP2PS	(Aberer, 2001), (Bonifati et al., 2004; Bonifati & Cuzzocrea, 2006), (Bremer & Gertz, 2003), (Clarke et al., 2000), (Crainiceanu et al., 2004), (Crespo & Garcia-Molina, 2002), (Gibbons et al., 2003), (Gupta et al., 2003), (Loo et al., 2004), (Ratnasamy et al., 2001), (Sartiani et al., 2004), (Stoica et al., 2001), (Zhao et al., 2001), (Kubiatowicz et al., 2000; Rhea et al., 2001)
DIRT	KbP2PS	(Callan, 2000), (Gauch et al., 1999), (Ogilvie & Callan, 2001), (Xu & Callan, 1998)
SemST	KbP2PS	(Cai & Frank, 2004), (Crespo & Garcia-Molina, 2003), (Deerwester et al., 1999), (Golub & Loan, 1996), (Halaschek et al., 2004), (Halevy et al., 2003), (Kokkinidis & Christophides, 2004), (Li et al., 2003), (Nejdl et al., 2003), (Tang et al., 2003), (Zhu et al., 2006)

which consists in propagating the query message from a peer to a randomly determined sub-set of its neighboring peers rather than all of them. A setting parameter establishes how many neighboring peers must be involved by the propagation of query messages (e.g., if the parameter is equal to 0.5, then the query message is propagated to half of all the neighboring peers, chosen at random). The major benefit of the RBFS approach consists in the fact that performance of the BFS approach is dramatically improved yet ensuring low computational overheads because of the random choice does not require any global knowledge. On the other hand, being RBFS a probabilistic technique, it could happen that large segments of the underlying P2P network are neglected by the random choice, thus reducing the efficiency of query tasks. Lv *et al.* (Lv et al., 2002) present the *Random Walkers Algorithm* (RWA), according to which each peer forwards the query message (called, in this context, *walker*) to another of its neighboring peers at random. To improve performance and reduce query time, the original idea of using one walker only is extended to the usage of $k > 1$ walkers, which are consecutively sent from the sender peer. RWA resembles RBFS but, indeed, in RBFS the query message is propagated to a sub-set of peers instead that at only one for time (as in RWA); as a consequence, in RBFS the number of service messages across the P2P network can become exponential, whereas in RWA such a number is bounded by a linear complexity (Lv et al., 2002). The *Adaptive Probabilistic Search* (APS), proposed by Tsoumakos and Roussopoulos (Tsoumakos & Roussopoulos, 2003b), is inspired from RWA with the difference that in APS each peer p_i implements a local data structure that captures the relative probability of each neighboring peer p_j to be chosen as the next hop for future requests. Furthermore, while RWA forwards walkers at random, APS exploits knowledge derived from previous searches to model the behavior of walkers on a probabilistic basis. In (Tsoumakos & Roussopoulos, 2003b), experimental results presented by authors show that APS outperforms RWA.

Intelligent Search Techniques

Beyond the previous basic approaches, another line of P2P IR research aims at integrating intelligent techniques, mainly inherited from similar experiences in related-but-different scientific disciplines, into P2P middleware in order to enforce the quality of the search task. We name such a class of proposals as *Intelligent Search Techniques* (IST). The *Intelligent Search Mechanism* (ISM), proposed by Zeinalipour-Yazti *et al.* (Zeinalipour-Yazti et al., 2005), belongs to the latter technique class, and represents a novel approach for supporting IR over P2P networks by (*i*) minimizing the number of messages sent among peers, and (*ii*) minimizing the number of peers that are involved for each search activity. To this end, ISM is composed by: (*i*) a *Profile Mechanism*, according to which each peer builds a "profile" for each of its neighboring peer; (*ii*) a *Query Similarity* function, which calculates the similarity queries to a new input query; (*iii*) a *Relevance Rank*, which realizes a ranking technique for peers – to this end, this component takes as input the (neighboring) peer profiles, and produces as output a ranked list of (neighboring) peers used to bias the search towards the most relevant peers; (*iv*) a *Search Mechanism*, which implements the ISM search policy. In (Zeinalipour-Yazti et al., 2005), authors show how ISM works well when peers hold some specialized knowledge about the P2P environment, and when P2P networks having high degrees of query locality are considered; in these particular conditions, ISM outperforms BFS as well as RBFS techniques. Other techniques that can be classified as belonging to the IST class are: (*i*) the P2P IR framework proposed by Gen Yee and Frieder (Gen Yee & Frieder, 2005), that combines ranking techniques and metadata management in order to efficiently support IR over P2P networks; (*ii*) *Metasearch Engines* by

Meng *et al.* (Meng et al., 2002), mainly focused on source selection and merging of results from independent sources; *(iii)* the system proposed by Sripanidkulchai *et al.* (Sripanidkulchai et al., 2003), which discriminates among peers based on their past behavior in order to form communities of peers having similar interests. The main limitation of IST is that, being usually implemented inside P2P middleware directly, they could become resource-consuming, and, in general, do not scale well on large and dynamic P2P networks.

Statistics-Based Search Techniques

Statistics-based Search Techniques (SST) are another important result for IR over P2P networks. These techniques use some aggregated statistics to forward queries towards a particular sub-set of peers, and, usually, the same statistics is maintained by mining results of past queries. Techniques belonging to such a class are: *(i)* the *Most Results in Past* (>RES) heuristic, proposed by Yang and Garcia-Molina (Yang & Garcia-Molina, 2002), where query messages are routed to those peers that returned the most results for the last *m* queries, being *m* a technique parameter (it should be noted that, in this case, the statistics employed is very simple being based on a "quantitative" approach); *(ii)* Galanis *et al.*'s data summaries and histograms (Galanis et al., 2003), which are built on each peer by means of data replication techniques, in order to exploit such information at query time to bias the search towards the most relevant peers; *(iii)* Gong *et al.*'s bloom filters (Gong et al., 2005), and Koloniari and Pitoura's multi-level bloom filters (Koloniari & Pitoura, 2004), which are statistics-inspired compressed data structures able to summarize the data of the neighborhood of a given peer, thus efficiently supporting query answering over P2P networks by means of probabilistic algorithms. Even if statistics allow performance of certain kinds of queries (e.g., *range-queries* (Gupta et al., 2003)) to be improved when compared against traditional approaches, maintaining summary data structures over P2P networks can become very resource-intensive, thus unfeasible in real-life scenarios.

Index-Based Search Techniques

Index-based Search Techniques (IndST) efficiently exploit the hierarchical nature of structured P2P networks, and extensively use and take advantages from well-known data indexing solutions coming from the RDBMS technology (e.g., B^+-trees and *R*-trees). Among IndST proposals, we recall: *(i)* Clarke *et al.*'s *Freenet* (Clarke et al., 2000), which uses an intelligent indexing scheme based on the *Depth-First-Search* (DFS) mechanism to locate objects (note that Freenet has not been properly proposed for P2P networks but, indeed, for a general "anonymous" information storage and retrieval system); *(ii)* Aberer's *P-Grid* (Aberer, 2001), which provides extensions to traditional DHTs in order to efficiently support scalability, which is recognized as one of the most critical factors for P2P systems; *(iii)* Ratnasamy *et al.*'s *Content-Addressable Network* (CAN) (Ratnasamy et al., 2001), which employs a *d*-dimensional Cartesian space to index resources on P2P networks; *(iv)* Stoica *et al.*'s *Chord* (Stoica et al., 2001), which uses a linear space of identifiers forming a ring, being such ring exploited to speed-up lookup operations over P2P networks; *(v)* Zhao *et al.*'s *Tapestry* (Zhao et al., 2001), which, based on the algorithm of Plaxton *et al.* (Plaxton et al., 1997), builds a randomized hypercube to near-by-cache copies of replicated objects in the P2P network; *(vi)* Kubiatowicz *et al.*'s *OceanStore* (Kubiatowicz et al., 2000; Rhea et al., 2001) that makes use of Tapestry to create a *global-persistent data store system* having the relevant feature of being scalable to *billions* of users, which is a critical requirement in large and dynamic P2P networks; *(vii)* the hybrid technique for building and maintaining local indices proposed by Crespo and Garcia-Molina (Crespo & Garcia-Molina, 2002), that present three different methods (namely *Compound Routing Index* (CRI), *Hop-Count Routing Index* (HRI), and *Exponentially Aggregated Routing Index* (ERI)) which generate indexing data structures able to store the "direction" towards relevant documents over P2P networks, by exploiting the original ideas about routing protocols developed and tested in *Arpanet*; (*viii*) Gibbons *et al.*'s *IrisNet* (Gibbons et al., 2003), which is an architecture for supporting IR over P2P networks storing XML data indexed by *XPath* (Berglund et al., 2007) expressions; (*ix*) the *Locality Sensing Hashing* (LSH) technique by Gupta *et al.* (Gupta et al., 2003), that propose using horizontal partitions of relational tables and extensions to the original DHT for supporting approximate range-query answering over P2P networks; (*x*) the Bremer and Gertz's distributed indexes (Bremer & Gertz, 2003), namely *P*-index, *A*-index, and *T*-index, which aim at building virtual XML repositories over P2P networks by encoding global path information, and efficiently support global query answering over them; (*xii*) *P-Trees* by Crainiceanu *et al.* (Crainiceanu et al., 2004), that propose augmenting the DHT with B^+-trees for supporting range-query answering on relational P2P databases; (*xii*) Loo *et al.*'s *PierSearch* (Loo et al., 2004), which exports RDBMS features in an Internet-scale P2P environment; (*xiii*) Sartiani *et al.*'s *XPeer* (Sartiani et al., 2004), which is targeted at XML data, and uses full tree-guides to perform query evaluation; (*xiv*) *XP2P*, proposed by us in (Bonifati et al., 2004; Bonifati & Cuzzocrea, 2006), where lightweight XPath expressions are encoded in few KB by means of Rabin's fingerprints in order to build a (lightweight) distributed index capable of efficiently supporting lookup queries over structured P2P networks. Just like SST, even if query capabilities are improved and well-supported, also including new aspects that have been neglected by first-generation P2P systems (such as range-query processing), IndST mainly suffer from scalability limitations, and updating distributed indexes over large P2P networks is still an open research problem.

Distributed Information Retrieval Techniques

The *Distributed Information Retrieval* (DIR) approach (Callan, 2000; Gauch et al., 1999; Ogilvie & Callan, 2001; Xu & Callan, 1998), first proposed in contexts different from P2P systems, assumes that peers have a global knowledge of the system, e.g. statistical knowledge about the content of each peer in the network, or intensional (i.e., schema-based) knowledge as in (Cai & Frank, 2004; Halaschek et al., 2004; Halevy et al., 2003; Nejdl et al., 2003; Tang et al., 2003). By contrary, most of actual P2P IR techniques assume that peers only have a *local knowledge* of the system, e.g. *knowledge about their neighboring peers*. This is mainly due to the fact that *Distributed Information Retrieval Techniques* (DIRT), being based on the assumption of holding (and maintaining) global views of the system across peers, could become very inefficient in large and dynamic P2P networks. As stated previously, DIRT are outside of the scope of this chapter.

Semantics-Based Search Techniques

Semantics-based Search Techniques (SemST) are the new frontier for IR over P2P networks. Such techniques aim at adopting formal semantics to both model and query distributed resources over P2P networks, in order to improve capabilities of traditional resource sharing P2P systems. The first advantage of SemST is the amenity of re-using and re-adopting well-founded results coming from semantic models and query languages, which have been intensively investigated in the context of relational database systems. Another advantage consists in the possibility of meaningfully integrating IR techniques in P2P network middleware by means of innovative research trends like *Ontologies* and *Semantic Web*. Since most papers are still focused on query performance of unstructured and structured P2P systems, in literature there are very few proposals addressing the described research challenges. However, it is expected that integrating semantics in P2P networks will be one of the most relevant research topic for next-generation P2P applications, as highlighted before.

First, Crespo and Garcia-Molina propose the notion of *Semantics Overlay Networks* (SON) (Crespo & Garcia-Molina, 2003), which are an efficient way of grouping together peers sharing the same schema information. Therefore, peers having one or more topics on the same *thematic hierarchy* belong to the same SON. This approach well-supports query routing as every peer p_i can quickly identify peers containing relevant information, namely the set $N(p_i)$, by avoiding network flooding. Here, "relevant" means that a certain semantic relation exists between information held in p_i and information held in peers belonging to $N(p_i)$. Such semantic hierarchies are naturally represented (and processed) via the *Resource Description Framework* (RDF) (Klyne & Carroll, 2004), by also taking advantages from several declarative languages for querying and defining views over RDF bases, such as *RDF Query Language* (RQL) (Karvounarakis et al., 2002) and *RDF View Language* (RVL) (Magkanaraki et al., 2003). In (Crespo & Garcia-Molina, 2003), authors demonstrate that SON can significantly improve query performance while at the same time allow users to decide what content to publish in their (peer) hosts, that is, how to form a SON.

The SON initiative has heavily influenced many P2P-focused research projects. Among all, some of them are focused on query route issues in SON, by meaningfully using the potentialities of RDF constructs: (*i*) *RDFPeers* by Cai and Frank (Cai & Frank, 2004), (*ii*) *SemDIS* by Halaschek *et al.* (Halaschek et al., 2004), (*iii*) *Piazza* by Halevy *et al.* (Halevy et al., 2003), (*iv*) *Edutella* by Nejdl *et al.* (Nejdl et al., 2003), and (*v*) *Self-Organizing SON* by Tang *et al.* (Tang et al., 2003). All these initiatives have in common the idea of propagating queries across a (semantic) P2P system by means of semantics-based techniques such as correlation discovering, containment etc, mainly working on RDF-modeled networks of concepts.

Another significant approach can be found in the *ICS-FORTH SQPeer Middleware* (Kokkinidis & Christophides, 2004), proposed by Kokkinidis and Christophides, that, starting from the same motivations of the SON initiative, propose more sophisticated information representation and extraction mechanisms by introducing (*i*) the concept of *active RDF schemas* in order to declare parts of a SON RDF schema that are *currently* of interest for a peer, via an *advertisement mechanism*, and (*ii*) the concept of *semantic query pattern* relying on query/view subsumption techniques that are able to drive query route on the basis of semantics.

A possible limitation of SON is represented by the overwhelming volume of messages that can be generated to support data object replications on peers, as required by SON design guidelines (Crespo & Garcia-Molina, 2003). Thus, P2P applications running on top of SON-based model for query route incur excessive overheads on network traffic. An interesting solution to this problem has been proposed by Li *et al.* (Li et al., 2003). They suggest using *signatures on neighboring peers* in order to direct searches along selected *network paths*, and introduce some schemes to facilitate efficient search of data objects. Signatures are a way of pushing semantics in data, by means of building a bit vector V; V is generated according to the following two steps: (*i*) hash the content of a data object into bit strings, said BS, and (*ii*) apply a bitwise OR operator on BS. So-built bit strings are used at query time via performing a bitwise AND operation on the *search signature* (i.e., the signature of the term used as search key) and the *data signature* (i.e., the signature stored on the *current* peer). In (Li et al., 2003), authors show how some proposed flooding-based search algorithms allow the signatures of neighboring peers to be efficiently exploited to enhance search results, and, moreover, an extensive experimental part clearly confirms the effectiveness of the neighborhood signature technique in comparison with existing P2P content search methods, including Gnutella (Gnutella, 2005), RWA (Lv et al., 2002), and the IndST of the systems *Morpheus* (Morpheus, 2005) and *OceanStore* (Kubiatowicz et al., 2000; Rhea et al., 2001).

Latent Semantic Indexing (LSI), first proposed by Deerwester *et al.* (Deerwester et al., 1999), is a state-of-the-art technique for supporting IR from collections of documents. It is based on the *Vector Space Model* (VSM), proposed by Salton *et al.* (Salton et al., 1975), that represent a document collection as a term-by-document matrix $A_{t\times d}$ such that each element of $A_{t\times d}$ is a weight w_{ij} of the corresponding term t_i in the specific document d_j. w_{ij} is computed by taking into account (*i*) the term frequency tf_{ij}, which captures the local relevance of t_i in d_j, and (*ii*) the inverted document frequency df_j, which models a sort of global statistical knowledge about d_j with respect to the whole document collection (Salton et al., 1975). As opposite to the original VSM approach, the main idea behind LSI is to compare user's queries and documents at the concept level (thus using semantics) rather than on the basis of simple keyword matching (as in VSM). In LSI, the VSM matrix $A_{t\times d}$ is factorized by the *Single Value Decomposition* (SVD) technique, first proposed by Golub and Loan (Golub & Loan, 1996), which, unfortunately, introduces an excessive computational cost when applied on huge document collections, as studied by Zhang *et al.* (Zhang et al., 2001). However, similarly to DIRT, LSI requires that each peer holds global knowledge about the system, thus it becomes ineffective for large P2P networks.

A possible solution to this problem can be found in the work of Zhu *et al.* (Zhu et al., 2006), which propose a novel query optimization scheme, called *Semantic Dual Query Expansion* (SDQE), where the lack of global knowledge is compensated by engaging ad-hoc query optimization plans implemented on peers locally. SDQE is in turn based on the *Query Expansion* (QE) technique, initially proposed by Salton and Buckley (Salton & Buckley, 1990), which consists in refining user's queries by adding to them other terms related to those expressed by original queries. Some works in the context of DIRT (e.g., (Gauch et al., 1999; Ogilvie & Callan, 2001; Xu & Callan, 1998)) show that DIRT performance can be improved thanks to QE. In other words, SDQE can reasonably be considered as a sort of advanced query engine for DIRT, which allows us to mitigate the requirement of global knowledge posed by DIRT. In any case, being SDQE directly related to DIRT, the comparison between SDQE and our work is outside the scope of this chapter.

XML-BASED P2P INFORMATION SYSTEMS

Despite more or less advanced query strategies, all today P2P systems are devoted to cover the initial resource sharing goal, and, as a consequence, there is a strength, effective demand for enriching P2P systems with functionalities that (*i*) are proper of information systems, such as *Knowledge Discovery* (KD)- and IR-style data object querying, and (*ii*) cannot be supported by current data representation and query models supported by P2P systems. Hence, IS_{P2P} represent an attempt to support even complex processes like knowledge representation, discovery, and management over P2P networks. More properly, knowledge representation and management techniques mainly concern with modeling IS_{P2P}, whereas knowledge discovery techniques (implemented via IR functionalities) mainly concern with querying IS_{P2P} (i.e., knowledge extraction from IS_{P2P}).

In literature, there are very few initiatives focused on these aspects. Present trend consists in extending current capabilities of P2P systems via nesting IR techniques inside P2P middleware directly (Gen Yee & Frieder, 2005; Meng et al., 2002; Sripanidkulchai et al., 2003). As an example, looking at the more specific data management perspective, (Gen Yee & Frieder, 2005) proposes implementing *headers* to be associated to data objects distributed across the P2P network, as a sort of metadata, in order to support IR processes like ranking of results. Scalability is an important limitation of these initiatives, as headers could require resource-intensive update procedures because of, typically, (*i*) peers are dispersed on the P2P environment and, above all, (*ii*) P2P networks are characterized by a continuously changing topology which can make the update task very problematic and resource-intensive.

All considering, we can claim that traditional P2P functionalities are inadequate to efficiently support innovative requirements of IS_{P2P}, whereas P2P systems relying on XML repositories, whose management has reached a sufficient maturity by now, offer from a side all the typical functionalities supported by a P2P system, such as information sharing, dynamism, and scalability, and from another side native support for real-life IT application scenarios, as XML data are semi-structured by definition and many of such scenarios perfectly cope with the semi-structured data model (e.g., *e*-commerce, *e*-government, *e*-procurement etc). Furthermore, by adopting XML as core data model, it is possible to meaningfully augment *semantics of data*, and support advanced KD- and IR-style functionalities. In fact, complex mining/reasoning models, like those based on graphs and trees, can be natively derived from the structure of XML data, which are intrinsically hierarchical, and used to infer knowledge via semantics, also adopting a large set of already-available algorithms and techniques coming from well-known, mature scientific disciplines like *Data Mining* (DM) and *Knowledge Discovery in Databases* (KDD).

As will be evident throughout the chapter, even if our proposal is targeted at XML documents, it can be extended to deal with different kinds of document (e.g., HTML pages on the Web). Therefore, in the rest of the chapter, due to its popularity, we assume of dealing with XML documents as a relevant case of interest, but it should be clear from here that models and algorithms proposed in this chapter can be straightforwardly extended to deal with other models for semi-structured and distributed databases, and the Web.

Based on these considerations, in this chapter we are interested in application scenarios drawn by IS_{P2P} whose participant peers contain XML repositories in form of collection of XML documents that are grouped on the basis of a *context*, thus building *clusters of resources* that are tightly semantically-related. We name these systems as XML-based P2P Information Systems (IS_{P2P}^{XML}). In such systems, "context" refers to the semantics of the content of related XML documents stored in P2P XML repositories. As an example, a peer p_j holding an XML repository concerning the "insurance" context could group XML documents storing data about insurance companies and their offers on several kinds of insurance contracts (e.g., life, homeowner, car etc). At the same time, the XML repository of p_j could also contain XML documents storing data about statistics on people of a certain urban area (e.g., salaries, compositions of families, people lifestyle etc), being the two clusters of documents semantically-related (e.g., statistics could be exploited to launch new insurance offers).

In more detail, as regards data modeling issues concerning XML repositories, we release the condition of holding DTDs of XML documents, as usually DTDs are missing in many real-life IT scenarios. To become convinced of this, it suffices to think of an *e*-commerce Web system, whose (XML-formatted) *e*-catalogues change rapidly and continuously over time, also in their structure, so that maintaining DTDs, besides XML documents, can involve in very problematic issues.

An instance of application scenarios we are interested in is depicted in Figure 1, which shows the data layer of an XML-based P2P Health Informa-

Figure 1. The data layer of an XML-based P2P health information system

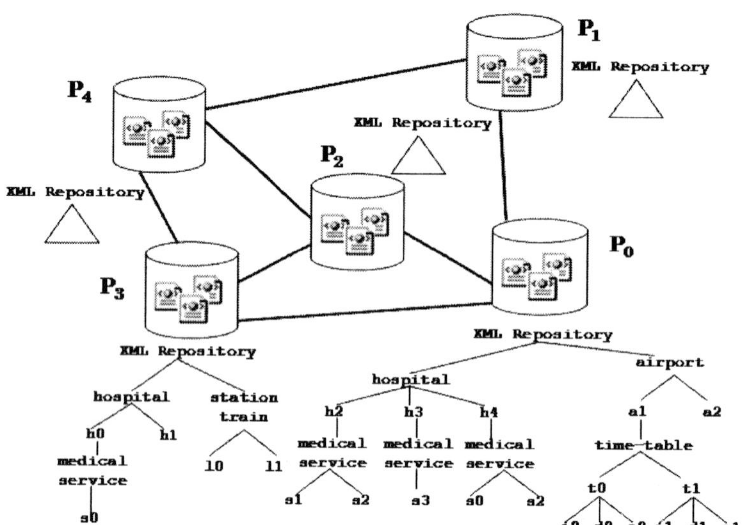

tion System. In such system, peers mainly contain information about hospitals and medical services in a certain urban area, and other related and useful information such as locations of airports and train stations, time-tables of public services, hotels and availabilities etc about the same area. Users of such system are interested in retrieving (useful) knowledge by means of join queries over (distributed) XML repositories. Although the described scenario is clearly independent of the specific query language used, join queries could be expressed in *XQuery* (Boag et al., 2007), a popular XML query language.

Join queries are widely-recognized as the most useful ones for users, mainly because (*i*) knowledge is typically distributed on different data sources rather than being centralized in a unique data provider, and (*ii*) join queries are just effective for extracting knowledge from distributed data sources. Specifically, with respect to specific goals of our work, join queries over distributed XML repositories effectively represent an adequate solution in order to support advanced KD- and IR-style functionalities within IS_{P2P}^{XML}, being knowledge production, processing, and fruition over P2P networks intrinsically decentralized and distributed processes.

On the other hand, XML is widely-recognized as the most important data interchange standard, because of its ability in representing data coming from a wide variety of sources (e.g., relational databases, text files, data stream sources etc). Hence, XML is likely to be the format through which data from multiple sources are integrated, thus overcoming data integration issues mentioned above. As a consequence, join queries over distributed XML repositories effectively represent a leading class of queries to support advanced KD- and IR-style functionalities within IS_{P2P}^{XML}, according to the previous guidelines. Another point in favor of this kind of queries is noticing that, in literature, there exist several, important solutions for supporting join queries over XML data, which remains a relevant research challenge. Among all, we recall: approximate matching in structure (Guha et al., 2002; Guha et al., 2003), synopsis data structures for approximate answers (Polyzotis et al., 2004), schema-based solutions (Schlieder, 2002), federating language/model for federated, distributed data sources (Gardarin et al., 1999) etc.

SEMANTICALLY-AUGMENTED XML-BASED P2P INFORMATION SYSTEMS: FOUNDATIONS AND DEFINITIONS

In $IS_{P2P}^{\langle XML,S\rangle}$ application scenarios such as those discussed in the previous Section, the most important research challenge is *pushing semantics in data and queries to support even complex knowledge representation and management processes, by improving IR-focused query capabilities (and performance) of* $IS_{P2P}^{\langle XML,S\rangle}$. Traditional query models of P2P systems, based on routing queries towards peers that contain the information of interest on the basis of a given *route policy* (e.g., random choices) can be sensitively improved by pushing semantics in both data and queries, and using semantics to *drive* query execution. According to this main intuition, our proposed framework introduces the concept of *Semantically-related Communities of Peers* (SCoP), which (*i*) store XML data about semantically-related concepts, and (*ii*) are used to drive query execution, by avoiding resource-intensive network flooding, thus reducing the required hop number during search operations. As we better motivate in the folloiwng, with respect to previous similar proposals, the most important innovation carried by SCoP is that SCoP are built *by taking into account the analysis of (past) query results only,* without consider pre-fixed schemes (e.g., knowledge representation schemes imposed by the system author) or intensional (i.e., schema-based) models (e.g., (Cai & Frank, 2004; Crespo & Garcia-Molina, 2003; Halaschek et al., 2004; Halevy et al., 2003; Nejdl et al., 2003)). From a theoretical point of view, this approach is just the opposite of the so-called *Distributed Information Retrieval* (DIR) approach (Callan, 2000), which assumes that peers have a *global knowledge* of the system (e.g., some statistical knowledge about the content of *each* peer). In other words, our framework assumes that peers only have a *local knowledge* of the system, i.e. *knowledge about queries flooded through their neighboring peers.* As a consequence, the comparison of our proposed framework against proposals adhering to the class of DIR techniques is outside of the scope of this chapter.

The described approach leads to the definition of $IS_{P2P}^{\langle XML,S\rangle}$, which allow the traditional functionalities of P2P systems to be improved via semantics. While SCoP are the "way" of *representing* knowledge in our proposed framework, some *graph-based computational models* and relative algorithms realize the way of *processing and extracting* knowledge from very large XML repositories, thus improving the semantic expressiveness of knowledge discovery tasks. Definitions 1 to 5 introduce foundations of $IS_{P2P}^{\langle XML,S\rangle}$, and clarify differences with precursor concepts and derived entities.

- **Definition 1: P2P System.** A P2P System P is a triple $P = \langle L,D,\Upsilon\rangle$, such that L is the set of participant peers, D is the overall data domain distributed across peers in L, and Υ is a set of primitive predicates supporting lookup mechanisms of data objects in D.
- **Definition 2: P2P Information System.** A P2P Information System IS_{P2P} is a pair $IS_{P2P} = \langle P,\Upsilon^{+}\rangle$, such that P is a P2P System, and Υ^{+} is a set of extended predicates supporting IR-focused knowledge extraction mechanisms from data in $D \in P$.
- **Definition 3: XML-based P2P Information System.** An XML-based P2P Information System IS_{P2P}^{XML} is a P2P Information System relying on a domain of distributed XML repositories D^{XML}.
- **Definition 4: Semantically-Augmented XML-based P2P Information System.** A Semantically-Augmented XML-based P2P Information System $IS_{P2P}^{\langle XML,S\rangle}$ is a pair $IS_{P2P}^{\langle XML,S\rangle} = \langle IS_{P2P}^{XML},S\rangle$, such that IS_{P2P}^{XML} is an XML-based P2P Information System, and S is a formal semantics used to optimize query

execution in Υ^{+}-based knowledge extraction processes, with $\Upsilon^{+} \in IS_{P2P}^{XML}$.

- **Definition 5: Semantic Community of Peers (SCoP).** Given a Semantically-Augmented XML-based P2P Information System $IS_{P2P}^{\langle XML,S\rangle}$, a Semantic Community of Peers C defined on $IS_{P2P}^{\langle XML,S\rangle}$ is a collection of peers in $L \in P$ that contains semantically-related (XML) data in $D^{XML} \in IS_{P2P}^{XML}$, whose relationships are built on the basis of the analysis of (past) query results, by exploiting local knowledge about neighboring peers.

Figure 2 shows the containment relationship among the classes of P2P systems we consider in this chapter. As shown in Figure 2, given two P2P systems P_i and P_j belonging to two different classes T_i and T_j, respectively, such that $P_i \in T_i$, $P_j \in T_j$, and T_i contains T_j (i.e., $T_j \subset T_i$), then P_i contains P_j (i.e., $P_j \subset P_i$) consequently. This means that P_i inherits all the functionalities/properties of P_j, and it also extends P_j with novel functionalities/properties not included in P_j. Finally, from Figure 2 it should be noted that semantics and semantic expressiveness are augmented from basic P2P systems to advanced $IS_{P2P}^{\langle XML,S\rangle}$.

A REFERENCE MULTI-LAYER ARCHITECTURE FOR SEMANTICALLY-AUGMENTED XML-BASED P2P INFORMATION SYSTEMS

The knowledge representation framework for $IS_{P2P}^{\langle XML,S\rangle}$ we propose is characterized by a multi-layer architecture (see Figure 3), mainly devoted to capture and support knowledge management and extraction tasks in such systems. In consequence of this, our architecture is composed by two main layers which, in turn, are composed by sub-components in a hierarchical fashion. This organization aims at maintaining the framework as more general and extensible as possible, in order to easily integrate new functionalities when available. These layers are:

- The *Knowledge Modeling Layer* (KML), which deals with the problem of modeling

Figure 2. Containment relationship among several classes of P2P systems

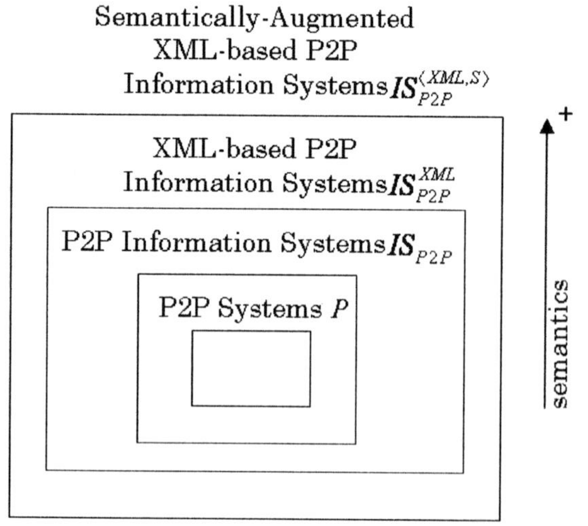

Semantically-Augmented XML-based P2P Information Systems $IS_{P2P}^{\langle XML,S\rangle}$

XML-based P2P Information Systems IS_{P2P}^{XML}

P2P Information Systems IS_{P2P}

P2P Systems P

\+

semantics

Figure 3. A reference knowledge representation-based multi-layer architecture for modeling and querying P2P IS

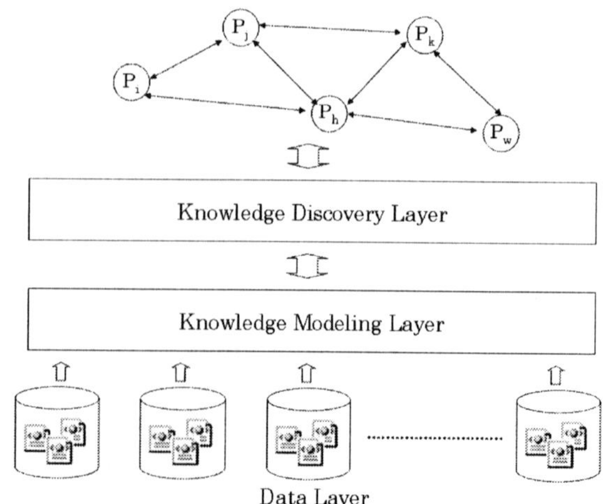

and representing the target $IS_{P2P}^{\langle XML,S\rangle}$ via knowledge representation and management techniques;

- The *Knowledge Discovery Layer* (KDL), which is concerned with query functionalities of $IS_{P2P}^{\langle XML,S\rangle}$ (i.e., knowledge extraction), being such functionalities the baseline for even complex IR methods.

As shown in Figure 3, KML interacts with XML repositories forming the *Data Layer* of our reference architecture, whereas KDL implements the knowledge-representation-based models mentioned above, and supports KD- and IR-style advanced functionalities in peers located in the *P2P Layer* of our reference architecture.

It should be noted that this vision resembles that of Aberer *et al.* (Aberer et al., 2004), that propose a general reference architecture for P2P IR according to which a P2P IR system is modeled by four different layers (in a bottom-up fashion): (*i*) the *Transport Communications* layer, which supports the physical access to peers; (*ii*) the *Structured Overlay Networks* layer, which provides a logical network independent by the physical one modeled in the first layer; (*iii*) the *Document and Content Management* layer, which associates documents and document management tasks to peer identifiers modeled in the second layer; (*iv*) the *Retrieval Models* layer, which supports keyword-based IR functionalities over documents modeled in the third layer. As a sketched comparison analysis, our KML can be intended as encapsulating the Aberer *et al.*'s *Structured Overlay Networks* and *Document and Content Management* layers enhanced by means of intelligent knowledge representation and management techniques. Similarly, our KDL resembles the Aberer *et al.*'s *Retrieval Models* layer enhanced via techniques more advanced than simple IR techniques (e.g., ranking). As regards the *Transport Communications* layer, our proposed framework is orthogonal to any network protocols (e.g., TCP/IP, UDP/IP etc), so that the communication layer is not handled in this chapter.

MODELING DOCUMENTS, REPOSITORIES AND QUERIES VIA SEMANTICS

In this Section, we introduce the XML data and query models supporting our proposed framework, which, as a consequence, should be considered as reference models for any $IS_{P2P}^{\langle XML,S\rangle}$.

The XML data model deals with the issues of modeling both XML documents and repositories stored in the Data Layer of our reference architecture (see Figure 3). In order to introduce it, we need to provide some fundamental definitions. First, we represent an XML document as a rooted, labeled *tree*, according to the widely-accepted assumption on XML data (e.g., W3C consortium (W3C, 2005)). Then, we introduce the concept of *forest* as the underlying XML data model for any XML repository stored in peers of a given $IS_{P2P}^{\langle XML,S\rangle}$. As a consequence, we define a forest as a rooted, unordered collection of XML documents that is dynamically produced on a peer via popular publisher-subscriber mechanisms of modern IT applications, like B2C and B2B *e*-commerce systems.

A critical point of our data model concerns with how concepts related to an XML document are represented and managed. Similarly, this affects how concepts are associated to an XML repository, due to the fact that the latter is defined, in turn, as a collection of documents. Given an XML document X, concepts held by X are represented as an ordered list of *terms* $\ell(X) = \{t_0, t_1, \ldots, t_{n-1}\}$, which are derived from the document according to an arbitrary procedure. Without loss of generality, we assume that $\ell(X)$ does not contain duplicated items. We point out that our framework is orthogonal to the particular procedure used to generate concepts, and any kind of solution can be applied to build the list (e.g., automatic or manual methods).

Following the approach above, we finally obtain a sort of *annotation of XML documents by concepts*, what annotation allows us to augment the semantics of documents and improve the capability of processing them. It should be noted that the described mechanism is similar to what happens with the classical use of keyword metadata used to describe documents, but targeted to capture semantics of documents. The derived benefits are mainly evident during the query execution phase, as, for instance, we can know the kind of data contained in an XML document without accessing the entire document, but accessing the annotated concepts only. Besides this, concepts are the basic entities for building SCoP over the target $IS_{P2P}^{\langle XML,S\rangle}$, as we better describe in the following Sections.

We highlight that semantic models more complex than lists, such as trees and graphs, and their variants, could be used in substitution of the former, thus achieving a greater semantic expressiveness in representing knowledge in form of related concepts. Nevertheless, we discard such models because of (*i*) they are computationally more "heavy" than lists, and, as a consequence, update procedures for our framework would be more resource-intensive and would reduce the scalability of the same framework, and (*ii*) since P2P users are usually interested in loose, incomplete query answers, lists efficiently fulfill this requirement with low computational overheads, yet preserving the scalability of the framework, which is a rigorous requirement for any P2P system and application.

In a similar spirit of what done for the general system-oriented framework related to $IS_{P2P}^{\langle XML,S\rangle}$, here we introduce the *semantically-augmented* "counterparts" for both the entities XML document and forest, that is, the *semantically-augmented XML document* and the *semantically-augmented XML forest*, which are used to build and maintain SCoP.

- **Definition 6: XML Document.** An XML document X is a rooted, labeled tree.
- **Definition 7: XML Forest.** An XML forest F is a rooted, unordered collection of XML documents.
- **Definition 8: Semantically-Augmented XML Document.** A semantically-augmented XML document X^* is a pair $X^* = \langle X,\ell(X)\rangle$, such that X is an XML document and $\ell(X)$ is the ordered list of concepts held by X.
- **Definition 9: Semantically-Augmented XML Forest.** A semantically-augmented XML forest F^* is a pair $F^* = \langle F,\ell(F)\rangle$, such that F is an XML forest and $\ell(F)$ is the list of concepts held by F, obtained by merging, without duplicates, the concept lists $\ell(X_k)$ of all the XML documents X_k in F, i.e., $\ell(F) = \bigcup_k \ell(X_k)$.

In the rest of the chapter, for the sake of simplicity, we denote the set of concepts held in a peer p_i, i.e. in its XML repository, as $\ell(p_i)$ (i.e., $\ell(p_i) \equiv \ell(F)$, such that $\ell(F) \in F^*(p_i)$).

Next, we describe how queries are modeled and evaluated in our proposed framework. Just like done with XML documents, we model queries as *collections of terms* representing the expressed (search) concepts. This approach quite resembles the LSI proposal by Deerwester *et al.* (1999).

Given a user query Q, the concepts expressed by Q are represented as an ordered list of terms $\varphi(Q) = \{u_0, u_1, \ldots, u_{m-1}\}$, and, formally, we name the couple $Q^* = \langle Q,\varphi(Q)\rangle$ as *semantically-augmented query*. Similarly to the list of terms of XML documents, without loss of generality, we assume that $\varphi(Q)$ does not contain duplicated items. Furthermore, like documents, lists of terms can be extracted according to any kind of procedure (e.g., external or built-in).

- **Definition 10: Semantically-Augmented Query.** A semantically-augmented query Q^* is a pair $Q^* = \langle Q,\varphi(Q)\rangle$, such that Q is a user query and $\varphi(Q)$ is the ordered list of concepts expressed by Q.

We evaluate a semantically-augmented query Q^* against a semantically-augmented XML document X^* by simply *matching* terms (i.e., concepts). In other words, we assume that the evaluation of Q^* against X^* produces a non-null answer if there exists at least a term u_j in $\varphi(Q)$ that matches with a term t_i in $\ell(X)$, otherwise the evaluation of Q^* against X^* fails. This is formally modeled by the following function *semEvalDoc*:

$$semEvalDoc(Q^*, X^*) = \begin{cases} TRUE & \ell(X) \cap \varphi(Q) \neq \varnothing \\ FALSE & \ell(X) \cap \varphi(Q) = \varnothing \end{cases} \quad (1)$$

The IR approach implemented by *semEvalDoc* can also be intended as a sort of *relaxation* of more strict query evaluation schemes such as that devised in the P2P IR framework proposed by Gen Yee and Frieder (2005). Here, fundamental entities of the P2P scenario are modeled via a metadata-based approach that provides *descriptors* for both data objects (via the set D_O, which is similar to the component $\ell(X)$ of our framework) and queries (via the set D_Q, which is similar to the component $\varphi(Q)$ of our framework). Given a query Q with descriptor D_Q and an object repository O with descriptor D_O, Q is evaluated against O by checking the non-strict containment between D_O and D_Q, that is, $D_O \supseteq D_Q$. In other words, Gen Yee and Frieder (2005) impose that the *whole* set D_Q must be contained by or must be equal to the set D_O. Contrarily to this, given a query Q^* and a document X^*, we evaluate Q^* against X^* via checking if a term u_j in $\varphi(Q)$ such that u_j is also contained in $\ell(X)$ exists. It should be noted that our approach takes into more consideration than (Gen Yee & Frieder, 2005) the imprecise nature of typical P2P queries and the strongly decentralized-and-dynamic nature of P2P systems, which have both been discussed in the first Section, via admitting that (*i*) approximate results are "reasonable" for P2P users, and (*ii*) content in P2P XML repositories can rapidly change during time.

The function *semEvalDoc* can be easily generalized in order to capture the case in which a query Q^* is evaluated against an XML repository instead of an XML document. In this case, the matching of terms in $\varphi(Q)$ is checked against the list of terms $\ell(F)$ of the XML forest F^* representing the target repository. This is formally modeled by the following function *semEvalRep*:

$$semEvalRep(Q^*, F^*) = \begin{cases} TRUE & \ell(F) \cap \varphi(Q) \neq \varnothing \\ FALSE & \ell(F) \cap \varphi(Q) = \varnothing \end{cases}$$

Now we highlight some advantages of the approach we use to model queries. First, since handling queries at the concept level is "orthogonal" to the particular XML query language, any language for XML data, such as XQuery and XPath, can be used on top of our framework, as ad-hoc *wrappers* can be designed and developed in order to efficiently codify/translate set of concepts into XML query statements, and vice-versa. Secondly, the usage of list of terms for both XML documents and repositories allows us to manage and evaluate queries against the two kinds of data sources in the *same* way, by providing facilities at the formal modeling level as well as the implementation level (thus, in turn, mitigating scalability issues). Moreover, for what regards the efficiency of our query evaluation scheme, it should be noted that the computational cost needed for evaluating queries against both XML documents and repositories is bounded by the logarithm (time) complexity. Finally, the query scheme we propose is also easily extendible. For instance, by exploiting the hierarchical nature of XML, we can provide an efficient support for the evaluation of *Semantic Tree-Pattern Queries* (see Schlieder, 2002), which allow us to express semantic queries more advanced (i.e., with a higher expressive power) than those presented previously. In a tree-pattern query Q_{TP}, concepts are organized according to a *hierarchical* fashion instead that in a *flat* one (like ours, based on lists), so that, in order to Q_{TP} against a given document X^*, we only need to simultaneously consider the matching between the *structure* of Q_{TP} and that of X^*, ahead of the matching between concepts in Q_{TP} and X^*. In this respect, the functions *semEvalDoc* (1) and *semEvalRep* (2) can be easily extended as to embed this novel feature, and provide efficient support to XML semantic tree-pattern queries.

REPRESENTING AND EXTRACTING KNOWLEDGE FROM SEMANTICALLY-AUGMENTED XML-BASED P2P INFORMATION SYSTEMS

In this Section, we describe the knowledge representation model and the knowledge extraction model of our framework. The first model is used to represent knowledge held in XML documents and repositories. The second one is instead used to extract knowledge from XML documents and repositories via elegant matrix-based Data Mining tools.

Knowledge Representation Model

Semantic Relationship Matrix (SRM) is the basic component of our knowledge representation model. SRM supports SCoP definition and management. Given a peer p_i of a $IS_{P2P}^{\langle XML,S\rangle}$, and the set of its neighboring peers $\Psi(p_i)$, the SRM defined on p_i, denoted by $M(p_i)$, is a two-dimensional matrix such that rows represent the *neighboring peers* $p_j \in \Psi(p_i)$ of p_i, and columns represent the set of *neighboring concepts* $\Omega(p_i)$ of p_i obtained by merging, without duplicates, the concepts held in the neighboring peers, that is:

$$\Omega(p_i) = \bigcup_{j=0}^{|\Psi(p_i)|-1} \ell(F_j)$$

being $\ell(F_j)$ the XML forest modeling the repository stored in p_j. It should be noted that $\Omega(p_i)$ models the local knowledge in our framework.

Each entry of $M(p_i)$, denoted by $M_i[p_h][t_k]$, contains the object NULL if the concept t_k is not held by the neighboring peer p_h or there is not any (semantic) relationship among concepts held in p_i and concepts held in p_h. Otherwise, $M_i[p_h][t_k]$ contains an object $m_{h,k} = \langle s_{h,k}, w_{h,k}\rangle$ such that $s_{h,k}$ is a percentage value, and $w_{h,k}$ is the list of the last N queries, being N a framework parameter that is empirically fixed.

In more detail, $s_{h,k}$ represents the percentage number of queries successfully completed by flooding the P2P network from p_i towards p_h in searching for XML data holding the concept t_k, with respect to the total number of queries posed to p_i and searching for the concept t_k. We assume that a query Q is successfully completed if the user, after having looked-up on the P2P network the location of the XML data belonging to the result of Q, denoted by $D^{XML}(Q)$, then accesses or downloads them. We highlight that this approach requires that the P2P middleware produces a notification message when the query answer is totally computed, in a similar way to what happens in Gnutella. Contrarily to Gnutella, our aim is that of reducing the whole message traffic, which, as widely-recognized, is instead relevant in Gnutella.

In a similar spirit, $w_{h,k}$ represents the list of the last N queries posed to p_i and which were routed towards p_h in searching for XML data holding the concept t_k. It should be noted that, in order to compute $s_{h,k}$, we take into account the *successfully* completed queries only, whereas $w_{h,k}$ is computed by also considering queries that were not successfully completed, but routed towards p_h. As we better explain in the remaining part of this Section, such an organization allows us to achieve several benefits, among which the amenity of efficiently performing SCoP maintenance operations.

- **Definition 11: Semantic Relationship Matrix.** Given a $IS_{P2P}^{\langle XML,S\rangle}$ P, a peer $p_i \in P$, the neighboring peer set $\Psi(p_i)$ *of* p_i, and the neighboring concept set $\Omega(p_i)$ of p_i, the Semantic Relationship Matrix $M(p_i)$ defined on p_i is a two-dimensional matrix having as rows the items belonging to the $\Psi(p_i)$ set, as columns the items belonging to the $\Omega(p_i)$ set, and containing as $M_i[p_h][t_k]$ entries $m_{h,k} = \langle s_{h,k}, w_{h,k}\rangle$ objects, where $m_{h,k}$ is a metrics reporting the percentage of successfully completed queries by flooding the P2P network from p_i to the neighboring peer p_h *in* searching for XML data holding the concept t_k, and $w_{h,k}$ is the list of the last N queries posed to p_i in searching for XML data holding the concept t_k.

We highlight that usually SRMs are sparse matrices (due to the typical nature and topology of P2P networks), so that we can adopt efficient techniques and algorithms for representing and processing them. Furthermore, it should be noted that we propose a very simple relationship description model (i.e., based on the existence of the direct relationship, without any inferred or derived relationship) instead of more complex models known in literature. This because of, as stated above, our main goal is building SCoP by considering the analysis of query results with respect to the neighboring peers only (thus, exploiting the local knowledge), without any pre-fixed scheme or intensional model. The most important benefit deriving from this approach is that our SCoP-based framework can be maintained very efficiently as SRMs are built incrementally, when queries are posed to peers, thus avoiding to introduce excessive computational overheads.

To adequately support our knowledge extraction models and algorithms, which are presented next, we need to introduce the definition of the so-called *RDF Schema Graph* (RSG), which is another component of our knowledge representation model. Given a peer p_i of a $IS_{P2P}^{\langle XML,S\rangle}$, the RSG defined on p_i, denoted by $R(p_i)$, is used to represent relationships among the neighboring concepts $\Omega(p_i)$ of p_i, by making use of the RDF. At query time, $R(p_i)$ allows us to discover relationships among (search) concepts.

The usage of RDF makes our proposed framework able to encapsulate and take advantage from some well-known RDF properties, which we briefly summarize next. First, RDF allows us to successfully represent networks of related classes/concepts, and efficiently supports the definition of predicates on these relationships. Secondly, RDF views can be easily derived starting from RDF schemas by using well-known declarative languages for processing RDF-based knowledge, such as RQL (Karvounarakis et al., 2002) and RVL (Magkanaraki et al., 2003). Furthermore, the namespace mechanism supported by RDF naturally marries the definition of SCoP on a $IS_{P2P}^{\langle XML,S\rangle}$, and can be efficiently used to improve the expressiveness in the knowledge representation task, as, for instance, we could define *hierarchies of SCoP* by significantly enhancing semantic capabilities and functionalities of P2P IS. Finally, it is easy to note that, like SRMs, RSGs can also be represented and managed very efficiently.

- **Definition 12: RDF Schema Graph.** Given a $IS_{P2P}^{\langle XML,S\rangle}$ P, a peer $p_i \in P$, the neighboring peer set $\Psi(p_i)$ *of* p_i, and the neighboring concept set $\Omega(p_i)$ of p_i, the RDF Schema Graph $R(p_i)$ defined on p_i is a triple $R(p_i) = \langle V,E,\zeta\rangle$, such that V is the set of nodes representing the concepts in $\Omega(p_i)$, E is the set of arcs representing the relationships among concepts in V, and ζ is a set of predicates defined on E, being ζ_k items in ζ of kind: $\zeta_k : C_i \xrightarrow{e} C_j$, where e is a property that establishes a relationship between the concept C_i and the concept C_j (i.e., $C_j = e(C_i)$).

It should be noted that, thanks to the functionalities offered by RVL, we can easily define and process views on RSGs, thus on SCoP or SCoP domains, by achieving the same semantic expressiveness in managing RDF views that SQPeer (Kokkinidis & Christophides, 2004).

Knowledge Extraction Model

As fundamental components of the knowledge extraction task implemented in our framework, in this Section we introduce a graph-based computational model and a cost-based algorithm for extracting useful knowledge by performing search on the domain D^{XML} belonging to a given $IS_{P2P}^{\langle XML,S \rangle}$. As stated in the first Section, recall that the main goal of our proposal is to drive query execution by semantics, thus reducing the hop number during search operations (i.e., reducing the P2P network flooding).

To this end, here we introduce a graph-based computational model founding on the so-called *Semantic Relationship Graph* (SRG). Given a peer p_i of a $IS_{P2P}^{\langle XML,S \rangle}$, the SRG defined on p_i, denoted by $G(p_i)$, is used to extract knowledge from p_i. In more detail, given a query Q, according to our knowledge extraction strategy, we dynamically build, for each peer p_i involved by search operations of Q, the SRG $G(p_i)$ starting from the SRM $M(p_i)$ and the RSG $R(p_i)$, and use it to bias the search towards relevant peers. SRG is a labeled graph, where each label on an arc a between two peers p_i and p_j is an object $l_{i,j} = \langle C_j, \vartheta_{i,j} \rangle$, such that (*i*) C_j is the concept retrieved by accessing p_j from p_i, and (*ii*) $\vartheta_{i,j}$ is a weight used to model the relevance and the goodness of biasing the search along a (furthermore, $\vartheta_{i,j}$ supports our cost-based algorithm for extracting (useful) knowledge from XML repositories). It should be noted that this approach allows us to achieve the important benefit of having a graph-based model for reasoning on knowledge held in peers, thus improving the expressiveness and the possibilities of the knowledge extraction phase. From a computational point of view, we highlight that the proposed approach does not introduce excessive computational overheads, as the SRG is built on top of the neighboring peers so that the numbers of nodes and arcs in SRG are, typically, bounded. As a consequence, SRG can be dynamically materialized in main memory, and, thus, good performances are usually obtained.

Given a peer p_i belonging to a $IS_{P2P}^{\langle XML,S \rangle}$, the SRG $G(p_i)$ represents semantic relationships among concepts (*i*) held in the neighboring peers of p_i (i.e., the set $\Psi(p_i)$), and (*ii*) that can be "reached" starting from p_i. In more detail, $G(p_i)$ is dynamically built starting from the SRM $M(p_i)$ and RSG $R(p_i)$ by *mining* both the entities, i.e. by discovering (*i*), from $M(p_i)$, *direct relationships* among the concepts held in $\Psi(p_i)$, and (*ii*), from $R(p_i)$, *indirect relationships* among the concepts held in $\Psi(p_i)$. In some sense, $G(p_i)$ *extends* the knowledge kept in the two entities (i.e., $M(p_i)$ and $R(p_i)$) by realizing an *instance of this knowledge* during the query execution task. For these reasons, in our framework, we distinguish between the so-called *static knowledge*, i.e., the knowledge kept in the entities SRM and the RSG, and the so-called *dynamic knowledge*, i.e. the knowledge kept in the entity SRG. The former describes knowledge represented *by* topological/semantic properties of the underlying P2P network. The latter describes knowledge that can be inferred *from* topological/semantic properties of the underlying P2P network.

Since the set $\Omega(p_i)$ is built by merging the concept sets held in the set $\Psi(p_i)$, we obtain that, in general, given a concept C_i and a peer p_i, C_i can be reached starting from p_i according to the following possibilities: (*i*) via a direct (semantic) path from p_i to $p_j \in \Psi(p_i)$, denoted by δ-*path*(*i,j*), or, alternatively, (*ii*) via an indirect (semantic) path from p_i to a peer p_j that, *in general*, could not belong to $\Psi(p_i)$, denoted by σ-*path*(*i,j*). δ- and σ-paths are discovered from p_i by mining the entities $M(p_i)$ and $R(p_i)$. In more detail, δ-paths are directly extracted from $M(p_i)$. On the contrary, to discover σ-paths, we adopt a Δ-*step propagation strategy*, such that Δ is an empirically set framework parameter. Given a search concept C_i and a *current* peer p_i

(i.e., the peer that is currently processed by our search algorithm), our strategy determines *how the corresponding search space $S(C_i)$ (i.e., the space of all the neighboring concepts) must be browsed.* The "result" of this relationship discovery task starting from p_i is "materialized" into the SRG $G(p_i)$. Particularly, we name the obtained mining structure as *Δ-degree SRG.*

The Δ-degree SRG $G(p_i)$ building process is as follows. Starting from p_i, we first derive all the relationships modeled by $M(p_i)$, thus adding an arc $\langle p_i,p_j\rangle$ for each peer p_j having a non-null entry in $M(p_i)$. Then, for each of the so-determined peer p_j, we access the SRM $M(p_j)$ and we add a new arc $\langle p_j,p_w\rangle$ for each peer p_w having a non-null entry in $M(p_j)$ in correspondence of concepts C_i modeled in the RSG $R(p_i)$. In turn, we iterate this process for other Δ-1 times (i.e., until the max depth from p_i to the actual p_w in the SRG $G(p_i)$ is Δ).

In this Section, we focus our attention on how to compute the weights $\vartheta_{i,j} \in l_{i,j}$ of the SRG (note that the concepts $C_j \in l_{i,j}$ are computed by mining the SRM and RSG, as described above), after that nodes and arcs of the SRG are determined according to the previous building process. Given two peers p_i and p_j, we compute the weight $\vartheta_{i,j}$ for the arc $\langle p_i,p_j\rangle$ of $G(p_i)$ as follows:

$$\vartheta_{i,j} = \frac{\Gamma(\delta - path(i,j))}{\sum_{k=i}^{j-1}\Gamma(\sigma - path(k,k+1))} \quad (3)$$

where Γ(δ-*path*(*i*,*j*)) is defined as follows:

$$\Gamma(\delta - path(i,j)) = s_{i,j} \in M(p_i) \quad (4)$$

and Γ(σ-*path*(*i*,*j*)) as follows:

$$\Gamma(\sigma - path(i,j)) = \sum_{k=i}^{j-1}\Gamma(\delta - path(k,k+1)) \quad (5)$$

such that Γ(•) is a function costing a given path in $G(p_i)$.

Selecting the "next" peer p_j to be processed starting from the "current" peer p_i in searching for XML data holding the concept C_j is the fundamental step of our cost-based knowledge extraction algorithm. We remark that our goal is to reduce the hop number during search operations, while at the same time extract useful knowledge. To this end, we devise a cost-based algorithm that tries to minimize σ-paths from the current peer p_i to the next peer p_j in the SRG, which is thus used as formal computational model.

In the more general case, starting from a peer p_i, we have a *set* of σ-paths that can be followed for accessing the XML data of interest (from the previous Section, note that δ-paths are particular instances of σ-paths). We denote the set of possible paths σ-paths in $G(p_i)$ that originate from p_i as follows:

$$\Phi(p_i) = \{\sigma_0, \sigma_1, \ldots, \sigma_{|\Phi(p_i)|-1}\} \quad (6)$$

The *best* σ-path σ* belonging to $\Phi(p_i)$ is the one definitively used to extract the XML data of interest, and it is obtained by minimizing the following cost function modeling the sum of all the weights $\vartheta_{i,j}$ belonging to σ*:

$$\Im(i,j) = \sum_{k=i}^{j-1}\vartheta_{i,j} : (i,j) \in \sigma^* \quad (7)$$

EXPERIMENTAL EVALUATION

In order to test the effectiveness and the reliability of our proposed knowledge-representation-based framework, we performed an experimental evaluation of our knowledge extraction algorithm against some most popular state-of-the-art P2P IR techniques.

In our experiments, the hardware infrastructure was composed by 10 workstations interconnected with a 10/100 LAN, each of them equipped with a processor *AMD Athlon XP 2600+* at 2.133 GHz and 1 GB RAM, and running *SUSE Linux*

9.1. On top of our experimental framework, we deployed 200 peers, each of them running like a single peer on a single host, thanks to the multi-thread programming environment offered by the underlying software platform. The data layer of our experimental setting was obtained by producing synthetic contents and concepts concerning with *e*-tourism P2P XML repositories. These repositories contained related data from which useful knowledge such as (*i*) information useful to reach tourist places, locations of hotels and restaurants, train and bus timetables, (*ii*) information related to historical/archeological sites, (*iii*) information related to gastronomic tours, (*iv*) information related to events and movies etc can be extracted. By means of specialized XML data set generators, we obtained several (synthetic) XML repositories having various structures and sizes. Specifically, the maximum depth and the maximum width of XML documents ranged in the intervals [5, 15] and [50, 650] respectively. Size of XML documents ranged in the interval [1, 45] MB. To model data-loads of the P2P network, we used (*i*) a Uniform distribution defined over the range [0, 199], and (*ii*) a Zipf distribution with characteristic parameter z equal to 0.5. Synthetic queries were generated by means of uniform extractions over the whole domain of concepts held in the generated synthetic XML repositories, by making use of concepts coming from the tourism context like as "destination", "holiday", "social event" etc.

As comparison techniques, we chose the following ones: Gnutella (Gnutella, 2005), RWA (Lv et al., 2002), ISM (Zeinalipour-Yazti et al., 2005), and the neighborhood signature technique (Li et al., 2003, particularly, in this case we use the PN-A scheme – see Li et al., 2003). Furthermore, we set the TTL parameter equal to 5. The goal of our experimental study is probing the quality of the IR support of our knowledge-representation-based framework against state-of-the-art techniques. On the other hand, the comparison between our approach and those proposed by SON (Crespo & Garcia-Molina, 2003), SQPeer (Kokkinidis & Christophides, 2004), and the neighborhood signature technique (Li et al., 2003) focusing on the semantic expressiveness and related scalability-and-maintenance issues is provided in the next Section.

In our experiments, we considered the following metrics:

- The *Average Message Number* (AMN), which measures the average number of messages used to retrieve documents of interest.
- The *Average Hop Number* (AHN), which measures the average number of hops needed to retrieve documents of interest.
- The *Recall Rate* (RR), which is the fraction of retrieved documents with respect to the collection of all the documents involved by a given search task.

It should be noted that AMN and AHN mainly test the efficiency of the target P2P IR technique, whereas RR is used to investigate on the accuracy of the target P2P IR technique. For what regards the independent parameters of the experimental evaluation (i.e., the parameters with respect to which the previous metrics are generated and observed), we considered the following ones:

- The *Number of Queries* (NoQ) used to retrieve documents of interest
- The *Number of Peers* (NoP) populating the network
- The "classical" TTL

It should be noted that, on a side, the parameter NoQ influences the quality of search results as, in general, the higher is the number of queries employed during the search task the higher is the quality of the retrieved results. On the other side, the parameter NoQ is also a way of evaluating the *reliability* of investigated techniques as, in general, the higher is the number of queries employed during the search task, the higher are the computational overheads introduced in the P2P network, since in this case a higher volume of query (route) messages is needed.

In addition to this, the parameter NoP allows us to study the performance of the target P2P IR technique under the ranging of the number of peers populating the network, i.e. to probe the *scalability*

Figure 4. Experimental results (TTL = 5): AMN w.r.t. NoQ for Uniform data-loads (a); AMN w.r.t. NoQ for Zipfian data-loads (b); AHN w.r.t. NoQ for Uniform data-loads (c); AHN w.r.t. NoQ for Zipfian data-loads (d); RR w.r.t. NoQ for Uniform data-loads (e); RR w.r.t. NoQ for Zipfian data-loads (f)

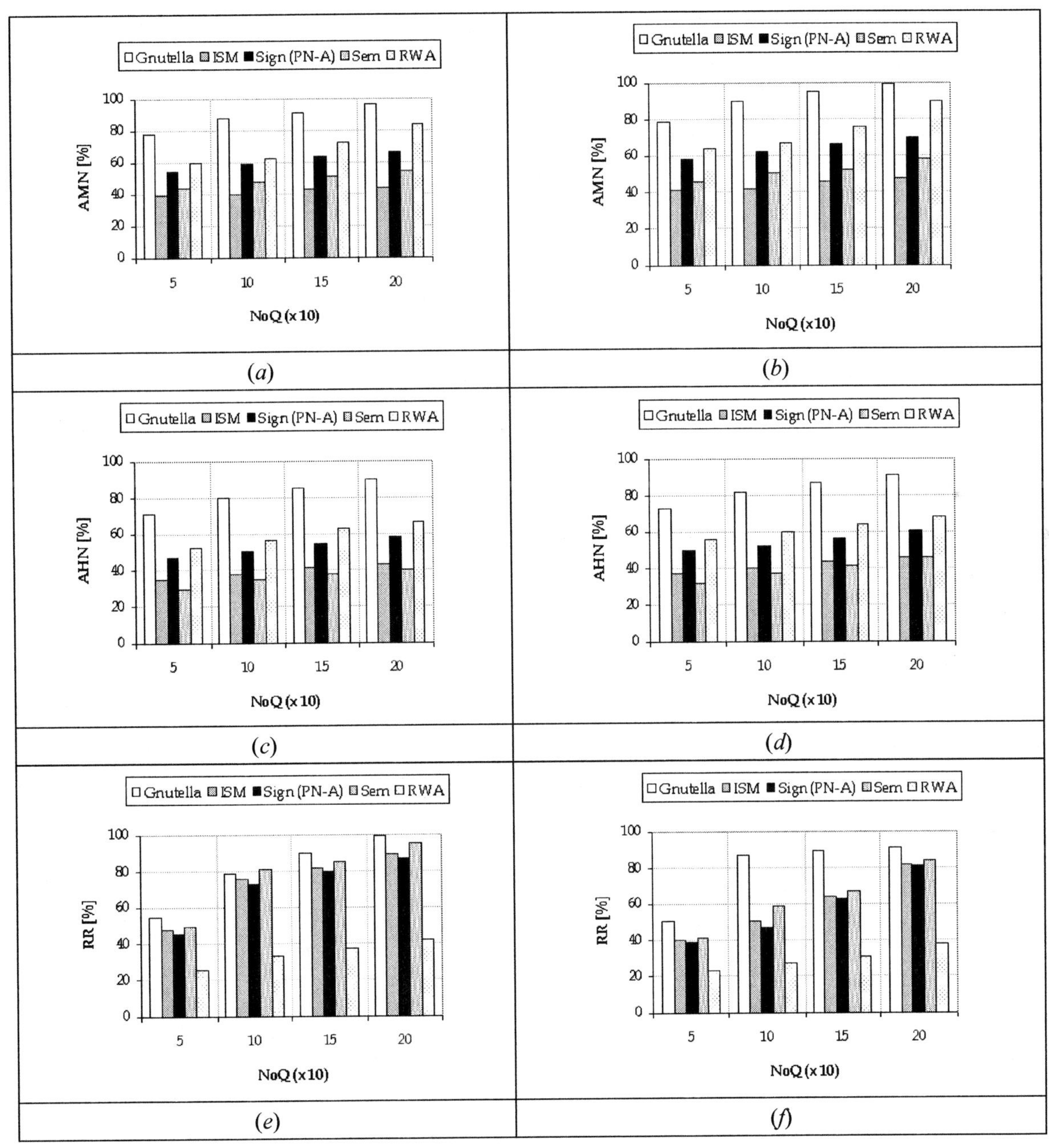

of the technique. Finally, the parameter TTL gives us the opportunity of studying how to efficiently bind the network flooding phenomenon that can occur in the target P2P IR technique.

Figure 4 shows the results of our experimental study for both Uniform and Zipfian data-loads. All considering, from the analysis of such results, it follows that ISM and our proposed semantic-based P2P IR retrieval technique (labeled as *Sem* in Figure 4) have the most convenient experimental behaviors. Before discussing our experimental results, we highlight that, overall, we obtain better performance for Uniform data-loads rather than for the Zipfian ones, as expected. In fact, Uniform data-loads avoid generating unreachable P2P network segments at query time, whereas Zipfian data-loads may cause this problem, as data following these distributions can be asymmetrically located in specific segments of the P2P network. In more detail, as regards the AMN-based metrics, ISM outperforms our technique. This is due to the fact that, in the average case, our technique requires a quite higher computational cost (in terms of query messages) to retrieve documents of interest rather than ISM. Contrarily, as regards the AHN-based metrics, our technique outperforms ISM; in other words, even if our technique introduces a little computational overhead when compared with ISM, it requires a smaller number of hops than ISM to retrieve documents of interest. This is due to the fact that our technique works better in forwarding query messages towards relevant peers rather than ISM. Therefore, our conclusion about the experimental study is that, depending on the particular application context, and by trade-offing the two benefits (i.e., low AMN, or low AHN), one can decide to choose between the two different most convenient solutions. Nevertheless, as regards the definitive goal of both the techniques (i.e., retrieving as more documents of interest as possible), the RR-based metrics confirms the superiority of our technique against ISM.

A THEORETICAL ANALYSIS OF THE SEMANTIC EXPRESSIVENESS AND RELATED SCALABILITY AND MAINTENANCE ISSUES OF SOME SEMST FOR INFORMATION RETRIEVAL OVER P2P NETWORKS

In this Section, we provide a theoretical analysis of our proposed approach against other similar techniques belonging to the SemST class: SON (Crespo & Garcia-Molina, 2003), SQPeer (Kokkinidis & Christophides, 2004), and the neighborhood signature technique by Li *et al.* (Li et al., 2003). The goal of this analysis is to put in evidence the semantic expressiveness of the investigated techniques by also looking at scalability and maintenance issues, which play a critical role in large and dynamic P2P networks. In this vest, this analysis completes the experimental evaluation of the performance of our framework provided in the previous Section.

When compared against SON and SQPeer, SCoP retain the important advantage of being a "low cost" solution. In fact, while RDF schemas allow the semantic expressiveness of the modeling and query phases (specifically, thanks to the solution of declaring RDF views on peer communities) to be significantly improved, system scalability results to be sensitively reduced because of schema and view replication across peers. Besides this, maintaining RDF schemas and views can become very resource-intensive due to specific properties of P2P systems, such as (quickly) changes in the topology, and strong delocalization of peers.

Also, SCoP can be represented and managed in a very efficient way, thus preserving network scalability, while at the same time ensuring a higher semantic expressiveness, via devising ad-hoc graph-based computational models for improving knowledge extraction via semantics, and (*ii*) supporting the mechanism of defining views over a single SCoP or a SCoP domain, in a similar way to the SQPeer proposal.

When compared with the Li *et al.*'s neighborhood signature technique, SCoP semantic expressiveness result to be higher, as search mechanisms supported by neighborhood signatures are efficiently but poor on the semantic level (in fact, there is not any semantic-based computational model besides simple bitwise operators), whereas update/maintenance overheads are low in both techniques.

Furthermore, with respect to previous experiences following the same direction, SCoP are built and maintained on the basis of the analysis of results of past user's queries through the neighboring peers (i.e., the local knowledge), without considering neither (*i*) any pre-fixed scheme, which is usually set by the system author, and, thus, could not fit the "real" evolution of the target $IS_{P2P}^{\langle XML,S\rangle}$, nor (*ii*) intensional models (i.e., schema-based reasoning), like in SON and SQPeer, which do not take into account query result analysis. On the contrary, in some sense, SCoP evolve *naturally* over time, according to the analysis of query results, i.e. user activities against the $IS_{P2P}^{\langle XML,S\rangle}$, thus meaningfully taking advantage from the local knowledge about neighboring peers.

CONCLUSION

In this chapter, we have presented a framework for pushing semantics in P2P IS relying on very large XML distributed repositories, called semantically-augmented XML-based P2P IS, by also inferring definitions and properties about them. Although centered to XML-formatted repositories, our framework can be extended to deal with data sources having different formats (e.g., HTML). A query-strategy-focused taxonomy of P2P IR techniques has been also proposed, what have to be considered as the background for our work. The (XML) data model, query model, knowledge representation model, and knowledge extraction model of the proposed framework have been rigorously defined and discussed in detail, by also inferring several definitions and properties about them. A cost-based algorithm for extracting (useful) knowledge by efficiently exploiting semantics has also been proposed, along with its detailed experimental evaluation, which has further confirmed the efficiency of our proposed framework against state-of-the-art techniques. Furthermore, we have presented a theoretical analysis (focusing on advanced aspects such as semantic expressiveness and related scalability-and-maintenance issues) of our proposed approach against similar techniques that make use of semantics to improve query performance and IR capabilities.

FUTURE RESEARCH DIRECTIONS

Efficiently querying P2P systems, which in this chapter has been addressed by means of a semantics-based approach, still poses several research challenges and open issues that need to be further investigated during next years. Among them, we list the following ones.

- *Schema-Aware Vs. Schema-Less Query Methods.* In a P2P network, data schemas may be available or not. This poses different requirements and problems concerning querying P2P data. For instance, if schemas are available, then queries can be posed accordingly, thus reducing many NULL values and false positives. If schemas are not available, then queries must be posed via keywords mainly, so that different query strategies capable of dealing with the lack of a fixed schema need to be devised.
- *Integration Issues in the Presence of Schemas.* If schemas are available, integration issues arise accordingly, as the strongly distributed and decentralized nature of P2P networks can cause the phenomenon of having peers that store similar information modeled according to even-very-different

schemas. This is a realistic bottleneck to be considered, as it can be source of performance decrease.

- *Network Flooding.* Network flooding refers to the phenomenon of moving from a peer to another in search for specific data objects. This phenomenon can easily become unbounded in large and highly-dynamic P2P networks, thus originating a great number of hops and, as a consequence, introducing excessive computational overheads that limit the effectiveness of the overall search task. Usually, query techniques for P2P networks aim at avoiding network flooding, and bounding the number of hops allowed during the search task.
- *Understanding the Semantics of Neighborhood.* Although very often neglected, the concept of neighborhood is critical for querying P2P systems, as it can affect query performance significantly. Usually, neighboring peers of a given peer p_i are defined as those peers connected to p_i directly, or whose distance from p_i is within a given threshold *E*. This "algorithmic" vision needs to be revised. As an example, exploiting semantics in order to model the *conceptual distance* among peers is a promising direction of research (e.g., Crespo & Garcia-Molina, 2003). Also, this approach allows us to move from "traditional" queries, i.e. queries looking for information content stored in peers, to *conceptual queries*, i.e. queries looking for concepts stored in peers (and related information content). Finally, semantics allows us to definitively devise intelligent techniques for routing queries across peers, beyond actual capabilities of DBMS-inspired solutions.
- *Query Classes.* Typical queries of P2P networks are very simple, and mainly focused to keyword-based search. Indeed, following innovative requirements posed by novel and emerging applications, there is a tough need for enriching the class of queries supported by P2P systems. To give examples, *range-queries*, *k-NN queries* and *top-k queries* are relevant classes of queries that, if embedded in P2P middleware, would allow us to improve the knowledge processing capabilities of P2P systems relaying on top of them.
- *Join Queries.* P2P users typically submit queries involving multiple peer data repositories. This because information is very often distributed, whereas users wish to access information in a centralized manner, in order to extract summarized knowledge, e.g. useful for decision making. The mechanism above is implemented-in-practice in terms of *join queries* over distributed peer data repositories. Join queries add to the actual result all data objects located in distributed peers such that these objects jointly satisfy a given set of predicates. Contrarily to classical join queries in distributed databases, in the P2P context these queries introduce novel and unrecognized challenges, such as the issue of defining the non-blocking semantics in the presence of missing data objects extracted from remote peers.
- *Dealing with Imprecise/Incomplete Information.* Peers may store imprecise/incomplete information. This because of the even-complex processes according to which knowledge is produced, processed and delivered across peers. The presence of such kind of information imposes us to consider innovative query models and algorithms able to provide *consistent* answers to such *inconsistent* information sources. Logic-based approaches are promising directions of research with respect to this specific goal.

Finally, for what particularly regards our proposed semantics-based framework, future work is mainly focused on (*i*) defining novel search functionalities for supporting more useful content-oriented KD- and IR-style queries, such as

Boolean, aggregate and range predicates, via innovative query paradigms like approximate query answering, in a similar spirit of the recent Gupta *et al.*'s proposal (Gupta et al., 2003), and (*ii*) studying the integration of our proposed framework with innovative paradigms such as the *Pervasive and Ubiquitous Computing*, which can be justly considered as one of the most relevant next-generation challenges for P2P system research.

REFERENCES

Aberer, K. (2001). P-Grid: A Self-Organizing Access Structure for P2P Information Systems. In C. Batini, F. Giunchiglia, P. Giorgini, M. Mecella (Eds.), *Proceedings of the 6th International Conference on Cooperative Information Systems, LNCS Vol. 2172* (pp. 179-194). Berlin, Germany: Springer.

Aberer, K., & Despotovic, Z. (2001). Managing Trust in a Peer-2-Peer Information System. In H. Paques, L. Liu, D. Grossman (Eds.), *Proceedings of the 10th ACM International Conference on Information and Knowledge Management* (pp. 310-317). New York, NY, USA: ACM.

Aberer, K., Hauswirth, M., Punceva, M., & Schmidt, R. (2002). Improving Data Access in P2P Systems. *IEEE Internet Computing, 6(1)*, 58-67.

Aberer, K., Klemm, F., Rajman, M., & Wu, J. (2004). An Architecture for Peer-to-Peer Information Retrieval. In J. Callan, N. Fuhr, W. Nejdl (Eds.), *Proceedings of the 2004 ACM International Workshop on Peer-to-Peer Information Retrieval* in conjunction with the *27th ACM International Conference on Research and Development in Information Retrieval* (online edition available at http://p2pir.is.informatik.uni-duisburg.de/16.pdf). New York, NY, USA: ACM.

Berglund, A., Boag S., Chamberlin, D., Fernández, M.F., Kay, M., Robie, J., & Siméon, J. (2007). XML Path Language (XPath) 2.0. *World Wide Web Consortium Recommendation.* Online edition available at http://www.w3.org/TR/2007/REC-xpath20-20070123/

Boag, S., Chamberlin, D., Fernández, M.F., Florescu, D., Robie, J., & Siméon, J. (2007). XQuery 1.0: An XML Query Language. *World Wide Web Consortium Recommendation.* Online edition available at http://www.w3.org/TR/2007/REC-xquery-20070123/

Bonifati, A., & Cuzzocrea, A. (2006). Storing and Retrieving XPath Fragments in Structured P2P Networks. *Data & Knowledge Engineering, 59(2)*, 247-269.

Bonifati, A., Cuzzocrea, A., Matrangolo, U., & Jain, M. (2004). XPath Lookup Queries in P2P Networks. In A.H.F. Laender, D. Lee, M. Ronthaler (Eds.), *Proceedings of the 6th ACM International Workshop on Web Information and Data Management* in conjunction with the *13rd ACM International Conference on Information and Knowledge Management* (pp. 48-55). New York, NY, USA: ACM.

Bremer, J.-M., & Gertz, M. (2003). On Distributing XML Repositories. In V. Christophides, J. Freire (Eds.), *Proceedings of the 6th ACM International Workshop on Web and Databases* in conjunction with the *2003 ACM International Conference on Management of Data* (pp. 73-78). New York, NY, USA: ACM.

Cai, M., & Frank, M. (2004). RDFPeers: A Scalable Distributed RDF Repository based on a Structured Peer-to-Peer Network. In S.I. Feldman, M. Uretsky, M. Najork, C.E. Wills (Eds.), *Proceedings of the 13rd International World Wide Web Conference* (pp. 650-657). New York, NY, USA: ACM.

Callan, J. (2000). Distributed Information Retrieval. In W.B. Croft (Ed.), *Advances in Information Retrieval* (pp. 127-150). Hingham, MA, USA: Kluwer Academic Publishers.

Callan, J., Powell, A.L., French, J.C., & Connell, M. (2000). *The Effects of Query-based Sampling on Automatic Database Selection Algorithms* (Tech. Rep. No. IR-181). Amherst, MA, USA: University of Massachusetts, Department of Computer Science, Center for Intelligent Information Retrieval.

Clarke, I., Sandberg, O., Wiley, B., & Hong, T.W. (2000). Freenet: A Distributed Anonymous Information Storage and Retrieval System. In H. Federrath (Ed.), *Proceedings of the ICSI Workshop on Design Issues in Anonymity and Unobservability, LNCS Vol. 2009* (pp. 311-320). Berlin, Germany: Springer.

Crainiceanu, A., Linga, P., Gehrke, J., & Shanmugasundaram, J. (2004). Querying Peer-to-Peer Networks Using P-Trees. In S. Amer-Yahia, L. Gravano (Eds.), *Proceedings of the 7th ACM International Workshop on Web and Databases* in conjunction with the *2004 ACM International Conference on Management of Data* (pp. 25-30). New York, NY: ACM.

Crespo, A., & Garcia-Molina, H. (2002). Routing Indices For Peer-to-Peer Systems. In L.E.T. Rodrigues, M. Raynal, W.-S.E. Chen (Eds.), *Proceedings of the 22nd IEEE International Conference on Distributed Computing Systems* (pp. 23-34). Los Alamitos, CA, USA: IEEE Computer Society.

Crespo, A., & Garcia-Molina, H. (2003). Semantic Overlay Networks for P2P Systems. In G. Moro, S. Bergamaschi, K. Aberer (Eds.), *Proceedings of the 3rd International Workshop on Agents and Peer-to-Peer Computing, LNAI Vol. 3601* in conjunction with the *3rd International Joint Conference on Autonomous Agents and Multi Agent Systems* (pp. 1-13). Berlin, Germany: Springer.

Deerwester, S., Dumais, S.T., Furnas, G.W., Landauer, T.K., & Harshman, R. (1999). Indexing by Latent Semantic Analysis. *Journal of the American Society for Information Science, 41(6)*, 391-407.

Ding, H., Solvberg, I.T., & Lin, Y. (2004). A Vision on Semantic Retrieval in P2P Networks. In L. Barolli (Ed.), *Proceedings of the 18th IEEE International Conference on Advanced Information Networking and Applications, Vol. 1* (pp. 177-182). Los Alamitos, CA, USA: IEEE Computer Society.

French, J.C., Powell, A.L., Callan, J., Viles, C.L., Emmitt, T., Prey, K.J., & Mou, Y. (1999). Comparing the Performance of Database Selection Algorithms. In F. Gey, M. Hearst, R. Tong (Eds.), *Proceeding of the 22nd ACM International Conference on Research and Development in Information Retrieval* (pp. 238-245). New York, NY, USA: ACM.

Galanis, L., Wang, Y., Jeffery, S.R., & DeWitt, D.J. (2003). Locating Data Sources in Large Distributed Systems. In J.C. Freytag, P.C. Lockemann, S. Abiteboul, M.J. Carey, P.G. Selinger, A. Heuer (Eds.), *Proceedings of the 29th International Conference on Very Large Data Bases* (pp. 874-885). San Francisco, CA, USA: Morgan Kaufmann.

Gardarin, G., Sha, F., & Ngoc, T.-D. (1999). XML-based Components for Federating Multiple Heterogeneous Data Sources. In J. Akoka, M. Bouzeghoub, I. Comyn-Wattiau, E. Métais (Eds.), *Proceedings of the 18th International Conference on Conceptual Modeling, LNCS Vol. 1728* (pp. 506-519). Berlin, Germany: Springer.

Gauch, S., Wang, J., & Rachakonda, S.M. (1999). A Corpus Analysis Approach for Automatic Query Expansion and its Extension to Multiple Databases. *ACM Transactions on Information Systems, 17(3)*, 250-269.

Gen Yee, W., & Frieder, O. (2005). On Search in Peer-to-Peer File Sharing Systems. In H. Haddad, L.M. Liebrock, A. Omicini, R.L. Wainwright (Eds.), *Proceedings of the 20th ACM Symposium on Applied Computing* (pp. 1023-1030). New York, NY, USA: ACM.

Gibbons, P.B., Karp, B., Ke, Y., Nath, S., & Seshan, S. (2003). IrisNet: An Architecture for a World-Wide Sensor Web. *IEEE Pervasive Computing, 2(4)*, 22-33.

Gnutella Group (2005). *The Gnutella File Sharing System*. Web pages available at http://gnutella.wego.com.

Golub, G.H., & Loan, C.F.V. (1996). *Matrix Computation*. Baltimore, MD, USA: The John Hopkins University Press.

Gong, X., Yan, Y., Qian, W., & Zhou, A. (2005). Bloom Filter-based XML Packets Filtering for Millions of Path Queries. In R. Agrawal, M. Kitsuregawa, K. Aberer, M. Franklin, S. Nishio (Eds.), *Proceedings of the 21st IEEE International Conference on Data Engineering* (pp. 890-901). Los Alamitos, CA, USA: IEEE Computer Society.

Gravano, L., & Garcia-Molina, H. (1995). Generalizing GlOSS to Vector-Space Databases and Broker Hierarchies. In U. Dayal, P.M.D. Gray, S. Nishio (Eds.), *Proceedings of the 21st International Conference on Very Large Data Bases* (pp. 78-89). San Francisco, CA, USA: Morgan Kaufmann.

Guha, S., Jagadish, H.V., Koudas, N., Srivastava, D., & Yu, T. (2002). Approximate XML Joins. In M.J. Franklin, B. Moon, A. Ailamaki (Eds.), *Proceedings of the 2002 ACM International Conference on Management of Data* (pp. 287-298). New York, NY, USA: ACM.

Guha, S., Koudas, N., Srivastava, D., & Yu, T. (2003). Index-based Approximate XML Joins. In U. Dayal, K. Ramamritham, T.M. Vijayaraman (Eds.), *Proceedings of the 19th IEEE International Conference on Data Engineering* (pp. 708-710). Los Alamitos, CA, USA: IEEE Computer Society.

Gummadi, P.K., Dunn, R.J., Saroiu, S., Gribble, S.D., Levy, H.M., & Zahorjan, J. (2003). Measurement, Modeling, and Analysis of a Peer-to-Peer File-Sharing Workload. In M.L. Scott, L. Peterson (Eds.), *Proceedings of the 19th ACM Symposium on Operating Systems Principles* (pp. 314-329). New York, NY, USA: ACM.

Gupta, A., Agrawal, D., & El Abbadi, A. (2003). Approximate Range Selection Queries in Peer-to-Peer Systems. In J. Gray, D. Dewitt, M. Stonebraker (Eds.), *Proceedings of the 1st Biennial Conference on Innovative Data Systems Research* (online edition available at http://www-db.cs.wisc.edu/cidr/cidr2003/program/p13.pdf). New York, NY, USA: ACM.

Halaschek, C., Aleman-Meza, B., Arpinar, I.B., & Sheth, A.P. (2004). Discovering and Ranking Semantic Associations over a Large RDF Metabase. In M.A. Nascimento, M.T. Özsu, D. Kossmann, R.J. Miller, J.A. Blakeley, K.B. Schiefer (Eds.), *Proceedings of the 30th International Conference on Very Large Data Bases* (pp. 1317-1320). San Francisco, CA, USA: Morgan Kaufmann.

Halevy, A.Y., Ives, Z.G., Mork, P., & Tatarinov, I. (2003). Piazza: Data Management Infrastructure for Semantic Web Applications. In G. Hencsey, B. White, Y.-F.R. Chen, L. Kovács, S. Lawrence (Eds.), *Proceedings of the 12nd International World Wide Web Conference* (pp. 556-567). New York, NY, USA: ACM.

Kalogeraki, V., Gunopulos, D., & Zeinalipour-Yazti, D. (2002). A Local Search Mechanism for Peer-to-Peer Networks. In C. Nicholas, D. Grossman, K. Kalpakis, S. Qureshi, H. van Dissel, L. Seligman (Eds.), *Proceedings of the 11st ACM International Conference on Information and Knowledge Management* (pp. 300-307). New York, NY, USA: ACM.

Karvounarakis, G., Alexaki, S., Christophides, V., Plexousakis, D., & Scholl, M. (2002). RQL: A Declarative Query Language for RDF. In D. Lassner, D. De Roure, A. Iyengar (Eds.), *Proceedings of the 11st International World Wide Web Conference* (pp. 592-603). New York, NY, USA: ACM.

KaZaA Group (2005). *The KaZaA File Sharing System.* Web pages available at http://www.kazaa.com.

Klyne, G., & Carroll, J.J. (2004). Resource Description Framework (RDF): Concepts and Abstract Syntax. *World Wide Web Consortium Recommendation.* Online edition available at http://www.w3.org/TR/2004/REC-rdf-concepts-20040210/.

Kokkinidis, G., & Christophides, V. (2004). Semantic Query Routing and Processing in P2P Database Systems: The ICS-FORTH SQPeer Middleware. In W. Lindner, M. Mesiti, C. Türker, Y. Tzitzikas, A. Vakali (Eds.), *EDBT 2004 Workshops – Proceedings of the 1st International Workshop on Peer-to-Peer Computing and Databases, LNCS Vol. 3268*, in conjunction with the *9th International Conference on Extending Database Technology* (pp. 486-495). Berlin, Germany: Springer.

Koloniari, G., & Pitoura, E. (2004). Content-Based Routing of Path Queries in Peer-to-Peer Systems. In E. Bertino, S. Christodoulakis, D. Plexousakis, V. Christophides, M. Koubarakis, K. Böhm, E. Ferrari (Eds.), *Proceedings of the 9th International Conference on Extending Database Technology, LNCS Vol. 2992* (pp. 29-47).

Kubiatowicz, J., Bindel, D., Eaton, P., Chen, Y., Geels, D., Gummadi, R., Rhea, S., Weimer, W., Wells, C., Weatherspoon, H., & Zhao, B. (2000). OceanStore: An Architecture for Global-Scale Persistent Storage. *ACM SIGPLAN Notices, 35(11)*, 190-201.

Li, M., Lee, W.-C., & Sivasubramaniam, A. (2003). Neighborhood Signatures for Searching P2P Networks. In B.C. Desai, W. Ng (Eds.), *Proceedings of the 7th IEEE International Database Engineering and Applications Symposium* (pp. 149-159). Los Alamitos, CA, USA: IEEE Computer Society.

Loo, B.T., Huebsch, R., Hellerstein, J.M., Stoica, I., & Shenker, S. (2004). Enhancing P2P File-Sharing with an Internet-Scale Query Processor. In M.A. Nascimento, M.T. Özsu, D. Kossmann, R.J. Miller, J.A. Blakeley, K.B. Schiefer (Eds.), *Proceedings of the 30th International Conference on Very Large Data Bases* (pp. 432-443). San Francisco, CA, USA: Morgan Kaufmann.

Lu, J., & Callan, J. (2004). Federated Search of Text-Based Digital Libraries in Hierarchical Peer-to-Peer Networks. In H. Nottelmann, K. Aberer, J. Callan, W. Nejdl (Eds.), *Proceedings of the 2004 ACM International Workshop on Peer-to-Peer Information Retrieval* in conjunction with the *27th ACM International Conference on Research and Development in Information Retrieval* (online edition available at http://p2pir.is.informatik.uni-duisburg.de/1.pdf). New York, NY, USA: ACM.

Lu, Z., & McKinley, K.S. (2000). The Effect of Collection Organization and Query Locality on Information Retrieval System Performance and Design. In W.B. Croft (Ed.), *Advances in Information Retrieval* (pp. 173-197). Hingham, MA, USA: Kluwer Academic Publishers.

Lv, Q., Cao, P., Cohen, E., Li, K., & Shenker, S. (2002). Search and Replication in Unstructured Peer-to-Peer Networks. In K. Ebcioglu, K. Pingali, A. Nicolau (Eds.), *Proceedings of the 16th ACM International Conference on Supercomputing* (pp. 84-95). New York, NY, USA: ACM.

Magkanaraki, A., Tannen, V., Christophides, V., & Plexousakis, D. (2003). Viewing the Semantic Web Through RVL Lenses. In D. Fensel, K. Sycara, J. Mylopoulos (Eds.), *Proceedings of the 2nd International Semantic Web Conference, LNCS Vol. 2870* (pp. 96-112). Berlin, Germany: Springer.

Meng, W., Yu, C., & Liu, K.-L. (2002). Building Efficient and Effective Metasearch Engines. *ACM Computing Surveys, 34(1)*, 48-84.

Morpheus Group (2005). *The Morpheus File Sharing System.* Web pages available at http://www.musiccity.com

Napster Group (2005). *The Napster File Sharing System.* Web pages available at http://www.napster.com

Nejdl, W., Wolpers, M., Siberski, W., Schmitz, C., Schlosser, M., Brunkhorst, I., & Loser, A. (2003). Super-Peer-based Routing and Clustering Strategies for RDF-based P2P Networks. In G. Hencsey, B. White, Y.-F.R. Chen, L. Kovács, S. Lawrence (Eds.), *Proceedings of the 12nd International World Wide Web Conference* (pp. 536-543). New York, NY, USA: ACM.

Ogilvie, P., & Callan, J. (2001). The Effectiveness of Query Expansion for Distributed Information Retrieval. In H. Paques, L. Liu, D. Grossman (Eds.), *Proceedings of the 10th ACM International Conference on Information and Knowledge Management* (pp. 183-190). New York, NY, USA: ACM.

Plaxton, C., Rajaram, R., & Richa, A. (1997). Accessing Nearby Copies of Replicated Objects in a Distributed Environment. In C.E. Leiserson, D.E. Culler (Eds.), *Proceedings of the 9th ACM Symposium on Parallel Algorithms ad Architectures* (pp. 311-320). New York, NY, USA: ACM.

Polyzotis, N., Garofalakis, M., & Ioannidis, Y. (2004). Approximate XML Query Answers. In G. Weikum, A.C. König, S. Deßloch (Eds.), *Proceedings of the 2004 ACM International Conference on Management of Data* (pp. 263-274). New York, NY, USA: ACM.

Powell, A.L., French, J.C., Callan, J., Connell, M., & Viles, C.L. (2000). The Impact of Database Selection on Distributed Searching. In E. Yannakoudakis, N.J. Belkin, M.-K. Leong, P. Ingwersen (Eds.), *Proceedings of the 23rd ACM International Conference on Research and Development in Information Retrieval* (pp. 232-239). New York, NY, USA: ACM.

Rabin, M.O. (1981). *Fingerprinting by Random Polynomials* (Tech. Rep. No. TR-15-81). Cambridge, MA, USA: Harvard University, Center for Research in Computing Technology.

Ratnasamy, P., Francis, P., Handley, M., Karp, R., & Shenker, S. (2001). A Scalable Content-Addressable Network. In R. Cruz, G. Varghese (Eds.), *Proceedings of the 2001 ACM Conference on Applications, Technologies, Architectures, and Protocols for Computer Communications* (pp. 161-172). New York, NY, USA: ACM.

Rhea, S., Wells, C., Eaton, P., Geels, D., Zhao, B., Weatherspoon, H., & Kubiatowicz, J. (2001). Maintenance-free Global Data Storage. *IEEE Internet Computing, 5(5)*, 40-49.

Salton, G., & Buckley, C. (1990). Improving Retrieval Performance by Relevance Feedback. *Journal of the American Society for Information Science, 41(4)*, 288-297.

Salton, G., Wang, A., & Yang, C.S. (1975). A Vector Space Model for Information Retrieval. *Journal of American Society for Information Science, 18(11)*, 613-620.

Sartiani, C., Manghi, P., Ghelli, G., & Conforti, G. (2004). XPeer: A Self-Organizing XML P2P Database System. In W. Lindner, M. Mesiti, C. Türker, Y. Tzitzikas, A. Vakali (Eds.), *EDBT 2004 Workshops – Proceedings of the 1st International Workshop on Peer-to-Peer Computing and Databases, LNCS Vol. 3268*, in conjunction with the *9th International Conference on Extending Database Technology* (pp. 456-465). Berlin, Germany: Springer.

Schlieder, T. (2002). Schema-driven Evaluation of Approximate Tree-Pattern Queries. In C.S. Jensen, K.G. Jeffery, J. Pokorný, S. Saltenis, E. Bertino, K. Böhm, M. Jarke (Eds.), *Proceedings of the 8th International Conference on Extending Database Technology, LNCS Vol. 2287* (pp. 514-532). Berlin, Germany: Springer.

Schmidt, A., Waas, F., Kersten, M., Carey, M., Manolescu, I., & Busse, R. (2002). XMark: A

Benchmark for XML Data Management. In F.H. Lochovsky, W. Shan, P.A. Bernstein, R. Ramakrishnan, Y. Ioannidis, (Eds.), *Proceedings of the 28th International Conference on Very Large Data Bases* (pp. 974-985). San Francisco, CA, USA: Morgan Kaufmann.

Sripanidkulchai, K., Maggs, B., & Zhang, H. (2003). Efficient Content Location using Interest-based Locality in Peer-to-Peer Systems. In F. Bauer, R. Puigjaner, J. Roberts, N. Shroff (Eds.), *Proceedings of the 22nd Annual Joint Conference of the IEEE Computer and Communications Societies, Vol. 3* (pp. 81-87). Los Alamitos, CA, USA: IEEE Computer Society.

Stoica, I., Morris, R., Karger, D., Frans Kaashoek, M, & Balakrishnan, H. (2001). Chord: A Scalable Peer-to-Peer Lookup Service for Internet Applications. In R. Cruz, G. Varghese (Eds.), *Proceedings of the 2001 ACM Conference on Applications, Technologies, Architectures, and Protocols for Computer Communications* (pp. 149-160). New York, NY, USA: ACM.

Tang, C., Xu, Z., & Dwarkadas, S. (2003). Peer-to-Peer Information Retrieval using Self-Organizing Semantic Overlay Networks. In A. Feldmann, M. Zitterbart, J. Crowcroft, D. Wetherall (Eds.), *Proceedings of the 2003 ACM Conference on Applications, Technologies, Architectures, and Protocols for Computer Communications* (pp. 175-186). New York, NY, USA: ACM.

Tsoumakos, D., & Roussopoulos, N. (2003a). A Comparison of Peer-to-Peer Search Methods. In V. Christophides, J. Freire (Eds.), *Proceedings of the 6th ACM International Workshop on Web and Databases* in conjunction with the *2003 ACM International Conference on Management of Data* (pp. 61-66). New York, NY, USA: ACM.

Tsoumakos, D., & Roussopoulos, N. (2003b). Adaptive Probabilistic Search for Peer-to-Peer Networks. In N. Shahmehri, R.L. Graham, G. Carroni (Eds.), *Proceedings of the 3rd IEEE International Conference on Peer-to-Peer Computing* (pp. 102-109). Los Alamitos, CA, USA: IEEE Computer Society.

World Wide Web Consortium (2005). *The World Wide Web Consortium.* Web pages available at http://www.w3.org/

Xu, J., & Callan, J. (1998). Effective Retrieval with Distributed Collections. In W.B. Croft, A. Moffat, C.J. van Rijsbergen, R. Wilkinson, J. Zobel (Eds.), *Proceedings of the 21st ACM International Conference on Research and Development in Information Retrieval* (pp. 112-120). New York, NY, USA: ACM.

Yang, B., & Garcia-Molina, H. (2002). Improving Search in Peer-to-Peer Networks. In L.E.T. Rodrigues, M. Raynal, W.-S.E. Chen (Eds.), *Proceedings of the 22nd IEEE International Conference on Distributed Computing Systems* (pp. 5-14). Los Alamitos, CA, USA: IEEE Computer Society.

Zeinalipour-Yazti, D., Kalogeraki, V., & Gunopulos, D. (2004). Information Retrieval Techniques for Peer-to-Peer Networks. *Computing in Science and Engineering, 6(4)*, 20-26.

Zeinalipour-Yazti, D., Kalogeraki, V., & Gunopulos, D. (2005). Exploiting Locality for Scalable Information Retrieval in Peer-to-Peer Systems. *Information Systems, 30(4)*, 277-298.

Zhang, X., Berry, M.W., & Raghavan, P. (2001). Level Search Schemes for Information Filtering and Retrieval. *Information Processing and Management, 37(2)*, 313-334.

Zhao, Y.B., Kubiatowicz, J., & Joseph, A. (2001). *Tapestry: An Infrastructure for Fault-Tolerant Wide-Area Location and Routing* (Tech. Rep. No. UCB/CSD-01-1141). Berkeley, CA, USA: University of California, Computer Science Division.

Zhu, X., Cao, H., & Yu, Y. (2006). SDQE: Towards Automatic Semantic Query Optimization in P2P Systems. *Information Processing and Management, 42(1)*, 222-236.

ADDITIONAL READING

Aberer, K., & Hauswirth, M. (2002). An Overview on Peer-To-Peer Information Systems. In W. Litwin, G. Lévy (Eds.), *Proceedings of the 4th International Workshop on Distributed Data and Structures* (pp.171-188). Waterloo, Ontario, Canada: Carleton Scientific.

Bernstein, P.A., Giunchiglia, F., Kementsietsidis, A., Mylopoulos, J., Serafini, L., & Zaihrayeu, I. (2002). Data Management for Peer-To-Peer Computing: A Vision. In M.F. Fernandez, Y. Papakonstantinou (Eds.), *Proceedings of the 5th ACM International Workshop on Web and Databases* in conjunction with the *2002 ACM International Conference on Management of Data* (pp. 89-94). New York, NY, USA: ACM.

Bharambe, A., Agrawal, M., & Seshan, S. (2004). Mercury: Supporting Scalable Multi-Attribute Range Queries.

In R. Yavatkar, E. Zegura, J. Rexford (Eds.), *Proceedings of the 2004 ACM Conference on Applications, Technologies, Architectures, and Protocols for Computer Communications* (pp. 353-366). New York, NY, USA: ACM.

Castro, M., Costa, M., & Rowstron, A. (2004). *Peer-To-Peer Overlays: Structured, Unstructured, or Both?* (Tech. Rep. MSR-TR-2004-73). Cambridge, England: Microsoft Research.

Daswani, N., Garcia-Molina, H., & Yang, B. (2003). Open Problems in Data-Sharing Peer-To-Peer Systems. In D. Calvanese, M. Lenzerini, R. Motwani (Eds.), *Proceedings of the 9th International Conference on Database Theory, LNCS Vol. 2572* (pp. 1-15). Berlin, Germany: Springer.

Datar, M. (2002). Butterflies and Peer-To-Peer Networks. In R.H. Möhring, R. Raman (Eds.), *Proceedings of the 10th Annual European Symposium on Algorithms, LNCS Vol. 2461* (pp. 310-322). Berlin, Germany: Springer.

Datta, A., Girdzijauskas, S., & Aberer, K. (2004). On de Bruijn Routing in Distributed Hash Tables: There and Back Again. In G. Caronni, N. Weiler, N. Shahmehri (Eds.), *Proceedings of the 4th IEEE International Conference on Peer-to-Peer Computing* (pp. 159-166). Los Alamitos, CA, USA: IEEE Computer Society.

Erice, L.G., Biersack, E., Felber, P., Ross, K.W., & Keller, G.U. (2003). Hierarchical Peer-To-Peer Systems. In H. Kosch, L. Böszörményi, H. Hellwagner (Eds.), *Proceedings of the 9th International Conference on Parallel Processing, LNCS Vol. 2790* (pp. 1230-1239). Berlin, Germany: Springer.

Ganesan, P., Gummadi, P.K., & Garcia-Molina, H. (2004). Canon in G Major: Designing DHTs with Hierarchical Structure. In M. Liu, Y. Matsushita (Eds.), *Proceedings of the 24th IEEE International Conference on Distributed Computing Systems* (pp. 263-272). Los Alamitos, CA, USA: IEEE Computer Society.

Gribble, S.D., Halevy, A.Y., Ives, Z.G., Rodrig, M., & Suciu, D. (2001). What Can Database Do for Peer-To-Peer? In G. Mecca, J. Siméon (Eds.), *Proceedings of the 4th ACM International Workshop on Web and Databases* in conjunction with the *2001 ACM International Conference on Management of Data* (pp. 31-36). New York, NY, USA: ACM.

Harvey, N., Jones, M.B., Saroiu, S., Theimer, M., & Wolman, A. (2003). Skipnet: A Scalable Overlay Network with Practical Locality Properties. In S.D. Gribble (Ed.), *Proceedings of the 4th USENIX Symposium on Internet Technologies and Systems* (online edition available at http://www.usenix.org/publications/library/proceedings/usits03/tech/harvey/harvey.pdf). Berkeley, CA, USA: USENIX Association.

Hellerstein, J.M. (2004). Architectures and Algorithms for Internet-Scale (P2P) Data Management. In M.A. Nascimento, M.T. Özsu, D. Kossmann,

R.J. Miller, J.A. Blakeley, K.B. Schiefer (Eds.), *Proceedings of the 30th International Conference on Very Large Data Bases* (pp. 1244). San Francisco, CA, USA: Morgan Kaufmann.

Kantere, V., Tsoumakos, D., & Roussopoulos, N. (2004). Querying Structured Data in an Unstructured P2P System. In A.H.F. Laender, D. Lee, M. Ronthaler (Eds.), *Proceedings of the 6th ACM International Workshop on Web Information and Data Management* in conjunction with the *13rd ACM International Conference on Information and Knowledge Management* (pp. 64-71). New York, NY, USA: ACM.

Jagadish, H.V., Ooi, B.C., & Vu, Q.H. (2005). BATON: A Balanced Tree Structure for Peer-To-Peer Networks. In In K. Böhm, C.S. Jensen, L.M. Haas, M.L. Kersten, P.-A. Larson, B.C. Ooi (Eds.), *Proceedings of the 31st International Conference on Very Large Data Bases* (pp. 661-672). San Francisco, CA, USA: Morgan Kaufmann.

Jagadish, H.V., Ooi, B.C., Vu, Q.H., Zhou, A.Y., & Zhang, R. (2006). VBI-Tree: A Peer-To-Peer Framework for Supporting Multi-Dimensional Indexing Schemes. In L. Liu, A. Reuter, K.-Y. Whang, J. Zhang (Eds.), *Proceedings of the 22nd IEEE International Conference on Data Engineering* (pp. 34). Los Alamitos, CA, USA: IEEE Computer Society.

Malkhi, D., Naor, M., & Ratajczak, D. (2002). Viceroy: A Scalable and Dynamic Emulation of the Butterfly. In A. Ricciardi (Ed.), *Proceedings of the 21st ACM Symposium on Principles of Distributed Computing* (pp. 183-192). New York, NY, USA: ACM.

Manku, G.S., Bawa, M., & Raghavan, P. (2003). Symphony: Distributed Hashing in a Small World. In S.D. Gribble (Ed.), *Proceedings of the 4th USENIX Symposium on Internet Technologies and Systems* (online edition available at http://www.usenix.org/publications/library/proceedings/usits03/tech/full_papers/manku/manku.pdf). Berkeley, CA, USA: USENIX Association.

Maymounkov, P., & Mazieres, D. (2002). Kademlia: A Peer-To-Peer Information System Based on the XOR Metric. In P. Druschel, M.F. Kaashoek, A.I.T. Rowstron (Eds.), *Proceedings of the 1st International Workshop on Peer-to-Peer Systems, LNCS Vol. 2429* (pp. 53-65). Berlin, Germany: Springer.

Montresor, A. (2004). A Robust Protocol for Building Superpeer Overlay Topologies. In G. Caronni, N. Weiler, N. Shahmehri (Eds.), *Proceedings of the 4th IEEE International Conference on Peer-to-Peer Computing* (pp. 202-209). Los Alamitos, CA, USA: IEEE Computer Society.

Petrakis, Y., & Pitoura, E. (2004). On Constructing Small Worlds in Unstructured Peer-To-Peer Systems. In W. Lindner, M. Mesiti, C. Türker, Y. Tzitzikas, A. Vakali (Eds.), *EDBT 2004 Workshops – Proceedings of the 1st International Workshop on Peer-to-Peer Computing and Databases, LNCS Vol. 3268*, in conjunction with the *9th International Conference on Extending Database Technology* (pp. 415-424). Berlin, Germany: Springer.

Ratnasamy, S., Handley, M., Karp, R., & Shenker, S. (2002). Topologically-Aware Overlay Construction and Server Selection. In P. Kermani, F. Bauer, P. Morreale, D. Lee, A. Orda (Eds.), *Proceedings of the 21st Annual Joint Conference of the IEEE Computer and Communications Societies, Vol. 3* (pp. 1190-1199). Los Alamitos, CA, USA: IEEE Computer Society.

Rowstron, A., & Druschel, P. (2001). Pastry: Scalable, Decentralized Object Location, and Routing for Large-Scale Peer-To-Peer Systems. In R. Guerraoui (Ed.), *Proceedings of the 2001 IFIP/ACM International Conference on Distributed Systems Platforms, LNCS Vol. 2218* (pp. 329-350), Berlin, Germany: Springer.

Schlosser, M.T., Sintek, M., Decker, S., & Nejdl, W. (2002a). A Scalable and Ontology-based P2P Infrastructure for Semantic Web Services. In M. Kamkar, R.L. Graham, N. Shahmehri (Eds.), *Pro-*

ceedings of the 2nd IEEE International Conference on Peer-to-Peer Computing (pp. 104-111). Los Alamitos, CA, USA: IEEE Computer Society.

Schlosser, M.T., Sintek, M., Decker, S., & Nejdl, W. (2002b). Hypercup – Hypercubes, Ontologies, and Efficient Search on Peer-To-Peer Networks. In G. Moro, M. Koubarakis (Eds.), *Proceedings of the 1st International Workshop on Agents and Peer-to-Peer Computing, LNCS Vol. 2530* (pp. 112-124). Berlin, Germany: Springer.

Valduriez, P., & Pacitti, E. (2004). Data Management in Large-Scale P2P Systems. In M.J. Daydé, J. Dongarra, V. Hernández, J.M.L.M. Palma (Eds.), *Proceedings of the 6th International Conference on High Performance Computing for Computational Science, LNCS Vol. 3402* (pp. 104-118). Berlin, Germany: Springer.

Section III

Chapter X
Applying Semantic Web to E-Tourism

Danica Damljanović
University of Sheffield, UK

Vladan Devedžić
University of Belgrade, Serbia

ABSTRACT

Traditional E-Tourism applications store data internally in a form that is not interoperable with similar systems. Hence, tourist agents spend plenty of time updating data about vacation packages in order to provide good service to their clients. On the other hand, their clients spend plenty of time searching for the 'perfect' vacation package as the data about tourist offers are not integrated and are available from different spots on the Web. We developed Travel Guides - a prototype system for tourism management to illustrate how semantic web technologies combined with traditional E-Tourism applications: a.) help integration of tourism sources dispersed on the Web b) enable creating sophisticated user profiles. Maintaining quality user profiles enables system personalization and adaptivity of the content shown to the user. The core of this system is in ontologies – they enable machine readable and machine understandable representation of the data and more importantly reasoning.

INTRODUCTION

A mandatory step on the way to the desired vacation destination is usually contacting tourist agencies. Presentations of tourist destinations on the Web make a huge amount of data. These data are accessible to individuals through the official presentations of the tourist agencies, cities, municipalities, sport alliances, etc. These sites are available to everyone, but still, the problem is to find useful information without wasting time. On the other hand, plenty of systems on the Web are maintained regularly to provide tourists with up-to-date information. These systems require a lot of efforts from humans - especially in travel agencies where they want to offer tourists a good service.

We present Travel Guides – a prototype system that is combining Semantic Web technologies with those used in mainstream applications (cp. Djuric, Devedzic & Gasevic, 2007) in order to enable data exchange between different E-Tourism systems and thus:

- Ease the process of maintaining the systems for tourist agencies
- Ease the process of searching for perfect vacation packages for tourists

The core of Travel Guides system is in ontologies. We have developed domain ontology for tourism and described the most important design principles in this chapter.

As ontologies enable presenting data in a machine-readable form thus offering easy exchange of data between different applications, this would lead to increased interoperability and decreased efforts tourist agents make to update the data in their systems. To illustrate increased interoperability we initialized our knowledge base using data imported from some other system. We built an environment to enable transferring segments of any knowledge base to the other by selecting some criteria - this transfer is possible even if the knowledge bases rely on different ontologies.

Ontology-aware systems provide the possibility to perform semantic search – the user can search the destinations covered by Travel Guides using several criteria related to travelling (e.g., accommodation rating, budget, activities and interests: concerts, clubbing, art, sports, shopping, etc.). For even more sophisticated search results we introduce user profiles created based on data that system possesses about the user. These data are analysed by a reasoner, and the heuristics is residing inside the ontology.

The chapter is organized as follows: in next section we describe different systems that are developed in the area of tourism which use semantic web technologies. In the central section we first discuss problems that are present in existing E-Tourism systems, and then describe how we solve some of these problems with Travel Guides: we give details of the design of the domain ontology, the creation of the knowledge base and finally system architecture. To illustrate Travel Guides environment we give an example of using this system by providing some screenshots. Finally, we conclude and give the ideas of future work and also future research directions in the field.

BACKGROUND

E-Tourism comprises electronic services which include (Aichholzer, Spitzenberger & Winkler, 2003):

- Information Services (IS), e.g. destination, hotel information.
- Communication Services (CS), e.g. discussion forums, blogs.
- Transaction Services (TS), e.g. booking, payment.

Among these three services *Information Services* are the most present on the Web. Hotels usually have their Web sites with details about the type of accommodation, location, and contact information. Some of these Web sites even offer *Transaction Services* so that it is possible to access the prices and availability of the accommodation for the requested period and perform booking and payment.

Transaction Services are usually concentrated on sites of Web tourist agencies such as Expedia, Travelocity, Lastminute, etc. These Websites sometimes include *Communication Services* in the form of forums where people who visited hotels give their opinion and reviews. With emerging popularity of social web applications many sites specialize in CS only (e.g., www.43places.com).

However, for complete details about a certain destination (e.g., activities, climate, monuments, and events) one often must search for several sources. Apparently all of these sources are dispersed on different places on the Internet and there is an "information gap" between them. The best way to bridge this gap would be to enable communication between different tourist applications.

For *Transaction Services* this is already partly achieved by using Web portals that serve as mediators between tourists and tourist agencies. These portals (e.g., Bookings.com) gather vacation packages from different vendors and use Web services to perform booking and sometimes payment. *Communication Services* are tightly coupled with *Information Services*, in a way that the integration of the first implies the integration of the latter. Henriksson (2005) discusses that the one of the main reasons for lack of interoperability in the area of tourism is the tourism product itself: immaterial, heterogeneous and non-persistent. Travel Guides demonstrates how Semantic Web technologies can be used to enable communication between *Information Services* dispersed on the Web. This would lead to easier exchange of communication services, thus resulting in better quality of E-Tourism and increased interoperability.

Hepp, Siorpaes and Bachlechner (2006) claim that "Everything is there, but we only have insufficient methods of finding and processing what's already on the Web" (p. 2). This statement reveals some of the reasons why Semantic Web is not frequently applied in real-time applications: Web today contains content understandable to humans hence only humans can analyse it. To retrieve information from applications using computer programs (e.g., intelligent agents) two conditions must be satisfied: 1) data must be in a machine-readable form 2) applications must use technologies that provide information retrieval from this kind of data.

Many academic institutions are making efforts to find methods for computer processing of human language. GATE (General Architecture for Text Engineering) is an infrastructure for developing and deploying software components that process human language (Cunningham, 2002). It can annotate documents by recognizing concepts such as: locations, persons, organizations and dates. It can be extended to annotate some domain-related concepts, such as hotels and beaches.

The most common approaches for applying Semantic Web in E-Tourism are:

1. Making applications from scratch using recommended standards
2. Using ontologies as mediators to merge already existing systems
3. Performing annotations in respect to the ontology of already existing Web content

One of the first developed E-Tourism systems was onTour (http://ontour.deri.org/) developed by DERI (Siorpaes & Bachlechner, 2006; Prantner, 2004) where they built a prototype system from scratch and stored their data in the knowledge base created based on the ontology. They developed domain ontology following the World Tourism Organization standards, although they considered a very limited amount of concepts and relations. Later on, they took over the ontology developed as a part of Harmonize project and now planning to develop an advanced E-Tourism Semantic Web portal to connect the customers and virtual travel agents (Jentzsch, 2005).

The idea of Harmonize project was to integrate Semantic Web technologies and merge tourist electronic markets yet avoiding forcing tourist agencies to change their already existing information systems, but to merge them using ontology as a mediator (Dell'erba, Fodor, Hopken, & Werthner, 2005).

The third approach is very challenging for researchers as with the current state of the Web it is not easy to add semantics to the data without changing the technologies used to develop the Web applications. Cardoso (2006) presents a system that creates vacation packages dynamically using previously annotated data in respect to the ontology. This is performed with a service that constructs itinerary by combining user preferences with flights, car rentals, hotel, and activities on-fly. In 2005, Cardoso founded a lab for research in the area of Semantic Web appliance in E-Tourism. The main project called SEED (Semantic E-Tourism Dynamic packaging) aims to illustrate the appliance of Web services and Semantic Web in the area of tourism. One of the main objectives of this project is the development of OTIS ontology (Ontology for Tourism Information Systems). Although they discuss the comprised concepts of this ontology, its development is not yet finished, and could not be further discussed in this chapter.

On the other side, Hepp et al. (2006) claim that there are not enough data in the domain of tourism available on the Web - at least for Tyrol, Austria. Their experiment revealed that existing data on the Web are incomplete: the availability of the accommodation and the prices are very often inaccessible.

Additionally, most of E-Tourism portals store their data internally, which means that they are not accessible by search engines on the Web. Using Semantic Web services, e.g. Web Service Modelling Ontology - WSMO (Roman et al., 2005) or OWL-based Web service ontology - OWL-S (Smith & Alesso, 2005) it would be possible to access data from data-intensive applications. SATINE project is about deploying semantic travel Web services. In (Dogac et al., 2004) they present how to exploit semantics through Web service registries.

Semantic Web services might be a good solution for performing E-Tourism *Transaction Services*, and also for performing E-Tourism *Information Services*, as they enable integrating homogenous data and applications. However, using Semantic Web services, as they are applied nowadays, will not reduce every-day efforts made by tourist agents who are responsible for providing current data about vacation packages and destinations. Data about different destinations are not static – they change over time and thus require E-Tourism systems to be updated. With the current state of the development of E-Tourism applications, each travel agency performs data update individually.

In Travel Guides we employ Semantic Web technologies by combining the first and the third approach. We use the first approach to build the core of the system, and to initialize the repository, whereas in later phase we propose using annotation tools such as GATE to perform semi-automatic annotation of documents and update of knowledge base accordingly. Some of the existing Knowledge Management platforms such as KIM (Popov, Kiryakov, Ognyanoff, Manov & Kirilov, 2004) use GATE for performing automatic annotation of documents and knowledge base enrichment. Due to the very old and well-known problem of syntactic ambiguity (Church & Patil, 1982) of human language widely present inside the Web content that is used in the process of annotation, we argue that the role of human is irreplaceable.

The core of the Travel Guides system is in ontologies. Many ontologies have been already developed in the area of tourism. Bachlechner (2004) has made a long list of the areas that need to be covered by E-Tourism relevant ontologies and made a brief analysis of the developed domain and upper level ontologies. Another good summary of E-Tourism related ontologies is given in (Jentzsch, 2005).

However, no ontology includes all concepts and relations between them in such a way that it can be used without any modifications, although some of them such as Mondeca's (http://www.mondeca.com) or OnTour's ontology (Prantner, 2004) are developed following World Tourism Organization standards. While developing Travel Guides ontology we tried to comprise all possible concepts that are related to the area of tourism and also - tourists. Concepts and relations that describe user's activities and interests coupled with built-in reasoner enable identifying the user as a particular type: some tourists enjoy comfort during vacation, whereas others don't care about the type of the accommodation but more about the outdoor activities or the scenery that is nearby.

Most of the developed ontology-aware systems nowadays propose using a RDF repository instead of using conventional databases (Stollberg, Zhdanova & Fensel, 2004). RDF repositories are not built to replace conventional databases, but to add a refinement which is not supported by conventional databases, specifically – to enable representing machine-readable data and reasoning. In Travel Guides system we distinguish between data that are stored in RDF repositories and those that are stored in conventional databases. In RDF repositories we store machine-understandable data used in the process of reasoning, and relational databases are used to store and retrieve all other data – those that are not important in this process and also being specific for each travel agency which means they are not *sharable*. We propose *sharable* data to be those that could be easily exchangeable between applications. This way, applications can share a unique repository which means that if, for instance, a new hotel is built on a certain destination and one tourist agency updates the repository, all others can use it immediately.

We suggest this approach as Semantic Web technologies nowadays are still weak to handle a huge amount of data, and could not be compared by performance with relational databases in the terms of transaction handling, security, optimization and scalability (cf. Guo, Pan & Heflin, 2004).

APPLYING SEMANTIC WEB TO E-TOURISM

E-Tourism Today

Searching for information on a desired spot for vacation is usually a very time-consuming. Figure 1 depicts the most frequent scenario which starts with the vague ideas of the user interested in travelling, and ends with the list of tourist destinations. In most of cases the user is aware of a few criteria that should be fulfilled (the distance from the shopping centre, sandy beach, a

Figure 1. The usual scenario of searching the Internet for a 'perfect' vacation package

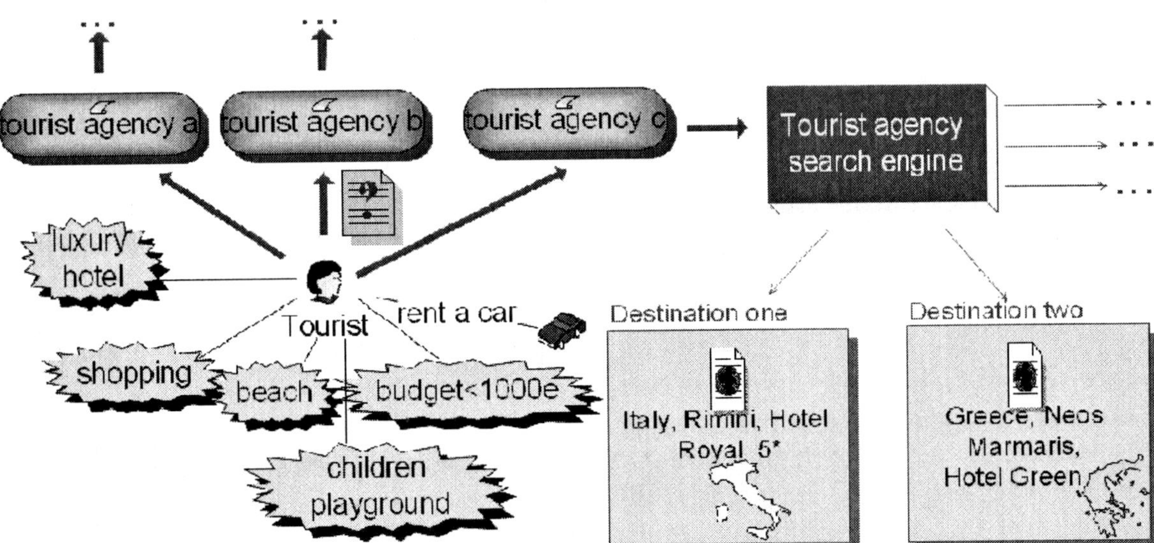

possibility to rent a car, etc.), as well as of some individual constraints (prices, departure times, etc.). After processing the user's query (using these criteria as input data), the search engine of a tourist agency will most likely return a list of vacation packages. It is up to the user to choose the most appropriate one. If the user is not satisfied with the result, the procedure is repeated, with another tourist agency. This scenario is restarted in N iterations until the user gets the desired result. The essential disadvantage of this system is a lack of the integrated and ordered collection of the tourist deals. Tourist deals are dispersed on the Web and being offered from different tourist agencies each of which maintain their system independently.

Additional problem with existing E-Tourism applications is the lack of interactivity. It is always the user who provides the criteria for the search/query and who analyzes the results returned.

The problem of dispersed information about tourist deals would be reduced totally if all vacation packages would be gathered at one place - the Web portal. This assumption could not be taken as realistic, but apparently the distribution of the tourist offers would be decreased by adding the tourist offers of each tourist agency into the portal. Although the portals are more sophisticated than simple Web applications, they usually do not compensate for the lack of interactivity.

Some of the popular Web tourist agencies, such as Expedia, expand their communication with the user by offering various services based on user selection during visiting their site. Namely, they track user actions (mouse clicks) so that when user browse throughout the site the list of user recently visited places is always available. In case the user provides his personal e-mail they send some special offers or advertisements occasionally. Although their intentions are to improve communication with their clients, this kind of service can be irritating sometimes. Developing more sophisticated user profiles would help developing more personalized systems thus avoiding spamming the user with an unattractive content.

Creating user profiles is widely used in many applications nowadays, not only in the area of tourism. In order to create his/her profile, the user is usually prompted to register and fill in few forms with some personal info such as location, year of birth, interests, etc. Filling these forms sometimes can take a lot of time and thus carries the risk of 'refusing' the user. The best way is to request a minimum data from the user on his first log in, and then update his data later step by step.

Travel Guides

Disadvantages of traditional E-Tourism systems imply requirements for a new system that is focusing on the integration of *Information Services* present on the Web and also on introducing sophisticated *user profiles*. Travel Guides prototype system has been developed to satisfy these requirements by combining semantic web technologies with those used in traditional E-Tourism systems.

Using semantic web technologies enables representing the data in machine-readable form. Such a representation enable easier integration of tourist resources as data exchange between applications is feasible. Integration of tourist resources would decrease efforts tourist agents make in tourist agencies to maintain these data. The final result would affect the tourist who will be able to search for details about destinations from the single point on the Web.

In Travel Guides we introduce more sophisticated user profiles – these are to enable personalization of the Web content and to act as agents who work for users, while not spamming them with commercial content and advertisements. For example, if during registration the user enters that he is interested in extreme sports, and later moves on to the search form where he does not specify any sport requirement, the return results could be filtered in a manner that the first listed are those that are flagged as "adventurer destinations".

Developing sophisticated user profiles requires analyse of the user behaviour while visiting the portal. This behaviour is determined by the data the system collects about the user: his personal data, interests, activities, and also the data that system tracks while 'observing' the user: user selection, mouse clicks, and the like. To be able to constantly analyze the user's profile the portal requires intelligent reasoning. To make a tourism portal capable of intelligent reasoning, it is necessary to build some initial and appropriate knowledge in the system, as well as to maintain the knowledge automatically from time to time and during the user's interaction with the system. Simply saving every single click of the user could not be enough to make a good-quality user profile. It is much more suitable to use a built-in reasoner to infer the user's preferences and intentions from the observations.

Any practical implementation of the aforementioned requirements leads to representing essential knowledge about the domain (tourism) and the portal users (user profiles) in a machine-readable and machine-understandable form. In other words, it is necessary to develop and use a set of ontologies to represent all important concepts and their relations.

When ontologies are developed, it is necessary to populate the knowledge base with instances of concepts from the ontology and with relevant relations. After some knowledge is created, it needs to be coupled with a built-in inference engine to support reasoning. Finally, it is essential to enable input in the system from the user as reasoning requires some input data to be processed.

In the next sections we describe the ontology we developed to satisfy the requirements, followed by the knowledge base creation and the architecture of the system that enables processing the input from end users.

Travel Guides Ontologies

The Travel Guides Ontologies are written in OWL (Antoniou & Harmelen, 2004) and developed using Protégé (Horridge, Knublauch, Rector, Stevens & Wroe, 2004). To develop a well-designed ontology, it was important to:

1. *Include all important terms in the area of tourism* to represent destinations in general, excluding data specific for any tourist agency. For instance, information about a city name, its latitude and longitude, and the country it belongs to is to be included here.
2. *Classify user interests and activities* so that they can be expressed in the manner of a collection of user profiles, and identify the concepts to represent them.
3. *Identify concepts to represent the facts about destinations* that are specific for each tourist agency. This information is extracted from expert knowledge, where an expert is a tourist agent who would be able to classify destinations according to the different criteria; for instance, if the destination is a family destination, a romantic destination, etc. After identifying these concepts they need to be connected with other relevant concepts, e.g. create relations between destination types and relevant user profile types.

Representing aforementioned three steps in a manner of a formal representation of concepts and relations results in the creation of the following:

1. *The World ontology*, with concepts and relations from the real world: geographical terms, locations with coordinates, land types, time and date, time zone, currency, languages, and all other terms that are expressing concepts that are in a way related

to tourism or tourists, but not to vacation packages that could be offered by some tourist agencies. This ontology should also contain the general concepts necessary for expression of semantic annotation, indexing, and retrieval (Kiryakov et al., 2003).

2. *The User ontology* containing concepts related to the users – the travellers who visit the Travel Guides portal. This ontology describes user interests and activities, age groups, favourite travel companies, and other data about different user profiles.
3. *The Travel (Tourism) ontology* contains concepts related to vacation packages, types of vacations, and traveller types w.r.t. various tourist destinations. It includes all terms being specific to vacation packages offered in tourist agencies and being important for travellers, like the type of accommodation, food service type, transport service, room types in a hotel, and the like. It is this ontology that makes a connection between users and destinations. This is accomplished by creating user profiles for the users, and determining the type of destination for each vacation package. Finally, user profiles are linked to relevant destination types (and vice versa).

After the evaluation of existing domain and upper-level ontologies, we have found that the one that suits the Travel Guides the best is the PROTON ontology (Terziev, Kiryakov and Manov, 2005). PROTON upper-level ontology includes four modules, each of which is a separate ontology. For the purpose of Travel Guides development, the Upper module of PROTON (Terziev et al., 2005) was used as *the World ontology*. This module was extended to fit *the Tourism (Travel) ontology*. The PROTON Knowledge management module (Terziev et al., 2005) was extended to serve as *the User ontology*.

Figure 2. The Location class and its subclasses in the PROTON Upper Level ontology

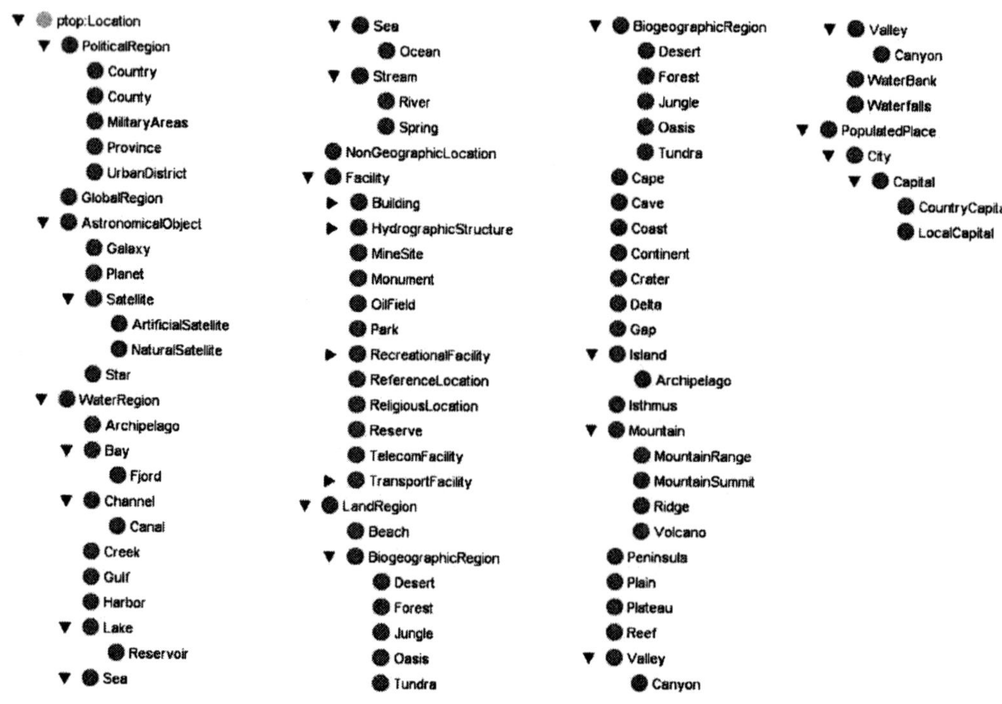

The World Ontology

The PROTON upper level ontology contains all concepts required by Travel Guides World ontology. In addition, it contains concepts and relations necessary for information extraction, retrieval and semantic annotation. PROTON class we used the most frequently in our World ontology is the class **Location**. Figure 2 depicts the hierarchy of the class **Location** and its subclasses in the PROTON Upper Level ontology.

The classes and properties from PROTON used in Travel Guides are shown in Figure 3. Following aliases have been used instead of full namespaces: pkm for PROTON Knowledge Management, psys for PROTON System Module, ptou for PROTON Upper Module, and ptop for Proton Top module.

For more information about PROTON ontology we refer reader to (Terziev et al., 2005).

The User Ontology

PROTON Knowledge Management (KM) ontology has been extended to suit *the User ontology* needs. The most frequently used classes are: **User**, **UserProfile**, and **Topic**. According to the PROTON documentation, **Protont:Topic** (the PROTON top module class) is "any sort of a topic or a theme, explicitly defined for classification purposes". For the needs of Travel Guides, **protont:Topic** class has been extended to represent user interests and activities. Its important relations and concepts are depicted in Figure 4.

For determining user profile types, the age and the user preferred travel company is of a great importance hence relevant concepts have been created inside the ontology: **AgeGroup** is a representation of the first and the **TravelCompany** is a representation of the latter (Figure 5). For example, if the user selects that he/she travels with family very often, he/she could be considered as a **FamilyType**.

The **UserProfile** class is extended to represent various types of tourists. These profiles are made based on user interests and activities. Figure 6 depicts various types of user profiles.

In practice, many tourists would be determined to belong to more than one type of user profiles. For this purpose, there is a property *weight* that could be assigned for each type of user profile. It is this property that reflects the importance of certain profiles. For example:

User *hasUserProfile* **Adventurer** (*weight* = 2),
User *hasUserProfile* **ClubbingType** (*weight* = 1).

Figure 3. The classes and properties from the PROTON ontology frequently used in Travel Guides

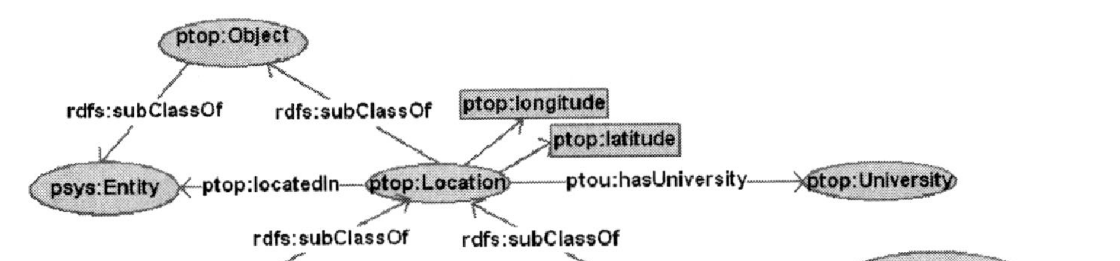

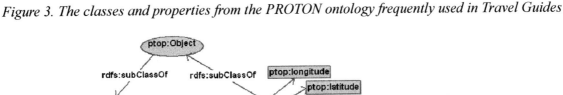

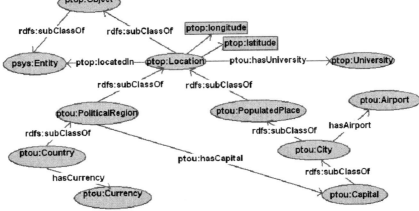

Figure 4. The most important concepts and their relation in the User ontology

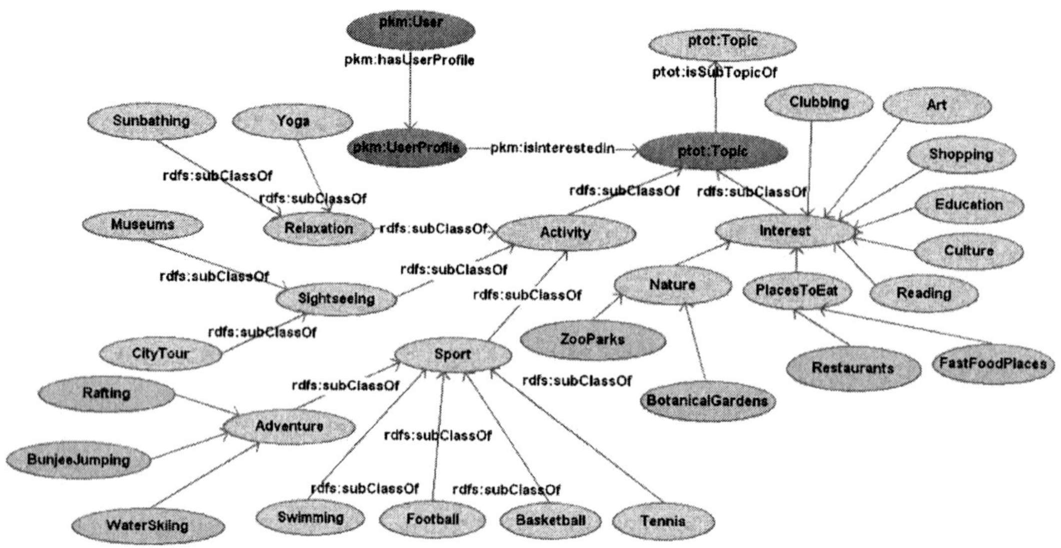

Figure 5. Extension of PROTON Group class

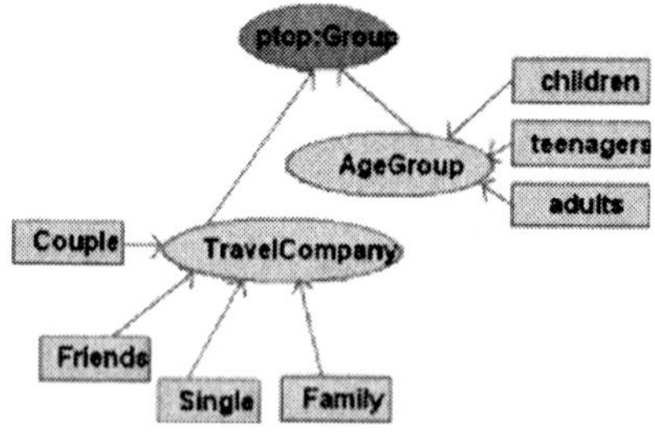

Figure 7. The extended ptou:Offer class in Travel Guides Tourism ontology

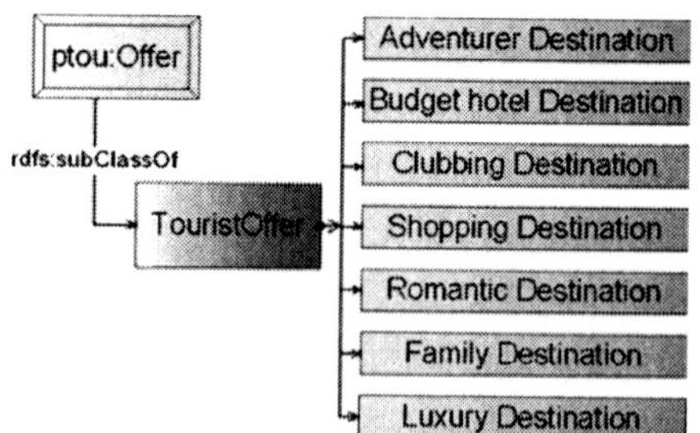

In this case the user profile is a mixture of the **Adventurer** and the **Clubbing** type, but due to the *weight* values adventure destinations have a priority over those that are "flagged" as great-night-life destinations.

Travel Guides User Ontology is available online at http:// goodoldai.org.yu/ns/upproton.owl.

Tourism (Travel) Ontology

In order to design the domain ontology for the area of tourism as well as to "link" tourist destination types to the user profile types, we extended the PROTON Upper module ontology. The class **Offer** is extended with the subclass of **TouristOffer** representing a synonym term for vacation package offered in a tourist agency. Figure 7 depicts the **TouristOffer** class and types of destinations assigned to tourist offers. These types are used as indicators of types of tourist offers which are later being assigned to relevant user profile types.

Figure 8 depicts classes and relations between them in *the Travel ontology.* Since the Travel ontology is an extension of the PROTON Upper module ontology, there are some concepts and relations from PROTON that are frequently used. They all have appropriate prefixes.

As shown on Figure 8, a vacation package being an instance of **TouristOffer** class *isAttractiveFor* certain type of **UserProfile**, where this type is determined by user's interests and activities.

Figure 6. Subclasses of PROTON UserProfile class

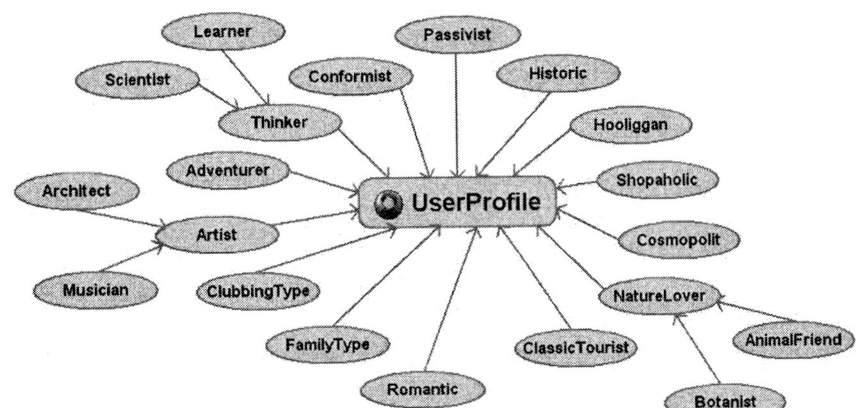

Figure 8. Concepts and relations in the Travel Guides Travel ontology

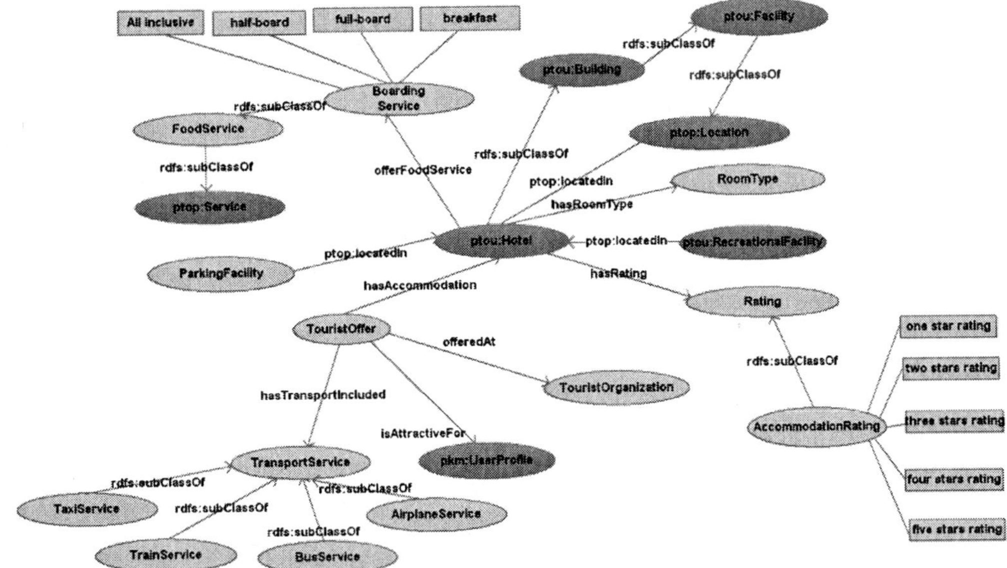

Travel Guides Travel Ontology is available online at http://goodoldai.org.yu/ns/tgproton.owl.

Travel Guides Knowledge Base

Due to a huge amount of data that is stored inside the knowledge base (KB), it is essential that its structure allows easy maintenance. To meet this requirement, we represent the KB as a collection of *.owl* files (Figure 9). The circle on the top represents the core and contains concepts such as continents and countries used by all other parts of the KB. The other parts are independent *.owl* files that are country specific and contain all destinations inside the country, all hotels on the destinations and finally all vacation packages related to the hotels. For the clarity of the presentation Figure 9 depicts only 3 elements of the KB apart from the core. Ideally, the number of these elements is equal to the number of existing countries.

To alleviate the creation, extensions, and maintenance of the KB, and also to address the

Figure 9. Organization of the knowledge base inside the Travel Guides system

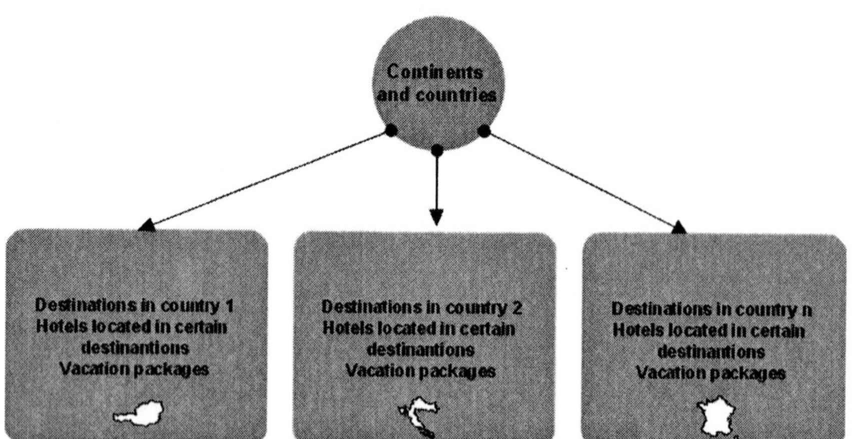

interoperability issue, we explored some other ontology-based systems that include instances of concepts that are of interest to Travel Guides system. We have built an environment that enables exploiting instances of classes (concepts) and relations of the arbitrary KB in accordance to the predefined criteria. We considered using KIM KB and also WordNet (Fellbaum, 1998). As KIM KB contains more data that are of interest to Travel Guides system and also is built based on the ontology whose core is PROTON ontology (Popov et al, 2004), we successfully exploited it to build our core (continents and countries). This core is available online at http:// goodoldai.org.yu/ns/travel_wkb.owl, and is used to initialize other elements of the KB.

This way we avoided entering permanent data about various destinations manually, and also showed that it is possible to share the knowledge between different platforms when it is represented using RDF structure and achieve interoperability - the content of one application can be of use inside the other application, even if they are based on different ontologies. Our environment for knowledge base exploitation is applicable for any knowledge base and ontology; the only precondition is selection of criteria that will define the statements to be extracted.

Apart from many concepts (e.g., organizations and persons), KIM Platform KB includes data about continents, countries and many cities. The environment created inside Travel Guides enables extracting of concepts by selecting some of the criteria, e.g., name of the property. We selected *hasCapital*, as this property has class **Country** as a domain and class **City** as a range. Our environment extracts not only the concepts that are directly related to the predefined property, but also all other statements that are the result of transitive relations of this property. For example, if defined relation **Country** ***isLocatedIn*** **Continent** exists, statements that represent this relation will also be extracted.

Figure 10 depicts some of the classes and relations whose instances are imported during the KB extraction.

Ideally, the knowledge base should contain descriptions of all destinations that could (but need not necessarily) be included in the offers of the tourist agencies connected to the portal.

The Portal Architecture

This section gives details about the architecture of Travel Guides system (Figure 11) and its design. The system comprises following four modules:

Figure 10. Classes and relations whose concepts are imported during KB extraction

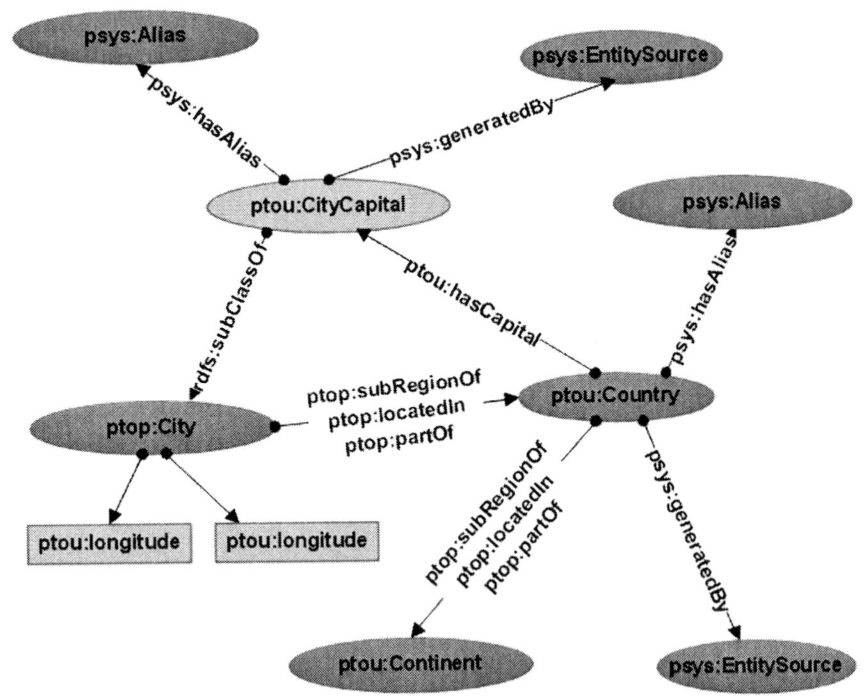

Figure 11. Travel Guides Architecture

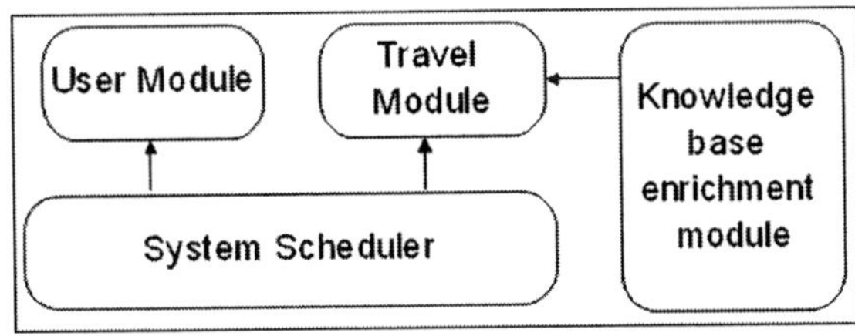

1. **User Module:** For generating user profiles and maintaining user data.
2. **Travel Module:** For generating and maintaining vacation packages and all other data related to vacation packages and destinations.
3. **System Scheduler Module:** For update of the knowledge base. It communicates with:
   - User Module when updating user profiles
   - Travel Module when updating data about vacation packages and destinations.
4. **Knowledge base enrichment module:** For knowledge base enrichment based on annotations in respect to the ontology. It communicates with Travel Module to update knowledge base with new instances and relations between them.

Following are details about key modules.

User Module

UserController (Figure 12) accepts requests from the user (via *User registration form*) and fires appropriate actions. Actions (at the presentation layer) are directly connected to the business layer of the system represented by *User Manager* (UM). The UM has the following roles:

- Store and retrieve data about the user.
- Observe and track the activities of the user during his visit to the portal.

For manipulation with data stored in the database UM uses the *User DAO* (User Data Access Object). These data are user details that are not subject to frequent changes and are not important for determining the user profile: the username, password, first name, last name, address, birth date, phone and email.

For logging user activities during visiting the portal UM uses *User Log DAO.*

When reasoning over the available data about the user and determining user profile types UM use the User Profile Expert. The *User Profile Expert* is aware of the *User ontology* and also of the User profile knowledge base (*User kb*) that contains instances of classes and relations from the User ontology.

The data about users are collected in two ways:

Figure 12. User module components

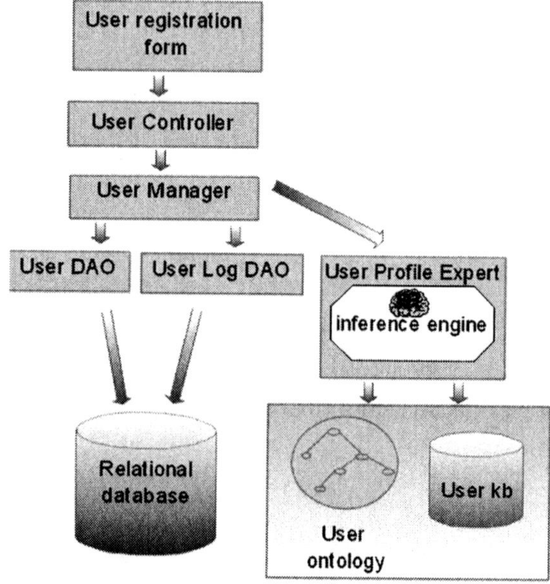

1. Using User interface: the user is prompted to fill the forms to input data about him/herself. These data are: gender, birth date, social data (single, couple, family with kids, friends), the user's location, profession, education, languages, interests and activities (art, museums, sightseeing, sports, exploring new places during vacation, animals, eating out, nightlife, shopping, trying local food/experiencing local customs/habits, natural beauties, books), budget, visited destinations.
2. The system collects data about the user's interests and preferences while the user is reading about or searching for vacation packages using the portal. Each time the user clicks on some of the vacation package details, the system stores his/her action in the database, and analyse it later on.

Travel Module

Travel Module generates and maintains data about vacation packages, destinations and related concepts. The User interface of Travel Module component comprises following forms (Figure 13):

1. *Recommended Vacation Packages* form: This form shows the list of vacation packages that the user has not explicitly searched for - system generates this list automatically based on the user profile.
2. *Vacation Packages Form*: This form is important for travel agents when updating vacation packages data.
3. *Vacation Package Semantic Search Form*: This form enables semantic search of vacation packages.

Each of the available forms communicates with the *Controller* who dispatches the requested actions to the *Travel Manager (TM).* The Travel Manager is responsible for fetching, storing and updating the data related to vacation packages. It includes a mechanism for storing and retrieving data from the database using *Vacation Package DAO* (Data Access Object). The data stored in the database are those that are subject to frequent changes and are not important in the process of reasoning: start date, end date, prices (accommodation price, food service price, and transport price), benefits, discounts and documents that contain textual descriptions with details about the vacation packages. Some of these data are used in the second phase of retrieving a 'perfect' vacation package, when the role of the inference engine is not important. Retrieving a 'perfect' vacation package is performed in two steps:

1. Matching the user's wishes with certain destinations – the user profile is matched with certain types of destinations. To perform this TM uses the *Travel Offer Expert* (TOE) and the *World Expert* (WE) components.
2. The list of destinations retrieved in the first step is filtered using the constraints the user provided (for example, the start/end dates of the vacation). TM filters retrieved result using the *Vacation Package DAO*.

Figure 13. Travel Module Components

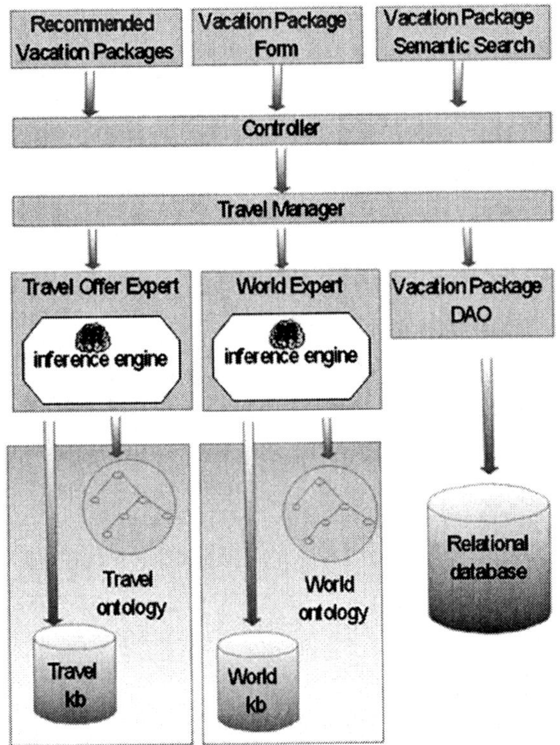

TOE and *WE* components include inference engines. These inference engines are aware of the ontologies and knowledge bases: TOE works with *Travel ontology* and a knowledge base (*Travel kb*) created based on this ontology. WE uses the *World ontology* and the knowledge base (*World kb*) created based on it.

After the initial knowledge base is deployed into Travel Guides application, its further update could be performed semi-automatically by *Knowledge base enrichment module (KBEM)* deployed inside Travel Guides. For example, when a new hotel is built, the knowledge base should be enriched with this information. This can be performed either by:

- Using the Travel Guides environment, where a tourist agent or administrator manually enters the name and other data about the new hotel (Figure 13).
- Performing annotation of the relevant content with regards to the Travel Guides ontology, semi-automatically (Figure 14).

Knowledge Base Enrichment Module (KBEM)

Semi-automatic annotation process starts with *Crawler* actions. Crawler searches the Internet and finds potentially interesting sites with details about destinations, hotels, beaches, new activities in a hotel, news about some destinations, popular events, etc. The result (HTML pages) is transformed into *.txt* format and redirected to JMS (Java Message Service) to wait in a queue for annotation process (*aQueue*). JMS API is a messaging

Figure 14. Knowledge base enrichment module inside the Travel Guides

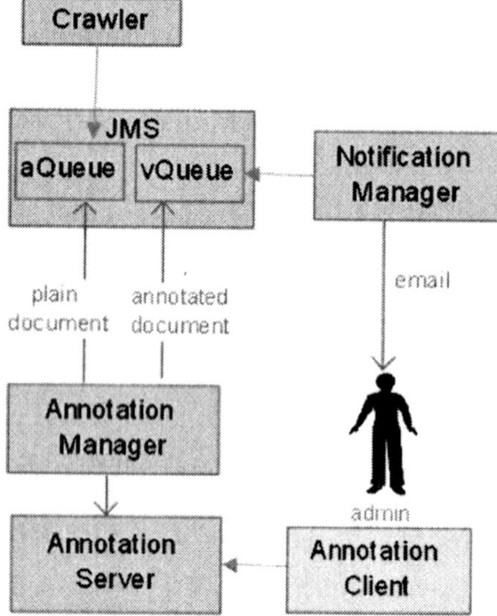

standard that allows application components based on the Java 2 Platform, Enterprise Edition (J2EE) to create, send, receive, and read messages. It enables distributed communication that is loosely coupled, reliable, and asynchronous.

Annotation Manager consumes these plain documents and connects to the *Annotation Server* to perform process of annotation with regards to Travel Guides ontologies. After the annotation process is completed, the annotated documents are sent to JMS to wait in a queue for verification (*vQueue*). The *Notification Manager* consumes these massages and sends an e-mail to the administrator with the details about annotated documents (e.g., location of the annotated documents). The administrator starts *Annotation Interface* and performs the process of verification. The output of the annotation process is correctly annotated documents.

Retrieved annotations that refer to the new concepts/instances could be further used to enrich the KB and also for semantic search over the knowledge store that includes processed documents. Similar approach uses KIM Platform: they provide querying of the knowledge store that includes not only the knowledge base created w.r.t. ontologies, but also annotated documents (Popov et al., 2004).

Annotation of documents performed by KBEM would be simplified in case that verification step is skipped. The implementation of the system would also be simpler. In addition, there would not be a human influence, but the machine would do everything by itself. This would lead to many missed annotations, though. A machine cannot always notice some "minor" refinements as humans can. For example, if in the title "Maria's sand" the machine notices "Maria" and finds it in the list of female first names, it will annotate it as an instance of a class **Woman**. "Maria" can be an instance of a woman, but in this context it is a part of the name of a beach. These kinds of mistakes would happen frequently, and the machine would annotate them in wrong ways, if it does it automatically without any verification.

An Example of Using Travel Guides

Travel Guides users are divided in 3 groups, each of which contributing to the knowledge base in its own way.

End users (i.e., tourists) visit this portal to search for useful information. They can feed the system with their personal data, locations, and interests, which then get analyzed by the system in order to create/update user profiles. Note that the system also uses logged data about each user's activities (mouse clicks) when updating the user's profile. User profile form for feeding the system with user personal information, activities and interests is depicted on Figure 15.

On the left hand side there is a section with results of system personalization. This section provides a list of potentially interested destinations for the tourist. The section is created based on the user profile analyse, which means that offered

Figure 15. The User profile form in Travel Guides

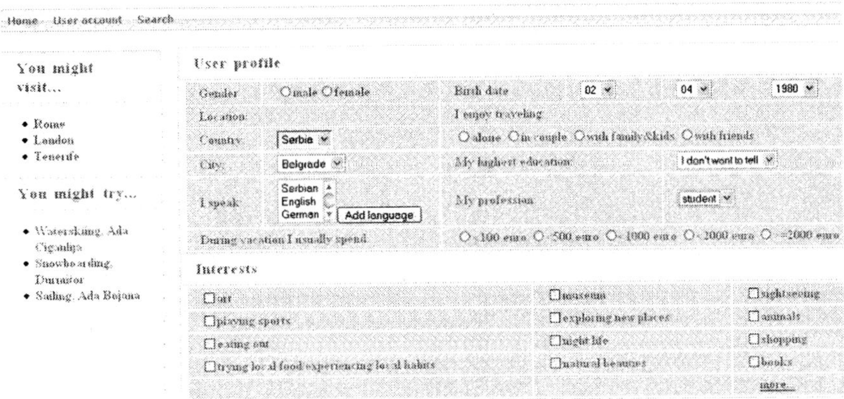

Figure 16. The Search form in Travel Guides

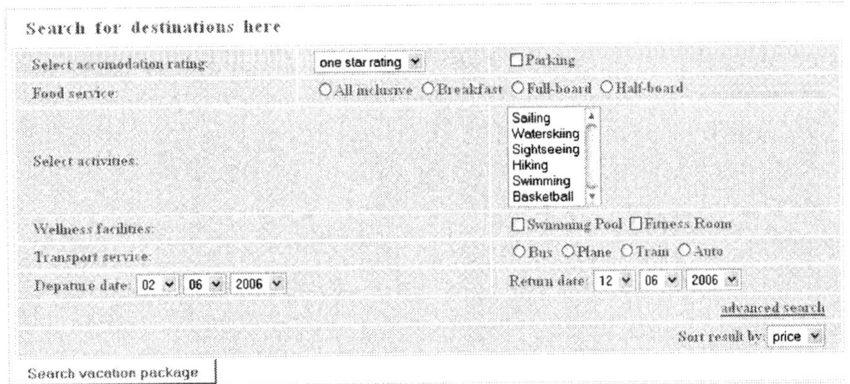

destinations should be matching user wishes, interests and activities. To explicitly search for a 'perfect' vacation package the user uses form shown on Figure 16.

Tourist agents create vacation packages and similar offers in tourist agencies. They feed and update the database with new vacation packages and also knowledge base with new information about destinations. To do this, they fill appropriate forms and save the filled-in information (Figure 17).

To successfully fill in this form and save the vacation package, the hotel has to be selected. If the hotel does not exist in the system, it has to be entered before creating the new vacation package. Figure 18 depicts a form for entering a new hotel into the KB.

Portal administrators mediate the knowledge base updates with destinations not covered by the tourist agencies connected to the portal. This process is very similar to the process conducted by tourist agents. The major difference is that this part of the knowledge base contains mostly static and permanent information about some geographical locations, such as countries, their capitals, mountains, rivers, seas, etc. all over the world. The idea is that tourist agents can use this part of the knowledge base as the basis for creating new vacation packages and other tourist offers.

Figure 17. The Vacation package form in Travel Guides

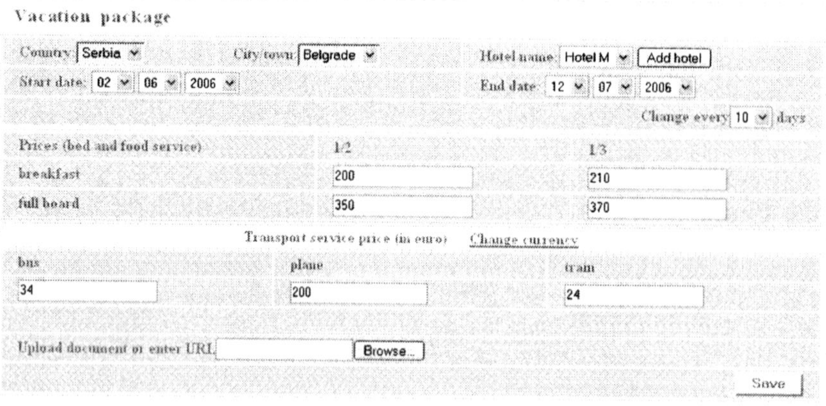

Figure 18. Entering a new hotel using the Travel Guides environment

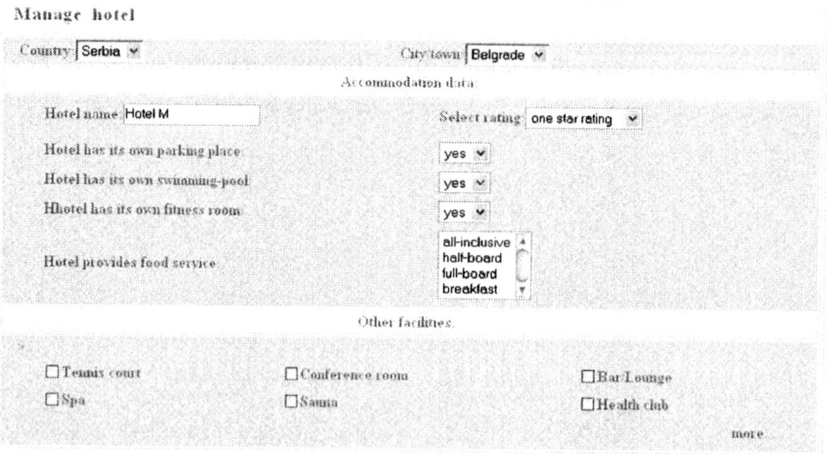

CONCLUSION

Representing tourism-related data in a machine-readable form can help the integration of E-Tourism Information Services. If tourism sources would be centralized in a unique repository, the maintenance efforts would be significantly decreased. Integration of all E-Tourism sources would result in the possibility to search for tourist deals from one place – this would drastically reduce the time tourists spend while searching various tourism-related Web sites.

Built-in heuristics inside ontologies and use of a reasoner enable implying the user profile types for different tourists w.r.t. their activities and interests. Coupled with the destination types which are derived from the specific vacation package descriptions, user profiles can improve the process of searching for the perfect vacation package. Additionally, building a good quality user profiles provides personalization of dynamically created content.

The system's prototype described here includes a limited collection of vacation packages. The main precondition for its evaluation and usability would be feeding it with vacation packages from real tourist agencies.

As Travel Guides focus on integration of Information Services, such as information about destinations, hotels and the like, it would be worth exploring the possibility to integrate such a system with existing applications that offer Transactional Services, so that it can be possible to book and pay for recommended vacation packages after searching repository with available tourist offers covered by Travel Guides. In addition, there are opportunities to extend Travel Guides or to develop an independent module for integration of Communication Services, so that tourists can contribute to the system knowledge about the destinations and express their experience as well.

Finally, as the current version of Travel Guides ontology supports only representing hotel accommodation, there is a space for future improvements that include extending types of accommodations with hostels, private apartments for rent, and campgrounds.

FUTURE RESEARCH DIRECTIONS

Integrating semantic web technologies in traditional existing Web applications has a lot of space for improvement. The most popular way to perform this integration is by employing ontologies as they enable presenting data in machine readable form, reasoning and running intelligent agents, semantic Web services and semantic search. Each of these is partly applied in E-Tourism applications nowadays. However, current state of the art in this field is not mature enough to be used in industry, meaning that there is lots of space for different research topics, some of which could be implied from reading this chapter.

Reasoning over ontologies is very expensive due to the state of development of current inference engines. Development of better and faster reasoner is a precondition for using ontologies in large scale applications. At the moment, only few ontology-based systems exist in the area of tourism, among which Mondeca (www.mondeca.com) is applying the most of them to tourism in different regions in France. Their ontologies define the structure of data they are working with but the use of a reasoner is on the minimum level.

Emerging popularity of social web applications raises another interesting field of research, specifically information retrieval from user created content. Existing Natural Language Processing Tools are still weak to extract and retrieve meaningful answers based on the understanding of the query given in a form of natural language. For example, searching a social web application (e.g., a forum with reviews of different hotels), it would be hard to find 'the hotel in the posh area' using mainstream search engines as some of the posts might talk about luxury hotels, but not using 'posh' to describe them. Developing Natural Language Processing tools that could analyse text so that machines can understand it is a field with lots of research opportunities that would contribute not only to the E-Tourism applications, but to all applications on the Web.

Improving the process of automatic annotation and developing algorithms for training such a process would be another important contribution. Up to date, only Named Entities (e.g., organisations, persons, locations) are known to be automatically retrieved to the reasonable level of accuracy. Additionally, as current systems for performing annotation process usually require the knowledge and understanding of the underlying software such as GATE, research in this field can lead to developing more user-friendly interfaces to allow handling annotations and verifications without any special knowledge of the underlying software. The most natural way would be that similar to using tags in Web 2.0 applications, or any other simple way that requires no training for the user.

REFERENCES

Aichholzer, G., Spitzenberger, M., Winkler, R. (2003, April). Prisma Strategic Guideline 6: eTourism. Retrieved January 13, 2007, from: http://www.prisma-eu.net/deliverables/sg6tourism.pdf

Antoniou, G., Harmelen, F. V. (2004). Web Ontology Language: OWL. In Staab, S., Studer, R. (Eds.): Handbook on Ontologies. International Handbooks on Information Systems, Springer, pp. 67-92.

Bachlechner, D. (October, 2004), D10 v0.2 Ontology Collection in view of an E-Tourism Portal, E-Tourism Working Draft. Retrieved January 15, 2007 from: http://138.232.65.141/deri_at/research/projects/E-Tourism/2004/d10/v0.2/20041005/#Domain

Cardoso, J. (2006). Developing Dynamic Packaging Systems using Semantic Web Technologies. Transactions on Information Science and Applications. Vol. 3(4). 729-736.

Cunningham, H. (2002). GATE, a General Architecture for Text Engineering. Computers and the Humanities. 36 (2). 223–254.

Church, K., Patil, R. (1982). Coping with Syntactic Ambiguity or How to Put the Block in the Box. American Journal of Computational Linguistics, 8(3-4).

Dell'erba, M., Fodor, O. Hopken, W., Werthner, H. (2005). Exploiting Semantic Web technologies for harmonizing E-Markets. Information Technology & Tourism. 7(3-4). 201-219(19).

Djuric, D., Devedzic, V. & Gasevic, D. (2007). Adopting Software Engineering Trends in AI. *IEEE Intelligent Systems*. 22(1). 59-66.

Dogac, A., Kabak ,Y., Laleci, G., Sinir, S., Yildiz, A. Tumer, A. (2004). SATINE Project: Exploiting Web Services in the Travel Industry . eChallenges 2004 (e-2004), 27 - 29 October 2004, Vienna, Austria.

Fellbaum, C. (1998). WordNet - An Electronic Lexical Database. The MIT Press.

Guo, Y; Pan, Z; and Heflin, J. (2004). An Evaluation of Knowledge Base Systems for Large OWL Datasets. The Semantic Web – ISWC 2004: The Proceedings of the Third International Semantic Web Conference, Hiroshima, Japan, November 7-11, 2004. Springer Berlin/Heidelberg. 274-288.

Henriksson, R., (November, 2005), Semantic Web and E-Tourism, Helsinki University, Department of Computer Science. [Online]. Available: http://www.cs.helsinki.fi/u/glinskih/semanticweb/Semantic_Web_and_E-Tourism.pdf

Hepp, M., Siorpaes, K., Bachlechner, D. (2006). Towards the Semantic Web in E-Tourism: Can Annotation Do the Trick? In Proc. of 14th European Conf. on Information System (ECIS 2006), June 12–14, 2006, Gothenburg, Sweden.

Horridge, M., Knublauch, H., Rector, A., Stevens, R., Wroe, C. (2004). A Practical Guide To Building OWL Ontologies Using The Protege-OWL Plugin and CO-ODE Tools Edition 1.0. The University of Manchester, August 2004. [Online]. Available: http://protege.stanford.edu/publications/ontology_development/ontology101.html

Jentzsch, A. (April, 2005) XML Clearing House Report 12: Tourism Standards. Retrieved September 6, 2007, from http://www.xml-clearinghouse.de/reports/Tourism%20Standards.pdf

Kiryakov, A., Popov, B., Ognyanoff, D., Manov, D., Kirilov, A., Goranov, M., (2003), Semantic Annotation, Indexing, and Retrieval, Lecture Notes in Computer Science, Springer-Verlag. Pages 484-499.

Popov, B., Kiryakov, A., Ognyanoff, D., Manov, D., Kirilov, A. (2004). KIM - A Semantic Platform For Information Extraction and Retrieval. Journal of Natural Language Engineering, Cambridge University Press. 10 (3-4). 375-392.

Prantner, K. (2004). OnTour: The Ontology [Online]. Retrieved June 2, 2005, from http://E-Tourism.deri.at/ont/docu2004/OnTour%20-%20The%20Ontology.pdf/

Roman D., Keller, U., Lausen, H., Bruijn J. D., Lara, R., Stollberg, M., Polleres, A., Feier, C.,Bussler, C., Fensel, D. (2005). Web Service Modeling Ontology. Applied Ontology. 1(1): 77 - 106.

Siorpaes, K., Bachlechner, D. (2006). OnTour: Tourism Information Retrieval based on YARS. Demos and Posters of the 3rd European Semantic Web Conference (ESWC 2006), Budva, Montenegro, 11th – 14th June, 2006.

Smith, C. F., Alesso, H. P. (2005). Developing Semantic Web Services. A K Peters, Ltd.

Stollberg, M., Zhdanova, A.V., Fensel, D. (2004). "h-TechSight - A Next Generation Knowledge Management Platform", Journal of Information and Knowledge Management, 3 (1), World Scientific Publishing, 45-66.

Terziev, I., Kiryakov, A., Manov, D. (2005). D1.8.1 Base upper-level ontology (BULO) Guidance, SEKT. Retrieved January, 15th, 2007 from: http://www.deri.at/fileadmin/documents/deliverables/Sekt/sekt-d-1-8-1-Base_upper-level_ontology__BULO__Guidance.pdf

ADDITIONAL READING

Bennett, J. (2006, May 25). The Semantic Web is upon us, says Berners-Lee. Silicon.com research panel: WebWatch. Retrieved January 3, 2007, from: http://networks.silicon.com/Webwatch/0,39024667,39159122,00.htm

Bussler, C. (2003). The Role of Semantic Web Technology in Enterprise Application Integration. IEEE Data Engineering Bulletin. Vol. 26, No. 4, pp. 62-68.

Cardoso, J. (2004). Semantic Web Processes and Ontologies for the Travel Industry. AIS SIGSEMIS Bulletin. Vol. 1, No. 3, pp. 25-28.

Cardoso, J. (2006). Developing An Owl Ontology For e-Tourism. In Cardoso, J. & Sheth, P. A. (Eds.). Semantic Web Services, Processes and Applications (pp. 247-282), Springer.

Davidson, C., Voss, P. (2002). Knowledge Management. Auckland: Tandem.

Davies, J., Weeks, R., Krohn. U. (2003a). QuizRDF: Search Technology for the Semantic Web. Towards the Semantic Web: Ontology-Driven Knowledge Management, pp. 133-43.

Davies, J., Duke, A., Stonkus, A. (2003b). OntoShare: Evolving Ontologies in a Knowledge Sharing System. Towards the Semantic Web: Ontology-Driven Knowledge Management, pp. 161-177.

Djuric, D., Devedžić, V.,Gašević, D. (2007). Adopting Software Engineering Trends in AI. IEEE Intelligent Systems. 22(1). 59-66.

Dzbor, M., Domingue, J., Motta, E. (2003). Magpie - Towards a Semantic Web Browser, In Proc. of the 2nd International Conference (ISWC 2003), pp. 690-705. Florida, USA.

Edwards, S. J., Blythe, P. T., Scott, S., Weihong-Guo, A. (2006). Tourist Information Delivered Through Mobile Devices: Findings from the Image. Information Technology & Tourism. 8 (1). 31-46(16).

Engels R., Lech, T. (2003). Generating Ontologies for the Semantic Web: OntoBuilder. Towards the Semantic Web: Ontology-Driven Knowledge Management, pp. 91-115.

E-Tourism Working Group (2004). Ontology Collection in view of an E-Tourism Portal. October, 2004. Retrieved January 13, 2007, from: http://138.232.65.141/deri_at/research/projects/e-tourism/2004/d10/v0.2/20041005/

Fensel, D., Angele, J., Erdmann, M., Schnurr, H., Staab, S., Studer, R., Witt, A. (1999). On2broker:

Semantic-based access to information sources at the WWW. In Proc. of WebNet, pp. 366-371.

Fluit, C., Horst, H., van der Meer, J., Sabou, M., Mika, P. (2003). Spectacle. Towards the Semantic Web: Ontology-Driven Knowledge Management, pp. 145-159.

Hepp, M. (2006). Semantic Web and semantic Web services: father and son or indivisible twins? Internet Computing, IEEE. 10 (2). 85- 88.

Heung, V.C.S. (2003). Internet usage by international travellers: reasons and barriers. International Journal of Contemporary Hospitality Management, 15 (7), 370-378.

Hi-Touch Working Group (2003). Semantic Web methodologies and tools for intraEuropean sustainable tourism [Online]. Retrieved April 6, 2004, from http://www.mondeca.com/article-JITT-hitouch-legrand.pdf/

Kanellopoulos, D., Panagopoulos, A., Psillakis, Z. (2004). Multimedia applications in Tourism: The case of travel plans. Tourism Today. No. 4, pp. 146-156.

Kanellopoulos, D., Panagopoulos, A. (2005). Exploiting tourism destinations' knowledge in a RDF-based P2P network, Hypertext 2005, 1st International Workshop WS4 – Peer to Peer and Service Oriented Hypermedia: Techniques and Systems, ACM Press.

Kanellopoulos, D. (2006). The advent of Semantic web in Tourism Information Systems. *Tourismos: an international multidisciplinary journal of* tourism. 1(2), pp. 75-91.

Kanellopoulos, D. & Kotsiantis, S. (2006). Towards Intelligent Wireless Web Services for Tourism. IJCSNS International Journal of Computer Science and Network Security. 6 (7). 83-90.

Kanellopoulos, D.,Kotsiantis, S., Pintelas, P. (2006), Intelligent Knowledge Management for the Travel Domain ,GESTS International Transactions on Computer Science and Engineering. 30(1). 95-106.

Kiryakov, A. (2006). *OWLIM: balancing between scalable repository and light-weight reasoner.* Presented at the Developer's Track of WWW2006, Edinburgh, Scotland, UK, 23-26 May, 2006.

Maedche, A., Staab S., Stojanovic, N., Studer, R., Sure, Y. (2001). SEmantic PortAL -

The SEAL approach. In D. Fensel, J. Hendler, H. Lieberman, W. Wahlster (Eds.) In Creating the Semantic Web. Boston: MIT Press, MA, Cambridge.

McIlraith, S.A., Son, T.C., & Zeng, H. (2001). Semantic Web Services. IEEE Intelligent Systems 16(2), 46-53.

Missikoff, M., Werthner, H. Höpken, W., Dell'Ebra, M., Fodor, O. Formica, A., Francesco, T. (2003) HARMONISE: Towards Interoperability in the Tourism Domain. In Proc. ENTER 2003, pp. 58-66, Helsinki: Springer.

Passin, B., T.(2004). *Explorer's Guide to the Semantic Web.* Manning Publications Co., Greenwich.

Sakkopoulos, E., Kanellopoulos, D., Tsakalidis, A. (2006). Semantic mining and web service discovery techniques for media resources management. International Journal of Metadata, Semantics and Ontologies. Vol. 1, No. 1, pp. 66-75.

Singh, I., Stearns, B., Johnson, M. and the Enterprise Team (2002): Designing Enterprise Applications with the J2EE Platform, Second Edition. Prentice Hall. pp. 348. Online: http://java.sun.com/blueprints/guidelines/designing_enterprise_applications_2e/app-arch/app-arch2.html

Shadbolt, N., Berners-Lee T., Hall, W. (2006). The Semantic Web Revisited. IEEE Intelligent Systems. 21(3). 96-101.

Stamboulis, Y. Skayannis P. (2003). Innovation Strategies and Technology for Experience-Based

Tourism. Tourism Management. Vol. 24, pp. 35-43.

Stojanovic, LJ., Stojanovic N.,Volz, R. (2002). Migrating data-intensive Web sites into the Semantic Web. Proceedings of the 2002 ACM symposium on Applied computing, Madrid, Spain, ACM Press. 1100-1107.

Sycara, K., Klusch, M., Widoff, S., Lu, J. (1999) Dynamic service matchmaking among agents in open information environments. ACM SIGMOD Record. Vol. 28(1), pp. 47-53.

World Tourism Organization, 2001, Thesaurus on Tourism & Leisure Activities: http://pub.world-tourism.org:81/epages/Store.sf/?ObjectPath=/Shops/Infoshop/Products/1218/SubProducts/1218-1

WTO (2002). Thesaurus on Tourism & Leisure Activities of the World Tourism Organization [Online]. Retrieved May 12, 2004, from http://www.world-tourism.org/

Chapter XI
Semantic Web in Ubiquitous Mobile Communications

Anna V. Zhdanova
The Telecommunications Research Center Vienna, Austria

Ning Li
University of Surrey, UK

Klaus Moessner
University of Surrey, UK

ABSTRACT

The world becomes ubiquitous, and mobile communication platforms become oriented towards integration with the web, getting benefits from the large amount of information available there, and creation of the new types of value-added services. Semantic and ontology technologies are seen as being able to advance the seamless integration of the mobile and the Web worlds. We provide background information on the Semantic Web field, discuss other research fields that bring semantics into play for reaching the ontology-enabled ubiquitous mobile communication vision, and exemplify the state of the art of ontology development and use in telecommunication projects.

INTRODUCTION

Nowadays, mobile and Web environments converge in one shared communication sphere. Technologies stemming from Semantic Web and Mobile Communication fields get combined to achieve this convergence towards the vision of ontology-enabled ubiquitous mobile communication. Knowledge Management and Semantic technologies fields produce ways to describe, specify and manage information in a machine processable form, in particular, acquire, evolve, reuse, and combine knowledge (Fensel, 2001). Certain formats and protocols stemming from these fields are already being applied to telecommunications: vCard[1], CC/PP[2], UAProf[3]. However, these specifications are only applicable to a limited number of telecommunication scenarios, and management of information about resources in mobile environment could be substantially improved, e.g., by alignment of heterogeneous information sources in knowledge-based service enablers.

Ontologies and architecture knowledge layers play an ever-increasing role in service platforms and mobile communications. As integration of Telco, Internet and the Web takes place, in order to achieve interoperability, telecommunication systems and services tend to rely on knowledge represented with the use of shared schema, i.e., on ontologies similar to as envisioned on the Semantic Web (Tarkoma et al., 2007). However, specific ontology-based implementation solutions for mobile systems are rare, and best practices for such interoperability are not established. In this chapter, we address a problem of ontology-based interoperation in order to integrate independent components in a system providing value-added mobile services.

We present the overall state of the art ontology-related developments in mobile communication systems, namely, the work towards construction, sharing and maintenance of ontologies for mobile communications, reuse and application of ontologies and existing Semantic Web technologies in the prototypes. Social, collaborative and technical challenges experienced in the project showcase the need in alignment of ontology experts' work across the mobile communication projects to establish the best practices in the area and drive standardization efforts. We indicate certain milestones in integration of Semantic Web-based intelligence with Mobile Communications, such as performing ontology construction, matching, and evolution in mobile service systems and alignment with existing heterogeneous data models.

The chapter is structured as follows. In Section 2 we provide a motivation for discussing the convergence between the areas of Semantic Web and ubiquitous mobile communications. Section 3 gives an overview of the core ontology technologies involved, related and relevant research and development fields and challenges in the area. In Section 4, two illustrative case studies for the converged area are described. Section 5 concludes the chapter and Sections 6 indicates future research directions.

WHY SEMATICS IN UBIQUITOUS MOBILE COMMUNICATIONS?

In this section we motivate why combination of Semantic Web technology with ubiquitous mobile communications is beneficial. Semantic technologies in mobile communication have been somewhat considered to the less extent comparing to other fields, such as semantics in e-sciences, e-government, e-enterprise, e-communities, etc. However, as the mobile world starts to integrate with the Web world in delivering new value-added services, the area of semantics ubiquitous mobile communication inevitably gains a larger importance and potential.

Ubiquitous computing, also referred to as pervasive computing, is the seamless integration of devices into the users every day life. Applications should vanish into the background to make the user and his tasks the central focus rather than computing devices and technical issues (Weiser, 1991). When applying to mobile communication scenarios, ubiquitous computing can be viewed as when user moves around and changes circumstances, he can always be connected and well served without being aware of the technical issues under the scene. To achieve the goal, information from all the involving participants, such as user, network, service provider etc., needs to be collected, shared and interoperable with each other, known by one or more operational agents but agnostic to the user. Such information is diverse in their language, format and lack of semantic meaning for autonomous processing by computer or operational agent. The Semantic Web can be a rescue with its vision to achieve global information sharing and integration.

An example of combination of the two fields can be a service enabler that could be used by other services and thus make their construction simpler. For example, such an enabler could access distributed information on user's location, availability and friends and inform other services about which groups of friends are available and located at the same place. Services that assist with scheduling business meetings or parties, or the ones that are targeted at selling products for groups of users can be among the services that need such information from the enabler. To achieve the output, the enabler would take external structured data represented in a formal way (e.g., in RDF): for instance, information about user's availability from PIDF files, information on who is a friend of whom from FOAF profiles, information about location from data stemming from such standards as IETF RFC4119, RFC4589. Then the enabler would combine the gathered information, apply certain rules to deduce the result and pass it to other mobile services via an interface.

GROUNDING FOR SEMANTICS IN UBIQUITOUS MOBILE COMMUNICATIONS

In this section, we describe existing developments relevant for the combined field of ubiquitous mobile communications and the Semantic Web.

Ubiquitous Mobile Communication Existing Developments

A lot of work has been undertaken to implement the vision of ubiquitous mobile communications by investigating the underlying technologies. Examples include, but not limited to, user-related context collection, such as sensor network, Bluetooth, GPS, user-related context modelling and transmission, such as CC/PP, UAProf, 3GPP, MPEG-21, multimedia content description, such as MPEG-7, service discovery and service context modelling, such as UPnP, Jini, Bluetooth SDP, agent technologies, such as FIPA, ACL. Network mobility, security and QoS management, such as Hierarchical mobile IP, IPSec, DiffServ etc. The combination of these technologies with Semantic Web has become an inevitable trend in a ubiquitous mobile communication environment. Some of such joint developments are presented later in Section: Relevant research fields.

Semantic Web Existing Developments

Existing developments of the Semantic Web include languages (i.e. core formalisms to specify domain knowledge or services), methodologies and tools. In this section we outline the major developments in these areas and indicate their role and contributions in the area of Semantic Web enabled mobile platforms.

Languages and Formalisms

RDF(S)

RDF (Lassila & Swick, 1999; Manola & Miller, 2004) became a W3C recommendation in 1999. It is a general-purpose language for representing resources on the web in terms of named properties and values (McBride, 2004). With RDF it is not possible to define the relationships between properties and resources. For this purpose, RDF Schema (Brickley & Guha, 2004) has been specified. It became a W3C recommendation in 2004 and is basically an extension of RDF. More specifically, it is a formal description language for eligible RDF expressions. In particular, a schema defines the kinds of properties available for resources (e.g., title, author, subject, size, colour, etc.) and the kind of resource classes being described (e.g., books, Web pages, people, companies, etc.). RDF Schema is a simple ontology and a simple ontology definition language. RDF and RDF Schema are usually denoted RDF(S).

RDF(S) bases on some syntactical principles of XML (e.g. URIs) and has been equipped with an XML syntax as well. The most basic Semantic Web language which provides the syntactical basis for all other Semantic Web languages is RDF(S). RDF(S) is not provided completely with a formal logical semantics, thus reasoning is only on partially supported.

Topic Maps

Topic Maps are a data modelling language and became an ISO standard (ISO/IEC 13250) in 2000. A Topic Map offers a means to create an index of information which resides outside of that information. It describes the information in documents and databases by linking into them using URIs. A Topic Map consists of topics, associations (relationships between topics), occurrences (information resources relevant to a topic). Topics and occurrences can by typed. Types in Topic Maps are themselves topics and thus there is no real difference between a topic and a type.

There exists SGML, XML and RDF language support for Topic Maps. However, they are very simple and do not have a formal semantics and thus no sophisticated inference support. Nevertheless, because of their simplicity, they are often used in industry applications.

OWL

OWL (Dean & Schreiber, 2004) became a W3C recommendation in 2004. OWL is mainly based on OIL and DAML+OIL, which are obsolete Semantic Web languages and therefore not mentioned further here. OWL is equipped by an RDF syntax and includes three sub languages:

OWL-Lite roughly consists of RDF(S) plus equality and 0/1-cardinality. It is intended for classification hierarchies and simple constraints. OWL-Lite corresponds semantically to the formal Description Logic *SHIF(D)* and cannot express the whole RDF vocabulary.

OWL-DL contains the language constructs of OWL-Lite. OWL-DL corresponds semantically to the Description Logic *SHOIN*(D). Although strictly more expressive than OWL-Lite, it still provides computational completeness and decidability.

OWL Full does not correspond to a formal logic anymore as it builds upon the complete RDF(S) vocabulary which also lacks a correspondence to a formal logic. The language incorporates maximum expressive power and syntactic freedom, but offers no computational guarantees.

Semantic Web Languages in Progress

In this subsection, we consider Semantic Web languages which have been submitted to the W3C and thus have communities promoting them. At least some of them can be expected to become W3C recommendations. Examples of such languages are:

- *Languages based on the Logic Programming Knowledge Representation paradigm*: The trend to the aforementioned paradigm exists already since the year 2000 when the development of RuleML[4] has started. RuleML is a set of languages revolving around the Logic Programming paradigm and being equipped with an RDF syntax. Other examples of Semantic Web Languages with Logic Programming semantics are WRL[5], a set of three layered rule languages of increasing expressivity, and SWRL[6], a language which combines OWL and RuleML but is computationally intractable. Furthermore, a W3C working group[7] has been formed for establishing standards for Semantic Web rule languages.
- *Semantic Web Service Modelling Languages*: Semantic Web Services will play an important role in the Semantic Web as they combine Web Services with semantics. Examples for Semantic Web Services Languages are WSML[8] and SWSL[9]. The

languages serve for the specification of ontologies describing Semantic Web Services. E.g., WSML is used to describe WSMO[10] and SWSL is used to describe SWSO[11].

Ontologies and Tools

Apart from the languages to describe data, specific ontologies related to the mobile communication domains and appropriate ontology management tools are necessary to implement the vision of ubiquitous mobile communications.

In a nutshell, the state of the art in development of the ontologies addressed by ubiquitous mobile communications comprises:

- Ad-hoc small-size schemata on certain general purpose topics are specified in ontology languages.
- Detailed, XML-based standards on certain narrow telecommunications topics.

Certain standardisation schemata and activities to be considered for the development of the ontology framework for mobile communications are listed later in Section: Mobile Ontology. Additional efforts coming from the Semantic Web community are listed in Table 1.

Typically, existing ontology management tools are adopted and explored in the semantic telecommunications projects. Stemming from the SPICE project (Zhdanova et al., 2006), examples of relevant and popular ontology management tools used, as well as encountered problems in their exploitation and an expected resolution times, are provided in Boxes 1 and 2.

As the ontology data are processed within the ubiquitous mobile communication applica-

Box 1.

Name............................ Protege
Website.......................... http://protege.stanford.edu/
White page.................... n/a
Main characteristics.......... Ontology editor

Open problems	Relevance					Term		
	1 Very low	2 Low	3 Normal	4 High	5 Very high	0-3 short	3-6 medium	6-12 long
Needs improvement of usability features, robustness		X					X	

Box 2.

Name............................ Jena
Website.......................... http://jena.sourceforge.net/
White page.................... n/a
Main characteristics.......... A Semantic Web Framework for Java. Ontology API and implementation, supports RDF(S), OWL, performs basic ontology management and reasoning (similar idea as Xerces for XML)

Open problems	Relevance					Term		
	1 Very low	2 Low	3 Normal	4 High	5 Very high	0-3 short	3-6 medium	6-12 long
Scalability: works slowly on large volumes of data					X		X	

Table 1. Ontologies Related to the Mobile Ontology

Ontology Name	Producer	URL	Description	Development Status
MeNow	Chris Schmidt	http://crschmidt.net/foaf/menow/menow.rdf	The motivation for the MeNow schema is to be able to describe a variety of aspects of the current status of someone, either online or off, in a way that the data can be easily aggregated or retrieved. This schema allows the definition of a variety of terms that would be common in many applications: describing the current book you are reading, music you are listening to, mood you are in, and more.	
Pervasive SO – Describing User Profile and Preferences	Harry Chen, UMBC	http://pervasive.semanticweb.org/doc/ont-guide/part1/	Pervasive Computing Standard Ontology (PERVASIVE-SO) is a set of RDF/OWL ontology documents. Each ontology document is identified by a unique XML namespace and defines the ontologies of a specific domain. In a pervasive computing environment, computer systems often need to access the profiles and the preferences of a user in order to provide services and information that are tailored to the user. The profile of a user includes typical contact information (telephone numbers, email addresses, name, etc.) and information that describe other computing entities that can act on the behalf of the user (e.g., the personal agent of a user). The preference of a user is a description of the environment state that the user desires the computer systems to honor or achieve whenever it is possible.	Frozen in 2004
Platform for Privacy Preferences	Brian McBride, HP	http://www.w3.org/TR/p3p-rdfschema/	The Platform for Privacy Preferences Project (P3P) enables Web sites to express their privacy practices in a standard format that can be retrieved automatically and interpreted easily by user agents. P3P user agents will allow users to be informed of site practices (in both machine- and human-readable formats) and to automate decision-making based on these practices when appropriate. Thus users need not read the privacy policies at every site they visit.	Frozen in 2002
Gadget	Morten Frederiksen	http://www.wasab.dk/morten/2004/10/gadget	Definitions of various terms related to (typically) electronic gadgets such as GPS receivers, cameras and mobile phones.	Frozen in 2004
ConOnto: Context Ontology	Mohamed Khedr	http://www.site.uottawa.ca/~mkhedr/contexto.html	ConOnto describes the different aspects of context-aware systems. ConOnto includes location, time, activities, software and hardware profiles. ConOnto also includes meta-information that describes negotiation and fuzzy ontologies to be used in systems that will negotiate and infer about context information.	
Ambient Networks: General, Cost, QoS Ontology	Anders Karlsson, TeliaSonera	http://kiwi.intra.sonera.fi/an_costs.owl		Created in 2005

tions, exploration and reuse of further ontology management technology is on the roadmap of the research and development field.

Major Challenges and Approaches

In this section, we define major challenges that are under development or need to be developed in the joint area. From ubiquitous mobile communication point of view, the challenges can be viewed from three perspective, i.e., from the user, the network operator, and the service provider. From user's point of view, there is an expectation of autonomous, non-stop service being provided with satisfying quality whatever terminal he/she uses, whenever he/she needs and wherever he/she goes without having to set the configuration. From network perspective, there is a challenge of ensuring the service delivery by providing a smooth handover, a guaranteed QoS and security level etc. when delivery circumstance changes, for example, from one type of network to another. From service provider point of view, the anticipation is to provide only one version of service, which, however, can be used by any device via any networks. To face these challenges, when designing a ubiquitous service delivery based on ontologies, the information from and about the user, network condition, the content/service being provided, together with any context information (to support personalization and service push to the user), need to be described in an unambiguous and interoperable manner in order to perform effective service delivery. Therefore, common ontologies describing such domain knowledge, as well as best practices in their reuse are required. Generally, challenges faced from ontology point of view include:

- **Heterogeneity:** Resolving inconsistencies, format differences (syntactic and semantic differences in formalization), business process mediation.
- **Versioning** when merging or combining ontologies representing different knowledge domains, ontology and instance data evolution and maintenance during updates.
- **Scalability:** Scalable repositories for ontology instance data (currently popular ontology management toolkits such as Jena and Sesame do not always meet industrial standards).
- **Ontology and instance data visualization**, user interfaces.
- **User/community generated content:** formalization, acquisition and employment (when building innovative mobile services in Web 2.0 style of social applications alike to YouTube, Flickr, LinkedIn, Google Base, etc.).
- **Semantically described mobile and web services** (no yet widely accepted "standard" solutions).
- **Service composition and discovery**, user-driven creation of new services by composing service enablers, mash-ups.
- **Integration with the non-semantic web services and formats**, which use traditional technologies such as WSDL, SOAP and UDDI, XML.
- **Integration with legacy applications**, which are not terminologically a service, but can be upgraded to be a service, e.g. MPEG codec.

Relevant Research Fields

The following research areas are related to, impact and will be potentially impacted by the described involvement of the Semantic Web in Mobile Communications.

Multimedia

Today, the amount of digital multimedia information is growing over the World Wide Web, in broadcast data streams and in personal and professional databases. One of the major challenges for ubiquitous mobile communication is to enable any mobile devices, e.g. mobile phone, PDA, to access, exchange and consume a rich set of multimedia content seamlessly over dynamic and heterogeneous networks. The need of semantic description of the multimedia information becomes apparent. The MPEG-7 and MPEG-21 are the dominant efforts for multimedia content and service description framework.

MPEG-7 is known as the multimedia description standard and offers several tools, i.e. Description Schemes, to annotate multimedia content at different levels. The main parts are: Description Definition Language (DDL), Visual, Audio and Multimedia Description Schemes (MDS). The DDL is a language that allows the creation of new Description Schemes and, possibly, Descriptors. It also allows the extension and modification of existing Description Schemes. The DDL is based on XML Schema Language, but with MPEG-7 extensions specifically for audiovisual description. The Visual description tools provide structures to describe basic visual features, such as color, texture, shape, motion and localization etc. The Audio description tools provides structures for the description of audio features that are common across many applications, such as spectral, parametric, and temporal features, and that are application-specific features, such as audio indexing, recognition and signature. MPEG-7 Multimedia Description Schemes provides the description tools for generic media entities, such as vector, time and more complex media entities. The latter can be grouped into 5 different classes according to their functionality: Content description, Content management, Content organization, Navigation and access and User interaction.

MPEG-21, the 21st century multimedia framework, goes further and provides tools to describe the environment to enable transparent multimedia creation, delivery and consumption between heterogeneous environments. The main parts are Digital Item Declaration (DID), Digital Item Identification (DII), Intellectual Property Managements and Protection (IPMP), Rights Expression Language (REL), Rights Data Dictionary (RDD) and Digital Item Adaptation (DIA). The Digital Item Declaration (DID) specification contains three normative sections, a model to describe a set of abstract terms and concepts to form a useful model for defining Digital Items, a representation to describe the syntax and semantics of each of the Digital Item Declaration elements, and a Schema comprising the entire grammar of the Digital Item Declaration representation in XML. The DII specification provides mechanisms to uniquely identify Digital Items, Intellectual Property related to the Digital Items such as abstractions, Description Schemes and types of Digital Items. IPMP is an extended efforts based on MPEG-4 to develop new systems and tools with enhanced interoperability. The REL, together with the RDD that supports the REL and provides extensive semantics, provides a universal method for specifying rights and conditions associated with the distribution and use of digital items and thus facilitates the creation of an open DRM architecture. DIA provides tools to describe the Digital Item usage environment including: Usage characteristics, such as user info, usage history, User preferences and physical characteristics such as disabilities, Device characteristics such as display, memory and battery, Network characteristics, such as error characteristics and bandwidth, and Natural environment characteristics such as noise and illumination. This is to facilitate transparent access to distributed digital items by shielding users from the technical complexity, such as network and terminal installation, management and implementation issues.

Web Service (SOA)

Service-Oriented Architecture (SOA), especially a Web service-based SOA, has the potential in speeding up the application development process and the agility in responding to the change of business needs. This is due to the loose coupling of client from service and the set of standard protocols and technologies used by the Web service, such as XML, WSDL, SOAP, and UDDI. The inherent features of SOA, i.e. reusability, interoperability, scalability and flexibility, can virtually meet the requirement of a supportive framework for ubiquitous mobile communication.

Coming along with Semantic Web is Semantic Web service, where Web service is described with added computer-processable semantics, and thus a number of services can be concatenated autonomously to compose a new service for a more complex task. This will benefit service provision in a ubiquitous environment where all information from user, network, together with the requested service and any intermediate service are required to make a delivery decision autonomously. In accordance with this advance, the set of standard protocols and technologies for Web services are evolving to reach their semantic counterparts or brand new standards are created. For example, the ontology languages, RDF, RDFS, and OWL are developed to add computer-processable semantics on top of the exiting syntax provided by XML. WSDL specifies a way to describe the abstract functionalities of a Web service and concretely how and where to invoke it. Semantic Annotations for WSDL (SAWSDL)[12] defines mechanisms using which semantic annotations can be added to WSDL components based on an earlier effort, namely WSDL-S[13], which adds semantic expressivity to the service description by extending original WSDL elements. SOAP, as the message exchange protocol and originally XML-based, can be combined with RDF and OWL in order to introduce semantics to assist the flexible service invocation (Zhao, 2004). Similarly, enabling UDDI to store semantic markup and handle semantic enquiries has been investigated in recent years (Luo et al., 2006). Correspondingly, service-oriented architectures require machine-processable semantics to achieve its full potential. In particular, DERI[14], targets this challenge by offering a set of tools and techniques ranging from ontology construction to description language. The later include Web Service Modelling Ontology (WSMO), Web Service Modelling Language (WSML) and a Web Service Execution Environment (WSMX)[15].

Security, Privacy, Trust

In recent years, the security and trust aspects of Web services are standardised by OASIS[16] with a WS-security specification released in 2004. WS-security insets security-related information to Web service messaging that provides for message integrity and confidentiality using security token and digital signatures. The use of Semantic Web technologies enables Web into a genuinely distributed and global content and service provider. Inherent with this are the issues of more widespread security, trust, information quality and privacy.

To achieve a security solution for Semantic Web service, the traditional security solutions can be described as one of the contextual information attached to the service and can be interpreted on the other end at semantic level. This solution has the advantage of not requiring to design a bottom-up Semantic Web service security architecture and thus provides the service provider with flexibility of control. However, embedding security and trust policies into every Web service may not appear to be an attractive solution and can result in tight coupling between services and particular security implementations. An alternative is to design an integrated Semantic Web security framework with security mechanisms available at various layers of the network. This may provide a comprehensive solution when more security and trust issues and challenges arise from the traditional communication domain. For example, when seamless interconnecting heterogeneous networks, particularly when security issue are jointly considered with other issues, such as QoS and mobility management, in the overall communication process.

Human Communication Interface

The design of the Human Communication Interface (HCI) for Web applications has always been of great importance. The Web technology is evolving with Semantic Web, the interaction must also evolve. With the emergence of the Semantic Web and Semantic Web services, which give information well-defined meaning and enable computer work in cooperation with humans, the interactions with Web-delivered information has become possible and thus the complexity of the human communication interface has increased. For example, instead of being an information receiver only, user can interact with information to construct new information and build knowledge. In addition, with the user terminal getting smaller and smaller in size like PDA, Pocket PC, together with the service being more customized to the user's personal need and preference, the human interface design becomes even more challenging than ever.

In ubiquitous mobile communication environment, human computing interfaces form one of the major contextual information of the user as well as one of the major component in the delivery path. Therefore, it is essential to bring interaction design principles with other contextual information into the semantically structured information in order to facilitate this evolution of the Web. On the other hand, with the popularity of Semantic Web and wide acceptance of its technology in integrating knowledge from various heterogeneous parties, embedding Semantic Web technology into the HCI design is envisioned to be a necessity for automating the deployment of rich user interfaces.

Lower Layer of Mobile Communication

One of the important contextual information to be included, and maybe semantically described, when customizing Semantic Web content and service to the user ubiquitously are the network conditions in the delivery path, e.g. bandwidth, QoS, Security, latency, jitter etc. Signalling and/or information exchange is required between the application layer and the underlying network layers for request and response. Enhancements to the communication protocols with semantic capabilities are envisaged to be required in order to assure user's satisfaction in ubiquitous service delivery. In addition, there have been extensive efforts to tackle the network layer integration of QoS, security and mobility management over heterogeneous network in a mobile environment.

Autonomous Computing

The vision of autonomous computing is to enable computing system operate in a fully autonomous manner. The challenges of autonomous computing are robustness, simplicity for the end-user and seamless integration (Hercock, 2002). With the vision of being a global information integrator by making information computer-interpretable, Semantic Web technologies can help realizing the vision of autonomous computing, particularly in a ubiquitous mobile communication environment where constant changes take place and autonomous process are expected.

Grid, Semantic Grid

Grid development is targeted at the problem of efficiently using computing power of distributed resources for achieving a common set of tasks. Typical Grid toolkits include GLOBUS[17]. Semantic Grid is oriented towards enhancing typical Grid services or processes with ontology-based descriptions (Goble et al., 2004). Different types of Grid resources can be used by ontology–enabled mobile services to reach their goals.

ONTOLOGY FRAMEWORK STUDIES

In this section, we describe ongoing research and development combining the areas of ubiquitous mobile communication and Semantic Web. One can view convergence of Semantic technologies with mobile communication from two sides: inclusion of the Semantic technologies in solutions delivered by mobile communication project from one side; and mobile communication use cases in core Semantic technology projects from the other side. On the one hand, work on development of mobile communication applications, enablers and services with involvement of ontologies has been carried out in the following mobile communication projects: SPICE[18], MobileVCE[19], Mobilife[20], OPUCE[21], Ambient Networks[22], etc. On the other hand, research and development involving mobile aspects has been carried out in the following Semantic Web projects: TripCom[23], SWING[24], ASG[25], SmartWeb: Mobile Access to the Semantic Web[26], etc. In this section, we provide detailed illustrating examples of the ontology work carried out for mobile communication solutions, specifically, mobile ontology (SPICE project) and an ontology solution for multimedia (MobileVCE project).

Mobile Ontology

Mobile environments and the Web converge forming a shared Distributed Communication Sphere (DCS). This causes the appearance of new settings to be supported, e.g., when the user utilizes mobile and fixed devices to interact with systems. Interaction and connectivity of mobile applications with the Internet increase. To ensure interoperation of mobile and Web services, applications and tools (running on heterogeneous various service platforms in such a sphere), developers need to have a shared specification of objects belonging to the sphere and their roles. Certain ontologies have already been developed for the mobile communication domain by employing area with employment of Semantic Web formalisms (Korpipää et al., 2004; Pfoser et al., 2002). However, widespread and global adoption of such ontologies remains a challenge.

Approaching the problem of interoperation between the Web and mobile service technologies, Mobile ontology, a comprehensive "higher-level" ontology for mobile communication domain, is being developed. Currently, definition and implementation of the Mobile ontology is managed as a collaborative effort amongst participants of the EU IST SPICE Integrated Project.

Mobile Ontology Introduction

What's Mobile Ontology for?

Mobile Ontology is being developed as a comprehensive "higher-level" ontology for mobile communication domain. The ontology is a machine readable schema intended for sharing knowledge and exchanging information both across people and across services/applications, and it covers domains related to mobile communications, specifically, addressing persons, terminals, services, networks.

The added values of Mobile Ontology are:

- Providing an easy and formal way to reference objects from the mobile communication domain (in particular, to serve as an exchange format between mobile service enablers).
- Providing an opportunity to implement enhanced, ontology-based reasoning.
- Providing a formal representation of the domain to be used in research and development projects, and for educational purposes.

Mobile Ontology Overview

DCS-related vocabulary terms, grouped in broad categories, are presented in Figure 1.

Mobile Ontology, in particular, its DCS Vocabulary (Zhdanova et al., 2006) definitions are written using RDF and OWL (Manola & Miller, 2004; Dean & Schreiber, 2006) that makes it easy for software (both Web-based and mobile-oriented) to process facts about the terms in the DCS vocabulary, and consequently about the

Figure 1. DCS-related Classes and Properties of Mobile Ontology

DCS Basics

- **CommunicationSphere**
- **AccessMethod**
- **Availability**
- **PhysicalLocation**
- **Modality**
- **InputModality**
- **OutputModality**
- **Cost**
- **Time**
- **AccessParameter**
- **consistsOf**
- **associatedWith**
- **characterizedBy**
- **providesAccessTo**
- **hosts**
- **PhysicalSpace**
- **Outdoors**
- **Indoors**
- **Building**
- **Roomspace**
- **Hall**
- **Floor**
- **Stairway**
- **isInsideOf**
- **hasInside**
- **isOnFloor**
- **isPhysicallyConnectedTo**
- **hasAboveFloor**
- **isAboveFloor**
- **isWithinRangeOf**
- **belongsTo**
- **owns**

Users and Groups, Personalization

- **Person**
- **UserGroup**
- **Mood**
- **UserRule**
- **CurrentActivity**
- **isUserDefaultActivity**
- **isWillingToCommunicate**
- **Recommendation**
- **RecommendedItem**
- **Feature**
- **hasWeight**
- **hasRelevanceScore**
- **hasSupport**
- **hasConfidence**
- **hasPreferred**
- **hasMeanRelevanceScore**
- **hasMeanSupport**
- **hasMeanConfidence**
- **Profile**
- **Subset**
- **hasType**
- **hasDescription**
- **hasSubset**

Devices

- **Terminal**
- **Device**
- **EmbeddedDevice**
- **SensorNode**
- **MultimodalityDevice**
- **ConfigurationElement**
- **DescriptionElement**
- **DataElement**
- **Datastore**
- **Module**
- **TerminalParameter**
- **hasParent**
- **hasModule**
- **hasAdditionalConfiguratio n**
- **hasAdditionalParameters**
- **hasAdditionalDescription**
- **hasData**
- **hasDescription**
- **hasConfiguration**
- **hasSize**
- **hasVersion**
- **hasName**
- **hasEncoding**
- **hasTStamp**
- **hasLocation**
- **hasDisplayName**
- **hasCategory**
- **hasMimeType**
- **hasVendor**
- **isEquippedWith**
- **isAvailableAt**

Services

- **Service**
- **QoS**
- **MultimodalityService**
- **InformationService**
- **KnowledgeService**
- **ContextService**

Networks

- **Network**
- **BluetoothNetwork**
- **WiFiNetwork**
- **GSMNetwork**
- **UMTSNetwork**
- **canBeAccessedVia**
- **isConnectedTo**
- **hostedBy**

things described in DCS documents. A DCS document/instance data can be combined with other DCS documents to create unified sources of information.

Example

A very basic annotation describing the state of the communication model is displayed in Box 3.

RDF/S and OWL have been chosen as formats to represent the mobile ontology, as they are current recommendation ontology languages of W3C and have a relatively large tool support for implementation of enablers and applications.

Starting from the DCS ontology, the Mobile ontology has developed a new structure and evolved in Mobile ontology Core and Mobile subontologies. Mobile ontology Core comprises the telecommunications domain concepts and properties that occur most commonly and in various subdomains or application types. Mobile subontologies contain further details related to specific topics in telecommunications, and its items are linked to the items of the Mobile ontology Core. The Mobile ontology Core overview is depicted at Figure 2.

Currently the subontologies on the following topics are being represented in the Mobile ontology infrastructure: Profile, Service, Service Context, DCS, Service Roaming, Rules and recommendations, Presence, Location, and Content. The up-to-date ontology versions and the status of the work are represented at the Mobile Ontology website[27].

Box 3.

```
<?xml version="1.0"?>
<rdf:RDF
    xmlns:rdf="http://www.w3.org/1999/02/22-rdf-syntax-ns#"
    xmlns:xsd="http://www.w3.org/2001/XMLSchema#"
    xmlns:rdfs="http://www.w3.org/2000/01/rdf-schema#"
    xmlns:owl="http://www.w3.org/2002/07/owl#"
    xmlns:p1="http://www.owl-ontologies.com/assert.owl#"
    xmlns="http://www.ist-spice.org/mobile_ontology/2006/5/26/mobile_ontology.owl#"
  xml:base="http://www.ist-spice.org/mobile_ontology/2006/5/26/mobile_ontology.owl">

...
<Device rdf:ID="BlueSonyEriccson">
    <belongsTo>
      <Person rdf:ID="AnnaZ">
        <owns rdf:resource="#BlueSonyEriccson"/>
        <rdfs:comment rdf:datatype="http://www.w3.org/2001/XMLSchema#string"
        ></rdfs:comment>
      </Person>
    </belongsTo>
  </Device>
...
</rdf:RDF>
```

Figure 2. Mobile Ontology Core Visualization

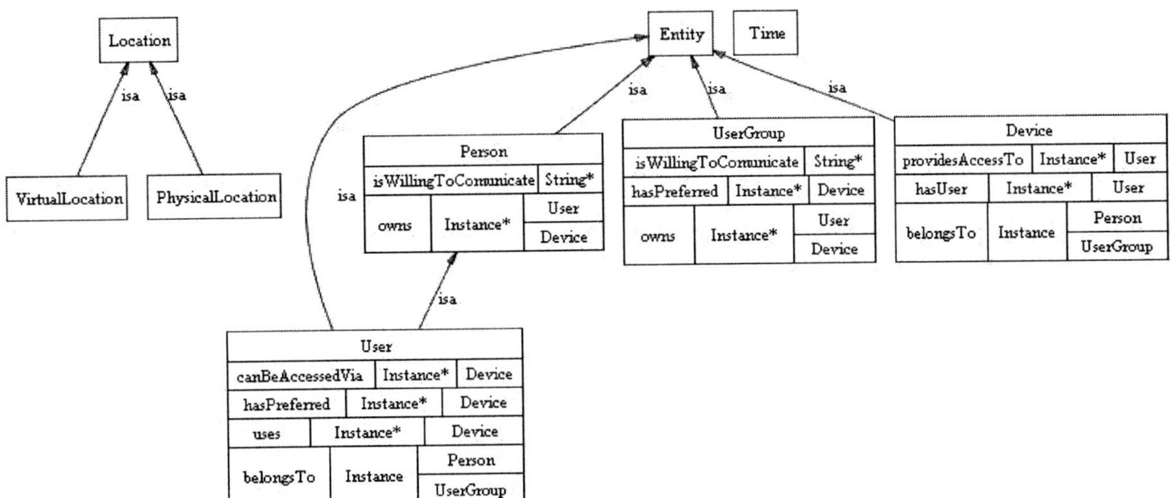

Reuse of Schemata and Ontologies

Certain schemata covering the domains of the Mobile ontology exist and have already acquired significant communities. Such schemata can be either an output of the standardization bodies or coming in a "bottom-up" manner from companies and individuals and being widely accepted by the masses. These schemata and ontologies can be specified in different knowledge representation formalisms. We address external sources represented via the most popular formats, namely OWL, RDF/S and XML/S.

Relating and mapping these schemata to the Mobile ontology is mainly beneficial for interoperation of the Mobile ontology community with other mobile communities. Thus:

- Mobile ontology developers and users benefit acquiring additional knowledge in the mobile communication domain captured in the existing OWL, RDF, XML schemas (i.e., reusing the present knowledge).
- Users of the related ontologies and schemas benefit from a straightforward mapping of their schemas to the Mobile ontology that enables a simpler move to/involvement or extension of the Semantic technologies for these communities.

Technically, two different approaches to combine the Mobile ontology with the existing common ontologies and schemata will be considered, depending on whether the data is encoded via an ontology language (such as PDF/S and OWL) or only via XML.

Approach 1: RDF/S or OWL Encoding
The following principles are valid when considering integration of Mobile ontology with ontologies of relevant topics expressed via RDF/S or OWL formalisms:

- When necessary directly reusing the agreed ontologies or their parts when modelling processes;
- Establishing and using the library of mappings of these ontologies with the "higher" level Mobile ontology classes and properties that have similar items as the used external ontology. Such a mapping library would not be re-modelling, but stating relations between items in a machine readable format. Equivalence, for example, can be stated

Table 2. OWL and RDFS -based Relevant Standards

Ontology name	Ontology Web address
UAProf	http://www.openmobilealliance.org/release_program/uap_v2_0.html
FOAF	http://www.foaf-project.org/
vCard	http://www.w3.org/TR/vcard-rdf

Table 3. XML-based Relevant Standards

Schema name	Schema Web address
Presence simple specification	http://www.openmobilealliance.org/release_program/Presence_simple_v1_0.html
Basic Presence Data model	http://www.ietf.org/rfc/rfc3863.txt
Generic Presence Data Model	http://www.rfc-editor.org/rfc/rfc4479.txt
Rich Presence Information	http://www.rfc-editor.org/rfc/rfc4480.txt
Location Types Registry	http://www.ietf.org/rfc/rfc4589.txt
A Presence-based GEOPRIV Location Object Format	http://www.ietf.org/rfc/rfc4119.txt

using constructions "owl:sameAs" so that applications and enablers can "understand" that an item from the Mobile ontology and an "imported" agreed upon ontology are the same.

The RDFS and OWL-based standard schemata considered for this approach are listed in Table 2.

Approach 2: XML Encoding

The following principles are valid when considering integration of Mobile ontology with schemata of relevant topics expressed via XML formalisms:

- Re-modelling XML schemata in OWL and providing the new sub-ontologies as relatively independent ontology sub-modules under the umbrella of the Mobile ontology;
- Creation of the converters lifting up the instance data represented solely in the XML format to RDF.

So the ontology work with the existing XML schemas would focus on ontologizing/considering the knowledge present these schemas, and combining it with the Mobile ontology, and not extending these schemata.

The XML-based standard schemata considered for this approach are listed in Table 3.

The following goals addressed by Mobile Ontology are open challenges for the current state of the art:

- The first comprehensive higher level ontology for mobile communication domain that is constructed with involvement/support of major players in mobile communication area, i.e. the ontology (i) responds to the needs of mobile service developers, (ii) is evolving, (iii) representatively captures the domain in an unbiased fashion.
- The most large scale international investigation on the use of Semantic technology in mobile communication domain.

Collaboration Aspects

Mobile Ontology construction has been initially implemented within two major deliverables of

SPICE EU project. 25 persons from 10 industry and research organizations stemming from 6 European countries have been initially involved in this specific cross issue. Therefore, apart from the definition of the up-to-date ontology infrastructure for Mobile services, the results of this study include observation of collaboration aspects of developers and users in the ontology construction.

Here we show how involved parties collaborated on the ontology construction, and what personal involvement expectations for a larger scale ontology infrastructure would be. In Figure 3, the extent to which the developers have been typically involved in initial definition of the ontology is demonstrated. The figure shows that most contributors tend to provide minor extensions to the ontology or choose a role of the user, which also confirms the previous research (Zhdanova, 2006).

Summarising, the main challenges identified in collaborative ontology construction as they have been observed are as follows:

- **Educational:** People with no/little knowledge on ontologies require *at least an introduction to the field.*
- **Methodology:** As of yet *no widely accepted or best practice solutions* on how to acquire ontologies from people in such a setting.
- **Basic technology:** Current ontology language standards (such as OWL) cause *confusion and awkward modelling solutions.*
- **Tool support:** *Better tools for ontology construction process coordination, documentation* would help to avoid ad-hoc solutions and manual work.

Ontology-Based Multimedia

Nowadays, network access technologies, such as Bluetooth, WiFi, WiMAX, are bringing the dream of ubiquitous service provision closer to reality. Ubiquitous service provision is of interest to service providers, telecommunication operators and technology manufactures for their future revenue prospect. However, the barriers to the delivery of ubiquitous services arise from the desire to deliver a wide service mix to users having a wide range of access devices via a multitude of heterogeneous access networks with different preferences and likings. Most of the existing applications and services are created and provided assuming a traditional pre-set delivery method and homogeneous transport media, which indicates a great importance and necessity for content and service adaptation in order to deliver them in such

Figure 3. Collaboration patterns in Mobile Ontology Construction

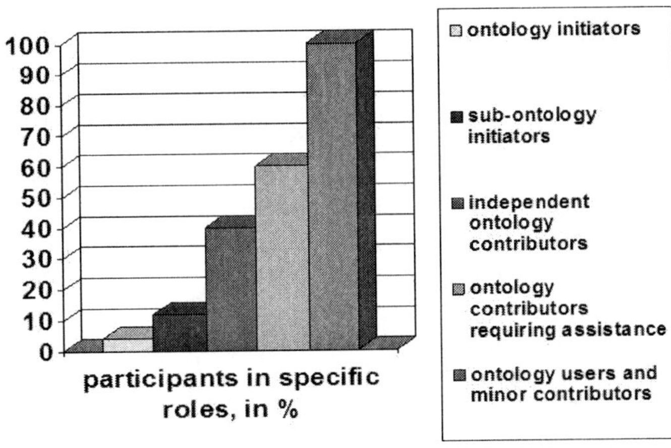

a ubiquitous environment. Such adaptation must be 'context-aware' and must facilitate user and situation specific content and service provision.

Therefore, the information from all the parties involved in the content and service delivery chain will form a contextual knowledge base that is shared by different operational agents in order to come up with a delivery or adaptation decision autonomously. These agents are generally heterogeneous in nature and distributed across networks. How to describe and represent such a knowledge base is fundamental to the development of a content and service adaptation framework which supports ubiquitous service delivery. This work has formed part of the Ubiquitous Services Core Research Programme of the Virtual Centre of Excellence in Mobile & Personal Communications, Mobile VCE.

Ontology has been recognized as the knowledge representation scheme and OWL as the knowledge representation language. However, to define a set of commonly-agreed vocabularies for the adaptation domain remains as a challenging issue. The ubiquitous content/service adaptation domain involves multiple sub-domains, i.e. the user domain, the content/service domain and the adaptation operation domain. Many efforts have been seen in recent years aiming to reach a description standard including vocabularies in order to achieve maximum acceptance and interoperability among communities. So far, the widely-acknowledged standards include usage environment description standards describing user information, device and network characteristics etc., such as CC/PP, UAProf and MPEG-21, and content description standards such as MPEG-7. Among those, MPEG-7 (ISO/IEC JTC1/SC29/WG11 N3752, 2000) and MPEG-21 DIA (ISO/IEC 21000-7, 2004) provide a good combination to linking content description with user environment description besides their well-established comprehensiveness in describing the respective domains. MPEG-7 offers several tools, i.e. Description Schemes (DS), to annotate multimedia content at different levels. These include Description Definition Language (DDL), Visual Schemes, Audio Schemes and Multimedia Description Schemes etc. MPEG-21 provides tools to describe the environment to enable transparent multimedia creation, delivery and consumption between heterogeneous environments. The most relevant part within MPEG-21 standard for the adaptation domain is Digital Item Adaptation (DIA). It provides tools to describe the user environment including: user characteristics, such as user info, preferences, usage history and physical characteristics, Device characteristics, such as display, memory and battery, Network characteristics, such as error characteristics and bandwidth, and Natural Environment characteristics such as noise and illumination.

Recent research efforts have reflected the recognition of using MPEG-7 and MPEG-21 DIA, together with ontology-based technologies, to construct an ontology to support the content/service adaptation (Soetens et al., 2004; Jannach et al., 2006). Though OWL has been chosen as the description language, Soetens et al. adopted limited usage of MPEG-21 vocabularies due to the immaturity of this standard at the time of writing (Soetens et al., 2004). In (Jannach et al., 2006), though MPEG vocabularies are adopted to form the domain ontology, the representation remains its original format of XML. With the actual adaptation operations being described in OWL-based language, this work realizes the integration of the different representation formats on the technical level using XML-based and logic-based technologies. Therefore, although MPEG-7 and MPEG-21 standards have been acknowledged for their strengths in multimedia domain description and delivery, their strengths can be still greatly enhanced by adding machine-processable semantics via ontology representation languages, such as OWL and RDF(S).

There exist several efforts to construct ontology representations of MPEG-7 and MPEG-21 (Hunter, 2001; Garcia, 2005). Those efforts construct ontology automatically by means of XSLT transformation according to the rules specified in (Garcia, 2005). By automatically converting the XML tree structure, the obtained ontology describes the relationship between the types of the tree element instead of describing the relationships between the semantics embodied by the tree elements. Although this approach expresses the XML-based standards in an OWL or RDF format, it does not add much semantic expressiveness to them. Such approach would be applied in any automatic XML schema to OWL conversion regardless of the semantics of the respective domain. In (Li et al., 2007), it argues that, for an expressive OWL representation of the XML-based standards, manual conversion is necessary. The manual conversion may result in some XML elements being discarded or treated with another XML construct as one OWL concept as a consequence of its semantic interpretation. There are no rules on how to manually convert an XML schema description into OWL ontology. Different from automatic conversion, which merely translates the XML syntax to OWL syntax, manual conversion has to examine the elements and the attributes of the XML schema, study their semantics, and translate them into OWL constructs.

CONCLUSION

State of the art and trends in convergence of the Semantic Web and mobile communication fields are presented in this article. Knowledge representation formalisms, relevant research fields, relevant ontologies are detailed, and the challenges of Semantic technology application to the mobile communications have been discussed. State-of-the-art examples of the work in this area have been outlined, including the development and use of ontology infrastructures that can serve as a semantic basis for applications and enablers within the convergence of the mobile and the Web worlds.

In a nutshell, one may conclude that (i) there exist a large number of ontologies addressing context-awareness and mobile communication issues, (ii) these ontologies are difficult to find and they are not or weakly linked and connected to each other. Factually, most of the time they do not form Semantic Web as the Web is about linking the data (and the users thus obtaining the typical Semantic Web benefits, such as interoperability), which is not the case for the current Semantic Mobile Communications.

FUTURE RESEARCH DIRECTIONS

The questions for the further research and development include: How to make these ontologies collaboratively constructed, linked to each other, easily found, used and evolved? And more specific, follow-up questions thus are:

1. How to involve developers and users in community-driven ontology construction and to what extent one should expect their involvement?
2. Which technical infrastructure is needed to implement this vision?

Ontologies are evolving as the domain is evolving and capturing the whole domain and all the needs by a (small) group of ontology developers alone is ineffective (Zhdanova, 2006). The ontology infrastructure for ubiquitous mobile communications should provide a user-friendly support to the ontology-based context-aware application and service developer with the following methods:

1. Key-word based ontology search (e.g., similar to OntoSelect[28], Swoogle[29])
2. Extraction and segmentation of the required ontology parts (e.g., operated on a level of triples and eventually on demand arranged in a stand-alone schemata)

3. In case no existing relevant ontology parts are found in the ontology platform infrastructure, possibility to plug in freshly developed ontologies and extensions
4. Simple ontology instantiation, with a subsequent simple discovery and use of the instance data
5. Ontology matching and alignment to the existing ontologies in case of duplicated modeling discovery, e.g., in a community-driven manner (Zhdanova & Shvaiko, 2006)
6. Search of relevant data within the instances (e.g., employing technologies such as YARS (Harth et al., 2006)
7. In case the developer made new ontology design/extensions, allow him/her easily plugging in the evolved versions of his/her ontologies/extensions, keeping up with the agreed ontology versioning practices

In conclusion, the starting points for the integration of the fields of Semantic Web and ubiquitous mobile communications exist both on the ontology schemata level as well as on the tools level. However, practices and processes for the common usage of the technologies originating from these two fields are still to be acquired. It is expected, that the new practices and processes are also to influence the future development of applications, services and tools appearing in the unified field.

REFERENCES

Brickley, D., & Guha, R.V. (Ed.) (2004 February). *RDF Vocabulary Description Language 1.0: RDF Schema.* W3C Recommendation. http://www.w3.org/TR/rdf-schema/

Dean, M., & Schreiber, G. (Ed.) (2004 February). *OWL Web Ontology Language Reference.* W3C Recommendation. http://www.w3.org/TR/owl-ref/

Fensel, D. (Ed.). (2001). *Ontologies: A Silver Bullet for Knowledge Management and Electronic Commerce*, Springer-Verlag.

Garcia, R., & Celma, O. (2005). Semantic integration and retrieval of multimedia metadata. In *Proceedings of the 5th International Workshop on Knowledge Mark-up and Semantic, Annotation at the 4th International Semantic Web Conference.*

Goble, C.A., De Roure, D., Shadbolt, N., & Fernandes, A.A.A. (2004). Enhancing services and applications with knowledge and semantics. In Foster, I. and Kesselman, C. (Ed.). *The Grid: Blueprint for a New Computing Infrastructure* (2nd. Ed., Ch. 23, pp. 431-458). Morgan Kaufmann.

Harth, A., Umbrich, J., & Decker, S. (2006). MultiCrawler: A pipelined architecture for crawling and indexing Semantic Web data. In *Proceedings of the 5th International Semantic Web Conference*, Athens, GA, USA.

Hercock, R.G. (2002). Autonomous Computing. In *Proceedings of the Workshop on Grand Challenges for Computing Research*, Edinburgh, UK.

Hunter, J. (2001). Adding multimedia to the semantic Web-building and MPEG-7 ontology. In *Proceedings of the 1st International Semantic Web Working Symposium.*

ISO/IEC JTC1/SC29/WG11 N3752, (2000). *Overview of the MPEG-7 Standard (version 4.0).*

ISO/IEC 21000-7, (2004). *Information Technology — Multimedia Framework (MPEG-21) — Part 7: Digital Item Adaptation* .

Jannach, D., Leopold, K., Timmerer, C., & Hellwagner, H. (2006). A knowledge-based framework for multimedia adaptation. *The International Journal of Artificial Intelligence, 24(2)*, pp. 109-125, Special Issue on Innovations in Applied Artificial Intelligence, Springer .

Korpipää, P., Häkkilä, J., Kela, J., Ronkainen, S., & Känsälä, I. (2004). Utilising context ontology in mobile device application personalization. *ACM International Conference Proceeding Series; Vol. 83 Proceedings of the 3rd international conference on Mobile and ubiquitous multimedia,* pp. 133-140, ACM Press.

Lassila, O., & Swick, R. (1999). *Resource Description Framework (RDF) Model and Syntax Specification.* W3C Recommendation. http://www.w3.org/TR/REC-rdf-syntax/

Li, N., Attou, A., & Moessner, K. (2007). A MPEG-based ontology for ubiquitous content/service adaptation. In *Proceedings of the 3rd Workshop on Context Awareness for Proactive Systems (CAPS'2007)*, Guildford, UK.

Luo, J., Montrose, B., Kim, A., Khashnobish, A., & Kang, M. (2006). Adding OWL-S support to the existing UDDI infrastructure. In *Proceedings of IEEE International Conference on Web Services (ICWS'06)* pp. 153-162.

Manola, F., & Miller, E. (2004). *RDF Primer.* W3C Recommendation. http://www.w3.org/TR/rdf-primer

Pfoser, D., Pitoura, E., & Tryfona, N. (2002). Metadata modeling in a global computing environment. *GIS'02*, November 8-9, 2002, McLean, Virginia, USA, ACM Press (2002).

Soetens, P., Geyter, M.D., & Decneut, S. (2004). Multi-step media adaptation with semantic Web services. In *Proceedings of International Semantic Web conference.*

Tarkoma, S., Prehofer, C., Zhdanova, A.V., Moessner, K., & Kovacs, E. (2007). SPICE: Evolving IMS to next generation service platforms. In *Proceedings of the 3rd Workshop on Next Generation Service Platforms for Future Mobile Systems (SPMS 2007) at the 2007 International Symposium on Applications and the Internet,* IEEE Computer Society Press.

Zhao, Y. X. (2004). Combining RDF and OWL with SOAP for Semantic Web Services. In *Proceedings of the 3rd annual Nordic Conference on Web Services (NCWS'04).*

Zhdanova, A.V. (2006 January). *An Approach to Ontology Construction and its Application to Community Portals.* PhD thesis, University of Innsbruck, Austria.

Zhdanova, A.V., Boussard, M., Cesar, P., Clavier, E., Gessler, S., Hesselman, C., Kernchen, R., Le Berre, O., Melpignano, D., Nani, R., Patrini, L., Räck, C., Strohbach, M., Sutterer, M., van Kranenburg, H., Villalonga, C., Vitale, A. (2006). *Ontology Definition for the DCS and DCS Resource Description, User Rules,* EU IST SPICE IP deliverable (D3.1).

Zhdanova, A.V., & Shvaiko, P. (2006). Community-driven ontology matching. In *Proceedings of the Third European Semantic Web Conference,* 11-14 June 2006, Budva, Montenegro, Springer-Verlag, LNCS 4011, pp. 34-49.

Weiser, M. (1991). *The Computer for the Twenty-First Century,* Scientific American, pp. 94-10.

ADDITIONAL READING

Cho, M. J., Kim, H., Kim, S. H., Lee, H. J., Hong, S. C., & Jung, M. J. (2007). *Context knowledge modelling method for sharing and reusing context knowledge in context-aware system,* vol. US2007038438, pp. 10.

De, S., & Moessner, K. (2007). Context gathering in ubiquitous environments: enhanced service discovery. In *Proceedings of the 3rd Workshop on Context Awareness for Proactive Systems (CAPS'2007)*, Guildford, UK.

Franz, B., Diego, C., Deborah, L. M., Daniele, N., & Peter, F. P.-S. (Eds.) (2003). *The description logic handbook: theory, implementation, and applications,* Cambridge University Press.

Kobeissy, N., Genet, M. G., & Zeghlache, D. (2007). Mapping XML to OWL for seamless information retrieval in context-aware environments. *Second IEEE International Workshop on Services Integration in Pervasive Environments (SEPS'07) at IEEE International Conference on Pervasive Services (ICPS'2007)*, pp. 349-354.

Li, N., & Moessner, K. (2007). The MVCE knowledge-based content and service adaptation management framework. In *Workshop on Applications and Services in Wireless Networks,* Santander, Spain.

Li, N., & Moessner, K. (2007). *Design of content/service adaptation framework*, Mobile VCE project Deliverable (D-U3.3).

Mukherjee, D., Delfosse, E., Jae-Gon, K., & Yong, W. (2005). Optimal adaptation decision-taking for terminal and network quality-of-service. *Multimedia, IEEE Transactions on*, vol. 7, pp. 454-462.

Noy, N. F., & Musen, M. A. (1999). An algorithm for merging and aligning ontologies: automation and tool support. *In Proceedings of the Workshop on Ontology Management at the Sixteenth National Conference on Artificial Intelligence (AAAI-99).*

Reif, G., Gall, H., & Jazayeri, M. (2005). WEESA - Web engineering for Semantic Web applications. *In Proceedings of 14th International World Wide Web Conference*, Chiba, Japan.

Smith, J. R., & Schirling, P. (2006). Metadata standards roundup. *IEEE Multimedia*, vol. 13, pp. 84-88.

Stamou, G., van Ossenbruggen, J., Pan, J. Z., Schreiber, G., & Smith, J. R. (2006). Multimedia annotations on the semantic Web. *IEEE Multimedia*, vol. 13, pp. 86-90.

Tsinaraki, C. et al. (2007). Interoperability support between MPEG-7/21 and OWL in DS-MIRF. *Knowledge and Data Engineering, IEEE Transactions on*, vol. 19, pp. 219-232.

Villalonga, C., Strohbach, M., Snoeck, N., Sutterer, M., Belaunde, M., Kovacs, E., Zhdanova, A.V., Goix, L.W., & Droegehorn, O. (2007). Mobile Ontology: Towards a standardized semantic model for the mobile domain. *In Proceedings of the 1st International Workshop on Telecom Service Oriented Architectures (TSOA 2007) at the 5th International Conference on Service-Oriented Computing,* Vienna, Austria.

Zhdanova, A.V., Du, Y., & Moessner, K. (2007). Mobile experience enhancement by ontology-enabled interoperation in a service platform. *In Proceedings of the 3rd Workshop on Context Awareness for Proactive Systems (CAPS'2007),* Guildford, UK, ISBN: 978-0-9556240-0-1.

ENDNOTES

1 vCard: http://www.w3.org/TR/vcard-rdf
2 CC/PP: http://www.w3.org/Mobile/CCPP/
3 UAProf: http://www.openmobilealliance.org/release_program/uap_v2_0.html
4 http://www.ruleml.org
5 http://www.w3.org/Submission/WRL/
6 http://www.w3.org/Submission/SWRL/
7 http://www.w3.org/2005/rules/wg
8 http://www.w3.org/Submission/WSML/
9 http://www.w3.org/Submission/SWSF-SWSL/
10 http://www.w3.org/Submission/WSMO/
11 http://www.w3.org/Submission/SWSF-SWSO/
12 http://www.w3.org/2002/ws/sawsdl/
13 http://www.w3.org/Submission/WSDL-S/
14 http://www.deri.org
15 http://www.w3.org/Submission/WSMX/
16 http://www.oasis-open.org/committees/wss/

[17] The GLOBUS Alliance: http://www.globus.org

[18] SPICE: http://www.ist-spice.org

[19] MobileVCE: http://www.mobilevce.com

[20] Mobilife: http://www.ist-mobilife.org

[21] OPUCE: http://www.opuce.tid.es

[22] Ambient Networks: http://www.ambient-networks.org

[23] TripCom: http://www.tripcom.org

[24] SWING: http://www.swing-project.org

[25] ASG: http://asg-platform.org

[26] SmartWeb: http://www.smartweb-project.de

[27] Mobile Ontology website: http://ontology.ist-spice.org

[28] OntoSelect: http://olp.dfki.de/ontoselect

[29] Swoogle: http://swoogle.umbc.edu

Chapter XII
Design Diagrams as Ontological Sources:
Ontology Extraction and Utilization for Software Asset Reuse

Kalapriya Kannan
IBM India Research Labs, India

Biplav Srivastava
IBM India Research Labs, India

ABSTRACT

Ontology is a basic building block for the semantic web. An active line of research in semantic web is focused on how to build and evolve ontologies using the information from different ontological sources inherent in the domain. A large part of the IT industry uses software engineering methodologies to build software solutions that solve real-world problems. For them, instead of creating solutions from scratch, reusing previously built software as much as possible is a business-imperative today. As part of their projects, they use design diagrams to capture various facets of the software development process. We discuss how semantic web technologies can help solution-building organizations achieve software reuse by first learning ontologies from design diagrams of existing solutions and then using them to create design diagrams for new solutions. Our technique, called OntExtract, extracts domain ontology information (entities and their relationship(s)) from class diagrams and further refines the extracted information using diagrams that express dynamic interactions among entities such as sequence diagram. A proof of concept implementations is also developed as a Plug-in over a commercial development environment IBM's Rational Software Architect.

INTRODUCTION

A Scientific American article describes evolution of Web that consisted largely of documents for humans to read and that included data and information for computers to manipulate. In order, to help the people and machines to communicate concisely, this huge repository of information (Web) have to be re-engineered to define shared and common domain theories that are machine processable. This is the precise aim of Semantic Web to build metadata – rich Web where presently human-readable content will have machine-understandable semantics. Semantic Web achieves the increased demand of shared semantic and a web of data and information derived from it through the adaptation of common conceptualizations referred to as Ontologies. Ontologies are fundamental building blocks of Semantic Web and therefore cheap and fast construction of domain-specific ontologies is crucial for the success and the proliferation of the Semantic Web. We explore how a semantic web may impact software engineering where common conceptualizations (e.g., software, work products, experience) from previous projects need to be reused in new projects.

The chapter will contribute in the following ways: (a) It will introduce an ontology learning technique from design diagrams (specifically UML) which is in line with the research direction of building ontologies from different sources to enable a rich semantic web; (b) It will show a concrete semantic web application how the semantic web technology of ontology can promote software reuse; (c) It will put recent research on transformations from UML to OWL and vice-versa in perspective; and (d) it will motivate more research effort in semi-automatically building integrated information models.

Ontology Learning and Sources

Ontology learning facilitates the construction of ontologies by ontology engineering. Ontology learning includes a number of complementary disciplines that feed on different types of unstructured, semi-structured and fully structured data in order to support a (semi -) automatic, cooperative ontology engineering process. Ontology learning is quiet a tedious task and often requires manual intervention. Ontology learning algorithms have concentrated in finding efficient methods of automatically extracting ontology information. Today, research apart from automatic ontology learning has also focused on finding sources (RDF, html, unstructured text etc) of ontological information. In our work we concentrate on identifying one such source i.e., design diagrams and provide an (semi-) automatic technique to extract (domain) ontological information. In the process of software solution development, large amount of ontological information is implicitly modeled in design diagrams. Our work aims at extracting this implicit ontology from the design diagrams. It largely helps reuse of the concepts in other software solutions.

In Figure 1, a simplified project cycle is shown. The project requirements are collected; the solution is developed and tested, and finally released to the customer. At the end of the project, a report is generated to capture the learning. However, it is rare that project-end deliverables or reports are explicitly used to improve the solution development process for new projects.

Our key observation is that the similarity among the projects alludes to the existence of a veritable domain of discourse whose ontology, if created, would make the similarity across the projects explicit. However, manually creating such domain ontologies is infeasible due to the training needed for the software professionals and the efforts required. Although many ontology engineering tools have matured over the last decade, manual ontology acquisition remains a tedious, cumbersome task that can easily result in domain knowledge acquisition bottleneck. We note that design diagrams are integral part of software project deliverables as they document

Figure 1. Custom Software Projects and the Impact of OntExtract

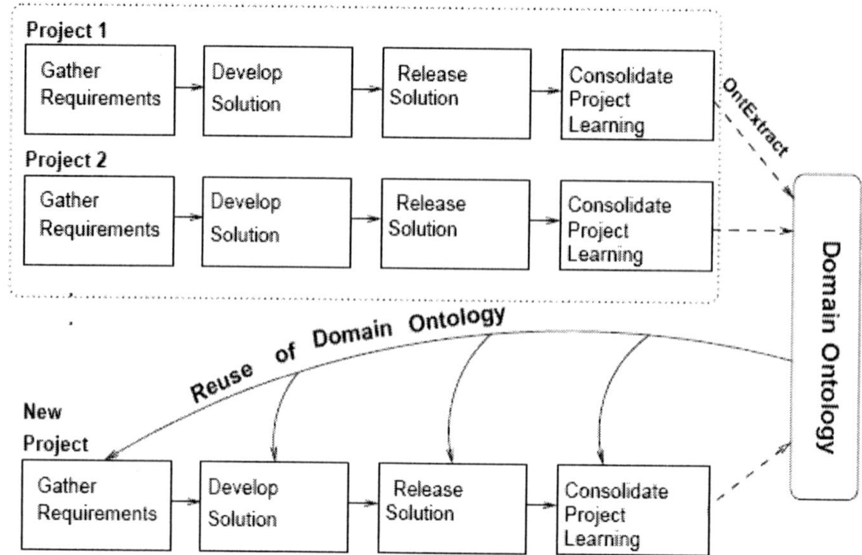

crucial facets of the solution dealing with software artifacts, their relationships and runtime behavior. Much, but not all, information in theses diagrams are ontological information. If one were to extract and explicitly represent them, they would enable shared and common domain theories that would not only enable better understanding of the domain but also allow software professionals to reuse the domain theories in creation of new solutions over their project cycle. This is illustrated in the lower half of Figure 1.

Using UML-2 as the design diagram representation, we present the OntExtract tool to extract ontologies from project deliverables and show that they can be reused for new projects. UML has become a de-facto standard for modeling software development activities. In UML, static behavior of the solution is captured by diagrams like the class diagram and dynamic behavior by diagrams like the sequence diagram. Two types of elements are present in UML diagrams: (a) those representing environmental artifacts representing characteristics of the problem space, and (b) those representing implementation artifacts introduced to ease a form of software implementation. We assume that the generated ontology should be general enough to span implementation trends. Our method, OntExtract, reads UML diagrams and proceeds by preserving the environmental artifacts, removing the implementation artifacts and maintaining the consistency of the resulting diagram. The output ontology is represented using UML class notations to ease the understanding by developers who may not be familiar with a new (ontology) representation language like OWL. However, using emerging UML to OWL (and vice-versa) transformation methods, the ontology can be maintained in multiple representations. Moreover, with UML diagrams from multiple projects, the emergent ontology can be refined. Over time, the ontology will capture the learning from previous projects.

The ontology can be used for any purpose including software reuse for new solution creation. For reuse, as the solution process is being followed, the initial UML diagrams for the new solution can be created by filtering the relevant content from the ontology. As an example, we show how the sequence diagram from the new solution can be used as a requirement over the ontology and an initial class diagram for the solution can be created.

Contributions

The main contributions of our work can be listed as follows:

1. Concept of Design diagrams (in specific UML diagrams) as sources of ontological information.
2. An automatic ontology extraction technique called 'OntExtract.
3. OntExtract Methodology from UML diagrams of a single solution of a specification:
   a. Concept of identifying the elements that relate to concepts in domain.
   b. Preserving those elements that express domain concepts.
   c. Eliminating and reducing the impact of elimination of components that doesn't relate to concepts.
4. Ontology aggregation methodology from Multiple UML diagrams.
5. The impact of extracted ontology in solution building. Hence, it is important to apply semantic techniques in this domain.
6. Relationship with approaches for information transformation: UML to OWL and vice- versa, UML as ontology language.
7. Challenges in extending information models with more ontological data sources.

We have implemented OntExtract as a plug-in using IBM Rational Software Architect. It benefits two groups of people: (a) Software professionals and (b) Ontology engineers. Software professionals benefit by using this tool to obtain domain models that allow reuse of design decisions at all stages of a new software project. Ontology engineers can use our tool to create/ maintain domain ontology considering design diagrams as a new source of information. Initial results show that the created ontologies are accurate and help in better software reuse for new solutions.

BACKGROUND

In this section we provide the background knowledge about the design diagrams and the standards used for creating and representing design diagrams and ontology. We also provide the same example considered in our work for evaluation purpose.

Design Diagrams and UML 2

Design Diagrams are used to represent visually software solution for a problem. They express environmental relationship (entities and relationship among entities that represent domain concept in domain ontology) among entities in the solution developed for requirement specification of a problem. In addition design diagrams express implementation artifact that model implementation entities and relationship needed for development of software solutions. We use UML 2 since it has become a de-facto standard for modeling software development activities. UML (Terry Quatrani, 2001), is a standard modeling language for specifying, constructing, visualizing and documenting artifacts of the software system. UML consists of 9 set of diagrams to model various software artifacts. In our work we use class diagram that belongs to the category of the structural diagrams that represents static behavior of the system to extract domain concepts. Sequence diagrams are used for further refining the extracted ontology. OCL is the constraint language with UML but it is not used widely in commercial projects.

Ontology

Ontologies are meta data schemes, providing controlled vocabulary of concepts, each with an explicitly defined and machine processable semantics and inter-relationships with other concepts.

Ontology uses the following elements to express environmental artifacts: Classes represents general things in the domain of interest, Individuals defines instance of an class and includes concrete objects such as people, animals etc., Attributes describes the general properties of the classes, Relationship represents the relationships in terms of subsumption (IS-A) relationship, meronymy (HAS-A) relationship that exists among things. The OWL language (Deborah, 2004) is a leading standard for ontology representation.

Example Domain

We use the case study of student course registration taken from the Rational tutorial (Terry, 2002) as the running example in the chapter:

At the beginning of each semester students may request a course catalogue containing a list of course offerings for the semester. Information about each course, such as professor, department, and prerequisites will be included to help students make informed decisions. The new on-line registration system will allow students to select four course offerings for the coming semester. In addition, each student will indicate two alternative choices in case a course offering becomes filled or canceled. No course offering will have more than ten students. No course offering will have fewer than three students. Once the registration process is completed for a student, the registration system sends information to the billing system, so the student can be billed for the semester. Professors must be able to access the on-line system to indicate which courses they will be teaching. They will also need to see which students signed up for their course offering. The billing system will credit all students for courses dropped during this period of time.

For purpose of experimentation and evaluation, in this work we consider several solutions for the above problem. Figure 3 gives the UML class diagram for a solution we have proposed. This solution is henceforth referred to as Solution A (SolA). We consider two other solutions (class diagrams) taken from tutorial website of Rational Software Corporation (Rational, 2000), (referred to as Solution B (SolB) and class room lecture of Prof. Dr. Bettina Berendt (Bettina, 2005), (referred as Solution C (SolC)). We assume that these input class diagrams are correct. We represent classes and association between two classes as nodes and edges, respectively.

We use the terms nodes and classes interchangeably, and similarly the terms edges and

Figure 2. System overview

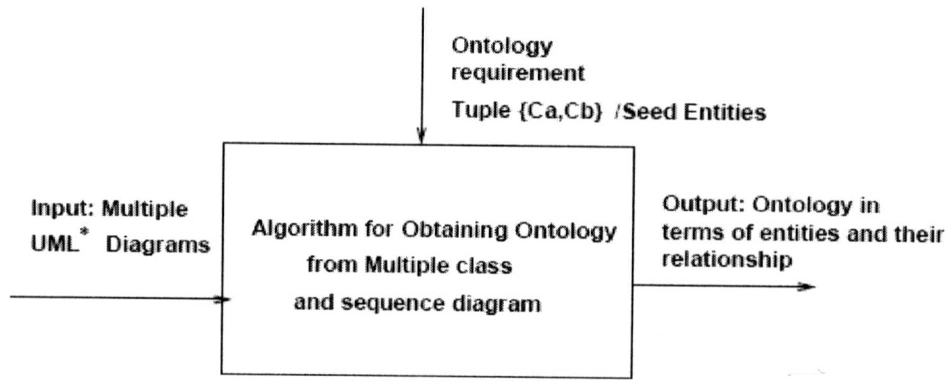

associations. The term Root node is used to refer to a node that is placed at the highest level of the tree and has no parents.

USING UML DIAGRAMS AS ONTOLOGICAL SOURCES

Figure 2 gives the system architecture of OntExtract. OntExtract takes UML diagrams (class and sequence diagram) of multiple projects and extracts the domain ontology. Domain requirements are taken as a tuple of keywords.

UML elements can be classified broadly into two categories: (a) Implementation Artifacts: They are introduced by the architect of the software solution to capture those elements that represent low-level details of the solution such as messages exchanged and their behavior. Such artifacts are either full-fledged classes or specific attributes of a class. (b) Environmental Artifacts: They include ontological entities and relationship among such entities. Relationship includes generalization (IS-A), aggregation/composition (HAS-A) and USING association. We use the stereotypes to identify UML elements. Implementation artifacts do not contribute to domain concepts while environmental artifacts such as IS-A, HAS-A, USING relationship and entities participating in such relationship reflects domain concepts. All UML diagrams have implementation or environmental artifacts. However, static information such as classes (concepts), attributes and relations (semantics) can be obtained from class diagrams. Therefore, in our we use class diagrams to extract domain information (ontol-

Figure 3. Ontology information from class diagram

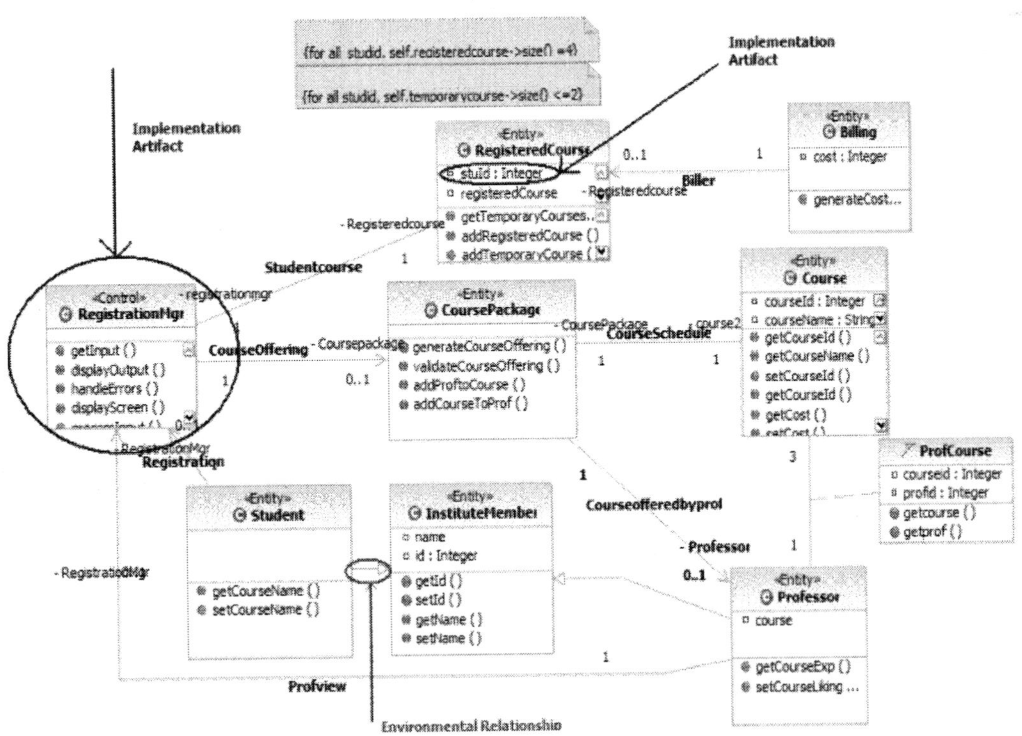

ogy) and explore whether interaction diagrams such as sequence diagram would help identify more domain concepts.

Ontology Extraction from Class Diagram

Class level implementation artifact: UML defines three types of stereotyped classes (a) Boundary class (b) Controller class and (c) Entity class. A boundary class models interaction between the software system and the environment. A control class acts as coordinator of activities. An entity class models information that has been stored by the system and its associated behavior. By and large, entity classes reflect real world entity and are part of environmental artifacts. Boundary and Controller classes are implementation artifacts, used to ease software development.

Attribute level implementation artifact: Attributes are storage elements of a class instance. Some attributes are introduced to maintain property values of an entity class while others are used purposes such as maintaining uniqueness, class level state, providing identities to entities. Attributes of the form of second category are implementation artifacts.

In Figure 3 we identify some of the implementation and environmental artifacts. In this Figure, the class RegistrationMgr is a class level implementation artifact (co-ordinates messages between other entities). Attribute 'stuID' in the class RegisteredClass is an attribute level implementation artifact introduced to maintaining uniqueness of the entity. Environmental artifacts such as class 'Student' inherits from 'InstituteMember' can also be seen in this Figure. Environmental artifacts reflecting domain concepts, OntExtract proceeds by removing implementation artifacts and preserving environmental artifacts.

OntExtract: Elimination of Implementation Artifact

Elimination of a class level attribute affects nodes that are associated with the eliminated node through inheritance, aggregation/composition and USING relationship. Nodes that are related to eliminated node through the above relationships is also eliminated. Links representing USING relationship between the neighbors of eliminated node result in dangling edges. In order to build relationship rich ontology, we aim to preserve this relationship by the process of propagation.

Figure 4. Elimination of a node and its dangling edges

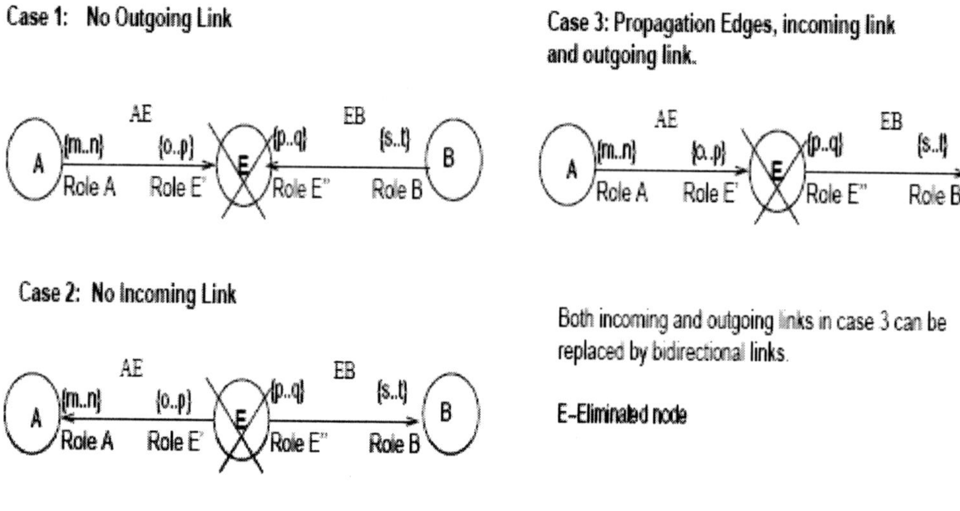

Case 1: No Outgoing Link

Case 2: No Incoming Link

Case 3: Propagation Edges, incoming link and outgoing link.

Both incoming and outgoing links in case 3 can be replaced by bidirectional links.

E-Eliminated node

Propagation results in new relationship (edges) among neighbors. The properties of the new relationship depends on the properties of two dangling edges that results in propagation. Figure 4 shows the nature of edges that are atypical of a relationship. In Figure 4, case 1 and case 2 do not have propagating links. We are interested in case 3 that has propagation edges where a new association is created between every incoming, bidirectional and outgoing links.

The attributes such as name, direction, cardinality, role names of the new association are obtained as follows: Direction: The direction of the new edge depends on whether the dangling edges were bidirectional or directed. New edge assumes the direction of the dangling edge(s) if the dangling edges were directed otherwise it is bidirectional. Role name: The new edges assume the role name of the nodes that the new edge connects. Cardinality: Cardinality of the new edge is obtained by finding the minimum and maximum number of instances of nodes that the new edge connects, can be associated through the node that is eliminated. In other words, the cardinality is calculated as the cross product of cardinality of the two links that results in propagation. Figure 5 (a) shows the propagation of cardinality constraints among the dangling edges.

Figure 5 (b) shows the new edges with the properties after elimination of a node (refer case 3 of Figure 4) and Figure 6 shows the class diagram of the student registration example after elimination of the class level implementation artifacts.

We leave the elimination of attribute level implementation artifacts as future work. Identifying these artifacts is difficult since there is no explicit notation is available in UML to annotate attributes according to intended usage and requires profiling of the code.

Algorithm 1 describes the steps for removing class level implementation artifact and propagating relationships. The algorithm gets and removes controller and boundary classes in the UML diagrams (line 1). A new association is created for every incoming (line 12), bidirectional edge (line 17) (to the controller/boundary class) to outgoing edge (from the controller/boundary class) line 4. The properties of the new association are obtained from the incoming/bidirectional - outgoing edge pair. In the algorithm, the terms 'this end' refers

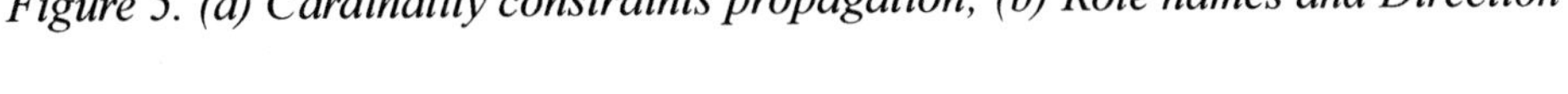
Figure 5. (a) Cardinality constraints propagation; (b) Role names and Direction

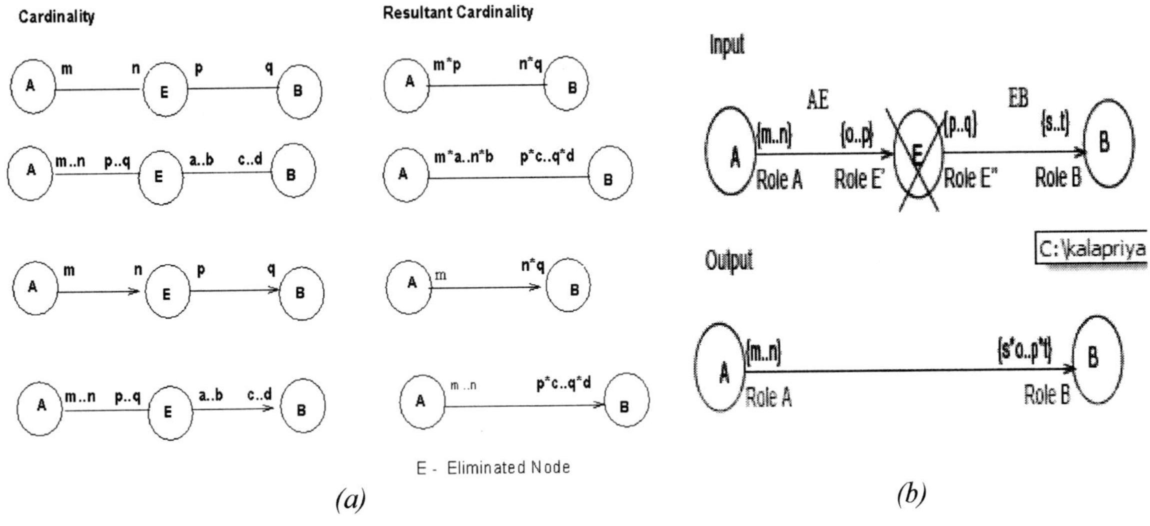

Algorithm 1.

Algorithm 1 : Elimination of Class Level Artifacts

```
List lst =getControllerAndBoundaryClasses();
for all (cls = classes) in lst do
    List lstIncoming = getIncomingLinks(cls);
    List lstOutgoing = getOutgoingLinks(cls);
    List lstbi = getBidirectionalLinks(cls);
    for all lnkIn = link in lstIncoming do
        node thisNode = getNode(lnkIn);
        thisProp = getLinkProperties(lnkIn);
        for all (lnkOut = link) in lstOutgoing do
            otherNode = getNode(lnkOut);
            otherProp = getLinkProperties(lnkOut);
            createNewDirectedEdge(thisNode, otherNode,thisProp,otherProp);
        end for
        for all (lnkbi=link) in lstbi do
            otherEndNode = getNode(lnkbi);
            otherProp = getLinkProperties(lnkbi);
            createDirectedNewEdge(thisNode, otherNode,thisProp, otherProp);
        end for
    end for
end for
```

Figure 6. Student registration class diagram after elimination of class level implementation artifacts

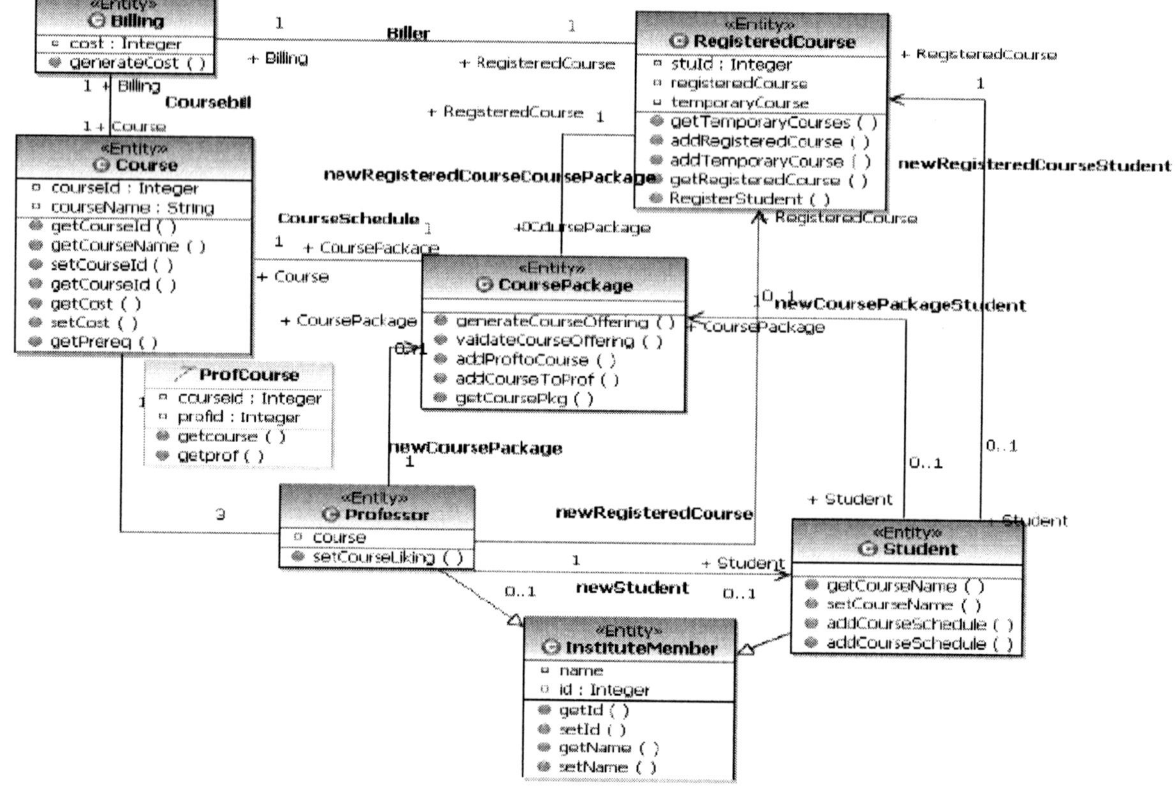

to the end associated with a neighbor nodes and 'other end' refers to the end associated with the other neighbor, between which a new association is created. Property role name, cardinality constraints are obtained in line 8 and 16. The new association assumes a new name for reference. The resultant class diagram is henceforth referred as Eliminated Entities Class Diagram (EECD).

OntExtract: Preserving Environmental Artifact

The EECD obtained as a result of elimination of implementation artifact represents in general all conceptual entities which can be directly reused in other similar software projects. In addition to this, we provide provisions for extraction of ontological information for specific domain requirements provided by the software professional. For example, in the context of 'professor' (in Figure 3) students billing information is not relevant.

The domain requirement is provided by the architect as a tuple of keywords. Let us consider an example in which we are interested in extracting student domain information i.e., input keyword is {student}. We assume that this input keyword directly maps to an entity class in EECD. This class is henceforth referred to as the candidate class. Preserving environmental artifact includes identifying those entities that reflect domain concepts in the resultant EECD. All entities that are related through inheritance (IS-A), aggregation/composition (HAS-A) and USING relationship (collectively known as environmental relationship) directly reflects domain information with respect to the input tuple.

For inheritance relationship, all ancestor classes influence the candidate class and all descendants classes are influenced by candidate class. Figure 7 (a) gives the generic graph of the candidate class and its neighbors in a class diagram. Therefore, with respect to inheritance relationship all ancestors and descendants of the candidate class are preserved. The siblings of the candidate class do not affect the candidate class and therefore do not reflect concepts of the domain represented by the candidate class. Algorithm 2 presents the algorithm to obtain all ancestors and descendants for the candidate class. To extract the nodes that are ancestors for the candidate

Figure 7. Generic Model (a) neighbors (b) inheritance output

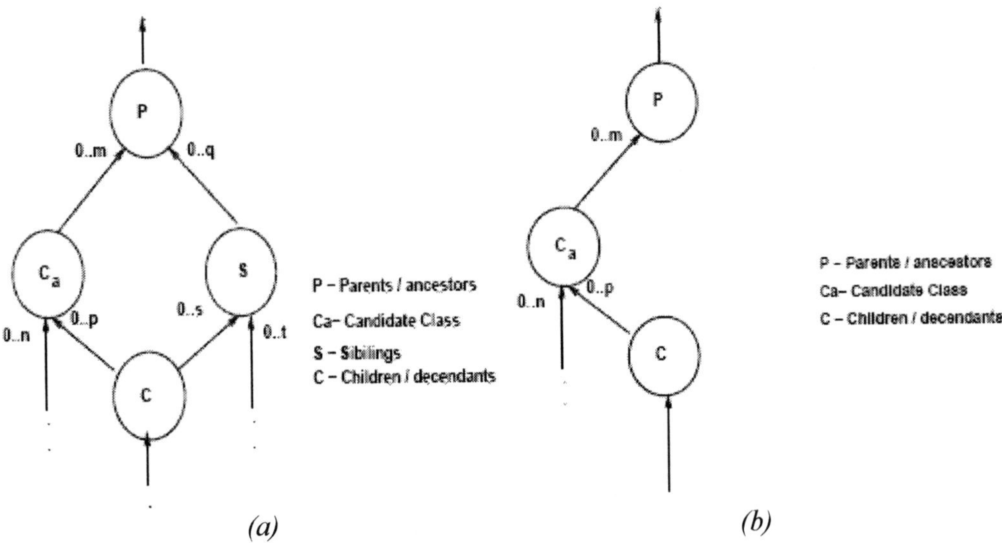

class, the algorithm finds all the paths from the candidate class to the root node (line 1). To find a descendant node the algorithm checks if a node has route to the candidate class in line 4. Figure 7 (b) gives the generic output structure (tree) after preserving inheritance relationship.

Preserving aggregation/composition relationship is similar to the technique presented for extracting inheritance relationship. 'USING' relationship is denoted by Directed and Bidirectional links. It represents exchange of messages between two classes during execution. We are interested in the classes that help to achieve the functionality (use case) by the relationship. Run time information such as classes related to candidate class through 'USING' relationship is not directly available from class diagram. The actual set of related classes can only be obtained from diagrams that reflect dynamic behavior (diagrams that describe the behavior of classes). Two UML diagrams, activity diagrams and sequence diagrams are candidates that provide dynamic information.

Ontology Refinement Using Sequence Diagram

Sequence diagrams describe the services provided by objects through exchange of messages.

Activity diagram describe sequence of activities and is generally more expressive than the state diagram. Based on the above comparison, we propose to use sequence diagram to extract classes that are related to the candidate class through 'USING' relationship. All sequence diagrams that has the candidate class are considered. Figure 8 gives the sequence diagram for the use case 'course registration'. Classes CoursePackage, Course, RegisteredCourse, Billing that are related to the candidate class {Student} through these sequence diagrams are preserved as ontological information.

Figure 9 gives the Ontology Diagram (OD) that represents the extracted ontology information for domain requirement {Student}.

Sequence diagrams acts as filters for extracting entities that are associated with the candidate class to achieve a certain functionality (use case) or to provide a service. Using Model Driven Architecture (MDA), the architects/professionals begin by describing the use cases (functionalities/services) from the functional requirements of a problem. By modeling these services into a set of sequence diagrams our approach can be used to obtain ontology customizable for the new problem. This helps to obtain existing solution approaches for the new problem and thereby largely help software reuse.

Algorithm 2.

Algorithm 2 Inheritance - obtaining neighbors for candidate class

```
1: ancestorNodes = getNodes(getallPathstoRoot(candidateClass)); {Get all ancestor nodes}
2: addNodestoInheritance (ancestorNodes, InheritanceRelationshipGraph);
3: for all (nodes) do
4:     if isPathtoCandidateClass(node,candidateClass) then
5:         addNodestoInheritance (nodes,InheritanceRelationshipGraph);
6:     end if
7: end for
```

Figure 8. Sequence diagram for functionality 'course registration'

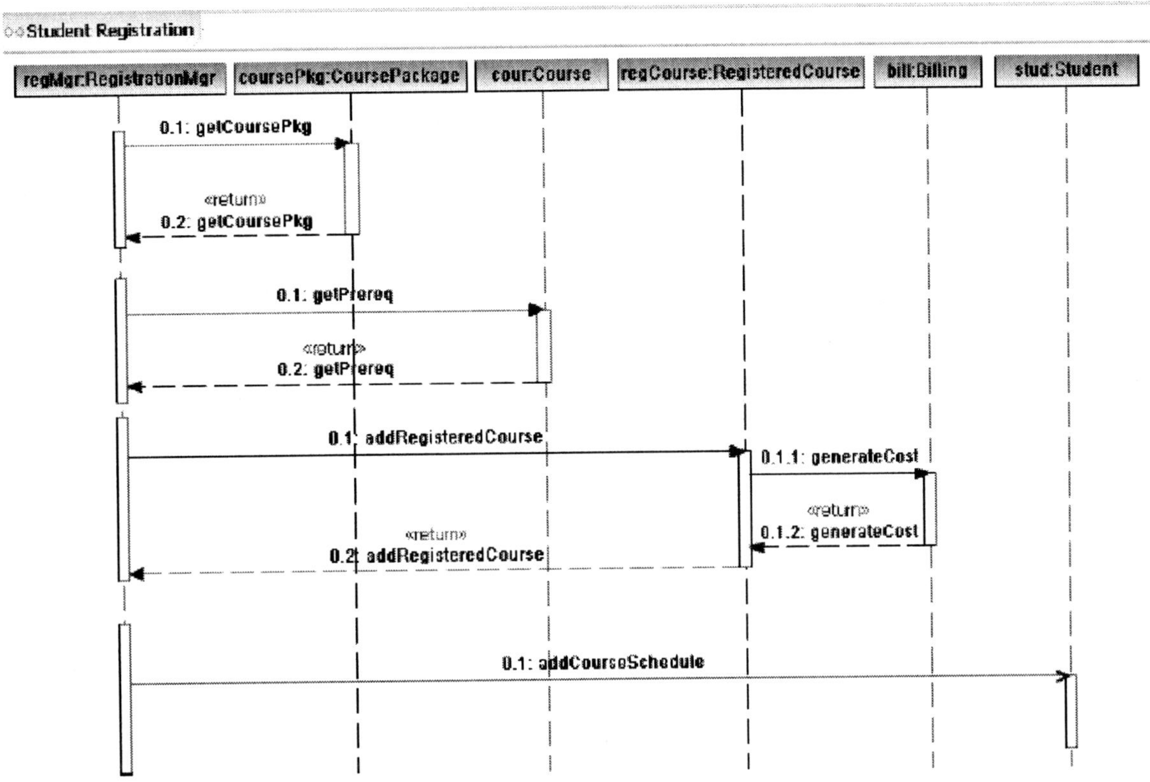

Figure 9. Extracted Ontology Diagram (OD)

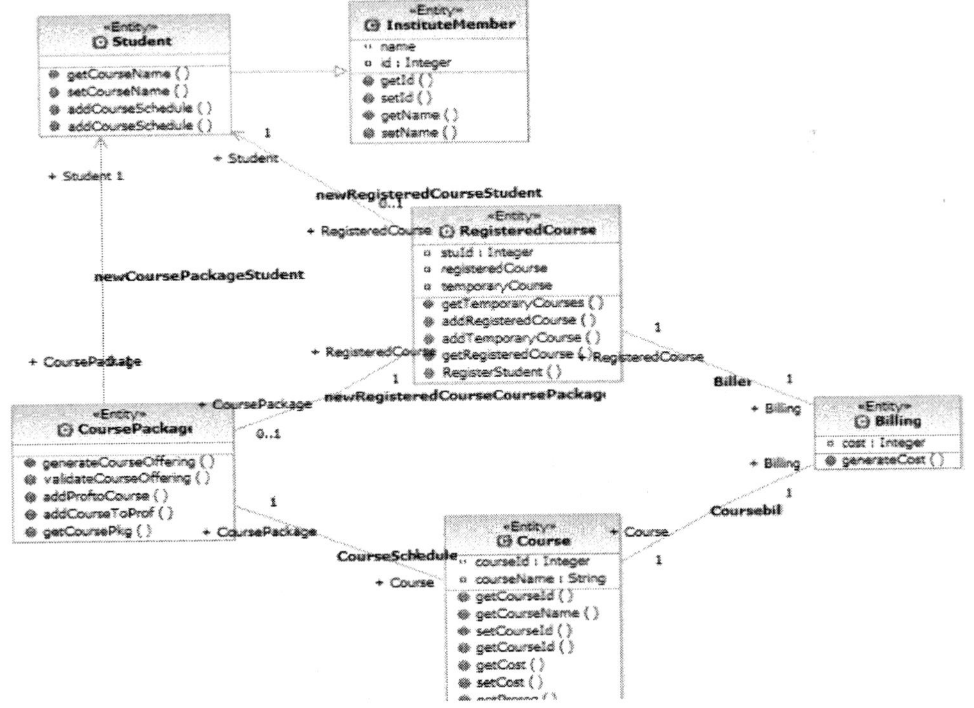

ONTOLOGY EXTRACTION FROM MULTIPLE UML DIAGRAMS

Methodology

With view of improving the quality of the extracted ontology, we propose an ontology refinement technique in which OntExtract extends to aggregate ontology from multiple Ontology Diagrams (OD) with respect to a domain requirement. The refinement process helps to correct/update/change to a fine granularity and increases the confidence of the correctness of the extracted ontology. These design diagrams can be different solution of same problem or solution(s) of different problem(s). Ontology aggregation from multiple OD can be done in two ways (a) Incremental approach, aggregates ontology by considering one relationship at a time, (b) Consolidated approach, aggregates ontology by considering all relationship in an ontology diagram. Consolidated approach increases the complexity of analysis of relationships since a single node can have multiple types of relationship. In addition, the consolidated approach does not handle propagation of relation inherently (explicit/ manual invention is required to handle propagation) whereas incremental approach handles propagation inherently (aggregation is based on all relationship but incrementally). Therefore, we use incremental approach by taking one relationship from multiple ontology diagrams to aggregate ontology.

Aggregation of ontology from multiple ontology diagrams requires adding/deleting/ updating ontology entities. We use the metric semantic distance to arrive at a decision whether to add/delete/update entities. Semantic distance measures the closeness of two entities in ontology diagram. Semantic Distance between nodes is reduced to distance between concepts in a graph. The distance between concepts is determined according to their positions (measured as levels). When a hierarchy is N = (n+1) layered, K/N nodes is connected to the class in the Kth level where (0 < K < N). Figure 10 (refer to output inheritance diagram Figure 9) diagram shows a sample inheritance graph in the ontology diagram with the candidate class in the Kth level. Value of K/N determines the characterization of the graph, if K/N is very low, then the relationship structure represents more generalization then specialization with respect to candidate class and vice-versa. The more general is the structure, the more re-usable is the extracted ontology. Therefore, our algorithm aims to keep the K/N as low as possible. More generalization the structure represents more re-usable is the extracted ontology. Therefore, our algorithm aims to keep the K/N as low as possible.

Figure 10. Semantic distance desired

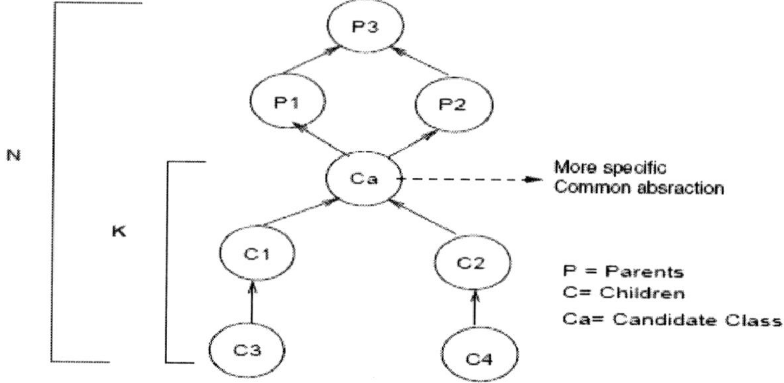

Aggregating Ontology from Multiple Inheritance/ Aggregation/ Composition Relationship Graph

We use the edge counting graph (Rada, 1989) method to calculate the semantic distance between the nodes since it gives a good estimate of how close two nodes are. In edge counting method, semantic distance between two nodes is measured as the number of edges between two nodes. In order to maximize generalization nodes, a smaller path between any two nodes in the levels above the level of the candidate class in a ontology diagram is replaced by a longer path (if one exists) from another ontology diagram(s). Figure 11(a) gives various input and output diagram for generalization nodes in an inheritance. The Figure shows the replacement of the smaller paths by longer paths if present in the input diagrams. The Figure also shows that if there are no common nodes, all the paths are preserved. In order to keep specialization nodes as low as possible, a longer path between two nodes below the level of the candidate class in a ontology diagram is replaced by a shorter path

Figure 11. Ontology Aggregation (a) Specialization (b) Generalization

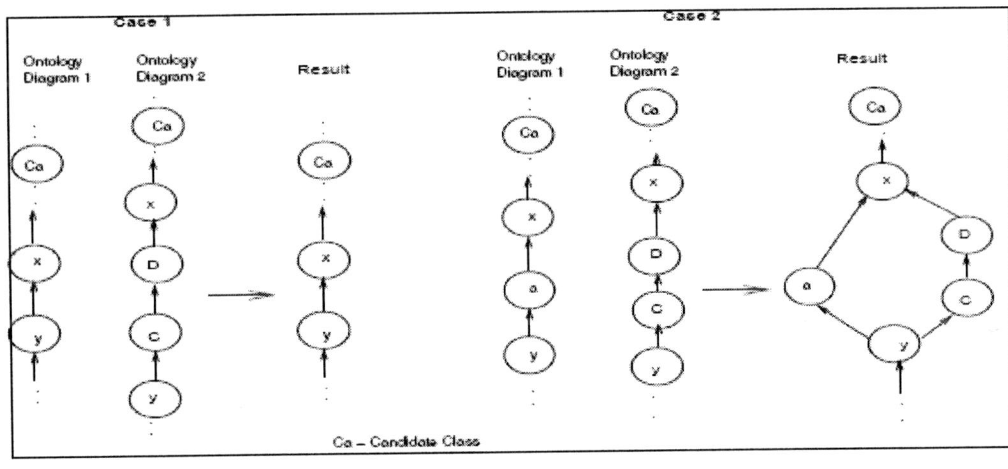

(a)

(b)

(if one exists) from another ontology diagram(s). Figure 11(b) shows the replacement of longer path(s) between any two nodes by shorter paths if available in the input diagrams. If no common nodes are present all the nodes in the ontology diagrams are preserved in the resultant structure. The resultant diagram obtained by aggregating inheritance/aggregation/composition relationship is referred to as the Partial Aggregated Relationship Diagram (PARD).

Aggregating Ontology from Multiple 'USING' Relationship Graphs

For aggregating 'USING' relationship, all the elements that are related to the candidate class through 'USING' relationship from the ontology diagram(s) are added to PARD. The resultant diagram is the final Aggregated Ontology Diagram (AOD).

Inconsistency

In general, aggregating information from multiple ontology diagrams would give rise to two kinds of inconsistencies: Class Level Inconsistency: This inconsistency arises when a class (identified by name) appears in multiple ontology diagrams but the attributes of the class are different in different in ontology diagrams. For example RegisteredCourse in an ontology diagram has {StudentId, CourseId} as two attributes and has {StudentId, CourseId, BillAmt} in another ontology diagram. Our aggregation algorithm handles this inconsistency by merging the list of attributes (attribute richness) in the resultant AOD. Association Level Inconsistency: This inconsistency arises when association between two nodes in one ontology diagram is different than in another ontology diagram. If such association exists between two nodes we preserve all the associations between the two nodes. In ontology each association is represented as a property. Properties are first class elements in ontology and therefore can exist independent (of the class). In ontology end points of the property are defined by defining the domain (source) and range (destination) for the property. This implies there can be multiple properties whose end points and range are same, but their utilization depends on the context. By maintaining these associations (as properties) we are precisely extracting the domain (context) in which a entity exits. This is one of the important benefits of aggregating domain information from multiple ontology diagrams.

ONTEXTRACT: IMPLEMENTATION, EVALUATION AND ASSESSMENT

To put our approach into practice, we have implemented our approach as a plug-in using IBM Rational Software Architect (IBM Enterprise Architect Kit for SOA, 2006) using Java language. The plug-in reads in the class and outputs an ontology diagram that is represented using UML notation. Our tool provides provisions for software professionals to extract relevant ontology as applicable to a new problem by providing two optional input holders: (a) sequence diagram holder and (b) domain requirement holder. Both these inputs help extract refined or customized ontology. We have evaluated two cases: (a) Sample Domain - Student course registration, (b) Large scale real world example from IBM. We refer to the extracted ontology of SolA as Base Ontology [BaseOnt] (Figure 6). In general ontology evaluation approaches are classified into four categories (i) those that evaluate the ontology by comparing it to the golden standard, (ii) those that evaluate the ontologies by plugging them in an application and measuring the quality of the results that the application returns, (iii) those that evaluate ontologies by comparing them to unstructured or informal data (e.g. text documents) and (iv) and those based on human interaction to measure ontology features not recognizable by machines. In our work we have used all the above mentioned work to prove two main aspects described as follows:

1. First we proceed to show that our extracted ontology by OntExtract is reasonable and correct.
2. The extracted ontology is reusable in new solutions (due to the fact that the created ontology overlaps with the design requirements of a new solution).

The first aspect evaluates the validity of the extracted ontology. We use the approach of comparing the extracted ontology with the golden standard to show that our algorithm extracts ontology similar to existing standard ontologies. In the second aspect, we use the approach of plugging the extracted ontology in an application and measuring the quality of results to evaluate the useful of the extracted domain ontology. Finally, we take the help of domain experts (humans) and bring out the importance of our tool in help them with defining better UML diagrams.

OntExtract Extracts Reasonable Ontology

The aim is to show that OntExtract extracts reasonably accurate ontology (serves the intended purpose of extracting ontology). By this we also show that our approach is correct.

Methodology

We evaluate our approach for correctness of is-a, has-a and other associations between entities relations by comparing the extracted ontology with manually built Golden standard (ontology). Golden standard ontology consists of set of entities and relationships that are considered as a good representation of the concepts of the problem domain under consideration. The golden ontology is often manually created by experts (Hassell, 2006) or obtained by merging multiple individual ontologies that are correct. We compare the extracted ontology to a golden ontology, considered as a good representation of the concepts of the problem domain under consideration. High values of matching entities between the two ontologies indicate that our approach OntExtract extracts similar ontology to existing ones.

In our case we consider domain 'University' (whose subset is the course registration) and obtain the golden standard ontology by aggregating several individual 'University' ontologies from (Jeff, 2000; University Ontology, 2002; Donnie Dorr, 2000). Let UML1, UML2 and UML3 be notations that represent these ontologies respectively. We first show that these individual ontologies are correct and therefore the aggregation of these ontologies results in golden standard ontologies. We use the evaluation method presented by Bruno et al (2005) to measure the correctness of individual ontologies. This method assigns grades (depending on the correctness) to individual ontologies and determines the corrections based on these grades. It uses the combined approaches proposed in (Gmez-Prez, 1994; Oltramari, 2002) considered as traditional evaluating methodologies. To begin with it assigns each ontology a grade starting at 20. For each error encountered the grade value is decreased.

Table 1 presents the various criteria s considered for assigning grades. Ontologies that have grades greater than 13 are considered to be satisfy correctness conditions.

Table 2 presents the consolidation of the grades obtained for individual ontology diagrams that we have considered to obtain the golden ontology. From Table 2 it can be seen that the UML diagrams that we have considered to obtain the golden ontology are correct (have grade points greater than 13). We aggregate these individual ontologies to obtain the golden standard. The reason why consider a golden ontology and not individual UML diagrams considered to aggregate is primarily because the individual ontologies considered might be not include all/most of the

Table 1. Criteria considered for grade assignment

Criteria	Points
Completeness Errors (not satisfying the requirements)	-1
Wrong usage of is-a relationship	-1
Wrong usage of has-a relationship	-1
Wrong usage of association	-1
Modeling errors	-2
Clarity errors	-1
Consistency errors	-10

Table 2. Grades for UML diagrams considered for merging

Criteria	UML 1	UML 2	UML 3
Completeness error	0	0	0
Wrong usage of is -a relationship	0	0	0
Wrong usage of has-a relationship	0	0	0
Modeling errors	-2	-2	-1
Clarity errors	-1	0	-1
Consistency errors	0	0	0
Total grade	**17**	**18**	**18**

components of the domain. Complete or partially complete domain ontology can be obtained by merging multiple ontologies.

We present the rules considered for aggregating these correct UML diagrams to obtain a golden standard. The aggregation of these individual ontologies is done using the following rules: (a) union of all relationships is considered between two similar classes (b) for any association all the classes that it connects are considered. A golden ontology thus obtained is shown in Figure 12.

For purposes of comparison, we define Entity Level Relationship Diagram (ELRD), which is a high level abstracted diagram of the extracted ontology containing only the entities and relationship after removing the properties of class and associations. The following rules are used to obtain ELRD from either EECD or OD.

(a) Properties of a class in a UML diagram (attributes) are specific to a specification. For example, property 'studentid' may appear in some university diagram. In some other university it may be 'studentName'. Since our aim is show that the extracted information is ontology we omit the properties and consider only the entity and relationships. Similarly, attributes of associations are omitted. (b) Inheritance link is replaced by a directed link; Aggregation, composition and using are replaced by just a link. (c) Inheritance is replaced by text 'is-a', Aggregation/compositions is replaced by text 'has-a', using is replaced by the appropriate verb (d) 'has-a' and 'is-a' relationship is given high priority. If two nodes are connected by has-a or is-a, then all other relationship is ignored. (e) Any variable containment is treated (including pointer containment) as 'has-a' relationship. (f) CASE is ignored (g) Naming conflicts are manually resolved through annotations using external sources. (h) Terms are extended with meanings to increase the scope of matching Figure 13 presents the ELRD of the BaseOnt. Base-ELRD is the term used to refer

Figure 12. Golden Ontology – University

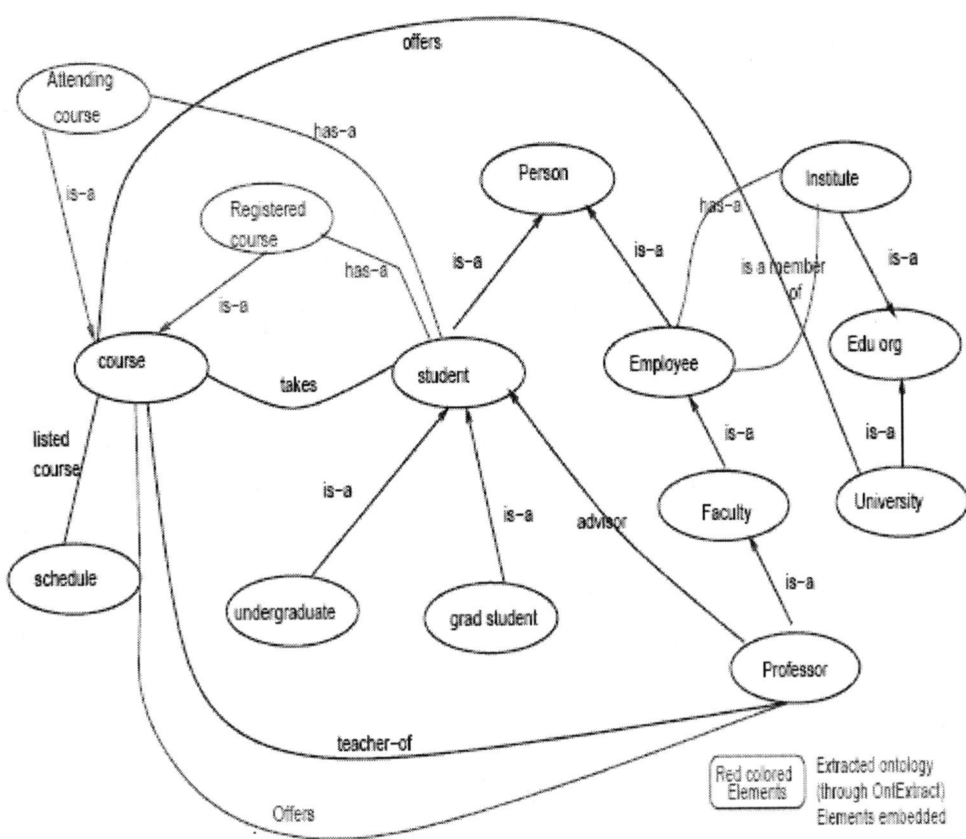

to this ELRD. We compare Base-ELRD with the golden ontology of university (Figure 12). Table 3 presents the inference criteria for determining matches between the golden ontology and the ELRD elements.

Results

Equation 1 gives the quantitative measure of entity level similarity (E_{sim}) observed as the ratio of the number of matching entities(s) between the golden ontology and Base-ELRD to the total number of entities present in the Base-ELRD of the extracted ontology:

$$E_{sim} = n^{E}_{match} / n^{E}_{ELRD} \quad (1)$$

where n^{E}_{match} is the matching entities between the golden ontology and Base-ELRD and n^{E}_{ELRD} give the number of total number of entities present in the Base-ELRD diagram. In the similar way, Equation 2 gives the quantitative measure of relationship level similarity (R_{sim}):

$$R_{sim} = n^{R}_{match} / n^{R}_{ELRD} \quad (2)$$

where n^{R}_{match} is the number of matching relationship(s) between the golden ontology and the Base-ELRD and n^{R}_{ELRD} gives the number of total number of relationship elements present in the Base-ELRD diagram.

Table 4 gives the number of matching entity and relationship elements between the golden ontology and Base-ELRD (Figure 12 and Figure 13). The class Course is related to registered course through

Figure 13. ELRD for student course registration

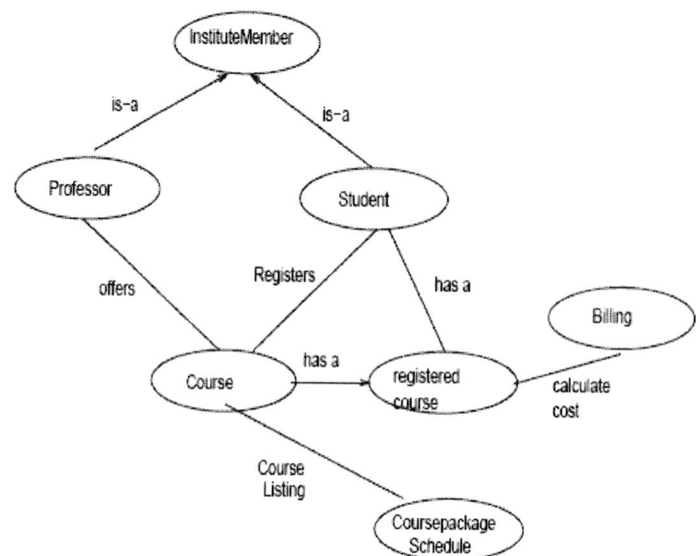

Table 3. Inference rules applicable for matching

Criteria	Name	Extensions to criteria
is-a, has-a		Matched as such
Other IS-A relation-ship(s)	Inference 1	A is-a B is-a C implies A is-a C
	Inference 2	In the above, Property of C is inherited by A
	Inference 3	A has-a B has-a C =) A has-a C
Using relationship	Offer	Matches offer of the standard ontology
	Registers	Since student has registered course and registered course has course, one can conclude that student has course

inference property of 'HAS-A' relationship. Using Table 4 and Equations 1 and 2, we calculate the matching (similarity) entities and relationships metrics as presented in Table 5.

The extracted ontology from the UML diagrams by preserving relationship and entities shows about 85.7% match with the golden standard and about 75% match with the relationships. High values of matching entities and relationships between the extracted ontology through OntExtract and golden ontology show that our approach extracts ontology similar to existing (golden) ontologies. In addition, our method detects other elements that do not have corresponding matches in the golden ontology thereby enriching the existing ontologies with additional elements. This directly proves that our OntExtract method is correct since otherwise there would have been large mismatch between the golden ontology and ontology extracted through OntExtract.

Reusability Evaluation

Design of software solutions is greatly enhanced if the software architect has/gets 'a-priori' knowl-

Table 4. Matching found for golden ontology and extracted ontology

Matching entities	Matching Relationship
Student, Professor, Course (registered course, through inference property of 'HAS-A' relationship), schedule/courselisting, Institutemember. Total: 6	is-a (Professor, institutemember), is-a(Student, institutemember) , has-a (student,course ;sub- Category registered course), Offer (professor, course) term 'offer' is matched with 'teacher-of', has-a (course, registered course), has-a (course [subcategory: registeredcourse], courselisting). Total:6

edge about concepts involved in the problem specification (Marcus A. Rothenberger, 1999). The aim is to show that the extracted ontology is reusable in a number of situations like: (a) Reuse in new solution development (b) Reuse in new problem scenario.

Reuse In New Solution Development

Let us consider a solution for a problem domain to be developed by different group of architects. A solution provided by a group will greatly help the other architects to detect artifacts and provide better solution in the problem. We illustrate this by showing that there exists large amount of common concepts among the solutions, if the solution is developed by different group of architects.

Methodology: We take two different solutions SolB and SolC provided by different group of experts for the course registration problem specification. Comparisons are made to determine the number of common matching entities between these solutions and the BaseOnt. High value of this metric indicates that the ontology from one solution is highly re-usable for new solutions of the problem.

We measure entity reuse (E_{reuse}) as the ratio of number of matching entities with the BaseOnt (n^{BE}_{match}) to total number of entities present in the solution (n^{SE}_{sol}) and is given by Equation 3. In the similar way, Equation 4 gives the relationship reuse R_{reuse}:

Figure 14. Sol B ELRD diagram

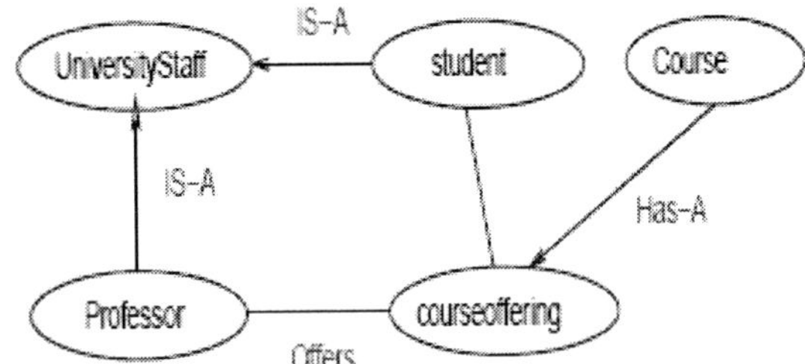

$$E_{reuse} = n^{BE}_{sim} / n^{SE}_{Sol} \quad (3)$$

$$E_{reuse} = n^{BR}_{sim} / n^{SR}_{Sol} \quad (4)$$

where n^{BR}_{sim} is the number of matching relationship(s) with the BaseOnt and n^{SR}_{Sol} is the number of relationship(s) present in the solution. Table 3 was used to obtain the matching entities.

SolB with Base Ontology: The ERLD of the extracted ontology for Solution 1 is provided in Figure 14.

Table 6 presents the matching elements between the ELRD of SolB and Base Ontology. In some cases, inference rules were extended to find similar relationships. For example has-a(course, courseoffering) in Solution 1 is similar to has-a(course, courseoffering) in the BaseOnt through 'courseSchedule'. Classes universityStaff in Solution 1 and instituteMember in BaseOnt represent the same entity and is resolved manually.

Equation 3 and 4 are used to measure re-usability as presented in Table 7. Reuse of entities and relationship(s) has been observed as high as 100% and 80% respectively.

Table 6. Matching for SolB and BaseOnt

Matching Entities	Matching Relationship
Course, Student, courseoffering, Professor, Universitystaff	is-a (professor,university staff),is-a(professor, univeristystaff), has-a(course, courseoffering), Using (Courselisting, student)

Table 7. Comparison of Solution 1 with BaseOnt

Criteria	Number value
Number of entities present in solution 1 ELRD Number of entities matching with base ontology Number of relationship(s) present in the solution 1 ELRD Number of relationship(s) matching with base ontology	5 5 5 4
Re-use of entities present E_{reuse} Re-use of relationship present R_{reuse}	5/5 * 100 = 100% 4/5*100 = 80%

Figure 15. Sol C ELRD diagram

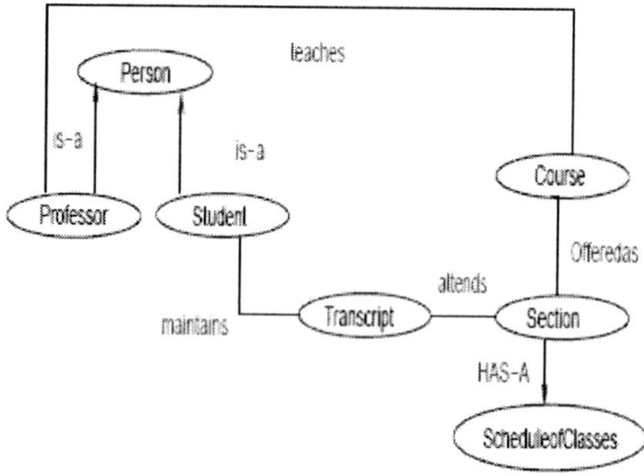

SolC with Base Ontology: Figure 15 gives the ELRD diagram for Solution 2. Table 8 gives the matching elements between ELRD of Sol2 and BaseOnt. Class person match is obtained using extended annotations using external source. Reusability is calculated as shown in Table 9.

Our results indicate that there is indeed great amount of reuse ranging from 70% -100% entity level and 57% to 80% relationship level reusable components. This shows OntExtract provides provisions for reusing previously available ontology to new solutions.

Table 8. Matching for Solution C and BaseOnt

Matching entities	Matching relationships
student, professor, person, course, scheduleclass	is-a(student, person), is-a(professor, person), teaches(professor,course), has-a(course, schedulecourse)

Reuse in New Problem Scenario

Our approach provides provisions for the software professionals to model the use cases of the new problem as sequence diagram and extract related ontology.

Methodology: The architect provides his solution as design diagrams. We extract the domain concepts through OntExtract and call the ontology as ArchitectOnt. We model the use-case requirement as a sequence diagram and use this as a filter to extract ontology from the BaseOnt. We call this ontology as NewScenarioOnt. We find the number of elements of NewScenarioOnt is present in the ArchitectOnt. High values of this metric indicate that large number of domain entities can be reused.

Table 9. Comparison of Solution 2 with BaseOnt

Criteria	Number value
Number of entities present in solution 2 ELRD Number of entities matching with base ontology Number of relationship(s) present in the solution ELRD Number of relationship(s) matching with base ontology	7 5 7 4
Re-use of entities present E_{reuse} Re-use of relationship present R_{reuse}	5/7 *100 = 71.4% 4/7*100 = 57.14%

Figure 16. Class diagram by architect

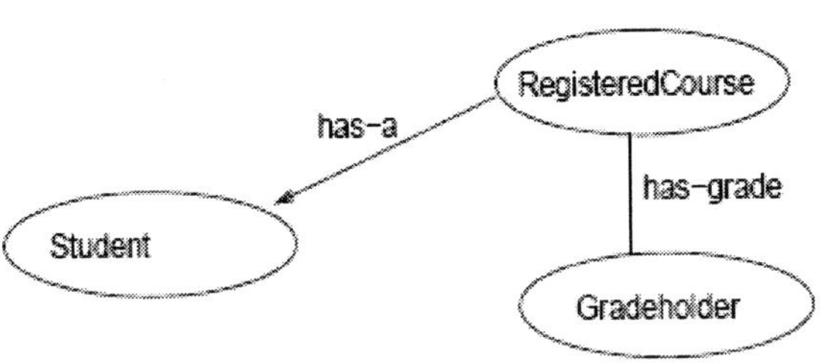

Figure 17. Relevant ontology extracted

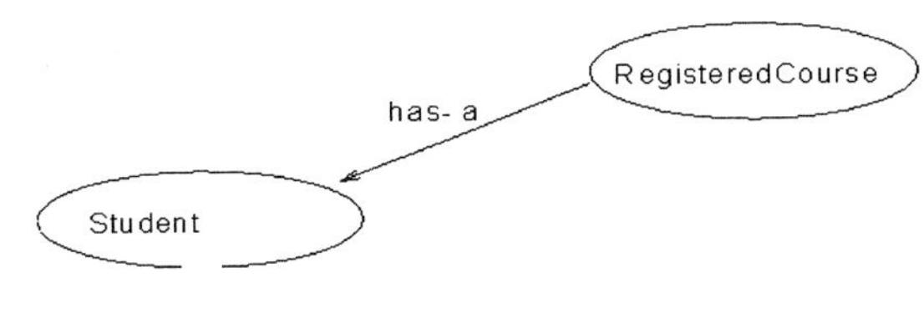

We take an example where the software architects want to design requirements to implement 'ClearDues' use-case of the administration department. The 'ClearDues' checks if the student is valid and have cleared all the courses with clear grades. The architect intends to design new classes and relationship with existing course registration system. For the sake of brevity, only the ELRD diagram (Figure 16) of the class diagram developed by the architect (ArchitectOnt) is provided.

We use the sequence diagram pertaining to 'ClearDues' (Figure 18) as a filter to extract ontology from Figure 6. This ontology extracted is henceforth referred to as the NewScenarioOnt. All the classes in the sequence diagram are considered to extract NewScenarioOnt. The NewScenarioOnt extracted in ELRD form is given in Figure 17.

The results presented in Table 10, indicates that the sequence diagram of a new functionality helps identifying reusable components from previously available solutions. Though this situation is ideal and has 100% reusable components, in practice the amount of re-usability might be less than the one presented here. However, the domain ontology is intended for reuse of domain concepts wherever required; one might expect high values of reusability.

Evaluation on Real World Example

We have taken a real world scenario called "Secure Trade Lanes" (Schaefer, 2006). The description is public but the design diagrams are confidential. It was made available from a business unit in IBM to evaluate our approach on a large scale problem. There were 25 component level diagrams, interaction diagrams (sequence diagram) for use cases. Practical limitations were observed in applying our approach to the real world scenario. The classes were not stereotyped. We had stereotyped the classes manually, since our tool relies on the stereotypes for identifying class level implementation artifacts. The sequence diagrams were at the component level. With the help of architects we had interpreted class level sequence diagrams before using our tool.

The work on real world problem was presented to a group of architects and developers to demonstrate the utility of our plug-in. Their feedbacks

Table 10. Reuse in similar but different domain

Criteria	Number value
Number of matching entities between the NewScenarioOnt and ArchitectOnt Number of matching relationship(s) between the NewScenarioOnt and ArchitectOnt Total number of entities present in the NewScenarioOnt Total number of relationship present in the NewscenarioOnt	2 1 2 1
Reuse of entities Ereuse Reuse of relationship Ereuse	2/2*100 = 100% 1/1*100 = 100%

Figure 18. Sequence diagram for Use case "ClearDues"

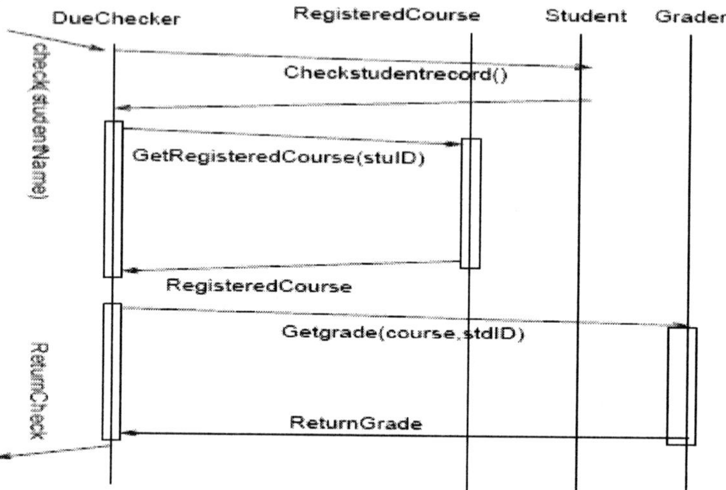

indicate that our tool will be useful to develop better software solution architecture.

Finally as a part of evaluation we present the practical usability of our tool. Table 11 provides the benefits of work for different category of people involved in design and development of software solutions.

CONTRIBUTIONS, LIMITATIONS, RELATED AND FUTURE WORK

We have introduced a novel automatic approach for extracting domain ontology for software asset reuse from multiple design diagrams like UML. We observe that dynamic behavior diagrams act as powerful filters in extracting customizable ontology for new scenario. Our OntExtract extends to aggregate ontology from multiple design diagrams. We have developed an ontology extraction plugin over IBM Rational. We have evaluated our work with a sample domain and a real world example. Our approach shows promising results to provide domain view and reuse of the domain theories to develop new scenarios.

Our main contribution in this article can be summarized as follows:

1. An approach for extracting ontology from UML class diagrams.
    - An approach to refine the extracted ontology using sequence diagram.
    - To obtain ontology relevant to a domain by specifying domain requirements as a set of key words.

Table 11. Advantages and relevance for practice of OntExtract

Users	Advantages	Impact on software development process
Architects	• Provides Domain View from previous knowledge base (rather than implementation) • Provides existing solution approaches for the new problem and helps extract customized ontology	• Obtaining complete domain prior to development is complicated. Our plug-in helps to provide domain view. • Better architectures by providing view of constraints, entities and relationships that would have been otherwise omitted.
Developer	Helps justify implementation decisions and model constraints from existing solutions	Re-usability
Reasoners	• Uniform understanding of the domain • Aggregation of ontology diagrams provides reuse through inference	• Aggregated Domain view from multiple design diagrams • Fosters reuse of components across different but related problems

- o To generate ontology customizable to a new problem domain.

2. An approach to aggregate the extracted ontology using multiple class diagrams of either same or different solutions.

Limitations

The following are the limitations of our work:

1. In our work we have shown extraction of ontology as relevant to a single domain requirement. An incremental approach of extracting ontology with respect to individual domain requirements followed by aggregation of these models will not satisfy the requirements of obtaining single unified ontology with respect to both domains. This is primarily due to fact that individual domain ontology can vary a lot. There will be missing associations between those entities that were extracted with respect to a domain requirement and those entities that were extracted with respect to other domain requirements. A different approach is required to capture more than one domain requirement and extract ontology with respect to both of them.
2. Although we have used analysis class diagram in our work, we are currently working on methodologies that would help identification of stereotypes for classes. For example, we are exploring methods such as code analysis, pattern analysis to categorize classes. In the code analysis methodology, we map the classes in UML diagram to specific stereotype based on the implementation. For example, entity beans can be categorized as entity class, session beans as controller class and servlets and JSPs are boundary class. In pattern based analysis, we analyze the interaction pattern among the class to arrive at a decision of the category of the classes. Such methodologies would enable and promote usage of more commonly available implementation class diagrams as sources of ontology.

Related Work

Significant work has been done in the area of ontology learning and extraction (Alexander, 2001). Various approaches have been used to extract and learn ontology: (a) pattern based approach (Morin, 1999) where a relation is recognized when a sequence of words in the text matches a pattern, (b) association rule approach (Adriaans,1996) where rules are used to match the query, typically used for data mining process, (c) conceptual pruning approach (Faure D, 2000) where the concepts are grouped according to semantic distance, (d) ontology pruning approach (Kietz, 2000), where the objective is to build a domain ontology based on different heterogeneous sources, (e) concept learning approach (Hahn, 2000), where the ontology is incrementally updated with new concepts. OntExtract is precisely an extraction technique that combines rule based approach along with conceptual pruning. Rules define the UML entities to be removed and preserved, while concept pruning groups entities based on semantic distance.

While the above-mentioned work concentrates on ontology sources and techniques to obtain ontological information, there has been significant amount of work done in using UML as an ontology language (Baclawski, 2002). Some work, such as presented in (Cranefield, 2001), aim at converting an UML specification to an Ontology language specification such as OWL (Deborah 2000). Our work does not concentrate on converting or mapping the UML notation (specification) to ontology language specification but concentrate on identifying and preserving elements that represents domain knowledge (ontology).

Close to our work along the lines of using UML diagrams in the field of domain engineering is the work presented in (Cranefield, 2003). The aim of their work is to express the ontology using UML and to automatically generate related ontology specific content language along with corresponding java classes and an RDF based serialization mechanism. The work in (Maurizio, 2000) aims at providing a domain engineering approach and the supporting tools to define software product lines. The approach concentrates on domain engineering (identifying domain, domain analysis, and reusable domain components) and expressing these entities using UML.

Future Work

The work presented in this article brings forward various promising areas as follow-up work which we have set as for exploring in the future. We present some of them below:

1. Exploring extraction of ontology by considering other UML diagrams such as object diagrams and use case diagrams has been left for future work. For example, object diagrams provide information about individuals which are one of the constituents of ontology. Time dependent activities can be captured as ontology from dynamic UML diagrams such as activity and use case diagrams. State diagrams are excellent sources of events that can be captured as ontology.
2. Our experience from the real world example that classes are not stereotyped point out that learning stereotype can also be a promising direction. Learning stereotypes are important not only in the context of ontology learning but also in the context of developing readable models.

Summary

Ontology extraction methods are of great importance to the Semantic Web, because it establishes (semi-) automatic methods of constructing fast and confident ontologies. We have presented a novel automatic ontology extraction methodology (OntExtract) that exploits commonalities in the domain software solutions to build ontologies which would not only help ontology engineers but greatly fosters software reuse. Our work uses design diagram as ontological sources to extract and explicitly represent these common domain concepts.

OntExtract tool provides software professionals a-priori information about domain theories thereby helping them to build faster and improved software solutions. With OntExtract, software professionals can extract domain ontology and ontologies customized to new scenarios. The prime target application of our ontology extraction being software reuse, it by itself serves as a measure for evaluating the resultant ontology. Evaluation results indicate that our method greatly promotes software reuse.

REFERENCES

Adriaans P & Zantinge D (1996), *Data Mining,* Addisson-Wesley.

Bettina Berndt (2005), UML II: Class diagrams, from UML to Java, other UML diagrams, Lecture Series Information systems, http://warhol.wiwi.huberlin.de/berendt/MEMS/information_systems_presentation_oct05.PPT

Bruno,G & Sofia,P. H (2005), *Experiences in Evaluation and Selection of Ontologies,* KCAP 05 workshop on Ontology Management, Oct. 2005 , pp. 25-32.

Baclawski, K. et al (2002), *Extending the Unified Modeling Language for ontology development,* Berlin, NewYork, Journal Software and Systems Modeling (SoSyM), Vol.1, No.2, pp. 142-156.

Cranefield, S (2001), *UML and the Semantic Web,* Palo Alto, Proceedings of the International Semantic Web Working Symposium (SWWS).

Cranefield,S. , Jin,P. & Martin., P. (2003), *A UML ontology and derived content language for a travel - Booking Scenario,* World Wide Web Consortium Web page, http://www.w3.org/RDF/

Donnie,D. (2000), *CS Dept Ontology in SHOE Ontologies in DAML Format,* http://www.cs.umd.edu/projects/plus/DAML/onts/cs1.0.daml

Faure D & Poibeau T (2000), *First experiments of using semantic knowledge learned by ASIUM for information extraction task using INTEX,* Berlin, Germany, Proceedings of the Workshop on Ontology Learning, 14th European Conference on Artificial Intelligence.

Gmez-Prez, A. (1994), *Some Ideas and Examples to Evaluate Ontologies,* tech. report KSL-94-65, Knowledge System Laboratory, Stanford Univ., 1994.

Hassell, J., Aleman-Meza, B., & Arpinar, I.B. (2006), *Ontology-Driven Automatic Entity Disambiguation in Unstructured Text,* th International Semantic Web Conference (ISWC 2006), Athens, GA, November 5–9, 2006, I, Lecture Notes in Computer Science, vol. 4273, Springer, 2006.

Hahn U & Schulz S (2000), *Towards Very Large Terminological Knowledge Bases: A Case Study from Medicine.* In Canadian Conference on AI 2000: 176-186.

IBM Enterprise Architect Kit for SOA (2006), http://www.ibm.com/developerworks/architecture/kits/archkit2/index.html?S_TACT=105AGX23&S_CMP=AKBDD

Jeff Heflin (2000), University Ontology, http://www.cs.umd.edu/projects/plus/SHOE/onts/univ1.0.html

Kietz JU, Maedche A & Volz R (2000), *A Method for Semi-Automatic Ontology Acquisition from a Corporate Intranet,* Juan-Les-Pins, Franc EKAW'00 Workshop on Ontologies and Texts.

Marcus A. Rothenberger, *System Development with Systematic Software Reuse: an Empirical Analysis of Project Success Factors,* Technical report, http://wi99.iwi.uni-sb.de/de/Doktoranden-Seminar_PDF/D_Rothenberger.pdf

Maurizio Morisio, Guilherme H. Travassos & Michael E. Stark (2000), "Extending UML to Support Domain Analysis", Proceedings of the 15th IEEE international conference on Automated software engineering, Page: 321.

Morin E (1999), *Automatic acquisition of semantic relations between terms from technical corpora*, TermNet-Verlag, Vienna, Proc. Of the Fifth Int. Congress on Terminology and Knowledge Engineering (TKE-99).

Oltramari, A. , Gangemi, A. , Guarino. N, & Masol.C (2002), *Restructuring WordNet's Top-Level: The OntoClean approach,* presented at LREC 2002.

Deborah L,M. , Frank,V. H., (2004) , OWL- Web Ontology Language (2004) , http://www.w3.org/TR/owl-features/

Rada.R, Hafedh Mili, Ellen Bicknell, & Maria Blettner (1989). *Development and Application of a Metric on Semantic Nets*, IEEE Transactions on Systems, Man and Cybernetics, 19:17-30.

Rational Software Corporation (2000), Rational Tutorial, www.ibm.com/developerworks

Schaefer,S., (2006), *Secure Trade Lane: A Sensor Network Solution for More Predictable and More Secure Container Shipments*, Portland, Oregon, USA, Dynamic Languages Symposium, Pages: 839 - 845.

Terry Quatrani (2001), *Introduction to the Unified Modeling Language*, Rational Developer Network, http://rational.net//

Terry Quatrani (2002) Visual Modeling with Rational Rose 2002 and UML, (pp 1-100), The Addison-Wesley Object Technology Series.

ADDITIONAL READING

Babenko. L. P. (2003), *Information Support of Reuse in UML-Based Software Engineering, Cybernetics and Systems Analysis,* Hingham, MA, USA, Kluwer Academic Publishers, Volume 39, Issue 1, PP: 65 - 70.

Benslimane, S. M, Malki .M., & Lehirech, A., (2006), *Towards ontology-based semantic web from data-intensive web: A reverse engineering approach,* International Conference on Computer Systems and Applications, pp. 771-778

Carlos,P., Amaia, B., Tim, S., Jessica, A.& Manuel, C., (2004), *A Framework for Ontology Reuse and Persistence Integrating UML and Sesame*, Springer Berlin / Heidelberg, Lecture Notes in Computer Science, Volume 3040/2004, pp: 37-46.

Daniel O, Andreas, E., Steffen,S & Raphael Volz (2004), *Developing and Managing Software Components In An Ontology-Based Application Server,* Toronto, Ontario, Canada, In 5th International Middleware Conference, volume 3231 of LNCS, pp. 459-478. Springer.

Falkovych, K. , Sabou, M. & Stuckenschmidt. H (2003), *UML for the Semantic Web: Transformation-Based Approaches,* Amsterdam, OS Press, Vol. 95 (2003) 92-106

Guizzardi, G., Herre, H. & Wagner G. (2002), *On the General Ontological Foundations of Conceptual Modeling.* Berlin, 21 Intl. Conf. on Conceptual Modeling (ER 2002). Springer-Verlag, Berlin, Lecture Notes in Computer Science, pp : 65—78

Guizzardi, G. & Wagner G. (2002), *Using Formal Ontologies to define Real-World Semantics for UML Conceptual Models.* In 1 Workshop on Application of Ontologies to Biology, European Media Laboratory, Heidelberg, Germany.

Happel, H.-J., Korthaus, A., Seedorf, S., & Tomczyk, P.(2006), *KOntR: An Ontology-Enabled Approach to Software Reuse,* San Francisco, In: Proc. of the 18th Int. Conf. on Software Engineering and Knowledge Engineering (SEKE).

Hyoil, H. & Ramez, E., (2003), *Ontology extraction and conceptual modeling for web information,* Hershey, PA, USA, Information modeling for internet applications, Pages: 174 - 188 .

Stephen,C., & Martin P., (1999), *UML as an Ontology Modelling Language*, Sweden, Workshop on Intelligent Information Integration, 16th International Joint Conference on Artificial Intelligence, volume 23, pp: 46-53

Szyperski. C (2002), *Component Software - Beyond Object- Oriented Programming*, London, 2nd edition, Addison-Wesley.

Odell, J. & Bock, C. (1998), *A More Complete Model of Relations and their Implications: Roles.* Journal of OO Programming, May, 51-54.

Uschold, M., Clark, P., Healy, M., Williamson, K., & Woods, S. (1998), *Ontology Reuse and Application.* Italy, Formal Ontology in Information Systems. IOS Press PP:179-192.

Welty, C.A. & Ferrucci, D.A.(1999) ,A formal ontology for re-use of software architecture documents, Cocoa Beach, FL, USA, Automated Software Engineering, PP: 259-262.

Yang, J. & Chung, I. (2006), *Automatic Generation of Service Ontology from UML Diagrams for Semantic Web Services* , Springer Berlin / Heidelberg, Lecture Notes in Computer Science, Volume 4185/2006, pp: 523-529.

Compilation of References

Aberer, K. (2001). P-Grid: A Self-Organizing Access Structure for P2P Information Systems. In C. Batini, F. Giunchiglia, P. Giorgini, M. Mecella (Eds.), *Proceedings of the 6th International Conference on Cooperative Information Systems, LNCS Vol. 2172* (pp. 179-194). Berlin, Germany: Springer.

Aberer, K., & Cudrè-Mauroux, P. (2005). Semantic Overlay Networks. In Proc. of the 31st International Conference on Very Large Data Bases (VLDB), Tutorial, 1367.

Aberer, K., & Despotovic, Z. (2001). Managing Trust in a Peer-2-Peer Information System. In H. Paques, L. Liu, D. Grossman (Eds.), *Proceedings of the 10th ACM International Conference on Information and Knowledge Management* (pp. 310-317). New York, NY, USA: ACM.

Aberer, K., & Hauswirth, M. (2002). An Overview on Peer-To-Peer Information Systems. In W. Litwin, G. Lévy (Eds.), *Proceedings of the 4th International Workshop on Distributed Data and Structures* (pp.171-188). Waterloo, Ontario, Canada: Carleton Scientific.

Aberer, K., Cudré-Mauroux, P., Hauswirth, M., & van Pelt, T. (2004). GridVine: Building Internet-Scale Semantic Overlay Networks. In Proc. of the 3rd International Semantic Web Conferenc (ISWC), 107-121.

Aberer, K., Datta, A., Hauswirth, M., & Schmidt, R. (2005). Indexing Data-Oriented Overlay Networks. In Proc. of the 31st International Conference on Very Large Databases (VLDB), 685-696.

Aberer, K., Hauswirth, M., & Cudrè-Mauroux, P. (2002). A Framework for Semantic Gossiping. ACM SIGMOD Record, 31(4), 48–53.

Aberer, K., Hauswirth, M., Punceva, M., & Schmidt, R. (2002). Improving Data Access in P2P Systems. *IEEE Internet Computing, 6(1)*, 58-67.

Aberer, K., Klemm, F., Rajman, M., & Wu, J. (2004). An Architecture for Peer-to-Peer Information Retrieval. In J. Callan, N. Fuhr, W. Nejdl (Eds.), *Proceedings of the 2004 ACM International Workshop on Peer-to-Peer Information Retrieval* in conjunction with the *27th ACM International Conference on Research and Development in Information Retrieval* (online edition available at http://p2pir.is.informatik.uni-duisburg.de/16.pdf). New York, NY, USA: ACM.

Abiteboul, S., Hull, R. & Vianu, V. (1995) *Foundations of Databases: The Logical Level.* Addison Wesley.

ACE: NIST, 2003, Automatic Content Extraction. www.nist.gove/speech/tests/ace

Adamic, L. A. & Adar, E. (2005). How to Search a Social Network. *Social Networks,* 27 (3), 187-203.

Adar, E., Karger, D., & Stein, L. A. (1999). Haystack: Per-user information environments. In *Proceedings of the Conference on Information and Knowledge Management.*

Adriaans P & Zantinge D (1996), *Data Mining,* Addison-Wesley.

Adwait, R. (1996). Maximum Entropy Model for POS tagging. In *Proceedings of the Conference on Empirical Methods in Natural Language Processing.* pp.133-142. Somerset, New Jersey, 1996.

Afsharchi, M. & Far, B. H. (2006). Improving Example Selection for Agents Teaching Ontology Concepts.

In Proceedings of the 10th International Workshop on Cooperative Information Agents, CIA '06, Edinburgh, UK, 228-242.

Agichtein, E. & Gravano, L. (2000). Snowball: Extracting Relations from Large Plain-Text Collections. In *Proceedings of the 5th ACM International Conference on Digital Libraries (JCDL'00).*

Ahmed, M., Hanh, H. H., Karim, S., Khusro, S., Lanzenberger, M., Latif, K., Michlmayr, E., Khabib, M., Nguyen, H. T., Rauber, A., Schatten, A., Nguyen, M. T., & Tjoa, A. M. (2004). Semanticlife — a framework for managing information of a human lifetime. In *Proceedings of the 6th International Conference on Information Integration and Web-based Applications and Services (IIWAS).*

Ahn, D. (2006). The Stages of Event Extraction. *In Proceedings of the Workshop on Annotating and Reasoning about Time and Events.* pp. 1–8. Sydney, July 2006.

Aichholzer, G., Spitzenberger, M., Winkler, R. (2003, April). Prisma Strategic Guideline 6: eTourism. Retrieved January 13, 2007, from: http://www.prisma-eu.net/deliverables/sg6tourism.pdf

Alani, H., Kim, S., Millard, D., Weal, M., Hall, W., Lewis, P., & Shadbolt, N. (2003). Automatic Ontology-Based Knowledge Extraction from Web Documents. *IEEE Intelligent Systems, 18*(1): 14-21.

Albertoni, R., Bertone, A., & Martino, M.D. (2004). Semantic Web and Information Visualization. *In Proceedings of Semantic Web Applications and Perspectives.* Italy, December 2004.

Aleman-Meza, B., Nagarajan, M., Ramakrishnan, C., Ding, L., Kolari P., Sheth, A.P., Arpinar, I. B., Joshi, A., & Finin, T. (2006). Semantic Analytics on Social Networks: Experiences in Addressing the Problem of Conflict of Interest Detection. *In Proceedings of the 15th International World Wide Web Conference.* pp.407-416. Edinburgh, UK, May 2006.

Alexaki, S., Christophides, V., Karvounarakis, G., & Plexousakis, D. (2001). On storing voluminous RDF descriptions: The case of web portal catalogs. In *Proceedings of the 4th International Workshop on the the Web and Databases.* ICSFORTH.

Alexaki, S., Karvounarakis, G., Christophides, V., Plexousakis, D., & Tolle, K. (2001). The ICS-FORTH RDFSuite: Managing Voluminous RDF Description Bases. *In Proceedings of 2nd International Workshop on the Semantic Web.* pp. 1-13. Hong Kong, May 2001.

Allen, J. (1994). Natural Language Understanding (2nd Edition). Addison Wesley. 1994

Altun, Y., Tsochantaridis, I., & Hofmann, T. (2003). Hidden Markov Support Vector Machines. *In Proceedings of the 20th International Conference on Machine Learning (ICML 2003).*

Anderson, M. L., Gomaa, W., Grant, J. & Perlis, D. (2005). On the Reasoning of Real-World Agents: Toward a Semantics for Active Logic. *In Proceedings of the 7th International Symposium on Logical Formalizations of Commonsense Reasoning, Corfu, Greece.*

Androutsellis-Theotokis, S., & Spinellis., D. (2004). A Survey of Peer-to-Peer Content Distribution Technologies. ACM Computing Surveys, 36(4), 335–371.

Angele, J., Boley, H., de Bruijn, J., Fensel, D., Hitzler, P., Kifer, M., Krummenacher, R., Lausen, H., Polleres, A. & Studer, R. (2005). *Web Rule language (WRL).* W3C Member Submission, from http://www.w3.org/Submission/WRL/

Antoniou, G. and Harmelen, F. V. (2003). *A Semantic Web Primer*, The MIT Press.

Antoniou, G., Harmelen, F. V. (2004). Web Ontology Language: OWL. In Staab, S., Studer, R. (Eds.): Handbook on Ontologies. International Handbooks on Information Systems, Springer, pp. 67-92.

Anyanwu, K. & Sheth, A.P. (2003). ρ-Queries: Enabling Querying for Semantic Associations on the Semantic Web. *In Proceedings of 12th International World Wide Web Conference.* pp.690-699. Budapest, Hungary, May 2003.

Anyanwu, K., Maduko, A., & Sheth, A.P. (2005). SemRank: Ranking Complex Relationship Search Results on the Semantic Web. *In Proceedings of 14th International World Wide Web Conference.* pp.117-127. Chiba, Japan, May 2005.

Appelt, D. E. (1999). Introduction to Information Extraction Technology. Tutorial. In *Proceedings of the International Joint Conference on Artificial Intelligence (IJCAI'1999).* August 2, 1999, Stockholm, Sweden.

Arenas, M., Kantere, V., Kementsietsidis, A., Kiringa, I., Miller, R.J., & Mylopoulos, J. (2003). The Hyperion Project: From Data Integration to Data Coordination. SIGMOD Record, 32(3), 53-58.

Aussenac-Gilles, N., Biebow, B., & Szulman, S. (2000). Revisiting ontology design: A methodology based on corpus analysis. In *Proceedings of the 12th European Workshop on Knowledge Acquisition, Modeling and Management EKAW '00*, 172-188. London, UK: Springer-Verlag.

Auxilio, M. & Nieto, M. (2003). *An Overview of Ontologies.* Technical Report, Center of Research in Information and Automation Technologies, Interactive and Cooperative Technologies Lab, Universidad de las Americas. Retrieved March 5th from http://www.starlab.vub.ac.be/teaching/ontologies_overview.pdf.

Baader, F., & Hanschke P. (1991). A scheme for integrating concrete domains into concept languages. In *Proc. of the 12th Int. Joint Conf. On Artificial Intelligence (IJCAI'91)*, pp. 452–457.

Baader, F., Calvanese, D., & McGuinness, D. (2003). *The Description Logic Handbook: Theory, Implementation and Applications.* Cambridge University Press.

Baader, F., Horrocks, I. & Sattler, U. (2003). Description Logics as Ontology Languages for the Semantic Web. In D. Hutter & W. Stephan (Eds.), *Festchrift in Honor of Jorg Siekmann, Lecture notes in Artificial Intelligence.* Springer.

Baader, F., Horrocks, I., & Sattler, U. (2005). Mechanizing Mathematical Reasoning. In *2605/2005 of Lecture Notes in Computer Science, chapter Description Logics as Ontology Languages for the Semantic Web,* 228-248. Berlin / Heidelberg, DE: Springer-Verlag.

Babenko. L. P. (2003), *Information Support of Reuse in UML-Based Software Engineering, Cybernetics and Systems Analysis,* Hingham, MA, USA, Kluwer Academic Publishers, Volume 39, Issue 1, PP: 65 - 70.

Bachlechner, D. (October, 2004), D10 v0.2 Ontology Collection in view of an E-Tourism Portal, E-Tourism Working Draft. Retrieved January 15, 2007 from: http://138.232.65.141/deri_at/research/projects/E-Tourism/2004/d10/v0.2/20041005/#Domain

Baclawski, K. et al (2002), *Extending the Unified Modeling Language for ontology development,* Berlin, NewYork, Journal Software and Systems Modeling (SoSyM), Vol.1, No.2, pp. 142-156.

Baeza-Yates, R. & Tiberi, A. (2007). Extracting Semantic Relations from Query Logs. In *Proceedings of KDD2007.*

Balmin, A., Hristidis, V., Papakonstantinou, Y. (2004). ObjectRank: Authority-Based Keyword Search in Databases. In *Proceedings of VLDB*, 2004. 564-575.

Balog, K. & de Rijke, M. (2006). Searching for People in the Personal Work Space. *In Proceedings of International Workshop on Intelligent Information Access.* pp.6-8. Helsinki, Finland, July 2006.

Banko, M., Cafarella, M. J., Soderland, S., Broadhead, M., & Etzioni, O. (2007). Open information extraction from the web. In *Proceedings of the 20th International Joint Conference on Artificial Intelligence*

Baral, C. (2003). *Knowledge Representation, Reasoning and Declarative Problem Solving.* Cambridge University Press.

Barkai, D. (2000). An Introduction to Peer-to-Peer Computing. Intel Developer Update Magazine, February 2000, 1-7.

Barwise, J. & Seligman, J. (1992). The rights and wrongs of natural regularity. In J. Tomberlin (ed.), *Philosophical Perspectives 8: Logic and language.* Atascadero, CA: Ridgeview.

Bastien, C. (1992). The shift between logic and knowledge. *Le courier du CNRS, Numéro Spécial "sciences cognitives"*, No 79, pp.38.

Baum, L. E. & Petrie, T. (1966). Statistical Inference for Probabilistic Functions of Finite State Markov Chains. *Annual of Mathematical statistics*, 37:1554-1563, 1966.

Bawa, M., Manku, G., & Raghavan, P. (2003). SETS: Search Enhanced by Topic Segmentation. In Proc. of the 26th ACM SIGIR Conference, 306-313.

Bechhofer, S., van Harmelen, F., Hendler, J., Horrocks, I., McGuinness, D. L., Patel-Schneider, P. F. & Stein, L. A. (2004). *OWL Web Ontology Language Reference*. W3C Recommendation, from http://www.w3.org/TR/2004/REC-owl-ref-20040210

Beliakov, G., Pradera, A., & Calvo, T. (2007). Aggregation Functions: A Guide for Practitioners. Berlin: Springer.

Bellifemine, F., Poggi, A. & Rimassa, G. (2000). Developing Multi-Agent Systems with JADE. *In Proceedings of the 7th International Workshop on Agent Theories, Architectures and Languages,* Boston, MA.

Ben-Akiva, M., & Lerman, S. (1985). Discrete Choice Analysis: Theory and Application to Travel Demand. Cambridge: MIT Press.

Ben-Ari, M. (2001). *Mathematical Logic for Computer Scientists.* Springer-Verlag.

Bennett, J. (2006, May 25). The Semantic Web is upon us, says Berners-Lee. Silicon.com research panel: WebWatch. Retrieved January 3, 2007, from: http://networks.silicon.com/Webwatch/0,39024667,39159122,00.htm

Benslimane, S. M, Malki .M., & Lehirech, A., (2006), *Towards ontology-based semantic web from data-intensive web: A reverse engineering approach,* International Conference on Computer Systems and Applications, pp. 771-778

Berendt, B., Hotho, A., Mladenic, D., Someren, M.V., Spiliopoulou, M., & Stumme, G. (2003). A Roadmap for Web Mining: From Web to Semantic Web. *In Proceedings of First European Web Mining Forum.* pp.1-22. Croatia, September 2003.

Berger, A., Pietra, S. D., & Pietra, V. D. (1996). A maximum entropy approach to natural language processing. In *Computational Linguistics, Vol.22*, 39-71. MA: MIT Press.

Berglund, A., Boag S., Chamberlin, D., Fernández, M.F., Kay, M., Robie, J., & Siméon, J. (2007). XML Path Language (XPath) 2.0. *World Wide Web Consortium Recommendation.* Online edition available at http://www.w3.org/TR/2007/REC-xpath20-20070123/

Berland, M. & Charniak, E. (1999). Finding parts in very large corpora. In *Proc. of the 37th Annual Meeting of the Association for Computational Linguistics.*

Bernaras, A., Laresgoiti, I., & Corera, J. M. (1996). Building and reusing ontologies for electrical network applications. *ECAI,* 298-302.

Berners-Lee, T. (2006). Artificial Intelligence and the Semantic Web, July, 2006. [online] Available: http://www.w3.org/2006/Talks/0718-aaai-tbl/Overview.html

Berners-Lee, T., Hendler, J., & Lassila, O. (2001). The Semantic Web. *The Scientific American*, 284 (5), 34- 43.

Bernstein, P.A., Giunchiglia, F., Kementsietsidis, A., Mylopoulos, J., Serafini, L., & Zaihrayeu, I. (2002). Data Management for Peer-To-Peer Computing: A Vision. In M.F. Fernandez, Y. Papakonstantinou (Eds.), *Proceedings of the 5th ACM International Workshop on Web and Databases* in conjunction with the *2002 ACM International Conference on Management of Data* (pp. 89-94). New York, NY, USA: ACM.

Bettina Berndt (2005), UML II: Class diagrams, from UML to Java, other UML diagrams, Lecture Series Information systems, http://warhol.wiwi.huberlin.de/berendt/MEMS/information_systems_presentation_oct05.PPT

Bharambe, A., Agrawal, M., & Seshan, S. (2004). Mercury: Supporting Scalable Multi-Attribute Range Queries.

Blaschke, C., Andrade, M. A., Ouzounis, C., & Valencia, A. (1999). Automatic extraction of biological information from scientific text: protein-protein interactions. In *Proceedings of International Conference on Intelligent Systems for Molecular Biology.*

Bloehdorn, S., Petridis, K., Saathoff, C., Simou, N., Tzouvaras, V., Avrithis, Y., Handschuh, S., Kompatsiaris, I., Staab, S., & Strintzis, M. G. (2005). Semantic Annotation of Images and Videos for Multimedia Analysis. In *Proceedings of the 2nd European Semantic Web Conference (ESWC 2005).*

Blythe, J., Chalupsky, H., Gil, Y. & MacGregor, R. (2004). *Ontology-Based Agent Communication with Rosetta.* USC/Information Sciences Institute. Retrieved March 12th from http://www.isi.edu/expect/projects/agents/rosetta.html.

Boag, S., Chamberlin, D., Fernández, M.F., Florescu, D., Robie, J., & Siméon, J. (2007). XQuery 1.0: An XML Query Language. *World Wide Web Consortium Recommendation.* Online edition available at http://www.w3.org/TR/2007/REC-xquery-20070123/

Bonifati, A., & Cuzzocrea, A. (2006). Storing and Retrieving XPath Fragments in Structured P2P Networks. *Data & Knowledge Engineering, 59(2)*, 247-269.

Bonifati, A., Cuzzocrea, A., Matrangolo, U., & Jain, M. (2004). XPath Lookup Queries in P2P Networks. In A.H.F. Laender, D. Lee, M. Ronthaler (Eds.), *Proceedings of the 6th ACM International Workshop on Web Information and Data Management* in conjunction with the *13rd ACM International Conference on Information and Knowledge Management* (pp. 48-55). New York, NY, USA: ACM.

Borst, W. N. (1997). *Construction of Engineering Ontologies.* Centre for Telematica and Information Technology, University of Tweenty. Enschede, The Netherlands.

Borthwick, A., Sterling, J., Agichtein, E., & Grishman, R. (1998). Exploiting Diverse Knowledge Sources via Maximum Entropy in Named Entity Recognition. *In Proceedings of the Sixth Workshop on Very Large Corpora New Brunswick*, New Jersey.

Boser, B. E., Guyon, I. M., & Vapnik, V. N. (1992). A training algorithm for optimal margin classifiers. In D. Haussler (Eds.), *5th Annual ACM Workshop on COLT* (pp. 144-152). Pittsburgh, PA: ACM Press.

Bosse, T., Jonker, C. M. & Treur, J. (2005). Requirements Analysis of an Agent's Reasoning Capabilities. *In Proceedings of the AOIS '05,* 48-63.

Bourret, R. (2001). *Mapping dtds to databases.* Technical report, from http://www.xml.com/lpt/a/2001/05/09/dtd-todbs.html

Bourret, R. (n.d.). *Xml-dbms.* Retrieved from http://www.rpbourret.com/xmldbms/readme.htm

Brachman, R. J. & Levesque, H. J. (2004). *Knowledge Representation and Reasoning.* Morgan Kauffman Publishers.

Branavan, S.R.K., Deshpande, P. & Barzilay, R. (2007). Generating a Table-of-Contents. In *Proceedings of the 45th Annual Meeting of the Association of Computational Linguistics*, pages 544–551, ACL2007

Brank, J., Grobelnik, M., & Mladenic, D. (2005). A survey of ontology evaluation techniques. *SIKDD 2005 at Multiconference IS.*

Bremer, J.-M., & Gertz, M. (2003). On Distributing XML Repositories. In V. Christophides, J. Freire (Eds.), *Proceedings of the 6th ACM International Workshop on Web and Databases* in conjunction with the *2003 ACM International Conference on Management of Data* (pp. 73-78). New York, NY, USA: ACM.

Brewster, C., Alani, H., Dasmahapatra, S. & Wilks, Y. (2004). Data Driven Ontology Evaluation. *Proceedings of Int. Conf. on Language Resources and Evaluation,* Lisbon.

Brézillon, P. (1993). *Context in Artificial Intelligence: II. Key elements of contexts.* Computer and AI.

Brézillon, P. (1999). *Context in problem solving: A survey.* The Knowledge Engineering Review, Volume: 14, Issue: 1, Pages: 1-34.

Brickley, D., & Guha, R.V. (Ed.) (2004 February). *RDF Vocabulary Description Language 1.0: RDF Schema.* W3C Recommendation. http://www.w3.org/TR/rdf-schema/

Brickley, D., & Miller, L. (2005). FOAF Vocabulary Specification. from http://xmlns.com/foaf/0.1/

Brin, S. (1998). Extracting Patterns and Relations from the World Wide Web. In *Proceedings of the 1998 International Workshop on the Web and Databases (WebDB'98)*

Brody, S. (2007). Clustering Clauses for High-Level Relation Detection: An Information-theoretic Approach. In *Proceedings of the 45th Annual Meeting of the Association of Computational Linguistics (ACL'2007)*, pp. 448–455.

Broekstra, J., Kampman, A., & Harmelen, F. (2002). Sesame: A generic architecture for Storing and Querying RDF and RDF Schema. In *Proceedings of International Semantic Web Conference.* Sardinia, Italy

Broekstra, J., Kampman, A., & van Harmelen, F. (2001). Semantics for the WWW. In *An Architecture for Storing and Querying RDF Data and Schema Information.* MIT Press, 2001, from http://www.cs.vu.nl/frankh/postscript/MIT01.pdf

Broekstra, J., Kampman, A., & van Harmelen, F. (2002). Sesame: A generic architecture for storing and querying rdf and rdf schema. In *ISWC 2002*, from http://www.openrdf.org/doc/papers/SesameISWC2002.pdf.

Brown, S., Peter, F., Della, P., Vincent, J. & Mercer Robert, L. (1991). Word sense disambiguation using statistical methods. *Proceedings of the 29th Annual Meeting of Association for Computational Linguistics*, Berkeley, California.

Bruandet, M.F. (1990). Domain Knowledge Acquisition for an Intelligent Information Retrieval System : Strategies and Tools. In *Expert Systems Applications EXPERSYS - 90*, Grenoble, pp231-235.

Bruno, G & Sofia, P. H (2005), *Experiences in Evaluation and Selection of Ontologies,* KCAP 05 workshop on Ontology Management, Oct. 2005 , pp. 25-32.

Buitelaar, P. & Declerck, T. (2003). Linguistic annotation for the semantic web. In *Annotation for the Semantic Web, Frontiers in Artificial Intelligence and Applications Series, Vol. 96.* IOS Press.

Buitelaar, P., Olejnik, D. & Sintek, M. (2004). *A protege plug-in for ontology extraction from text based on linguistic analysis.* ESWS.

Bunescu, R. & Mooney, R. J. (2005b). Statistical relational learning for natural language information extraction. In Getoor, L., & Taskar, B. (Eds.), *Statistical Relational Learning*, forthcoming book

Bunescu, R. C. & Mooney, R. J. (2005a). Subsequence Kernels for Relation Extraction. In *Proceedings of the 19th Annual Conference on Neural Information Processing Systems*, Vancouver, British Columbia

Bunescu, R.C. & Mooney, R.J. (2004). Collective Information Extraction with Relational Markov Networks. *In Proceedings of Association of Computing Linguistics (ACL'2004).*

Bunescu, R.C. & Mooney, R.J. (2007). Learning to Extract Relations from the Web using Minimal Supervision. In *Proceedings of the 45th Annual Meeting of the Association of Computational Linguistics* (ACL2007), pp. 576-583.

Bush, V. (1945). As we may think. *The Atlantic Monthly, 176(7)*,101–108.

Bussler, C. (2003). The Role of Semantic Web Technology in Enterprise Application Integration. IEEE Data Engineering Bulletin. Vol. 26, No. 4, pp. 62-68.

Buyukkokten, O., Garcia-Molina, H. & Paepcke, A. (2001). Accordion summarization for end-game browsing on PDAs and Cellular Phones. In *Proc. Of Conference on Human Factors in Computing Systems (CHI01).*

Cafarella, M.J., Downey, D., Soderland, S., & Etzioni, O. (2005). KnowItNow: Fast, Scalable Information Extraction from the Web. In *Proceedings of Human Language Technology Empirical Methods in Natural Language Processing (HLT/EMNLP'2005).*

Cai, D., Yu, S., Wen, J. & Ma, W. (2004). Block-based web search. *Proceedings of the 27 Annual International ACM SIGIR Conference on Research and Development in Information Retrieval*, pages 456-463.

Cai, M., & Frank, M. (2004). RDFPeers: A Scalable Distributed RDF Repository based on a Structured Peer-to-Peer Network. In S.I. Feldman, M. Uretsky, M. Najork, C.E. Wills (Eds.), *Proceedings of the 13rd International World Wide Web Conference* (pp. 650-657). New York, NY, USA: ACM.

Cai, M., Frank, M., Chen, J., & Szekely, P. (2004). Maan: a Multi-Attribute Addressable Network for Grid Information Services. Journal of Grid Computing, 2(1), 3-14.

Cali, A. & Lukasiewicz, T. (2007). *Tightly Integrated Probabilistic Description Logic Programs.* Technical Report, Institut für Informationssysteme, TU Wien.

Cali, A., Lukasiewicz, T., Predoiu, L. & Stuckenschmidt, H. (2008). Tightly Integrated Probabilistic Description Logic Programs for Representing Ontology Mappings. In *Proceedings of the International Symposium on Foundations of Information and Knowledge Systems (FOIKS).*

Califf, M. E., & Mooney, R. J. (1998). Relational learning of pattern-match rules for information extraction. In *Working Notes of AAAI Spring Symposium on Applying Machine Learning to Discourse Processing.* pp. 6-11.

Califf, M. E., & Mooney, R. J. (2003). Bottom-up relational learning of pattern matching rules for information extraction. *Journal of Machine Learning Research, Vol.4,* pp.177-210.

Callan, J. (2000). Distributed Information Retrieval. In W.B. Croft (Ed.), *Advances in Information Retrieval* (pp. 127-150). Hingham, MA, USA: Kluwer Academic Publishers.

Callan, J., Powell, A.L., French, J.C., & Connell, M. (2000). *The Effects of Query-based Sampling on Automatic Database Selection Algorithms* (Tech. Rep. No. IR-181). Amherst, MA, USA: University of Massachusetts, Department of Computer Science, Center for Intelligent Information Retrieval.

Calvanese, D., de Giacomo, G., Lembo, D., Lenzerini, M., & Rosati, R. (2005). DL-Lite: Tractable description logics for ontologies. In *Proceedings 20th AAAI conference on Artificial Intelligence.*

Cardoso, J. (2004). Semantic Web Processes and Ontologies for the Travel Industry. AIS SIGSEMIS Bulletin. Vol. 1, No. 3, pp. 25-28.

Cardoso, J. (2006). Developing An Owl Ontology For e-Tourism. In Cardoso, J. & Sheth, P. A. (Eds.). Semantic Web Services, Processes and Applications (pp. 247-282), Springer.

Cardoso, J. (2006). Developing Dynamic Packaging Systems using Semantic Web Technologies. Transactions on Information Science and Applications. Vol. 3(4). 729-736.

Carlos,P., Amaia, B., Tim, S., Jessica, A.& Manuel, C., (2004), *A Framework for Ontology Reuse and Persistence Integrating UML and Sesame*, Springer Berlin / Heidelberg, Lecture Notes in Computer Science, Volume 3040/2004, pp: 37-46.

Castillo, E., Gutierrez, J. M. & Hadi. A. S. (1997). *Expert systems and probabilistic network models.* Springer-Verlag

Castro, M., Costa, M., & Rowstron, A. (2004). *Peer-To-Peer Overlays: Structured, Unstructured, or Both?* (Tech. Rep. MSR-TR-2004-73). Cambridge, England: Microsoft Research.

Chalendar, G. & Grau, B. (2000). SVETLAN A system to classify nouns in context. *Proceedings of the ECAI 2000 Workshop on Ontology Learning.*

Chang, M., Ratinov, L., & Roth D. (2007). Guiding Semi-Supervision with Constraint-Driven Learning. In *Proceedings of the 45th Annual Meeting of the Association of Computational Linguistics (ACL2007),* pages 280–287

Chen, H., Finin, T. & Joshi, A. (2003). Using OWL in a Pervasive Computing Broker. *In Proceedings of the Workshop on Ontologies in Agent Systems, AAMAS '03, Melbourne, Australia.*

Chen, S. F. & Rosenfeld, R. (1999). A Gaussian prior for smoothing maximum entropy models. *Technical Report CMU-CS-99-108*, Carnegie Mellon University.

Chieu, H.L. (2002). A Maximum Entropy Approach to Information Extraction from Semi-Structured and Free Text. *In Proceedings of the Eighteenth National Conference on Artificial Intelligence (AAAI'2002)*. pp.786-791.

Chirita, P. A., Costache, S., Nejdl, W., & Paiu, R. (2006). Beagle++: Semantically Enhanced Searching and Ranking on the Desktop. Proceedings of The Semantic Web: Research and Applications. Springer Berlin / Heidelberg, 2006. 348–362.

Cho, M. J., Kim, H., Kim, S. H., Lee, H. J., Hong, S. C., & Jung, M. J. (2007). *Context knowledge modelling method for sharing and reusing context knowledge in context-aware system*, vol. US2007038438, pp. 10.

Chu-Carroll, J. & Prager, J. An Experimental Study of the Impact of Information Extraction Accuracy on Semantic Search Performance. In *Proceedings of Conference on Information and Knowledge Management (CIKM2007)*.

Church, K., Patil, R. (1982). Coping with Syntactic Ambiguity or How to Put the Block in the Box. American Journal of Computational Linguistics, 8(3-4).

Cilibrasi, R. & Vitanyi, P. (2006). Automatic Extraction of Meaning from the Web. *The IEEE International Symposium on Information Theory*, Seattle, WA.

Cimiano, P. & Volker, J. (2005). *Towards large-scale, open-domain and ontology-based named entity classification*. RANLP.

Cimiano, P., Handschuh, S., & Staab, S. (2004). Towards the self-annotating web. In *Proceedings of the Thirteenth International Conference on World Wide Web*. pp. 462-471.

Cimiano, P., Ladwig, G., & Staab, S. (2005). Gimme' the context: context-driven automatic semantic annotation with C-PANKOW. In *Proceedings of the 14th World Wide Web Conference*.

Ciravegna, F. (2001). $(LP)^2$, an adaptive algorithm for information extraction from Web-related texts. In *Proceedings of the IJCAI-2001 Workshop on Adaptive Text Extraction and Mining held in conjunction with 17th International Joint Conference on Artificial Intelligence (IJCAI)*, Seattle, USA.

Clarke, I., Sandberg, O., Wiley, B., & Hong, T.W. (2000). Freenet: A Distributed Anonymous Information Storage and Retrieval System. In H. Federrath (Ed.), *Proceedings of the ICSI Workshop on Design Issues in Anonymity and Unobservability, LNCS Vol. 2009* (pp. 311-320). Berlin, Germany: Springer.

Claveau, V., Sebbillot, P., Fabre, C.& Bouillon, P. (2003). Learning Semantic Lexicons from a Part-of-Speech and Semantically Tagged Corpus using Inductive Logic Programming. *Journal of Machine Learning Research, special issue on ILP.*

Collins, M. (2002). Discriminative Training Methods for Hidden Markov Models: Theory and Experiments with Perceptron Algorithms. In *Proceedings of the Conference on Empirical Methods in Natural Language Processing (EMNLP'2002)*. pp.1-8, July 06, 2002.

Comito, C., Patarin, S., & Talia, D. (2005). PARIS: A Peer-to-Peer Architecture for Large-Scale Semantic Data Integration. In Proc. of the International Workshop on Databases, Information Systems, and Peer-to-Peer Computing (DBISP2P), 163-170.

Compton, P. & Jansen R. (1988). Knowledge in context: a strategy for expert system maintenance. In J.Siekmann (Ed), *Lecture Notes in Artificial Intelligence, Subseries in computer sciences*, Vol. 406.

Cooper, B. (2004). Using Information Retrieval Techniques to Route Queries in an InfoBeacons Network. In Proc. of the International Workshop on Databases, Information Systems, and Peer-to-Peer Computing (DBISP2P), 46-60.

Cooper, B. F., & Garcia-Molina, H. (2005). Ad Hoc, Self-Supervising Peer-to-Peer Search Networks. ACM Transactions on Information Systems, 23(2), 169-200.

Costa, P. C. G. & Laskey, K. B. (2006). *PR-OWL:* A Framework for Probabilistic Ontologies. In *Proceedings of the International Conference on Formal Ontology in Information Systems (FOIS).*

Cowell, R. G., Dawid, A. P., Lauritzen, S. L. & Spiegelhalter, D. J. (1999). *Probabilistic Networks and Expert Systems*. Springer-Verlag.

Crainiceanu, A., Linga, P., Gehrke, J., & Shanmugasundaram, J. (2004). Querying Peer-to-Peer Networks Using P-Trees. In S. Amer-Yahia, L. Gravano (Eds.), *Proceedings of the 7th ACM International Workshop on Web and Databases* in conjunction with the *2004 ACM International Conference on Management of Data* (pp. 25-30). New York, NY: ACM.

Cranefield, S (2001), *UML and the Semantic Web*, Palo Alto, Proceedings of the International Semantic Web Working Symposium (SWWS).

Cranefield, S., Jin, P., & Martin, P. (2003), *A UML ontology and derived content language for a travel - Booking Scenario*, World Wide Web Consortium Web page, http://www.w3.org/RDF/

Crescenzi, V, Mecca, G., & Merialdo, P. (2001). RoadRunner: Towards Automatic Data Extraction from Large Web Sites. In *Proceedings of the 27th International Conference on Very Large Data Bases* (VLDB'2001). pp. 109-118.

Crespo, A., & Garcia-Molina, H. (2002). Routing Indices For Peer-to-Peer Systems. In L.E.T. Rodrigues, M. Raynal, W.-S.E. Chen (Eds.), *Proceedings of the 22nd IEEE International Conference on Distributed Computing Systems* (pp. 23-34). Los Alamitos, CA, USA: IEEE Computer Society.

Crespo, A., & Garcia-Molina, H. (2002). Routing Indices for Peer-to-Peer Systems. In Proc. of the 22nd IEEE International Conference on Distributed Computing Systems (ICDCS), 23-34.

Crespo, A., & Garcia-Molina, H. (2003). Semantic Overlay Networks for P2P Systems. In G. Moro, S. Bergamaschi, K. Aberer (Eds.), *Proceedings of the 3rd International Workshop on Agents and Peer-to-Peer Computing, LNAI Vol. 3601* in conjunction with the *3rd International Joint Conference on Autonomous Agents and Multi Agent Systems* (pp. 1-13). Berlin, Germany: Springer.

Cuenca-Acuna, F.M., Peery, C., Martin, R.P., & Nguyen, T.D. (2003). PlanetP: Using Gossiping to Build Content Addressable Peer-to-Peer Information Sharing Communities. In Proc. of the 12th International Symposium on High-Performance Distributed Computing (HPDC), 236-249.

Culotta, A. & Sorensen, J. (2004). Dependency tree kernels for relation extraction. In *Proceedings of the 42nd Annual Meeting of the Association for Computational Linguistics* (pp. 423-429). Barcelona, Spain

Culotta, A., McCallum, A., & Betz, J. (2006). Integrating Probabilistic Extraction Models and Data Mining to Discovering Relations and Patterns in Text. In *Proceedings of the Human Language Technology Conference of the North American Chapter of the ACL* (pp. 296-303). New York.

Cunningham, H. (2002). GATE, a General Architecture for Text Engineering. Computers and the Humanities. 36 (2). 223–254.

Cunningham, H., Maynard, D. & Tablan, V. (2000). JAPE: A Java annotation patterns engine. Department of Computer Science, University of Sheffield

Cunningham, H., Maynard, D., Bontcheva, K., & Tablan, V. (2002). GATE: a framework and graphical development environment for robust NLP tools and applications. In *Proceedings of the 40th Anniversary Meeting of the Association for Computational Linguistics (ACL'02)*

Daniel O, Andreas, E., Steffen,S & Raphael Volz (2004), *Developing and Managing Software Components In An Ontology-Based Application Server*, Toronto, Ontario, Canada, In 5th International Middleware Conference, volume 3231 of LNCS, pp. 459-478. Springer.

Dar, S., Franklin, M. J., Jónsson, B. T., Srivastava, D., & Tan, M. (1996). Semantic Data Caching and Replacement. *In Proceedings of 22nd International Conference on Very Large Data Bases*. pp.330-341. Bombay, India, September 1996.

Darroch, J. N., & Ratcliff, D. (1972). Generalized iterative scaling for log-linear models. *The Annals of Mathematical Statistics, 43 (5)*, 1470-1480.

Daswani, N., Garcia-Molina, H., & Yang, B. (2003). Open Problems in Data-Sharing Peer-To-Peer Systems. In D. Calvanese, M. Lenzerini, R. Motwani (Eds.), *Proceedings of the 9th International Conference on Database Theory, LNCS Vol. 2572* (pp. 1-15). Berlin, Germany: Springer.

Datar, M. (2002). Butterflies and Peer-To-Peer Networks. In R.H. Möhring, R. Raman (Eds.), *Proceedings of the 10th Annual European Symposium on Algorithms, LNCS Vol. 2461* (pp. 310-322). Berlin, Germany: Springer.

Datta, A., Girdzijauskas, S., & Aberer, K. (2004). On de Bruijn Routing in Distributed Hash Tables: There and Back Again. In G. Caronni, N. Weiler, N. Shahmehri (Eds.), *Proceedings of the 4th IEEE International Conference on Peer-to-Peer Computing* (pp. 159-166). Los Alamitos, CA, USA: IEEE Computer Society.

Davidov, D., Rappoport, A., & Koppel, M. (2007). Fully Unsupervised Discovery of Concept-Specific Relationships by Web Mining. In *Proceedings of the 45th Annual Meeting of the Association of Computational Linguistics* (ACL2007), pp. 232–239.

Davidson, C., Voss, P. (2002). Knowledge Management. Auckland: Tandem.

Davies, J., Duke, A., Stonkus, A. (2003). OntoShare: Evolving Ontologies in a Knowledge Sharing System. Towards the Semantic Web: Ontology-Driven Knowledge Management, pp. 161-177.

Davies, J., Weeks, R., Krohn. U. (2003). QuizRDF: Search Technology for the Semantic Web. Towards the Semantic Web: Ontology-Driven Knowledge Management, pp. 133-43.

Davulcu, H., Vadrevu, S. & Nagarajan, S. (1998). OntoMiner: Boostrapping ontologies from overlapping domain specific web sites. In AAAI'98/IAAI'98 *Proceedings of the 15th National Conference on Artificial Intelligence* and the *10th Conference on Innovative Applications of Artificial Intelligence.*

de Bruijn & J., Heymans, S. (2007). Logical Foundations of (e)RDF(S): Complexity and Reasoning. In *Proceedings of the International Semantic Web Conference (ISWC).*

De Jong, K.A. (1994). Genetic Algorithms: A 25 Year Perspective. *Computational Intelligence Life,* 68, 125-134.

De Raedt, L., Kimmig, A. & Toivonen, H. (2007). ProbLog: A Probabilistic Prolog and Its Application in Link Discovery. In *Proceedings of the 20th International Joint Conference on Artificial Intelligence.*

De, S., & Moessner, K. (2007). Context gathering in ubiquitous environments: enhanced service discovery. In *Proceedings of the 3rd Workshop on Context Awareness for Proactive Systems (CAPS'2007),* Guildford, UK.

Dean, M., & Schreiber, G. (Ed.) (2004 February). *OWL Web Ontology Language Reference.* W3C Recommendation. http://www.w3.org/TR/owl-ref/

Deborah L.M., Frank,V. H., (2004) , OWL- Web Ontology Language (2004) , http://www.w3.org/TR/owl-features/

Decker, S., Melnik, S., van Harmelen, F., Fensel, D., Klein, M. C. A., Broekstra, J., Erdmann, M., & Horrocks, I. (2000). The Semantic Web: The Roles of XML and RDF. IEEE Internet Computing, 4(5), 63-74.

Decker, S., Melnik, S., van Harmelen, F., Fensel, D., Klein, M., Broekstra, J., et al. (2000). The Semantic Web: The roles of XML and RDF. *IEEE Internet Computing,* 4(5), 63-67.

Deen, S. M. & Ponnaperuma, K. (2006). Dynamic Ontology Integration in a Multi-agent Environment. *In Proceedings of the 20th International Conference on Advanced Information Networking and Applications (AINA '06),* 373-378.

Deerwester, S., Dumais, S.T., Furnas, G.W., Landauer, T.K., & Harshman, R. (1999). Indexing by Latent Semantic Analysis. *Journal of the American Society for Information Science, 41(6),* 391-407.

Dell'erba, M., Fodor, O. Hopken, W., Werthner, H. (2005). Exploiting Semantic Web technologies for harmonizing E-Markets. Information Technology & Tourism. 7(3-4). 201-219(19).

Dietterich, T. (2002). Machine Learning for Sequential Data: A Review. In *Proceedings of the Joint IAPR International Workshop on Structural, Syntactic, and Statistical Pattern Recognition.* pp. 15–30. 2002. Springer-Verlag.

Dijkstra, E. (1959). A Note on Two Problems in Connexion with Graphs. *Numerische Mathematik*, 1, 269-271.

Dill, S., Gibson, N., Gruhl, D., Guha, R., Jhingran, A., Kanungo, T., Rajagopalan, S., Tomkins, A., Tomlin, J. A., & Zien, J.Y. (2003). SemTag and Seeker: bootstrapping the semantic web via automated semantic annotation. In *Proceedings of the Twelfth International World Wide Web Conference.* pp. 178-186.

Dillon, S. (2005). Which storage xml? *Oracle Magzine, April 2005*, from http://www.oracle.com/technology/oramag/oracle/05mar/o25xmlex.html.

Ding, H., Solvberg, I.T., & Lin, Y. (2004). A Vision on Semantic Retrieval in P2P Networks. In L. Barolli (Ed.), *Proceedings of the 18th IEEE International Conference on Advanced Information Networking and Applications, Vol. 1* (pp. 177-182). Los Alamitos, CA, USA: IEEE Computer Society.

Ding, L. & Finin, T.W. (2005). Boosting Semantic Web Data Access Using Swoogle. *In Proceedings of the 20th National Conference on Artificial Intelligence.* pp.1604-1605. Pittsburgh, Pennsylvania, July 2005.

Ding, L., Finin, T., Joshi, A., Cost, R. S., Peng, Y., Reddivari, P., Doshi, V., Sachs, J. (2004). Swoogle: a search and metadata engine for the semantic web. In *Proceedings of the thirteenth ACM international conference on Information and knowledge management*, New York, NY, USA: ACM Press, 2004. 652–659.

Ding, L., Kolari, P., Ding, Z. & Avancha, S. (2006). BayesOWL: Uncertainty Modeling in Semantic Web Ontologies. In *Soft Computing in Ontologies and Semantic Web.* Springer Verlag..

Ding, L., Pan, R., & Finin, T., Joshi, A., Peng, Y., & Kolari, P. (2005). Finding and Ranking Knowledge on the Semantic Web. In *Proceedings of ISWC*, 2005. 156–170.

Dingli, A., Ciravegna, F., & Wilks, Y. (2003). Automatic semantic annotation using unsupervised information extraction and integration. In *Proceedings of K-CAP 2003 Workshop on Knowledge Markup and Semantic Annotation.*

Dinh-Khac, D., Hölldobler, S. & Tran, D. K. (2006). The fuzzy linguistic description logic ALC_{FL}. *Proceedings of the 11th International Conference on Information Processing and Management of Uncertainty in Knowledge-Based Systems,* 2096-2103.

Djuric, D., Devedzic, V. & Gasevic, D. (2007). Adopting Software Engineering Trends in AI. *IEEE Intelligent Systems.* 22(1). 59-66.

Do, H. & Rahm, E. (2002). Coma: A System for Flexible Combination of Schema Matching Approaches. *In Proceedings of 28th International Conference on Very Large Data Bases.* pp.610-621. Hong Kong, August 2002.

Doan, A., Madhavan, J., Domingos, P. & Halevy, A. (2003). Ontology Matching: A Machine Learning Approach. In *Handbook on Ontologies in Information Systems* (pp 397-416), Springer-Verlag.

Doan, A.H., Madhavan, J., Domingos, P., & Halevy, A. (2002). Learning to Map Between Ontologies on the Semantic Web. *In Proceedings of the 11th World Wide Web Conference.* pp.662–673. Hawaii, USA, May 2002.

Dogac, A., Kabak ,Y., Laleci, G., Sinir, S., Yildiz, A. Tumer, A. (2004). SATINE Project : Exploiting Web Services in the Travel Industry . eChallenges 2004 (e-2004), 27 - 29 October 2004, Vienna, Austria.

Donaldson, I., Martin, J., Bruijn, B., Wolting, C., Lay, V., Tuekam, B., Zhang, S., Baskin, B., Bader, G., Michalickova, K., Pawson, T., & Hogue, C. W. (2003). PreBIND and Textomy – mining the biomedical literature for protein-protein interactions using a support vector machine. *BMC Bioinformatics*, 4:11.

Donnie,D. (2000), *CS Dept Ontology in SHOE Ontologies in DAML Format*, http://www.cs.umd.edu/projects/plus/DAML/onts/cs1.0.daml

Dou, D., McDermott, D. V. & Peishen, Q. (2002). Ontology Translation by Merging Ontologies and Automated Reasoning. *In Proceedings of the EKAW2002, Workshop on Ontologies for Multi-Agent Systems,* 3-18.

Doulkeridis, C., Nørvåg, K., & Vazirgiannis, M. (2007). DESENT: Decentralized and Distributed Semantic Overlay Generation in P2P Networks. IEEE Journal on Selected Areas in Communications, 25(1), 25-34.

Downey, D., Etzioni, O., & Soderland, S. (2005). A probabilistic model of redundancy in information extraction. In *Proceedings of the 19th International Joint Conference on Artificial Intelligence*. Edinburgh, Scotland.

Dubois, D., & Prade, H. (2004). On the use of aggregation operations in information fusion processes. Fuzzy Sets and Systems, 142(1), 143-161.

Duchi, J., Tarlow, D., Elidan, G. & Koller, D. (2006) Using Combinatorial Optimization within Max-Product Belief Propagation. In *Proceedings of Advances in Neural Information Processing Systems (NIPS2006)*

Durbin, R., Eddy, S., Krogh, A., & Mitchison, G. (1998). Biological sequence analysis: Probabilistic models of proteins and nucleic acids. Cambridge University Press, 1998.

Durfee, E. H., & Lesser, V. (1989). Negotiating Task Decomposition and Allocation Using Partial Global Planning. In *L.* Gasser & M. Huhns (eds), *Distributed Artificial Intelligence, Vol. 2, 229-244.* San Francisco, CA: Morgan Caufmann.

Dzbor, M., Domingue, J., Motta, E. (2003). Magpie - Towards a Semantic Web Browser, In Proc. of the 2nd International Conference (ISWC 2003), pp. 690-705. Florida, USA.

Ebbinghaus, H.-D., Flum, J. & Thomas, W. (2007) *Mathematical Logic*. Springer-Verlag.

Edwards, D. (2000). *Introduction to Graphical Modelling*, 2nd ed. Springer-Verlag.

Edwards, S. J., Blythe, P. T., Scott, S., Weihong-Guo, A. (2006). Tourist Information Delivered Through Mobile Devices: Findings from the Image. Information Technology & Tourism. 8 (1). 31-46(16).

Eikvil, L. (1999). Information Extraction from World Wide Web - A Survey. Rapport Nr. 945, July, 1999.

Eiter, T., Lukasiewicz, T., Schindlauer, R. & Tompits, H. (2004). Combining answer set programming with description logics for the Semantic Web. In *Proceedings of the 9th international conference on the Principles of Knowledge Representation and Reasoning* (KR-2004).

Elmore, M. T., Potok, T. E. & Sheldon, F T. (2003). Dynamic Data Fusion Using An Ontology-Based Software Agent System. *In Proceedings of the 7th World Multiconference on Systemics, Cybernetics and Informatics.*

Embley, D.W. (2004). Toward Semantic Understanding - An Approach Based on Information Extraction. In *Proceedings of the Fifteenth Australasian Database Conference*, 2004.

Enderton, H. B. (2002). *A mathematical Introduction to Logic*, 2nd edition, Academic Press.

Engels R., Lech, T. (2003). Generating Ontologies for the Semantic Web: OntoBuilder. Towards the Semantic Web: Ontology-Driven Knowledge Management, pp. 91-115.

Erice, L.G., Biersack, E., Felber, P., Ross, K.W., & Keller, G.U. (2003). Hierarchical Peer-To-Peer Systems. In H. Kosch, L. Böszörményi, H. Hellwagner (Eds.), *Proceedings of the 9th International Conference on Parallel Processing, LNCS Vol. 2790* (pp. 1230-1239). Berlin, Germany: Springer.

Eriksson, H., Fergerson, R., Shahar, Y., & Musen, M. (1999). Automatic Generation of Ontology Editors. In *Proceedings of the 12th Banff Knowledge Acquisition Workshop.* Banff Alberta, Canada

E-Tourism Working Group (2004). Ontology Collection in view of an E-Tourism Portal. October, 2004. Retrieved January 13, 2007, from: http://138.232.65.141/deri_at/research/projects/e-tourism/2004/d10/v0.2/20041005/

Etzioni, O., Cafarella, M., Downey, D., Kok, S., Popescu, A., Shaked, T., Soderland, S., Weld, D., & Yates, A. (2004). Web-scale information extraction in KnowItAll.

In *Proceedings of the 13th International World Wide Web Conference* (pp. 100-110). New York City, New York

Euzenat, J. & Shvaiko, P. (2007). *Ontology Matching.* Springer Verlag.

Fagin, R. (1999). Combining fuzzy information from multiple systems. *Journal of Computer and Systems Sciences*, 58:83-99.

Fagin, R. (2002). Combining Fuzzy Information: an Overview. SIGMOD Record, 31(2), 109-118.

Fagin, R., & Wimmers, E. L. (2000). A formula for incorporating weights into scoring rules. Theorethical Computer Science, 239(2), 309-338.

Falkovych, K., Sabou, M. & Stuckenschmidt. H (2003), *UML for the Semantic Web: Transformation-Based Approaches,* Amsterdam, OS Press, Vol. 95 (2003) 92-106

Faure D & Poibeau T (2000), *First experiments of using semantic knowledge learned by ASIUM for information extraction task using INTEX,* Berlin, Germany, Proceedings of the Workshop on Ontology Learning, 14th European Conference on Artificial Intelligence.

Faure, D., Nedellec, C. & Rouveirol, C. (1998). *Acquisition of semantic knowledge uing machine learning methods: the system ASIUM.* Technical report number ICS-TR-88-16, inference and learning group, University of Paris-sud.

Fellbaum, C. (Ed.). (1998). *Wordnet: An Electronic Lexical Database.* MA: MIT Press.

Felzenszwalb, P. F., & Huttenlocher, D. P. (2006). Efficient Belief Propagation for Early Vision. *International Journal of Computer Vision*, Vol. 70, No. 1, October 2006.

Fensel, D. (2000). The Semantic Web and its Languages. *IEEE Computer Society, 15(6),* 67-73.

Fensel, D. (Ed.). (2001). *Ontologies: A Silver Bullet for Knowledge Management and Electronic Commerce,* Springer-Verlag.

Fensel, D., Angele, J., Erdmann, M., Schnurr, H., Staab, S., Studer, R., Witt, A. (1999). On2broker: Semantic-based access to information sources at the WWW. In Proc. of WebNet, pp. 366-371.

Fensel, D., Decker, S., Erdmann, M., & Studer, R. (1998). Ontobroker: Or how to enable intelligent access to the WWW. In *Proceedings of 11th Banff Knowledge Acquisition for Knowledge-Based SystemsWorkshop.* Banff, Canada, 1998.

Fernandez, M., Gomez-Perez, A., & Juristo, N. (1997). Methontology: from ontological art towards ontological engineering. In *Proceedings of the AAAI97 Spring Symposium Series on Ontological Engineering,* 33-40. Stanford, USA.

Fikes, R. & McGuinness, D. (2001). *An Axiomatic Semantics for RDF, RDF-S and DAML+OIL.* W3C Note from http://www.w3.org/TR/daml+oil-axioms

Fine, S., Singer, Y., & Tishby, N. (1998). The Hierarchical Hidden Markov Model: Analysis and Applications. In *Machine Learning, Vol.32, Issue 1,* 41-62

Finin, T., Fritzson, R., McKey, D. & McEntire, R. (1994). KQML as an Agent Communication Language. *In Proceedings of the 3rd International Conference on Information and Knowledge Management,* 456-463.

Finin, T., Mayfield, J., Fink, C., Joshi, A. & Cost., R.S. (2005). Information Retrieval and the Semantic Web. In *Proceedings of the 38th Annual Hawaii International Conference on System Sciences* (HICSS'05) - Track 4, Washington, DC, USA: IEEE Computer Society, 2005. 113.1.

Finkel, J. R., Grenager, T., & Manning, C. D. (2005). Incorporating non-local information into information extraction systems by gibbs sampling. In *Proceedings of the 43rd Annual Meeting of the Association for Computational Linguistics (ACL-2005).* pp. 363-370.

Finn, A. (2006). *A multi-level boundary classification approach to information extraction.* Phd thesis, University College Dublin.

Finn, A., & Kushmerick, N. (2004). Information extraction by convergent boundary classification. In *AAAI-04 Workshop on Adaptive Text Extraction and Mining.* San Jose, USA.

FIPA (2002). *FIPA ACL Message Structure Specification*. Retrieved March 12th from http://www.fipa.org/specs/fipa00061/SC00061G.html

Fluit, C., Horst, H., van der Meer, J., Sabou, M., Mika, P. (2003). Spectacle. Towards the Semantic Web: Ontology-Driven Knowledge Management, pp. 145-159.

Franconi, E., *Description Logics Course Information*. http://www.cs.man.ac.uk/~franconi/dl/course/

Franklin, S. & Graesser, A. (1997). Is It an Agent, or Just a Program?: A Taxonomy for Autonomous Agents. In Müller, J.P., Wooldridge, M.J. & Jennings, N.R. (Eds), *Intelligent Agents III*. Springer-Verlag, Berlin.

Franz, B., Diego, C., Deborah, L. M., Daniele, N., & Peter, F. P.-S. (Eds.) (2003). *The description logic handbook: theory, implementation, and applications,* Cambridge University Press.

Freitag, D. (1998). Information extraction from HTML: Application of a general machine learning approach. In *Proceedings of the 15th Conference on Artificial Intelligence (AAAI'98).* pp. 517-523.

Freitag, D., & Kushmerick, N. (2000). Boosted wrapper induction. In *Proceedings of 17th National Conference on Artificial Intelligence*. pp. 577-583.

French, J.C., Powell, A.L., Callan, J., Viles, C.L., Emmitt, T., Prey, K.J., & Mou, Y. (1999). Comparing the Performance of Database Selection Algorithms. In F. Gey, M. Hearst, R. Tong (Eds.), *Proceeding of the 22nd ACM International Conference on Research and Development in Information Retrieval* (pp. 238-245). New York, NY, USA: ACM.

Fuhr, N. (2000). Probabilistic Datalog: Implementing Logical Information Retrieval for Advanced Applications. *Journal of the American Society for Information Science*, 51(2): 95-110.

Fukushige, Y. (2005). *Representing Probabilistic Knowledge in the Semantic Web.* From http://www.w3.org/2004/09/13-Yoshio/PositionPaper.html

Furche, T., Linse, B., Bry, F., Plexousakis, D., & Gottlob, G. (2004). RDF Querying: Language Constructs and Evaluation Methods Compared. In *Proceedings of Reasoning Web*, 2006. 1-52.

Fuxman, A., Kolaitis, P. G., Miller, R. J., & Tan, W. C. (2006). Peer Data Exchange. ACM Transactions on Database Systems, 31(4), 1454-1498.

Galanis, L., Wang, Y., Jeffery, S.R., & DeWitt, D.J. (2003). Locating Data Sources in Large Distributed Systems. In J.C. Freytag, P.C. Lockemann, S. Abiteboul, M.J. Carey, P.G. Selinger, A. Heuer (Eds.), *Proceedings of the 29th International Conference on Very Large Data Bases* (pp. 874-885). San Francisco, CA, USA: Morgan Kaufmann.

Gale, W.A., Church, K.W., & Yarowsky, D. (1992a). Using bilingual materials to develop word sense disambiguation methods. *Proceedings of the International Conference on Theoretical and Methodological Issues in Machine Translation*, 101-112.

Gamallo, P., Gonzalez, M., Agustini, A., Lopes, G. & de Lima, V. S. (2002). Mapping syntactic dependencies onto semantic relations. *ECAI Workshop on Machine Learning and Natural Language Processing for Ontology Engineering*, Lyon, France.

Ganesan, P., Gummadi, P.K., & Garcia-Molina, H. (2004). Canon in G Major: Designing DHTs with Hierarchical Structure. In M. Liu, Y. Matsushita (Eds.), *Proceedings of the 24th IEEE International Conference on Distributed Computing Systems* (pp. 263-272). Los Alamitos, CA, USA: IEEE Computer Society.

Garcia, R., & Celma, O. (2005). Semantic integration and retrieval of multimedia metadata. In *Proceedings of the 5th International Workshop on Knowledge Mark-up and Semantic, Annotation at the 4th International Semantic Web Conference.*

Gardarin, G., Sha, F., & Ngoc, T.-D. (1999). XML-based Components for Federating Multiple Heterogeneous Data Sources. In J. Akoka, M. Bouzeghoub, I. Comyn-Wattiau, E. Métais (Eds.), *Proceedings of the 18th International Conference on Conceptual Modeling, LNCS Vol. 1728* (pp. 506-519). Berlin, Germany: Springer.

Gatterbauer, W., Bohunsky, P., Herzog, M., Kr¨ upl, B. & Pollak B. (2007). Towards Domain Independent Information Extraction from Web Tables. In *Proceedings of World Wide Web Conference (WWW2007).*

Gau, W. L. & Buehrer, D. J., (1993) Vague sets. *IEEE Transactions on Systems, Man, and Cybernetics,* 23 (2), 610-614.

Gauch, S., Wang, J., & Rachakonda, S.M. (1999). A Corpus Analysis Approach for Automatic Query Expansion and its Extension to Multiple Databases. *ACM Transactions on Information Systems, 17(3)*, 250-269.

Geerts F, Mannila H, Terzi E. (2004) Relational link-based ranking. In *Proceedings of VLDB*, 2004. 552-563.

Gemmel, J., Bell, G., Lueder, R., Drucker, S., & Wong, C. (2002). Mylifebits: Fulfilling the memex vision. In *ACM Multimedia '02, December*, 235–238.

Gen Yee, W., & Frieder, O. (2005). On Search in Peer-to-Peer File Sharing Systems. In H. Haddad, L.M. Liebrock, A. Omicini, R.L. Wainwright (Eds.), *Proceedings of the 20th ACM Symposium on Applied Computing* (pp. 1023-1030). New York, NY, USA: ACM.

Georgii, H.-O. (2008). *Stochastics.* de Gruyter Verlag.

Ghahramani, Z. & Jordan, M. I. (1997). Factorial Hidden Markov Models. *Machine Learning, Vol.29*, 245-273

Gibbons, P.B., Karp, B., Ke, Y., Nath, S., & Seshan, S. (2003). IrisNet: An Architecture for a World-Wide Sensor Web. *IEEE Pervasive Computing, 2(4)*, 22-33.

Girju, R., Badulescu, A. & Moldovan, D. (2003). Learning semantic constraints for the automatic discovery of part-whole relations. In *Proc. of the HLT- NAACL.*

Giugno, R. & Lukasiewicz, T. (2002). P-SHOQ(D): A Probabilistic Extension of SHOQ(D) for Probabilistic Ontologies in the Semantic Web. In *Proceedings Logics in Artificial Intelligence, European Conference, JELIA.*

Gmez-Prez, A. (1994), *Some Ideas and Examples to Evaluate Ontologies,* tech. report KSL-94-65, Knowledge System Laboratory, Stanford Univ., 1994.

Gnutella Group (2005). *The Gnutella File Sharing System.* Web pages available at http://gnutella.wego.com.

Gnutella. [Online]. Available: http://www.gnutella.com.

Goble, C.A., De Roure, D., Shadbolt, N., & Fernandes, A.A.A. (2004). Enhancing services and applications with knowledge and semantics. In Foster, I. and Kesselman, C. (Ed.). *The Grid: Blueprint for a New Computing Infrastructure* (2nd. Ed., Ch. 23, pp. 431-458). Morgan Kaufmann.

Goh, C.H., Madnick, S.E. & Siegel, M.D (1994). Context interchange: overcoming the challenge of large-scale interoperable database systems in a dynamic environment. In *proceedings of the third international conference on information and knowledge management*, Gaithersburg (USA), pp. 337-346.

Golub, G.H., & Loan, C.F.V. (1996). *Matrix Computation.* Baltimore, MD, USA: The John Hopkins University Press.

Gomez-Perez, A. (1996). A framework to verify knowledge sharing technology. *Expert Systems with Application,* 11(4), 519-529.

Gomez-Perez, A., Fernandez-Lopez, M. & Corcho, O. (2004). *Ontological Engineering.* Springer-Verlag (2nd printing).

Gong, X., Yan, Y., Qian, W., & Zhou, A. (2005). Bloom Filter-based XML Packets Filtering for Millions of Path Queries. In R. Agrawal, M. Kitsuregawa, K. Aberer, M. Franklin, S. Nishio (Eds.), *Proceedings of the 21st IEEE International Conference on Data Engineering* (pp. 890-901). Los Alamitos, CA, USA: IEEE Computer Society.

Gravano, L., & Garcia-Molina, H. (1995). Generalizing GlOSS to Vector-Space Databases and Broker Hierarchies. In U. Dayal, P.M.D. Gray, S. Nishio (Eds.), *Proceedings of the 21st International Conference on Very Large Data Bases* (pp. 78-89). San Francisco, CA, USA: Morgan Kaufmann.

Grefenstette, G. (1992). Use of syntatic context to produce terms association list for text retrieval. In *Conference in*

Researche and Developement in Information Retrieval (SIGIR'92), Copenhagen, Denmarke, pages 89-97.

Grefenstette, G. (1994). Explorations in Automatic Thesaurus Discovery. Kluwer Academic Publishers, Norwell, MA, USA.

Gribble, S.D., Halevy, A.Y., Ives, Z.G., Rodrig, M., & Suciu, D. (2001). What Can Database Do for Peer-To-Peer? In G. Mecca, J. Siméon (Eds.), *Proceedings of the 4th ACM International Workshop on Web and Databases* in conjunction with the *2001 ACM International Conference on Management of Data* (pp. 31-36). New York, NY, USA: ACM.

Grishman, R. & Sundheim, B. (1996). Message Understanding Conference–6: A Brief History. In *Proceedings of the 16th International Conference on Computational Linguistics*, Copenhagen, June 1996.

Grosof, B., Horrocks, I., Volz, R. & Decker, S. (2003). Description Logic Programs: Combining Logic Programs with Description Logic. In *Proceedings of 12th International Conference on the World Wide Web.*

Gruber, T. R. (1993). A Translation Approach to Portable Ontology Specification. *Knowledge Acquisition, 5(2)*, 199-220.

Gruber, T.R. (1993). Towards Principles for the Design of Ontologies used for Knowledge sharing. In N. Guarino & R. Poli (Eds), *Formal Ontology in Conceptual Analysis and Knowledge Representation.* Deventer, the Netherlands: Kluwer Academic Publishers.

Guan, S. & Zhu, F. (2004). Ontology Acquisition and Exchange of Evolutionary Product-brokering Agents. *Journal of Research and Practice in Information Technology, 36(1)*, 35-46.

Guarino, N. (1998). Formal Ontologies and Information Systems. *FOIS'98*. Trento, Italy: IOS Press.

Guha, R., Kumar, R., Raghavan, P., & Tomkins, A. (2004). Propagation of Trust and Distrust. *In Proceedings of the 13th international Conference on World Wide Web.* pp.403-412. NY, USA, May 2004.

Guha, R.V., McCool, R., & Miller, E. (2003). Semantic Search. *In Proceedings of the 12th International World Wide Web Conference.* pp.700-709. Budapest, Hungry, May 2003.

Guha, S., Jagadish, H.V., Koudas, N., Srivastava, D., & Yu, T. (2002). Approximate XML Joins. In M.J. Franklin, B. Moon, A. Ailamaki (Eds.), *Proceedings of the 2002 ACM International Conference on Management of Data* (pp. 287-298). New York, NY, USA: ACM.

Guha, S., Koudas, N., Srivastava, D., & Yu, T. (2003). Index-based Approximate XML Joins. In U. Dayal, K. Ramamritham, T.M. Vijayaraman (Eds.), *Proceedings of the 19th IEEE International Conference on Data Engineering* (pp. 708-710). Los Alamitos, CA, USA: IEEE Computer Society.

Guizzardi, G. & Wagner G. (2002), *Using Formal Ontologies to define Real-World Semantics for UML Conceptual Models.* In 1 Workshop on Application of Ontologies to Biology, European Media Laboratory, Heidelberg, Germany.

Guizzardi, G., Herre, H. & Wagner G. (2002). *On the General Ontological Foundations of Conceptual Modeling.* Berlin, 21 Intl. Conf. on Conceptual Modeling (ER 2002). Springer-Verlag, Berlin, Lecture Notes in Computer Science, pp : 65-78

Gummadi, P.K., Dunn, R.J., Saroiu, S., Gribble, S.D., Levy, H.M., & Zahorjan, J. (2003). Measurement, Modeling, and Analysis of a Peer-to-Peer File-Sharing Workload. In M.L. Scott, L. Peterson (Eds.), *Proceedings of the 19th ACM Symposium on Operating Systems Principles* (pp. 314-329). New York, NY, USA: ACM.

Guo, Y; Pan, Z; and Heflin, J. (2004). An Evaluation of Knowledge Base Systems for Large OWL Datasets. The Semantic Web – ISWC 2004: The Proceedings of the Third International Semantic Web Conference, Hiroshima, Japan, November 7-11, 2004. Springer Berlin/Heidelberg. 274-288.

Gupta, A., Agrawal, D., & El Abbadi, A. (2003). Approximate Range Selection Queries in Peer-to-Peer Systems. In J. Gray, D. Dewitt, M. Stonebraker (Eds.),

Proceedings of the 1st Biennial Conference on Innovative Data Systems Research (online edition available at http://www-db.cs.wisc.edu/cidr/cidr2003/program/p13.pdf). New York, NY, USA: ACM.

Haarslev V., Lutz C., & Möller R. (1999). A description logicwith concrete domains and role-forming predicates. *J. of Logic and Computation*, 9(3), 351–384.

Haase, P., Siebes, R., & van Harmelen, F. (2004). Peer Selection in Peer-to-Peer Networks with Semantic Topologies. In Proc. of the 1st International Conference on Semantics of a Networked World: Semantics for Grid Databases (ICSNW), 108-125.

Haddad, M-H. (2002). *Extraction et impact des connaissances sur les performances des systèmes de recherche d'information.* Doctoral thesis, université joseph Fourier.

Haghighi, A. & Klein, D. (2007). Unsupervised Coreference Resolution in a Nonparametric Bayesian Model. In *Proceedings of Association of Computing Linguistics (ACL2007).*

Hahn U & Schulz S (2000), *Towards Very Large Terminological Knowledge Bases: A Case Study from Medicine.* In Canadian Conference on AI 2000: 176-186.

Halaschek, C., Aleman-Meza, B., Arpinar, I.B., & Sheth, A.P. (2004). Discovering and Ranking Semantic Associations over a Large RDF Metabase. In M.A. Nascimento, M.T. Özsu, D. Kossmann, R.J. Miller, J.A. Blakeley, K.B. Schiefer (Eds.), *Proceedings of the 30th International Conference on Very Large Data Bases* (pp. 1317-1320). San Francisco, CA, USA: Morgan Kaufmann.

Halevy, A., Franklin, M.J., & Maier, D. (2006). Principles of Dataspace Systems. In Proc of the 25th ACM SIGACT-SIGMOD-SIGART Symposium on Principles of Database Systems (PODS), 1-9.

Halevy, A.Y., Ives, Z., Madhavan, J., Mork, P., Suciu, D., & Tatarinov, I. (2004). The Piazza Peer Data Management System. IEEE Transactions on Knowledge and Data Engineering. 16(7), 787-798.

Halevy, A.Y., Ives, Z., Suciu, D., & Tatarinov, I. (2005). Schema Mediation for Large-Scale Semantic Data Sharing. VLDB Journal. 14(1), 68-83.

Halevy, A.Y., Ives, Z.G., Mork, P., & Tatarinov, I. (2003). Piazza: Data Management Infrastructure for Semantic Web Applications. In G. Hencsey, B. White, Y.-F.R. Chen, L. Kovács, S. Lawrence (Eds.), *Proceedings of the 12nd International World Wide Web Conference* (pp. 556-567). New York, NY, USA: ACM.

Halevy, A.Y., Tatarinov, I., Ives, Z., Madhavan, J., Suciu, D., Dalvi, N., Dong, X., Kadiyska, Y., Miklau, G., & Mork, P. (2003). The Piazza Peer Data Management Project. SIGMOD Record, 32(3), 47-52.

Hamasaki, M., Matsuo, Y., Nishimura, T. & Takeda, H. (2007). Ontology Extraction Using Social Network. *In Proceedings of the 20th International Joint Conference on Artificial Intelligence, Workshop on Semantic Web for Collaborative Knowledge Acquisition, Hyderabad, India.*

Hammersley, J. & Clifford, P. (1971). *Markov fields on finite graphs and lattices.* Unpublished manuscript.

Hammond, B., Sheth, A., & Kochut, K. (2002). Semantic enhancement engine: a modular document enhancement platform for semantic applications over heterogeneous content. In: V. Kashyap & L. Shklar (Eds.), *Real World Semantic Web Applications*, 29-49. IOS Press

Han, H. & Elmasri, R (2000). *Architecture of WebOntEx: A system for automatic extraction of ontologies from the Web.* WCM 2000.

Han, H., Giles, L., Manavoglu, E., Zha, H., Zhang, Z., & Fox, E. A. (2003). Automatic document metadata extraction using support vector machines. In *Proceedings of 2003 Joint Conference on Digital Libraries (JCDL'03).* pp. 37-48

Handschuh, S., Staab, S., & Ciravegna, F. (2002). S-CREAM — semi-automatic creation of metadata. In *Proceedings of the 13th International Conference on Knowledge Engineering and Management.* pp. 358-372

Handschuh, S., Staab, S., & Maedche, A. (2001). CREAM—Creating relational metadata with a component-based, ontology driven framework. In *Proceedings of K-Cap 2001*, Victoria, BC, Canada

Hanschke P. (1992). Specifying role interaction in concept languages. In *Proc. of the 3rd Int. Conf. on the Principles of Knowledge Representation and Reasoning (KR'92)*, Morgan Kaufmann, Los Altos, pp. 318–329.

Happel, H.-J., Korthaus, A., Seedorf, S., & Tomczyk, P.(2006), *KOntR: An Ontology-Enabled Approach to Software Reuse,* San Francisco, In: Proc. of the 18th Int. Conf. on Software Engineering and Knowledge Engineering (SEKE).

Harth, A., Umbrich, J., & Decker, S. (2006). MultiCrawler: A pipelined architecture for crawling and indexing Semantic Web data. In *Proceedings of the 5th International Semantic Web Conference*, Athens, GA, USA.

Harvey, N., Jones, M.B., Saroiu, S., Theimer, M., & Wolman, A. (2003). Skipnet: A Scalable Overlay Network with Practical Locality Properties. In S.D. Gribble (Ed.), *Proceedings of the 4th USENIX Symposium on Internet Technologies and Systems* (online edition available at http://www.usenix.org/publications/library/proceedings/usits03/tech/harvey/harvey.pdf). Berkeley, CA, USA: USENIX Association.

Hassell, J., Aleman-Meza, B., & Arpinar, I.B. (2006), *Ontology-Driven Automatic Entity Disambiguation in Unstructured Text,* th International Semantic Web Conference (ISWC 2006), Athens, GA, November 5–9, 2006, I, Lecture Notes in Computer Science, vol. 4273, Springer, 2006.

Hatcher, E., & Gospodneti, O. (2004). *Lucene in Action.* Manning Publications Corporation. 2004.

Hayes, J. (2004). A Graph Model for RDF: [Master Thesis]. August, 2004.

Hearst, M-A. (1992). Automatic acquisition of hyponyms from large text corpora. In *proceedings of the fourteenth international conference on computational linguistics*, Nantes, France, pages 539-545.

Heflin, J. & Hendler, J. (2000). Searching the Web with SHOE. *Proceedings of the AAAI 2000 Workshop on Artificial Intelligence for Web Search.* pp.35-40. Austin, Texas, July 2000.

Heflin, J., Hendler, J. A., & Luke, S. (2003). SHOE: a blueprint for the semantic web. In: D. Fensel, J. A. Hendler, H. Lieberman, & W. Wahlster (Eds.), *Spinning the Semantic Web* (pp. 29-63). MA: MIT Press.

Heinsohn, J. (1991). A Hybrid Approach for Modeling Uncertainty in Terminological Logics. In *Proceedings of the European Conference on Symbolic and Qualitative Approaches to Reasoning with Uncertainty.*

Hellerstein, J.M. (2004). Architectures and Algorithms for Internet-Scale (P2P) Data Management. In M.A. Nascimento, M.T. Özsu, D. Kossmann, R.J. Miller, J.A. Blakeley, K.B. Schiefer (Eds.), *Proceedings of the 30th International Conference on Very Large Data Bases* (pp. 1244). San Francisco, CA, USA: Morgan Kaufmann.

Hendler, J. & McGuinness, D. (2000). The DARPA Agent Markup Language. *IEEE Intelligent Systems, 15,* No. 6:67-73.

Hendler, J. (2001). Agents and the Semantic Web. *IEEE Intelligent Systems,* 30-37.

Henriksson, R., (November, 2005), Semantic Web and E-Tourism, Helsinki University, Department of Computer Science. [Online]. Available: http://www.cs.helsinki.fi/u/glinskih/semanticweb/Semantic_Web_and_E-Tourism.pdf

Hepp, M. (2006). Semantic Web and semantic Web services: father and son or indivisible twins? Internet Computing, IEEE. 10 (2). 85- 88.

Hepp, M., Siorpaes, K., Bachlechner, D. (2006). Towards the Semantic Web in E-Tourism: Can Annotation Do the Trick? In Proc. of 14th European Conf. on Information System (ECIS 2006), June 12–14, 2006, Gothenburg, Sweden.

Hercock, R.G. (2002). Autonomous Computing. In *Proceedings of the Workshop on Grand Challenges for Computing Research*, Edinburgh, UK.

Heung, V.C.S. (2003). Internet usage by international travellers: reasons and barriers. International Journal of Contemporary Hospitality Management, 15 (7), 370-378.

Hi-Touch Working Group (2003). Semantic Web methodologies and tools for intraEuropean sustainable tourism [Online]. Retrieved April 6, 2004, from http://www.mondeca.com/articleJITT-hitouch-legrand.pdf/

Holi, M. & Hyvönen, E. (2006). Modeling Uncertainty in Semantic Web Taxonomies. In Z. Ma (Ed.), *Soft Computing in Ontologies and Semantic Web*. Springer-Verlag.

Hölldobler, S, Störr, H. P. & Tran, D. K. (2003). The fuzzy description logic ALC_{FH} with hedge algebras as concept modifiers. *Journal of Advanced Computational Intelligence and Intelligent Informatics*, 7 (3), 294-305.

Hölldobler, S., Khang, T.D., & Störr, H.P. (2002) A fuzzy description logic with hedges as concept modifiers. In *Proceedings In Tech/VJFuzzy'2002*. pp. 25–34.

Hölldobler, S., Nga, N. H. & Khang, T. D. (2005). The fuzzy description logic ALC_{FLH}. *Proceedings of the 9th IASTED International Conference on Artificial Intelligence and Soft Computing*, pp. 99-104.

Hölldobler, S., Störr, H. P., & Khang, T. D. (2004). The subsumption problem in the fuzzy description logic ALC_{FH}. *Proceedings of the 10th International Conference on Information Processing and Management of Uncertainty in Knowledge-Based Systems*, pp. 243-250.

Holsapple, C. & Joshi, K.D. (2005). A collaborative approach to ontology design. *Communications of ACM*, Vol. 45(2) pp. 42-47.

Horridge, M., Knublauch, H., Rector, A., Stevens, R., Wroe, C. (2004). A Practical Guide To Building OWL Ontologies Using The Protege-OWL Plugin and CO-ODE Tools Edition 1.0. The University of Manchester, August 2004. [Online]. Available: http://protege.stanford.edu/publications/ontology_development/ontology101.html

Horrocks I., & Sattler, U. (2001). Ontology reasoning in the SHOQ(D) description logic. *Proceedings of the 17th International Joint Conference on Artificial Intelligence (IJCAI 2001)*, pp. 199–204.

Horrocks, I. & Patel-Schneider, P. F. (2004). Reducing OWL entailment to description logic satisfiability. *Journal of Web Semantics*, 1(4):345-357.

Horrocks, I. & Patel-Schneider, P. F., van Harmelen, F. (2003). From SHIQ and RDF to OWL: The making of a web ontology language. *Journal of Web Semantics*, 1(1):7-26.

Horrocks, I. (2005). OWL Rules, OK? In *Proceedings of W3C Workshop on Rule Languages for Interoperability*.

Horrocks, I., Patel-Schneider, P. F., Bechhofer, S. & Tsarkov, D. (2005). OWL rules: A proposal and prototype implementation. *Journal of Web Semantics*, 3(1):23-40.

Horrocks, I., Sattler, U. & Tobies, S. (1999). Practical Reasoning for Expressive Description Logics. *In Proceedings of LPAR '99, number 1705 in LNAI, Springer-Verlag*, 161-180.

Hotho, A., Maedche, A., & Staab, S. (2001). Ontology-based Text Clustering. *In Proceedings of the IJCAI-2001 Workshop on Text Learning: BeyondSupervision*. Seattle, USA, August 2001.

Howell, F.W. (1997). The SimJava Home Page [Online]. Available: http://www.dcs.ed.ac.uk/home/hase/simjava.

Hu, Y., Li, H., Cao, Y., Meyerzon, D., Teng, L., & Zheng, Q. (2006). Automatic Extraction of Titles from General Documents using Machine Learning. *Information Processing and Management*. pp.1276-1293, 2006

Huebsch, R., Hellerstein, J.M., Lanham, N., Thau Loo, B., Shenker, S., & Stoica, I. (2003). Querying the Internet with PIER. In Proc. of the 29th International Conference on Very Large Data Bases (VLDB), 321-332.

Huffman, S.B. (1995). Learning Information Extraction Patterns from Examples. In *Proceedings of Learning for Natural Language Processing'1995*. pp. 246-260.

Huhns, M. & Stephens, L. M. (2004). Multiagent Systems for Internet Applications. In M. P. Singh (Ed.), *Practical Handbook of Internet Computing.* Chapman Hall and CRC Press.

Hunter, J. (2001). Adding multimedia to the semantic Web-building and MPEG-7 ontology. In *Proceedings of the 1st International Semantic Web Working Symposium.*

Hustadt, U., Motik, B. & Sattler, U. (2005). Data complexity of reasoning in very expressive description logics. In *Proceedings of the 19th International Joint Conference on Artificial Intelligence.*

Hyoil, H. & Ramez,E., (2003), *Ontology extraction and conceptual modeling for web information*, Hershey, PA, USA, Information modeling for internet applications, Pages: 174 - 188 .

IBM Enterprise Architect Kit for SOA (2006), http://www.ibm.com/developerworks/architecture/kits/archkit2/index.html?S_TACT=105AGX23&S_CMP=AKBDD

Iria, J. & Ciravegna, F. (2005). Relation Extraction for Mining the Semantic Web. *Dagstuhl Seminar on Machine Learning for the Semantic Web,* Dagstuhl, Germany.

ISO/IEC 21000-7, (2004). *Information Technology —Multimedia Framework (MPEG-21)—Part 7: Digital Item Adaptation .*

ISO/IEC JTC1/SC29/WG11 N3752, (2000). *Overview of the MPEG-7 Standard (version 4.0).*

Jackson, P. & Moulinier, I. (2002). Natural Language Processing for Online Applications. John Benjamins, 2002.

Jaeger, M. (1994). Probabilistic Reasoning in Terminological Logics. In *Proceedings of the 4th international Conference on Principles of Knowledge Representation and Reasoning.*

Jagadish, H. V., Ooi, B. C., Tan, K. L., Vu, Q. H., & Zhang, R. (2006). Speeding Up Search in Peer-to-Peer Networks with a Multi-Way Tree Structure. In Proc. of the ACM SIGMOD International Conference on Management of Data (SIGMOD), 1-12.

Jagadish, H.V., Ooi, B.C., & Vu, Q.H. (2005). BATON: A Balanced Tree Structure for Peer-To-Peer Networks. In In K. Böhm, C.S. Jensen, L.M. Haas, M.L. Kersten, P.-A. Larson, B.C. Ooi (Eds.), *Proceedings of the 31st International Conference on Very Large Data Bases* (pp. 661-672). San Francisco, CA, USA: Morgan Kaufmann.

Jagadish, H.V., Ooi, B.C., Vu, Q.H., Zhou, A.Y., & Zhang, R. (2006). VBI-Tree: A Peer-To-Peer Framework for Supporting Multi-Dimensional Indexing Schemes. In L. Liu, A. Reuter, K.-Y. Whang, J. Zhang (Eds.), *Proceedings of the 22nd IEEE International Conference on Data Engineering* (pp. 34). Los Alamitos, CA, USA: IEEE Computer Society.

Jannach, D., Leopold, K., Timmerer, C., & Hellwagner, H. (2006). A knowledge-based framework for multimedia adaptation. *The International Journal of Artificial Intelligence, 24(2)*, pp. 109-125, Special Issue on Innovations in Applied Artificial Intelligence, Springer .

Janssens, F., Glänzel, W. & Moor, B. D. (2007). Dynamic Hybrid Clustering of Bioinformatics by Incorporating Text Mining and Citation Analysis. In *Proceedings of ACM SIGKDD2007.*

Jeff Heflin (2000), University Ontology, http://www.cs.umd.edu/projects/plus/SHOE/onts/univ1.0.html

Jennings, N. R. & Wooldridge, M. (1998). Applications of Intelligent Agents. In N. R. Jennings & M. J. Wooldridge (eds), *Agent Technology: Foundations, Applications and Markets.* Springer-Verlag: Heidelberg, Germany.

Jennings, N. R. & Wooldridge, M. (1998). Applications of Intelligent Agents. In N. R. Jennings and M. J. Wooldridge (eds), *Agent Technology: Foundations, Applications and Markets.* Springer-Verlag: Heidelberg, Germany.

Jensen, F. V. (2001). *Bayesian Networks and Decision Graphs.* Springer-Verlag.

Jentzsch, A. (April, 2005) XML Clearing House Report 12: Tourism Standards. Retrieved September 6, 2007, from http://www.xml-clearinghouse.de/reports/Tourism%20Standards.pdf

Jeremy, J. Carroll, J.J., Dickinson, I., Dollin, C., Reynolds, D., Seaborne, A., & Wilkinson, K. (2004). Jena: Implementing the Semantic Web Recommendations. *In Proceedings of the 13th International World Wide Web Conference on Alternate Track Papers & Poster.* pp.74-83. NY, USA, May 2004.

Jian, N., Hu, W., Cheng, G., & Qu, Y. (2005). Falcon-AO: Aligning Ontologies with Falcon. *In Proceedings of the K-CAP Workshop on Integrating Ontologies.* Canada, October 2005.

Jiang, J. & Zhai. C. (2007). A Systematic Exploration of the Feature Space for Relation Extraction. In *Proceedings of the Human Language Technology Conference of the North American Chapter of the ACL.*

Jiao, F., Wang, S., & Lee, C. (2006). Semi-supervised conditional random fields for improved sequence segmentation and labeling. In *Proceedings of the 21st International Conference on Computational Linguistics and the 44th annual meeting of the ACL.* pp. 209-216

Jin, W., Ho, H., & Wu, X. (2007). Improving Knowledge Discovery by Combining Text Mining and Link Analysis Techniques. In *Proceedings of International Conference on Data Mining (ICDM2007).*

Jordan, M. I. & Weiss, Y. (2002). Graphical Models: Probabilistic Inference. In M. Arbib (Eds.), *The Handbook of Brain Theory and Neural Networks, 2nd edition.* Cambridge, MA: MIT Press, 2002.

Joseph, S. (2002). NeuroGrid: Semantically Routing Queries in Peer-to-Peer Networks. In Proc. of the International Workshop on Peer-to-Peer Computing (NETWORKING), 202-214.

Kahan, J. & Koivunen, M. R. (2001). Annotea: an open RDF infrastructure for shared web annotations. In *Proceedings of the 10th International World Wide Web Conference (WWW 2005).* pp. 623-632

Kalogeraki, V., Gunopulos, D., & Zeinalipour-Yazti, D. (2002). A Local Search Mechanism for Peer-to-Peer Networks. In C. Nicholas, D. Grossman, K. Kalpakis, S. Qureshi, H. van Dissel, L. Seligman (Eds.), *Proceedings of the 11st ACM International Conference on Information and Knowledge Management* (pp. 300-307). New York, NY, USA: ACM.

Kambhatla, N. (2004). Combining Lexical, Syntactic, and Semantic Features with Maximum Entropy Models for Extracting Relations. In *Proceedings of the 42nd Annual Meeting of the Association for Computational Linguistics.*

Kamvar, S.D., Schlosser, M.T., & Garcia-Molina, H. (2003). The Eigen Trust Algorithm for Reputation Management in P2P Networks. *In Proceedings of the 12th International World Wide Web Conference.* pp.640–651. Budapest, Hungry, May 2003.

Kanellopoulos, D. & Kotsiantis, S. (2006). Towards Intelligent Wireless Web Services for Tourism. IJCSNS International Journal of Computer Science and Network Security. 6 (7). 83-90.

Kanellopoulos, D. (2006). The advent of Semantic web in Tourism Information Systems. *Tourismos: an international multidisciplinary journal of* tourism. 1(2), pp. 75-91.

Kanellopoulos, D., Panagopoulos, A. (2005). Exploiting tourism destinations' knowledge in a RDF-based P2P network, Hypertext 2005, 1st International Workshop WS4 – Peer to Peer and Service Oriented Hypermedia: Techniques and Systems, ACM Press.

Kanellopoulos, D., Panagopoulos, A., Psillakis, Z. (2004). Multimedia applications in Tourism: The case of travel plans. Tourism Today. No. 4, pp. 146-156.

Kanellopoulos, D.,Kotsiantis, S., Pintelas, P. (2006), Intelligent Knowledge Management for the Travel Domain ,GESTS International Transactions on Computer Science and Engineering. 30(1). 95-106.

Kantere, V., Tsoumakos, D., & Roussopoulos, N. (2004). Querying Structured Data in an Unstructured P2P System. In A.H.F. Laender, D. Lee, M. Ronthaler (Eds.), *Proceedings of the 6th ACM International Workshop on Web Information and Data Management* in conjunction with the *13rd ACM International Conference on Information and Knowledge Management* (pp. 64-71). New York, NY, USA: ACM.

Karoui, L. & Aufaure, M-A (2007). Revealing Criteria for the Ontology Evaluation Task. *Special Issue of Journal of Internet Technology (JIT) on Ontology Technology and Its Applications.*

Karoui, L. & El Khadi, N. (2007). Relation Extraction and Validation Algorithm. *4th International Conference on Distributed Computing and Internet Technology,* LNCS volume 3347.

Karoui, L. (2006). Intelligent Ontology Learning based on Context: Answering Crucial Questions. *The IEEE International Conference on Computational Intelligence for Modelling, Control and Automation - CIMCA06,* Sydney.

Karoui, L., Aufaure, M-A. & Bennacer, N. (2007). Analyses and Fundamental ideas for a Relation Extraction Approach. *The IEEE proceedings of the Workshop on Data Mining and Business Intelligence in conjunction with the IEEE 23rd International Conference on Data Engineering (ICDE'07),* Turkey.

Karoui, L., Bennacer, N. & Aufaure, M-A. (2006). Extraction de concepts guidée par le contexte. *XIIIème Rencontres de la Société Francophone de Classification SFC'06,* pp 119-123.

Karvounarakis, G., Alexaki, S., Christophides, V., Plexousakis, D., & Scholl, M. (2002). RQL: A Declarative Query Language for RDF. In D. Lassner, D. De Roure, A. Iyengar (Eds.), *Proceedings of the 11st International World Wide Web Conference* (pp. 592-603). New York, NY, USA: ACM.

Kauchak, D., Smarr, J., & Elkan, C. (2004). Sources of success for boosted wrapper induction. *The Journal of Machine Learning Research, Vol.5,* 499-527. MA: MIT Press.

Kautz, H., Selman, B., & Shah, M. (1997). ReferralWeb: Combining Social Networks and Collaborative Filtering. *Communication of the ACM, 40* (3), 63-65.

KaZaA Group (2005). *The KaZaA File Sharing System.* Web pages available at http://www.kazaa.com.

Kazaa. [Online]. Available: http://www.kazaa.com.

Kersting, K. & De Raedt, L. (2001). *Bayesian Logic Programs.* Technical Report No. 151, Institute for Computer Science, University of Freiburg, Germany.

Kersting, K. & De Raedt, L. (2007). Bayesian Logic Programs: Theory and Tool. In Getoor, L. & Taskar, B. (Ed.), *Introduction to Statistical Relational Learning.* MIT Press.

Kersting, K. & Dick, U. (2004). Balios – The Engine for Bayesian Logic Programs. In *Proceedings of Knowledge Discovery in Databases (PKDD).*

Kersting, K. (2006). An Inductive Logic Programming Approach to Statistical Relational Learning. In *Frontiers in Artificial Intelligence,* Volume 148, IOS Press, Amsterdam, The Netherlands.

Khambatti, M., Ryu, D. K., & Dasgupta, P. (2002). Efficient Discovery of Implicitly Formed Peer-to-Peer Communities. International Journal of Parallel and Distributed Systems and Networks, 5(4), 155-164.

Kida, K. & Shimazu, H. (2002). Ubiquitous Knowledge Management - Enabling an Office-work Scheduling Tool for Corporate Knowledge Sharing. *In Proceedings of Workshop on Knowledge Media Networking.* pp.99-104. Kyoto, Japan, Jul 2002.

Kietz JU, Maedche A & Volz R (2000), *A Method for Semi-Automatic Ontology Acquisition from a Corporate Intranet,* Juan-Les-Pins, Franc EKAW'00 Workshop on Ontologies and Texts.

Kiryakov, A. (2006). *OWLIM: balancing between scalable repository and light-weight reasoner.* Presented at the Developer's Track of WWW2006, Edinburgh, Scotland, UK, 23-26 May, 2006.

Kiryakov, A., Popov, B., Ognyanoff, D., Manov, D., Kirilov, A., Goranov, M., (2003), Semantic Annotation, Indexing, and Retrieval, Lecture Notes in Computer Science, Springer-Verlag. Pages 484-499.

Kiyakov, A. K., IV. Simov, K., & Dimitrov, M. (2001). *Ontomap: Ontologies for lexical semantics.* Technical report, OntoText Lab, Sirma AI EOOD, from http://www.ontotext.com/publications/ranlp01.pdf.

Kiyota, Y. & Kurohashi, S. (2001). Automatic summarization of Japanese sentences and its application to a WWW KWIC index. *Proceedings of the 2001 Symposium on applications and the internet*, page 120.

Klein, D. & Manning, C. (2002). Conditional Structure Versus Conditional Estimation in NLP Models. In *Proceedings of the Conference on Empirical Methods in Natural Language Processing (EMNLP'2002)*, Philadelphia.

Klein, M., Broekstra, J., Fensel, D., van Harmelen, F. & Horrocks, I. (2003). Ontologies and Schema Languages on the Web. In D. Fensel. J. Hendler, H. Lieberman & W. Wahlster (eds), *Spinning the Semantic Web: Bringing the World Wide Web to its Full Potential.* Cambridge, MA: The MIT Press.

Kleis, M., Lua, E.K., & Zhou, X. (2005). Hierarchical Peer-to-Peer Networks Using Lightweight SuperPeer Topologies. In Proc. of the 10th IEEE Symposium on Computers and Communications (ISCC), 143-148.

Klir, G. J., & Yuan, B. (1995). Fuzzy Sets and Fuzzy Logic: Theory and Applications. Upper Saddle River: Prentice Hall.

Klyne, G., & Carroll, J.J. (2004). Resource Description Framework (RDF): Concepts and Abstract Syntax. *World Wide Web Consortium Recommendation.* Online edition available at http://www.w3.org/TR/2004/REC-rdf-concepts-20040210/.

Kobeissy, N., Genet, M. G., & Zeghlache, D. (2007). Mapping XML to OWL for seamless information retrieval in context-aware environments. *Second IEEE International Workshop on Services Integration in Pervasive Environments (SEPS'07) at IEEE International Conference on Pervasive Services (ICPS'2007)*, pp. 349-354.

Kogut, P. & Holmes, W. (2001). AeroDAML: Applying Information Extraction to Generate DAML Annotations from Web Pages. In *Proceedings of the First International Conference on Knowledge Capture.*

Kokkinidis, G., & Christophides, V. (2004). Semantic Query Routing and Processing in P2P Database Systems: The ICS-FORTH SQPeer Middleware. In W. Lindner, M. Mesiti, C. Türker, Y. Tzitzikas, A. Vakali (Eds.), *EDBT 2004 Workshops – Proceedings of the 1st International Workshop on Peer-to-Peer Computing and Databases, LNCS Vol. 3268*, in conjunction with the *9th International Conference on Extending Database Technology* (pp. 486-495). Berlin, Germany: Springer.

Koller, D., Levy, A. & Pfeffer, A. (1997). P-CLASSIC: A tractable probabilistic description logic. In *Proceedings of the 14th AAAI Conference on Artificial Intelligence (AAAI-97).*

Koloniari, G., & Pitoura, E. (2004). Content-Based Routing of Path Queries in Peer-to-Peer Systems. In E. Bertino, S. Christodoulakis, D. Plexousakis, V. Christophides, M. Koubarakis, K. Böhm, E. Ferrari (Eds.), *Proceedings of the 9th International Conference on Extending Database Technology, LNCS Vol. 2992* (pp. 29-47).

Korpipää, P., Häkkilä, J., Kela, J., Ronkainen, S., & Känsälä, I. (2004). Utilising context ontology in mobile device application personalization. *ACM International Conference Proceeding Series; Vol. 83 Proceedings of the 3rd international conference on Mobile and ubiquitous multimedia,* pp. 133-140, ACM Press.

Kossmann, D. (2000). The state of the art in distributed query processing. ACM Computing Surveys, 32(4), 422-469.

Kotis, K. & Vouros, G. A. (2004). The HCONE Approach to Ontology Merging. *In Proceedings of the 1st European Semantic Web Symposium,* Heraclion, Greece, 137-151.

Kou, Z. & Cohen, W. W. (2007). Stacked Graphical Models for Efficient Inference in Markov Random Fields. In *Proceedings of SIAM Conference on Data Mining (SDM2007).*

Krishnan, V. & Manning, C. D. (2006). An Effective Two-Stage Model for Exploiting Non-Local Dependencies in Named Entity Recognition *Proceedings of the 21st International Conference on Computational Linguistics and 44th Annual Meeting of the ACL*, pages 1121–1128, ACL2006

Krohn, U., & Davies, J. The Search Facility RDFferret. *On-To-Knowledge Deliverable D11*, from http://www.ontoknowledge.org .

Kschischang, F. R., Frey, B. J., & Loeliger, H. (2001). Factor Graphs and the Sum-Product Algorithm. *IEEE Transitions on Information Theory*, VOL. 47, No. 2, February, 2001.

Kubiatowicz, J., Bindel, D., Eaton, P., Chen, Y., Geels, D., Gummadi, R., Rhea, S., Weimer, W., Wells, C., Weatherspoon, H., & Zhao, B. (2000). OceanStore: An Architecture for Global-Scale Persistent Storage. *ACM SIGPLAN Notices, 35(11)*, 190-201.

Kuckelberg, A., & Krieger, R. (2003). *Efficient structure oriented storage of xml documents using ordbms*. Technical report, RWTH Aachen.

Kushmerick, N. (2000). Wrapper induction: Efficiency and expressiveness. *Artificial Intelligence, Vol.118*, 15-68.

Kushmerick, N., Weld, D. S., & Doorenbos, R. (1997). Wrapper induction for information extraction. In *Proceedings of the International Joint Conference on Artificial Intelligence (IJCAI'97)*. pp. 729-737.

Lacher, M. & Groh, G. (2001). Facilitating the Exchange of Explicit Knowledge through Ontology Mapping. *American Association for Artificial Intelligence, 2001.*

Laender, A.H.F., Ribeiro-Neto, B.A., da Silva, A.S., & Teixeira, J.S. (2002). A Brief Survey of Web Data Extraction Tools. *Journal of ACM SIGMOD Record*, 2002.

Lafferty, J., McCallum, A., & Pereira, F. (2001). Conditional Random Fields: Probabilistic models for segmenting and labeling sequence data. In *Proceedings of the 18th International Conference on Machine Learning (ICML'01)*. pp. 282-289.

Lafferty, J., Zhu, X., & Liu, Y. (2004). Kernel conditional random fields: representation and clique selection. In *Proceedings of the 21st International Conference on Machine Learning.*

Lambrix, P. & Padgham, L. (1998). Using Knowledge Representation for Agent World Model. *In Proceedings of the International Conference on Multi-agent Systems, France,* 443-444.

Laskey, K. B & Costa, P. C. G. (2005). Of Klingons and Starships: Bayesian Logic for the 23rd Century. In *Proceedings of the 21st Conference of Uncertainty in AI (UAI).*

Laskey, K. B. (2006). *MEBN: A Logic for Open-World Probabilistic Reasoning.* Technical Report C4106-01, George Mason University, USA.

Lassila, O. & Swick, R. (1999). *Resource Description Framework (RDF) Model and Syntax Specification.* W3C Recommendation, from http://www.w3.org/TR/REC-rdf-syntax/

Lawrence, S., Giles, C.L., & Bollacker K. (1999). Digital libraries and autonomous citation indexing. *IEEE Computer, Vol.32(6)*, 67-71.

Leek, T.B. (1997). Information Extraction Using Hidden Markov Models. M.S. thesis.

Leighton, H. V. & Srivastava, J. (1999). First 20 precision among World Wide Web search services (search engines). *Journal of the American Society for Information Science*, 1999, 50(10):870–881.

Lenat, D.B. & Guha, R.V. (1990). Building Large Knowledge Based Systems Reading, Massachusetts: Addison Wesley.

Li, J. & Yu, Y. (2001). Learning to generate semantic annotation for domain specific sentences. In *Proceedings of the Knowledge Markup and Semantic Annotation Workshop in K-CAP'2001.* Victoria, BC.

Li, J., Tang, J, Zhang, J., Luo, Q., Liu, Y., & Hong, M. (2007). EOS: expertise oriented search using social networks. *In Proceedings of the 16th International Conference on World Wide Web.* pp.1271-1272. Alberta, Canada, May 2007.

Li, L., Wu, B. & Yang, Y. (2005). Agent-Based Ontology Integration for Ontology-Based Applications. *In Proceedings of the 2005 Australasian Ontology Workshop, Sydney, Australia,* 53-59.

Li, L., Yang, Y. & Wu, B. (2005). Agent-Based Ontology Mapping Towards Ontology Interoperability. *In Proceedings of the 18th Australian Joint Conference on Artificial Intelligence (AI '05), LNAI 3809, Springer-Verlang, Sydney, Australia,* 843-846.

Li, M., Lee, W. C., & Sivasubramaniam, A. (2004). Semantic Small World: An Overlay Network for Peer-to-Peer Search. In Proc. of the 12th IEEE International Conference on Network Protocols (ICNP), 228-238.

Li, M., Lee, W.-C., & Sivasubramaniam, A. (2003). Neighborhood Signatures for Searching P2P Networks. In B.C. Desai, W. Ng (Eds.), *Proceedings of the 7th IEEE International Database Engineering and Applications Symposium* (pp. 149-159). Los Alamitos, CA, USA: IEEE Computer Society.

Li, N., & Moessner, K. (2007). *Design of content/service adaptation framework*, Mobile VCE project Deliverable (D-U3.3).

Li, N., & Moessner, K. (2007). The MVCE knowledge-based content and service adaptation management framework. In *Workshop on Applications and Services in Wireless Networks,* Santander, Spain.

Li, N., Attou, A., & Moessner, K. (2007). A MPEG-based ontology for ubiquitous content/service adaptation. In *Proceedings of the 3rd Workshop on Context Awareness for Proactive Systems (CAPS'2007)*, Guildford, UK.

Li, W. (2002). Intelligent Information Agent with Ontology on the Semantic Web. *In Proceedings of the 4th World Congress on Intelligent Control and Automation, 2(2),* 1501-1504.

Li, Y. & Bontcheva K. (2007). Hierarchical, Perceptron like Learning for Ontology Based Information Extraction In *Proceedings of World Wide Web (WWW2007).*

Li, Y., Bontcheva, K., & Cunningham, H. (2005). Using Uneven-Margins SVM and Perceptron for Information Extraction. In *Proceedings of Ninth Conference on Computational Natural Language Learning (CoNLL-2005).* pp.72-79

Liang B., Tang J., & Li J. (2005). Association search in Semantic Web: search + inference. (Poster Paper). *Proceedings of the 14th International World Wide Web Conference, Chiba, Japan, 10-14 May, 2005,* 992-993

Liang, B., Tang J., Li J., & Wang K. (2006). Semantic Similarity Based Ontology Cache. *In Proceedings of the 8th Asia Pacific Web Conference.* pp.250-262. Harbin, China, January, 2006.

Liang, B., Tang, J., Li, J., & Wang, K. (2005). SWARMS: A Tool for Exploring Domain Knowledge on Semantic Web. *In Proceedings of the AAAI'05 workshop on Contexts and Ontologies: Theory, Practice and Applications.* pp.120-123. Pittsburgh, USA, July 2005.

Liang, B., Tang, J., Li, J., & Wang, K. (2006). SWARMS: A Tool for Domain Exploration in Semantic Web and its Application in FOAF Domain. *In Proceedings of the 1st Asia Semantic Web Conference on Demo Track.* Beijing, China, September 2006.

Linari, A., & Weikum, G. (2006). Efficient Peer-to-Peer Semantic Overlay Networks Based on Statistical Language Models. In Proc. of the ACM CIKM International Workshop on Peer-to-Peer Information Retrieval (P2PIR), 9-16.

Liu, D. (2003). *Agents and Web Services.* SENG609.22 Tutorial.

Lloyd, J. W. & Topor, R. W. (1984). Making Prolog more Expressive. *Journal of Logic Programming,* 3:225-240.

Lloyd, J. W. (1987). *Foundations of Logic Programming.* Springer-Verlag.

Lodi, S., Mandreoli, F., Martoglia, R., Penzo, W., & Sassatelli, S. (2008). Semantic Peer, Here are the Neighbors You Want! In Proc. of the 11th International Conference on Extending Database Technology (EDBT), 26-37.

Loh, S., Wives, L. & Oliveira, J.P. (2000). Concept-based knowledge discovery in texts extracted from the web. In *SIGKDD Explorations.* Volume 2, Issue 1, Page 29.

Loo, B.T., Huebsch, R., Hellerstein, J.M., Stoica, I., & Shenker, S. (2004). Enhancing P2P File-Sharing with an Internet-Scale Query Processor. In M.A. Nascimento, M.T. Özsu, D. Kossmann, R.J. Miller, J.A. Blakeley, K.B.

Schiefer (Eds.), *Proceedings of the 30th International Conference on Very Large Data Bases* (pp. 432-443). San Francisco, CA, USA: Morgan Kaufmann.

Lu, J., & Callan, J. (2004). Federated Search of Text-Based Digital Libraries in Hierarchical Peer-to-Peer Networks. In H. Nottelmann, K. Aberer, J. Callan, W. Nejdl (Eds.), *Proceedings of the 2004 ACM International Workshop on Peer-to-Peer Information Retrieval* in conjunction with the *27th ACM International Conference on Research and Development in Information Retrieval* (online edition available at http://p2pir.is.informatik.uni-duisburg.de/1.pdf). New York, NY, USA: ACM.

Lu, Z., & McKinley, K.S. (2000). The Effect of Collection Organization and Query Locality on Information Retrieval System Performance and Design. In W.B. Croft (Ed.), *Advances in Information Retrieval* (pp. 173-197). Hingham, MA, USA: Kluwer Academic Publishers.

Lukasiewicz, T. (2005). Probabilistic Description Logic Programs. In *Proceedings of the 8th European Conference on Symbolic and Quantitative Approaches to Reasoning with Uncertainty.*

Lukasiewicz, T. (2005). Stratified Probabilistic Description Logic Programs. In *Proceedings of the ISWC-2005 Workshop on Uncertainty Reasoning for the Semantic Web (URSW).*

Lukasiewicz, T. (2007). A Novel Combination of Answer Set Programming with Description Logics for the Semantic Web. In *Proceedings of the 4th European Semantic Web Conference (ESWC 2007).*

Luke, S., Spector, L. Rager, D. & Hendler, J. (1997). *Ontology-Based Web Agents. In Procedings of the 1st International Conference on Autonomous Agents, USA, 59-66.*

Luo, J., Montrose, B., Kim, A., Khashnobish, A., & Kang, M. (2006). Adding OWL-S support to the existing UDDI infrastructure. In *Proceedings of IEEE International Conference on Web Services (ICWS'06)* pp. 153-162.

Lutz, C. (1999). *Reasoning with concrete domains.* In Proc. of the 16th Int. Joint Conf. on Artificial Intelligence (IJCAI'99), Stockholm, Sweden, pp. 90–95.

Lutz, C. (2001). NEXPTIME-complete description logics with concrete domains. In *Proc. of the Int. Joint Conf. on Automated Reasoning (IJCAR 2001),* volume 2083 of Lecture Notes in Artificial Intelligence, Springer, pp. 45–60.

Lv, Q., Cao, P., Cohen, E., Li, K., & Shenker, S. (2002). Search and Replication in Unstructured Peer-to-Peer Networks. In K. Ebcioglu, K. Pingali, A. Nicolau (Eds.), *Proceedings of the 16th ACM International Conference on Supercomputing* (pp. 84-95). New York, NY, USA: ACM.

Ma. Z. M. (2006) *Soft Computing in Ontologies and Semantic Web.* Springer-Verlag.

MacQueen, J. (1967). Some methods for classification and analysis of multivariate observations. *Proceedings of 5th Berkeley Symposium on Mathematics, Statistics and Probability,* 1:281- 298, 1967.

Madhavan, J., Bernstein, P. A., Doan, A., & Halevy, A. Y. (2005). Corpus-based Schema Matching. In Proc. of the 21st International Conference on Data Engineering (ICDE), 57-68.

Maedche, A. & Staab, S. (2000). Discovering Conceptual Relations from Text. In *Proceedings of European Conference on Artificial Intelligence (ECAI'2000).*

Maedche, A. & Staab, S. (2004). Ontology Learning. In Staab, S. & Studer, R. (Eds.) *Handbook on Ontologies.* Springer 2004.

Maedche, A. (2002). *Ontology Learning for the Semantic Web.* Norwell, MA: Kluwer Academic Publishers. 2002.

Maedche, A., Staab S., Stojanovic, N., Studer, R., Sure, Y. (2001). SEmantic PortAL -

Maedche, A., Staab, S., Studer, R., Sure, Y., & Volz, R. (2002). *SEAL – Tying up Information Integration and Web Site Management by Ontologies.* from http://lsdis.cs.uga.edu/SemNSF/Studer-SemWebPosition.pdf

Magkanaraki, A., Karvounarakis, G., Anh, T. T., Christophides, V., & Plexousakis, D. (2002). Ontology Storage and Querying. Technical Report 308, Foundation for

Research and Technology Hellas, Institute of Computer Science, Information System Laboratory, April, 2002.

Magkanaraki, A., Tannen, V., Christophides, V., & Plexousakis, D. (2003). Viewing the Semantic Web Through RVL Lenses. In D. Fensel, K. Sycara, J. Mylopoulos (Eds.), *Proceedings of the 2nd International Semantic Web Conference, LNCS Vol. 2870* (pp. 96-112). Berlin, Germany: Springer.

Magnini, B., Negri, M., Pianta, E., Romano, L., Speranza, M. & Sprugnoli, R. (2005). From Text to Knowledge for the Semantic Web: the ONTOTEXT Project. *SWAP 2005, Semantic Web Applications and Perspectives*, Trento.

Malkhi, D., Naor, M., & Ratajczak, D. (2002). Viceroy: A Scalable and Dynamic Emulation of the Butterfly. In A. Ricciardi (Ed.), *Proceedings of the 21st ACM Symposium on Principles of Distributed Computing* (pp. 183-192). New York, NY, USA: ACM.

Mandreoli, F., Martoglia, R., Penzo, W., & Sassatelli, S. (2006). SRI: Exploiting Semantic Information for Effective Query Routing in a PDMS. In Proc. of the 8th ACM CIKM International Workshop on Web Information and Data Management (WIDM), 19-26.

Mandreoli, F., Martoglia, R., Penzo, W., Sassatelli, S., & Villani, G. (2007). SRI@work: Efficient and Effective Routing Strategies in a PDMS. In Proc. of the 8th International Conference on Web Information Systems Engineering (WISE), 285-297.

Mani, I & Maybury, M. (1999). *Advances in Automatic Text Summarization.* Cambridge, MA: MIT Press. 1999.

Mani, I. (2001). *Automatic Summarization. Amsterdam.* AMSTERDAM, The Netherlands: John Benjamins Publishing Company. 2001.

Manku, G.S., Bawa, M., & Raghavan, P. (2003). Symphony: Distributed Hashing in a Small World. In S.D. Gribble (Ed.), *Proceedings of the 4th USENIX Symposium on Internet Technologies and Systems* (online edition available at http://www.usenix.org/publications/library/proceedings/usits03/tech/full_papers/manku/manku.pdf). Berkeley, CA, USA: USENIX Association.

Manning, C., & Schutze, H. (1999). Markov Models. In Book: Foundations of Statistical Natural Language Processing. The MIT Press. 1999.

Manola, F. & Miller, E. (2004). *RDF Primer.* W3C Recommendation, from http://www.w3.org/TR/rdf-primer/

Marcus A. Rothenberger, *System Development with Systematic Software Reuse: an Empirical Analysis of Project Success Factors*, Technical report, http://wi99.iwi.uni-sb.de/de/DoktorandenSeminar_PDF/D_Rothenberger.pdf

Martin, D. L., Cheyer, A. J. & Moran D. B. (1998). The Open Agent Architecture: A Framework for Building Distributed Software Systems. *Applied Artificial Intelligence, 1998.*

Martin, P. & Eklund, P. (1999). Embedding knowledge in web documents. In *Proceedings of the 8th International World Wide Web Conference* (pp. 1403-1419). Toronto

Maurizio Morisio, Guilherme H. Travassos & Michael E. Stark (2000), "Extending UML to Support Domain Analysis", Proceedings of the 15th IEEE international conference on Automated software engineering, Page: 321.

Maymounkov, P., & Mazieres, D. (2002). Kademlia: A Peer-To-Peer Information System Based on the XOR Metric. In P. Druschel, M.F. Kaashoek, A.I.T. Rowstron (Eds.), *Proceedings of the 1st International Workshop on Peer-to-Peer Systems, LNCS Vol. 2429* (pp. 53-65). Berlin, Germany: Springer.

Maynard, D. (2003). Multi-Source and Multilingual Information Extraction. In *BCS-SIGAI Workshop.* Nottingham Trent University, Sep. 12th

McCallum, A. (2003). Efficiently inducing features of Conditional Random Fields. In *Proceedings of the 19th Conference in Uncertainty in Artificial Intelligence.* pp. 403-410.

McCallum, A., Freitag, D., & Pereira, F. (2000). Maximum Entropy Markov Models for information extraction and segmentation. In *Proceedings of the 17th International Conference on Machine Learning (ICML'00).* pp. 591-598.

McCarthy, J. (1993). Notes on formalization context. *Proceedings of the 13th IJCAI*, Vol. 1, pp. 555-560.

McDonald, R., Pereira, F., Kulick, S., Winters, S., Jin, Y. & White, P. (2005). Simple Algorithms for Complex Relation Extraction with Applications to Biomedical IE. *43rd Annual Meeting of the Association for Computational Linguistics (ACL-2005)*, Ann Arbour, Michigan, pp. 491-498.

McIlraith, S.A., Son, T.C., & Zeng, H. (2001). Semantic Web Services. *IEEE Intelligent Systems* 16(2), 46-53.

Meadche, A & Staab, S. (2002). Measuring similarity between ontologies. *Proc. CIKM 2002*. LNAI vol.2473.

Meadche, A. & Staab S. (2001). Ontology learning for the semantic Web. *IEEE Journal on Intelligent Systems*, Vol. 16, No. 2, 72-79.

Meadche, A. & Staab, S. (2002). Measuring similarity between ontologies. *Proc. CIKM 2002*. LNAI vol.2473.

Meghini, C., Sebastiani F. & Straccia, U. (1997). Reasoning about the form and content for multimedia objects. *Proceedings of AAAI 1997 Spring Symposium on Intelligent Integration and Use of Text, Image, Video and Audio*, pp. 89-94.

Melnik, S., Bernstein, P. A., Halevy, A. Y., & Rahm, E. (2005). Supporting Executable Mappings in Model Management. In Proc. of the ACM SIGMOD International Conference on Management of Data, 167-178.

Melnik, S., Molina-Garcia, H., & Rahm, E. (2002). Similarity Flooding: A Versatile Graph Matching Algorithm. *In Proceedings of the 18th International Conference on Data Engineering*. pp.117-128. CA, USA, February 2002.

Meng, W., Yu, C., & Liu, K.-L. (2002). Building Efficient and Effective Metasearch Engines. *ACM Computing Surveys, 34(1)*, 48-84.

Michel, S., Bender, M., Triantafillou, P., & Weikum, G. (2006). IQN Routing: Integrating Quality and Novelty in P2P Querying and Ranking. In Proc. of the 10th International Conference on Extending Database Technology: Advances in Database Technology (EDBT), 149-166.

Michelet, B. (1988). *L'analyse des associations*. Doctoral thesis, Université de Paris VII, UFR de Chimie, Paris.

Mika, P. (2004). Social Networks and the Semantic Web. In Proc. of the IEEE/WIC/ACM International Conference on Web Intelligence (WI), 285-291.

Mika, P. (2005). Flink: Semantic Web Technology for the Extraction and Analysis of Social Networks. *Journal of Web Semantics 3*(2), 211-223.

Miller, R. J., Haas, Laura M., & Hernández, M. A. (2000). Schema Mapping as Query Discovery. In Proc. of the 26th International Conference on Very Large Data Bases (VLDB), 77-88.

Missikoff, M., Werthner, H. Höpken, W., Dell'Ebra, M., Fodor, O. Formica, A., Francesco, T. (2003) HARMONISE: Towards Interoperability in the Tourism Domain. In Proc. ENTER 2003, pp. 58-66, Helsinki: Springer.

Mitra, P., Noy, N. F. & Jaiswal, A. R. (2004). OMEN: A Probabilistic Ontology Mapping Tool. *In Proceedings of the 3rd International Conference on the Semantic Web (ISWC-2004), Workshop on Meaning Coordination and Negotiation, Hiroshima, Japan.*

Mittal, V.O & Paris, C.L. (1995). Use of context in explanations systems. *International Journal of Expert Systems with Applications*, Vol.8 No. 4, pp. 491-504.

Mittermeier (2003). Naiv nativ. *iX, 42(8)*.

Moens, M. (2006). Information Extraction: Algorithms and Prospects in a Retrieval Context. Springer press

Montresor, A. (2004). A Robust Protocol for Building Superpeer Overlay Topologies. In G. Caronni, N. Weiler, N. Shahmehri (Eds.), *Proceedings of the 4th IEEE International Conference on Peer-to-Peer Computing* (pp. 202-209). Los Alamitos, CA, USA: IEEE Computer Society.

Morin, E. (1999), *Automatic acquisition of semantic relations between terms from technical corpora*, TermNet-Verlag, Vienna, Proc. Of the Fifth Int. Congress on Terminology and Knowledge Engineering (TKE-99).

Morin, E. (1999). Using Lexico-Syntactic Patterns to Extract Semantic Relations between Terms from Technical Corpus. In *Proceedings, 5th International Congress on Terminology and Knowledge Engineering (TKE)*, 268–278. TermNet, Innsbruck, Austria.

Morpheus Group (2005). *The Morpheus File Sharing System*. Web pages available at http://www.musiccity.com

MUC: NIST, 1999, Message Understanding Conference. http://www.itl.nist.gov/iaui/894.02/related_projects/muc/proceedings/ie_task.html

Mukherjee, D., Delfosse, E., Jae-Gon, K., & Yong, W. (2005). Optimal adaptation decision-taking for terminal and network quality-of-service. *Multimedia, IEEE Transactions on*, vol. 7, pp. 454-462.

Mukherjee, S., Yang, G., & Ramakrishnan, I. (2003). Automatic annotation of content-rich HTML documents: structural and semantic analysis. In *Proceedings of the Second International Semantic Web Conference* (pp. 533-549). Sanibel Island, Florida

Muller, J. P. (1998). Architectures and Applications of Intelligent Agents: A Survey. *The Knowledge Engineering Review, 13(4),* 353-380. Cambridge University Press.

Muslea, I. (1999). Extraction patterns for information extraction tasks: A survey. In *Proceedings of AAAI-99: Workshop on Machine Learning for Information Extraction*. Orlando.

Muslea, I., Minton, S., & Knoblock, C. (1998). STALKER: Learning extraction rules for semistructured, web-based information sources. In *AAAI Workshop on AI and Information Integration*. pp. 74-81.

Muslea, I., Minton, S., & Knoblock, C. (1999). Hierarchical wrapper induction for semistructured information sources. *Autonomous Agents and Multi-Agent Systems, Vol.4*, pp. 93-114.

Muslea, I., Minton, S., & Knoblock, C. A. (2003). Active learning with strong and weak views: A case study on wrapper induction. In *Proceedings of the International Joint Conference on Artificial Intelligence (IJCAI)*. Acapulco, Mexico.

Nakache, J.P. & Confais, J. (2005). *Approche pragmatique de la classification : arbres hiérarchiques, partitionnements*. Editions Technip, Paris.

Napster Group (2005). *The Napster File Sharing System*. Web pages available at http://www.napster.com

Napster. [Online]. Available: http://www.napster.com.

Nardi, D. & Brachman, R. J. (2003). An Introduction to Description Logics. In F. Baader, D. Calvanese, D. L. McGuinness, D. Nardi & P. F. Patel-Schneider (eds), *The description Logic Handbook: Theory, Implementation, and Applications*. Cambridge University Press.

Navigli, R. & Velardi, P. (1998). Learning domain ontologies from document warehousees and dedicated web sites. In *AAAI'98/IAAI'98 Proceedings of the 15th National Conference on Artificial Intelligence* and the *10th Conference on Innovative Applications of Artificial Intelligence*.

Navigli, R., Velardi, P., Cucchiarelli, A. & Neri, F. (2004). Quantitative and qualitative evaluation of the ontolearn ontology learning system. In *Proc. Of ECAI-2004 Workshop on Ontology Learning and Population*, Valencia, Spain.

Nazarenko, A. (1994). *Compréhension du langage naturel : le problème de la causalité*. Doctoral thesis.

Neches, R., Fikes, R. E., Finin, T., Gruber, T. R., Senator, T. & Swarout, W. R. (1991). Enabling Technology for Knowledge Sharing. *Artificial Intelligence Magazine, 12(3),* 36-56.

Nejdl, W., Siberski, W., & Sintek, M. (2003). Design Issues and Challenges for RDF- and Schema-based Peer-to-Peer Systems. ACM SIGMOD Record, 32(3), 41-46.

Nejdl, W., Wolf, B., Staab, S., & Tane, J. (2002). EDUTELLA: Searching and Annotating Resources within an RDF-based P2P Network. In Proc. of the WWW International Workshop on the Semantic Web, pp.19-26.

Nejdl, W., Wolpers, M., Siberski, W., Schmitz, C., Schlosser, M., Brunkhorst, I., & Loser, A. (2003). Super-Peer-based Routing and Clustering Strategies for RDF-based P2P Networks. In G. Hencsey, B. White, Y.-F.R. Chen, L. Kovács, S. Lawrence (Eds.), *Proceedings of the 12nd International World Wide Web Conference* (pp. 536-543). New York, NY, USA: ACM.

Ng, W.S., Ooi, B.C., Tan, K., & Zhou, A. (2003). PeerDB: A P2P-based System for Distributed Data Sharing. In Proc. of the 19th International Conference on Data Engineering (ICDE), 633-644.

Nie, Z., Ma, Y., Shi, S., Wen, J., & Ma., W. (2007). Web Object Retrieval. In *Proceedings of World Wide Web (WWW2007).*

Nie, Z., Zhang, Y., Wen, J. R., & Ma, W. (2005). Object-level ranking: bringing order to Web objects. In *Proceedings of WWW,* 2005. 567-574.

Nocedal, J. & Wright, S. J. (1999). *Numerical optimization.* New York: Springer press.

Nottelmann, H. & Fuhr, N. (2006). Adding Probabilities and Rules to OWL Lite Subsets based on Probabilistic Datalog. *International Journal of Uncertainty, Fuzziness and Knowledge-Based Systems,* 14(1):17-41.

Nottelmann, H. (2005). *Inside PIRE: An extensible, open-source IR engine based on probabilistic logics.* Technical Report, University of Duisburg-Essen, Germany.

Noy, F. N. & McGuinness, D. L. (2001). *Ontology Development 101: A Guide to Creating Your First Ontology.* Stanford Knowledge Systems Laboratory Technical Report KSL-01-05 and Stanford Medical Informatics Technical Report SMI-2001-0880, March.

Noy, N. F. & Musen, M. A. (1999). SMART: Automated Support for Ontology Merging and Alignment. *In Proceedings of the 12th Workshop on Knowledge Acquisition, Modelling and Management,* Banff, Canada.

Noy, N. F. & Musen, M. A. (2000). PROMPT: Algorithm and Tool for Automated Ontology Merging and Alignment. *In Proceedings of the National Conference on Artificial Intelligence,* Austin, Texas.

Noy, N. F., & Musen, M. A. (1999). An algorithm for merging and aligning ontologies: automation and tool support. *In Proceedings of the Workshop on Ontology Management at the Sixteenth National Conference on Artificial Intelligence (AAAI-99).*

Noy, N.F., Sintek, M., & Decker, S. (2001). Creating Semantic Web Contents with Protégé-2000. *IEEE Intelligent Systems, 16*(2), 60-71.

Nwana, H. S. (1996). Software Agents: An Overview. *The Knowledge Engineering Review, 11(3),* 1-40.

Nwana, H. S., Ndumu, D. T. & Lee L. C. (1998). ZEUS: An Advanced Toolkit for Engineering Distributed Multi-Agent Systems. *In Proceedings of the PAAM '98,* London, UK, 377-391.

O'Madadhain, J. (2003). *JUNG: A Brief Tour.* From http://jung.sourceforge.net/presentations/jung4.ppt

Odell, J. & Bock, C. (1998), *A More Complete Model of Relations and their Implications: Roles.* Journal of OO Programming, May, 51-54.

Ogilvie, P., & Callan, J. (2001). The Effectiveness of Query Expansion for Distributed Information Retrieval. In H. Paques, L. Liu, D. Grossman (Eds.), *Proceedings of the 10th ACM International Conference on Information and Knowledge Management* (pp. 183-190). New York, NY, USA: ACM.

Oltramari, A. , Gangemi, A. , Guarino. N, & Masol.C (2002), *Restructuring WordNet's Top-Level: The OntoClean approach,* presented at LREC 2002.

Oyama, S. (2002). *Query Refinement for Domain-Specific Web Search.* (Doctoral dissertation, Kyoto University, 2002). From http://www.lab7.kuis.kyoto-u.ac.jp/publications/02/oyama-kyotou-doctorthesis.pdf

Padmini, S. (1992). Thesaurus construction. In William B. Frakes & Ricardo Baeza-yates (Eds.), *Information retrieval: data structures and algorithms,* 161-218. New York: Prentice-Hall.

Pan, J. Z. & Horrocks, I. (2006). OWL-Eu: Adding Customised Data types into OWL. *Journal of Web Semantics,* 4(1), 29-49.

Pan, R., Ding, Z., Yu, Y. & Peng, Y. (2005). A Bayesian Approach to Ontology Mapping. *Proceedings of the 4th International Semantic Web Conference,* Galway, Ireland.

Pan, Z. & Heflin, J. (2004). DLDB: Extending Relational Databases to Support Semantic Web Queries. Technical Report LU-CSE-04-006, Dept. of Computer Science and Engineering, Lehigh University, 2004.

Pan., J. Z. (2007). A Flexible Ontology Reasoning Architecture for the Semantic Web. *IEEE Transaction on Knowledge and Data Engineering.* 19(2), 246 - 260.

Park, M. J., Lee, J., Lee, C. H., Lin, J., Serres, O., & Chung, C. (2007). An Efficient and Scalable Management of Ontology. In *Proceedings of DASFAA*, 2007. 975-980.

Parreira, J. X., Michel, S., & Weikum, G. (2007). P2P-Dating: Real life inspired semantic overlay networks for Web search. Information Processing & Management, 43(3), 643-664.

Paslaru Bontas, E. (2005). Using context information to improve ontology reuse. Doctoral Workshop at the *17th Conference on Advanced Information Systems Engineering CAiSE'05.*

Passin, B., T.(2004). *Explorer's Guide to the Semantic Web.* Manning Publications Co., Greenwich.

Patel, C., Supekar, K., Lee, Y., & Park, E. K. (2003). OntoKhoj: a semantic web portal for ontology searching, ranking and classification. In *Proceedings of the 5th ACM international workshop on Web information and data management*, New York, NY, USA: ACM Press, 2003. 58–61.

Pazienza, M.T. (1999). Information Extraction: Towards Scalable, Adaptable Systems. Springer press.

Pearl, J. (1988). *Probabilistic Reasoning in Intelligent Systems: Networks of Plausible Inference.* Morgan Kaufmann.

Peng, F. (2001). *Models for Information Extraction.* Technique Report.

Pennacchiotti, M. & Pantel, P. (2006). A Bootstrapping Algorithm for Automatically Harvesting Semantic Relations. In *Proceedings of Inference in Computational Semantics (ICoS-06)*, Buxton (England)

Petrakis, Y., & Pitoura, E. (2004). On Constructing Small Worlds in Unstructured Peer-To-Peer Systems. In W. Lindner, M. Mesiti, C. Türker, Y. Tzitzikas, A. Vakali (Eds.), *EDBT 2004 Workshops – Proceedings of the 1st International Workshop on Peer-to-Peer Computing and Databases, LNCS Vol. 3268*, in conjunction with the 9th *International Conference on Extending Database Technology* (pp. 415-424). Berlin, Germany: Springer.

Pfoser, D., Pitoura, E., & Tryfona, N. (2002). Metadata modeling in a global computing environment. *GIS'02*, November 8-9, 2002, McLean, Virginia, USA, ACM Press (2002).

Pham, T. T, Maillot, N., Lim, J. H., & Chevallet, J. P. (2007). Latent Semantic Fusion Model for Image Retrieval and Annotation. In *Proceedings of Conference on Information and Knowledge Management (CIKM2007)*

Pinto, H. S. (1999). Some Issues on Ontology Integration. *IJCAI 1999, Workshop on Ontologies and Problem Solving Methods.*

Plaxton, C., Rajaram, R., & Richa, A. (1997). Accessing Nearby Copies of Replicated Objects in a Distributed Environment. In C.E. Leiserson, D.E. Culler (Eds.), *Proceedings of the 9th ACM Symposium on Parallel Algorithms ad Architectures* (pp. 311-320). New York, NY, USA: ACM.

Polyzotis, N., Garofalakis, M., & Ioannidis, Y. (2004). Approximate XML Query Answers. In G. Weikum, A.C. König, S. Deßloch (Eds.), *Proceedings of the 2004 ACM International Conference on Management of Data* (pp. 263-274). New York, NY, USA: ACM.

Poole, D. (1997). The independent choice logic for modelling multiple agents under uncertainty. *Artificial Intelligence*, 94(1-2):7-56.

Popov, B., Kiryakov, A., Kirilov, A., Manov, D., Ognyanoff, D., & Goranov, M. (2003). KIM – semantic annotation platform. In *Proceedings of 2nd International Semantic Web Conference* (pp. 834-849). Florida, USA.

Popov, B., Kiryakov,A., Ognyanoff, D.,Manov, D., Kirilov, A. (2004). KIM - A Semantic Platform For Information Extraction and Retrieval. Journal of Natural Language Engineering, Cambridge University Press. 10 (3-4). 375-392.

Powell, A.L., French, J.C., Callan, J., Connell, M., & Viles, C.L. (2000). The Impact of Database Selection on Distributed Searching. In E. Yannakoudakis, N.J. Belkin, M.-K. Leong, P. Ingwersen (Eds.), *Proceedings of the 23rd ACM International Conference on Research and Development in Information Retrieval* (pp. 232-239). New York, NY, USA: ACM.

Prantner, K. (2004). OnTour: The Ontology [Online]. Retrieved June 2, 2005, from http://E-Tourism.deri.at/ont/docu2004/OnTour%20-%20The%20Ontology.pdf/

Prasad, S., Peng, Y. & Finin, T. (2002). Using Explicit Information to Map Between Two Ontologies. *In Proceedings 2nd International Workshop on Ontologies in Agent Systems,* Bologna, Italy.

Predoiu, L. & Stuckenschmidt, H. (2007). A probabilistic Framework for Information Integration and Retrieval on the Semantic Web. In *Proceedings of the 3rd International Workshop on Database interoperability (InderDB).*

Predoiu, L. (2006). Information Integration with Bayesian Description Logic Programs. In *3rd IIWeb Interdisciplinary Workshop for Information Integration on the Web.*

Probabilistic Datalog

Prud'hommeaux, E. & Seaborne, A. (2007). *SPARQL Query Language for RDF.* From W3C. http://www.w3.org/TR/rdf-sparql-query/

Punyakanok, V. & Roth, D. (2001). The Use of Classifiers in Sequential Inference. In *Proceedings of NIPS'01.* pp.995-1001.

Quellet, R. & Ogbuji, U. (2002). Introduction to DAML: Part I & Part II. *O' Reilly xml.com.* Retrieved March 12th from http://www.xml.com/pub/a/2002/01/30/daml1.html

Rabin, M.O. (1981). *Fingerprinting by Random Polynomials* (Tech. Rep. No. TR-15-81). Cambridge, MA, USA: Harvard University, Center for Research in Computing Technology.

Rabiner, L. A. (1989). Tutorial on Hidden Markov Models and Selected Applications in Speech Recognition. In *Proceedings of the IEEE'1989.*

Rada.R, Hafedh Mili, Ellen Bicknell, & Maria Blettner (1989). *Development and Application of a Metric on Semantic Nets*, IEEE Transactions on Systems, Man and Cybernetics, 19:17-30.

Rational Software Corporation (2000), Rational Tutorial, www.ibm.com/developerworks

Ratnasamy, P., Francis, P., Handley, M., Karp, R., & Shenker, S. (2001). A Scalable Content-Addressable Network. In R. Cruz, G. Varghese (Eds.), *Proceedings of the 2001 ACM Conference on Applications, Technologies, Architectures, and Protocols for Computer Communications* (pp. 161-172). New York, NY, USA: ACM.

Ratnasamy, S., Handley, M., Karp, R., & Shenker, S. (2002). Topologically-Aware Overlay Construction and Server Selection. In P. Kermani, F. Bauer, P. Morreale, D. Lee, A. Orda (Eds.), *Proceedings of the 21st Annual Joint Conference of the IEEE Computer and Communications Societies, Vol. 3* (pp. 1190-1199). Los Alamitos, CA, USA: IEEE Computer Society.

Reif, G., Gall, H., & Jazayeri, M. (2005). WEESA - Web engineering for Semantic Web applications. *In Proceedings of 14th International World Wide Web Conference,* Chiba, Japan.

Reinberger, M.L., Spyns, P. & Pretorius, A.J. (2004). Automatic initiation of an ontology. *On the Move to Meaningful Internet Systems 2004: CoopIS, DOA, and ODBASE*, LNCS 3290, Napa, Cyprus, pp. 600-617.

Renda, M.E., & Callan, J. (2004). The Robustness of Content-based Search in Hierarchical Peer to Peer Networks In Proc. of the 2004 ACM CIKM International Conference on Information and Knowledge Management, 562-570.

Resnik, P. (1999). Semantic Similarity in a Taxonomy: An Information-Based Measure and Its Application to Problems of Ambiguity in Natural Language. *Journal of Artificial Intelligence Research,* 11, 95-130.

Reticular Systems (1999). *AgentBuilder – An Integrated Toolkit for Constructing Intelligence Software Agents.* http://www.agentbuilder.com.

Rhea, S., Wells, C., Eaton, P., Geels, D., Zhao, B., Weatherspoon, H., & Kubiatowicz, J. (2001). Maintenance-free Global Data Storage. *IEEE Internet Computing, 5(5),* 40-49.

Richardson, R., Smeaton, A.F., & Murphy, J. (1994). *Using WordNet as a Knowledge Base for Measuring Semantic Similarity.* From http://www.computing.dcu.ie/research/papers/1994/1294.ps

Riloff, E. (1993). Automatically Constructing a Dictionary for Information Extraction Tasks. In *Proceedings of the Eleventh National Conference on Artificial Intelligence.* pp. 811-816.

Robison, H.R. (1970). Computer detectable semantic structures. *Information Storage and Retrieval, 6,* 273-288.

Roelleke, T., Lübeck, R., Kazai, G. (2001). The HySpirit Retrieval Platform. In *Proc. of the 24th International ACM SIGIR Conference on Research and Development in Information Retrieval, SIGIR.*

Roman D., Keller, U., Lausen, H., Bruijn J. D., Lara, R., Stollberg, M., Polleres, A., Feier, C.,Bussler, C., Fensel, D. (2005). Web Service Modeling Ontology. Applied Ontology. 1(1): 77 - 106.

Rosenfeld, B. & Feldman, R. (2007). Using Corpus Statistics on Entities to Improve Semi-supervised Relation Extraction from the Web. In *Proceedings of the 45th Annual Meeting of the Association of Computational Linguistics (ACL2007),* pp. 600-607.

Ross, S. M. (2005). *A first course in Probability.* Prentice Hall.

Roth, D. & Wen, T. Y. (2002). Probabilistic Reasoning for Entity & Relation Recognition. In *Proceedings of the 19th International Conference on Computational linguistics, Vol.1.* 1-7. Taipei, Taiwan

Rowstron, A., & Druschel, P. (2001). Pastry: Scalable, Decentralized Object Location, and Routing for Large-Scale Peer-To-Peer Systems. In R. Guerraoui (Ed.), *Proceedings of the 2001 IFIP/ACM International Conference on Distributed Systems Platforms, LNCS Vol. 2218* (pp. 329-350), Berlin, Germany: Springer.

Russel, S. & Norvigm P. (1995). *Artificial Intelligence: A Modern Approach.* Prentice Hall, Inc.

Sabou, M. (2004). Extracting ontologies from software documentation: a semi-automatic method and its evaluation. *In Proceedings of the ECAI-2004 Workshop on Ontology Learning and Population (ECAI-OLP).*

Sakkopoulos, E., Kanellopoulos, D., Tsakalidis, A. (2006). Semantic mining and web service discovery techniques for media resources management. International Journal of Metadata, Semantics and Ontologies. Vol. 1, No. 1, pp. 66-75.

Salton, G., & Buckley, C. (1990). Improving Retrieval Performance by Relevance Feedback. *Journal of the American Society for Information Science, 41(4),* 288-297.

Salton, G., Wang, A., & Yang, C.S. (1975). A Vector Space Model for Information Retrieval. *Journal of American Society for Information Science, 18(11),* 613-620.

Sánchez, D. & Tettamanzi, G. (2006). Reasoning and quantification in fuzzy description logics. *Lecture Notes in Artificial Intelligence,* 3846, pp. 81-88.

Sánchez, D., & Tettamanzi, G. (2004). Generalizing quantification in fuzzy description logic. In *Proceedings 8th Fuzzy Days in Dortmund.*

Sanchez, E. & Yamanoi, T. (2006). Fuzzy ontologies for the Semantic Web. *Lecture Notes in Artificial Intelligence,* 4027: pp. 691-699.

Sanchez, E., (2006). *Fuzzy Logic and the Semantic Web.* Elsevier.

Sartiani, C., Manghi, P., Ghelli, G., & Conforti, G. (2004). XPeer: A Self-Organizing XML P2P Database System. In W. Lindner, M. Mesiti, C. Türker, Y. Tzitzikas, A. Vakali (Eds.), *EDBT 2004 Workshops – Proceedings of the 1st International Workshop on Peer-to-Peer Computing and Databases, LNCS Vol. 3268*, in conjunction with the *9th International Conference on Extending Database Technology* (pp. 456-465). Berlin, Germany: Springer.

Schaefer,S., (2006), *Secure Trade Lane: A Sensor Network Solution for More Predictable and More Secure Container Shipments*, Portland, Oregon, USA, Dynamic Languages Symposium, Pages: 839 - 845.

Schlieder, T. (2002). Schema-driven Evaluation of Approximate Tree-Pattern Queries. In C.S. Jensen, K.G. Jeffery, J. Pokorný, S. Saltenis, E. Bertino, K. Böhm, M. Jarke (Eds.), *Proceedings of the 8th International Conference on Extending Database Technology, LNCS Vol. 2287* (pp. 514-532). Berlin, Germany: Springer.

Schlosser, M.T., Sintek, M., Decker, S., & Nejdl, W. (2002). A Scalable and Ontology-based P2P Infrastructure for Semantic Web Services. In M. Kamkar, R.L. Graham, N. Shahmehri (Eds.), *Proceedings of the 2nd IEEE International Conference on Peer-to-Peer Computing* (pp. 104-111). Los Alamitos, CA, USA: IEEE Computer Society.

Schlosser, M.T., Sintek, M., Decker, S., & Nejdl, W. (2002). Hypercup – Hypercubes, Ontologies, and Efficient Search on Peer-To-Peer Networks. In G. Moro, M. Koubarakis (Eds.), *Proceedings of the 1st International Workshop on Agents and Peer-to-Peer Computing, LNCS Vol. 2530* (pp. 112-124). Berlin, Germany: Springer.

Schmid, H. (1994). *Probabilistic Part-of-Speech Tagging Using Decision Trees*. IMS-CL, Institut Für maschinelle Sprachverarbeitung, Universität Stuttgart, Germany.

Schmidt, A., Waas, F., Kersten, M., Carey, M., Manolescu, I., & Busse, R. (2002). XMark: A Benchmark for XML Data Management. In F.H. Lochovsky, W. Shan, P.A. Bernstein, R. Ramakrishnan, Y. Ioannidis, (Eds.), *Proceedings of the 28th International Conference on Very Large Data Bases* (pp. 974-985). San Francisco, CA, USA: Morgan Kaufmann.

Schoening, U. (1994). *Logic for Computer Scientists*. Birkhaeuser Verlag.

Schölkopf, B., Burges, C. JC, & Smola, A. J. (1999). *Advances in kernel methods: Support vector learning*. MA: MIT Press.

Schutz, A. & Buitelaar, P. (2005). RelExt: A Tool for Relation Extraction from Text in Ontology Extension. In *Proceedings of International Semantic Web Conference (ISWC'05)*. pp. 593-606.

Sciore, E., Siegel, M. & Rosenthal, A. (1992). Context interchange using meta-attributes. *Proceedings of the 1st International Conference in Information and knowledge Management*, pp. 377-386.

Seaborne, A. (2001). *RDQL: A Data Oriented Query Language for RDF Models*. From http://jena.sourceforge.net/tutorial/RDQL/

Searle, J. (1969). *Speech Acts*. Cambridge University Press.

Sebastiani, F. (2002). Machine learning in automated text categorization. *ACM Computing Surveys*, 34(1):1-47.

Sha, F. & Pereira, F. (2003). Shallow parsing with Conditional Random Fields. In *Proceedings of Human Language Technology, NAACL*. pp. 188-191.

Shadbolt, N., Hall, W. & Berners-Lee, T. (2006). The Semantic Web revisited. *IEEE Intelligent Systems*, 21 (3), 96-101.

Shapire, R. E. (1999). A brief introduction to Boosting. In *Proceedings of the 16th International Joint Conference on Artificial Intelligence (IJCAI-1999)*. pp. 1401-1405.

Shawe-Taylor, J. & Cristianini, N. (2000). Introduction to Support Vector Machines. Cambridge University Press, 2000

Sheth, A., Aleman-Meza, B., Arpinar, I.B., Halaschek, C., Ramakrishnan,C., Bertram, C., Warke,Y., Avant, D., Arpinar, F.S., Anyanwu, K., & Kochut, K. (2004). Semantic Association Identification and Knowledge Discovery for National Security Applications. *Journal of Database Management*, *16*(1), 33-53.

Shewchuk, J. R. (1994). *An introduction to the conjugate gradient method without the agonizing pain*, from http://www-2.cs.cmu.edu/.jrs/jrspapers.html#cg.

Sheykh, Esmaili, K. & Abolhassani, H. (2006). A Categorization Scheme for Semantic Web Search Engines. In *Proceedings of 4th ACS/IEEE International Conference on Computer Systems and Applications* (AICCSA-06), Sharjah, UAE, 2006. 171–178.

Siebes, R. & van Harmelen, F. (2002). Ranking Agent Statements for Building Evolving Ontologies. *In Proceedings of the Workshop on Meaning Negotiation, in conjunction with the 18th National Conference on Artificial Intelligence,* Edmonton, Canada.

Siefkes, C., & Siniakov, P. (2005). An overview and classification of adaptive approaches to information extraction. *Journal on Data Semantics IV.* Berlin, Germany: Springer.

Singh, I., Stearns, B., Johnson, M. and the Enterprise Team (2002): Designing Enterprise Applications with the J2EE Platform, Second Edition. Prentice Hall. pp. 348. Online: http://java.sun.com/blueprints/guidelines/designing_enterprise_applications_2e/app-arch/app-arch2.html

Siorpaes, K., Bachlechner, D. (2006). OnTour: Tourism Information Retrieval based on YARS. Demos and Posters of the 3rd European Semantic Web Conference (ESWC 2006), Budva, Montenegro, 11th – 14th June, 2006.

Skounakis, M., Craven, M., & Ray, S. (2003). Hierarchical Hidden Markov Models for Information Extraction. In *Proceedings of the 18th International Joint Conference on Artificial Intelligence.* Acapulco, Mexico.

Smith, B. (2003). Ontology. In L. Floridi (ed.), *Blackwell Guide to the Philosophy of Computing and Information.* Oxford: Blackwell, pp. 155–166.

Smith, C. F., Alesso, H. P. (2005). Developing Semantic Web Services. A K Peters, Ltd.

Smith, J. R., & Schirling, P. (2006). Metadata standards roundup. *IEEE Multimedia*, vol. 13, pp. 84-88.

Smith, M. K., Welty, C. & McGuiness, D. L. (2004). *OWL Web Ontology Language Guide.* W3C Recommendation, from http://www.w3.org/TR/2004/REC-owl-ref-20040210/

Soderland, S. (1999). Learning information extraction rules for semi-structured and free text. *Machine Learning.* Boston: Kluwer Academic Publishers

Soderland, S., Fisher, D., Aseltine, J., & Lehnert, W. (1995). CRYSTAL: Inducing a conceptual dictionary. In *Proceedings of the Fourteenth International Joint Conference on Artificial Intelligence (IJCAI'95).* pp. 1314-1319.

Soetens, P., Geyter, M.D., & Decneut, S. (2004). Multi-step media adaptation with semantic Web services. In *Proceedings of International Semantic Web conference.*

Somani, A., Agrawal, R., & Xu, Y. (2001). Storage and querying of e-commerce data. In *Proceedings of VLDB* , Rome, Italy. From http://www.vldb.org/conf/2001/P149.pdf.

Soni, A. (2006) Protein Interaction Extraction from Medline Abstracts Using Conditional Random Fields. Technical Report, from http://www.cs.wisc.edu/~apirak/cs/cs838/soni_report.pdf

Soo-Guan Khoo, C. (1995). *Automatic identification of causale relations in text and their use for improving precision in information retrieval.* PhD thesis.

Sproat, R., Black, A., Chen, S., Kumar, S., Ostendorf, M., & Richards, C. (1999). Normalization of Non-Standard Words, WS'99 Final Report.

Spyns, P. (2005). *Evalexon: Assessing triples mined from texts.* Technical report 09, STAR Lab, Brussels, Belgium.

Sripanidkulchai, K., Maggs, B., & Zhang, H. (2003). Efficient Content Location using Interest-based Locality in Peer-to-Peer Systems. In F. Bauer, R. Puigjaner, J. Roberts, N. Shroff (Eds.), *Proceedings of the 22nd Annual Joint Conference of the IEEE Computer and Communications Societies, Vol. 3* (pp. 81-87). Los Alamitos, CA, USA: IEEE Computer Society.

Stamboulis, Y. Skayannis P. (2003). Innovation Strategies and Technology for Experience-Based Tourism. Tourism Management. Vol. 24, pp. 35-43.

Stamou, G., van Ossenbruggen, J., Pan, J. Z., Schreiber, G., & Smith, J. R. (2006). Multimedia annotations on the semantic Web. *IEEE Multimedia*, vol. 13, pp. 86-90.

Steels, L. (1998). The Origins of Ontologies and Communication Conventions in Multi-Agent Systems. *Journal of Autonomous Agents and Multiagent Systems, 1(1)*, 169-194.

Stephen, C., & Martin P., (1999), *UML as an Ontology Modelling Language*, Sweden, Workshop on Intelligent Information Integration, 16th International Joint Conference on Artificial Intelligence, volume 23, pp: 46-53

Stephens, L. & Huhns, M. (2001). Consensus Ontologies – Reconciling the Semantics of Web Pages and Agents. *IEEE Internet Computing*, 92-95.

Stevenson, M. & Greenwood, M. (2005). A Semantic Approach to IE Pattern Induction. *43rd Meeting of the Association for Computational Linguistics (ACL-05)*, Ann Arbour, Michigan, p. 379-386.

Stoica, I., Morris, R., Karger, D., Frans Kaashoek, M, & Balakrishnan, H. (2001). Chord: A Scalable Peer-to-Peer Lookup Service for Internet Applications. In R. Cruz, G. Varghese (Eds.), *Proceedings of the 2001 ACM Conference on Applications, Technologies, Architectures, and Protocols for Computer Communications* (pp. 149-160). New York, NY, USA: ACM.

Stoilos, G., Simous, N., & Stamou, G. (2006), Uncertainty and the Semantic Web. *IEEE Intelligent Systems*, 21 (5), 84-87.

Stoilos, G., Stamou, G. & Pan, J. Z., (200b) Handling imprecise knowledge with fuzzy description logic. *Proceedings of the 2006 International Workshop on Description Logics.*

Stoilos, G., Stamou, G., & Tzouvaras V. (2005) The fuzzy description logic f-SHIN. *Proceedings of the International Workshop on Uncertainty Reasoning for the Semantic Web*, pp. 67-76.

Stoilos, G., Stamou, G., & Tzouvaras, V. (2005) A fuzzy description logic for multimedia knowledge representation. *Proceedings of the 2005 International Workshop on Multimedia and the Semantic Web.*

Stoilos, G., Stamou, G., & Tzouvaras, V. (2005) Fuzzy OWL: Uncertainty and the Semantic Web. *Proceedings of the 2005 International Workshop on OWL: Experience and Directions.*

Stoilos, G., Straccia, U., & Stamou, G. B. (2006). General concept inclusions in fuzzy description logics. *Proceedings of the 17th European Conference on Artificial Intelligence*, pp. 457-461.

Stojanovic, LJ., Stojanovic N.,Volz, R. (2002). Migrating data-intensive Web sites into the Semantic Web. Proceedings of the 2002 ACM symposium on Applied computing, Madrid, Spain, ACM Press. 1100-1107.

Stojanovic, N., Studer, R., & Stojanovic, L. (2007). An Approach for the Ranking of Query Results in the SemanticWeb. In *Proceedings of International Semantic Web Conference*, 2003. 500-516.

Stollberg, M., Zhdanova, A.V., Fensel, D. (2004). h-TechSight - A Next Generation Knowledge Management Platform, *Journal of Information and Knowledge Management*, 3 (1), World Scientific Publishing, 45-66.

Straber, M., Baumann, J. & Hohl, F. (1997). Mole – A Java based Mobile Agent System. In M. Muhlhauser (eds), *Special Issues in Object Oriented Programming.* Dpunkt Verlag, 301-308.

Straccia, U. & Troncy, R. (2006). Towards Distributed Information Retrieval in the Semantic Web: Query Reformulation Using the oMAP Framework. In *Proceedings of the 3rd European Semantic Web Conference (ESWC).*

Straccia, U. (1998). A fuzzy description logic. In *Proc. of the 15th Nat. Conf. on Artificial Intelligence (AAAI-98)*, pp. 594–599 Madison, USA.

Straccia, U. (2001) Reasoning within fuzzy description logics. *Journal of Artificial Intelligence and Research*, 14(1), 137–166

Straccia, U. (2004). Transforming fuzzy description logics into classical description logics. *Proceedings of the 9th European Conference on Logics in Artificial Intelligence*, pp. 385-399.

Straccia, U. (2004). Fuzzy ALC with fuzzy concrete domains. *Proceedings of the 9th European Conference on Logics in Artificial Intelligence*, pp. 385-399.

Straccia, U. (2005). Towards a fuzzy description logic for the semantic web. In *Proceedings of the 2nd European Semantic Web Conference*.

Stuckenschmidt, H. & Timm, I. J. (2002). Adapting Communication Vocabularies Using Shared Ontologies. *In Proceedings of the 2nd International Workshop on Ontologies in Agent Systems, in conjunction with the AAMAS '02,* Bologna, Italy, 6-12.

Stumme, G. & Meadche, A. (2001). Ontology Merging for Federated Ontologies on the Semantic Web. *In Proceedings of the International Workshop on Foundations of Models for Information Integration,* Viterbo, Italy.

Stumme, G. (2005). Ontology Merging with Formal Concept Analysis. In Kalfoglou Y., Schorlemmer M., Sheth A., Staab S. & Uschold (eds), *Semantic Interoperability and Integration,* Internationales Begegnungs – und Forschungszentrum fuer Informatik (IBFI), Dagstuhl, Germany.

Stumme, G., Hotho, A., & Berendt, B. (2006). Semantic Web Mining: State of the Art and Future Directions. *Web Semantics: Science, Services and Agents on the World Wide Web*, *4*(2), 124-143.

Suchanek, F.M., Ifrim, G., & Weikum, G. (2006). Combining Linguistic and Statistical Analysis to Extract Relations from Web Documents. In *Proceedings of the 12th ACM SIGKDD*. pp.712-717.

Sutton, C. & McCallum A. (2005). Composition of Conditional Random Fields for Transfer Learning. In *Proceedings of Human Language Technology Empirical Methods in Natural Language Processing (HLT/EMNLP2005).*

Sutton, C. & McCallum, A. (2006). An introduction to Conditional Random Fields for relational learning. In L. Getoor & B. Taskar (Eds.), *Statistical Relational Learning*, forthcoming book.

Sutton, C. & McCallum, A. (2007). Piecewise Pseudo-likelihood for Efficient Training of Conditional Random Fields. In *Proceedings of International Conference on Machine Learning (ICML2007).*

Sutton, C., Rohanimanesh, K., & McCallum, A. (2004). Dynamic conditional random fields: factorized probabilistic models for labeling and segmenting sequence data. In *Proceedings of ICML'2004*. pp. 783-790.

Sycara, K. & Paolucci, M. (2003). Ontologies in Agent Architectures. In S. Staab & R. Stuber (eds), *Handbook on Ontologies in Information Systems.* Springer-Verlag.

Sycara, K., Klusch, M., Widoff, S., Lu, J. (1999) Dynamic service matchmaking among agents in open information environments. ACM SIGMOD Record. Vol. 28(1), pp. 47-53.

Sycara, K., Pannu, A., Williamson, M. & Zeng, D. (1996). Distributed Intelligent Agents. *IEEE Expert, 11(6),* 36-46.

Szyperski. C (2002), *Component Software - Beyond Object- Oriented Programming*, London, 2nd edition, Addison-Wesley.

Tang, C., Xu, Z., & Dwarkadas, S. (2003). Peer-to-Peer Information Retrieval using Self-Organizing Semantic Overlay Networks. In A. Feldmann, M. Zitterbart, J. Crowcroft, D. Wetherall (Eds.), *Proceedings of the 2003 ACM Conference on Applications, Technologies, Architectures, and Protocols for Computer Communications* (pp. 175-186). New York, NY, USA: ACM.

Tang, J., Hong, M., Li, J., & Liang, B. (2006). Tree-structured conditional random fields for semantic annotation. In *Proceedings of 5th International Conference of Semantic Web* (*ISWC'2006*), pp. 640-653.

Tang, J., Hong, M., Zhang, D., Liang, B., & Li, J. (2007). Information extraction: methodologies and applications. In Hercules A. Prado & Edilson Ferneda (Ed.), *Emerging Technologies of Text Mining: Techniques and Applications,* (pp. 1-33). Hershey: Idea Group Inc.

Tang, J., Li, J., Liang, B., Huang, X., Li, Y., Wang K. (2006). Using Bayesian Decision for Ontology Mapping. *Web Semantics: Science, Services and Agents on the World Wide Web, 4* (4), 243-262.

Tang, J., Li, J., Lu, H., Liang, B., & Wang, K. (2005). iASA: learning to annotate the semantic web. *Journal on Data Semantic, IV,* 110-145. Springer Press.

Tang, J., Zhang, D., & Yao, L. (2007). Social Network Extraction of Academic Researchers. In *Proceedings of 2007 IEEE International Conference on Data Mining (ICDM'2007).*

Tang, J., Zhang, D., Zhang, D., Yao, L., & Zhu, C. (2007). ArnetMiner: An Expertise Oriented Search System for Web Community. Semantic Web Challenge. In *Proceedings of the 6th International Conference of Semantic Web* (*ISWC'2007*).

Tarkoma, S., Prehofer, C., Zhdanova, A.V., Moessner, K., & Kovacs, E. (2007). SPICE: Evolving IMS to next generation service platforms. In *Proceedings of the 3rd Workshop on Next Generation Service Platforms for Future Mobile Systems (SPMS 2007) at the 2007 International Symposium on Applications and the Internet,* IEEE Computer Society Press.

Taskar, B., Guestrin, C., & Koller, D. (2003) Max-Margin Markov Networks. In *Proceedings of Annual Conference on Neural Information Processing Systems.* Vancouver, Canada

Tatarinov, I., & Halevy, A. Y. (2004). Efficient Query Reformulation in Peer-Data Management Systems. In Proc. of the ACM SIGMOD International Conference on Management of Data, 539-550.

Tempich, C., Staab, S., & Wranik, A. (2004). REMINDIN': Semantic Query Routing in Peer-to-Peer Networks Based on Social Metaphors. In Proc. of the 13th World Wide Web Conference (WWW), 640-649.

Terry Quatrani (2001), *Introduction to the Unified Modeling Language*, Rational Developer Network, http://rational.net//

Terry Quatrani (2002) Visual Modeling with Rational Rose 2002 and UML, (pp 1-100), The Addison-Wesley Object Technology Series.

Terziev, I., Kiryakov, A., Manov, D. (2005). D1.8.1 Base upper-level ontology (BULO) Guidance, SEKT. Retrieved January, 15th, 2007 from: http://www.deri.at/fileadmin/documents/deliverables/Sekt/sekt-d-1-8-1-Base_upper-level_ontology__BULO__Guidance.pdf

The DAML Services Coalition (2001). *DAML-S: Semantic Markup for Web Services.* Retrieved March 12th from http://www.daml.org/services/daml-s/2001/05/daml-s.html.

The European On-To-Knowledge project (IST-1999-10132), from http://www.ontoknowledge.org.

The SEAL approach. In D. Fensel, J. Hendler, H. Lieberman, W. Wahlster (Eds.) In Creating the Semantic Web. Boston: MIT Press, MA, Cambridge.

Thesauus on tourism and leisure activities (1999). First edition copyright Secretariat of state for tourism of France and World Tourism Organisation.

Ting, K.M., & Witten, I.H. (1999). Issues in Stacked Generalization. *Journal of Artificial Intelligence Research,* 10, 271-289.

Torra, V., & Narukawa, Y. (2007). Modeling Decisions. Information Fusion and Aggregation Operators. Berlin: Springer.

Tresp, C., & Molitor, R. (1998). A description logic for vague knowledge. In *Proc of the 13th European Conf. on Artificial Intelligence (ECAI-98).* Brighton, England.

Triantafillou, P., Xiruhaki, C., Koubarakis, M., & Ntarmos, N. (2003). Towards High Performance Peer-to-Peer Content and Resource Sharing Systems. In Proc. of the 1st Biennial Conference on Innovative Data Systems Research (CIDR), 2003. Online proceedings.

Tsinaraki, C. et al. (2007). Interoperability support between MPEG-7/21 and OWL in DS-MIRF. *Knowledge and Data Engineering, IEEE Transactions on*, vol. 19, pp. 219-232.

Tsoumakos, D., & Roussopoulos, N. (2003). A Comparison of Peer-to-Peer Search Methods. In V. Christophides, J. Freire (Eds.), *Proceedings of the 6th ACM International Workshop on Web and Databases* in conjunction with the *2003 ACM International Conference on Management of Data* (pp. 61-66). New York, NY, USA: ACM.

Tsoumakos, D., & Roussopoulos, N. (2003). Adaptive Probabilistic Search for Peer-to-Peer Networks. In N. Shahmehri, R.L. Graham, G. Carroni (Eds.), *Proceedings of the 3rd IEEE International Conference on Peer-to-Peer Computing* (pp. 102-109). Los Alamitos, CA, USA: IEEE Computer Society.

Turney, P. (1996). The management of context-sensitive features: A review of strategies. *Proceedings of the ICML-96 Workshop on Learning in Context-Sensitive Domains*, pp. 53-69.

Udrea, O., Subrahmanian, V. S., & Maijkic, Z. (2006). Probabilistic RDF. In *Proceedings of the Conference on Information reuse and integration.*

Ullman, J. D. (1988). *Principles of Database and Knowledge-Base Systems, Volume I.* Computer Science Press.

Uschold, M. & Gruninger, M. (1996). *ONTOLOGIES: Principles, Methods and Applications,* Knowledge Engineering Review, *11(2),* 93-155.

Uschold, M., Clark, P., Healy, M., Williamson, K., & Woods, S. (1998), *Ontology Reuse and Application.* Italy, Formal Ontology in Information Systems. IOS Press PP:179-192.

Valduriez, P., & Pacitti, E. (2004). Data Management in Large-Scale P2P Systems. In M.J. Daydé, J. Dongarra, V. Hernández, J.M.L.M. Palma (Eds.), *Proceedings of the 6th International Conference on High Performance Computing for Computational Science, LNCS Vol. 3402* (pp. 104-118). Berlin, Germany: Springer.

Vallet, D., Fern'andez, M., & Castells, P. (2005). An Ontology-Based Information Retrieval Model. In *Proceedings of ESWC*, 2005. 455-470.

Van Aart, C. Pels, R., Caire, G. & Bergenti, F. (2002). Creating and Using Ontologies in Agent Communication. *In Proceedings of the Workshop on Ontologies in Agent Systems, AAMAS '02,* Bologna, Italy.

Van. Rijsbergen, C.J. (1979). *Information Retrieval.* London: Butterworths.

Vapnik V. (1999). *The Nature of Statistical Learning Theory.* New York: Springer Verlag

Vapnik, V. (1998). Statistical Learning Theory. New York: Springer Verlag

Vargas-Vera, M., Motta, E., Domingue, J., Lanzoni, M., Stutt, A., & Ciravegna, F. (2002). MnM: ontology driven semi-automatic and automatic support for semantic markup. In *Proceedings of the 13th International Conference on Knowledge Engineering and Management.* pp. 379-391.

Vazirgiannis, M., Halkidi, M. & Gunopoulos, D. (2003). *Uncertaintly handling and quality assessmen in data mining.* Springer.

Villalonga, C., Strohbach, M., Snoeck, N., Sutterer, M., Belaunde, M., Kovacs, E., Zhdanova, A.V., Goix, L.W., & Droegehorn, O. (2007). Mobile Ontology: Towards a standardized semantic model for the mobile domain. *In Proceedings of the 1st International Workshop on Telecom Service Oriented Architectures (TSOA 2007) at the 5th International Conference on Service-Oriented Computing,* Vienna, Austria.

Vishwanathan, S.V. N., Schraudolph, N. N., Schmidt, M. W., & Murphy, K. P. (2006). Accelerated Training of Conditional Random Fields with Stochastic Gradient Methods. In *Proceedings of the 23 rd International Conference on Machine Learning (ICML2006)*

Voorhes, E-M. (1993). Using WordNet to disambiguate word senses for text retrieval. *ACM SIGIR Conference on Research and Development in Information Retrieval,* Pittsburgh, Pennsylvania, 171-180.

W3C (2002). *Web Services Activity.* Available at http://www.w3.org/2002/ws.

W3C (2004a). OWL – Web Ontology Language Overview. *W3C Recommendation.* Retrieved March 12th from http://www.w3.org/TR/owl-features/

W3C (2004). RDF Primer. *W3C Recommendation, eds F. Manola & E. Miller.* Retrieved March 12th from http://www.w3.org/TR/rdf-primer/

W3C (2004). *OWL-S: Semantic Markup for Web Services.* Retrieved March 12th from http://www.w3.org/Submission/OWL-S

W3C . RDF Semantics, 2004. [online] Available: http://www.w3.org/TR/rdf-mt/.

W3C . SPARQL Query Language for RDF, 2007. [online] Available: http://www.w3.org/TR/rdf-sparql-query/.

Wainwright, M. J., & Jordan, M. I. (2005). A Variational Principle for Graphical Models. Chapter 11 in New Directions in Statistical Signal Processing. In Haykin, S., Principe, J., Sejnowski, T., & McWhirter, J. (Eds.). MIT Press.

Wainwright, M. J., Jaakkola, T. S., & Willsky, A. S. (2003). Tree-based reparameterization framework for analysis of sum-product and related algorithms. *IEEE transaction on Information Theory*, 49:1120-1146

Wainwright, M., Jaakkola, T., & Willsky, A. (2001). Tree-based reparameterization for approximate estimation on loopy graphs. In *Proceedings of Advances in Neural Information Processing Systems (NIPS'2001).* pp. 1001-1008.

Walther, E., Eriksson, H. & Musen, M.A. (1992). Plug-and-play: Construction of task-specific expert-system shells using sharable context ontologies. *Proceedings of the AAAI Workshop on knowledge Representation Aspects of Knowledge Acquisition*, San Jose, CA, pp. 191-198.

Wang, R. C. & Cohen, W. W. (2007). Language-Independent Set Expansion of Named Entities using the Web. In *Proceedings of International Conference on Data Mining (ICDM2007).*

Wang, X. (2007). SHINE: Search Heterogeneous Interrelated Entities. In *Proceedings of Conference on Information and Knowledge Management (CIKM2007).*

Watche, H., Vogele, T., Viser, U., Stuckenschmidt, H., Schuster, G., Neumman, H. & Hubner, S. (2001). Ontology-Based Integration of Information – A Survey of Existing Approaches. *In Proceedings of the 17th International Joint Conference on Artificial Intelligence (IJCAI 2001), Workshop: Ontologies and Information Sharing,* Seattle, Washington, 108-117.

Weinstein, P. & Birmingham, W. (1999). *Agent Communication with different ontologies: height new measures of description compatability*, Technical Report CSE-TR-383-99, 7.

Weippl, E. R., Klemen, M., Linnert, M., Fenz, S., Goluch, G., and Tjoa, A. M. (2005). Semantic storage: A report on performance and Flexibility. *Submitted to DEXA 2005.*

Weiser, M. (1991). *The Computer for the Twenty-First Century*, Scientific American, pp. 94-10.

Weisman, F., Roos, N. & Vogt, P. (2002). Automatic Ontology Mapping for Agent Communication. *In Proceedings of the 1st International Joint Conference on Autonomous Agents and Multiagent Systems,* Bologna, Italy, 563-564.

Welty, C.A. & Ferrucci, D.A.(1999) ,A formal ontology for re-use of software architecture documents, Cocoa Beach, FL, USA, Automated Software Engineering, PP: 259-262.

Widhalm, R., & Mueck, T. (2002). *Topic Maps: Semantische Suche im Internet.* Springer Verlag.

Widmer, G. (1996). Recognition and exploitation of contextual clues via incremental meta-learning. *Oesterreichisches Forshungsinstitut fuer artificial intelligence*, Wien, TR-96-01.

Williams, A.B. & Tsatsoulis, C. (2000). An Instance-based Approach for Identifying Candidate Ontology Relations within a Multiagent System. *In Proceedings of the First Workshop on Ontology Learning.* Berlin, Germany, August 2000.

Wooldridge, M. & Jennings, N. R. (1995). Intelligent Agents: Theory and Practice. *The Knowledge Engineering Review, 10(2),* 115-152.

Wooldridge, M. J., & Jennings, N. R. (1995). Agent Theories, Architectures, and Languages: A Survey. *In Intelligent Agents: ECAI-94 Workshop on Agent Theories, Architectures, and Languages, eds. M. J. Wooldridge & N. R. Jennings, 1–39.* Berlin: Springer-Verlag.

World Tourism Organization, 2001, Thesaurus on Tourism & Leisure Activities: http://pub.world-tourism.org:81/epages/Store.sf/?ObjectPath=/Shops/Infoshop/Products/1218/SubProducts/1218-1

World Wide Web Consortium (2005). *The World Wide Web Consortium.* Web pages available at http://www.w3.org/

WTO (2002). Thesaurus on Tourism & Leisure Activities of the World Tourism Organization [Online]. Retrieved May 12, 2004, from http://www.world-tourism.org/

Xu, J., & Callan, J. (1998). Effective Retrieval with Distributed Collections. In W.B. Croft, A. Moffat, C.J. van Rijsbergen, R. Wilkinson, J. Zobel (Eds.), *Proceedings of the 21st ACM International Conference on Research and Development in Information Retrieval* (pp. 112-120). New York, NY, USA: ACM.

Xun, E., Huang, C., and Zhou M. (2000). A Unified Statistical Model for the Identification of English baseNP. In *Proceedings of the 38rd Annual Meeting of the Association for Computational Linguistics* (*ACL'2000*).

Yang, B., & Garcia-Molina, H. (2002). Improving Search in Peer-to-Peer Networks. In L.E.T. Rodrigues, M. Raynal, W.-S.E. Chen (Eds.), *Proceedings of the 22nd IEEE International Conference on Distributed Computing Systems* (pp. 5-14). Los Alamitos, CA, USA: IEEE Computer Society.

Yang, J. & Chung, I. (2006), *Automatic Generation of Service Ontology from UML Diagrams for Semantic Web Services*, Springer Berlin / Heidelberg, Lecture Notes in Computer Science, Volume 4185/2006, pp: 523-529.

Yang, Y. & Calmet, J. (2006). OntoBayes: An Ontology-Driven Uncertainty Model. In *Proceedings of the International Conference on Computational Intelligence for Modelling, Control and Automation and International Conference on Intelligent Agents, Web Technologies and Internet Commerce (CIMCA-IAWTIC'06).*

Yangarber, R., Grishman, R. & Tapanainen, P. (2000). Unsupervised Discovery of Scenario-Level Patterns for Information Extraction. *6th ANLP,* Seattle, pp. 282-289.

Yarowsky, D. (1992). Word sense disambiguation using statistical models of Roget's categories trained on large corpora. *Proceedings of the 14th International Conference on Computational Linguistics, COLING'92,* Nantes, France, 454-460.

Yarowsky, D. (1993). One sense per collocation. *Proceedings of ARPA Human Language Technology Workshop,* Princeton, New Jersey, 266-271.

Yedidia, J. S., Freeman, W. T., & Weiss, Y. (2003). Understanding Belief Propagation and its Generalization. In: G. Lakemeyer & B. Nebel (Eds.), Exploring Artificial intelligence in the new millennium (pp. 239-269). San Francisco: Morgan Kaufmann Publishers Inc.

Yelland, P.M. (2000). An Alternative Combination of Bayesian Networks and Description Logics. In *Proceedings of the 7th international Conference on Knowledge Representation (KR).*

Yen, J. (1991). Generalising term subsumption languages to fuzzy logic. In *Proc of the 12th Int. Joint Conf on Artificial Intelligence (IJCAI-91),* pp: 472-477, Sydney, Australia

Zadeh, L. A. (1965). Fuzzy sets. *Information and Control,* 8(3), 338-353.

Zadeh, L.A. (1978) Fuzzy sets as a basis for a theory of possibility, *Fuzzy Sets Systems,* 1(1), pp. 3-28.

Zaniolo, C., Ceri, S., Faloutsos, C., Snodgrass, R. T., Subrahmanian, V. S. & Zicari, R. (1997). *Advanced Database Systems.* Morgan Kaufmann.

Zeinalipour-Yazti, D., Kalogeraki, V., & Gunopulos, D. (2004). Information Retrieval Techniques for Peer-to-Peer Networks. *Computing in Science and Engineering, 6(4),* 20-26.

Zeinalipour-Yazti, D., Kalogeraki, V., & Gunopulos, D. (2005). Exploiting Locality for Scalable Information Retrieval in Peer-to-Peer Systems. *Information Systems, 30(4)*, 277-298.

Zelenko, D., Aone, C., & Richardella, A. (2003). Kernel Methods for Relation Extraction. *Journal of Machine Learning Research. Vol. 3*, 1083- 1106.

Zhang, J., Tang, J., & Li, J. (2007). Expert Finding in a Social Network. *In Proceedings of Database Systems for Advanced Applications.* pp.1066-1069. Bangkok, Thailand, April 2007.

Zhang, L., Yu, Y., Zhou, J., Lin, C., & Yang, Y. (2005). An enhanced model for searching in semantic portals. In *Proceedings of the 14th international conference on World Wide Web*, New York, NY, USA: ACM Press, 2005. 453–462.

Zhang, M., Zhang, J., & Su, J. (2006). Exploring Syntactic Features for Relation Extraction using a Convolution Tree Kernel. In *Proceedings of the Human Language Technology Conference of the North American Chapter of the ACL (HLT-NAACL'2006)*. pp. 288-295. New York.

Zhang, W., Liu, S., Sun, C., Liu, F., Meng, W., & Yu. C. T. (2007). Recognition and Classification of Noun Phrases in Queries for Effective Retrieval. In *Proceedings of Conference on Information and Knowledge Management (CIKM2007).*

Zhang, X., Berry, M.W., & Raghavan, P. (2001). Level Search Schemes for Information Filtering and Retrieval. *Information Processing and Management, 37(2)*, 313-334.

Zhang, Y., Vasconcelos. W., & Sleeman, D. (2004). OntoSearch: An Ontology Search Engine. In *Proceedings of Proceedings The Twenty-fourth SGAI International Conference on Innovative Techniques and Applications of Artificial Intelligence* (AI-2004), Cambridge, UK, 2004.

Zhang, Z. (2004). Weakly-Supervised Relation Classification for Information Extraction. In *Proceedings of the Thirteenth ACM International Conference on Information and Knowledge Management (CIKM'2004).* pp581-588.

Zhao, B.Y., Kubiatowicz, J., & Joseph, A.D. (2001). Tapestry: An Infrastructure for Fault-tolerant Wide-area Location and Routing. Technical Report UCB/CSD-01-1141, UC Berkeley.

Zhao, S. & Grishman, R. (2005). Extracting relations with integrated information using kernel methods. In *Proceedings of the 43rd Annual Meeting of the Association for Computational Linguistics* (*ACL'2005*).

Zhao, Y. X. (2004). Combining RDF and OWL with SOAP for Semantic Web Services. In *Proceedings of the 3rd annual Nordic Conference on Web Services (NCWS'04).*

Zhao, Y., Karypis, G., & Fayyad U. M. (2005). Hierarchical Clustering Algorithms for Document Datasets. *Data Mining and Knowledge Discovery,* 10(2), 141-168.

Zhao, Y.B., Kubiatowicz, J., & Joseph, A. (2001). *Tapestry: An Infrastructure for Fault-Tolerant Wide-Area Location and Routing* (Tech. Rep. No. UCB/CSD-01-1141). Berkeley, CA, USA: University of California, Computer Science Division.

Zhdanova, A.V. (2006 January). *An Approach to Ontology Construction and its Application to Community Portals.* PhD thesis, University of Innsbruck, Austria.

Zhdanova, A.V., & Shvaiko, P. (2006). Community-driven ontology matching. In *Proceedings of the Third European Semantic Web Conference*, 11-14 June 2006, Budva, Montenegro, Springer-Verlag, LNCS 4011, pp. 34-49.

Zhdanova, A.V., Boussard, M., Cesar, P., Clavier, E., Gessler, S., Hesselman, C., Kernchen, R., Le Berre, O., Melpignano, D., Nani, R., Patrini, L., Räck, C., Strohbach, M., Sutterer, M., van Kranenburg, H., Villalonga, C., Vitale, A. (2006). *Ontology Definition for the DCS and DCS Resource Description, User Rules*, EU IST SPICE IP deliverable (D3.1).

Zhdanova, A.V., Du, Y., & Moessner, K. (2007). Mobile experience enhancement by ontology-enabled interoperation in a service platform. *In Proceedings of the 3rd Workshop on Context Awareness for Proactive Systems (CAPS'2007),* Guildford, UK, ISBN: 978-0-9556240-0-1.

Zhou, G., Su, J., Zhang, J., & Zhang, M. (2005). Exploring Various Knowledge in Relation Extraction. In *Proceedings of the 43rd Annual Meeting of the Association for Computational Linguistics.*

Zhou, Q., Wang, C., Xiong, M., Wang, H., & Yu, Y. (2007). SPARK: Adapting Keyword Query to Semantic Search. In *Proceedings of ISWC*, 2007.

Zhu, J. (2001). *Non-classical Mathematics for Intelligent Systems.* Wuhan: HUST Press. 2001.

Zhu, J., Nie, Z., Wen, J., Zhang, B., & Ma, W. (2005). 2D Conditional Random Fields for Web information extraction. In *Proceedings of 22nd International Conference on Machine Learning.* pp. 1044-1051.

Zhu, J., Nie, Z., Zhang B., & Wen J. (2007). Dynamic Hierarchical Markov Random Fields and their Application to Web Data Extraction. In *Proceedings of ICML2007.*

Zhu, X., Cao, H., & Yu, Y. (2006). SDQE: Towards Automatic Semantic Query Optimization in P2P Systems. *Information Processing and Management, 42(1),* 222-236.

Zini, F. & Sterling, L. (1999). On Designing Ontologies for Agents. *In Proceedings of Appia-Gulp-Prode '99: Joint Conference on Declarative Programming,* L' Aquila, Italy.

About the Contributors

Zongmin Ma (Z. M. Ma) received the PhD degree from the City University of Hong Kong in 2001 and is currently a full professor in College of Information Science and Engineering at Northeastern University, China. His current research interests include intelligent database systems, knowledge management, the Semantic Web and XML, knowledge-bases systems, engineering database modeling, and enterprise information systems. Dr. Ma has published over 60 papers in international journals, conferences, edited books and encyclopedias in these areas since 1998. He also edited and authored several scholarly books published by Idea Group Publishing and Springer-Verlag, respectively.

Huaiqing Wang is a professor at the Department of Information Systems, City University of Hong Kong. He is also the honorary dean and a guest professor of the School of Information Engineering, Wuhan University of Technology, China. He received his PhD in computer science from University of Manchester, UK, in 1987. Dr. Wang specializes in research and development of business intelligence systems, intelligent agents and their applications (such as multi-agent supported financial information systems, virtual learning systems, knowledge management systems, conceptual modeling and ontology). He has published more than 40 international refereed journal articles.

* * *

Jingwei Cheng, is a PhD student at the Northeastern University, China. He received his bachelor's degree from the College of Information Science and Engineering, Jilin University, China. His research interests include fuzzy description logics and Semantic Web, intelligent information processing, and fuzzy query answering over tractable fuzzy description logics.

Alfredo Cuzzocrea received the Laurea Degree in computer science engineering on April 2001 and the PhD Degree in computer science and systems engineering on February 2005, both from the University of Calabria. Currently, he is a researcher at the Institute of High Performance Computing and Networking of the Italian National Research Council, and adjunct professor at the Department of Electronics, Computer Science and Systems of the University of Calabria. His research interests include multidimensional data modeling and querying, data warehousing and OLAP, data stream modeling and querying, XML data management, Web information systems modeling and engineering, knowledge representation and management models and techniques, Grid and P2P computing. He is author or co-author of more than 70 papers in referred international conferences (including SSDBM, WISE, DEXA, DaWaK, DOLAP, IDEAS, SEKE, FQAS, SAC) and journals (including JIIS, DKE, WIAS, JDIM). He serves as program committee member of referred international conferences (including ICDM, CIKM, ICDCS, PAKDD, ECAI, WISE, DEXA, DaWaK, DOLAP, ADMA, IDEAS, FQAS, SAC, APWeb,

WAIM) and as review board member of referred international journals (including TODS, TKDE, IS, DKE, INS, IJSEKE, FGCS, JDIM, JCST, IJKESDP). Up-to-date information is available at http://si.deis.unical.it/~cuzzocrea

Danica Damljanovic is a research associate in GATE team, Natural Language Processing Group, Department of Computer Science at the University of Sheffield, UK. Her scientific interests include knowledge sharing, ontologies, natural language processing, software engineering and application of artificial intelligence to tourism, specifically development of expert systems and semantic web applications. Currently she is working on semantically-enabled knowledge technologies by combining natural language processing with ontologies and knowledge discovery from structured content.

Vladan Devedzic is a professor of computer science at the University of Belgrade, FON - School of Business Administration, Department of Information Systems and Technologies. His long-term professional goal is to bring close together the ideas from the broad fields of intelligent systems and software engineering. His current professional and scientific interests include knowledge modeling, ontologies, intelligent reasoning techniques, Semantic Web, software engineering, and application of artificial intelligence to education and medicine.

Stathes Hadjiefthymiades received his BSc, MSc and PhD degrees in informatics from the Dept. of Informatics and Telecommunications, University of Athens (UoA). He also received a joint engineering-economics MSc from the National Technical University of Athens. In 1992 he joined the Greek consulting firm Advanced Services Group. In 1995 he joined the Communication Networks Laboratory (CNL) of UoA. During the period 2001–2002, he served as a visiting assistant professor at the University of Aegean, Dept. of Information and Communication Systems Engineering. On the summer of 2002 he joined the faculty of the Hellenic Open University, Patras, Greece, as an assistant professor. Since December 2003, he is in the faculty of the Dept. of Informatics and Telecommunications, University of Athens, where he is presently an assistant professor. He has participated in numerous EU & National projects. His research interests are in the areas of web engineering, mobile/pervasive computing and networked multimedia. He has contributed to over 100 publications in these areas. Since 2004 he co-ordinates the Pervasive Computing Research Group of CNL.

Kalapriya Kannan is a technical staff member at the IBM India research laboratory in Bangalore. Kalapriya has obtained her PhD from Indian Institute of Science, Bangalore and has been working in IBM for about 1 year. Her research interests spans systems and networks modeling and analysis, pervasive computing, streaming applications and systems management. Currently she has been working in the area of semantic web and knowledge extraction techniques and its applicability to reuse.

Lobna Karoui received a Master's in intelligent systems from the University Paris-Dauphine. She is currently a PhD student at the engineering school 'Supélec' and the University Paris-11 in France and teaches at the University Paris-Sorbonne. Her research interests include artificial intelligence, data mining and semantic web. She is working on research into ontology learning, knowledge acquisition and evaluation and has published in national and international conferences and journals. She has served on review committees and delivered presentations concept extraction and evaluation. Currently, she is participating in a national project related to two domains: ontology information retrieval and annotation.

Markus Klemen is lecturer at the Technical University of Vienna and Managing Director of Secure Business Austria. His research focuses mainly on applied concepts of IT-security and semantic database solutions. Markus graduated with a Master's degree in International Business Administration from the University of Vienna. During 10 years of work as IT-Security consultant and software project manager he carried out various customer projects. He introduced and thought several lectures on IT-Security at the Technical University of Vienna and was responsible for the IT-Management of the Institute for Software Technology and Interactive Systems.

Kostas Kolomvatsos received his BSc in informatics from the Department of Informatics at the Athens University of Economics and Business in 1995 and his MSc in computer science - new technologies in informatics and telecommunications from the Department of Informatics and Telecommunications at the National and Kapodistrian University of Athens (UoA) in 2005. He is now a PhD candidate in the National and Kapodistrian University of Athens – Department of Informatics and Telecommunications under the supervision of assistant professor Stathes Hadjiefthymiades. His research interests are in the areas of Semantic Web technologies, ontological engineering, agent technologies and pervasive computing.

Juanzi Li is now an associate professor at the Department of Computer Science and Technology (DCST), Tsinghua University. She got PhD degree from DCST, Tsinghua in January, 2000. Her research areas are Semantic Web and Semantic Web Services, Text Mining and Knowledge Discovery including Semantic Content Management, News Mining, and Semantic based Service Discovery and Composition. She is the principal investigators of and joins in many projects supported by Natural Science Foundation of China, National Basic Science Research Program, and International Cooperation Projects. She has published more than ninety papers on international journals/conferences such as WWW, SIGIR, ISWC, SIGKDD, CIKM, JoDS and JoWS. More information can be found on his homepage: http://juanzili.arnetminer.org/

Ning Li received her BEng degree in computer science and engineering department from Shandong University, China in 1997, and PhD degree in computer science from the University of Manchester, UK in 2002. She currently works as a research fellow at Centre for Communication System Research (CCSR) at the University of Surrey, UK. She is a work package coordinator for the UK DTI-funded ubiquitous services research programme. Her research interests include ubiquitous computing, Semantic Web and Web service.

Yi Li is now a third year master candidate in Department of Computer Science and Technology (DCST), Tsinghua University. He received his BE degree from the same department of Tsinghua University in 2005. His research interests include Semantic Web, ontology mapping. He had participated in the international ontology alignment contest (OAEI) in 2006 and 2007 and obtained good results.

Bangyong Liang is now an associate researcher in NEC Labs. China. He was born in 1978 and got PhD degree from Department of Computer Science and Technology, Tsinghua University in Jul, 2006. His research directions are ontology management, information retrieval and text processing. He has published more twenty research papers in conferences/journals such as ISWC, ASWC and WWW. More information can be found on his homepage: http://keg.cs.tsinghua.edu.cn/persons/lby

Federica Mandreoli is a research associate at the Department of Information Engineering of the University of Modena and Reggio Emilia, Italy. She holds a Laurea degree in computer science and a PhD in electronics engineering and computer science from the University of Bologna. Her scientific interests are in the field of information and knowledge management and, currently, mainly concerns data sharing in P2P networks and query processing over graph-structured data. As to those research themes, she is author of publications dealing with query processing in P2P networks, structural disambiguation for semantic-aware applications and personalized accesses to XML and ontologies and she joined national and international projects.

Riccardo Martoglia is a research associate at the Faculty of Mathematical, Physical and Natural Sciences of the University of Modena e Reggio Emilia. He received his Laurea Degree (*cum Laude*) and his PhD in computer engineering from the same university. He teaches a number of subjects in the area of databases, information systems, information retrieval and Semantic Web. His current research is about studying new methodologies for efficiently and effectively searching large and distributed (P2P) data repositories. He is author of many publications and book chapters about the above mentioned topics. He is a member of ACM and IEEE Computer Society.

Klaus Moessner is a senior research fellow in the Mobile Communications Research Group, at the Centre of Communication Systems Research (CCSR) at the University of Surrey. He earned his Dipl-Ing (FH) at the University of Applied Science in Offenburg, Germany, an MSc from Brunel University, UK and his PhD from the University of Surrey (UK). His main responsibilities within CCSR include conducting research, managing and co-ordinating different research contracts and projects, supervision of PhD and MSc students and teaching courses at postgraduate student level. He leads a research team on Software based systems and IP based internetworking technologies in CCSR. Klaus is responsible for the content and service adaptation work package in the Mobile VCE core 4 research programme Ubiquitous Services.

Wilma Penzo received the MS degree in computer science in 1993 from the University of Bologna, Italy, and the PhD degree in electronic and computer engineering from the same University in 1997. Since 1996, she has been a research associate at the Department of Electronics and Computer Science (DEIS), University of Bologna, and at the IEIIT Institute of Italian CNR (National Council of Research). Her main research interests include query processing in the Semantic Web, semantic peer-to-peer systems, fuzzy query languages for multimedia databases, semistructured databases, indexing and query processing in XML digital libraries. She has served as a reviewer for several international journals and conferences in the database area.

Livia Predoiu is a PhD student at the University of Mannheim, Germany, and has received her master degree from the University of Freiburg, Germany. Her research interests include probabilistic knowledge representation formalisms and distributed reasoning for the purpose of information integration on the Semantic Web. More information can be found on her homepage: http://webrum.uni-mannheim.de/math/lpredoiu/

Stefan Raffeiner completed his Master's in computer science at the Vienna University of Technology and focused on IT-security and data storage.

Simona Sassatelli is a PhD Student in computer science at the International Doctorate School in Information and Communication Technologies of the University of Modena and Reggio Emilia. She received her Laurea degree *cum laude* and her Laurea Magistralis degree *cum laude* in computer engineering from the same University. Her scientific interests are in the field of information and knowledge management and mainly concern data sharing and retrieval in P2P networks. She is author of publications about the above mentioned topics, with particular reference to semantic query routing and network organization. She is a member of ACM and IEEE Computer Society.

Biplav Srivastava is a research staff member at the IBM India research laboratory in New Delhi and Bangalore, India. Biplav has over 12 years of research experience of which 7 is in IBM Research (industrial setting). Biplav's research interests are in planning, scheduling, policies, learning and information management, and their practical applications in services -- infrastructure and software (web services), semantic web, autonomic computing and societal domains. Biplav has extensive research experience in web services and semantic web, and lead the influential Synthy http://domino.research.ibm.com/comm/research_people.nsf/pages/biplav.Synthy.html web services composition technology which was piloted at a major telecommunication company. Biplav has a PhD and Master's from Arizona State University, USA and a Bachelor's from IT-BHU, India, all in computer science. Biplav is the author of over 50 refereed papers and has over 20 patent filings and awards.

Heiner Stuckenschmidt is professor of computer science at the University of Mannheim where he leads the research group on knowledge representation and knowledge management. His research interests include distributed and large scale knowledge representation for semantic web applications and intelligent information systems. He received his PhD from the Vrije Universiteit Amsterdam in 2003 for a thesis on ontology-based information sharing. He is author of a book on information sharing on the semantic web and has published more than 50 papers in international journals and conferences. He served as member of the programme committee for the most important conference on semantic web technologies and is member of the editorial board of the Journal on Data Semantics.

Jie Tang is now an assistant professor in Department of Computer Science and Technology (DCST), Tsinghua University. He was born in 1977 and got Ph.D. degree from DCST, Tsinghua in Jul, 2006. His research directions are semantic annotation, ontology interoperability, text mining, and machine learning. He has published more than forty research papers in international conferences/journals, such as SIGKDD, ISWC, ASWC, ACL, ICDM, and WWW. He is the principal investigator of NSFC project, Minnesota/China Collaborative project, IBM innovative joint-research project, etc., and also took part in research projects including National Foundational Science Research (973), NSFC and several international cooperation projects. More information can be found on his homepage: http://keg.cs.tsinghua.edu.cn/persons/tj

Giorgio Villani is a PhD student in computer science at the International Doctorate School in Information and Communication Technologies of the University of Modena and Reggio Emilia. He received his Laurea degree and Laurea Magistralis degree *cum laude* in engineering management from the University of Bologna. His research focuses primarily on information retrieval and dataspace systems and, currently, mainly concerns query processing over graph-structured data.

Hailong Wang is a PhD student at the Northeastern University, China. He received his bachelor's degree from the College of Computer Science and Technology, Shandong University, China. His research interests include fuzzy knowledge representation formalisms, fuzzy rule reasoning, fuzzy extensions to OWL and the implementation technologies of the rule reasoning machine on the Semantic Web.

Edgar R. Weippl (CISSP, CISA, CISM) is science director of Secure Business Austria and university assistant at the Vienna University of Technology. His research focuses on applied concepts of IT-security and e-learning. Edgar has taught several tutorials on security issues in e-learning at international conferences, including ED-MEDIA 2003-2007 and E-Learn 2005. In 2005, he published *Security in E-Learning* with Springer. After graduating with a PhD from the Vienna University of Technology, Edgar worked for two years in a research startup. He then spent one year teaching as an assistant professor at Beloit College, WI. From 2002 to 2004, while with the software vendor ISIS Papyrus, he worked as a consultant for an HMO (Empire BlueCross BlueShield) in New York, NY and Albany, NY, and for Deutsche Bank (PWM) in Frankfurt, Germany.

Li Yan, is an associate professor at the College of Information Science and Engineering, Northeastern University, China. Her research interests include XML databases, intelligent information processing and fuzzy database modeling.

Limin Yao is a third year master candidate in Department of Computer Science and Technology, Tsinghua University. She earned her BE degree from Department of Computer Science in Xi'an Jiaotong University in 2005. Her research interests cover information extraction, semantic annotation, natural language processing, and information retrieval. She was an intern at Microsoft Research Asia. She had published several academic papers. For more details, please refer to her homepage http://keg.cs.tsinghua.edu.cn/persons/lmyao/

Duo Zhang is now a PhD candidate in Department of Computer Science at UIUC. He obtained his bachelor degree and master degree from Department of Computer Science at Tsinghua University respectively in 2005 and 2007. His research interests include information extraction, data mining, information retrieval, and statistical machine learning. He was a visiting student in Microsoft Research Asia from 2004 to 2006. For more details, please refer to his homepage: http://keg.cs.tsinghua.edu.cn/persons/duozhang

Anna V. Zhdanova is a senior researcher at ftw. – Telecommunications Research Center Vienna, Austria. Earlier she worked as a researcher at the University of Surrey, UK, and at DERI, University of Innsbruck, Austria. Anna has been a doctoral student in Informatics at the University of Innsbruck and has defended her PhD thesis "An approach to ontology construction and its application to community portals" in 2006. She has received a diploma in mathematics and computer science equivalent to the Master's degree in 2003 from Novosibirsk State University, Russia. She is an author of more than 30 refereed papers in international journals, conference and workshop proceedings.

Index

I

K

M

O

P

Q

R

S

T

U

W